A DIGEST

OF THE

EARLY CONNECTICUT

PROBATE RECORDS.

❦

COMPILED BY

CHARLES WILLIAM MANWARING,

Member Connecticut Historical Society.

Vol. I.

HARTFORD DISTRICT,

1635—1700.

Volumes I and II were originally published
in 1904, Volume III in 1906.
Reprinted 1995 by Genealogical Publishing Co., Inc.
Baltimore, Maryland 21202
Library of Congress Catalogue Card Number 94-74584
International Standard Book Number, Volume I: 0-8063-1469-9
Set Number: 0-8063-1472-9
Made in the United States of America

PREFACE.

It seems appropriate, when a book has been prepared for publication, in offering it to the public, that the author or compiler should state clearly and concisely its purpose. The late Hon. Charles J. Hoadly, LL.D., once said to the writer: "People looking up their ancestry come back to Hartford." This indicates not only the value for research of the early records to be found here, but as well the numerous and widely distributed descendants of the men who settled upon the "Great River," at Hartford, Wethersfield, and Windsor, 1634-1636. To preserve the essential part of these *Probate Records;* to arrange them in form to be more available for reference; to arrest their constant wear and rapidly accelerating destruction; to marshal the *parents* and *children* of these early families by name, place, and collateral relationship, with incidental historical matter, giving volume, page and date for reference to the original writings; with a *copious index* in a book the reader may hold in hand, whether living near or remote from Hartford—is here offered as a reason for this Digest.

In the volumes of Probate Records the wills and inventories are entered upon one side and indexed. Upon the other side are entered the (Acts), or *Court Records,* also indexed. The wills, inventories, and some distributions of estates, are kept on file, in boxes—*each separate*—wills in one box, inventories in another, and the distributions in a third box. There being from 100 to 150 papers in each box, the wear, by frequent examinations of the frail old papers, tends to ultimate destruction.

Vol. I of this Digest is made up from the first six original volumes of Probate Records, and each volume is indicated by roman numerals in the *running title,* except the Appendix to Vol. I, which is composed of miscellaneous matters. Throughout the work, page and figures in the center of the line indicate wills and inventories in the volume shown in the running title, unless otherwise stated. Page numbers following the words "Court Record," refer only to the acts of the Court in the volumes of original record.

Wills and inventories have been copied from the pages in the several volumes, or from the original papers on file. Wills and distributions, with some inventories, found upon file (not recorded) have received careful attention. Among this class are found some valuable and interesting papers.

Court Records are not put upon file. As the acts of Court are sometimes found in several volumes, continued many years before the final settlement of an estate, errors in names or otherwise occur, which cause much care and labor to adjust.

Inventories—These were taken under such varying conditions, that their value is not an essential factor. They may represent the remainder of an estate, a large part of which had been given during the life-time of the testator, or be only the personal estate, or taken as valued in country pay; or, if as money, in the depreciated ills of the Colony, as compared with the pound sterling in silver.

Distributions have a special value in revealing changes by marriage, or other changes following from childhood to adult age.

Contractions, so common in the early records, usually represented by superior letters or by a line over the contracted word, were introduced in the copy for printing; but it was found inexpedient to follow this, except as modified in the text. The capitalization and spelling of every word exactly as recorded was not undertaken, for the sufficient reason that in most cases the language is not that of a testator, but of another who writes, and of still another who records, with differences between them. But withal, the effort has been to give a correct Digest of every paper in such language as is found in it, in every important particular. Contractions for economy of space have been used, the meaning of which will be suggested by their connections—as Invt., for Inventory; Adms., for Administration, and derivatives; Dist., for Distribution, etc.; Recog.,. for Recognizance; W. R., Windsor Records; P. C., Private Controversies.

The word "cousin" usually means nephew, or niece; X indicates his or her mark; Ls., the seal.

Many names appear with only a prefix to surname. All such, as Goodman, Goody, Deacon, Corpll, Lieut., Capt., Major, Col., etc., are indexed as Mr. or Mrs. Also, Jr. and Sen., and similar designations, are omitted in the index, as liable to mislead unless extended beyond allowed limits.

In most cases the Court Record of acceptance of inventory has been omitted, as well as the formal granting of letters of administration; this, being in the ordinary course of business, may be assumed; *to whom* letters were granted, and *date*, being the essential matter. Neither has it been considered as necessary to record every date and report of an administrator to the Court, as the payment of some debts, or for an extension of time. But in all Court cases in the settlement of any estate (testate or intestate), that which adds any information of value has been sought for with untiring zeal. That some desired items could not be found, the work must show. The conception and arrangement being mine, so must be its errors or shortcomings.

My thanks are due, and are here extended, to all who have given aid or encouragement in its preparation, and especially to those who have so generously financed its publication.

C. W. Manwaring

INTRODUCTION.

COURT RECORDS IN THE OFFICE OF THE SECRETARY OF STATE.

Of the Records of the General Court or Assembly of the Colony of Connecticut, which in early times was also a Court of Appeals and had original jurisdiction in the more important equity cases, it is not necessary to say much, because they are in print from April, 1636, to April, 1775, inclusive *(see Colonial Records of Connecticut)*. The records of the Particular Court were kept in the same book with those of the General Court until 1649. (See 1st Vol. Colonial Records of Connecticut). This Court had jurisdiction over every subject of judicial controversy throughout the Colony. It was succeeded in 1666 by the County Courts. The second volume of these records, which is the first kept in a separate book, is thus lettered: *"Particular Court, Vol. II, Probate Records,"* and begins with a Court held at Hartford, March 7, 1649-50, and ends with one held May 16, 1663. There are 196 pages of Court proceedings, and 185 pages of wills and inventories. This volume, after a disappearance for many years, was recovered in the City of New York in December, 1861. The third volume is lettered: *"Probate Records, Book III, County Court."* It begins with Hartford, Quarter Court, June 4, 1663, and extends to a County Court held at Hartford by adjournment, December 6, 1677. It contains 167 pages of Court records, 199 pages of wills and inventories, and three pages of land records. Both these volumes are well indexed for names in the Court proceedings. Vols. IV, V, and VI, in continuation of the preceding, are in the Hartford Probate Office. The General Assembly, at its session in May, 1666, established the four Counties of Hartford, New London, New Haven, and Fairfield, which included all the towns then organized and settled, and ordered that wills and inventories of persons deceased within any of the Counties of the Colony shall be exhibited and proved at the County Court to which the deceased did appertain by his habitation. This was the first actual division of the State into Probate Districts, although Probate Courts, as such, were not established and separated from the County Courts until 1698, and the limits of the Counties and Probate Districts remained coterminous until 1719.

Under the jurisdiction of the Particular Court, County Court and Court of Probates were entered estates from towns in the district of Hartford now known by the following names: Andover, Ashford, Avon, Barkhamsted, Berlin, Bloomfield, Bolton, Bristol, Burlington, Canaan, Canton, Colchester, Colebrook, Cornwall, Coventry, Cromwell, Glastonbury, Goshen, Haddam, Haddam (East), Hartford, Hartford (East), Hartland, Hebron, Kent, Mansfield, Middletown, New Hartford, New

INTRODUCTION.

London, Norwich, Rocky Hill, Saybrook, Simsbury, Southington, Tolland, Vernon, Waterbury, Wethersfield, Willington, Winchester, Windsor Locks, and others for a longer or shorter period.

The establishment of Windham District in May, 1719, took the towns of Windham and Mansfield from Hartford District. Woodbury District, in October of the same year, took away the towns of Litchfield and Waterbury. And East Haddam District, in October, 1741, took off the towns of East Haddam, Haddam, Colchester and Hebron, with the parish of Middle Haddam. The District of Litchfield, in October, 1742, of Middletown, in May, 1752, of Stafford, in May, 1759, Farmington, in January, 1769, and Simsbury, in May of the same year, further diminished the size of the Hartford District, and the process of division has been continued until that district now embraces but eight towns, while the four districts into which the Colony was divided in 1666 have been multiplied twenty-eight fold—numbering one hundred and twelve at the present time, 1904.

COURT OF ASSISTANTS.

The Records of the Acts of the Court of Assistants in the Colony of Connecticut, beginning 11 May, 1669, and extending to 7 October, 1686, and of the same Court from 1 October, 1696, to 3 October, 1701, fill 137 pages of a volume lettered *"Colonial Records, New England, 1659-1701."* This Court was established in October, 1665, and the records prior to 1669 are in Book III of the County Court. The continuation is found in a large parchment-bound book entitled: "No. 2—*Records Court of Assistants, Superior Court, Began 1687, Ends in 1715.*" It begins with the record of a special Court of Assistants, 15 February, 1686-7. At page 4 is this memorandum by Caleb Stanly, Jr.:

"Now in the moneth of October, anno Dom. 1687, Sir Edmund Andross, Knight, Governor of New England, received and took upon him the government of this his Majesties Colony of Connecticut, and therefore there was no Court of Assistants holden in this Colony in the year 1688, nor in May, anno Dom. 1689; and the Court book containing the records of the Court of Assistants holden at Hartford in October, 1689 (if any Court was then held*), can't be found."

The record then goes on from a Court held 27 May, 1690, to one held 11 May, 1696, and the reverse of the volume contains the records of the Court of Assistants from 7 May, 1702, and of its successor, the Superior Court, to 8 November, 1715. A large folio, 423 36 pages. Both these volumes are indexed for names.

*That there *was* a session of the Court of Assistants in October, 1689, appears from the printed "Colonial Records," Vol IV, page 25.

LIST OF

PROBATE DISTRICTS AND TOWNS,

Showing the Districts in which they are
or have been included.

———

Compiled by ALBERT C. BATES, Librarian of the Connecticut
Historical Society,

And reprinted, by permission of the Society, from its
Annual Report for 1897.

LIST OF PROBATE DISTRICTS.

(To avoid frequent repetition, the names of districts are printed in small capitals and the names of towns in lower case letters.)

ANDOVER—Includes Andover, Bolton, and Columbia.
Constituted June 27, 1851, from HEBRON.
Contains the records of HEBRON from May session, 1789, to June 27, 1851.

ASHFORD—Includes Ashford.
Constituted June 4, 1830, from POMFRET.

AVON—Includes Avon.
Constituted May session, 1844, from FARMINGTON.

BARKHAMSTED—Includes Barkhamsted.
Constituted June 5, 1834, from NEW HARTFORD.
Contains the records of NEW HARTFORD from May 27, 1825, to June 5, 1834.

BERLIN—Includes Berlin and New Britain.
Constituted June 2, 1824, from FARMINGTON, HARTFORD, and MIDDLETOWN.

BETHANY—Includes Bethany.
Constituted July 4, 1854, from NEW HAVEN.

BETHEL—Includes Bethel.
Constituted July 4, 1859, from DANBURY.

BOZRAH—Includes Bozrah.
Constituted June 3, 1843, from NORWICH.

BRANFORD—Includes Branford.
Constituted June 21, 1850, from GUILFORD.

BRIDGEPORT—Includes Bridgeport, Easton, Monroe, and Trumbull.
Constituted June 4, 1840, from STRATFORD.
Contains the records of STRATFORD from May session, 1782, to June 4, 1840; and the records of EASTON, which include the records of WESTON.

BRISTOL—Includes Bristol.
Constituted June 4, 1830, from FARMINGTON.

BROOKFIELD—Includes Brookfield.
Constituted June 19, 1850, from NEWTOWN.

BROOKLYN—Includes Brooklyn.
Constituted June 4, 1833, from POMFRET and PLAINFIELD.

BURLINGTON—Includes Burlington.
Constituted June 3, 1834, from FARMINGTON.

CANAAN—Includes Canaan and North Canaan.
Constituted June 6, 1846, from SHARON.

CANTERBURY—Includes Canterbury.
Constituted May 27, 1835, from PLAINFIELD.

CANTON—Includes Canton.
Constituted June 7, 1841, from SIMSBURY.

CHAPLIN—Includes Chaplin.
Constituted June 7, 1850, from WINDHAM.

CHATHAM—Includes Chatham and Portland.
Constituted June 1, 1824, from MIDDLETOWN and EAST HADDAM.

CHESHIRE—Includes Cheshire and Prospect.
Constituted May 27, 1829, from WALLINGFORD.

CLINTON—Included Clinton and Killingworth.
Constituted May 28, 1838, by change of name from KILLINGWORTH;
name changed back to KILLINGWORTH, June 1, 1842.

CLINTON—Includes Clinton.
Constituted July 5, 1862, from KILLINGWORTH.

COLCHESTER—Includes Colchester.
Constituted May 29, 1832, from EAST HADDAM.
Contains the records of EAST HADDAM from October session,
1741, to May 29, 1832.

CORNWALL—Includes Cornwall.
Constituted June 15, 1847, from LITCHFIELD.

COVENTRY—Includes Coventry.
Constituted June 19, 1849, from HEBRON.

DANBURY—Includes Danbury and New Fairfield.
Constituted May session, 1744, from FAIRFIELD.

DERBY—Includes Ansonia and Derby.
Constituted July 4, 1858, from NEW HAVEN.

EAST GRANBY—Includes East Granby.
Constituted July 4, 1865, from GRANBY.

EAST HADDAM—Includes East Haddam.
Constituted October session, 1741, from HARTFORD.
The records of EAST HADDAM previous to May 29, 1832, are in
COLCHESTER.

EAST HARTFORD—Includes East Hartford.
  Constituted May, 1887, from HARTFORD.

EAST HAVEN—Included East Haven.
  Constituted August, 1868, from NEW HAVEN.
    Annexed to NEW HAVEN, January 3, 1883. The records of
    EAST HAVEN are at NEW HAVEN.

EAST LYME—Includes East Lyme.
  Constituted June 2, 1843, from NEW LONDON.

EAST WINDSOR—Includes East Windsor and South Windsor.
  Constituted May session, 1782, from HARTFORD and STAFFORD.

EASTFORD—Includes Eastford.
  Constituted June 21, 1849, from ASHFORD.

EASTON—Included Easton.
  Constituted July 22, 1875, from WESTON.
    Contained the records of WESTON from May 22, 1832, to July
    22, 1875.
    EASTON was annexed to BRIDGEPORT March 4, 1878, and the
    records of EASTON, including the records of WESTON to July
    22, 1875, are in BRIDGEPORT.

ELLINGTON—Includes Ellington and Vernon.
  Constituted May 31, 1826, from EAST WINDSOR and STAFFORD.

ENFIELD—Includes Enfield.
  Constituted May 26, 1831, from EAST WINDSOR.

ESSEX—Includes Essex.
  Constituted July 4, 1859, from OLD SAYBROOK.
    Contains the records of OLD SAYBROOK from July 4, 1853, to
    July 4, 1859.

FAIRFIELD—Includes Fairfield.
  Constituted May session, 1666, as a County Court; the records in the
  probate office, however, contain some probate proceedings as early
  as 1649.

FARMINGTON—Includes Farmington and Plainville.
  Constituted January, 1769, from HARTFORD.

GRANBY—Includes Granby.
  Constituted May session, 1807, from SIMSBURY and HARTFORD.

GREENWICH—Includes Greenwich.
  Constituted July 4, 1853, from STAMFORD.

GROTON—Includes Groton.
  Constituted May 25, 1839, from STONINGTON.

GUILFORD—Includes Guilford and North Branford, except the Society of
  Northford.
    Constituted October session, 1719, from NEW HAVEN and NEW
    LONDON.

HADDAM—Includes Haddam.
   Constituted June 3, 1830, from MIDDLETOWN and CHATHAM.

HAMPTON—Includes Hampton.
   Constituted June 2, 1836, from WINDHAM.

HARTFORD—Includes Bloomfield, Glastonbury, Hartford, Newington,
   Rocky Hill, West Hartford, Wethersfield, and Windsor Locks.
   Constituted May session, 1666, as a County Court.

HARTLAND—Includes Hartland.
   Constituted June 3, 1836, from GRANBY.

HARWINTON—Includes Harwinton.
   Constituted May 27, 1835, from LITCHFIELD.

HEBRON—Includes Hebron.
   Constituted May session, 1789, from WINDHAM, EAST HADDAM,
   and EAST WINDSOR.
   The records of HEBRON previous to June 27, 1851, are in
   ANDOVER.

HUNTINGTON—Includes Huntington.
   Constituted May, 1889, from BRIDGEPORT and DERBY.

KENT—Includes Kent.
   Constituted May 26, 1831, from NEW MILFORD.

KILLINGLY—Includes Killingly.
   Constituted June 4, 1830, from POMFRET and PLAINFIELD.

KILLINGWORTH—Includes Killingworth.
   Constituted June 3, 1834, from SAYBROOK.
   Name changed to CLINTON, May 28, 1838, and changed back
   to KILLINGWORTH, June 1, 1842.

LEBANON—Includes Lebanon.
   Constituted June 2, 1826, from WINDHAM.

LEDYARD—Includes Ledyard.
   Constituted June 6, 1837, from STONINGTON.

LITCHFIELD—Includes Litchfield, Morris, and Warren.
   Constituted October session, 1742, from HARTFORD, WOODBURY,
   and NEW HAVEN.

LYME—Included in 1868 Lyme and Old Lyme (South Lyme).
   Constituted June 4, 1830, from NEW LONDON.
   Name changed to OLD LYME, July 24, 1868. (See OLD LYME.)

LYME—Includes Lyme.
   Constituted July 5, 1869, from OLD LYME.

MADISON—Includes Madison.
   Constituted May 22, 1834, from GUILFORD.

MANCHESTER—Includes Manchester.
   Constituted June 22, 1850, from HARTFORD.
MANSFIELD—Includes Mansfield.
   Constituted May 30, 1831, from WINDHAM.
MARLBOROUGH—Includes Marlborough.
   Constituted June 11, 1846, from COLCHESTER.
MERIDEN—Includes Meriden.
   Constituted June 3, 1836, from WALLINGFORD.
MIDDLETOWN—Includes Cromwell, Durham, Middlefield, and Middletown.
   Constituted May session, 1752, from HARTFORD, GUILFORD, and
   EAST HADDAM.
MILFORD—Includes Milford.
   Constituted May 22, 1832, from NEW HAVEN.
MONTVILLE—Includes Montville.
   Constituted June 27, 1851, from NEW LONDON.
NAUGATUCK—Includes Beacon Falls and Naugatuck.
   Constituted July 4, 1863, from WATERBURY.
NEW HARTFORD—Includes New Hartford.
   Constituted May 27, 1825, from SIMSBURY.
      The records of NEW HARTFORD previous to June 5, 1834, are in
      BARKHAMSTED.
NEW HAVEN—Includes East Haven, Hamden, New Haven, North Haven,
   Orange, Seymour, and Woodbridge.
   Constituted May session, 1666, as a County Court, soon after the
   union of the Connecticut and New Haven colonies. Probate pro-
   ceedings of the towns comprising the New Haven Colony before
   the union with Connecticut, are to be found with that Colony's
   records or with the records of the town where the deceased resided.
NEW LONDON—Includes New London and Waterford.
   Constituted May session, 1666, as a County Court.
NEW MILFORD—Includes Bridgewater and New Milford.
   Constituted May session, 1787, from WOODBURY, SHARON, and
   DANBURY.
NEWTOWN—Includes Newtown.
   Constituted May session, 1820, from DANBURY.
NORFOLK—Includes Norfolk.
   Constituted May session, 1779, from SIMSBURY and LITCHFIELD.
NORTH STONINGTON—Includes North Stonington.
   Constitued June 4, 1835, from STONINGTON.
NORWALK—Includes New Canaan, Norwalk, and Wilton.
   Constituted May session, 1802, from FAIRFIELD and STAMFORD.

NORWICH—Includes Franklin, Griswold, Lisbon, Norwich, Preston, Sprague, and Voluntown.
  Constituted October, 1748, from NEW LONDON.
  Contains the records of VOLUNTOWN.

OLD LYME—Includes Old Lyme.
  Name changed from LYME to OLD LYME July 5, 1869.
  Contains the records of LYME from June 4, 1830, to July 24, 1868.

OLD SAYBROOK—Includes Old Saybrook.
  Constituted July 4, 1853, from SAYBROOK.
  The records of OLD SAYBROOK previous to July 4, 1859, are in ESSEX.

OXFORD—Includes Oxford.
  Constituted June 4, 1846, from NEW HAVEN.

PLAINFIELD—Includes Plainfield.
  Constituted May session, 1747, from WINDHAM.

PLYMOUTH—Includes Plymouth.
  Constituted May 31, 1833, from WATERBURY.

POMFRET—Includes Pomfret.
  Constituted May session, 1752, from WINDHAM and PLAINFIELD.
  The records of POMFRET were burned January 5, 1754.

PUTNAM—Includes Putnam.
  Constituted July 5, 1856, from THOMPSON.

REDDING—Includes Redding.
  Constituted May 24, 1839, from DANBURY.

RIDGEFIELD—Includes Ridgefield.
  Constituted June 10, 1841, from DANBURY.

ROXBURY—Includes Roxbury.
  Constituted June 6, 1842, from WOODBURY.

SALEM—Includes Salem.
  Constituted July 9, 1841, from COLCHESTER and NEW LONDON.

SALISBURY—Includes Salisbury.
  Constituted June 16, 1847, from SHARON.

SAYBROOK—Includes Chester and Saybrook.
  Constituted May session, 1780, from GUILFORD.

SHARON—Includes Sharon.
  Constituted October session, 1755, from LITCHFIELD.

SHERMAN—Includes Sherman.
  Constituted June 4, 1846, from NEW MILFORD.

SIMSBURY—Includes Simsbury.
  Constituted May session, 1769, from HARTFORD.

SOMERS—Includes Somers.
Constituted June 3, 1834, from ELLINGTON.

SOUTHINGTON—Includes Southington.
Constituted May 24, 1825, from FARMINGTON.

STAFFORD—Includes Stafford and Union.
Constituted May session, 1759, from HARTFORD and POMFRET.

STAMFORD—Includes Darien and Stamford.
Constituted May session, 1728, from FAIRFIELD.

STERLING—Includes Sterling.
Constituted June 17, 1852, from PLAINFIELD.

STONINGTON—Includes Stonington.
Constituted October session, 1766, from NEW LONDON.

STRATFORD—Includes Stratford.
Constituted May session, 1782, from FAIRFIELD.
The records of STRATFORD previous to June 4, 1840, are in BRIDGEPORT.

SUFFIELD—Includes Suffield.
Constituted May session, 1821, from HARTFORD and GRANBY.

THOMASTON—Includes Thomaston.
Constituted June, 1882, from WATERBURY.

THOMPSON—Includes Thompson.
Constituted May 25, 1832, from POMFRET.

TOLLAND—Includes Tolland and Willington.
Constituted June 4, 1830, from STAFFORD.

TORRINGTON—Includes Goshen and Torrington.
Constituted June 16, 1847, from LITCHFIELD.

VOLUNTOWN—Included Voluntown.
Constituted June 4, 1830, from PLAINFIELD.
VOLUNTOWN was annexed to NORWICH April 3, 1889. The records of VOLUNTOWN are in NORWICH.

WALLINGFORD—Includes the Society of Northford in North Branford and Wallingford.
Constituted May session, 1776, from NEW HAVEN and GUILFORD.

WASHINGTON—Includes Washington.
Constituted May 22, 1832, from LITCHFIELD and WOODBURY.

WATERBURY—Includes Middlebury, Waterbury, and Wolcott.
Constituted May session, 1779, from WOODBURY.

WATERTOWN—Includes Watertown.
Constituted June 3, 1834, from WATERBURY.

WESTBROOK—Includes Westbrook.
Constituted July 4, 1854, from OLD SAYBROOK.

WESTON—Included in 1875, Easton and Weston.
> Constituted May 22, 1832, from FAIRFIELD.
>> Weston was annexed to WESTPORT and the town of Easton constituted as the district of EASTON July 22, 1875. The records of WESTON were to remain in EASTON, and with the EASTON records, are now in BRIDGEPORT.

WESTPORT—Includes Weston and Westport.
> Constituted May session, 1835, at the time of the incorporation of the town of Westport. The territory was taken from FAIRFIELD, NORWALK, and WESTON.

WINCHESTER—Includes Colebrook and Winchester.
> Constituted May 31, 1838, from NORFOLK.

WINDHAM—Includes Scotland and Windham.
> Constituted October session, 1719, from HARTFORD and NEW LONDON.

WINDSOR—Includes Windsor.
> Constituted July 4, 1855, from HARTFORD.

WOODBURY—Includes Bethlehem, Southbury, and Woodbury.
> Constituted October session, 1719, from HARTFORD, FAIRFIELD, and NEW HAVEN.

WOODSTOCK—Includes Woodstock.
> Constituted May 30, 1831, from POMFRET.

WESTMORELAND—Included Westmoreland.
> Constituted May session, 1775, probably from LITCHFIELD.
>> The decree of Trenton, December 30, 1782, declared that Westmoreland was under the jurisdiction of Pennsylvania.

LIST OF TOWNS.

Showing Districts in which they are or have been included.

(To avoid frequent repetition, the names of districts are printed in small capitals and the names of towns in lower case letters. The dates of incorporation or naming of towns are taken from the State Register.)

Andover.—Incorporated May, 1848, from Hebron and Coventry.
In HEBRON until June 27, 1851 ; since then in ANDOVER.

Ansonia.—Incorporated May, 1889, from Derby.
In DERBY since incorporation.

Ashford.—Named October, 1710.
In HARTFORD until October session, 1719; then in WINDHAM until May session, 1752; then in POMFRET until June 4, 1830; since then in ASHFORD.

Avon.—Incorporated May, 1830, from Farmington.
In FARMINGTON until May session, 1844; since then in AVON.

Barkhamsted.—Named May session, 1732; incorporated October, 1779.
In HARTFORD until May session, 1769; then in SIMSBURY until May 27, 1825; then in NEW HARTFORD until June 5, 1834; since then in BARKHAMSTED.

Beacon Falls.—Incorporated May, 1871, from Bethany.
In NAUGATUCK since its incorporation.

Berlin.—Incorporated May, 1785, from Farmington, Wethersfield, and Middletown.
In FARMINGTON, HARTFORD and MIDDLETOWN, partly in each, until June 2, 1824; since then in BERLIN.

Bethany.—Incorporated May, 1832, from Woodbridge.
In NEW HAVEN until July 4, 1854; since then in BETHANY.

Bethel.—Incorporated May, 1855, from Danbury.
In DANBURY until July 4, 1859; since then in BETHEL.

Bethlehem.—Incorporated May, 1787.
In WOODBURY since its incorporation.

Bloomfield.—Incorporated May, 1835, from Windsor.
  In HARTFORD since its incorporation.

Bolton.—Incorporated October, 1720.
  In HARTFORD until May session, 1782; then in EAST WINDSOR
  until May session, 1789; then in HEBRON until June 27, 1851; since
  then in ANDOVER.

Bozrah.—Incorporated May, 1786, from Norwich.
  In NORWICH until June 3, 1843; since then in BOZRAH.

Branford.—Settled in 1644, under New Haven jurisdiction.
  In NEW HAVEN until October session, 1719; then in GUILFORD
  until June 21, 1850, except that the Society of Northford was in
  WALLINGFORD from May session, 1776, until its incorporation in
  North Branford in May, 1831; since then in BRANFORD.

Bridgeport.—Incorporated May, 1821, from Stratford.
  In STRATFORD until June 4, 1840; since then in BRIDGEPORT.

Bridgewater.—Incorporated May, 1856, from New Milford.
  In NEW MILFORD since its incorporation.

Bristol.—Incorporated May, 1785, from Farmington.
  In FARMINGTON until June 4, 1830; since then in BRISTOL.

Brookfield.—Incorporated May, 1788, from Danbury, New Milford, and
  Newtown.
  In DANBURY until May session, 1820; then in NEWTOWN until June
  19, 1850; since then in BROOKFIELD.

Brookhaven.—See Setauket.

Brooklyn.—Incorporated May, 1786, from Pomfret and Canterbury.
  In POMFRET and PLAINFIELD, partly in each, the part taken from
  Canterbury being in PLAINFIELD, until June 4, 1833; since then
  in BROOKLYN.

Burlington.—Incorporated May, 1806, from Bristol.
  In FARMINGTON until June 3, 1834; since then in BURLINGTON.

Canaan.—Incorporated October, 1739.
  In HARTFORD until October session, 1742; then in LITCHFIELD until
  October session, 1755; then in SHARON until June 6, 1846; since
  then in CANAAN.

Canterbury.—Incorporated October, 1703, from Plainfield.
  In NEW LONDON until October session, 1719; then in WINDHAM
  until May session, 1747; then in PLAINFIELD until May 27, 1835;
  since then in CANTERBURY.

Canton.—Incorporated May, 1806, from Simsbury.
  In SIMSBURY until June 7, 1841; since then in CANTON.

Chaplin.—Incorporated May, 1822, from Mansfield and Hampton.
  In WINDHAM until June 7, 1850; since then in CHAPLIN.

Chatham.—Incorporated October, 1767, from Middletown.

In MIDDLETOWN and EAST HADDAM, partly in each, the part south of Salmon river being in EAST HADDAM until June 1, 1824; since then in CHATHAM.

Cheshire.—Incorporated May, 1780, from Wallingford.

In WALLINGFORD until May, 27, 1829; since then in CHESHIRE.

Chester.—Incorporated May, 1836, from Saybrook.

In SAYBROOK since its incorporation.

Clinton.—Incorporated May, 1838, from Killingworth.

In CLINTON (the old district) until June 1, 1842; then in KILLINGWORTH until July 5, 1862; since then in CLINTON (the new district).

Colchester.—Named October, 1699.

In NEW LONDON until October session, 1708; then in HARTFORD until October session, 1741; then in EAST HADDAM until May 29, 1832; since then in COLCHESTER.

Colebrook.—Named May session, 1732; incorporated October, 1779.

In HARTFORD until May session, 1769; then in SIMSBURY until May session, 1779; then in NORFOLK until May 31, 1838; since then in WINCHESTER.

Columbia.—Incorporated May, 1804, from Lebanon.

In WINDHAM until May session, 1808; then in HEBRON until June 27, 1851; since then in ANDOVER.

Conway.—Incorporated May session, 1841, from Chatham. Name changed to Portland during the same session of the legislature (see Portland).

Cornwall.—Incorporated May, 1740.

Probably in HARTFORD until October session, 1742; then probably in LITCHFIELD until June 15, 1847; since then in CORNWALL. (Cornwall was annexed to Hartford County, May session, 1738. It is not named in the act constituting Litchfield probate district, October session, 1742, but in the edition of the Colony laws printed in 1750 it is named as being in Litchfield district.)

Coventry.—Named October, 1711.

In HARTFORD until October session, 1719; then in WINDHAM until May session, 1789; then in HEBRON until June 19, 1849; since then in COVENTRY.

Cromwell.—Incorporated May, 1851, from Middletown.

In MIDDLETOWN since its incorporation.

Danbury.—Named October, 1687.

In FAIRFIELD until May session, 1744; since then in DANBURY.

Darien.—Incorporated May, 1820, from Stamford.

In STAMFORD since its incorporation.

Derby.—Named May, 1675.
  In NEW HAVEN until July 4, 1858; since then in DERBY.

Durham.—Incorporated May, 1708.
  In NEW HAVEN until October session, 1719; then in GUILFORD until May session, 1752; since then in MIDDLETOWN.

East Granby.—Incorporated June, 1858, from Granby and Windsor Locks.
  In GRANBY until July 4, 1865; since then in EAST GRANBY.

East Haddam.—Incorporated May, 1734, from Haddam.
  In HARTFORD until October session, 1741; since then in EAST HADDAM, except that a small part of the town was in CHATHAM from May session, 1830, to June 2, 1831.

East Hampton (N. Y.)—In Connecticut from 1658 to 1664.
  Probably under jurisdiction of the Particular Court.

East Hartford.—Incorporated October, 1783, from Hartford.
  In EAST WINDSOR until May session, 1797; then in HARTFORD until May, 1887; since then in EAST HARTFORD.

East Haven.—Incorporated May, 1785, from New Haven.
  In NEW HAVEN until August, 1868; then in EAST HAVEN until January 3, 1883; since then in NEW HAVEN.

East Lyme.—Incorporated May, 1839, from Lyme and Waterford.
  In NEW LONDON until June 2, 1843; since then in EAST LYME.

East Windsor.—Incorporated May, 1768, from Windsor.
  In HARTFORD and STAFFORD, partly in each, the parish of Ellington being in STAFFORD, until May session, 1782; since then in EAST WINDSOR, except that the small portion of Ellington Parish lying east of a meridian line drawn from the northwest corner of Tolland remained in STAFFORD.

Eastford.—Incorporated May, 1847, from Ashford.
  In ASHFORD until June 21, 1849; since then in EASTFORD.

Easton.—Incorporated May, 1845, from Weston.
  In WESTON until July 22, 1875; then in EASTON until March 4, 1878; since then in BRIDGEPORT.

Ellington.—Incorporated May, 1786, from East Windsor.
  In EAST WINDSOR and STAFFORD, partly in each, "that part lying east of a meridian line drawn from the northwest corner of Tolland" being in STAFFORD, until May 31, 1826; since then in ELLINGTON.

Enfield.—Named and granted by Massachusetts, May, 1683; annexed to Connecticut, May, 1749.
  In HAMPSHIRE COUNTY (Northampton, Mass.) until May, 1749; then in HARTFORD until May session, 1782; then in EAST WINDSOR until May 26, 1831; since then in ENFIELD.

Essex.—Incorporated May, 1854, from Old Saybrook.
In OLD SAYBROOK until July 4, 1859; since then in ESSEX.

Fairfield.—Settled, 1639; named, 1645.
Under the jurisdiction of the Particular Courts until May session, 1666; since then in FAIRFIELD.

Farmington.—Incorporated December, 1645.
Under the jurisdiction of the Particular Court until May session, 1666; then in HARTFORD until January, 1769; since then in FARMINGTON.

Franklin.—Incorporated May, 1786, from Norwich.
In NORWICH since its incorporation.

Glastonbury.—Incorporated May, 1690, from Wethersfield.
In HARTFORD until May session, 1782; then in EAST WINDSOR until May session, 1797; since then in HARTFORD.

Goshen.—Incorporated October, 1739.
In HARTFORD until October session, 1742; then in LITCHFIELD until May 13, 1895; since then in TORRINGTON.

Granby.—Incorporated October, 1786, from Simsbury.
In SIMSBURY until May session, 1807; since then in GRANBY.

Greenwich.—Settled 1640.
The settlement was made under authority of the New Haven Colony; but in 1642 the inhabitants claimed the protection of the Dutch government at New Netherlands, and so remained until 1656, when they returned to the New Haven Colony. In 1662 they submitted to the authority of the Connecticut Colony. Probably in NEW HAVEN from 1656 until 1662; then probably under the jurisdiction of the Particular Courts until May session, 1666; then in FAIRFIELD until May session, 1728; then in STAMFORD until July 4, 1853; since then in GREENWICH.

Griswold.—Incorporated October, 1815, from Preston.
In NORWICH since its incorporation.

Groton.—Incorporated May, 1705, from New London.
In NEW LONDON until October session, 1766, then in STONINGTON until May 25, 1839; since then in GROTON.

Guilford.—Settled 1639.
In NEW HAVEN until October session, 1719; since then in GUILFORD.

Haddam.—Incorporated October, 1668.
In HARTFORD until October session, 1741; then in EAST HADDAM until May session, 1752; then in MIDDLETOWN, except that the part lying east of the Connecticut river was annexed to CHATHAM June 1, 1824, until June 3, 1830; since then in HADDAM.

Hamden.—Incorporated May, 1786, from New Haven.
In NEW HAVEN since its incorporation.

Hampton.—Incorporated October, 1786, from Windham, Pomfret, Brooklyn, Canterbury, and Mansfield.
In WINDHAM until June 2, 1836; since then in HAMPTON.

Hartford.—Settled 1635.
Under the jurisdiction of the Particular Court until May session, 1666; since then in HARTFORD.

Hartland.—Incorporated May, 1761.
In HARTFORD until May session, 1769; then in SIMSBURY until May session, 1807; then in GRANBY until June 3, 1836; since then in HARTLAND.

Harwinton.—Incorporated October, 1737.
In HARTFORD until October session, 1742; then in LITCHFIELD until May 27, 1835; since then in HARWINTON.

Hebron.—Incorporated May, 1708.
In HARTFORD until October session, 1741; then in EAST HADDAM until May session, 1789; since then in HEBRON.

Huntington (N. Y.)—In Connecticut from 1660 to 1664.
Probably under jurisdiction of the Particular Court.

Huntington.—Incorporated January, 1789, from Stratford.
In STRATFORD until June 4, 1840; then in BRIDGEPORT, except that the "first voting district" was annexed to DERBY March 25, 1880, until May, 1889; since then in HUNTINGTON.

Kent.—Incorporated October, 1739.
In HARTFORD until October session, 1742; then in LITCHFIELD until October session, 1755; then in LITCHFIELD and SHARON, partly in each, the Society of East Greenwich remaining in LITCHFIELD, and being incorporated into the town of Warren in 1786, and the remainder of the town being in SHARON, until May session, 1787; then in NEW MILFORD until May 26, 1831; since then in KENT.

Killingly.—Incorporated May, 1708.
In NEW LONDON until October session, 1719; then in WINDHAM until May session, 1747; then in PLAINFIELD, except that the two north societies were annexed to POMFRET May session, 1752, until June 4, 1830; since then in KILLINGLY.

Killingworth.—Named May, 1667.
In NEW LONDON until October session, 1719; then in GUILFORD until May session, 1780; then in SAYBROOK until June 3, 1834; then in KILLINGWORTH until May 28, 1838; then in CLINTON until June 1, 1842; since then in KILLINGWORTH.

Lebanon.—Incorporated October, 1700.

In NEW LONDON until October session, 1719; then in WINDHAM until June 2, 1826, except that the part of the parish of Andover belonging to Lebanon was in HEBRON from May session, 1790, until about 1820; since then in LEBANON.

Ledyard.—Incorporated May, 1836, from Groton.

In STONINGTON until June 6, 1837; since then in LEDYARD.

Lisbon.—Incorporated May, 1786, from Norwich.

In NORWICH since its incorporation.

Litchfield.—Incorporated May, 1719.

In WOODBURY until October session, 1742; since then in LITCH-FIELD.

Lyme.—Named May, 1667.

In NEW LONDON until June 4, 1830; then in LYME (the old district) until July 24, 1868; then in OLD LYME until July 5, 1869; since then in LYME (the new district).

Madison.—Incorporated May, 1826, from Guilford.

In GUILFORD until May 22, 1834; since then in MADISON.

Manchester.—Incorporated May, 1823, from East Hartford.

In HARTFORD until June 22, 1850; since then in MANCHESTER.

Mansfield.—Incorporated May, 1702, from Windham.

In HARTFORD until October session, 1719; then in WINDHAM until May 30, 1831; since then in MANSFIELD.

Marlborough.—Incorporated October, 1803, from Colchester, Glastonbury, and Hebron.

In EAST HADDAM until May 29, 1832; then in COLCHESTER until June 11, 1846; since then in MARLBOROUGH.

Meriden.—Incorporated May, 1806, from Wallingford.

In WALLINGFORD until June 3, 1836; since then in MERIDEN.

Middlebury.—Incorporated 1807, from Waterbury.

In WATERBURY since its incorporation.

Middlefield.—Incorporated May, 1866, from Middletown.

In MIDDLETOWN since its incorporation.

Middletown.—Incorporated September, 1651.

Under jurisdiction of the Particular Court until May session, 1666; then in HARTFORD until May session, 1752, except that the part included in the parish of Middle Haddam was in EAST HADDAM from October session, 1741, until May session, 1752, and the part south of Salmon river was in EAST HADDAM from May session, 1742; then in MIDDLETOWN and EAST HADDAM, partly in each, until October session, 1767, when the part south of Salmon river which had been in EAST HADDAM was incorporated as Chatham; since then in MIDDLETOWN.

Milford.—Settled 1639.
>   In NEW HAVEN until May 22, 1832; since then in MILFORD.

Monroe.—Incorporated May, 1823, from Huntington.
>   In STRATFORD until June 4, 1840; since then in BRIDGEPORT.

Montville.—Incorporated October, 1786, from New London.
>   In NEW LONDON until June 27, 1851; since then in MONTVILLE.

Morris.—Incorporated May, 1859, from Litchfield.
>   In LITCHFIELD since its incorporation.

Mortlake.—Never was incorporated as a distinct town, although it was frequently spoken of as such. It became a part of Pomfret.
>   In WINDHAM until May session, 1752; after that in POMFRET.

Naugatuck.—Incorporated May, 1844, from Waterbury, Bethany, and Oxford.
>   In WATERBURY until July 4, 1863; since then in NAUGATUCK.

New Britain.—Incorporated May, 1850, from Berlin.
>   In BERLIN since its incorporation.

New Canaan.—Incorporated May, 1801, from Norwalk and Stamford.
>   In FAIRFIELD and STAMFORD, partly in each, until May session, 1802; since then in NORWALK.

New Fairfield.—Incorporated 1740.
>   In FAIRFIELD until May session, 1744; since then in DANBURY, except that the north society was in NEW MILFORD from May session, 1787, until it was incorporated as the town of Sherman in October, 1802.

New Hartford.—Incorporated October, 1738.
>   In HARTFORD until January, 1769; then in FARMINGTON until October session, 1808; then in SIMSBURY until May 27, 1825; since then in NEW HARTFORD.

New Haven.—Settled 1638.
>   In NEW HAVEN since its settlement.

New London.—Settled 1646.
>   Under the jurisdiction of the Particular Courts until May session, 1666; since then in NEW LONDON.

New Milford.—Incorporated October, 1712.
>   In NEW HAVEN until October session, 1719; then in WOODBURY until May session, 1787; since then in NEW MILFORD.

Newington.—Incorporated July 11, 1871, from Wethersfield.
>   In HARTFORD since its incorporation.

Newtown.—Incorporated October, 1711.
>   In FAIRFIELD until May session, 1744; then in DANBURY until May session, 1820; since then in NEWTOWN.

Norfolk.—Incorporated October, 1758.
In LITCHFIELD until May session, 1779; since then in NORFOLK.

North Branford.—Incorporated May, 1831, from Branford.
In GUILFORD and WALLINGFORD, partly in each, since its incorporation, the Society of Northford being in WALLINGFORD.

North Canaan.—Incorporated May, 1858, from Canaan.
In CANAAN since its incorporation.

North Haven.—Incorporated October, 1786, from New Haven.
In NEW HAVEN since its incorporation.

North Stonington.—Incorporated May, 1807, from Stonington.
In STONINGTON until June 4, 1835; since then in NORTH STONINGTON.

Norwalk.—Incorporated September, 1651.
Under the jurisdiction of the Particular Courts until May session, 1666; then in FAIRFIELD until May session, 1802; since then in NORWALK.

Norwich.—Settled 1660.
Under the jurisdiction of the Particular Courts until May session, 1666; then in NEW LONDON until October, 1748; since then in NORWICH.

Old Lyme.—Incorporated as South Lyme May, 1855, from Lyme; name changed in 1857.
In LYME (the old district) until July 24, 1868; since then in OLD LYME.

Old Saybrook.—Incorporated May, 1852, from Saybrook.
In SAYBROOK until July 4, 1853; since then in OLD SAYBROOK.

Orange.—Incorporated May, 1822, from Milford and New Haven.
In NEW HAVEN since its incorporation.

Oxford.—Incorporated October, 1798, from Derby and Southbury.
In NEW HAVEN until June 4, 1846; since then in OXFORD.

Plainfield.—Incorporated May, 1699.
In NEW LONDON until October session, 1719; then in WINDHAM until May session, 1747; since then in PLAINFIELD.

Plainville.—Incorporated May, 1869, from Farmington.
In FARMINGTON since its incorporation.

Plymouth.—Incorporated May, 1795, from Watertown.
In WATERBURY until May 31, 1833; since then in PLYMOUTH.

Pomfret.—Named 1713.
In NEW LONDON until October session, 1719; then in WINDHAM until May session, 1747; then in PLAINFIELD until May session, 1752; since then in POMFRET.

Portland.—Incorporated May, 1841, from Chatham.
    In CHATHAM since its incorporation.

Preston.—Named October, 1687.
    In NEW LONDON until October, 1748; since then in NORWICH.

Prospect.—Incorporated May, 1827, from Cheshire and Waterbury.
    In WALLINGFORD until May 27, 1829; since then in CHESHIRE.

Putnam.—Incorporated May, 1855, from Thompson, Pomfret, and Killingly.
    In THOMPSON until July 5, 1856; since then in PUTNAM.

Redding.—Incorporated May, 1767, from Fairfield.
    In FAIRFIELD until January session, 1782; then in DANBURY until
    May 24, 1839; since then in REDDING.

Ridgefield.—Incorporated October, 1709.
    In FAIRFIELD until May session, 1728; then in STAMFORD until
    October session, 1746; then in DANBURY until June 10, 1841; since
    then in RIDGEFIELD.

Rocky Hill.—Incorporated May, 1843, from Wethersfield.
    In HARTFORD since its incorporation.

Roxbury.—Incorporated October, 1796, from Woodbury.
    In WOODBURY until June 6, 1842; since then in ROXBURY.

Rye (N. Y.)—In Connecticut from 1665 to 1683.
    Probably under the jurisdiction of the Particular Courts until May
    session, 1666; then probably in FAIRFIELD until 1683.

Salem.—Incorporated May, 1819, from Colchester, Lyme, and Montville.
    In NEW LONDON and EAST HADDAM, partly in each, the part taken
    from Lyme being in NEW LONDON until July 9, 1841; the part
    taken from Montville being in NEW LONDON from June 3, 1824,
    until July 9, 1841 (previous to June 3, 1824, it had apparently been
    overlooked and not assigned to any probate district); the part
    taken from Colchester being in EAST HADDAM until May 29, 1832,
    then in COLCHESTER until July 9, 1841. In SALEM since July 9,
    1841.

Salisbury.—Incorporated October, 1741.
    In NEW HAVEN until October session, 1742; then in LITCHFIELD
    until October session, 1755; then in SHARON until June 16, 1847;
    Since then in SALISBURY.

Saybrook.—Settled 1635, and was a separate colony until it united with
    Connecticut in 1644.
    Under the jurisdiction of the Particular Courts from 1644, until
    May session 1666; then in NEW LONDON until October session,
    1719; then in GUILFORD until May session, 1780; since then in SAY-
    BROOK.

Scotland.—Incorporated May, 1857, from Windham.
In WINDHAM since its incorporation.

Setauket (now Brookhaven, N. Y.)—In Connecticut from 1661 to 1664.
Probably under jurisdiction of the Particular Court.

Seymour.—Incorporated May, 1850, from Derby.
In NEW HAVEN until 1899; since then in DERBY.

Sharon.—Incorporated October, 1739.
In NEW HAVEN until October session, 1742; then in LITCHFIELD
until October session, 1755; since then in SHARON.

Sherman.—Incorporated October session, 1802, from New Fairfield.
In NEW MILFORD until June 4, 1846; since then in SHERMAN.

Simsbury.—Named May session, 1670.
In HARTFORD until May session, 1769; since then in SIMSBURY.

Somers.—Incorporated 1734. In Massachusetts until 1749.
In HAMPSHIRE COUNTY (Northampton) until 1749; then in HART-
FORD until May session, 1759; then in STAFFORD until May 31,
1826; then in ELLINGTON until June 3, 1834; since then in SOMERS.

South Lyme.—Incorporated May, 1855, from Lyme. Name changed to
Old Lyme in 1857.
In LYME until after the change of name.

South Windsor.—Incorporated May, 1845, from East Windsor.
In EAST WINDSOR since its incorporation.

Southampton (N. Y.)—In Connecticut from 1645 to 1664.
Probably under jurisdiction of the Particular Court.

Southbury.—Incorporated May, 1787, from Woodbury.
In WOODBURY since its incorporation.

Southington.—Incorporated October, 1779, from Farmington.
In FARMINGTON until May 24, 1825; since then in SOUTHINGTON.

Southold (N. Y.)—Settled 1640. In Connecticut, New Haven Colony,
until 1664.
In NEW HAVEN.

Sprague.—Incorporated May, 1861, from Lisbon and Franklin.
In NORWICH since its incorporation.

Stafford.—Settled 1719.
In HARTFORD until May session, 1759; since then in STAFFORD.

Stamford.—Settled 1640.
In NEW HAVEN until May session, 1666; then in FAIRFIELD until
May session, 1728; since then in STAMFORD.

Sterling.—Incorporated May, 1794, from Voluntown.
> In PLAINFIELD until June 17, 1852; since then in STERLING.

Stonington.—Incorporated October, 1658, by Massachusetts.
> Was for some years claimed by both Connecticut and Massachu-
> setts, and the location of its early probate records is doubtful;
> perhaps a part will be found in Massachusetts and a part in the
> records of Particular Courts in Connecticut; then in NEW LONDON
> until October session, 1766; since then in STONINGTON.

Stratford.—Settled 1639.
> Under jurisdiction of the Particular Courts until May session,
> 1666; then in FAIRFIELD until May session, 1782; since then in
> STRATFORD.

Suffield.—Incorporated by Massachusetts, May, 1674; annexed to Connecticut, May, 1749.
> In HAMPSHIRE COUNTY (Northampton, Mass.) until May, 1749;
> then in HARTFORD, except that the part lying west of the mountain
> was annexed to GRANBY May session, 1807, until May session,
> 1821; since then in SUFFIELD.

Thomaston.—Incorporated May, 1875, from Plymouth.
> In WATERBURY until June, 1882; since then in THOMASTON.

Thompson.—Incorporated May, 1785, from Killingly.
> In POMFRET until May 25, 1832; since then in THOMPSON.

Tolland.—Named May, 1715.
> In HARTFORD until May session, 1759; then in STAFFORD until June
> 4, 1830; since then in TOLLAND.

Torrington.—Incorporated October, 1740.
> In HARTFORD until October session, 1742; then in LITCHFIELD
> until June 16, 1847; since then in TORRINGTON.

Trumbull.—Incorporated October, 1797, from Stratford.
> In STRATFORD until June 4, 1840; since then in BRIDGEPORT.

Union.—Incorporated October, 1734.
> In WINDHAM until May session, 1752; then in POMFRET until May
> session, 1759; since then in STAFFORD.

Vernon.—Incorporated October, 1808, from Bolton.
> In HEBRON until May session, 1814; then in STAFFORD until May
> 31, 1826; since then in ELLINGTON.

Voluntown.—Named May, 1708.
> In NEW LONDON until May session, 1726; then in WINDHAM until
> May session, 1747; then in PLAINFIELD until June 4, 1830; then in
> VOLUNTOWN until April 3, 1889; since then in NORWICH.

Wallingford.—Named May, 1670.
In NEW HAVEN until May session, 1776; since then in WALLING-FORD.

Warren.—Incorporated May, 1786, from Kent.
In LITCHFIELD since its incorporation.

Washington.—Incorporated January, 1779, from Woodbury, Litchfield, Kent, and New Milford.
In LITCHFIELD and WOODBURY, partly in each, the parts taken from Woodbury and New Milford and known as the Society of Judea being in WOODBURY, until May 22, 1832; since then in WASHINGTON.

Waterbury.—Named May, 1686.
In HARTFORD until October session, 1719; then in WOODBURY until May session, 1779; since then in WATERBURY.

Waterford.—Incorporated October, 1801, from New London.
In NEW LONDON since its incorporation.

Watertown.—Incorporated May, 1780, from Waterbury.
In WATERBURY until June 3, 1834; since then in WATERTOWN.

West Hartford.—Incorporated May, 1854, from Hartford.
In HARTFORD since its incorporation.

Westbrook.—Incorporated May, 1840, from Saybrook.
In SAYBROOK until July 4, 1853; then in OLD SAYBROOK until July 4, 1854; since then in WESTBROOK.

Westmoreland (Penn.)—Incorporated January, 1774.
Probably in LITCHFIELD until May session, 1775; then made a distinct district by the name of WESTMORELAND.

Weston.—Incorporated October, 1787, from Fairfield.
In FAIRFIELD until May 22, 1832; then in WESTON until July 22, 1875; since then in WESTPORT.

Westport.—Incorporated May, 1835, from Fairfield, Norwalk, and Weston.
In WESTPORT since its incorporation.

Wethersfield.—Settled 1635.
Under the jurisdiction of the Particular Court until May session, 1666; since then in HARTFORD.

Willington.—Incorporated May, 1727.
In HARTFORD until May session, 1759; then in STAFFORD until June 4, 1830; since then in TOLLAND.

Wilton.—Incorporated May, 1802, from Norwalk.
 In NORWALK since its incorporation.

Winchester.—Named 1733. Incorporated May, 1771.
 In HARTFORD until May session, 1769; then in SIMSBURY until May
 session, 1779; then in NORFOLK until May 31, 1838; since then in
 WINCHESTER.

Windham.—Incorporated May, 1692.
 In HARTFORD until October session, 1719; since then in WINDHAM.

Windsor.—Settled 1637. (1634.—C. W. M.)
 In HARTFORD until July 4, 1855, except that Ellington Parish, which
 was included in East Windsor at the incorporation of that town,
 was set off to STAFFORD, May session, 1759; since then in WINDSOR.

Windsor Locks.—Incorporated May, 1854, from Windsor.
 In HARTFORD since its incorporation.

Wolcott.—Incorporated May, 1796, from Waterbury and Southington.
 In WATERBURY since its incorporation.

Woodbridge.—Incorporated January, 1784, from New Haven and Milford.
 In NEW HAVEN since its incorporation.

Woodbury.—Named May, 1674.
 In FAIRFIELD until October session, 1719; since then in WOODBURY.

Woodstock.—Incorporated by Massachusetts March, 1690; annexed to
 Connecticut May, 1749.
 Probably in SUFFOLK COUNTY (Boston, Mass.) until 1731; then
 in WORCESTER COUNTY until May, 1749; then in WINDHAM until
 May session, 1752; then in POMFRET until May 30, 1831; since then
 in WOODSTOCK.

BOOK NO. A,

OR THE

FIRST BOOK OF THE RECORDS

OF THE

COLONY OF CONNECTICUT.

Wherein is Recorded the first Acts and Lawes of the
Said Colony; and the first acts of the General Courts
of the Same.　　　　And this is also the first book
of the Records of the County Courts and Courts of probates,
and of Wills and Inventories, Especially in the County
of Hartford, in which said County Courts are Somtimes
Stiled perticular Courts, and Somtimes Quarter Courts.

NO. I.

COLONIAL RECORDS.

(Volume I.)

[1]   A Corte holden att Newton, 26 Apr. 1636.

Roger Ludlowe, Esqr.,   Mr. Westwood,
Mr. Steele,   Mr. Warde.
Mr. Phelps,

Constables sworne, for Dorchester, Newtowne & Watertowne, for this next yeere and vntill newe be chosen, are Henry Walcott for Dorchester, Samuell Wakema for Newtowne & Daniell Finch for Watertowne.

21 Febr. 1636.

Mr. Ludlowe,   Mr. Phelps,
Mr. Steele,   Mr. Westwoode.
Mr. Swaine,

Whereas, it was ordered yt Samuel Wakeman, Geo: Hubbert, & Anncient Stoughton were to consider of the boundes of Dorchester towarde the Falls & of Watertowne towards the mouth of the River; The saide Samuel Wakeman & [Geo:] Hubberd thinkes meete yt the plantacon of Dorchester shall extend towards the Falls, on the same side the Plantacon standes, to a Brooke called Kittle Brooke, & soe over the greate River vppon the same line that Newe Towne & Dorchester doth betweene them. And soe it is ordered by the Corte.

It is ordered that the plantacon nowe called Newtowne shall be called & named by the name of Harteford Towne, likewise the plantacon now called Watertowne shalbe called & named Wythersfeild.

Samuell Wakeman & Ancient Stoughton doe thinke meete that the boundes of Wythersfeild shalbe extended toward the Rivers mouth, in the same side it standes in, to a Tree six miles downeward from the boundes between them & Harteford [marked wth] N :F : & to [runn in an east] & west line, [& over] the great River, the saide Wythersfield to begin att [4] the mouth of Pewter pott Brooke & there to runn due east into the Countrey 3 miles & downeward sixe miles in breadth, wch is ordered accordingly.*

---

*The words in brackets (now illegible in the original Record) are here supplied from a certified copy of this and the next preceding order, made in 1708.

It is ordered yt the plantacon called Dorchester shalbee called Windsor.

The boundes betweene Wethersfeild & Harteford are agreed on the side wherein they stand to be att a Tree mrked N :F : & to wch the Pale of the saide Harteford is fixed, to goe into the Countrey due east & on the other side of the greate River from Pewter pott Brook att the lower side of Hocanno due east into the Countrey, wch is nowe ordered accordingly.

The boundes betweene Harteford & Windsor is agreed to be att the vpper end of the greate meadowe of the saide Harteford toward Windsor att the Pale that is nowe there sett vpp by the saide Harteford wch is abuttinge vppon the great River vppon a due east line, & into the Countrey from the saide Pale vppon a due west line as paralell to the saide east line as farr as they have now paled, & afterward the boundes to goe into the Countrey vppon the same west line.   But it is to be soe much shorter towards Windsor as the place where the Girte that comes alonge att th' end of the saide meadowe & falls into the saide greate River is shorter then their Pale, & over the saide great Riuer the saide Plantacon of Windsor is to come to the Riveretts* mouth that falls into the saide great River of Conectecott, and there the saide Harteford is to runn east into the Countrey, wch is ordered accordingly.

[2]   Page 5.

Guilford, June 16: 1665†

This is to certify unto all whom it may concerne, that vpon his certaine knowledge, by the advice of the Court, Wethersfeild men gaue so much unto Sowheag as was to his sattisfaction for all their plantations lyeing on both sides the great Riuer, wth the Islands, viz. six miles in bredth on both sides the Riuer, & six miles deep from the River westward, and three miles deep from the Riuer eastward.   Thus testifyeth George Hubbard.   By me GEORGE HUBBARD.

Taken upon oath Before me, Wilm Leete;

This is a true coppy of the originell, being examined & compared therewith this 18 of May, 1667, pr me

John Allyn: Secretry.

---

* ·(*In margin*) The Riuerett on the other side by the Indians is called Podanke.

†This certificate is inserted at the foot of the 2d Page of the original in the handwriting of Mr. Allyn.

PROBATE RECORDS.

VOLUME I.

1635 to 1650.

[269] Page 505.

Allyn, Samuel, Wyndsor. (Buried 28 April, 1648.—W. R.). Invt. £76-18-08. Taken 8th September, 1648, by Henry Clarke and David Wilton.

The Inventory of the Estate of Samuel Allyn, late of Windsor, Dec'd, is as followeth:

	£ s d
Imp. The Howsing and Home lottes, £11	) 18-00-00
It. 4 acres of Meadow, £7	)
It. 15 acres ouer the Great Riuer,	) 15-00-00
It. 18 acres of Vpland,	) 04-10-00
It. In Goodes; one Bed with his Furniture,	) 05-00-00
It. two beds more, &c	) 02-14-00
It. one pillowbeere, one table cloath & Napkins,	) 00-10-08
It. his wearing apparrell,	) 05-05-00
It. 3 Iron potts, £2-05; in brass, £1-10; in pewter £1	) 04-15-00

Henry Clarke   £76-18-08
Dauid Wilton.

Page 115.

Bedle, Robert, is adiudged to restore double for the seuerall thefts acknowledged by him, and to be seuerly whipped, and branded in the hand, vppo Wensday next. Bedle stole fro Mr. Blakman, of gunpowder, ij pownd: Fro wydowe Foote, of Rye, iiij bush; Fro Tho: Welles, 2 sacks; Fro Rich: Mylls, 1 blanket: Fro Tho: Tracy, 1 sacke.

[70] Page 444.

Brundish, John, Wethersfield. Invt. £174-06-00 in Goods & Cattle, & £130 in Lands. Taken 27 October, 1639, by Andrew Ward, Richard

Gyldersly. Shee hath 5 Children: the 2 eldest, girls; the next, a boy; the other 2, girls. A noate brought in Court since the Inuentry, as followeth: Rachell Brundishe hath 14 acres of meadow, her howse lott 3 acres, and wt vpland belongs thereunto in euery diuysion, saueing wt her husband and shee hath sould, vizt: her shaire beyond the Riuer and 6 acres in Penny wise.

Court Record, Page 40—7 November, 1639. Adms. to the Widow. Decree, Page 45—2 Aprill, 1640; To the Widow, £90-05-04. The Land and House to be for the Children's portions, vizt: £30 to the sonne, and £25 apeice to each of the 4 daughters; to be payd into the Court for their Use when each of them come to the age of 16 years, and in the meane tyme the Widow to haue the Use of the Land for the bringing vp the Children.

[251]   Page 482.

Butler, William, Hartford. Invt. £429-03. Taken by John Cullick, and William Gibbins. Will dated 11 May, 1648.

I William Butler, of Hartford, in Conectecot; doe meake and ordayne this my last will and testament wherein I give my earthly goods as followeth: And first I meake my brother Richard Butler, dwelling in Hartford, my sole Executor. All that is left of my lands and goods, when he hathe payd all the legeses vnder ritene, I give to him. It. I give my Sister Weste's Children, that ear now living in olld Ingland, five pounds apese. It. I give my Sister Winter's Childrene, that eare nowe living in Ingland, five pounds apese. It. I give my loveing frendes of Hartford, Mr. Stone and Mr. Goodwin and Mr. Hoker and Mr. John Stelle, ten pounds apese. It. I give to the Churtche of Hartford, three Schore pounds; and farther I doe earnestly desier my tow frendes, Mr. John Colicke and William Gibbince, both of Hartford, to see that this my last will and testament be follfiled, and for there lowe and paynes I doe bequeath to etche of them thre pounds apes.

In Witness wherof I, the said Will Butler, have set tow my hand this Eleventh of May, 1648.   WILLIAM X BUTLER.

(This will copied from original paper on file.)

[69]   Page 457.

Cattell, John, Hartford. Invt. £69-00-00. Taken 17 July, 1644, by John Coleman and Samuel Hales.

Court Record, Page 110, September, 1644. The Inventory of John Cattell was brought into Court by Will' Gybbins & his widdowe, to administer.

Witness: *Thos. Coleman.*
            Sam. Hale.
            Tho. Thompson.

[259]   Page 492.

Chalkwell, Edward. Invt. £13-07-08. Taken 5 December, 1648. Will dated 17 October 1648. Imprimis: I doe bequeath vnto Nicholas Sension, my gunn and sword and bandaleers and best hatt and 40 shillings: Item. to John Moses, my best Sute and Coate and Stockings and Shoes: Item. to Mr. Warham, 40 Shillings, according as my Goods doe hould out, after my debts bee paid: Item. to George Phelps, £3, and if anything bee left I giue it to the poore of the Church. And I do make George Phelps Executor to this my Will and Testament.   (Not signed.)

Witness: *Henry Woollcott,*
            Nicholas Sension.

[From the Original Copy on File.]

Clarke, Joseph, Windsor. Died 19 April, 1641. (W. R.) Invt. £44-00-00. Taken by Henry Clarke and William Gaylord. Will dated 1st December, 1640. I, Joseph Clarke, of Windsor, being somewhat weake but of prfect memory, doe make and ordayne this my last Will & Testament: First, I bequeath my Soule to God, waiting for his Salvation through ye alone merit of Jesus Christ, and my Body to Christian Buriall at ye discretion of my Executors. And as for my worldly Goods, I thus dispose of ym: I bequeath my Estate in Lands and Goods to my two Children in ye Discretion of mine Executors, ye wch office I desire ye Church by ye ministers & ye Deacons & Oversight of ye Elders to vndertake; and my desire is yt my House and Lott should be Let and Farmed at Rent for 10 or 12 years & ye Rent yearly to goe towards ye maintenance of ye Children so long; and if yt will not suffice ym maintenance, & ye Church see it meete, my desire is yt my Lott joyning to ye Great River above sequestered Meadow bee go to for supply if need require; and ye sd. 10 or 11 years my desire is yt my 2 Children be sett forth in some Godly family for 6 or 7 years or more, in ye Churches Wisdome, and duringe ye sd. terme my desire is yt ye Rent of my House and Land bee resarved by ye deacons for to make portion for my daughter, to be paid unto her at ye age of 21 years; at wch time also my desire is my house and Land bee delivered to my sonne, to whome (in case it bee not otherwise in ye meantime disposed of by ye Church) I bequeath it forever; provided yt in case of sickness or any other disaster, my desire is yt ye Church doe dispose of my Estate otherwise as in yt discretions may best Conduce to ye Comfort of my Children.

                                         JOSEPH CLARKE.

Witness: *John Warham, Ephraim Huit,*
John Witchfield, Wm Hosford, William Gaylord.

(This Will is on Record in Vol. II, Page 64, Probate Records.)

Page 122.

Crumpe, Thomas, Hartford—Andrew Bacon and George Graues, on the 5th day of March, 1644, testified in Court, that they being wth Tho: Crumpe, when he was sicke, not long before his death, asking him how he would dispose of his Estate, he said, his debts being paid, he desired his master would doe wth yt as he pleased.

Ed: Hopkins Esqr, Govr, is admitted to administer the Estate of Tho: Crumpe, late of Hartford, Deceased.

---

[255]   Page 487.

Day, Robert, Hartford. Invt. £142-13-06. Taken 14 October, 1648, by John Tailecoate, Gregory Wilterton and Edward Stebbing. Will dated 20 May, 1648.

The Will of Robert Day, hee being sick and weake, yet in perfect memory, doth order and dispose of his Estate to his wife and Children, in the manner following:

I give unto my beloued wife, Edatha Day, my now dwelling house and Howsing thereto adjoyning, houselott. Also all my Land whereof I stand possessed, or that of Right doth belong to mee, lying in Hartford, during the tearme of her natural life; And at the end of her life, my Will is that the sd. house and Land shall bee for the vse of my Children that then shall bee liuing, to be divided in an equall proportion: my Will also is that all my howshold Stuff, and Cattle and other moueable Goods, shall bee my wiue's, to bring vp my Children: And in case my wife should be married to another man, then my survivors of my Will shall haue power, if they thinke good, to take security for the bringing vp of the Children, and for soe much Estate as shall bee thought meete by them; and to this my last Will and Testament I make my wife Executrix, and I doe desire my Deare Brethren Mr. Tailecoate, Wilterton and Stebbing to take Care of and Assist my wife in the ordering herselfe and my Children; and I give them power to doe what in their judgements may be for the Best, to bring vp my Children and dispose of them, and that I leave for their Good. And to this my Will I sett to my hand the day above written.

Witness: *Edward Stebbing,*   ROBERT DAY.
            Walter Gaylord.

---

[249]   Page 480.

Dewey, Thomas, Windsor (who married Frances Clarke, 22 March, 1638) Buried 27 April, 1648—(W. R.) Invt. £213-00-00. Taken 19 May, 1648, by David Wilton and Robert Winchell. Six Children, 4 Boyes and two girles: Mary Clarke, 12 years old; Thomas Dewey, 8, Josiah, 7; Annah, 5; Israel, 3; Jydidiah Dewey, ¾ of a year old.

Court Record, Page 168—17 October, 1648. Dist. of the Estate of
Thomas Dewey was ordered as followeth:

	£ s d
To the Relict,	60-00-00
To his eldest son by name Thomas Dewey,	30-00-00
And to the other 5 children, £20 apeice,	100-00-00
	190-00-00

The daughters' portions of £20 to be paid them at the age of 18 years,
and the seuerall sons' portion at the age of 21 years; the Relict giving in
sufficient security to the Children for their several portions.   George
Phelps and Frances Dewey were married 30 November, 1648 (W. R.)
   Court Record, Vol. II, Page 9—6 June, 1650: It is agreed and con-
cluded betwixt this Court, in the behalf of the Children of Thomas Dewey,
and Geo: Phelps, of Wyndsor, that the whole of the Land, both Meadow
and Upland, mentioned in sd. Dewey's Inventory, amounting to the sum of
£78, shall be sequestered for the Children's portions so farr as it goes,
and the remainder, being £52, hee Ingages himself to give into the Court
sufficient security for the payment thereof, according to the Will of the
Court.   The House and peice of Land belonging to it, valued at £40, the
sd. Phelps accepts upon his wive's part of the Estate.
   Page 2 (Vol. III) 4 June, 1663: Upon the Request of George Phelps
and Frances, his wife, this Court do appoint Lt. Fyler, Robert Winchell
and Matthew Grant to judge of the difference of the Land of Thomas
Dewey, Deceased, for an equal Division amongst the children of sd.
Dewey.

---

[247]   Page 479.

   Elsen, Abraham, Wethersfield. Invt. £99-11-00. Taken 8 May, 1648,
by Sa: Smith, Nath: Dickinson, Tho: Hurlebutt.

	£ s d
Impris his apparell att	9-00-00
Ite: in wheat & pease,	3-05-00
It: in Indean, att	1-10-00
It: in meale & molte,	1-00-00
It: one bed & Bedding,	5-00-00
It: his Husbandry Tooles	3-10-00
It: Chests & a bed ticke, & wooden vessell,	2-10-00
It: his brasse, in potts & kettells,	2-10-00
It: his arms & amunition	1-15-00
It: his house, homelotte & mea: att	40-08-00
It: his Cattell, att	18-10-00
It: his hoggs, att	5-10-00
It: that wch is due to him fro other,	5-03-00
Som:	99-11-00

The Wyddow is admitted to administer. She hath two daughters, on 3 years old and the other a yeare & ½. Hannah, the daughter of Abraham Elsen and Rebeckah his wife, was born 1 August, 1646. Sarah, the daughter of Abraham Elsen and Rebeckah his wife, was born——— (Wethersfield's Records.)

Court Record, Page 162—9 March, 1647: The Inventory of Abraha Elsen was brought into Court. Page 202—6 December, 1649: This Court doth sequester the Howse, Homelott and Meadow of the Relict of Abraham Elsing, now the wife of Jaruis Mudge, wch is mentioned and valued in the Inventory of Abraham Elsing's Estate £40-08-00, for the Vse and Benefit of the two daughters of the sd. Abraham Elsing; and the whole rent of the aforesd. premises shall bee reserued for the vse of the sd. Children from this present yeare vntill the Rent of the sd. Land shall make vpp the sd. £40-08-00 to bee 2-3 of the sum of the whole Estate that the sd. Inventory doth ammount vnto.

(This Item, following, appears on the Inventory side, Page 479):

This 6th of June, 1655: An Account of ye House and Land of ye Heirs of Abraham Elsen, deceased, in Wethersfield, rented out by us, Nath: Dickinson and Sam: Smith, foure years, for ye raising of ye Children's portions, according to ye appointment of this Court, unto Thomas Hurlbutt, at £4-10-00 ye year, voth ye use of £4-10-00 for 3 years: yt is to say, ye Rent is £10-00-00 yee Use is   £2-01-07.

	£ s d
Ye Rent is	18-00-00
Ye Use is	2-01-07
	20-01-07
Laid out for Ground selling ye House	20-01-07
And for necessary Charges layd out of Purse	1-10-00
There remains	18-11-07

For wch £18-11-07, Wee, sd. Nath: Dickinson and Sam: Smith, doth by our Hands ye day and yeare above said, secure the sd. portions for ye Children, either till they come of age or till the Court be pleased to call us to accot.   PR NATH: DICKINSON.
                                                SAMUEL SMITH.
(See Nathaniel Greensmith, Vol. II.)

[249]   Page 480.

Elsen, John, Wethersfield. Invt. of the Goods & Land of John Elsen of Wethersfield, on Connecticott River, wch he was cesed on when he dyed. Prysed the sixteenth of May, by Sa. Smith and Nath. Dickinson:

	£ s d
Imp. his Apparrell,	6-18-00
Ite. his Cattell, hoggs & a mare,	67-10-00
Ite. his cart, and plows, wth husbandry tooles,	8-10-00
Ite. his brasse, and pewter, and iron vessell,	5-00-00
Ite. his tables, and forms, chests, & tubbs, and other wooden vessell, and some other things,	5-10-00
Ite. his corne, and meat, and molte,	6-00-00
Ite. his bedds, and bedding, woollen & lynin, with some leather,	14-10-00
Ite. his arms and ammunition,	2-00-00
Ite. his corn vppon the ground,	8-13-04
Ite. his howse & barne & homelott, and other land,	87-00-00
Ite. debts wch were owing him,	8-10-00
Ite. his books,	1-00-00
	£221-01-04

A coppy of the dispose of his estate, before Mr. Smith: To my B. Gardner's children, land att the meadowe gate; to my Br'. Gardner. my coate; to Mr. Smith, £5; My loveing wife, all the rest. Only the howse and land to her two sons, after her life; 11 acres of meadowe, howse & lotte, 3 roods of meadowe to B. Gardner's boy. The howse & home lott to Ben; the meadowe to be divided between him & Job.

Witness: *Henry Parke.*   JOHN X. ELSIN.
    Henry Smith.

Wethersfield Records, Vol. I, Page I. (1640) 16 March, 1641.

Hillyard's Bond: This present writing witnesseth, that I, Benjamin Hillyard, of Wethersfield, on Connecticut River, being fined by the Cou(rt) ten pounds, and caused by the Court to pro(cure) a bond of ten to be of good behavior for twelve months after the prticular Court, being the first thursday of this Instant March, my father-in-law, Tho Wright, being bound for me for my good behavior in ten pounds, as also for and in consideratio for the paym for me the first ten pounds, I do bind me, my heirs, executs or assigns, to fully satisfy or cause to fully satisfy my father, Tho. Wright, the ten pounds in currant pay within a twelve month after the day of the date hereof, and do further ingage me, my exse and assigns, to keep harmless or warrant my said father for his bond of ten pounds wch he is Ingaged for me unto Court and County, standing bound in the ten pounds in the Court Roules, and (for the) better securing of my said father-in-law,(trans)fer my house, and barne, and home lot, that was given me by my father-in-law, John Elsen, in his last will & Testament, in (re) version after the decease of my mother, and if the said Benjamin Hillyard preserve these covenants according as he ingages himself, then this obligation to be void and of none effect.
Witness: *Nath. Dickinson of Wethersfield,*
    Keeper of the Records.

Page 162—Ante. At a Court held 9 March 1647.
The Inventories of John Elsen & Abraha Elsen are brought into Courte.
A Caueat put agt both Wills by Sam: Gardner.
The Wyddow of John Elsen is allowed to administer.
Sa: Smith giueth security for the Estate.
Tho: Coleman vndertakes the Estate of Abraham Elsen shall be presearued vntil the Court settle the Adms.
The entries which follow in relation to the Estates of John and Abraham Elsen are in a different handwriting from the rest of the page, and were probably made some weeks subsequently.
Invt. of John Elsen was taken 16 May (Probably 1648.)

---

[246]   Page 477.

Fenner, Thomas. Died 15 May, 164(7). Invt. of the Goods taken 17 May by Gn Luffun & Gn Northam:

	£ s d
Imprs. a peece of Trucking Cloath of about 4 yards,	00-32-00
A Jackette, a pre of breches,	30-00
1 Fowleing peece,	30-00
1 Racoone skine coate,	12-00
11 Beauer skins atte 8 Shillings pr pd,	08-00
21 kniues att 4 shillings a dozen,	07-00
2 lookeing glasses,	00-08
An old Hatt, stockings & shues,	03-00
a little iron potte,	06-00

Prysed by Gn Luffun & Gn Northam:.

A prcell of wooden ware, about	06-00-00

Ite: his boate & lyne wch he brought vp, a prcel of wampu, 16 peeces of Dutch mony in Mr. Whitings hand, the Boate & loading, Goods att Totokett of the sd. Tho:Fenners,   20-00-00

Prysed by Robert Rose & Jo: Plum:

Imprs. 1 peece of Trucking Cloth con. 24 yards at £0-7-6 pr yard,	9-01-10
Ite: 1 peece more of Vyolet cullered trucking cloath of 21 yards, at £0-7-6 pr yard,	7-17-06
Ite: On other peece of damask coulered trucking cloath. con. 13 yards, at £0-6-6 the yard,	4-04-06
Ite: 1 smale & course featherbed tecke & Boulster, wth some feathers put into them,	2-00-00
Ite: 1 course Courlette,	0-12-00
Ite: 2 Blanketts, 1 Cotton, the other cotton & lynen,	0-14-00
Ite: 1 weareing Coate,	1-05-00

Ite: 1 coate made of Catte skins,   0-10-00
Ite: 1 Coate made of Racoone skins,   0-10-00
Ite: 2 deer skins,1 foxe skin,& a pair of Indean stockins,   0-11-00
Ite: 1 old Sword £0-05 Ite:1 pair of shues,   0-05-06
Ite: 11 traplines £0-01- It: a litle oyle, in a half firkin,   0-01-06
Ite: A smale kettle, he vsed to boyle tar in,   0-02-00
Ite: 1 short coate made of darnixe,   0-06-00
Ite: 1 Portingale cap begun,made & unlyned, wth a smale
    peice of Cloth of the same,   0-04-00
Ite: in wampum,   1-00-00
Ite: 2 yards of blewe lynen, £0-06- Ite: 4 Bands,   0-04-00
Ite: 4 handkerchiefs, cut out, unmade,   0-06-00
Ite: 1 Kettell wch will hold about a pint,   0-02-00
Ite: 2 dozen & ½ of Jues trumps, £0-04- It: his Chest,   0-04-00
Ite: 3 yards & ½ of red broad cloth, at £0-18 pr yard,   3-03-00
Ite: 24 Bush :of Indean trucked wth Indeans at £0-2-6 pr Bush: 3-00-00

                              ROBERT ROSE.
                              JO: PLUM.

- - - - - - - - - - - - - - - - - - - -

[68]   Page 445.

Finch, Abraham. Invt. of Goods, Corne & Cattle, £137-17-00. Taken
3 September, 1640, by Sam: Smith, Nathaniel Foote.

                                                         £   s   d
Imprs. his Apparell,   2-06-00
Ite: one Cow,   20-00-00
Ite: one Heifer,   10-00-00
Ite: four swyne shoats,   2-00-00
Ite: one Cutting saw, one axe,   0-10-00
Ite: 3 prre of Sheets, 2 prre of pilloberes.   1-10-00
Ite: 5 Napkins,   0-03-00
Ite: 2 Kettles and 1 potte,   1-08-00
Ite: his howse lott, wth all deuisions belonging thereto, 100-00-00
                                                        ──────────
                    The some: £137-17-00

It (is) Ordered, that the Relike of Abraham Finch, deceased, shall
administer & possesse the Estate lefte in Goods, and also hold the Land
& Howseing untill the Child com to the age of 21 years, and then the Child
of the sd. Abraham to have 2 parts, and the sd. Relick duering her naturall
life the third ; the sd. Relick is to mayntayne the Child, or to comitte him to
his Grandfather Abraha Fynch, who tenders to educate yt at his owne
Coste ────── 3 December, 1640.

[115]   Page 461.

Foote, Nathaniel, Wethersfield. Invt. £380-17-00. Taken 20 November, 1644, by Richard Tratte, Samuel Smith and Nath: Dickinson.

		£ s d
The Children: Nathaniel Foote, about 24 years, to have		148-00-00
Robert Foote, " 17 " " "		74-00-00
Frances Foote, " 15 " " "		74-00-00
Sarah Foote, " 12 " " "		74-00-00
Rebeckah Foote, " 10 " " "		74-00-00
The Wyddow of sd. Nathaniel Foote Adms.her portion,		212-00-00

	£ s d
Imprs His purse and apparrell,	7-16-00
It. In neat Cattell and in Hay,	93-00-00
It. in horsse fleshe,	34-00-00
It. in hoggs,	66-60-00
It. in debts,	29-03-04
It. in Englishe Corne,	70-00-00
It. in goats,	3-15-00
It. in Carts, ploughs, etc.	6-00-00
It. in nayles,	1-10-00
Ite. Indean Corne,	8-00-00
It. in old Wheat and pease,	6-06-00
It. for certain things in the chamber,	2-00-00
It. for amunition,	5-00-00
Ite. for fouer beds wth the furniture,	13-06-08
It. in fyne lynen,	5-10-00
Ite. 2 table boards,2 chests,1 Trunke, wth other Implts.	5-00-00
It. pewter & brasse and other vseful vessells,	12-00-00
It. in husbandry tooles,	3-00-00
It. in beife, butter, and cheese and other neces- sary prvision for the howse.	8-10-00
It. in poultry,	1-00-00
somm :	£380-17-00

The Land:

Ten acres of home lotts wth one dwelling howse and 2 barnes wth other buildings therevppon,————
4 acres of home lotts,————
6 acres of meadow wth an acre of swampe,
20 acres of plaine fenced in being 14 ac. broke vp,
7 acres of plaine meadow plowed vp,
20 acres in the great meadow of hay ground,
4 acres in bever meadow,

27 acres of Swampe Ground,
81 Acres of Vpland in the Weste field
32 Rod broad beyond the River, being 3 Miles in length,

RICHARD TROTT, SAMUEL SMITH,
NATHANIEL DICKINSON.

Court Record, Page 115—11 December, 1644.' Mr. Heynes & Mr. Willis are desired to consider of the Estate of Nath: Foote, decd, and to take in what helpe they please fro any of the neighbours to advise how yt may be disposed of, and to report their apprehensions to the next Court.

P. C. No. 63-4-5.

Fokes, Henry, Windsor, had land set to him 16 May, 1640. He deceased & his widow married Mr. Hosford, who took possession of the place (23 Acres).

[230]   Page 465.

ffroste, William. (*Copy of the original paper on file*). His Last Will and Testament, where in The Said William Doth Give and Be Qeth All his Lands and Goods now in joying the sixt daye off Jenuary, one Thousand six hundred fforty ffouer.

I Give and Be queth tto My Eldest Sonn, Danill ffrost, Tooe partts of my medow and upland laid outt and To Laye outt, & the Home Loott Exsepted; And Also to the saide Daniell ffroste All my parts of The swampe And Redye ponds, and allso ffiffteene Eakers of medow That I bought of John Gray, Linge att Machuncohs,—or Sasgug, Comonly so Called ; And allso my Clloke and warmeing pan I give to ye saide Danill ffroste, his Aires, for Ever.—I Give—And Bequeth to Rebecker and Sarah ffroste That Blacke heffer that Danill ffroste Hath to winter. I give and Beqeth to my sonn Abraham ffroste All that Lotte and House, with All The Land Laid outt and to be Laid outt, that I Bought off John Sticklin with those mouveabls I boutt of him, And Also those Clothes one my Bead, And my Leettell Chest, and Allso my Tooe grett oxen, And my Tooe gret yerling Calffes, with all that is in mve Leettel chest, and one Third part of my housuld Goods. I give And Be queth to my Daughter Elisebeth and John Gray the Sowe that he hath to winter, And all hur increase, The third partt of my housuld Goods; And to Luke Wattson my Tooe yere ould black heffer that Goodman Close hatth tto the haffes ffor ffouer yeers, The profett to be fore the said Luke; And tto Susana and Johana Wattson, Daughters tto Elisabeth Grey, one Black hefer that John Gray hath tto the Haffes ffor ffouer yers, and the profit——tto Them Booth Equaly; and the Reade hefer that danill ffrost wintereth I Give to John Grays owne Tooe children, and The proffet Equaly tto Them Booth.

I Give And Beqeth to Henry Gray And Ledyee Gray ffor Their Lives, And affter them to Jacob, their sonn, all my house and home Lotte with that part that I changed with John ffoster, And The Third partt of my medoe and upland Laid outt and tto Lay ought; And tto Mary Gray, Daughter tto Henry Gray, I Give and bequeth my Reede heffer that Goodman Close hath tto wintter; And to Mary Rylie and hur children I Give and Beqeth all my Goods and Lands that I have in ould ingland. And to the Towne of uncowah I give and Beqeth Tene pounds in good paye Towards the building of a meeting house; to Be paide when itt is Halff Bultt; fferdermore I ordayne and make henry Gray of uncoway my Lafful Exsectore tto pay and discharge my Legacis and duttes and allso power tto reseve what is doue tto mee, and I give the fore said henry Gray ffull power tto sue and discharge ffor my dutes, or goodes that those presenc should stand in force affter my deses and nott befoar, and I Inttreatt Effrem Wheeller and danill ffrost tto be my ourseers tto se my will purfformed acording tto the inttentt Thereoff. They are tto have ten shillings ffor their pain; where tto I have put my hand and sell the day and dat hereof WILLIM FFROST LS

Witness: *Ephraim Wheeler,*
frances purdie,
Mary Purdie.

This explanation was written upon the reverse side of Frost's Will:
These are to explayne my meaneing of howshold goods; all my moveable goods or tables, excepte corne and Cattell and swyne. Further I would have Abraham, my sonne, to receave to his vse the rent of all howsing and land that I bought of John Sticklin; further, I will that Abraha, my sonne, pay no rent to Henry Greye, my sonne, nor Henry to him, but all former ingadgements to be voyd betwixt the in or about the lease. I will that two third prts of my land be devided as soone after my death as may be, yet so that my sonne Henry his lease be not disturbed.

Witness my (hand) WILLIAM FROST.

Witness: *Ephraim Wheeler, Frances Purdy, Mary Purdy.*

[268] Page 504.

Gibbs, Gyles, Wyndsor.—Know all men by these presents, that I, Gyles Gibbs, of Wyndsor, on Connecticutt, *yeoman,* being weake in body but of perfect understanding and memory, doe ordaine this my last will and testament as followth:

Impr. my will is that my sonne Gregory bee put forth an Apprentice to some Godly man for the space of five years at the discretion of my execut. and the overseers of this my last will; and if hee submitt there vnto and stay out his time to the likinge of my overseers, I doe then bequeath vnto him my lott ouer the great River, to him and his heires forever; in case my overseers have any incouragement to judge him worthy, otherwise at their discretion, I bequeath him £5 to bee paid him at the age of 21 yeares. Also, I give to my two sonnes, Samuel & Benjamin, £20 apeece; to my daughter Sarah, £20; to bee paid at the age of 21 years. And to Jacob, my sonne, I give my howse and lotts, meadows, home lotte, and great lott and lottes whatsoever, on this side the great Riuer, after his mothers life. And to my wife I give all my lottes, howses, all my househould goods, Cattells, & Chattells, my debts being discharged; provided that in case my said overseers have no good incouragement concerning the disposition of my sonne Gregory, but doe judge him unworthy a fathers blessing vnder their hands, my will is that my exceut: shall have the said lotte towards the Education of my children vntil my sonne Jacob shall attain the age of 21 yeares, and then my will is that my sonne Jacob shall have it to him and his heires for ever. And Executrixe, of this my last Will, I appointe Katharine my wife. And overseers of this my Will and Testament, I appointe the Deacons of the Church of Wyndsor, at all times in being. Blessed bee God.   GYLES GIBBS.

Witness: 18 May, 1641.
John Warham
Ephraim Huitt.

Postscript: I giue to Elizaphatt Gregory 10 bushells of Corne in case hee discharge the debt I gave my worde for him to Mr. Huitt. And to Richard Wellar I give 40s by 20s a yeare, beginninge from September next.

Witness: John Warham
        Ephraim Huitt.

---

[250]   Page 481.

Grant, Seth. A trew and prfecte Inventory of the goods and Chattells of Seth Grant, of Hartford, Deceased. Invt. £141-10-08. Taken 4 March, 1646:

	£ s d
Impris *In the parlowre:* one great table iο; ʔ iσ˙ ʾed	
stooles, 6s; two chaire, 4s 6d; on ˙l.e˙ι ˙	1-06-06
It. *in the lodgeing roome:* 1 fetherbed ὰ · pillowes,	3-10-00
It. one rugge 20s; one flock bolster, 10s ; ʒ · .etts &	
one couerlett, £1-10,-	3-00-00
It. 5 Curtens, 12s 6d; one bedsted and strawe bedd, £1,	1-12-06
It. one trundle bed, 7s; fower sheets & one board cloath, £3-10s,	3-17-00
It. 3 sheets, £3-10s; fower sheets, £1; 5 perre of pillobers, £1-10s.	6-00-00
It. a parcell of linen cloath, £2-0; one table cloath	
& 3 napkins, 12s,	2-12-00

It. 1 graue cloath 3s; three towells, 4s 6d; smale boxe
    wth some child bed linnen,   0-12-06
It. 2 Chests, 4 boxes, 13s4d; one cubberd, 5s; one warmeing
    panne, 6s8d,   1-05-00
It. *in the Hall:* one Table, 2 forms, 1 chaire, one muskett,
    bandaleers & sowrd,   1-11-08
It. 1 paire of cobirons, 1 slyce, 1 paire of tongs,
    1 prre of bellows, 2 perre of Tramells,   0-14-00
It. 7 smale books, 8s; one spit & Gridiron, 4s; 2 brasse
    kettles, £1-5s; three brasse posnetts, 10s,   2-07-00
It. on paile wth an iron baile, 1s 6d; 2 Iron potts &
    pott hooks, £1; one bell mettell morter & iron pestel,   1-06-06
It. 2 smale bear vessels, 4s; a cowl, 2s 8d; an hower
    glasse, 2s,   0-08-08
It. 2 wedges, 2 axes, 2 betel rings, 8s. It. 10 pewter
    dishes, £2-4s; 4 smale dishes, 4s,   2-16-00
It. 1 pewter quart, 1 halfe pinte, 1 beker, 1 Candlestick,
    2 salts, 3 porringer, 2 saucers & basan,   0-15-10
It. 2 pair of new shoos, 10s; one peir of boots, 7s; 4
    cushions & his weareing apparrell,   3-03-08
It. *in the chambers;* 29 bush of wheate, £5-16s; 10 bush.
    of pease, £1-10s; To 7 Bushels of Indean Corne, £0-17s,   8-03-00
It. two bush. of Indean molt, 5s; 7 bush. of oats, 12s;
    13lb. of towe, 6s:4d; 25 pownd of hempe teare, £1-5s.   2-08-04
It. *in the yards:* 1 Cowe, £6; two hoggs, £1-10s,   7-10-00
It. on dwelling howse wth the barne, & home lott Cont
    1 acre, 1 rood,   40-00-00
It. *in the north meadow:* 1 prcell of meado Cont 3 roods.
    on prsell of meadow & swampe Cont :3 ac-3 roods &
    27 prches,   24-10-00
It. 2 roods, 4 prches, of meadow on the east side of the
    great River, £2; 1 acre of swampe, £2; and 32 acres of
    vpland, £30,   34-10-00
                                                            _____
4th March, 1646.   The total sume as ther cast vppe   £141-10-08

---

[263]   Page 498.

Hooker, Thomas, Hartford. Invt. £1136-15-00. Taken 21st April,
1644, by Nathaniel Ward & Edward Stebbing. Will dated 7 July, 1647.

I, Thomas Hooker, of Hartford, uppon Connecticutt, in New England, being weakened in my body through the tender visitation of the
Lord, but of sound & prfect memory, doe dispose of that outward estate
I have been betrusted withall by him, in maner following: I doe give unto
my sonne Jno. Hooker, my housing and Lands in Hartford aforesaid, both
that wch is on the west and also that wch is on the east syde of ye River,

to be injoyed by him and his heires for ever, after the death of my wife Susannah Hooker, provided he be then att. the age of one & twenty yeares. It being my will that my sayd deare wiefe shall injoy and possess my sayd Howsing & Lande during her naturall life, and yf she dy before my sonne Jno come to the aforesaid age of one & twenty yeares, that the same bee improved by the overseers of this my will for the maintenence and education of my children not(   )disposed of, according to their best discretion. I doe also give unto my sonne Jno my Library of printed books and manuscripts, under the limittations and provisoes hereafter expressed. It is my will that my sonne Jno. deliver to my sonne Samuel Soe many of my books as shall be valued by the overseers of this my will to be worth fifty pounds sterling, or that he pay him the summe of fifty pounds Sterling to buy such books as may be useful to him in thee way of his studdyes, att such tyme as the overseers of this my will shall Judge meett. But if my sonne Jno. doe not goe on to the prfecting of his Studdyes, or shall not give up himselfe to the service of the Lord in the worke of the ministry, my will is that my Sonne Samuel enjoy and possesse the whole Library and manuscripts to his proper use forever; onely, it is my will that whatever manuscripts shall be Judged meett to be printed, the disposall thereof and advantage that may come thereby I leave wholy to my executrix; and in case she depart this life before the same be Judged of and Settled, then to my overseers to be improved by them in their best discretion, for the good of myne, according to the trust reposed in them. And however I doe not forbid my sonne Jno from seeking and takeing a wife in England, yett I doe forbid him from marrying and tarying there. I doe give unto my sonne Samuel, in case the whole Library come not to him, as is before expressed, the summe of Seventy pounds, to be payd unto him by my Executrix att such tyme and in such maner as shall be judged meetest by the overseers of my will. I doe also give unto my daughter Sarah Hooker, the summe of one hundred pounds Sterling, to be payd unto her by my Executrix when she shall marry or come to the age of one and twenty years, wch shall first happen; the disposall and further education of her and the rest, I leave to my wife, advising them to attend her counsell in the feare of the Lord. I doe give unto the two children of my daughter Joanna Sheperd, deceased, and the child of my daughter Mary Newton, to each of them the summe of tenn pounds, to be payd unto them by my son John within one year after he shall come to the possession and injoyment of my Houseing & Lands in Hartford, or my Son Samuell, if by the decease of Jno he come to injoy the same. I doe make my beloved wiefe Susannah Hooker, Executrix of this my Last will and Testament, and (my just debts being payd) doe give and bequeath unto her all my estate and goodes, moveable and immoveable, not formerly bequeathed by this my last will. And I desire my beloved friends, Mr. Edward Hopkins and Mr. William Goodwyn, to affoard their best assistence to my wife, and doe constitute and appoint them the overseers of this my will. And itt haveing pleased the Lord now to visitt my wife with a sickness, and know not how itt may please his Matie to dispose of her, my mind &

will is, that in case she depart this life before she dispose of the estate bequeathed her, my aforesaid beloved friends, Mr. Edward Hopkins and Mr. William Goodwyn, shall take charge both of the education and dispose of my children (to whose love and faithfullness I comend them) and of the estate left & bequeathed to my wiefe, and doe comitt itt to their best judgement and discretion to manage the sayd estate for ye best good of mine, and to bestow itt uppon any or all of them in such a proportion as shall be most suitable to their owne apprehensions. Being willing onely to intimate my desire that they wch deserve best may have most, but nott to Lymett them, but leave them to the full scope and bredth of their owne Judgement; in the dispose whereof, they may have respect of ye forementioned children of my two daughters, if they see meete. It being my full will that what trust I have comitted to my wife, either in matter of estate or such manuscript as shall be judged fitt to be printed, in case she live not to order the same herselfe, be wholly transferred and past over from her to them for ye ende before specifyed. And for mortality sake I doe putt power into the hands of the forementioned Beloved friends to constitute and appoint such other faithfull men as they shall judge meett (in case they be deprived of life or libberty to attend the same in their owne persons), to manage, dispose, and performe the estate and trust comitted to them in as full maner as I have comitted it to them for the same ende.   THOS. HOOKER

This was declared to be the last will and testament of Mr. Thomas Hooker, the seventh day of July, 1647, in the presence of *Henry Smith, Sam. Stone, John White.*

[252]   Page 483.

Horskins, John, Windsor. Invt. £338-06-08. Taken 20 June, 1648, by Will Gaylord, Thomas Stoughton, David Willton. Will dated 1st May, 1648.

I give to the Church £3, to be distributed by the Deacons unto the poor, to be paid in wheat or pease, as wee are able. My Servant, Sammuel Rockwell, if he be willing to Serve in my house one quarter of a year after his covenant is out which he hath formerly made, my will is that at the end of his service he shall have £6 of mee; if not willing, then he shall receive £4 at the completion of his term of service already covenanted. Some persons owe mee small sums of Corn: Robert Winchell, Thomas Hollcombe, Samuel Gaylord, Abraham Randall; I leave all to my wife and Son Thomas, they to collect debts & make payments.   JOHN HORSKINS.

Witness: *Thomas Hoskins,
Samuel Rockwell, Abraham Randall.*

[54]   Page 457.

Hunt, Blaynch. Invt. £43-16-03. Taken 20 September, 1644, by Andrew Ward and Will Gybbins.

I, Blaynch Hunt, doe make my last will: Imprs: I give my best suite of weareing Cloathes to my Cossen Mary Robins, & a prre of my best blanketts; Ite: I give my Cossens in the howse twenty Shillings a peece, in gold or sylver, if yt can be made upp att my decease. Ite: For the rest of my estate in howsehold stuffe & debts I comitt to the dispose of my Vnckle Welles, only I remit 40s I lent my Cossen Mary Robins; I make my Vnckle Welles my Executor. I give my Cossen Mary Baylding VI yards of Kersey.

                                        BLAYNCH HUNT.

---

[297]   Page 458.

Huit, Ephraim, Wyndsor. Invt. £633-19-01. Taken 9 November, 1644, by Will Gaylord, Will Hill, Henry Clarke.

I give to my wife my dwelling house and home lott down to the Swamp, with all the howseing thereon; My meadow lott of 14 acres more or less, my lott of 15 acres with the swampe adjoyneing thereto; also I give unto her Tho. Stairs, his house, and the square plot of gardens lying beyond the Swamp to the highway. I give to my daughter Susanna & dau. Mercy my great lott lying behind the hogpen, adjoyning to Daniel Clarke & Humphrey Hide. I give to my two younger daughters, Lydea & Mary, my great lott at the Falls, containing fower score and two rodde in breadth, to make them two lotts together. I give to my daughters, Susanna & Mercy, my right and Interest in the Grant of the towne made me of 15 acres of meadow when yt shall com. first into their hands, about Pequanucke. My great Island at the Falls I give to the Court at Hartford for the use of the Country, my debts to be paid out of my personal estate; and all the rest, both wth in dores and wth out, I give to my wife, whether Lands or Goods. I appoint David Wilton and Daniel Clarke to be Executors, only they shall not meddle wth anything wth in dores; and the Overseers of this my will I intreat the Deacons of our Church to be.

                                        EP. HUIT.

Vol. 1, Page 59, of Lands, Sec. State's Office:

Henry Clarke, of Windsor, hath by Purchase of Isabell Huit, Widow of Ephraim Huit, deceased, & wth thee consent of the Administrators & Overseers of the Estate of the said Ephraim, his dwelling house, out housing, wth appurtenances belonging to it, his home Lott containing Sixe acres more or lesse, as it takes in two acres one quarter purchased by the said Ephraim of David Wilton, who sold it as hee was Agent for Thomas Stayers, & is bounded West by the street called the Pallisado, North by

George Phillips, South by the Land of the said Henry, East by a high way that devided it, and the meadow of Job Drake (with 3 other parcells).

Henry Clarke hath purchased of Major John Mason, his mansion house, out housing, orchard, wth all appurtenances, the land in quantity three acres one quarter upon the hill & running downe into the meadow, in breadth thirteen rods, & is bounded east & west by high wayes, & south in part as upon the hill, & running downe by Samuel Marshall, North by Land that was Ephraim Huits, deceased, with 3 other Parcells of Land.

Dates wanted not found. The latest date by subsequent insertion is 1680. This Vol. No. 1 appears to be made up of several parts of Records of Land: Hartford 2 parts, each part indexed separately: Windsor, one part, Wethersfield one part, Stamford one part & Farmingtown one part, Saybrook one part & Pequat one part.

Page 468.

Ierland, Samuel. Died 20 May, 1639. Invt. £70-00-00. Taken by Tho. Vffoote, Jo. Edwards.

(Report) : A trewe Inventory, as neere as we can find out, of all goods, corne, and Cattle and Lands, of Samuel Ierland. His Howse and lotts wth 8 acres of meadowe & all dividents vnsold, prysed at £40-00-00. His Apparell and prsonall Estate, £10-00-00. His Hoggs, £20-00-00. Som, £70-00-00.

Court Record, Page 137. 5 March, 1645: (The) Inventory of sd. Ierland is brought into Court by Jo. Edwards, And the wife of Robert Burrows, who was wife to (the) deceased, is to administer & to have the thirds, the other two prts to be for the Children.

---

[75]   Page 453.

Johnson, Thomas. Invt. per sale, £10-13-05, per Andrew Bacon & John Barnard, who were appointed by the Court to sell them.

Page 49: 11 April, 1640. Andrew Bacon & John Barnard have returned into the Court an Inventory of the goods of Tho. Johnson, deceased, to the some of £11-05-10.

Page 55: 2 July, 1640. Andrew Bacon & John Barnard are appointed to sell the goods of the Cobler (Thomas Johnson), deceased, formerly taken by Inventory given into Courte by the said partys—and due £10 from Goodman Hill.

---

[240]   Page 473.

Lotham, William. 20th March, 1645. A prticular of all debts oweing & also by him oweing:

Impr. Debts to him oweing, first from Mr. Robins for
   deliuring Robert Bedle at Fishers Iland, accor-   £ s d
   ding to Mr. Robins desire,   1-14-00
Ite. to him due fro Walter baker, for tobaco,   06-00
Ite. to him due fro Goodman Comstocke, for tobaco,   06-00
Fro Seargent Bryan, for transporting 2 butts of Sacke
   from Mr. Leches,   16-00
   also fro Seargent Bryan vppon Mr. Tapens account, 1-09-00
Fro. Seargent Bryan, more in sope,   3-00-00
from Henry Townsend, £1. Ite. fro John Ogden,   1-15-00
fro Mr. Mitchell, for carrieing goods,   3-19-00
fro Goodma Carman, 0-6s. Ite. fro Mr. Olderton,   1-00-00
fro Frances Homes, 36 pound of Iron
        Debts by him oweing to the prsons following:
Imprs. To one Elias, his servant formerly, about   3-00-00
   To Michaell Chatterton,   0-10-00
   To Frances Homes,   0-06-00
to Latha as long as he is myne after, sixe and twenty Shillings a month.
         A prticular of his goods, as followeth:
   Imprs. 3500 of planke, 6000 Trunnells, 500 of Iron, part att Frances
Homes, part att Mr. Tappings, the rest in a grapnell lying att the Water-
side.
   Ite. a barrell and three quarters of tarre and pitch, lying att the water-
side.
   Ite. a sow in Edmund Sticlins hands.
   Ite. a boate of tenn tun, wth two owres, an anker, a grapnell, maine-
sale and fore sale, a iron pott, a new sute of cloathes, shues, hatt, stockins,
three shirts, 6 hand charses, 2 bands, a gunn, one hundred nynty three
pickes, on auger, one draweing knife.

---

   2 Chessells, 2 Cauking irons, some heads for clinke worke, a scraper,
a breast wimble, one iron wedge, a frying pan, a skellette, a sacke wth
some biskitt in yt, another old Sacke vsed for a bedd, an axe, a perre of
pinsers, 2 hamers, a gymlett, 2 Indean baggs, a file, a butter tube, a powder
horne, a prre of old Stockings, an old Buckett, an old Kettell to make fyer
in, a Mallett, a wooden dishe, a platter, a little box, on gouge, on narowe
chessell, a chest, an iron candle sticke, 2 owers, 2 setting poles an hales
peare, a pocket compasse, a skefe & two Owyres.
   These severall prticulars appeareing under the lyne were added vppon
a vewe taken in the Boate the same morneing the Testator dyed, by others
& Will Wells. [241] Whereas on the other side hereof there is prticulars
of the Debts & Credits and Goods of Willia Lotha, wch appears best vnder
each prticular matter, and thereunto as his memory may be [   ]
being he was now visited by the Hand of the Almighty Jehovah wth sickness, having, in prsence of vs whose names are hereunder subscribed, declared his mynd and Will to be, that in Case a period be put to his days

before alteratio hereof, then, his just Debts being defrayed out by his prsonal Estate, the remaynder hereof is by him given & bequeathed to John Clarke and John Ogden, who he maks joynt Executors of this his last Will & Testament, equally to be divided betwixt them. Witness my Hands the day and year wth in written.

In presence of vs

Will' Wells, Ed: More,
Isacke Nicholls, George Allsoope.

September the 27th, 1645.

An Inventory of the Goods of Will' Lotha, late Decd:

	£ s d
Imprs a Boat 8 tun more or lesse valued at £0-30 pr tun,	12-00-00
One grapnell, on anker about a C. and ¼,	3-10-00
Mayn sale & fore Sale,	5-10-00
About the boat, ½ a C. wayght of rigging, wth the oares,	1-00-00
a Skife, £1-10; for old Tooles & Nayles, £0-10; sum,	2-00-00
Also a Chest, £0-03 ; a Coat, drawers & Cap, a doublet, Breeches,	
Stockins, shues, an iron pott & Hatt, & some other clothes,	3-15-00

Prised by Thomas Burchwood, Ed: More, Will' Carrose, Tho: Tracy, Stephen Poste.

---

[52]   Page 442-3.

Lyman, Richard. Invt. of Goods, £83-16-02. Taken 6 September, 1641, by John Moodie, Andrew Bacon, John Barnard. Will dated 22 April, 1640.

I give unto my wife all my houseing and Lands during her life, and 1/3 parte of my Lands to dispose of at her death amongst my Children as she pleaseth, and I give her all my moveable goods, as Cattell and howsehold stuffe, and all other implements or moveables. And the other two prts of my land & Howse, I give to my Elder sonne Richard, and to his heires forever ; and if he dy wthout an heir, then I give yt to my sonne Robert, and to his heirs forever. To my dau. Sarah, besides the Cattell I formerly have given her, my will is, that my wife shall pay her £20, two yeres after my death. To my sonne, John Lyman, I give him £30, to be paid by my wife att 22 years of age. To my sonne Robert, I give £24 at 22 years of age ; and to my dau. Fillis, the wife of Willia Hills, I give tenne shillings ; and I make my wife sole Executrixe to this my last will.

RICHARD LYMAN.

Witness : *Thomas Bull, John Moodie, Andrew Bacon.*

Court Record, Page 81—27 January, 1642 (Particular Courte).
The Will and Invt. of Richard Lyman, Decd., is brought into Court.

John Moody makes oath that yt is the Last Will of the said Rich., and the noate that was brought in is the noate of the Widdow Lyman, Decd. The several prtyes prsent at the prsenting of the said Will agree that John Lyman, if he live, will be 22 yere ould in Septe, 1645; Robert Lyman, 22 in Sept. 1651.

24 July.

The wydowe Lymans mynd is that her sonne Richard Lyman should prforme her husbands will, and that her son Robert should live wth him till he be 22 yeares of age; and she gives Robert Lyman the third prrte of the howsen & grounds; & for the prformence of her husbands will she gives Richard all her moveable goods, both wth out the howse and wth in, only her wearing Clothes and some of her lining She will dispose of.

John Moodie. Andrew Bacon.

Page 57.

Mason, Ed: 4th September, 1640. A true Inventory of the Goods & Chattells of Edward Mason, of Wethersfyeld, late deceased, vizt:

	£ s d
Imprs the Cloathes of the said Edward,	4-00-00
Ite. *in Halle,* brasse, Pewter, etc.	7-16-00
Ite. *in the parlor,* a featherbed wth chests, lynen, and other things,	13-00-00
Ite. *in the celler,*	2-00-00
Ite. Englishe Corne, wth Indean Old and New	41-00-00
Ite. *in the chamber,* a featherbedde wth others	9-10-00
Ite. twenty sixe barrowe hoggs, stores, & Sowes,	31-00-00
Ite. 3 Ewes, one Ewe kydd, 2 weathers,	8-00-00
Ite. Tooles & all other Implyments belonging to the trade of said Edward	4-15-00
Som totalis, (Except Lands)	£121-01-00

Valued pr
Willia Swayne,
George Hubbard.

Som totalis,
(Except Lands)
Test: Leo Chester.

His Lands in Wethersfield:

One pece whereon a house standeth, con. by estimatio three acres. The ends abutt against the landing place east and the land of Jo. Plum west; the sides against Conectecutt north, and Jo Plum his swampe south.

One pece whereon a barne standeth, con. by estimatio twelve Rods. The ends abutte against the landing place north and the howse lott of George Hubbard, south; the sids, against the west landing place east, the above. said howse lott of Edward Mason, west.

One pece lying in the great meadow, con. by estimatio fouer acres. The ends against the hie weae west, and a pece of meadow that was the fore said Edwards, east; the sids against the meadow of Jonas wod South, and the reres of the little lotts North.

One pece also lying in the great meadow, con. by estimatio two acres. It abutts against the river east, and land of his owne & Sam. Sharemans west, and Jonas Weed north, and Lyslie Broadfield South.

One pece in Pennywise, con. by estimatio Six acres two roods. The ends abutt against the hie waie west, and Conecticutt river east; the sids against the land of Jo. Reinnolds north, and Jeffrey fferris south.

One pece also in pennywise, con. by estimatio two acres, two roods. The ends abutte against the hie weae west, and Conecticutt River east; the sids against the land of Jeffrey fferris north, and that somtymes Jo. Sharemans south.

One pece lying in the Island, con. by estimatio three acres. The ends abutt against the river end west, and sids against the land of Jer. Gager, and that lately Tho. Wilcox, his land, south.

One pece lying in the little west field, con. by estimatio seven acres, one halfe, and thirty pole. The end abutt against the hie waye north, and the land of Mr. Smith south; the sids, against the land of Tho. Wetmore east, and Jacob Waterhouse west.

One other pece in the little west field con. by estimatio seven acres one halfe and thirty pole. The ends abutt against the waie north, and the land of Mr. Smith south; the sids against the land of Tho. Wetmore west, and Richard Wastcoat east.

(From Records of Lands, office Sec. State, Hartford, Vol. I. Page 51.)

Page 44.

5th March, 1639.　　　　A Particular Court.

Jno. Haynes, Esq., Governor.　　　Roger Ludlow, Esq., Deputy.
Mr. Hopkins, Mr. Wells, Mr. Webster, Mr. Phelpes.

Newbery, Thomas. This present day there was returned into the Court by Mr. Gaylard, one of the overseers, a Coppy of the estate of the

Children of Thomas Newbery, deceased, dated the 10th of February, 1639, subscribed by Mr. Ludlow, Mr. Phelpes, Mr. Huett, Mr. Hill, George Hull and Wm. Hosford.

[270]   Page 506-7.

(This Will was copied from File.)

Nowell, Thomas, Wyndsor.   Invt.   £368-11-01.   Taken 22 February, 1648/9, by Henry Clarke, David Wilton, John Moore.   Will dated 3 November, 1648.

I, *Thomas Nowell,* of Windsor, on Connecticutt, being right in understanding and of perfect memory in regard of my age and weakeness, desyring to sett my howse in order, as my Last Will and testament and as a token of my Love and respect, doe bequeath unto Robert Willson, my Kinsman, one Steere and one Cow; and unto Isable Phelps, my Kinswoman, one cowe; and in Case my wife shall, after my decease, marry agayne, then it is my will and testament that at the time of marriage fore specified the sd. Elizabeth, over and above my foresd. gifts, shall pay to the sd Robert and Isable, each of them, tenne pounds a peece.

It. As a token of my lowe, I bequeath unto my wife Elizabeth all the rest of my Estate in goods, debts or dues, of what kind soever, to her full and finall dispose as shee shall see best, as allso I bequeath unto her my dwelling howse, with all my Lands thereto prtayning, in Windsor aforesd, for and during the terme of her life; and after her decease, as a token of my Love, I bequeath my sd. howse and land unto Christopher Nowell, sone of Edward Nowell, of Wakefield, in Yorkeshyre, in England, deceased; to him and his heyres forever; & to this my last will and testament Witness my hand subscribed this prsent November, 3d, Anno domm. 1648.

                                                    THOMAS NOWELL.
Witness: *Isable X Phelps.*
          Bray Rosseter.

                              Page 3.

[2]   A Corte held att Watertowne 10 7br, 1636.

Roger Ludlowe Esqr.,   Mr. Wm. Phelps,
Mr. Jo: Steele,   Mr. Wm. Westwoode,
Mr. Wm. Swaine,   Mr. Andr: Warde.

Oldame, John. Whereas, there was tendered to vs an Inventory of the Estate of Mr. Jo: Olda wch seemed to bee somewhat vncerteinely valued, wee therefore thinke meete to, & soe it is ordered, that Mr. Jo: Plum & Rich: Gildersleeue, togeather wth the Constable, shall survey the saide Inventory and prfect the same before the next Corte, & then to deliur it into the Corte.

It is ordered, yt Thurston Rayner, as he hath hitherto done soe, shall continue to looke to & prserve the Corne of Mr. Olda, & shall inn the same in a seasonable tyme, & shall bringe an Accompt the next Cort what quantitie there is of it, as alsoe of his labor, & then the Corte will, out of the same, allott unto him soe many byshells as shall be reasonable for his paines & labor. And in the meane, if he hath use of some for his owne spendinge, to take some, wch shalbe then deducted out of what Wilbe due to him. And then the Corte will give finall order concerninge the same.

Page 5.

[3]   A Corte held att Newe Towne, 8br 4to, 1636.

Mr. Ludlowe,   Mr. Phelps,
Mr. Swaine,   Mr. Westwoode,
Mr. Steele,   Mr. Warde.

It is ordered, that a Warrant be directed to Daniell Finch to sumon Rich: Gildersleeue to appr the next Corte or other meetinge of the Comrs, to bringe in an Inventory of Mr. Oldames estate wch was sometyme in his handes, as alsoe to sumon any other to appr that hath in his handes or canne declare where any of th' estate of the saide Mr. Olda is yt is not as yet revealed.

Page 5.

[3]   A Corte held att Newe Towne 10 Novembr, 1636.

Mr. Ludlowe,   Mr. Phelps,
Mr. Pyncheon,   Mr. Westwoode,
Mr. Swaine,   Mr. Warde.
Mr. Steele,

It is ordered, that Srieant Seely shall, betweene this & the next Corte, consider of such noates & Inventories as haue come to his handes or knowledge concerninge the estate of Mr. Oldam, & then deliuer them into the Corte vppon oath, & in the meane to prduce any noate or Inventory to Mr. Swayne & Mr. Warde that he hath or cann come by yt may make for the furtherance of the discouery of the estate of the saide Mr. Olda, to th' end the Cort may then prceede in yt business as they shall see cause.

Page 6.

A Corte at New Towne 27 Decr., 1636.

Mr. Ludlowe,   Mr. Westwoode,
Mr. Swaine,   Mr. Phelps,
Mr. Steele,   Mr. Warde.

It is ordered yt Daniell Finch shall haue for sixe dayes imploymt about Mr. Oldames estate & a Corte, 13s.-6.

Page 6.

It is ordered, that Mr. Clement Chaplin shall take into custody the goodes of Mr. Oldam, deceased, according to an Inventory in Corte, & in the Custody of Daniell Finch, & he the saide Mr. Chaplin is to be responsible for them. He may sell them or any of them.

It is ordered yt all the Creditors of Mr. Olda in the River of Connectecott bring in their debts before the next Corte or E(ls) he shall not be deemed as a Creditor in the estate that is now extant.

Page 43-44.

[35]   Febr. the 6th, 1639. A Prticular Court.

Mr. Oldams Estate being examined, the account of it as it stands in this Jurisdiction is as followeth:

Estate Mr. Oldam, deceased, is debtor:

	£	s	d
To Matthew Marvine,	1	06	08
to Richard Lord,	5	05	00
to Wm. Lewis,	9	12	03
to Edward Mason,	3	03	00
to Jeffrey Feris,	3	15	00
to Henry Browning,	11	00	00
to Thomas Stanton,	03	05	00
to Thomas Scott,	00	18	00
to Mr. Chapleyn,	146	18	00
to Mr. Pincheon,	022	19	09
to Andrew Warner,	009	19	00
to Edwa. Stebbing,	002	13	04
to Mr. Talcott,	021	06	03
to Mr. Jno. Haynes,	002	00	00
to Matthew Allen,	020	15	00
to Lieftenant Seely,	010	13	00
to Edward Hopkins & Mr. Matthew Craddocke,	229	00	00

£504-09-03

Pr contra Credit:

	£	s	d
By Lieftenant Seely,	28	15	02
by Jno Chapman,	4	15	00
by Rich. Lawes,	6	04	11

by Mr. Chapleyne,   89-15-02
by Thomas Allen,   6-16-06
                                                        ──────────
                                                        £136-66-21
Jan. the 6th, 1640.

Wm. Lewis abated out of his debt £2-16 wch he was to allow for a
hogg he bought of Mr. Oldam.

It was thought fit, and ordered, that the Accot be sent to the Bay and
yf a just accot be also returned from thence in a reasonable tyme,
an equal division may be made of the whole; yf not, the estate here
shall be divided among the Creditors here.

Page 48.

11 April, 1640.

Mr. Steele is returned Recorder for the Towne of Hartford, and hath
brought into the Courte 114 coppyes of the severall prcells of land belonging to & conserneing 114 prsons.

Mr. Rocester is returned Recorder for the Towne of Wyndsor.

Mr. Michell is returned Recorder for the Towne of Wethersfyeld,
but he is found vncapable of the place, lying vnder censure of the Courte,
and was fyned twenty Nobles for vndertaking the office. That prte of
the Town of Wethersfylde who chose him were fyned £5.

Page 446.

Olmstead, James, Hartford. Invt. £397-19-02. Taken 28 September, 1640, by John Steele, Edward Stebbing.

Will: It is my will to give my estate betweene my two sonns, that is
to say, the on halfe to my son Nicholas, and the other halfe to my sonne
Nehemiah, equally divyded betweene the both, wth this reservation, that if
my brother Lymus doe make his word good to make my sonne Nicholas
wifes portion as good as any child he hath, for so I understand his prmise
is, but if he shall refuse so to doe, I shall then refuse to give my sonne any
prte of my moveable goods, cattell or debts; but my will is to leave the
thing wth Richard Webb and William Wodsworth to see my Brother
Lumus doe prforme his prmise, and as the said Richard Webb and Will
Wodsworth shall doe I shall be content. And if my brother Lumus doe
prforme his prmise, then my will is their portions shall be a like, only
Nicholas shall abate so much as I have given him before. And my will is
that my sonne Nehemiah shall give out of his portion ten pound to my
Cossen Rebeca Olmstead that now dwelleth wth me, and he shall pay yt
her wth in three yeares after my decease, and I leave her to be disposed
by Richard Webb and Will Wadsworth, and as shee shall carry herselfe

yt shall be in their power ether to give her the ten pound or to detayne yt fro her. I doe give my servant Will Corby five pound, to be paid when his tyme comes forth, and I doe will my sonne Nehemyah to pay him out of his owne portion ; And I doe will that Will Corby doe searve his tyme wth my sonne Nehemiah. And I leave my sonne Nehemiah wth Richard Webb and Will Wadsworth, intreating the to have the ouer sight of him and the disposeing of him as their owne child. But if my sonne Nehemiah shall goe contrary in Bestowing himselfe any way contrary to the judgement of my two friends, Rich. Webb and Will Wadsworth, then yt shall be in their power to comannd and take a hundred pound of his estate and dispose of yt as they thinke fitt. I give to my two frynds, Richard Webb and Will Wadsworth, wch I put in trust, six pounds and a marke to be paid equally betwixt the, and my two sonnes shall pay the, the one pay the one halfe and the other pay the other halfe.   JA. OLMSTEAD.

Witness : *Richard Webb*
     Will Wadsworth.

A Decision and an Agreement by Richard Webb & Will Wadsworth with Nicholas Olmstead & Nehemiah Olmstead, that is to say, to his Kynsman Richard Olmstead, £5, and to his Kynsman John Olmstead, £5, to be paid within 3 yeares after his decease. And unto the church of Christ in Hartford, £20, to be paid at the same tyme of 3 years after the decease of their said Father.

Will Wadsworth.   NICHOLAS OLMSTEAD.
     NEHEMIAH OLMSTEAD.

[50]   Page 56.

Packs, Henry, his will, dated 4 September, 1640.
It is my will to bestow uppon the Church the Clocke that Brother Thornton had bought ; to Mr. Wichfyeld, my best Coate and whoight (?) Cappe ; to Mr. [   ] my best dublets.

[244]   Page 475.

Porter, John, Windsor. Invt. £470-17-00. Taken 27 April, 1648, by Henry Clarke, David Wilton, William Phelps, Thomas Ford. Will dated 20 April, 1648.
Imprimis. This is the last will and Testament made by mee, John Porter, of Wyndsor, allthough now weake and sick in body, yet in prfect memory, doe bequeath my soule to God that gave it, and my Body to be buried, and my goods as followeth :
Ite. I give to my eldest sonne, John Porter, £100 ; and to my second sonne, Jeames Porter, I give £60 ; and to my other six children, to witt, Samuel Porter, Nathaniel, Rebeka, Rose, Mary & Anne Porter, to each

£30, wch is to be raised out of my whole estate, as howseing, lands, cattell, and household goods, and is to be paid as they come to be twenty yeares of age, or sooner if my overseers sees just cause, without whose consent I would not have them marrye, wch if they doe it shall bee in the power of my ourseers to abate their portions and give it to the other that are more deserveing. And in case any of my children dye before they be married, or be twenty yeares of age, their portion shall be equally divided amongst the rest, unless the ourseers see cause to abate it uppon the eldest. In case my estate shall bee founde uppon perticular view to arise to be more in valew than these portions above given, or less than the summe, my will is that it shall bee proportionally added or abated to my childrens severall portions, except my ourseers see cause to abate my eldest, that hath the bigger portion, or likewise my second. The particular goods wherein each child shall have his portion paid out of my whole estate I leave to the discretion of my ourseers. My sonne Joseph Judgson is to take twenty shillings of Thomas Thornton, the next winter; also I give fifty shillings to the pore of Wyndsor Church. My desire is that these my beloved friends would bee the ourseers of this my last will and testament: Mr. Warham of Wyndsor, Mr. Goodwyn of Hartford, Goodman White of Hartford, Matthew Grant of Wyndsor. JOHN PORTER.

Witness: *Henry Clarke*
Abigaill Branker.

Court Record, 7 March, 1650. One of the younger daughters had died, and there was an adjustment of the Elder daughters' Portions. 7 June, 1649, Will Proven. *John Taillcott*
Will Westwood.
J. C. Secry

[231] Page 466-7-8.

Purkas, John. Invt. £30-15-00. Taken October, 1645. I, John Purkas, doe appoynt my wife to be sole executor to administer vppon my whole estate, to bring up my children, and it is my mynd & will that my wife shall possesse my house and land for her prper vse for the whole tyme of her life, pruided that shee shall have noe power to alienate yt or make sale of my howse or any of my land wth out the consent of John Talcotte and Richard Goodman, or one of them if ether of them shall dy. If my wife beare me a son and (he) survive until the death of my wife, then he shall possesse my howse and all my land in Hartford, for himselfe and heires; but if the Lord give me noe son, my mynd is that my howse and land be equally divided among my daughters that shall survive after the death of my wife. My daughters Mary & Elizabeth shall have ech of the a whole and serviceable pear of sheets, and ech of the a pewter platter, at the age of eighteen yeares. And if God give me a sonne wch my wife goeth with all, my mynd is that if my sonne shall live to the age of eighteen yeares that he shall have my gunne, wch is a fire locke, and my sword and bandaleres and rest, and my long crosscut sawe, and my betell rings, and three wedges. Also, my mynd is that my howshold stuff shall be devided to my daughters after the death of my wife, only the bedde and blanketts and one pair of sheets and one trunke I leave wholy to my wife to dispose on at her death. 15th of October, 1645.

Jo. PURKAS.

Witness: *Jo. Talcott.*
Rich. Goodman

November 26, 1663. Know all men by these presents, that I, Jeret Spicke, doe acknowledg my self received of Nicholas Palmer the full and just summe of tenn pounds, which is the acquitting all accots between us two concerning my wiues portion which was due to her by her father, John Parkas, his will. JERET SPECK.

Witness: *Thomas Butler, Robert Sanford.*

Whereas, there have bin an appoyntment that Nicholas Palmer was to pay his daughter in lawe Elizabeth Purkass, tenn pounds, these presents doe testify that I, Richard Case, of Windsor, doe acknowledg that I have received of Nicholas Palmer, of Windsor, a foar sayd, ten pounds in pay to my content and sattisfaction, & doe hereby acquitt & discharge the sd. Nicho of all debts and demands, as witness my hand this 17 December, 1663.

RICHARD X CASE

Signed and delivered in the presence & Witness of us

John Moore, Antho X Hoskins.

These are True coppyes of the originall receipts, being compared therewith October 20th, '64, pr. me. John Allyn Secretry.

[254] Page 486.

Rissley, Richard, Hockanum. Invt. £135-05-16. Taken by John Cullick, Will Gibbins.

3 Children: one daughter, Sarah Rissly, betweene 7 and 8 years old; one sonne by name Samuell Risley, about 2 yeares old: and one sonne, by name Rich. Risley, about 3 months old. The distribution of the estate by the Courte, the 7th of December, 1648, is: To the 3 children £16 a peece, to bee pd. to the daughter at the age of 18 yeares, and to the sonnes at the age of 21 yeares. William Hill, bringing of ym vpp to write and read, and giving security to the Courte for the payment of the severall childrens portions.

[255] Debts owing pr the estate of Richard Risly, deceased, to

	£	s	d
Mr. Olcott,	09	01	09
Rich. Lord,	00	13	00
Sam. Smith, Weth.,	01	04	00
Will Gibbens,	00	04	00
Mr. Moody,	00	03	00
Will Houghton,	00	12	06
John Lyman,	00	06	00
Mr. Stone & Mr. Hooker,	00	11	00
———Knott,	00	10	06
Patience Smith,	00	09	00
John Sabell,	10	00	00
Joseph Mygatt,	02	06	05
Thomas Selden,	01	13	11
Capt. Cullick,	00	17	10
Phillip Dauis,	00	13	10
Rich. Fellowss,	00	15	00
Will Wessly,	03	08	00
Andr. Warner,	01	03	00
Robt. Ely,	01	12	00
Mr. Edw. Hopkins,	16	15	08
John Hopkins,	00	04	00
Thomas Woodford,	00	03	00

£53-07-05

[253]   Page 485.

Sawyer, Richard. Died 24 July, 1648. Invt. of goodes and estate, £7-17-10 ½. Taken by John Bernard, Arthur Smith.

Court Record, Page 169: 17 October, 1648. The Courte gives Mr. Cullick order to administer vppon the estate of his man Richard Sawyer, deceased, there being evidence in Courte that Richard Sawyer said before his death that hee would leave all that he had to the dispose of his Mar Cullick.

Page 453.

[71]   The 6th of November, 1643.

Scott, Thomas, Hartford. Invt. £174-12-04. Taken 6 January, 1643. The last Will and Testament of Tho Scott, of Hartford, deceased, as yt was spoken by him to Edward Stebbing and Tymothy Standly, who were sent for by him for that end, to who he expressed his Will as followeth:

I doe give to my wife and to my sonne Thomas, the one halfe of my howse and halfe of my barne and halfe of my howselott, my two lotts in the North meadow, my lott in the little meadow, also the swampe at both ends, also all my corne in my howse and barne, both here at Hartford and at Tunxis Cepus, as also two Cowes and my two elder Steeres, and fiue Hoggs, wth halfe my howshold stuffe. I doe also give them my Carts and ploughs, and the tacklin belonging to the. His howseing & Lands to come to the rest of his children after the death of his wife & son Thomas. And my mynd is that if my sonne Tho. depart this life before my wife, at his death that the one halfe of the meadow & catle and howshold stuff before given to him and my wife shall be equally divided betwixt my other children then living, and my mynd is that my wife shall have power at her death to dispose of, and give away, the other halfe of that wch is given to her and my sonne, as shee seeth fitt, except my howseing and Land, wch my mynd is, shall then com. to the rest of my children at the death of the longest liver of my wife or my sonne Thomas. I doe also make my wife Executrix. My mynd is, that my youngest daughter doe remayne wth my wife so long as shee seeth meet, & wth the advice of those that oversee my will. My mynd also is, that all my daughters be disposed of both in service and mariedge by my wife and overseers, and that my daughters shall receive their portions ether at the day of their mariedge or at twenty years of age. My will is, that all the remaynder of my estate wch is not given to my wife and sonne Thomas, after my debts are discharged, shall be equally divided among them. The youngest daughter to remain with her Mother, and the boy Servant to continue with the Relict & son Thomas.

Dist. to the 3 daughters.

The Relict of the said Thomas, with the apprbacon of the Court, hath desired John Talcott, Wm. Westwood, Ed Stebbing and Andrew Warner to assist in seeing the Will performed. And these Ouerseers vnderstanding fro these that are the witnesses of his will, &c.

In March, 1652 (see Vol. II, Page 123 of Lands, Sec. State's office) :

The copy of a Deed of Sale made and recorded from Mary Porter and Sarah Standly and Elizabeth Standly, all of Farmingtown, of Severall Prcells of Land, wth a dwelling howse & other outhouses & home lott, unto Thomas Cadwell, of Hartford, wthin the Jurisdiction of Connecticut, & his heyres for ever :

This prsent writing, made the ninth of March, in the yeare of or Lord one thousand Six hundred fifty two, Wittnesth : That whereas, Thomas Scott, sometime of Hartford, upon Connecticute Ryver, did give & bequeath unto his wife & unto his sonne Thomas Scott, by his Last will & testament, one message or tenement wth a barne & other out houses, & also a house wth the yard or garden therein contained, wch house lott is esteemed two acres (bee it more or less) abutting the highway Leading from the little river to the North meadow on the East, & on a highway Leading from that highway to the meeting house on the North, & on John Pantress Land on the South, & on Thomas Mason Land on the west ; And one prcell of meadow wth the swamp adjoyning. Lying in the North meadow, esteemed two acres two roods & twenty Seven perches (bee it

more or lesse), abutting on John Mainards Land on the south, & on the
great river on the East; And one prcell more Lying in the North meadow,
of meadow & swamp, esteemed twenty & one acres three rood & eighteen
perches (more or lesse), abutting on Bartholomew Barnards Land on the
south, & on William Wadsworth Land on the North; And one prcell of
meadow, esteemed one acre (bee it more or lesse) abutting on the highway
Leading to the Landing place on the North, & on John Pantrees Land on
the South; And one prcell Lying in the old oxe pasture, esteemed eighteen
acres, abutting Thomas Stantons Land on the North, & on Matthew
Marvins Land on the south; And one prcell lying for cowe pasture, esteemed thirty acres (bee it more or lesse), abutting on the widdow Standlys
Land on the South, & on John Pantrees Land on the North; And one
prcell Lying in the Venturer feild, esteemed sixe acres twenty eight
perches (bee it more or lesse), abutting on Thomas Standlyes Land on the
North, on the highway Leading to the Brick Kell on the South; And one
prcell Lying in the neck of Land, esteemed five acres twenty foure perches
(bee it more or lesse), abutting on Richard Webb's Land on the south,
& on William Westwood's Land on the North; All wch prcells of Land
& halfe the building, & halfe the howse lott, the said Thomas Scott bequeathed to his said wife & to his sonne Thomas Scott during the time
of the naturall life of both of them, & after their decease unto his daughters, Mary Scott, Sarah Scott & Elizabeth Scott, to them & their heirs
forever.

Now know yee, that these prsents wittnesseth, that the day of the
date hereof the said Mary Porter, & Sarah Standly, & Elizabeth Loomis,
wth the consent of every of their husbands, viz., Robert Porter, John Standly, & John Loomis, all now or late of ffarmington, in consideration of the
summe of forty five pounds by us in hand received, & a bill of debt given
to us bearing date the day of the date of these prsents, have given, granted,
bargained and sold all and singular those prcells of Land, dwelling house
& other buildings on the premises before expressed, and were given to us
by our ffathers will, is in reversion after the death of our mother, now
Anne fford, & after the decease of our said Brother Thomas Scott, unto
Thomas Cadwell, of Hartford, for ever without molestation from the said
Robert Porter or Mary his wife, or from John Standly or Sarah his wife,
or from John Loomys or Elizabeth his wife, or from any other person or
persons, from the time of the decease of our said mother & Brother for
ever.

It is also agreed upon by the prties abovesaid, that if the said Thomas
Scott shall survive his mother, Ann fford, & that the said Thomas Scott
shall be left by the overseers of the Will to be paid for and maintained
by his Brothers & Sisters, either, all, or by any of them, & that the said
Thomas Cadwell shall pay eight pounds by the yeare during the terme

of his naturall life for every yeare or part of a yeare, then we doe bind ourselves to free the Land from any charges or claymes for the maintenance
of the said Thomas Scott during the terme of his naturall life.

Signed

JOHN LOOMIS
ELIZABETH X LOOMIS
ROBERT PORTER
MARY X PORTER
JOHN STANDLY
SARAH X STANDLY

Witness : *Edward Stebbin & John Steele.*

---

[266]   Page 502.

Smith, Henry, Wethersfield.   Invt.   £370-18-06.   Taken by James
Boosey, Samuel Smith.   Will dated 8 May, 1648.

I Henry Smith, of Wethersfield, being at present in health of body
and soundness of minde, considering my mortality, and knoweing it to be
my duty to provide for my family and settle my estate, that I may leave
no occasion of trouble to my children when I am gone, and that I may be
free my self from distractions of this kind, if it shall please God to visit
mee with sickness before I dye ; I doe therefore leave this testimony vppon
Record as my last Will and Testament. Then, for my outward estate, wch,
because it is little and I have well proved the difficultyes of this Country,
how hard a thinge it will be for a woman to manage the affaires of so
great a family as the Father of Mercyes hathe blessed me withall, and
have had allso experience of the prudence and faithfullness of my deare
wife, who shall, in parting with me, parte with a great parte of her liveli-
hood, I give to my wife full power to dispose of all my estate in howses,
Lands, Cattell and Goods whatsoever, within dores and without, only providing if she marry again, or otherwise be able comfortably to spare it
from her owne necessary maintenance, that she give to my sonne Samuell
that part of my howselott which was intended for my sonne Peregrine,
lyinge next to the burying place, and the land I have beyond the great
River eastward, and also to him and my 2nd sonne Noah, 5 acres apeece
of meadow, with upland proportionable thereunto ; and to the rest of my
children unmarried, £20 apeece at the age of 21 yeares, or at the time of
her death wch shall come the soonest ; and for my two daughters that bee
married, my desire is that they have £20 apeece, and every one of their
children £5 apeece, either in books or such other thing as my wife shall
best please to parte withall. And I desire the Church, whose serviant I
now am, to take an ouersight of my family, that they may be brought vp
in the true feare of God, and to see that this my will bee faithfully
prformed.   HENRY SMITH.

[257]   Page 489.

Standly, Timothy. Hartford. Invt. £332-18-10. Taken 16 October, 1648, by John Tailecoate, Edward Stebbing, Will Westwood, Thomas Standly.

Court Record, 7 December, 1648. Dist: To the two eldest daughters, £50 out of the moveables; to the eldest son Calib, the howses and lands in Hartford, at the age of 21 years, Hee paying to the youngest dau. £30 if she lives; to the youngest son Isaack, after the decease of his mother, the land and howsing at Farmington.

1670, December 1st. Thomas Porter & Lois Porter give Receipt to Calib Standly that they have fully received that portion that was allotted by the Courte as her portion due to her of her father Timothy Standly estate.   THOMAS PORTER.

Witness: *Samuel Cowles,*
         Abigail Cowles.   *Test* 5 *January,* 1670.
                                        Pr me, John Allyn, Secrtry.
              (*A true copy of the original.*)

---

[60]   Page 449.

Spencer, Willia. Invt. £231-12-02.

A coppy of the will & testament of Willia Spencer, late of Hartford, deceased, prsented in Court vpon oath by John Taylcott & John Pratt, of the said towne. A noate of the mynd and will of Willia Spencer, for prsent the 4th of May, 1640.

Imprs. His will is that the estate that he hath in New Ingland, and also that wch may com to his wife hereafter, that is, any prte of his wifes portion yf any doe com, that all the estate be dyuyded as followeth :

I give to my wife one third prte of all my estate.

I give to my sonne Samuell one third prte :

I give to my two daughters, Sarah and Elizabeth, one third partte.

The children to be brought vppe wth the improvement of the whole estate that I leaue both to my wife and children.

Also my mynd is, my Cosen Matthew Allyn, my brother John Pratt, and John Taylcoate, that these three partyes or any two of them shall haue the Ouersight of my Estate ; and in case that they shall see in theire judgement the Estate to be wasted, that they shall haue power to take the children and their portions (   ) for their bringing vppe, and to pay the Children their portions that remayne at the severall tymes above written.

Also my mynd is, that my wife shall have no power to alienatt or make sale of my howse or any prte of my land I leaue wthout the consent of two of the prtyes that are to ouersee my Estate.

These last three lines were added subsequently in the hand writing of Secretary John Allyn. The distribution of the estate appeares in the

Records of the perticular Courte, the 24th June, 1650, fol. 10, and the Coppyes of the bills given to the Courte for the payment of the £30 to the children are in the Booke of Records of Lands for the Severall townes, at ye other end of it. The original Bills are vppon fyle of wills & Inventories.

Land Records. Vol. II, Page—(Not paged in this side of the Book). Know all men by these prss, that I, John Tayllcott, of Hartford, upon Connecticut River, do hereby Bynde my selfe, my Heires, Executors, Administers and Assigns, to pay or cause to be paid unto Sara Spencer, and to Elizabeth Spencer, the full value of tenn pounds when they shall bee of full age of eighteen yeares, in some pay that is Current for so much when the said payments are to be made.   JOHN TALLCOTT.

Witness: *Richard Lord.*
John Steele   14 March, 1650.

It is also agreed, that if either of the children dye before the time that they are of age, then the survivour & survivours shall receive it at the time when it should have been paid to the deceased, if he or she had lived. And if they all dye before the said time, then it shall bee paid to Agnes Edwards, or her Lawfull Attorney of the said Agnes, the mother of the said children.   JOHN TALLCOTT, JOHN STEELE.

March the twelfth, one thousand Six hundreth and fifty. Know all men by these prsents, that I, Richard Lord, of Hartford, doe owe and confess my self to be Indebted unto the Executors & supervisors of William Spencers Last will and Testament, the full sum of Twenty pounds Sterling for the aloane use of Samuel Spencer and Sara Spencer, to be paid as follows: fifteene pounds when the said Samuel shall be of full age, which will bee in the yeare 1660, in any pay that shall be Current in the Country at that time for so much; and five pounds unto Sara Spencer, at the age of eighteen yeares, wch will be in the yeare 1653.   RICHARD LORD.

Witness: *John Steele.*
William Edwards.

Court Record, Page 10—(Vol. II) 24 June, 1650.
With the Information of the Overseers, in presence of Thomas Spencer, the brother of sd. Decd, with the Consent of the wife of William Edwards, this Court do judge that £30 is as much as the Estate here will bear to be sequestered for the Use of the Children, also provided that what shall be paid here or in England of any Estate due to the wife of the sd. William Spencer, 2-3 shall be and remain to the Children.

-----

[228]   Page 463.

Veir, Ed., Wethersfield. Invt. £33-08-00. Taken 2 December, 1645, by Richard Trotte & Nathaniel Dickinson.

Will—19 July, 1645: I give to Mr. Shareman, of Totokot, £4; to Mr. Smith of Wethersfield, £4, made up in part in a cow at Totocott; I give to Lysly Bradfield and his wife, £3; to Mary & Hannah, the daughters of John Robins, £3; to John Robins, my two acres of meadows wch I had of John Robins in exchange for my Howse and home lott. My mynd is, that John Carrington and Tho. Kirkeman shall be no loosers by the bargaine of pease and wheat they bought of me. I make Mr. Shareman and Mr. Smith my executors, to who I give the rest of my estate. Memorand: yt is my mynd that John Carrington and Tho. Kirkeman shall use their indeavor they loose not anything in their Corne, through their owne default. My mynd is, that John Carrington and Tho. Kirkman shall have 20s for making my Coffen. My mynd is, that there shall be 20s bestowed uppon pruissions of wyne, bear, caks, and such like of what may be had for my buriall. I give to Mr. Swayne all my workeing tooles.   ED. VEIR.
In presence of *Nathaniel Dickinson.*

Page 145. 29 October, 1646: Kircu & Carrington are to pay 30s to the Adms. of Veir for their bargaine of Corne.

Court Record. 10th of July, 1645—Page 129: Will presented in Court.

[62]   Page 451.

Ward, Joyce, Wethersfield. Invt. £52-15-06. Taken 24th February, 1640-1, by George Hubbard & Leonard Chester. Will dated 15th November, 1640:

I, Joyce Ward, of Wethersfield, being sicke in body but whole in mynd, doe make my last will & Testament this 15th day of November, in this prsent yeare of the Lord Christ 1640, in manner and forme as followeth:

Imprs. I give to foure of my sonnes, that is to say, Anthony Ward, to Willie Ward, Robert Ward, & John Ward, ech of the a pare of sheets, and to my eldest sonne Edward, I give unto him twelve pence of mony; furthermore, I make my sonne in law John Flecher my whole and sole Executor, to pay and discharge all those debts, legaces wch I am bownd to prforme, and for to see my body brought to the ground in a decent manner. Memorand: that I, Joyce Ward, have left my sonne Roberts portion wch his father gave him, wch is (£20) twenty pound, in England, in the hands of my sonne Edward Ward; I have made Mr. Wollersloue, of Clipsum, in England, in the County of Rutland, my Atturny, for to receave yt for my vse; if he have gott yt there, my son Robert shall have the whole twenty pound; but if yt be not gotten, then the six pound wch I paid for the putting out of the saide Robert Ward to Apprentice, shall be prte of that twenty pound.   JOYCE WARD   her mark

Witness: *Nathaniel Dickinson*
            Roger Prichat

An Inventory of all and singular the goods, Chattells, cattle, belonging to Joyce Ward, wydow, late of Wethersfield, made, taken and found the 24th of February, by George Hubbard and Leonard Chester:

	£ s d
Imprs 7 yards of Hemppen cloath at 2s pr yard,	0-14-00
It. four prrs of Hemppen Sheets,	2-00-00
It. one prre of flaxen sheets,	1-00-00
It. her apparell, vist, 2 gowns, one hatt, one pre of bodyes, wth other,	5-00-00
It. one bedd, two boulsters, two pillows, two Coverings, two Curtains,	10-00-00
It. one boxe, wth a little hand Trunke.	0-03-06
one brasse pott, 16s; one brasse panne, £1,	1-16-00
one iron potte, one chamber pott, 2s,	0-04-00
one brasse coal dish,	0-02-00
one sowe wth three piggs,	1-00-00
two table cloathes, wth 4 napkins,	0-16-00
one Bond or Specialty	30-00-00
	£52-15-06

Pr Leonard Chester,
George Hubbard.

Page 135.

Wakeman, Sam: Court Record, 4 December, 1645. The estate of Sam. Wakeman, deceased, is setled on Nath. Willette, in consideratio whereof he is to pay £40 to the eldest sonne wn he shall attayne 21 years of age, and £20 apeece to the three daughters wn they shall attayne the age of 18 yeares. If any dy in the meane, the portio is to be devided betwix the survivors, the land to stand ingadged for the prformance thereof; and if any debts more shall appeare than are nowe knowne, to be equally borne by him & the children, and if any estate more appeare, that also is to be devided. The children's receipts of their portions is record in Book D. Fol. 21, Decembr. 23 : 1673.

(1657.)

I, Ezbon Wakeman, doe acknowledge to have received of my father-in-law, Nath. Willett, the full and just summe of forty pounds, which was allowed me as my portion of my deceased fathers estate. I say received by me   EZBON WAKEMAN

Witness: *John White.*   *Test pr me, John Allyn Secrtry.*

Know all men, that I, John Kelly, have received of my father-in-lawe, Nath. Willett, the full just summe of moneys that was due from him to my wife as the portion which was allowed her, & doe by these presents give unto my aforesaid father a discharge from all and whatsoever from the beginning of the world to this day, as witness my hand June 10, 1663.

JOHN X KELLEY.

Witness: *Joseph Smith.*
Ezekell Sanford.

6th September, 1662. I, Joseph Arnold, & Elizabeth his wife, who was the daughter of Samull Wakeman, deceased, have received from my father-in-law, Nathll. Willett, twenty pounds in full sattisfaction, which was allowed to me for my portion. I say received by us.

JOSEPH ARNOLD.
ELIZABETH X ARNOLD.

Witness: *John Richards.*
Ezbon Wakeman.

6 September, 1662. I, Hanna Hackelton, doe acknowledge to have received the full and just summe of twenty pounds, which was allowed me by the court, being the daughter of Samuell Wakeman, deceased. I say received by me from my father-in-law, Nath. Willett,

HANNA X HACKLETON.

Witness: *John Richards*
Ezbon Wakeman.

This writing witness that I, James Wakely, doe give to Nath. Willette acquittance from demands of Bill or Bills of all debt & damage from the beginning of the world to this day, as witness my hand this 26th of October, 1655.   JAMES X WAKELEY.

Witness: *Thomas Bull.*

The above written is a true coppy of the original record, 23 December, 1673, pr me, John Allyn, Secretary.

I, Elizabeth Wakeman, as also Hanna Hackleton, did hear that Francis Hackleton did acknowledge that he had received his full due, that was due to his wife, & halfe a crown more.

ELIZABETH X ARNOLD,
HANNA X HACKLETON.

[260]   Page 493-495.

Whiting, William, Hartford. Invt. £2854-00-00. Taken 20 April, 1643. I, William Whiting, doe intend a voyage presently unto sea. I give to my wife halfe my household stuffe of all kinds, and one fourth parte of my personal estate, and her widdowes estate in my now dwelling house and lands at Hartford untill my sonne William be 21 years of age; and after, if she continue a widow, I give her the halfe of my sd. howse and land for life. I give to my sonne William £100 more than I give to either my sonne John or Samuel; I give to John & Samuel £100 more to each than I give to my daughter Sarah or Mary. I give £20 to Mr. Hooker, £10 to Mr. Stone, £5 to mending the Highway betwixt my howse and the meeting house, also £5 to some godly poore of the towne. I desire Mr. John Haynes, Mr Edward Hopkins, Mr. John Webster, with Mr. Hooker & Mr. Stone, to be Overseers. I give to my father & mother £20.

WILLIAM WHITING.

2 April, 1646.

Intending another voyage, my will is, my son Joseph shall have an equal portion with sonnes John & Samuel. I give William £50 more; to Mary, £10 more; to my sister Wiggin, £5; and to each of her children, £3; I give to Margery Parker £10, my former will to remain in force.

WILLIAM WHITING.

In presence of *Edward Hopkins.*

William Whiting, upon his death bed: It is my minde that the children which God hath given me since the will was made wch I have in Mr. Hopkins hands, shall have an equal portion in all my estate together with the rest of my children as I have to these devised. Also I confirme £10 given to Mr. Hopkins, £10 to Mr. Webster, £10 to Mr. Hooker's Children, £10 to Mr. Stone's Children, £10 to the poor, £5 to Hartford, & £5 to the other two towns, Wyndsor & Wethersfield, and £5 to Mr. Smith's Children, of Wethersfield.

WILLIAM WHITING.

In presence of *Henry Smith.*
James Cole.

24th July, 1647.
Paper on file compared with original.
Court Record, 24 April, 1649. Then the Court Ruled upon a Construction of the will.

Page 157.

2 September, 1647, Mrs. Whiting is admitted to Adms. according to the will.

Page 262.

3 October, 1654. Mr. Webster, Mr. Stone, Mr. Fitch, Mr. Will Whiting, John Whiting, presenting to this Court a distributiyon of Mr.

Whitings estate agreed upon by them (signed & sealed), bearing date 30
Sept. 1654, this Court allowes to be recorded.

Page 69—(Vol. III).

29 October, 1667. Whereas, Mr. Alexander Briant and Mrs. Susannah Fitch have, by an Instrument of Resignation bearing date 27 June,
1662, resigned their Interest in and unto the estate of Mr. William Whiting, Decd, that hath bee in ye possession and Improvement of sd. Susannah in the time of her Widowhood, unto the Children of ye sd. Mr.
Whiting, and they desire the favor of the Court to have Deacon Edward
Stebbing & Thomas Bull as Adms. on the remayning part of ye Estate.

Williams, Amos. Court Record, Page 396—11 March, 1662-3. The
Magestrates order Sam: Boreman to deliver the little Bible and a paper
book vnto Amos Williams, wch was given to him by his Mother, and that
he and Will: Goodrich dist. the Estate to ye Creditors.

Williams, Matt: Court Record, Page 433—13 October, 1664. This
Court orders Sam: Boreman, Mr. Chester & Samll Welles to dispose of
the Estate of Matt: Williams, his wife, for the payment of what debts are
due from the Estate, so farr as it will goe.

---

[233]   Page 468.

Wyllys, George. Died 9 March, 1644-5. Will dated 14 December,
1644. I, George Wyllys, of Hartford, do make my last will & Testament.
I give all my buildings, lands, tenements and heredetaments in Hartford
bounds and at Tunxis Cepus, vnto my beloved wife Mary Willis (as
spelled through the will) and unto my sonne Samuell, etc. I doe give to my
son George all my Land and buildings upon the west side of the River,
in the bownds of Wethersfield, now in the occupation of divers men,
prvided he doe com over into New England and settle himselfe and family heere according as I have wrote him by letter dated 28th October laste.
If he doe not come, the buildings & Land aforesaid shall be and remain at
the whole dispose of my wife Mary Willis. My will is that my sonne
George injoy and possesse my Land and buildings att Fenny Compton.
in Old England, according to a Deed made to him by my feoffees; for
want of heirs, then to my son Samuel; or, this failing, to the right heirs
of me George Willis. I give to my dau. Hester £400; to my dau. Amy,
£350. My wife Mary shall have and injoy to her own prper use, and to
her assigns, the lease of the moiety of Fenny Compton for one and twenty
yeares, she to pay to my dau. Hester £10 pr year, and to my sd. Amy £10

a year, for the sd. terme of the lease, provided they live so long; if not, then the annuity to cease. I doe give my son Samuel all my land on the east side of the River wthin the bownds of Wethersfield, he paying to my daughters Hester and Amy £40 apeece sixe years after my decease. I give to Mr. Fenwicke, Mr. Heynes, Mr. Hopkins, Mr. Webster, Mr. Whiting, Capten Mason, Mr. Hooker, Mr. Stone & Mr. Warham, twenty shillings apeece as a token of my love. I give Mrs. Huet £5 out of the debts due to me fro her deceased husband; and to Mr. Smith £5 out of the debts he oweth me; and to William Gybbins, £10 out of Mr. Smiths debt.   GEORGE WILLIS

I doe further give my sonne Samuel £10 money, all my Books, and my watch. I doe give unto ech of my two daughters a bedde & furniture, wch I leave to the ordering of my wife. I doe give to my wife all my debts, cattell, chattells, utensels, mony, plate, wth all moveables not otherwise disposed of by this my will. I make her sole Executrixe.
                                                        GEORGE WILLIS.
Witness: 14 December: *Ed Hopkins,*
                 Will. Gybbins.

Note was added 22 February, 1644, & change of date. Samuel now to pay the £40 to his sisters within one year after he come to the age of 21 yeares.
4 March, 1644 (5). Another change was made relating only to Hester, Amy or Samuel in kind, or in the case of death of either. I doe further give & bequeath twenty Nobles to the poore in the towne of Hartford, five marke to the poore in Wethersfield, forty shillings to the poore att Windsor, and forty shillings to the poore at Tunxis Cepus, to be paid in County Comadits and disposed according to the discretion of my Executrixe.
                                                        GEORGE WILLIS.
Ed. Hopkins.
Will Whiting.

APPENDIX TO VOLUME I.

1635 to 1700.

Some Wills, and other papers of a miscellaneous character, gathered from the volumes entitled Private Controversies (P. C.), or other volumes not conveniently accessible, mostly at the State Library or the Office of the Sec. of State, are here assembled, it appearing that they have a bearing upon some matters, near or remote, giving value to them.

(Vol. IV)   P. C. No. 63.

Augur, Nicholas, New Haven. Will dated 20th September, 1669.
Know all men by these presents, that I, Nicholas Augur, of New Haven, being bound on a voyage to Boston, & not knowing the end of my appointed time, do make and ordain this my last Will & Testament in manner and forme following: Imprimis: I give & bequeath unto my beloved sister, Hester Coster, what Money & Estate I have in the house, as a token of my love. 2ly, My Debts being paid, I give unto Katharine Reeston £5. 3ly, I give unto my mayd Servant, Mercy Willmet, £20. My Debts & Legacies being paid, I order & dispose of my Estate as followeth: I give unto my Brother John Augur, £20. I give unto my sister, Hester Coster, £300. I give unto Robert Augur £150. I give unto my Cousin Nicholas Augur, ye son of my Brother John Augur, £100. I make my sister sole Executrix.

Witness: *John Nash,*   Nicholas Augur.
        Sam: Whitehead.

Baret, Peter. The following letter from Peter Baret discloses some exceedingly interesting historical facts connecting the families of Baret in England, Thomas Stoughton at Windsor, and Huntington of Saybrook and Norwich, Connecticut. Also, difficulties of trade with England, with an allusion to happenings in the time of Oliver Cromwell.

Land Records, Sec. State's office, Vol. II, Page 4 by Count.

Norwich, England, 20 April, 1650.
Cosen Christopher Huntington: Your letter, date about the 20th September, 1649, from Seabrook, I Received, & doe pereseve that you

have & shall receive to the value of 140 pounds of my Brother Sawton, which, when you have Received, & Securitee for what shall be behinde unpaide, then give him and my sister an acquittance as from me, in full Discharge of all matters & Demands that I can or may Lay claim unto from them soe. The devision of this £140, it shall be thus done: Whatever is Lost, as ox or a Cowe, or by Reason the Comodities may not be altogether worth soe much as you took them for, shall be first deducted, only the £140, & then the rest shall be thus devided: You shall take out £5 in the first place, And then devide the rest into five parts, whereof take too to yourselfe, one to Symon, one to Thomas, & one to Ann, wch will be all the five parts; & then give to Symon the other five pound, for my Intent is that hee shall have £5 more than one fifth part; & I suppose you now know my Intent & meaning herein, & Let it be thus done. I well remember I told you that my Cousin Ann should have £20 because that her preferment by way of mariag; but I gave you noe Comission to dispose of the money but by my order. Let Tho: his first part be put into Good hands & Security taken for it, with allowance for the forbearance that when he shall come to be capable to imploy it he may receive it with the Increase. Let me know what you doe herein, & sende me an acquittance under your hand for your parts as a gift given you by me, one under Symon's hand for his as a gift given him by me, also Ann her hand or marke as a gift given her by me. If shee cannot write doe you wittness it; & for Tho. Likewise a receipt under his hand as a gift given him also. Let me receive these 4 acquittances by the next Letters. Let the security for Tho. his part be taken in his owne name, & the yearly increase that shall be allowed him for it putt into the Securitie also. My father it hath pleased God to take away out of this world in August Last. I pray God fitt us all for the Like change. My mother is made Executrix, but I cannot heare that any of you are mentioned in his will. For holding in the Barbadoss my father hath nothing to show of any debt due to my Brother Huntington, but the Debt which he owes is £17, which is my debt, made over to mee under his hand & seale before he wentt away; & £12 he owes me uppon a bond to myself, so the whole debt is £29, which hath been my Loss. All this while the parliament hath taken all the King's officers places away, all England over, and I have hereupon Lost £20 a yeare by this Act. that now I am removing myselfe towards London, & so cannott (by reason of these distractions) think of Sending you any Merchandising Comodities. Let this inclosed be conveiyed to My Brother Stawton. If I have time & Leisure, I will against the next spring send you over some Comodities, but for Dutch cloath cannot accomodate you with, for I shall not have any ways of or means to gett them upon good tearms. I should think our North County Cloath should sell best, or these best Course cloths which you send me a patterne of. You mention in your letter of Shott, but not what sortes & for what use, for thereby we may guess at the sortes you should have. With the price of this kind of cloath & the bredth, I should have there by knowne the better what to have done therein; you must hereafter write more particularly ye thinge. I shall not further inlarge myselfe, but my love to yourselfe & your Brothers, & Sister Remembered. Comitting you to the prtection of the almighty & Rest.

Your Loving unckle

Norwich the 20th aprill, 1650.   PETER BARET.

Sende your Letters to me by Mr. Edward French at his ware howse in the George Yard in Lumbard Street in London.

Blackleach, Elizabeth. The following Plea of Mrs. Blackleach, before the Court of Assistants, relates to a will made by a married woman, and to an error of the Court admitting it to Probate:

(Vol. III)   P. C., No. 211.

An Appeal to the Court of Assistants now sitting at Hartford, the Humble Application of Elizabeth Blackleach. Whereas, the Reverend John Whiting, in the absence of my Husband, at a late County Court in Hartford, did exhibit a certain Writing as the last Will of Christian Harbert, late wife of Benjamin Harbert, which that Court was pleased to accept as her will approved by her husband, Etc., I was necessitated to this Application for an alteration of that conclusion, and do therefore present the following considerations: 1st, Whereas, the said paper is presented as a will, It is evident thereby that the estate therein bestowed was originally Benjamin Harberts, and there is, nor indeed could be, no alienation of it to his wife to make it hers to dispose of. That the woman therein undertaking was a *feme Covert* is plain, and that the whole estate of a feme Covert (while so) is her husbands right, is as undeniable a principal as any in law, and the sole and one ground of the Husbands enjoying what comes in his wives right; nor can any man lift his wife out of the Coverture the Law puts her under, and the consequents of it, for the Law is above all in those things, so that she being no person in law to take the right, but that still remaining by law in her husband, she cannot will what in Law shee can have no right personally and seperately in. That which is aleadged from her husbands witnessing the will, and by a will of his owne, as giveing her a right, is unsufficient; for 1st, as aforesaid, he could not do it; 2nd, hee hath not done it, for 1st, to her will he is but a witness at most, the extent of which is only that he testifies this is to be his wives will. A party or testator to the will hee cannot bee and a witness two, for Testatorship therein in any degree requires others to bee witnessess, and as to his will so caled of 6th June, 1684, it was revoked 7 Feb. following. Besides, to the passing the Land by Law, there must be som writing, record or Act passing it, but none such appears, nor are a few words sufficient thereunto without any other Conveyance. 2ndly, the said woman, being *Covert feme,* is absolutely incapable also, persons not of sound memory or not Compos mentis of makeing a will to dispose of Lands, by the 38 of King Hen. 8, which is well knowne; and no *feme Covert* is inabled to make a will wch was the Confusion of Mr. Warams will, nor can her husband Capacitate her without the Law, nor is there need or room for it, because the Husband

may, ought, and only can, in person, give what he hath a mind anyone should have. So that if a womans will be any thing, yt is So not as her will properly and formaly but as it is her husbands will, having the ruling power in the case, hath actually overruled his wives will, nullfying his owne of 6 June, 1684, wch gave all the strength to his wives will by his act to Mr. Blackleach 7 Feb. 1684, and so nulled his wives will. 4thly, this was done by her husband 7 Feb. 1684, uppon necessity of maintaining himself and wife, wch is a good call and warrant by al Laws to alter his owne and wives will too, for it had been meer unrighteous profusion for him to give away his estate, and the providence of God caled for it to be used to feed and cloath himself and wife, so that as his circumstances went hee had been worse than an infidell had he not so provided. 5thly, Just debts notwithstanding must be paid, yea, and by All those mentioned wills are exprest or implyed to be paid. Now this estate is a debt contracted after those wills so called as by that writing of 7 Feb. 1684, and to take it from him is to take away his due which hee hath sufficiently paid for, and might have paid dearer for. For Mr. Blackleach paid all his debts, wch were considerable, tooke him and his wife in a miserable condition, Mantained them well all their days to his no little cost, and that Mr. Whiting should now indeavor in Mr. Blackleach absence to deprive us of so great a part of the just repavment of our real expense, hath to me no good Aspect. 6thly, Whereas, Jos. Bull and Sam. Steele give testimony that what is a Bond written is a true paragraph of my Father Harberts last will, etc., And thereupon I suppose on a promiscuous view it may seem proved that such a will of my father was and still is in force, and ratifying his first wifes will, etc., and so the Court had ground to act as they did. I pray the Court to Consider that there is no such will in force, nor proved; for had it been so, then should it have come from the Court Records, and not be brought in by a back dore, as it were, from witnesses; but the wors Capt. Allyn can Certify that there is no such will of my Father Harberts on record, and I pray the Court to distinguish between a will only tittular, or such, in the nameing of two witnesses, and a will proved and of efficacy, for the one sort, and such is the one they testify to, is only tittularly so, and is clearly revoked by his act of 7 Feb. 1684; and if the Court had been pleased as well to say they found his revocation as his approbation, I had not given this trouble. I could do no less than acquaint this Worshipful Court with these things in my husbands absence, and thereupon to desire, as I do, either the rejection of said will as disallowed by my Father Harbert, or such a suspension of the case as may save my husbands claims unhurt till the next session of this worsp Court, I having daily expectations of his return, and for this worsp Court I shall ever pray.　　　　　　　　　　　　ELIZABETH X BLACKLEACH.
　　　　　　　　　　　　　　　　　　　　　　　　　　her marke.
May 31, 1687.

　　See P. C., No. 201, for the Bond of John Blackleach to support his father Benjamin Harbert & his Mother Jane Harbert, 7 February, 1684.

(Vol. II) P. C. No 180.

[See Will of James Boosey, in Book II.]

Boosey, James. A Court of Election held at Hartford 14th May, 1668. Upon the Petition of Ensign Steele, John Pratt & Nathaniel Stanley, etc., this Court do hereby order, that the Children of James Boosey, or their heirs, shall not be prejudiced or disenabled by the law for Claime of Land, & prosecution within a twelve moneth & a day to sue for or recover any Right they have or ought to have in any land in Reversion after the death of the Mother, either by Will or heirship at Common law. Extracted out of the Court Records of 4th March, 1683-4.

No. 181—Nathaniel ffoot testifieth as followeth: He being in Company with Enoch Buck, and entering into Discourse about ye Dry Swampe which he bought of Jehu Burr, which is now in controversy, the said Buck told me yt Mr. Burr came to him and offered to sell him the said swamp, and after some discourse about it he said he bought it, and he said yt after they or he had bought ye Land some considerable time, then arose a doubt whether Jehew Bur could give them a good assurance off the said land, and soe there was a delay made for a little time, and then the said Bur came again to ye said Buck and said now he had gott goodwiff Wakely to Record the land to Joseph Boosey, and gott her to sett her hand to the Record, and now he thought he could give good Assurance of it, And yt Goodm Griswold and himself bought the said Land. Testimony of Mary Steele testifieth yt she heard Enoch Buck speak the substance of what is in the above written testimony, in their house, to her husband and her Bro. Stanly. Nath. ffoote testifieth that the above written is truth according to his best remembrance, or the substance of it. Nath. ffoot & Mr. Steele gave their respective oaths to the above written testimonys Octobr 11, 1684, before me

Samll Talcott Adms

No. 182—Testimony of Mary Steele, aged about 50 years, yt her Father James Boosey did give some of the Lott yt he bought of Robert Cooe, which pease is ye Upland Lott in ye West Field, and yt shee, with William Smith which dyed att Farmington, did have the sd. pease, and yt to ye best of her rememberance there was between two and three acres of them. She further testifieth yt she did often hear her mother say that the Land in the Dry Swamp which her father bought of Robert Cooe did belong to her, and her sister Stanly of Hartford after her decease. This she saith she heard her say often of late days. Given upon Oath 11th October, 1684.

before Samll Tallcott Comer.

No. 186 shows that the Widow, name Esther, of Joseph Boosey, sone of James Boosey, late of Fairfield, Decd, had become the wife of Jehu Burr: Emanuel Buck & Michael Griswold, Defts., they having bought the Land in Controversy (a question of Title); also the Will of Joseph Boosey, proven in Fairfield, his wife being the only Legatee.

(Vol. IV) P. C. No. 188.

Chesbrough, Nathaniel, sometime of Stonington. 25 May, 1698. Joseph Saxton, you, as Adms. in the Right of your wife Hannah Saxton to the Estate of Nathaniel Chesbrough, sometime of Stonington, Decd, and Nathaniel Chesbrough, son of sd. Decd, you are both required to appear at the County Court to be held at New London on the 1st Tuesday in June next, then and there to answer the Complaint of Elihu Chesbrough, son of Elisha Chesbrough, sometime of sd. Stonington, also decd, in an Action on the Case for that you doe refuse and have refused & neglected to divide between him & you certain Lands & Appurtenances lying in sd. Stonington, given & devised by the last Will & Testament of Mr. William Chesbrough, sometime of sd. Stonington, Decd, unto his two sones, the aforesd Nathaniel Chesbrough and Elisha Chesbrough, both Decd, and soe of Right to be divided equally between the respective heirs of the sd. deceased brother. Unto the County Marshall, and return to the Court or Clerk before the Corte or Constable of Stonington.

Pr Samuel Mason, Assistant.

Pr Samuel Frink, Constable.

A true Copy.

(Vol. II) P. C. No. 157.

Cole, James. One parcel of Land in Hartford belonging to James Cole and his Heirs, lying by Wethersfield Bounds, being an Island containing by Estimation 4 acres more or less, abutting on Wethersfield Bounds on the South End, and on the Great River on the East, and on a Creek from the Great River compassing it.

Recorded 30 August, 1684. Per *John Allyn, Register.*

No. 165—Testimony of William Williams, that James Cole owned the Island at Wethersfield, wherein is also mentioned John Cole, son of James Cole, late of Hartford.

No. 158—24 July, 1654, Land in Hartford belonging to Daniel Sillivant and his heirs forever, by Gift from his Father-in-law, James Cole, according to the Cautions and provisions made in his Will.

More: One parcel by Gift also from his aforsd. father, neare Wethersfield Bounds, which was sometimes the Land of Mr. Hollister of Wethersfield, containing by Estimation five acres more or less, abutting upon Penny Wise on the South, and on John Wilson's Land West, and on Land of the aforsd. James Cole north, and the Great River East. Recorded 3 September, 1684. *John Allyn, Register.*

A true Copie from Hartford Records.

(Vol. II.) Land Records, Sec. State's office.

On the 17th day of August, 1650—I, Andrew Munroe, of Appamatticke, marriner, have bargained, sold and delivered to Robert Lord and

Daniel Sullivane, of New England, Marriners. And on the 25th of August, 1652, Daniel Sullivane of Hartford makes Mr. William Gibbins his lawfull Attorney.

Test: *ffra Barnard,*   DANIEL SULLIVANE.
       Samuel X Gardner.

(Vol. II)   P. C. No 156.

Cole, John, Hartford. 3rd October, 1655. This Indenture wittnesseth that I, Elizabeth Sillivant, of New Haven, Widow, do by these presents alien, bargain and sell, and by these presents have bargained and sold unto John Cole, of Hartford, all that my house and houselott with all Meadow and Land & Accomodations belonging and appertaining unto the same. In consideration hereof I, the sd. John Cole, hereby promise to pay, or cause to be paid, to the sd. Elizabeth or her Assigns, the just and full sume of £58 in Wheat and pease, And the sd. payment of £58 to be fully satisfieid and paid in manner and form following, that is to say: £29 at or before the 20th day of April next ensuing the date hereof, & the other £29 at or before the 20th day of April, 1657; & for the sume & true payment hereof we have thereunto set our Hands this 3rd day of October, 1655.

With the sd. House & Accommodations   ELIZABETH SILLIVANT.*
is also, at the same price of £58, is allowed
a bed-sted & a table.   JOHN COLE.

Received of the sume above specified, by order from Mr. Goodyear and upon his Account, the sume of £49-10, this 3rd July ('57).

Pr me, HENRY WOLCOTT.

A certified copy, compared 3rd of September, 1684.

Pr me, JOHN ALLYN, Secrty

(Vol. II) Land Records, Sec. State's office, Page 22 by Count.

Edwards, William, Cooper, Hartford. I, William Edwards, of Hartford, Cooper, for good Consideration, acquit and discharge John Packer of Pequett, shipwrighte, from all Debts, and more particularly

---

*Elizabeth Sillivant, Widow of Daniel Sillivant, late of New Haven, was daughter of Mr. George Lamberton, the Capt. lost in the Phantom ship. Her husband died in Virginia in the summer of 1655. His Will was testified to upon Oath before Obedience Robbins, a Magistrate of Northampton Co., Va., June 4th, 1655. As Mr. Stephen Goodyear married Lamberton's Widow, Elizabeth Sillivant is called, on the New Haven Record, Goodyear's daughter. She was Daniel Sillivant's 2nd wife; his 1st wife was Abigail Cole, daughter of James Cole of Hartford. After Daniel Sillivant's death, his Widow Elizabeth Sillivant married at Milford 9 June, 1656, William Trowbridge, Assistant.

and especially doe acquit and discharge the sd. John Packer from a certain Bill from him to mee for about £5-14, which hee the sd. Packer hath paid by my Order to John Pickett of Pequett, for which I acknowlege myself fully satisfied, and therefore the sd. Bill ought to bee delivered in unto the sd. John Packer, but, being lost, cannot be delivered and cancelled as it ought to bee; but I, the sd. William Edwards, doe hereby ingage to secure and save harmless the sd. John Packer.
27th June, 1654.
Witness: *John Cullick,*   WILLIAM EDWARDS.
      Samuel Smith.

Fenwicke, George, Saybrook. The Will of George Fenwick is that of an historic personage, giving glimpses of an English gentleman's home and estate. Also, an intimation of a fact that tribute must be paid at the mouth of Connecticut River. (To the Saybrook Company?)

Inventory from File. *Will,* P. C., Vol. I, No 9.

Invt. £941-15-00. Taken by Robert Chapman, William Parker & William Waler.

Delivered in the General Courte at Hartford, 18th day of May, 1660, by Mr. John Cullick. Inventory as followeth:

	£	s	d
Items. in Cattle at six Mile Island, taken 12 May, 1660, by Thomas Bull and Robert Lay, with farme buildings, fences upon it, and Implements of husbandry belonging to it,		432-15-00	
the land at Oyester river quarter, £30-00-00; the Land at black hall quarter, £60-00-00,		90-00-00	
the land at pottapoge quarter with the meadow belonging unto it,		25-00-00	
the land in the towne of Seabrook with all the housing and buildings thereupon, all the Orchard, and house lott belonging thereunto,		80-00-00	
the hundred acres and the meaddow belonging to the thousand pound Lott, Corne field being about twentie acres, and one hundred acres of Land adjoyning,		60-00-00	
the westerne acres at Seabrook, £60-00-00; one yoke of oxen in Mr. James Fitch his hands £14; in debts belonging unto the estate about one hundred pounds, several of them being uncertain,		74-00-00	
besides the arrears in the several towns by yon the river for the fort, etc.,		100-00-00	
Total,		941-00-00	

the mares and horses in the woods, the number and value of them unknown.
Debts oweing by the estate, about sixty pounds.

Note: all the Land at Seabrook, with the yoake of oxen, was appraysed by John Clark, Senior, and William Pratt, with John Lay.

The Will of George Fenwick was extracted out of ye Regisrt of ye Court of Probate of Wills & grantinge Administrations:

The Councell which the Prophet gave to King Hezekiah upon ye Lords Message to him, that he should die and not live, is seasonable for all, it being as true of all others as of him, that they must dye & not live, the truth of which is not more certain than the time uncertain, whereof by mercy being sensible, though at present in good health, I make this my Last Will & Testament as followeth: First, I bequeath unto my dearly beloved wife Katharine all remainder of terme for years that shall beeto come at ye time of my decease, in Worminghurst, with all ye Appurtenances to it belonging, in lieu of that part of her joynture in Morton, in ye County of Durham, which is yett in lease for about five or six years. Item. I give unto my saide wife two suites of Hangings, ye one of Caesar, ye other of Diana, as also ye Greene imbroydered bed & ye brocond Cloth bed lyned with Sarsnett, with Chairs & Stoles, & all belonging to them, with ye best bed quilt, blanketts, & two paire of holland sheetes for her owne bed, And two other beds, blanketts, foure pairs of Sheets, & other necessaries to them, for two servants' beds. Item. I give unto my said wife all ye plate & pewter that is marked with our Armes; Also ye blew Damaske Couch & Chairs, & all ye lining wee bought since marriage, and all ye pictures & such Books as shee will chuse; Also ye Coach horses. I mention not her Towells, or a bed of her owne working, or other things that are her owne which she brought with her. But if there be any question of them, I intend her them all, as alsoe the best looking glasse & another Lesee. Item. I give unto my most Naturall & dear Mother, Mrs Dorothy Clavering, ten pounds per Annum, to bee paid quarterly to her during her life by my Executrix. Item. I give unto my Brother Claudius & to ye heirs, males of his body, Lawfully begotten, after ye decease of my wife, All my Landes in Brenck bourne and nether ffarmington, in the county of Northumberland, with theire appurtenances. And if my said brother shall dye without an heire, male of his body, and leave daughters, then my will is that my heirs to whom ye reversion of ye said devised Lands shall come shall pay to ye said daughters, if two, each of them five hundred pounds; if three, four hundred pounds a piece; if above three, then to each one three hundred pounds apiece, the first payment to beginne according as ye propprtion shall happen to bee paid yearly from the time that my heires shall enter upon & receive ye profitt of ye said Land. Item. I give unto my Nephew Thomas Ledgard, & to ye heirs males of his body lawfully to bee begotten, all my Lands in Thirston & Tillington, in the County of Northumberland, after ye decease of my wife; and if my said nephew shall dye without heirs, males, Then my will is, That my heirs shall pay to such daughters as hee shall leave, three hundred pounds by one hundred pounds per Annum, ye first payment to beginne from ye time that my heirs enter into and receive the profitts of ye said Land. Item. I give to my sister Ledgard & my sister Cullick each fifty pounds; to my brother Ledgard & Brother Cullick each Ten pounds; to my sister Cullick's children One hundred pounds a peece; to my neece Clifton fifty pounds, And my neece Bootflower's boy fifty pounds. Item. I give to my Daughter Elizabeth ye suite of Landskipp hangings & to my Daughter Dorothy that of Susanna. The remainder of my houshold stuffe not devised I leave to be divided between them. Lastly, I make my daughter Elizabeth sole Executrix of this my last will & Testament, and doe give unto her ye remainder of all my personal estate and Chattells, my debts & Legacies paid, onely I give unto my daughter Dorothy one hundred pounds per Annum out of my Lease of ye Lands in Sussex. Item. I give unto Ralph Fenwick, now Schollar of Christ Church in Oxford, Tenne pounds per Annum, to bee paid quarterly for ye terms of Six yeares from ye date hereof. Alsoe, I give to every servant Twenty shillings for every year they have been in my service before ye day of my death. Lastly, whereas there are besides those Lands in the North, which will descend to my daughter from myselfe, certain Lands in Sussex after a few yeares that discends unto them from their Uncle Edward Apsley, Esquire, deceased, as also some houses in Hartshene, Land in Middlesex, & some Salt Marsh in Kent neare Epr church, after ye Lease expired, My advice unto them is, that by ye Councill of some Judicious & indifferent friends, ye Lands in ye North & South may be balanced & divisions equally made, soe that if it may bee ye one may have ye Lands in ye North for her part & ye other those in ye south, And yt my daughter Elizabeth, being ye Elder Sister, may have her Choice.

In witness heereto I have set my hand & Seale this second of ffebruary, One thousand Six hundred & fifty Six.   G. FFENWICKE.

And I purpose, if God give life, to adde a Codicill in remembrance of some friends which now I could not perfect. This I declare and publish to bee my last Will & Testament.
Sealed the 8th day of March, 1656.
In presence of *Robert Leeues,*   G: FFENWICKE.
       Moses ffryer.

       I, George ffenwicke, of Warminghust, in ye County of Sussex, Esquire, doe make & appoint these prsents to bee my true & proper Codicil to my Will & Testament, this Ninth day of March, One thousand six hundred & fifty six. And first of all I doe hereby revoke and renounce fifty pounds by ye yeare, given in my will to Dorothy my daughter out of ye Lands in Sussex during my terme in them, and also I revoke £500 of ye Legacy, one thousand pounds, which I give by my will to her my said daughter Dorothy, And I doe hereby give & bequeath the summe of five hundred pounds to Katharine ffenwicke, my deare & loveing wife. I doe also hereby revoke & make voyd ye gift of wt ever sum or Summes of money are given formerly by my will to my Sister Cullick & her Children, or to all or any of them, And I doe give & bequeath to her my Said Sister and her Children all my Lands, Chattells, reall & personall, that are in New England, and my debts that are oweing thereunto mee, to be

54 APPENDIX.

divided amongst them into soe many parts as there are persons of them, & in such manner as yt her Eldest sonne may have a double portion. And likewise that out of itt may bee had Five Hundred pounds which I doe give to ye publique use of that Country of New England, if my loveing friend Mr. Edward Hopkins think it fitt, And to be employed and used to that end as my said Loveing friend Mr. Edward Hopkins Shall order and direct. Alsoe, I doe hereby give & bequeath to my Loveing friend Mr. Robert Leeues ye summe of Twenty pounds to buy him Books. I doe also desire ye said Robert Leeues to be Assistinge to my Executrix, And to take care of and helpe her in ye management of her estate in ye Countyes of Sussex, Middlesex & Kent. And I will that ye charges which he shall bee at therein be Allowed him by my Executrix, And alsoe Consideration for his paines. I alsoe give and bequeath to my Servant Moses ffryer soe much as will make up the Legacye given him by my will Ten pounds, which I will to bee employed by my Executrix to ye payment of his debts soe farr as it will extend, and the remainder to be paid to himselfe if any bee. I give and bequeath to dame Eleanor Selby, of Barwick, Tenne pounds. I doe alsoe hereby desire her my much honored goodfriend Eleanor Selby of Barwicke to undertake ye care and education of my daughter Dorothy. I also desire my deare friend & ffather-in-law, Sr Arthur Haslerigge, to accept ye meane remembrance of forty shillings to buy a ringe, which I doe hereby will & bequeath unto him. And likewise forty shillings a peice to every one of his Children for the like purpose.

I desire my very good freinds, my Cosen Lawrence and his wife, And my Cosen Strickland and his Lady, to accept as the remembrance of an affectionate friend, of ye sum of forty shillings a piece to buy them rings, which I doe hereby give & bequeath unto them. I alsoe give & bequeath to my Ancient Acquaintance and dearly beloved friend Sr Thomas Widdrington the sum of five pounds which I desire him to accept to buy a ringe. I give also & bequeath to my deare & good friend Mr. Edward Hopkins, late warden of ye ffleete, forty Shillings, to buy a ringe. I give & bequeath to my good friend Aaron Gourdon, Dr. of phisick, Ten pounds. I give and bequeath to my good friends Mr. Tempest Milner, Alderman, of London, & to his kinsman Mr. Robert Key, five pounds to buy what they please in remembrance of mee. I also give to my father-in-Law, Mr. Claveringe, and to Thomas Burrell, Brinkebarne, in ye County of Northumberland, forty shillings a peice to buy them rings. And in witness of all this I have hereunto Set my hand & Seale & published & declared this to be my true & proper Codicil, to be annexed to my Will, ye day & yeare first before mentioned. Before Sealing I will that Six pounds per Annum bee paid to Tristram ffenwicke during his life, forty Shillings by the yeare to Mr. Ogle of Leith in Scotland, And Twenty Shillings a yeare to ye widdowe Clarke of Weldon, during their severall lives.

In presence of *John Straford,*   G: FFENWICKE.
Ro: Leeues, George Largripe.

This was declared by George ffenwicke, Esqr, to be his Act, True Intent & meaning, a Codicil added and annexed to ye within closed Will, to which wee that set our hands to this as Witnesses did also set our hands witnessing his declaration of that and publication of it And this hee added to itt.

In presence of *Ro: Lewes,*
John Straford, George Largripe.

This Will and Codicil annexed was proved at London the 27th day of April, in the yeare of our Lord 1657, before the Judges for Probate of Wills and grantinge Administrations, lawfully authorized by the Oath of Elizabeth ffenwicke, the daughter & Executrix named in ye Will of the sd. Decd, To whom *Adscon* of all and singular the Goods, Chattells & debts of ye sd. Decd was committed, she being first sworn by Commission well & truly to administer ye same.

This is a true Copie of ye originall Will & Codicil of ye sd. George ffenwicke, Esqr, decd, which is truly & faithfully examined and collated

Pr me, *Leonard Brown, Notary Publique.*

This is a true Coppy of the aforesd. attested Coppy, examined together with him whose name is hereunder written as Attest.

Pr me, *Robert Howard, Notary Publique.*

Massachusetts Collonee, Novae Angle 10 March, 1658.

THOMAS WALKER.

(Vol. III)   P. C. No 50.

Goodrich, John. You are hereby in his magesties named required to attach 2 peeces or parcels of Meadow Land, containing about 8 acres, in Wethersfield meadow, such as you shall be directed unto, which belonged to the estate of John Goodrich Sen., late of Wethersfield, deceased, and secure the same to be responsible at the County Court to be held at Hartford on the first Thursday in September next to the complaint of Wm. Pitkin as Attorney to Thomas Tracy, of Norwich, and Mary his wife, in an action of the case for that fower pounds by the year since the decease of the sd. John Goodrich hath not been paid unto the said Mary Tracy, according to a Covenant made to that intent by the said Goodrich, dated April 4th, 1674, and for payment of which said Land was bound, whereof remains unpaid thirteen pounds two shillings, besides part of a years due unto the payment of the said summe, and you are to give notice hereof to Lt. Samuel Steele, Daniell Rose and Joseph Goodrich, Administrators to the said John Goodrich his estate, and warn them to, or so many of them as you can warn, to appear at said Court to answer the action and defend the estate, and make return of serveing hereof to the Court or to the clerk thereof before the Court, the Plaintif having given Security according to Law to prosecute his action to effect and answer all damages in case he make not his plea good. Hereof fail not. To the Marshall George Grave to serve.

John Allyn, Secrtry.

No 51—Mr. Pitkin: That which my wife have reseved of her legesy that her husband Goodrich gave her during life, the 1st year she reseved £4, the 2nd year she reseved £2-18, and that is all that have been reseved.   THOMAS TRACY.

	£ s d
Dyed April, 1680—5 years,	20-00-00
Paid	6-18-00
Due	13-02-00

No. 52—There is a description of Land that John Goodrich made over to his wife Mary, which now is the wife of Lt. Thomas Tracy, by way of Joynture.   JOHN GOODRICH.

(Vol. V)   P. C. No 239.

Goodrich, William, Hegessett. Will dated 12 May, 1677. I, William Goodrich, of Hegessett, in the County of Suffolk, Clerk, being through the Mercy of God of sound mind and good health and disposeing memory, doe make and ordain this my last Will in manner and form following: Imprimis: I give unto Rebeckah, my loving wife, all my Messuage (   ) wherein I now dwell in Hegessett, with all the houses, out: houses, Gardens, Lands and Appurtenances thereunto belonging, to hold to her and her assigns for and during the term of her naturall life, she keeping the same from time to time in good repair; and after my sd wifes decease I give the same Messuage or Tenement houses, outhouses, Yards, Orchards, Lands and Appurtenances thereunto belonging, unto Joseph, the Eldest son now living of my Brother John Goodrich, and his heirs forever; but in case he dyes and have no naturall issue from his own body,I give all the aforesd. houses, etc., Lands with all their Appurtenances before mentioned, belonging to me in Hegessett, To my Brothers next son Jonathan, and his heirs; and if he be dead before my wife and have no Naturall issue of his own body, I give the abovesaid houses and Lands, with all the Appurtenances named or not named, belonging to me in Hegessett, unto my Brother Johns Eldest daughter and her heirs that shall then be Living. Also I give unto Rebecca, my Loveing wife, all that Coppy hold Close Called by the name of Robletts, Containing by Estimation Seven Acres more or Less, Lying in Chilton Hamlet, in Stow. Market, in the County of Suffolk, holden on the Mannor of Dagworth Cum Sorrells, To hold to her and her assigns for and during the Term of her naturall Life; and after my Said Wifes decease, I give the aforesaid Close, with all the Appurtenances thereof, to John, the Eldest Son of my Brother William Goodrich, and his heirs forever; and if he dye before my wife and leave no naturall issue, I give the aforesaid Close to William, the next Son of my Brother William Goodrich, and his heirs

forever. Also, I give unto Rebecca, my wife, all the Closes Mortgaged
To me by John Tillott, of Bayton, now deceased, for fifty pounds, and
seized upon by me for the Lack of the payment of the principall. All these
Closes they are mentioned in the Indenture made to me, with their Appurtenances, I give to the said Rebecca, my wife, during the Term of
her naturall Life; but in Case the Land be Redeemed, and the fifty pounds
paid, with the Interest that is or Shall be due to me, my will is, that my
wife shall have the Interest and Improvement thereof towards her maintenance during her Life; but my will is, that after her decease that all the
Closes of the aforesaid John Tillott, Mortgaged to me and Seized upon
by me for the want of the payment of the aforesaid Principall, Shall
descend to John Goodrich, the Eldest Son of my Brother William Goodrich, and to his heirs: but if Redeemed, I will and devise to the aforesaid
John and his heirs, after my wifes decease, fifty pounds of Lawfull
English money in the Roome of the Land. And whereas, I have Sundry
Sums of money abroad in Severall hands, I will and devise Concerning
the same that my said wife shall have the Interest and Improvement thereof Towards her Maintenance during her Life; but my will is that the
aforesaid fifty pounds, in Case paid and the aforesaid Land of John Tillott
be Redeemed, and besids that an hundred and fifty pounds more, which
I have abroad, be well secured by my wife within three months after my
decease, the above named fifty pounds for the use (   ) forenamed
John Goodrich, Eldest Son of my Brother William, and his heirs (   )
forever. Out of the hundred and fifty pounds after my wifes decease, I
will and devise one fifty pounds to the above said John, Eldest Son of my
Brother William Goodrich, and his heirs forever. And as for the other
hundred pounds, I will and devise the Same unto Joseph, the Eldest Son
now Living of my Brother John Goodrich, and his heirs forever. after the
decease of my wife. And I further will, that whenever Mr John Tillotts
Land be Redeemed and the fifty pounds paid in, That the said fifty pounds
Shall be put out for the better Improvement for my wifes maintenance;
but no part nor parcell of it but by and with the Consent of my kinsman
Henry Bull, Sen., of Bury Malster, and John Goodrich, Eldest son now
living of my Cozen Robert Goodrich, of Hawlsigh Chirurgeon. And after
the Same manner shall the hundred and fifty pounds before mentioned,
to be disposed for the maintenance of my Said wife, no part of the Same
to be put out or altered & out of the present hands where it is but by and
with the Consent of Henry Bull, of Bury, and John Goodrich of Hawlsigh,
that so the principal Sum may be preserved for the aforesaid John Goodrich, Eldest Son of my Brother William Goodrich, and his heirs, and Joseph
Goodrich, Eldest Son of my Brother John Goodrich, and his heirs. And
in Case of her disposal of the Said Two Hundred pounds or any part
thereof without the Consent of the aforesaid Henry Bull and John Goodrich, Then I will that my sd 2 Brothers Children, Joseph and John, or
their heirs Liveing, Shall Immediately, from and after Such disposal, have
and Injoy the Two Hundred pounds according to my mind and purpose
abovesaid, either of them their appoynted Part and Share. And 'tis

further my will, that my Said wife doe, before She injoy any benefit of this my will, first enter into Bond in four hundred pounds to the Said Henry Bull and John Goodrich, that her Executors & Administrators shall duly pay to the above named Joseph and John, within three months after her decease, ye Two hundred pounds In Case the Land of Mr. Tillott be Redeemed and the principall paid, or else One hundred and fifty pounds if they shall Come so Soon out of New England to Receive the Same, or by sufficient and undoubted authority Send for the Same, or else as soon as they shall Come for it. Item: It is my will that all the over plus of my Estate, either goods or money or household Stufe or Chattells whatsoever, Shall be and for the Sole use and benefit of my wife, and at her disposall; to whom I give the Same. And I Constitute and appoynt ye Said Rebecca, my wife, Sole Executrix of this my last will & testament, and I Nominate ye said Henry Bull and John Goodrich Supervisors thereof. Also, my mind and will is, that Mr. John Bull, now Reader of Bury in the Parish of St. James, and the Son of Henry Bull abovesaid, shall have these books named by mine own hand in the Margin* of my will, which my Executrix after my decease Shall deliver unto him. In witness of all this I, the said William Goodrich, have to this my last will and Testament, Contained in one Sheet of paper, Set my hand and Seale, dated the twelveth of May, in the year of our Lord 1677.

WILLIAM GOODRICH.

A True Coppy, attested by *Edward Oxbrough, Notary.*

No. 240.—A letter from Henry Bull, dated 23 November, 1692, to Cozen Goodrich: Suggest your Aunt is in good health. My own son John, a minister, and my son-in-law, Thomas Winlock, who married my daughter, are intrusted according to your desire to look after your Estate.

Your loving friend & Kinsman, HENRY BULL.

No 241.

Bury, 24 November, 1698.

Dear Brother: John: My kind Love to you and yours. This is to desire you to send to my Cousens, the Goodriches, to let them know that their Aunt is dead and was buried the 18th day of this instant November.

Your loving brother, HENRY BULL.

No. 242.

From Bury ye 16th of July, 1678.

Cozen Goodrich:

This is to inform you that your brother William is lately dead. He dyed in Hegessett, near Bury, in the County of Suffolk, and left no children. The sum of his last will and testament is this: He has given to his wife all during her naturall life. After her decease he has bequeathed to your Relations as followeth, viz: To Joseph, the eldest son

*The titles of these books, which were written in the margin, were not legible.

C. W. M.

of his brother John, he has given his howse and ground at Hegesett above-said, and one hundred pounds in money, if the Joseph shall then be living; else to 2nd son; failing this, to the eldest daug. of his Brother John. He has also given one coppy hold ground, in value neare £100, and £100 in money, to John, the Eldest sone of his brother William, after the decease of his wife, if then living, & next, this failing, to William, the son of his brother William, and his heirs forever; all to be enjoyed after the death of his wife, whom he has appointed sole executrix; myself and one Mr. John Goodrich, of Hawlsigh, to be supervisers.

my Wife is yet living, who was your Cozen Jane Coates, and desires to be kindly remembered to you. I am also your loving Kinsman,

HENRY BULL.

No. 243. Be it know unto all men by these presents: that I, Jonathan Goodrich, of Wethersfield, Taylor, one of the sons of John Goodrich, late of Wethersfield aforesd., Husbandman, decd, for divers good causes have constituted & appointed my friend Nicholas Hallam, of New London, in the County of New London, Mariner, my true and lawful atty. to act for me in the realm of England to enter into and upon one certain Messuage or Tenement lying and being in Hegesett, in the County of Suffolk, in the Kingdom of England, formerly belonging to and in the possession of William Goodrich, of Hegesett aforesd., Clerke, and now of Right belonging to me, to do, execute and accomplish all and whatsoever I myself might or could do personally.

Witness: *Hez: Willis,*   JONATHAN GOODRICH.
    Caleb Stanly, Jr.   18 May, 1703.
Test: Eleazer Kimberly, Sec.   By the Command J. Winthrop.

No. 243. John Wintrop, Esq., Governor of his Magesties Colony of Con. in New England, greeting: The 20th May, 1703, appeared before me, sd. John Winthrop, in Hartford, William Warner, age about 57 years, And Thomas Welles, aged about 41 years, both of Wethersfield, to testify from personal knowledge and acquaintance with John Goodrich, late of Wethersfield, Husbandman, deceased, living & converseing with him many years; and that sd John Goodrich had a Reputed son named Joseph Goodrich, who hath been dead for about 22 yr. and died without issue.

And the said William Warner & Thomas Welles further declare that the sd John Goodrich left another son at his decease named Jonathan Goodrich, who now (since the sd. Joseph his death) is reputed only son surviving lawfully begotten, and that Jonathan Goodrich aforesd., Taylor, a person who was present at the time of takeing the Oath, upon whose Request this Certificate is granted, Claims estate lying in Hegesett, County Suffolk, England, devised to him by the last will of William Goodrich, sometime of sd. Hegesett, Clerke. Said Jonathan Goodrich, about 38 years of age, married and has several children living.

                                        (COLONY SEAL)
Eleazer Kimbaly, Sect.   J. WINTHROP.

(Vol. II)   P. C. No 203.

Griswold, Edward. The statement of Edward Griswold reveals an ebb-tide in the affairs and settlement of Windsor.

The Testimony of Edward Griswold, aged about 77 years, is that about the year 1639 Mr. William Whiting, Decd, was Undertaker for a shipp in England, in which Shipp I came to New England. The sd Mr. Whiting borrowed of one Mr. John Saint Nicholas about two hundred pounds, wch I had the Bill to receive here, wch money reced. against Mr. Whiting by Mr. Nicholas order here. And at the time many passengers came over, severall of which settled in Windsor, and a gennerall expectation there was at that time, as appeared by discourse of many more passengers to come, and some of note, as the said Mr. St. Nicholas for one, by which means Land at Windsor near the towne and ready for improvement was at a high price; and about that time the said Mr. Whiting bought, as was Commonly reported, Mr. Ludlow's Land at Windsor, that is, when Land was dear, and I know Mr. Ludlow went away then in a short time after. But afterwards people that were Expected out of England, not Comeing in Such numbers as was looked for, Mr. Ludlow (   ) to England, and others removeing to the Sea Side, the Lands at Windsor fell very much in price from what they were at when Mr. Ludlow sold to Mr. Whiting, So that Generally, to my Observance, Lands were not sold but at half the price as before or about half the price. Further, I testifie that the above said Mr. St. Nicholas, living near Mr. Hewett in England, did manifest his desire to settle by Mr. Hewett in New England, and by my observance of Mr. St. Nicholas words and actions and also Mr. Whiting, did apprehend that Mr Whiting bought Mr. Ludlow's Lands to accomodate the said Mr. St Nicholas. Mr. Edward Griswold personally appeared this 15 May, 1684, & made oath to the above written before me.

John Allyn, Assist.

At Perticular Court, Page 98.

Howell, Mr. 11th May, 1657. Upon Examination of Wignagub, he confessed that he was hyred to burn Mr. Howell's house by 2 Indians, one Anabayn-hoe prmised him one gun, and Agagon agu, who promised him £7-06; and hee said Auwegenum did know hee was to burne the house two dayes before it was done, and that himselfe and the three Indians were together when he was hyred, but Auwegenum did not hear their discourse; but Anwabeg told Anwegenum of it afterwards. Upon consideration of the motion made from our ffreinds at South Hampton for the prsence, countenance and assistance of 20 men from us, and considering their Sad distressed prsent State by reason of the insolent & insufferable outrage of some heathen upon that Island & neare that Plantation by fyering several dwellings houses to the undoeing of severall members of this Collony, this Court doth order, that there shall be 20 men prssed forthwith to goe over to their assistance, as the case may require, together with necessary prvisions and Ammunition, wch are to be taken out of the Severall Towns in the prportion following:

Hartford,   :
Windsor,   :   these men to have 25 lbs. of powder
Wethersf.,   :   & 50 lbs of Bullets.
ffarmington, :
Middletown,   :
Sea Brooke,   :
Pequott.   :

Page 196. John Cooper, 6 May, 1663, makes appearance at this Court to answer the Appeal of Joseph Reiner, Richard Howell, Thomas Cooper & Samuel Dayton, according to his bond. The Pltf. appeare not to prosecute according to their Bond of £20.

(Vol II)   P. C. No. 146.

Latham, Thomas. We, Andrew Davis and John Bailey, being employed as Carpenters by John Packer, sen., for the finishing of the House of Thomas Latham, Decd, the sd. Packer marrying the Widow of the sd. Latham, And being since desired to give the best of our judgement concerning the frame of that house as to value & worth thereof, and alsoe sd. frame & house wch frame shingles & Clapboards did once belong unto John Morgan and was by him sold unto Cary Latham, we finde the length of the sd. howse to be 28 foote and the breadth Eighteen foote, and (9*feet & ½ between joynts) & 9 ½ foot between ye Joynts; being all slitt worke, wee vallue the sd. frame to be really worth £16, & the Clapboards & Shingles to be £6-18; all, £22. So much new, doe really judge the Frame, Clapboards & Shingles to be really worth at our Finishing of the sd. House. And if need shall require, we shall make oath to the truth hereof; & in Testimony wee have hereunto sett our Hands, in New London, the 9th of May, 1683.
Sworn October 4th, 1683, before me,   Daniel Witherell. Commissioner.

(Vol. III)   P. C. No. 26.

Mason, John. Dist. of the Estate of Capt. John Mason, of Norwich: To Abigail, sometime the wife of Capt. Mason of Norwich, the Stock of Cattle of what kinds soever, also the 200 acres of Land already laid out in the western side of Norwich Bounds, and halfe of that Mile of Land given by Joshua Sachem of such Lands as are not yet disposed of, & likewise from allottments willed by Joshua the Sachem.

---

*This was blotted and the words set in the margin probably by Daniel Witherell, as the writing indicates.   C. W. M.

Inventory as distributed: To the Mother, £169; To John, the son, £255; and to the daughter, £110. John Mason, brother to Ann Mason, is ordered to pay to her £23 to make up her proportion according to the Court.

JAMES FITCH,
SAMUEL MASON.

Order of Court, 12 May, 1685.

(Vol. IV)   P. C. No 38.

Pigg, Robert, New Haven. Will dated 28th March, 1660:

I, Robert Pigg, being in perfect health and memory, doe make this my last will and testament: I give unto my daughter Alice my greate brass Kettle and a brass pott and a pewter platter that was her mother's, and shee is to have them after the death of my wife. I give unto Thomas Jenner, my daughter's sonne, my house and home lotte and foure acres and a halfe of land that lieth next the lott that was Mr. Malbones towards the mill, to him and to his heirs after the death of my wife; and if yt my wife should remove from New Haven and doth sell the house and land, yt Thomas Jenner shall have the half that it is soulde for, and his mother shall have the disposeing of it for him; and if yt shee be living. And I did give them a mare colt but it is lost. And I give unto my daughter by my life time two cowes worth £10. And I give unto my daughter's other children 2 ewes and one ewe lamb, to be equally divided amongst the other children, and they to be one another's heires.

This is a true Copy as it stands upon Record in the Book of Wills. Examined pr me,   *James Bishop, Clerk.*

No 39. John Bishop, of New Haven, acknowledging his indebtedness to Thomas Jenner, of Brookhaven, in ye County of Suffolk, on Long Island, is as followeth: £60 to be paid in good winter Wheat at 5 shillings per Bushell, & good Marchantable pork at £3-10-00 a barrell; & in failure thereof, in other good Marchantable provision equivalent thereto at price current wt yt marchant, ye place of paymt to be at New Haven; also for a certain dwelling house, Barne & Homelott, & 4 acres of Land, which I have bought of ye sd. Thomas Jenner and am to have possession thereof in November next, & not before ye present Crop is off from ye ground. 20th June, 1687.

Witness: *Samuel Ells, sen.*)   JOHN BISHOP, Ls.
) of Milford.
        Samuel Ells, Jr.)
                              before me, *Jno Beard, Commissioner.*
                                         James Bishop, Clerk.

No. 40. 4 June, 1690. Simon Simons, aged near 38, testifieth yt upward of 2 years past having lived sometime before wth ye Widow

Thorpe, decd, he had ye Land & house lott of her, & wth her consent improved it; & having a crop on ye ground, John Bishop of New Haven came to him & told him he had bought ye land and must have ye possession of it, & bid ye deponent take of his crop, which he did, & told him ye land was ready for him. After this, on ye day Mr. Trowbridge was buried, which was ye spring after ye sd. Jno. Bishop came to deponent & told him he must take ye land again, & before Jno. Roo did deliver up possession of it, & accordingly he took possession & hath had it ever since, & further saith not. Ye sd. Simon sworne ye day & year above written.

before me, *Wm Jones, Assist.*

Copies as   *James Bishop, Cler.*

(Vol. II)   P. C. No 100.

Richardson, Stephen. To the Honoured the General Assembly of Connecticut Colony now sitting in Hartford, the Humble Application of Stephen Richardson, showing: That whereas, my Hond Father Mr. Amos Richardson, of Stonington, by the all-disposing Providence of God is lately decd, and did before his death make his Will, wherein he constituted my Hond Mother Executrix, giving her power to dispose of part of his Estate; since which it hath pleased God to take away my mother also by death, who hath also left her last Will in writing, wherein she hath made mee and my brother, Samuel Richardson, Executors of her last Will, we, according to the Trust therein reposed in us, would have proved the sd. Will at the County Court at New London, that we might have been in a legal capacity to have administered the Estate and have executed the Wills: but it hath pleased God to visit the Magestracy of New London County that there were not so many as to constitute a Court at the usual time, and so all business at that Court, and ours among the rest, was unatended, nor can we learn that there will & certainly be any Court soon held there; and so it is that much of the Estate being in stock of Cattell which are given immediately to be paid on proveing my Mothers Will, & other Estate that requires a present Care & Dispose of, & which we are unwilling to run the Hazzard of if it should be lost, I do for and by order of my Brother, the Co-Executor wth me, and for myself, Humbly beseech this Honourable Court to appoint persons that may speedily hold a Court at New London, or at least that this Court, as your Wisdom shall see best, do appoint some means whereby there may be opportunity given us for a lawful probation of sd. Wills so far as shall appear to be just, that so wee may be capable of Disposeing the Estate as willed by our parents, & not exposed to any Hazzard of Loss of what we can now discharge ourselves if the sd. Wills were proved, nor bear the further charge of it, which is considerable; or if the Honoured Court please to take Cognisance of it and settle the Will, we shall rest satisfied therein; & for this Honoured Court we ever pray, etc.

Hartford, 11 October, 1683.   STEVEN RICHARDSON.

64 APPENDIX.

(Vol. II)   P. C. No. 50.

Russell, John. May the 16th, 1660. Lands of Mr. John Russell, Jr., which he bought of John Fletcher of Milford, lying in Wethersfield on Connecticut River: One pece of Upland and Swamp in the South Field, Containing 16 acres more or lesse. The ends abutt against a Highway leading to Middletown West, & the Plaine East; the sides against lands that was formerly Richard Belding's, Decd, South; on Land that was formerly Lissley Bradfield's, North. One peice lying in the South Field, containing 12 acres more or lesse. The end abutts against a Hieway West, and beaver Brook East; the Sids against the Lands of Nathaniel ffoot, decd, or his heirs, North, and John Lattimer South. The above written are true Coppies of the Records of the abovesd. parcells of Land as they stand recorded unto me.

JOHN RUSSELL, JUNR.

In the 79th page of the 1st Booke of Wethersfield Records, 28 February, 1682, pr me   *John Welles, Recorder.*

No. 51. 26 of December, 1648. Lands of Robert Foote, which he bought of Samuel Gardner of Wethersfield: Another pece of Homelott, containing 3 acres more or lesse. The ends abutts on the Way South, and the Plaine North; the sids against the Lands of Nathaniel Foot, East & West.

The above written is a true coppie of the Records of the parcell of Land as it stands recorded to Robert Foote in the 19th page of the 1st Book of the Wethersfield Records.

Per John Welles, Recorder.

(Vol. I)   Windsor Lands, Page 16, Sec. State's office.

Stoughton, Thomas, sen. 11th January, 1640, Thomas Stoughton, sen., hath granted to him from the Plantation an Homelott whereon his Dwelling House now stands, wch together wth the Additions and Meadow adjoyning conteynes in yt 52 acres more or less, vizt, 25 acres of Meadow wch is in breadth by the Great River 39 Rods wide; at the head next the Upland, by reson of exchange wth George Gunne, 53 ½ Rodd; the Upland at the Head of the sd. Meadow being in breadth, by reson of Purchase fro John Lykins, 34 ½ Rodd; and in breadth next the Street by addition to George Gunne 27 Rodd; and on the West side of the sd. Street the remainder of the before sd. 52 acres in breadth, by addition fro the Towne, 74 ½ Rodd; bounded on the West by a Highway appointed betwixt yt and the Lotts of David Wilton & Nicholas Denslow, & on the South Side bounded at the West & by Tho: Dewey & fro him to the sd. great River to the aforementioned Highway at the West End. Also, over the Great River, next unto the same, the breadth 50 Rodd more or less, to run the same breadth 3 Myles to the East, bounded on the South by

Ephraim Huet, on the North by Stephen Terry. Also, towards Plmo Mead 69 acres more or less, in breadth 69 Rodd, in Length northward 160, bounded on the north by John Lykin, on the South by Thomas Gunn. (See Stiles's History of Windsor, Vol. II, Page 722):

We learn from tradition that the brothers, Thomas and Israel, were accompanied to New England by their father, Thomas, Senior. Thomas the Elder, as he is designated on the Land Rec. of Windsor, in a deed date 14 July, 1645, makes over to "Thomas, my son," all his ppty in W. except his home lott, well court, and court before the house, and orchard, evidently reserved for his own use. Afterwards Thomas Stoughton the Elder sold to Thomas the younger his dwelling house and outhouses, orchard and courts, formerly exempted, provided the said Thomas the younger shall afford convenient maintenance to the said Thomas his ffather, and his mother-in-law, that is, the former widow Huntington, during the time of their lives, and in case Mr. Stoughton dyes first, then to all (   ) his mother-in-law the third part of a hundred pounds which the said particulars were prized at, or to allow the said convenient maintenance with himself during her life (being her choice), provided she live with the said Thomas, otherwise not. The founders of this family in the United States were, as we have seen, two brothers, Thomas and Israel, who came over in 1630 or 1633 with their father, Thomas the Elder.

Sunckquasson Indian Treaty.—"Whereas our predecessor Sunck-quasson, sachem of Suckiage, alias Hartford, did about the yeare sixteen hundred thirty six, by a writeing under his hand, pass over unto Mr. Samuel Stone and Mr. Wm. Goodwin, in the behalfe of the present pro-prietors and owner of the lands belonging to the township of Hartford, all that part of his country from a tree marked N. F. which is the dividend between Hartford and Wethersfield—we say from the afoarsayd tree on the south, till it meet with Windsor bounds on the north, and from the great river on the east, the whole bredth to run into the wilderness to-wards the west full six miles, which is to the place where Hartford and Farmington bounds meet; which grant of Sunckquasson, as occasion hath been, was by him renewed to the honoured John Haines, Esqr. and other the first magistrates of this place, and enlarged to the westward so far as his country went; which enlargement as well as his former grant was made in presence of many of the natives of the place and English in-habitants; and severall yeares after, about the time of the planting of Farmington in the yeare one thousand six hundred and forty, in a write-ing made between the English and Pethus the sachem or gentleman of that place, there is a full mention of the afoarsayd Sunckquasson his grant of his country to the magistrates of this place, which grant we are privy too; and we being the onely successors of Sunckquasson and pro-prietors (before the forementioned sale) of the lands belonging to the township of Hartford on the west side of the great river, being desired to confirm and pass over all our right and interest in the afoarsayd lands to the present possessors of them, they informeing us that those writeings made by Sunckquasson before recited are at present out of the way, knowing what our predecessor hath done, and what consideration he hath received for the same,—

We, Masseeckcup and William squa in behalf of ourselves and Wawarme the sister and onely heire of Sunckquasson, and Keepequam, Seacutt, Jack Spiner, Currecombe, Wehassatuck squa and Seacunck squa, the onely inhabitants that are surviveing of the afoarsayd lands, doe by these presents owne, acknowledge and declare, that Sunckquasson whoe was the sachem of Suckiage alias Hartford, and grand proprietor of the lands adjacent, did with the consent of those of us whoe were of age to declare our consent, and with the consent of the rest of the inhabitants of this place, about the year 1636, pass over unto Mr. Samuel Stone and Mr. Wm. Goodwine, in behalfe and for the use of themselves and their company, all the land from Wethersfield bounds on the south, to Windsor bounds on the north, and the whole bredth from Connecticutt river on the east six large miles into the wilderness on the west, which sayd grant was afterwards upon further consideration renewed and enlarged by the sayd Sunckquasson, upon the desire of the honoured Mr. Haines and the rest of the magistrates of this place: but we being informed that on the removeall of some of the gentlemen afoarmentioned, the papers and writeings before specifyed are out of the way, and haveing now received of Mr. Samuel Willys, Capt. John Tallcott, Mr. John Allyn and Mr. James Richards, a farther grattification of near the value the land was esteemed at before the English came into these parts—to prevent all farther trouble between ourselves and the inhabitants of Hartford, we the sayd Masseeckcup, Wm. squa as afoarsayd, and Seacutt, Keepequam, Jack Spiner, Currecombe, Wehassatuck squa and Seacunck squa, upon the Consideration forementioned, by these presents have and doe fully, clearly and absolutely give, grant, bargain, sell, alien, enfeoffe and confirme unto Mr. Samuel Willys, Capt. John Tallcott, Mr. John Allyn, and Mr. James Richards, in behalfe of the rest of the proprietors of the land belonging to the township of Hartford, their heires and assignes forever, all that parcell of land from a tree marked N. F. being a boundary between Wethersfield and Hartford on the south, to Windsor bounds on the north, and the whole bredth of land from Wethersfield to Windsor bounds from the great river on the east to runn into the wilderness westward full six miles, which is to the place where Hartford and Farmington bounds meet,—To have and to hold all the afoarsayd parcell of land as it is bounded, with all the meadowes, pastures, woodes, underwood, stones, quarries, brookes, ponds, rivers, profitts, comodities and appurtenances whatsoever belonging thereto, unto the sayd Mr. Samuel Willys, Capt. John Tallcott, Mr. James Richards and Mr. John Allyn, in behalfe of themselves and the rest of the inhabitants of the towne of Hartford, whoe are stated proprietors in the undivided lands, their heires and assignes, to the onely proper use and behoofe of the sayd Mr. Samuel Willys, Capt. John Tallcott, Mr. John Allyn and Mr. James Richards as afoarsayd, their heires and assignes forever; and the sayd Massecup and Wm. squa in behalf of themselves and Wawarme the sister of Sunckquasson and Seacutt, Keepequam, Jack Spiner, Currecombe, Wehassatuck squa, and Seacunck squa, doe covenant to and with the sayd Mr. Samuel Willys, Mr. John Tallcott, Mr. James Richards and Mr. John Allyn, that after and next unto the afoarsayd Sunckquasson, they the said Masseeckcup, Wm. squa, Seacutt, Keepequam, &c. have onely full power, good right, and lawfull authority to grant, bargain, sell and convey all and singular the before hereby granted or mentioned to be granted premises with their and every of their appurtenances, unto the sayd Mr. Samuel Willys, Mr. John Tallcott, Mr. John Allyn and Mr. James Richards as afoarsayd, their heires and assignes forever, and that they the sayd Mr. Samuel Willys, Mr. John Tallcott, Mr. John Allyn and Mr. James Richards, and the rest of the proprietors of the undivided lands within the bounds of the township of Hartford, their heires and assignes, shall and may by force and vertue of these presents, from time to time and all times forever hereafter, lawfully have, receive and take the rents, issues and profitts thereof to their owne proper use and behoofe forever, without any lett, suit, trouble or disturbance whatsoever of the heires of Sunckquasson or of us the sayd Massecup, Wm. Squa, Seacutt, Keepequam, Jack Spiner, Currecombe, Wehassatuck squa, and Seacunck squa, our heires or assignes, or of any other person or persons whatsoever clayming by, from or under us or any of us or by our meanes, act, consent, priority or procurement, and that free and clear and freely and clearly acquitted, exonerated and discharged or otherwise from time to time, well and sufficiently saved and kept harmless by the sayd Massecup, William—squa, Seacutt and Keepequam, &c., their heires, executors and administrators, from all former and other grants, guifts, bargains, sales, titles, troubles, demands, and incumbrances whatsoever had, made, committed, suffered or done by the afoarsayd Massecup, William squa, Keepequam, Seacutt, &c.

"In Witness whereof, they have signed, sealed and delivered this writing with their own hands, this fifth of July, one thousand six hundred and seventy.

Signed, sealed and delivered in
presence of
Arramamatt, his mark,
Mamanto, his mark,
Neschegen, his mark,
Attumtoha, his mark,
Wennoe, his mark,
Will. Wadsworth,
John Addams,
John Strickland,
Giles Hamlin,
Masseeckcup, his mark,   L. S.
Seacutt, his mark,   L. S.
Jack Spiner, his mark,   L. S.
Seacunck squa's mark,   L. S.

Currecombe, his mark,   L. S.
Keepequam, his mark,   L. S.
William squa's mark,   L. S.
Wehassatuck squa's mark,   L. S.
Nesacanett gives consent to this
    grant and bargain, as he witness-
    eth by subscribing
Nesacanett, his mark,   L. S.

The original marks or signatures of the Indians are singular and gro-
tesque. Some represent implements of war, some wild beasts, &c.

This treaty with Sunckquasson, sachem, and the sale of land by
Joshua Sachem, included all the land upon both sides of the Connecticut
River within the original bounds of the Township of Hartford except that
portion lying between the Township of Windsor on the north and Glastonbury upon the south, upon the Connecticut River west, and extending
eastward three miles, and commonly called the Three Mile Lotts. For this
land no deed is known to be in existence. No doubt can with reason be
held that title was acquired by the English settlers in as equit-
able and peaceful a manner as were those aforementioned. An inference
may be drawn from the action of Wethersfield men in obtaining title to
their three miles east side of the Great River, as testified to by George
Hubbard. See page 2 Ante:

Sachem, Joshua.* The following Deed was a conveyance of Land
which is now included in the Town of Manchester, it being all the Land
in that Town except about ½ mile in width taken off the East side of the
Original 3 miles. This ½ mile given over to Manchester seems to have
been an unjust act of the General Assembly of Conn. Frequent reference
having been made to the five miles in Wills. The Survey is given following this Deed:

(Vol. I)   Hartford Lands, Fol: 6, Town Clerk's office.

Will on Record, Book D: Fol: 184, Colony Records of Deeds.

Whereas, Joshua Sachem, some short time before his death, did make
a Sale of a Parcel of Land to Major Talcott, of Hartford, for the Use &
behoofe of the Town of Hartford, & the sd. Joshua Sachem Deceasing
before he had made conveyance of sd. Land by writeing, & the said Joshua
Sachem by his Will reciteing his said bargain & disposeing of the said
pay agreed on for the said Lands for the use of the children of him the
said Joshua, as more at length is expressed in the said Will, and the child
of the said Joshua now needing the purchase money for the said Land to
be improved for the use of the said child, we the underwritten, Mr. James

---

*Attawanhood, Son of Uncas, was called by the English Joshua; probably
given as a baptismal name. He appears to have been generally known as Joshua
Sachem.

Fitch of Norwich, in the Colony of Connecticut, & Mr. Thomas Buckingham of Saybrook, in the colony of Connecticut, Administrators to the
Estate of the said Joshua Sachem, deceased, for a Valuable consideration
to us secured by Mr. Siborn Nichols, Sargt Caleb Stanly, & John Marsh,
Select men of the town of Hartford, by these presents hath given, granted,
aliened, Bargained & sold, Enfeoffed & Confirmed, & by these presents
doth fully, Clearly, Absolutely Give, grant, Bargain, Sell, alien, Enfeoffe
& Confirm unto the said Mr. Seaborn Nichols, Sargt. Caleb Stanly &
John Marsh, in the behalf & for the only proper use & behoofe of the sayd
town of Hartford, one Parcell of Land Lying on the East Side of the
Connecticut River, the Western Side being three miles from the Connecticut River, & is abutted on Land belonging to the Town of Hartford on the
West, & the bredth of the Bounds of Hartford Township, Three miles
Eastward from Connecticut River, & Runs toward the East five Miles in
Length, & abutts on the Commons East, and on Windsor bounds on the
North, where it was last stated by the Court, & on Wethersfield bounds on
the South, to have and to hold all the aforesayd parcell of Lands, with
all its appurtenances & privleges, from the day of the date hereof forever
unto the said Mr. Seaborn Nichols, Sargt Caleb Stanly & John Marsh,
for the use and behoofe of the Town of Hartford & their successors forever ; & the sayd Capt. James Fitch & Mr. Thomas Buckingham have full
power, Good right & lawfull authority to Grant, Bargain, Sell & Convey
all & singular the before hereby granted premises with their and every
of their appurtenances (only reserveing to the heirs & Successors of the
sayd Joshua Sachem Liberty of Hunting & fishing in such of the aforesaid
Lands as Lye in Common without fence), unto the sayd Mr. Seaborn
Nichols, Sargt. Caleb Stanly & John Marsh, for the use and behoofe of
the said Towne of Hartford & their Successors in manner and form aforesaid, & that the sayd Towne of Hartford & their Successors shall & may,
by force and virtue of these presents, from time to time and at all times
forever hereafter, have, use, occupy, possess, & Enjoy the sayd Parcell of
Land with all and Singular its rights, members, and appurtenances, &
have, receive, & take the rents, Issues & profits thereof to them & their
own proper use & behoofe forever without any Lawful Let, Sute, Trouble,
Tryall, Interuption, Eviction or disturbence of the sayd Capt. James Fitch.
(and) Mr. Thomas Buckingham, administrators aforesaid, or of the heirs
of the aforesaid Joshua Sachem, or of the heirs of either of them, or assigns, or of any other person or persons claiming by, from or under them,
Every of them, or by them or their means, act, Consent, title, interest,
privity or procurement that free & Clear, freely & Clearly acquitted, exonerated & discharged, or otherwise from time to time Well and Sufficiently saved, kept harmless by the sayd Capt. James Fitch & Mr. Thomas
Buckingham, their heirs, Executors or Administrators, of and from all
manner and Former and other Gifts, Grants, Bargains, Sales, Legacies,
Mortgages, Joyntures, & from all Extents, Judgement, Executions, uses,
forfeitures, fines, & of & from all and singular other titles, troubles,
Charges & demands had, made, Committed, Suffered, omitted, done, by

the sayd Capt. James Fitch & Mr. Thomas Buckingham, administrators aforesaid, our heirs, assigns, or by any other person or persons whatsoever claiming by, from, or under them, or of them, or by, from, or under his or their means, act, consent, title, interest, privity or procurement. In witness whereof, we doe hereunto set our hands & seals, this thirteenth day of May, One Thousand Six hundred & Eighty two.

Witness: *Richard Edwards,*   JAMES FITCH, LS.
       John Coals.   THOMAS BUCKINGHAM, LS.

Capt. James Fitch & Mr. Tho: Buckingham personally appeared & acknowledged the abovesd. Instrument of Deed to be their Act & Deed, on the 13th of May, 1682, before me,

William Leete, Governor.

The above written is a true Copy of the Original, being examined and Compared there wth this 21st of January, 1683, by me,

John Allyn, Recorder.

And is left in the Hands of Major Talcott with the former Deed which Mr. Richards sometime had. Recorded 21st January, 1683.

See Vol. V, Hartford Land Records, Page 690-699 inclusive:

We, the Subscribers, being appointed a Committe by the Proprietors of the Undivided Five Miles of Lands lying on the East Side of the Great River, to lay out Three Miles and One Hundred Rodds of said Land on the East Side, next to Bolton, from Windsor to Glastonbury Bounds, to be divided to the Original Proprietors or their heirs according to their Rate as it stands Recorded in the Towne Book, including necessary Ways, accordingly Wee Proceeded as followeth: Beginning at the South East Corner, extending West upon the Line divideing between Glastonbury and Hartford Two Hundred and Fourty Rods to a Highway Thirty Rods wide, said Highway extending that width due North to Windsor Bounds, said Highway being the Butment of the West End of the Eastermost Tier of Lotts, and butting East upon Bolton Bounds, Wee began first at Glastonbury and laid out, beginning at No. 1 as they are drawn by Vote of the Proprietors:

No.		Chains.	Links.
1.	To Thomas Thornton, bounded South upon Glastonbury Bounds and North upon Henry Graham,	4	60
2.	To Henry Graham, bounded South upon Thomas Thornton and North upon Benjamin Adams,	14	66
3.	To Benjamin Adams, bounded South upon Henry Graham and North upon John Tuller,	1	44
4.	To John Tuller, bounded South upon Benjamin		

No.		Chains.	Links.
	Adams and North upon Samuel Hooker,	1	73
5.	To Samuel Hooker, bounded South upon John Tuller and North upon Daniel Crow,	10	12
6.	To Daniel Crow, bounded South upon Samuel Hooker and North upon Widow Goodman,	3	06
7.	To Widow Goodman, bounded South upon Daniel Crow and North upon John Skinner,	31	41
8.	To John Skinner, bounded South upon Widow Goodman and North upon William Burnham,	6	30
9.	To William Burnham, bounded South upon John Skinner and North upon Deacon Butler,	6	73
10.	To Deacon Butler, bounded South upon William Burnham and North upon James Forbes,	14	66
11.	To James Forbes, bounded South upon Deacon Butler and North upon Obadiah Wood,	8	08
12.	To Obadiah Wood, bounded South upon James Forbes and North upon Mr. Webster,	2	12
13.	To Mr. Webster, bounded South upon Obadiah Wood and North upon Jonathan Ashley,	11	68
14.	To Jonathan Ashley, bounded South upon Mr. Webster and North upon a Highway,	6	21
	To the Highway, bounded South upon Jonathan Ashley and North upon Land set out to Hartford Mills,	2	50
15.	To Hartford Mills, bounded South upon Highway and North upon Thomas Dickinson,	3	97
16.	To Thomas Dickinson, bounded South upon Hartford Mills and North upon Jeremy Addams,	3	97
17.	To Jeremy Addams, bounded South upon Thomas Dickinson and North upon John Marsh,	8	92
18.	To John Marsh, bounded South upon Jeremy Addams and North upon Paul Peck,	7	59
19.	To Paul Peck sen., bounded South upon John Marsh and North upon John Meakins,	6	67
20.	To John Meakins, bounded South upon Paul Peck sen. and North upon Mr. Wyllys,	9	02
21.	To Mr. Wyllys, bounded South upon John Meakins and North upon John Watson,	21	62
22.	To John Watson, bounded South upon Mr. Wyllys and North upon Jonathan Gilbert,	4	64
23.	To Jonathan Gilbert, bounded South by John Watson and North upon Joseph Whaples,	17	94
24.	To Joseph Whaples, bounded South upon Jonathan Gilbert and North upon Joseph Andruss,	1	67
25.	To Joseph Andruss, bounded South upon Joseph Whaples and North upon Richard Edwards,	3	40

No.		Chains.	Links.
26.	To Richard Edwards, bounded South upon Joseph Andruss and North upon Sergt. John Shepherd,	2	36
27.	To Sergt. John Shepherd, bounded South upon Richard Edwards and North upon Thomas Adkins,	7	76
28.	To Thomas Adkins, bounded South upon Sergt. John Shepherd and North upon Robert Shurley,	2	19
29.	To Robert Shurley, bounded South upon Thomas Adkins and North upon William Hills,	5	41
30.	To William Hills, bounded South upon Robert Shurley and North upon David Ensign,	6	44
31.	To David Ensign, bounded South upon William Hills and North upon Thomas Kilbourn,	9	09
32.	To Thomas Kilbourn, bounded South upon David Ensign and North upon Mr. Foster,	4	37
33.	To Mr. Foster, bounded South upon Thomas Kilbourne and North upon Stephen Kelsey,	2	38
34.	To Stephen Kelsey, bounded South upon Mr. Foster and North upon a Highway or Country Road,	4	72
	To the Highway or Country Road, bounded South upon Stephen Kelsey and North upon William Williams,	3	00
35.	To William Williams, bounded South upon the Highway or Country Road and North upon Samuel Gains,	10	12
36.	To Samuel Gains, bounded South upon William Williams and North upon Capt. Watts,	3	62
37.	To Capt. Watts, bounded South upon Samuel Gains and North upon Daniel Butler,	11	32
38.	To Daniel Butler, bounded South upon Capt. Watts and North upon Joseph Easton, Jr.,	13	34
39.	To Joseph Easton, Jr., bounded South upon Daniel Butler and North upon Nathaniel Crow,	8	97
40.	To Nathaniel Crow, bounded South upon Joseph Easton Jr. and North upon John Kelley,	3	10
41.	To John Kelley, bounded South upon Nathaniel Crow and North upon Henry Arnold,	1	96
42.	To Henry Arnold, bounded South upon John Kelley and North upon Samuel Olcott,	2	36
43.	To Samuel Olcott, bounded South upon Henry Arnold and North upon John Blackledge,	3	34
44.	To John Blackledge, bounded South upon Samuel Olcott and North upon George Stocking,	5	47
45.	To George Stocking, bounded South upon John Blackledge and North upon Jno Webster,	3	91
46.	To John Webster, bounded South upon George Stocking and North upon a Highway,	4	54

No.		Chains.	Links.
	To the Highway, bounded South upon John Webster and North upon William Goodwin,	2	50
47.	To William Goodwin, bounded South upon a Highway and North upon Sergt. Sandford,	2	53
48.	To Sergt. Sanford, bounded South upon William Goodwin and North upon Sergt. Buckland,	3	40
49.	To Sergt. Buckland, bounded South upon Sergt. Sanford and North upon Thomas Bunce, Jr.,	2	30
50.	To Thomas Bunce, Jr., bounded South upon Sergt. Buckland and North upon Thomas Bunce,	8	74
51.	To Thomas Bunce, bounded South upon Thomas Bunce, Jr., and North upon William Pitkin,	8	57
52.	To William Pitkin, bounded South upon Thomas Bunce and North upon Andrew Benton,	13	06
53.	To Andrew Benton, bounded South upon William Pitkin and North upon Thomas Standish,	2	24
54.	To Thomas Standish, bounded South upon Andrew Benton and North upon James Steele,	1	09
55.	To James Steele, bounded South upon Thomas Standish and North upon Samuel Cole,	17	59
56.	To Samuel Cole, bounded South upon James Steele and North upon Thomas Vigar,	3	10
57.	To Thomas Vigar, bounded South upon Samuel Cole and North upon Andrew Stephens,	1	44
58.	To Andrew Stephens, bounded South upon Thomas Vigar and North upon Windsor Bounds,	1	42

AN ACCOUNT OF THE SECOND TIER OF LOTTS, BEGINNING AT WINDSOR BOUNDS.

No.		Chains.	Links.
59.	To John Merrells, bounded North upon Windsor Bounds and South upon Mr. John Talcott,	11	gone
60.	To Mr. John Talcott, bounded North upon John Merrells and South upon Thomas Burnham,	7	65
61.	To Thomas Burnham, bounded North upon Mr. John Talcott and South upon Thomas Cadwell,	0	81
62.	To Thomas Cadwell, bounded North upon Thomas Burnham and South upon John Dyx,	11	96
63.	To John Dyx, bounded North upon Thomas Cadwell and South upon John Grave,	3	40
64.	To John Grave, bounded North upon John Dyx and South upon Stephen Hopkins,	3	16
65.	To Stephen Hopkins, bounded North upon John Grave and South upon John Richards,	11	21
66.	To John Richards, bounded North upon Stephen Hopkins and South upon John Mitchell, Jr.,	5	69
67.	To John Mitchell, Jr., bounded North upon John Richards and South upon John Pratt,	1	44

No.		Chains.	Links.
68.	To John Pratt, bounded North upon John Mitchell, Jr., and South upon a Highway,	13	11
	To a Highway, bounded North upon John Pratt and South upon Bevel Waters,	2	50
69.	To Bevel Waters, bounded North upon a Highway and South upon Samuel Steele,	9	83
70.	To Samuel Steele, bounded North upon Bevel Waters and South upon Stephen Brace,	4	06
71.	To Stephen Brace, bounded North upon Samuel Steele and South upon Richard Gilman,	4	03
72.	To Richard Gilman, bounded North upon Stephen Brace and South upon John Catlin,	2	76
73.	To John Catlin, bounded North upon Richard Gilman and South upon Charles Barnard,	11	10
74.	To Charles Barnard, bounded North upon John Catlin and South upon Thomas Long,	1	50
75.	To Thomas Long, bounded North upon Charles Barnard and South upon Benjamin Harbott,	2	99
76.	To Benjamin Harbott, bounded North upon Thomas Long and South upon George Knight,	4	48
77.	To George Knight, bounded North upon Benjamin Harbott and South upon Richard Risley,	3	51
78.	To Richard Risley, bounded North upon George Knight and South upon Arthur Smith,	5	12
79.	To Arthur Smith, bounded North upon Richard Risley and South upon John Cole,	3	74
80.	To John Cole, bounded North upon Arthur Smith and South upon Josiah Arnold,	7	07
81.	To Josiah Arnold, bounded North upon John Cole and South upon a Country Road,	1	44
	To a Country Road, bounded North upon Josiah Arnold and South upon Thomas Wadsworth,	3	00
82.	To Thomas Wadsworth, bounded North upon a Country Road and South upon Joseph & John Easton,	10	99
83.	To Joseph & John Easton, bounded North upon Thomas Wadsworth and South upon Widow Wyard,	12	13
84.	To Widow Wyard, bounded North upon Joseph & John Easton and South upon Richard Blancher,	1	61
85.	To Richard Blancher, bounded North upon Widow Wyard and South upon John Mason,	4	89
86.	To John Mason, bounded North upon Richard Blancher and South upon John Sadd,	2	76
87.	To John Sadd, bounded North upon John Mason and South upon a Highway,	4	78

No.		Chains.	Links.
	To the Highway, bounded North upon John Sadd and South upon Joseph Olmsted,	2	00
88.	To Joseph Olmsted, bounded North upon a Highway and South upon Stephen Hosmer,	5	06
89.	To Stephen Hosmer, bounded North upon Joseph Olmsted and South upon John Bidwell,	12	76
90.	To John Bidwell, bounded North upon Stephen Hosmer and South upon Joell Marshall,	12	65
91.	To Joell Marshall, bounded North upon John Bidwell and South upon Joseph Peck,	1	84
92.	To Joseph Peck, bounded North upon Joell Marshall and South upon Capt. Cooke,	2	40
93.	To Capt. Cooke, bounded North upon Joseph Peck and South upon Daniel Clarke,	10	12
94.	To Daniel Clarke, bounded North upon Capt. Cooke and South upon Nathaniel Ruscoe,	3	79
95.	To Nathaniel Ruscoe, bounded North upon Daniel Clarke and South upon James Gordon,	5	02
96.	To James Gordon, bounded North upon Nathaniel Ruscoe and South upon Thomas Humphries,	2	86
97.	To Thomas Humphries, bounded North upon James Gordon and South upon Jacob Johnson,	1	48
98.	To Jacob Johnson, bounded North upon Thomas Humphries and South upon Edmund O'Neal,	1	50
99.	To Edmund O'Neal, bounded North upon Jacob Johnson and South upon Mr. Harris,	1	72
100.	To Mr. Harris, bounded North upon Mr. O'Neal and South upon Mrs Holyoake,	3	86
101.	To Mrs. Holyoake, bounded North upon Mr. Harris and South upon (the) Mine Lott,	1	96
	To the Mine Lott, bounded North upon Mrs. Holyoake and South upon Samuel Benton,	1	63
102.	To Samuel Benton, bounded North upon the Mine Lott and South upon Obadiah Spencer,	2	13
103.	To Obadiah Spencer, bounded North upon Samuel Benton and South upon Cyprian Nichols,	2	76
104.	To Cyprian Nichols, bounded North upon Obadiah Spencer and South upon John Church,	15	41
105.	To John Church, bounded North upon Cyprian Nichols and South upon Mr. Roberts,	7	76
106.	To Mr. Roberts, bounded North upon John Church and South upon John Wilson,	4	89
107.	To John Wilson, bounded North upon Mr. Roberts and South upon the Highway,	6	21
	To the Highway, bounded North upon John Wilson and South upon Hannah Wells,	2	50

No.		Chains.	Links.
108.	To Hannah Wells, bounded North upon the Highway and South upon Samuel Andrews,	22	94
109.	To Samuel Andrews, bounded North upon Hannah Wells and South upon Sergt. Spencer,	3	79
110	To Sergt. (Benj:) Spencer, bounded North upon Samuel Andrews and South upon John Hills,	2	47
111.	To John Hills, bounded North upon Sergt. Spencer and South upon Thomas Clark,	2	93
112.	To Thomas Clark, bounded North upon John Hills and South upon Mr. Barnard,	6	79
113.	To Mr. Barnard, bounded North upon Thomas Clark and South upon John Perry,	18	17
114.	To John Perry, bounded North upon Mr. Barnard and South upon Walter Hay,	2	04
115.	To Walter Hay, bounded North upon John Perry and South upon George Ash,	1	70
116.	To George Ash, bounded North upon Walter Hay and South upon Glastonbury Bounds,	1	44
	To the Highway, Fourty Rods wide between the Second and Third Tier of Lotts, from Glastonbury to Windsor,	10	00

AN ACCOUNT OF THE THIRD TIER OF LOTTS, BEGINNING AT GLASTONBURY BOUNDS.

No.		Chains.	Links.
117.	To Thomas Whaples, bounded South upon Glastonbury Bounds and North upon John Bunce,	1	72
118.	To John Bunce, bounded South upon Thomas Whaples and North upon Jno Bigelow,	4	95
119.	To John Bigelow & Nicholas Olmsted, bounded South upon John Bunce and North upon John Pantry,	15	13
120.	To John Pantry, bounded South upon Jno Bigelow and Nicholas Olmsted and North upon Mr. Way,	9	72
121.	To Mr. Way, bounded South upon John Pantry and North upon a Highway,	21	28
	To the Highway, bounded South upon Mr. Way and North upon Sergt. Stanly,	2	00
122.	To Sergt. Stanly, bounded South upon the Highway and North upon Capt. Lewis,	11	79
123.	To Capt. Lewis, bounded South upon Sergt. Stanly and North upon Joseph Whiting,	9	66
124.	To Joseph Whiting, bounded South upon Capt. Lewis and North upon John Mitchell,	2	53
125.	To John Mitchell, bounded South upon Joseph Whiting and North upon Capt. Allyn,	1	67

No.		Chains.	Links.
126.	To Capt. Allyn, bounded South upon John Mitchell and North upon William Warren,	21	34
127.	To William Warren, bounded South upon Capt. Allyn and North upon Thomas Olcutt,	7	76
128.	To Thomas Olcott, bounded South upon William Warren and North upon Joseph Mygatt,	4	14
129.	To Joseph Mygatt, bounded South upon Thomas Olcott and North upon Marshall George Grave & Philip Davis,	5	00
130.	To Marshall George Grave & Philip Davis, bounded South upon Joseph Mygatt and North upon a Highway,	14	84
	To a Highway, bounded South on Marshall George Grave & Philip Davis and North upon Jared Spencer,	2	00
131.	To Jared Spencer, bounded South upon a Highway and North upon Nicholas Disbrow,	4	78
132.	To Nicholas Disbrow, bounded South upon Jared Spencer and North upon Jehoida Bartlett,	4	20
133.	To Jehoida Bartlett, bounded South upon Nicholas Disbrow and North upon Thomas Wells,	1	90
134.	To Thomas Wells, bounded South upon Jehoida Bartlett and North upon Daniel Pratt,	5	00
135	To Daniel Pratt, bounded South upon Thomas Wells and North upon Jonathan Bigelow,	11	56
136.	To Jonathan Bigelow, bounded South upon Daniel Pratt and North upon Corpll Butler,	5	06
137.	To Corpl Butler, bounded South upon Jonathan Bigelow and North upon Samuel Burr,	13	11
138.	To Samuel Burr, bounded South upon Corpl Butler and North upon a Country Road,	8	74
	To the Country Road, Twelve Rods wide, bounded South upon Samuel Burr and North upon Richard Case,	3	00
139.	To Richard Case, bounded South upon the Country Road and North upon William Edwards,	4	48
140.	To William Edwards, bounded South upon Richard Case and North upon Paul Peck, Jr.,	1	50
141.	To Paul Peck, Jr., bounded South upon William Edwards and North upon Samuel Spencer,	6	04
142.	To Samuel Spencer, bounded South upon Paul Peck, Jr., and North upon Ichabod Wells,	4	43
143.	To Ichabod Wells, bounded South upon Samuel Spencer and North upon Thomas Burr,	5	00
144.	To Thomas Burr, bounded South upon Ichabod Wells and North upon Ensign Stanly,	3	51

No.		Chains.	Links.
145.	To Ensign Stanly, bounded South upon Thomas Burr and North upon John Seymour,	19	96
146.	To John Seymour, bounded South upon Ensign Stanly and North upon Edward Cadwell,	4	95
147.	To Edward Cadwell, bounded South upon John Seymour and North upon Capt. Thomas Bull,	6	50
148.	To Capt. Thomas Bull, bounded South upon Edward Cadwell and North upon the Highway,	13	45
	To the Highway, bounded South upon Capt. Thomas Bull and North upon Joseph Smith,	2	00
149.	To Joseph Smith, bounded South upon the Highway and North upon Richard Lord,	5	48
150.	To Richard Lord, bounded South upon Joseph Smith and North upon Widow Andrews,	30	48
151.	To Widow Andrews, bounded South upon Richard Lord and North upon Ozias Goodwin,	5	00
152.	To Ozias Goodwin, bounded South upon Widow Andrews and North upon Joseph Strickland,	1	96
153.	To Joseph Strickland, bounded South upon Ozias Goodwin and North upon Jonathan Webster,	1	78
154.	To Jonathan Webster, bounded South upon Joseph Strickland and North upon Widow Burr,	3	22
155.	To Widow Burr, bounded South upon Jonathan Webster and North upon Joseph Bull,	1	84
156.	To Joseph Bull, bounded South upon Widow Burr and North upon John Shepherd,	6	67
157.	To John Shepherd, bounded South upon Joseph Bull and North upon Thomas Loveman,	3	40
158.	To Thomas Loveman, bounded South upon John Shepherd and North upon Joseph Garrett,	4	89
159.	To Joseph Garrett, bounded South upon Thomas Loveland and North upon George Hall,	1	44
160.	To George Hall, bounded South upon Joseph Garrett and North upon John Barnard,	5	69
161.	To John Barnard, bounded South upon George Hall and North upon Robert Bell,	6	24
162.	To Robert Bell, bounded South upon John Barnard and North upon Thomas Swetman	1	42
163.	To Thomas Swetman, bounded South upon Robert Bell and North upon Gilbert Forsyth,	1	70
164.	To Gilbert Forsyth, bounded South upon Thomas Swetman and North upon Thomas Bennett,	1	72
165.	To Thomas Bennett, bounded South upon Gilbert Forsyth and North upon Thomas Tomlins,	1	42
166.	To Thomas Tomlins, bounded South upon Thomas Bennett and North upon a vacant Lot near Windsor Bounds,	2	44

No.		Chains.	Links.
	To the Vacant Lot, bounded South upon Thomas Tomlins and North upon Windsor Bounds,	5	06

AN ACCOUNT OF THE FOURTH TIER OF LOTTS, BEGINNING AT WINDSOR BOUNDS.

No.		Chains.	Links.
167.	To Major Talcott, bounded North on Windsor Bounds and South upon Mr. Richards,	24	84
168.	To Mr. Richards, bounded North upon Major Talcott and South upon Benjamin Hills,	28	93
169	To Benjamin Hills, bounded North upon Mr. Richards and South upon Nathaniel Cole,	2	76
170.	To Nathaniel Cole, bounded North upon Benjamin Hills and South upon Nathaniel Willett,	4	03
171.	To Nathaniel Willett, bounded North upon Nathaniel Cole and South upon Henry Howard,	2	76
172.	To Henry Howard, bounded North upon Nathaniel Willett and South upon John White,	16	39
173.	To John White, bounded North upon Nathaniel Willett and South upon Noah Cook,	3	40
174.	To Noah Cook, bounded North upon John White and South upon a Highway,	6	38
	To the Highway, bounded North upon Noah Cook and South upon Texell Ainsworth,	2	00
175.	To Tickzell Ainsworth, bounded North upon the Highway and South upon Thomas Trill,	1	44
176.	To Thomas Trill, bounded North upon Tickzell Ainsworth and South upon Thomas Marshall,	2	07
177.	To Thomas Marshall, bounded North upon Thomas Trill and South upon Mrs. Gardner,	5	00
178.	To Mrs. Gardner, bounded North upon Thomas Marshall and South upon William Goodwin Jr.,	1	27
179.	To William Goodwin, Jr., bounded North upon Mrs. Gardner and South upon Jacob White,	2	53
180.	To Jacob White, bounded North upon William Goodwin and South upon Jared Spikes,	8	62
181.	To Jared Spikes, bounded North upon Jacob White and South upon John Camp,	2	88
182.	To John Camp, bounded North upon Jared Spikes and South upon Caleb Watson,	4	54
183.	To Caleb Watson, bounded North upon John Camp and South upon Martin More,	2	07
184.	To Martin More, bounded North upon Caleb Watson and South upon Nathaniel Goodwin,	1	50
185.	To Nathaniel Goodwin, bounded North upon Martin More and South upon John Andrews, "Poke Hill,"	6	21

No.		Chains.	Links.
186.	To John Andrews, "Poke Hill," bounded North upon Nathaniel Goodwin and South upon Alexander Douglass,	2	99
187.	To Alexander Douglass, bounded North upon John Andrews and South upon Mr. John Whiting,	2	88
188.	To Mr. John Whiting, bounded North upon Alexander Douglass and South upon John Crow,	3	74
189.	To John Crow, bounded North upon Mr. John Whiting and South upon Mr. Haynes,	18	58
190.	To Mr. Haynes, bounded North upon John Crow and South upon Country Road,	19	44
	To the Country Road, bounded North upon Mr. Haynes and South upon Mr. Olcott,	3	00
191.	To Mr. Olcott, bounded North upon the Country Road and South upon Andrew Benton,	10	52
192.	To Andrew Benton, bounded North upon Mr. Olcott and South upon William Williams, Jr.,	9	55
193.	To William Williams, Jr., bounded North upon Andrew Benton and South upon Richard Burnham,	1	84
194.	To Richard Burnham, bounded North upon William Williams, Jr., and South upon Robert Sanford,	3	22
195.	To Robert Sanford, bounded North upon Richard Burnham and South upon Thomas Hosmer,	13	28
196.	To Thomas Hosmer, bounded North upon Robert Sanford and South upon Joseph Collyer,	15	52
197.	To Joseph Collyer, bounded North upon Thomas Hosmer and South upon John Day,	3	45
198.	To John Day, bounded North upon Joseph Collyer and South upon Daniel Bidwell,	4	69
199.	To John & Daniel Bidwell, bounded North upon John Day and South upon Jonathan Bull,	9	89
200.	To Jonathan Bull, bounded North upon John & Daniel Bidwell and South upon John Williams,	7	93
201.	To John Williams, bounded North upon Jonathan Bull and South upon a Highway,	1	44
	To the Highway North, bounded North upon John Williams and South upon Nathaniel Sanford,	2	00
202.	To Nathaniel Sanford, bounded North upon the Highway and South upon Mr. Wilson,	11	85
203.	To Mr. Wilson, bounded North upon Nathaniel Sanford and South upon John Gilbert,	13	17
204.	To John Gilbert, bounded North upon Mr. Wilson and South upon Joseph Wadsworth,	7	13
205.	To Joseph Wadsworth, bounded North upon John Gilbert and South upon Mr. Gibbons,	14	26

No.		Chains.	Links.
206.	To Mr. Gibbons, bounded North upon Joseph Wadsworth and South upon Samuel Wadsworth,	10	12
207.	To Samuel Wadsworth, bounded North upon Mr. Gibbons and South upon John Holloway,	12	19
208.	To John Holloway, bounded North upon Samuel Wadsworth and South upon John Baker,	1	50
209.	To John Baker, bounded North upon John Holloway and South upon a vacant Lot, to Glastonbury Bounds,	7	30
	To a vacant Lot, bounded North upon John Baker and South upon Glastonbury Bounds,	55	13

7$\frac{92}{100}$ inches, one Link.
25 Links, one Rod.
4 Rods or 66 Ft., one Chain.
80 Chains, one Mile.

CYPRIAN NICHOLS,
JONATHAN STEELE,
Signed, JOHN CHURCH,   Committee.
THOMAS WELLS,
JONATHAN BUTLER,
JAMES BUNCE,

Returned Signed: 5 July, 1731.

The remaining portion of the five-mile purchase was termed Commons and Grants before 1753, when the boundary lines were run by William Wells, surveyor. From the 3 miles to the 4th tier of lotts, measured along the line of Glastonbury, 547 rods; thence north from Glastonbury to Windsor upon the line of the 4th tier of lotts, 4½ miles one degree east (1°); thence west along the south line of Windsor 410 rods, there meeting the east line of the 3 mile lots. During the next year this tract of land was laid out in six tiers of lots to the original proprietors or to their legal representatives.

The whole Commons and Grants contain 4428 acres of land; the Grants contain 1305 acres and 100 rods; there remains 3122 acres and 60 rods to be divided.

Page 72.

The Returne of Saybrook & Pequott Bounds:

Whereas, there was an agreement in Court that some of Sea Brooke and Pequott should in convenient time Lay out the bounds betwixt Sea Brook and Pequott belonging to each towne, as also the bounds of Pequott beyond Pequott River, according to an order of Court, Sept. 11,-'50;

We, whose names are underwritten, being appointed for ye end aforesaid by the towns, having improved our utmost endeavor, doe give in as followeth:

For the bounds of Pequott, the east side the River, we began the line opposite to ye dwelling house of John Winthrop, Esq. Running a line due east foure miles, we fell short, as we conceive, halfe one mile of the head of Mistick River, at a little Brook where is a tree marked with an M. and foure marks upon a tree, from wch place, running ye line East, we came one mile Six score and twelve Rodds to ye Noeward about the como wadeing place on Paukatuck River, wch wadeing place is to ye North-ward of Thomas Stanton's tradeing house.

Alsoe, the foure miles from Pequott River doe come to Sea Brooke bounds and 40 Rods neerer to Sea Brook, upon Niantic plaines where the marked tree stands neere the Indian fforte, but the Bounds betwixt the Towne of Sea Brooke and Pequott are to Stand as they are now Set out, viz., at ye marked tree neere Niantick ffort as aforesaid.

The quantity of meadow betwixt Mistick and Paukatuck, as we con-ceive, having viewed according to our best Skill, good and bad, doth not amount to above Three hundred and Eighty Acres.

the mark of

THOMAS LEFFINGWELL,
REYNOLD MARVIN,
THOMAS MINOR,
HUGH X CAULKIN,
ROBERT HEMPSTED.

EARLY LAND OWNERS.

The early landholders in the following lists had their holdings recorded in Hartford, at the *County Seat*. The *form of record* used in the Colony until about 1700 may be seen under the name of *Edward Mason*, where his lands are given, on pages 23-4, to which reference is here made.

HARTFORD.

Owners of Land before 1653. *See Vol. I of Lands, in Office of Secretary of State.*

Allen (Allyn), Matthew,
Addams, Jeremie,
Andrews, William,
Andrews, Francis,
Arnold, John,
Bartlett, Robert,
Baysey, John,
Bacon, Andrew,
Barnard, John,
Barnes, Tho:
Berding, Nath:

Burre, Ben:
Butler, Will:
Burchard, Tho:
Bliss, Tho: Sen.
Bliss, Tho: Jr.
Blufield, Will:
Burr, Tho:
Butler, Rich:
Bridgeman, James,
Bull, Thomas,
Byddell, John, (Bidwell)
Brunson, John,

Chester, Dorothy,
Church, Rich:
Clarke, Nich:
Clarke, John,
Cornwall, Will:
Coall, Jeames, (Coale)
Crow, John,
Day, Robert,
Disborow, Nicholas,
Easton, Joseph,
Ely, Nath:
Elmer, Ed:
Elmer, Richard,
Ensign, James,
Field, Zach:
Garrad, Samuel,
Gibbins, Will:
Goodwyn, Will:
Goodwing, Ozias,
Graves, George,
Greenhill, Tho:
Greenhill, Rebeckah,
Grant, Seth:
Gynnings, John,
Goodman, Rich:
Hart, Stephen,
Hall, Jo: Sen.
Hill, Will:
Hide, Will:
Hooker, Thomas,
Hopkins, Edward,
Hopkins, John,
Heynes, John,
Heyton, Will:
Holton, Will:
Hubbard, George,
Hosmore, Tho:
Keeler, Ralph,
Kelsey, Will:
Kellogg, Nathaniel,
Lewis, Will:
Lord, Tho: Sen.
Lord, Tho: Jr.

Lord, Rich:
Lyman, Rich:
Maynard, John,
Marven, Nath:
Moody, John,
Marsh, John,
Munn, Ben:
Morris, John,
Mygatt, Joseph,
Olmsted, Rich:
Olmsted, John,
Olmsted, James,
Olcott, Tho:
Parker, Will:
Pantry, Will:
Peck, Paul,
Perce, John,
Perce, John, (2d?)
Pratt, John,
Phillips, Will:
Pratt, Will:
Porter, Thos:
Purkas, John,
Post, Stephen,
Richards, Nath:
Roote, Tho:
Rusco, Will:
Semer, Rich:
Selden, Tho:
Skinner, John,
Smith, Arthur,
Smith, Gyles,
Spencer, Tho:
Spencer, Will:
Stebbing, Ed:
Steele, John,
Steele, George,
Stocking, George,
Standly, Tho:
Standly, Tym:
Stone, Samuel,
Taylcoat, John,

Thornton, Tho:
Trott, Tho:
Upson, Tho:
Wadsworth, Will:
Wade, Robert,
Warner, John,
Warner, Andrew,
Wa(i)rd, Nath:
Watts, Richard,
Wakely, James,
Wakeman, Sa:
Watts, John,

Webb, Rich:
Westwood, Will:
Webster, John,
Welles, Thomas,
Westly, Ric:
Westly, Will:
White, John,
Whiting, Will:
Willis, George,
Wilterton, Gregory,
Wilcocks, John,
Woodruff, Tho:

WINDSOR.

Owners of Land before 1653. *See Vol. I of Lands, in Office of Secretary of State.*

Allen, Samuel,
Bascom, Tho:
Bassett, Tho:
Bartlett, John,
Bissill, John,
Buckland, Tho:
Buell, Will:
Branker, John,
Burge, John,
Burge, Richard,
Burg, Richard,
Carter, Joseph,
Clarke, Henry,
Clarke, Joseph,
Cooke, Aaron,
Collins, Mary,
Diament, John,
Denslow, Nicholas,
Drake, John,
Eggleston, James,
Eggleston, Begget,
Elssin, Lawrence,
Filley, William,
ffouks, Henry,
Fyler, Walter,
Ford, Tho:

Gaylord, Will: Sen.
Gaylord, Will: Jun.
Grant, Matthew,
Gybbs, Francis, (Gibbs)
Gyllett, Nathan, (Gillet)
Gunn, Tho:
Hamun, William,
Heynes, John,
Hill, Will:
Hillier, John,
Howkins, Anthony,
Howkins, John,
Hoyte, Symon,
Horsford, Will:
Holcomb, Tho:
Holbard, Will:
Hopkins, John,
Hull, George,
Hull, Josias,
Lumas, Joseph Jr.
Marshfield, Tho:
Marshall, Samuel,
Mills, Symon,
Moore, Tho:
Nubery, Joseph,

Nubery, Benjamin,
Nubery, John,
Nubery, Sarah,
Nubery, Mary,
Nubery, Rebecah,
Nubery, Hannah,
Oldage, Richard,
Palmer, Nicholas,
Parkman, Elias,
Parsons, Richard,
Pinney, Humphrey,
Phillips, George,
Phelps, Will: Sen.
Phelps, Will:
Phelps, George,
Pomeroy, Edward,
Porter, John,
Randall, Philip,
Randall, Abraham,
Rockwell, Will:
Rockwell, John,
Rasseter, Bray,
Samos, Richard,
Sammis,
Samwis,
Samwise,

Sension, Matthew,
Staynes, Tho:
Styles, Tho:
Styles, Henry,
Styles, John,
Stoughton, Tho:
Stuckey, George,
Talcott, John,
Terry, Stephen,
Taylor, John,
Thornton, Tho:
Tilly, Eady,
Thrall, Will:
Voare, Richard,
Warham, John,
Weller, Rich:
Wichfield, John,
Wilton, David,
Williams, Rodger,
Williams, Arthur,
Wynchell, Robert, (Winchell)
Woolcott, Christopher,
Woolcott, Henry, Sen.
Wolcott, Henry, Jr.

WETHERSFIELD.

Owners of Land before 1653. *See Vol. I of Lands, in Office of Secretary of State.*

Abbotte, Robert,
Alcoke, Tho: (Olcott?)
Bates, Robert,
Baydon, Richard,
Boosey, James,
Brundish, Wyd:
Butler, Will:
Chester, Leonard,
Churchill, Josias,
Chaplin, Clem:
Comstocke, Will:
Coe, Robert,

Crabbe, Richard,
Demon, John, (Deming)
Deynton, Richard,
Edwards, John,
Ferris, Jeffrey,
Finch, Abra:
Fletcher, John,
Gayer, Jer: (Gager?)
Goodrich, John,
Gybbs, John, (Gibbs)
Gybbins, Will: (Gibbins)
Gyldersleive, Richard,

Hubbard, George,
Ierland, Sam:
Mitchell, Matthew,
Myller, Jo:
Northend, John,
Notte, John,
Palmer, Will:
Plum, Jo:
Raynolds, John,
Rawlings, Jasper,
Rayner, Thurston,
Robbins, John,
Rose, Robert,
Shareman, Sam:
Smith, Samuel,

Standish, Tho:
Swayne, Will:
Talcoate, John,
Tinker, John,
Tomson, John,
Uffoute, Tho:
We(a)tt, Richard,
Waterhouse, Jacob,
Wastecoat, Richard,
Wa(i)rd, Andrew,
Weede, Jonas,
Whitmore, Jo:
Willis, Geo:
Wright, Tho:

FARMINGTON.

Owners of Land, 1648 *to* 1657. *See Vol. I of Lands, in Office of Secretary
of State.*

Addams, William,
Andrews, John,
Barnes, Thomas,
Brunson, John,
Brunson, Richard,
Clarke, John,
Demon, Thomas,
Graves, George,
Haynes, John,
Hart, Stephen,
Hart, John,
Judd, Thomas,
Kellogg, Nathaniel,
Kellogg, Joseph,
Lancton, John,
Lewis, William,
Loomis, Samuel,
Lee, John,
Newell, Thomas,
Newton, Roger,
North, John,
Olmsted, Nehemiah.

Orton, Thomas,
Porter, Daniel,
Porter, Robert,
Porter, Thomas,
Smith, William,
Stebbing, Edward,
Steele, John,
Steele, Samuel,
Steele, John, Jr.
Standly, John,
Upson, Thomas,
Ventrus, Moses.
Warner, Andrew,
Warner, John,
Warner, John, Jr.
Wadsworth, John,
Webster, Thomas,
Webster, Nathaniel,
Wilson, Robert,
Welles, Thomas,
Woodruff, Matthew,
Wyatt, John.

FAIRFIELD.

Owners of Land, 1649 to 1652. See Vol. II of Lands, Page 43, in Office of Secretary of State.

Addams, Edward,
Bateman, William,
Banker, John,
Baxter, Thomas,
Bennet, James,
Drake, Samuel,
Dun, Thomas,
Everts, James,
Everts, John,
Fossacar, John,
Grumman, John,
Hedges, Steven,
Henderson, Hendrick,
Hide, Humphrey,
Jennings, Joshua,
Jones, John,
Jones, Thomas,
Knowles, Alexander,
Lancaster, Walter,

Lyon, Henry,
Lyon, Richard,
Middlebrooke, Joseph,
Osborne, Richard,
Patchen, Joseph,
Perry, Richard,
Pell, Thomas,
Pinckney, Philip,
Rowland, Henry,
Sherington, Thomas,
Sherwood, Thomas,
Staples, Thomas,
Staples, Thomas,
Squire, George,
Vouke, Richard,
Williams, Richard,
Wheeler, Ephraim,
Wheeler, John,
Wheeler, Thomas.

STRATFORD.

See Vol. I of Lands, in Office of Secretary of State.

Beardsley, John,
Beardsley, William,
Beach, John,
Coe, Robert,
Curtis, William,
Griffin, Hugh,
Hawley, Joseph,
Judson, Joseph,

Knoll(s), Nicholas,
Nichols, Joseph,
Peacock, John,
Peack, John,
Reader, John,
Uffoot, Thomas,
Wells, John.

VOLUME II.

March, 1649-50, to May, 1663.

This is the Second Book of the Records
of the Acts of the County Courts and
Courts of Probates in the County of
Hartford, and of Wills and Inventories
which Said County Courts are Called Somtimes
Quarter Courts, Somtimes a Court of Magistrates
and Somtimes perticular Courts.

No. 2.

This volume, after having disappeared for
many years, was discovered by me, in the
City of New York, on Friday the sixth
day of December, eighteen hundred sixty one.

CHARLES J. HOADLY.

PROBATE RECORDS.

VOLUME II.

1650 to 1663.

Abercrombe, Davie. Court Record, Page 166—7 March, 1661-2: Robert Loveland Contra the Estate of Davie Abercrombie, in an Act of ye Case for detaining Goods shipped aboard ye sd. Crombe to ye value of £150, the Jury find for Plntf. Abercrombie. Page 177—4 September, 1662: On ye Action depending betwixt George Tong & ye Estate of Abercrombe, the Court find for the defendant Cost of Court. Page 178—4 September, 1662: Robert Loveland is apointed Adms. to ye Estate of Abercrombe, & Mr. George Tonge is ordered to surrender wt Estate or Specialties are in his Custody, of Abercrombe's, to Mr. Loveland.

	£ s d
George Tonge Recd of James Morgan,	7-15-00
of John Elderkin,	3-06-00
pr Cowdals Howse Morgaged,	20-00-00
pr due from G: Rice,	7-05-00
pr Samuel Martin,	10-00-00
pr Henry Grimes,	2-08-00
	19-13-00

by *Josiah Rockwell, Mr. Wm Thomson.*

Addams, John. Court Record, Page 104—26 August, 1657: A Coppy of a Certificate undr the names of these subscribed. These are to certify any to whom it may come, that our Children John Addams & Abigail Smith have our full Consent to be marryed together, & wee know no engagemt of either party to any other. As witness our Hands:

RICH: SMITH,
JER: ADDAMS.

These may certify whom it may concerne, that John Addams and Abigail Smith are lawfully marryed, by Order from their parents.

As Witness our Hands in the pressence of

> Thomas Newman,
> Magistrate:
> John Lord.
> Richard Smith,
> Secretary:
> Josias Gilbert.

Page 76.

Addams, William, Farmington. Invt. £36-03-00. Taken 6 September, 1655, by Stephen Hart, Thomas Newell, Thomas Judd & John Hart. The children: Benjamin, age 6 years; Elizabeth, 3 years; Samuel Heacock, 12; and Joseph Heacock, 10 years of age. This Court desires Mr. Steele and Thomas Judd to preserve the Estate and to place out ye Children as well as they can, and make Return to ye Court in May next.

Court Record, Page 79—1st Tuesday in December, 1655: Exhibited an Invt.

Page 129-30.

Andrews, William, Hartford. Invt. £211-14-00. Taken 8 August, 1659, by Edward Stebbing, George Grave, John Barnard. Will dated 1 April, 1659; I, William Andrews, being sick and weak, but of perfect memory, do in this my last Will & Testament give & bequeath to Abigail, my wife, my House, Barne & House Lott as it is Inclosed between my son Edward Grannis and mee; allsoe, I doe give & bequeath to Abigail, my wife, all my Meadow & Swamp Land lieinge in the South Meadow and that lieth in the place called Hockanum, and all my Upland Ground elsewhere, during the time of her naturall life; allsoe, I give to the sd. Abigail 2 Cowes, one yearling Calf; also I give to Abigail, my wife, fower yards of Kersey with 3 dozen of Buttons and silke, and all other of my Moveable Goods, during the time that she liveth unmarried. If she marry (again), then my Will is, that such of the Moveables as shee can conveniently spare shall be disposed off amonge our Children as shee seeth meete, with the advice of the Overseers. My Will is, to give to my son John one workinge steer; alsoe, that Abigail, my wife, shall dispose of my Land, Meadow, Swamp, Howsing and Homelott amonge our Children, to every one of them some, as shee shall think fitt with the advice and Consent of the Overseers. I doe make Abigail, my wife, Executrix, and I doe Intreat my friend Edward Stebbinge and my Brother George Grave to assist and to see this my Will performed.

Witness: *Edward Stebbing,*   (Not signed.)
         George Grave.

Court Record, Page 32—1st Thursday, 1651: This Court confirms Mr. Andrews Recorder.

Page 151.

Armstrong, Avis. Died 25 December, 1660. Invt. £16-06-02. Taken 19 February, 1661-2. by *John Allyn.* Court Record, Page 152—7 March, 1661-2 ; Adms. to Nathaniel Ruscoe in his own behalf.

Page 12-13.

Ayres, Nicholas (Seaman). Invt. £7-18-00. Taken 9 May, 1651, by John Pratt and Jasper Gunn. Testimony of Robert Codman on the 25th of April, 1651, with Bill of Account of Expense in the Sickness and Death of Ayres, due to Robert Codman at Mattabeseck, on a voyage from Nansemun in Virginia ; that this is a true Inventory of the whole Estate of the Decd so farre as the deponent knoweth and as came into his custody (except his wearing Apparrell being divided amongst those that laid him forthe and buried him). And hee further saith and affirmeth in Court, that Nicholas Ayres, decd, tould him that Mr. Damrell, Marriner in the Bay, had a Chest of his in his Hands with some Goods in it.

Court Record, Page 23—14 May, 1651 : This day there was exhibited into the Courte by Robert Codman an Invento : of the Estate of Nicholas Aires, Marriner, decd, being sumed up £7-18-00, and a Bill of Charges of £3-10-00. This Court grants Mr Ollcott Libberty and power to Administer upon the aforesd. Estate, hee paying to Codman the Bill of Charges out of the aforesd. Estate, and the remainder to bee Responsible for to this Jurisdiction whenever required thereto.

Page 65.

Baker, Jeffrey, Windsor. Invt. £101-15-10. Taken 13 August, 1655, by William Gaylord, Matthew Grant, Henry Wolcott. The widow, Joane. The children : Samuel, eldest son, age 11 years ; Hepsibah, 9 years ; Mary, 6 years ; Joseph, 18 days.

Court Record, Page 79—20 December : Invt. exhibited. (See Page 65, Probate Side) : This Court grants Adms. to the Widow, and also orders that the estate be Dist., the Widow to administer the Estate and to pay to the Heirs as they attain to lawful age. William Gaylord and Matthew Grant, by request, are appointed to assist the Adms.

Page 104.

Banckes, Ezekiel. Invt. £29-18-00. Taken 18 December, 1655, by John Cowles and John Rootes.

6 June, 1656 : Margaret Hutchins renounceing Adms., this Court commits the Care of the Estate for the Good of the Creditors to Gregory

Woolterton and Lt. William Lewis, they to give an Account to the Court when called for.

Page 166.

Bancroft, John. Died 6 August, 1662 (W. R.) Invt. £110-14-00. Taken 22 August, 1662, by Matthew Grant. The children: John Bancroft, 12 ¾ years of age; Nathaniel, 9 years; Ephraim, 8; Hannah, 3 & 5 months, and Sarah 3 months (W. R.)

Court Record, Page 178—10 September, 1662: Order to Dist. the Estate:

	£ s d
To the Widow,	37-10-00
To the Eldest son,	14-11-00
To each of the others,	12-00-00

To be paid them at lawfull age.   (This Dist. on Page 166, Probate Side.)

Page 184.

Barber, Thomas, Windsor. Invt. £132-14-00. Taken 20 October, 1662, by Benjamin Newbery and John Moore.

Court Record, Page 187—4 February, 1662-3: Invt. approved. Samuel was placed with his brother Thomas Barber to learn a Trade; Mercy Barber was placed with Lt. Walter Fyler and his wife until 18 years of age, unless she marry before with her Master & Dame and Eldest brother's Approbation; Josias Barber was placed with Deacon John Moore until 21 years of age, to learn a Trade; Thomas Barber doth engage to take Samuel Barber's portion, and after 2 years from the present to allow 6 per cent. Simple Interest per annum; John Barber took Josias' portion upon the same terms.   Page 188—6 June, 1662: Dist. to John & Sarah Joyntly:

	£ s d
The House & Homelott as their Father Willed,	126-13-04
To Thomas Barber by Guift & his portion,	13-00-00
To Samuel, Mercy, Josias, to each,	36-15-00

By Capt. Newbery, Deacon Moore & Sergt. Alvord.

Page 57.

Barnes, John. Hartford. Invt. £7-14-08. Taken 18 April, 1654, by James Northam, Samuel Gardner.

Court Record, Page 50—2 March, 1653-4: Proclamation to the Creditors to appear at the next Quarter Court. Adms. to James Northam. Page 53—16 May, 1654: Creditors: Sam: Gardner, Tho: Edwards, John Sadler, Matthias Sension, James Northam. The Town of Hartford proved that their Charge of John Barnes' Burial was £00-13-02.

Page 112-113.

Bartlett, William, New London. Invt. £250-15-04. Taken 29 August, 1658, by Jonathan Brewster, Robert Royce. Nuncupative Will, dated 6 August, 1658: I, William Bartlett , of New London, do make and ordain this my last Will & Testament: I give to my wife all my Goods in my House, with House and Lott; and to my Brother Robert all my Outlands; and when my wife dies Robert shall have all my Goods and Lands. Testimony of Jonathan Brewster and Elizabeth Brawley. Will approved and the wife named Executrix. The Will of William Bartlett, of New London, by Word of Mouth in presence of Jonna Brewster and Elizabeth Brawley. The Oath of Jonnah Brewster and Elizabeth Brawley, taken by me who sayeth that William Bartlett spoke (not being very well & fearing his death), that whether I live or dye I give to my wyfe all my Goods in my House wth House & Lott, and to my Brother Robert all my Out lands; and when my wife dyes Robert shall have all my Goods & Lands.

JONNA BREWSTER.

There was 2 men more present wth my self, & whose Testimonies shall if required be sent up to the Courte.

Page 80.

Basly, John, Hartford. Invt. £14-09-00. Taken 4 December, 1655, by John White and Andrew Bacon. Inventory as followeth:

	£ s d
In Wearing Apparell,	2-00-00
In Debts owing to him,	13-15-00
	15-15-00

Testimony of John White, 10 March, 1654-5 (This date on the original Paper on File) : John Basly, of Hartford, late deceased, in his last sickness wherof hee dyed, while hee had his memory and understanding did by Word of Mouth express it as his last Will & Testament yt ye ½ of ye Estate hee dyed seized of hee gave to his wife, ye other halfe hee gave to his Master Nathaniel Ward and to William Markham to bee divided betweene ym in an equal proportion. In Case his wife bee dead yt yn yt halfe hee gave to his wife hee gave to his next Kinsman in Case hee have any living and it can bee safely conveyed to her or ym; if yt his wife and kindred all faile, yn it was his Will yt ye aforesd. Nathaniel Ward and William Markam shall enioy and possess his whole Estate aforesd. Witness: *John White.*

Page 110.

Beardsley, Thomas, Fairfield. Invt. £30-00-06. Taken ye 5th July, 1656, by Anthony Wilson, Humphrey Hide, Alexander Knowles.

Court Record, Page 32—19 May, 1652: Acknowledgement of Debt to Richard Lettin.

Page 20-21.

Beebye, John. Invt. £73-02-05. It being agreable to Civil and Religious Custom, as requyered by God upon the occation of his Hand upon the sonnes of Men as a fore runner of Death unto ym therefore to sett theyr howse in Order, wherefore I, John Beebe, Husbandman, late of Broughton in the County of Northampton, being by God's good hand brought on a voyadge towards New England to Sea, and there smitten by the Good Hand of God so as that my expectation is for my chaynge, yet throughe mercy as yet in perfect Memory and understanding, doe here by (my Just Debts and dewe debts being fully and dewly discharged) give and bequeath unto my 7 Children, to say: John Beebe, Thomas Beebe, Samuel, Nathaniell, Jeames, Rebecca and Mary Bebe, all and every such monnyes or Goods of what spetia or kynde some ever, as all the proper Estate belonging unto me the abovesd. John Beebe, to be equally divided betweene the sd. John, Thomas, Samuel, Nathaniell, Jeames, Rebecca and Mary Beebe, in equal pts & portions. Further, I, the sd. John Beebe, doe Will that my ffoure elder Children, to say: John, Thomas, Samuel and Rebecca, shall have that sayd pts of the monnyes & Goods belonging unto the three younger, to say: Nathaniell, Jeames and Mary, in theyer hands as well as theyr owne proportions, and that the sayd John, Thomas, Samuel and Rebecca shall take Care for the provition of the 3 younger till they the sd. Nathaniell, Jeames and Mary be of adge, at wch tyme they are to have theyr pportions payde in unto ym by my sd. sonnes & Daughter, John, Thomas, Samuel and Rebecca Beebe; whome I appoynt as Executors of this my last Will. Further, I, John Beebe, doe Will and deseyer my Loveing ffriends, Mr. William Lewis and John Cole, be overseers of this my last Will, and that all my sayd Children be advised and Counselled by my sayd overseers for their future dispose by marriage or otherwise. That this is my last Will & Testament I have this 18th day of May, 1650, sett to my Hand and Seale.

Witness: *William Partridge,*   JOHN BEEBE. Ls.
   John Partridge.

Page 58.

Belden, Richard, Wethersfield. Invt. £111-19-00. Taken 22 August, 1655, by John Talcott, John Nott.

Court Record, Page 82—2 October, 1655: Division of the Estate defered.

Page 69-70.

Belden, William, Wethersfield. Invt. £142-06-08. Taken 1st June, 1655, by Nathaniel Dickinson, Samuel Smith, John Deming. Will dated 27 March, 1665. The last Will & Testament of William Belden, late of Wethersfield: Imprimis: I give to my Sonne Sam: £15 when he shall com to the age of 21 years. Item: I give to my son Daniell Belden £15. I give to my son John Belden £15. I give to my daughter Susannah Belden £15 when she shall com to the Age of 18 yeares. I give to my daughter Mary Belden £15. I give to my son Nath: Belden £15. I make Commisin Belden my whole & sole Executrix. I doe also Desire Sam: Smith and Nath: Dickinson, senior, to be supervisors of this my Will, to doe wt they can to Advice and Counsell my wife, & to doe their best to take Care of my Little ones, and to see my Body to be honourably Buried.

Witness: *Thomas Wright,*   WILL X BELDEN.
          Samuel Wright.

Page 176.

Bird, Thomas. Invt. £149-05-10. Taken 10 August, 1662, by Thomas Bunce & John Coale.

	£ s d
(Order of Court) To Distribute to ye Relict ye Widow,	34-00-00
to be paid her presently, & John Belden promist to look	
to her to see her provided for. To James Bird,	20-00-00
To Joseph the House & Land prsently,	40-00-00
to Mary Northe,	32-00-00
To Hannah Scott,	4-00-00

Court Record, Page 178—4 September, 1662: Invt. exhibited and approved.

Page 14—(Vol. III) 3 March, 1663-4: Thomas Bunce and Thomas Watts present a Dist. of the Estate of Thomas Bird:

	£ s d		£ s d
To the Relict,	34-00-00	To Hanna Scott,	4-00-00
To Joseph Bird,	40-00-00	To Goodwife Northe,	18-00-00
To James Bird,	29-08-04	(Proximately.)	

And in Case there appears to be any Estate to remayne when Debts are paid out of ye hops and ye £10 sequestered to pay Debts, it shall be divided betwixt Goodwife Northe and James Bird. Thomas Bunce & Sergt. Hart and Sergt. Watts are desired and appointed to set out ye Estate and to ordr it according to ye Courts Dist. and to see Debts paid.

Page 34-5-6.

Birge, Richard, Windsor.   Invt.   £174-00-00.   Taken October, 1651, by Danuell Clarke & John Moore. The children: Daniel, b. 24 November, 1644; Elizabeth, 28 July, 1646; Jeremiah, 6 May, 1648; John, 14 January, 1649; & Joseph, bapt. 2 November, 1651. (W. R.) Nuncupative Will, dated 10 September, 1651. The last Will & Testament of Richard Birge, late of Windsor, Decd: I give to my wife Elizabeth Birge 1-3 part of my Estate, and the other 2 parts to my Children, only my son Danyell a double portion. William Gaylor, Jr., also Benedictus Alford & Robert Haward, to be Overseers.

Witness: *Robert Hawarth,*   RICHARD BIRGE.
   William Phelps.

Court Record, Page 33—19 May, 1652: Adms. granted to the Relict.

Page 28.

Bliss, Thomas, Hartford.   Invt.   £86-12-08.   Taken 14 February, 1650, by Nathaniel Ward, Joseph Mygatt. Nuncupative Will. Testimony of John Pinchon & Hen: Smith gives property to his wife. Mary Parsons, a daughter, of Springfield, doth Testify to the same.

Court Record, Page 17—20 February, 1650-1: Adms. to the Relict, She to keep the whole Estate in her Hands for her Use and the Education of the Children during her life, then to be divided among the Children, viz: to Lawrence, to John, to Samuel, to Hester, to Elizabeth, to Hannah, and to Sarah Bliss.

Page   17-18-19.

[See Private Controversies, Nos. 180-1-2, in Appendix to Vol. I.]

Boozey, James, Wethersfield.   Died 22 June, 1649.   Invt. £983-08-00. Taken 4 August, 1649, by Samuel Smith sen., Nath: Dickinson. Will dated 21 June, 1649: I, James Boozey, of Wethersfield, do make and confirme this as my last Will & Testament: Imprimis: I give to my eldest Sonne Joseph Boosey £200, to be paid him when he shall com to the age of 21 years, in manner as followeth: I give Him my Homelott, wth a Barne standing upon it, wch I bought of Mr. Alcot, wch was Thomas Sherwood's, the younger, con. 6 acres more or lesse, wch I price at £50; 17 acres of my Plaine, that is to say the Little Plaine running into the Great Plaine, of a true Square, making up his 17 acres, price at £50; and 7 acres in the Great Meadow wch I bought of Robrt Coe, price £45; and 5 acres in Beauer mea at £15; and all my Upland wch I bought of Robrt Coe, price £20 and £29, in such pay as his Mother can conveniently pay him in. When my sonne Joseph Coms to the Injoyment of his Land according to this my Will, he (Joseph) shall repay back the £29 again unless it be paid in Land. I give to my son James Boosey £100, to be paid him at 21 years of age. I give to my daughter Mary Boosey £50 at the age of 21 years or at the day of her maridge. I give to my daughter Hannah Boosey £50 at the age of 21 years or at the day of her marridge. I give to my daughter Sarah Boosey £50 at the age of 21 years or at the day of her marridge. Further, it is my Will that my two sons Joseph & James Boosey shall have all my Lands after the Death of their Mother. Joseph shall have all my Purchased Land except 4 acr in Beauer mea, wch is 20 acr on the Great Plain and 4 acrres in the Great Mea wch was John Simonsis & Jeremy Jaggers. This, wth that before mentioned, is the whole of my purchased Land, except 4 acr in Beaver mea before excepted. My sonne James shall have my now Dwelling House & House Lott, and Barnes & Houses standing thereon, wth all the Land wch was given me by the Towne that is now in my possession, wch is 12 acres in the Great Mea, 56 acr of Upland & Swamp, wth 4 acr in Beaver Mea wch was named before. ——It is also my Will that what this Land shall amount to above these 2 Legacies of £300, the value of it shall be divided amongst my 5 Children proportionably according to their portions. If the Land is prised at £400, wch we Conceive, this £100 which surmounts to be divided:

	£ s d		£ s d
To Joseph,	44-08-02	To Hannah,	11-02-02
To James,	22-04-05	To Sarah,	11-02-02
To Mary,	11-02-02		

It is my Will, that if any of my Children shall prove undutifull or stubborne, and will not be ruled by their Mother, it shall be in the power of their mother to take from those wch is the undutifullest as she shall see cause. And as for the rest of my Goods, I doe bequeath to my wife as my whole and sole Executrix, and do intreat Mister Welles, Brother Smith, sen., & Brother Dickinson to be the supervisors of this my Will & Testament.

Witness: *Sam: Smith, senior,*   (Not signed.)
          Nath: Dickinson.

P. C. Page 79.

Boosey, Joseph, Deceased in Westchester. Invt. £504-10-00. Taken 24 July, 1655, by Thomas Wheeler, William Newman and Josias Gilbert.

Nuncupative Will of Joseph Boosey: that which was spoken by Joseph Boosey as his last Will before his wife Esther and Josias Gilbert, being in his perfect senses the sd. Joseph Boosey now decd he gave his wife Esther his whole Estate, and the sd. Esther is to pay out of the Estate 2 Oxen to James Wakeling of Wethersfield, being his free Gift to the sd. Wakeling; they are to bee the same Oxen that was bought of James Wakeling by Joseph Boosey upon Consideration that the sd. James Wakeling must acquit all Account between them. And the remainder of the Estate, in Case he left his wife with Child, the sd. Esther is to give half of his Estate to the Child when the Child is of age, provided that all Debts that doth appear upon Just Accounts doe be satisfied in the 1st place.

Page 151-2.

Boswell, James, Wethersfield. Invt. £162-07-00. Taken 27 December, 1660, by Samuel Welles and John Goodrich:

september 24: 1660.

i ieames buswell ofe wethe theres feld felenge my selefe ve ry ele thenkes it is my du ty ha uenge my ri te sen ses and re sene to sete my estate that god haue geuen me in ordere and thes is my wele i haue giuene my uncell and ante and io nathane smethe my foure catetele ate good mane wrytes i land more ouerre i haue giuen theme my tou yonge marese   more ouere thes is my wele i haue geuen my cos sen ri richard smethe and my cos sene iosephe sun smethe ale my land in nawbuck my cous sene mr richard shale haue hes halefe ofe my lote nuexth good mane bonces lote more ouere i haue guene my cus sen richard smethe my ould mare ande here coulte and my ould coue and my yonge seege i had ofe iohne adomes thate i cote sence i hade heme ofe iohn addames and a wethere shepe i giue hime and my house ale soe   more ouere i make my cos sene richard smith and Thomas edwardes my ouere serese to prouid for my honeuorabell buryable ife ite ples god i dy and in con sederacyon fore there care and payenes i geue them ale kyndes ofe my were renge clos and heed clos and hates and shoues and towe yonger hogs i haue ate nawbuk they are to haue thes theuyes alyke i geue them to be deuided to bothe alyke more ouer this is my wele i haue guen toe Thomas edwardes my coulte and a shepe he has them booth aleredy in hes kepenge & thes i geue hem fre ly be seyd othere chere ges he have bene oute one me these my estate most paye moste pay these i leue in the handes ofe my 2 cus sene richard smethe & ale soee i make my cos sene richard smethe my ex seckeetore toe pay ale my detes and receyue ale my dates

JAMES BUSWELL
Thomas Edwardes
richard smith Junr.

Court Record, Page 152—7 March, 1660-1: Will proven.

Page 148.

Branke, John, Windsor. Died 27 May, 1662. Invt. £502-00-00. Taken 17 June, 1662, by Matthew Grant, John Moore, Benjamin Newbery. Will dated 26 May, 1662. He doth bestow all his estate unto Abigail Branke, his wife, and doth make her sole executrix.

Witness: *John Warham,   Richard Vore,*   JOHN BRANKE. Ls.

Court Record, Page 179, 11 Sept., 1662: Will Proven.

Page 159.

Brawley, Peter, (probably a Seaman of New London). Invt. £59-01-00. Taken 19 June, 1662, by Obadiah Bruen, Samuel Smith and John Smith.

An Inventory of Peter Brawley's Estate taken 19 June, 1662:

	£ s d
Impr. House & Lott with 4 Acrs Mead, £30; 1 Gunn, £1,	31-00-00
In Bedding, £5; A Shute of Clothes, £1,	6-00-00
Chest, Trunk, Boxes, £0-12; Half a Boat, A Cow, £28-08,	29-00-00
A Jarr, Stilliards, Sea Clothes, £1-03,	1-03-00
28 Acrs Land in ye Neck, £0-18; 6 acrs more, £1,	1-18-00
	69-01-00

Browne, Henry. Court Record, Page 23—14 May, 1651 (Particular Courte). Henry Browne testified upon Oath in Court that Elizabeth Turner and James Jupp were dd to him in London by a man from the Mother of Robert Chapman who tould him that the sd. Mother of Chapman did desire the sd. Browne to dd the sd. Turner and Jupp to her sd. sonne Robert Chapman in New England and that hee had heard the sd. Turner and Jupp Severall times say that they were to goe to Robert Chapman.

Page 114-115.

Browne, Nathaniel, Middletown. Invt. £96-02-04. Taken 26 August, 1658, by Robert Webster, Nathaniel White, Thomas Wetmore. (No Court Record.)

Page 160.

Buckland, Thomas, Hartford. Died 28 May, 1662. (W. R.) Invt. £343-06-04. Taken 20 June, 1662, by Deacon Gaylord, Deacon Moore, Matthew Grant.

Court Record, Page 168—10 September, 1662: Adms. to the Widow and an Order for Dist.

	£ s d		£ s d
To the Widow,	118-00-00	To Sarah,	30-00-00
To Nicholas,	30-00-00	To Hannah,	30-00-00
To Thomas,	30-00-00	To Timothy,	30-00-00
To Temperance			
(m. John Ponder),	30-00-00		

To each, with what they have already received, £30 from the Estate when they attain to lawful age, the sons at 21 and the daughters at 18 years of age. This Court also orders that the Estate dist. to Elizabeth the wife of Edward Adams shall so remain to her and to her heirs, and that he shall give security that it shall not be alienated.

Note: (See Vol. III, No. 142 P. C.) Sarah m. John Phelps. See Will of Elizabeth Denslow, Gr. Mother to these Children.

Page 146-7.

Bushnell, Richard, Norwalk. Invt. £212-08-08. Taken 17 July, 1660, by Matthew Marvin, Nathaniel Richards & Richard Olmsted. Will dated 1st December, 1659:   In the name of God, Amen. I Richard Bushnell of Norwalk, being of perfect memory though weake in Body, do make this my last Will & Testament. I doe give and bequeath unto my dearly beloved wife Marcy Bushnell the ½ of whatsoever shall remain, & the other half I doe give and bequeath to my 4 children, allowing my 2 sones each of them £5 more than to my 2 daughters, & this I desire may be imployed for them until they shall bee of sufficient age or marryed, wch soever shall first come to passe. I request Matthew Marvin, sen., Nathaniel Richards & Richard Olmsted of Norwalk to be Overseers.

Witness: *Alice Marvin,*   RICHARD BUSHNELL, Ls.
              Jas: Cornish.

Court Record, Page 167—6 March, 1661-2. Will proven. And ye Relict being again married to William Adgate, Adms. is granted to ye sd. Adgate, he giving to the Overseers sufficient Security to discharge the Legacies to the Bushnell Children.

Page 142.

Carmackle, William. Died 27 July, 1666. Invt. £4-05-06. Taken by Francis Bushnell, Thomas Dunk.

Impr pr one Wastcoat,	0-04-00
In sutes of Cloathes, Shirts, Boots, Shoes, and other	
Appurtenances to his wearing apparrell,	4-01-06

4-05-06

Townsmen.   Robert Chapman,
John Clark,
Robt Chapman and William Parker are appointed to administer to ye Estate abovesd.

Page 33.

Carpenter, David, Farmington. Invt. £76-00-00. Taken 18 May, 1652. Will dated 20 January, 1650-1. The last Will & Testament of David Carpenter, late of Farmington, Decd: I give to my wife Elizabeth the Celler that I live in and all my Household Stuff and half my Estate abroad. And I give to my children, Elizabeth, David and Mary, the other half of my Estate abroad, viz., all besides the Celler and Household Stuff. And I comitt the Care and Oversight of my Children and Estate and Buildings wholly to my Master, John White of Hartford.

Testimony of Stephen Hart and Thomas Judd in Court.

Witness: *Roger Newton,*
Stephen Hart, Thomas Judd.

Court Record, Page 33—19 May, 1652: Will & Invt. exhibited. Adms. to John White.

Carrington, John. Court Record, Page 17—20 February, 1650-1. A Particular Courte in Hartford upon the Tryall of John Carrington and his wife.

Edw. Hopkins, Gov; John Haynes, Dept. Governor.
Magistrates:
Mr. Welles, Mr. Wolcott, Mr. Webster, Mr. Cullick, Mr. Clarke.
Jury:
Mr. Phelps, Mr. Tailcoat, Mr. Hollister, David Wilton, John White, Will: Lewis, Samll Smith, John Pratt, John Moore, Edw: Griswold, Steph: Hart, Tho: Judd.

Indightment: John Carrington, thou art indighted by the name of John Carrington of Wethersfield, Carpenter, that not having the Fear of God before thine eyes, thou hast Intertained familarity with Sattan, the great Enemy of God and Mankind, and by his help has done works above the Course of nature, for wch, both according to the Laws of God and the Established Laws of this Common Wealth, thou deservest to Dye.

The Jury finds this Inditem against John Carrington the 6th of March 1650-1. Att the same Court, Time and Place, was found an Indightment also against Joanne Carrington, wife of John Carrington, with the same Verdict.

Page 40—1st Thursday in March, 1652-3. There was presented to this Court an Invt. of John Carrington's Estate, *which is ordered to be filed but not recorded.* The Estate presented being £23-11-00, and the Debts specified therein oweing by the Estate is sumed up to £13-01-06.

(See Book II of Lands, at Sec. State's Office, Hartford.)

Case, John, Mashpath Killes, New Netherlands, 17 August, 1656. A Letter giving power of Attorney:

Know all Men by these prsents, that I John Case, now Inhabiting in Mashpath Kills in the new Netherlands, have constituted and made my Father William Edwards, inhabitant in Hartford in New England, my true and lawfull Attorneye to demand, recouver and receive in my name and for my vse of Mr. Richard Lord of Hartford in New England, mrcht, £6 which the sd. Mr. Richard Lord was assigned by the ourseers to pay unto my wife in Pease and Wheat when shee was 18 yeares of Age, in Pease at 3 Shillings the Bushell, and Wheat at 4 Shillins the Bushell. Also I doe Authorise my Attornye, with as full power as if myselfe was existant, to demand, recouer and receive of the sd. Mr Lord all other Debts or Dues which shall bee found to bee owing unto mee from him. I say I doe Authorise, Ratifie and Confirme my Attornye with as full power in this Case as if myselfe was existant. Upon the Refusall to pay, I doe Authorise my Attorney to Arrest, Sue, Recouver, and upon receipt to give discharge, or if occasion bee to plead or implead in my name and place, and what Attornye shall see Cause to doe in this Case I Will Ratifie and Confirme as done by myselfe.

Witness: *Joseph Langdon,*   JOHN X CASE.
       Thomas Casse.

Note: On the back side was written to his loving ffather William Edwards, living at Hartford in New England this prsent.

The above written is a true Coppie of an original writing Recorded this 18th Aprill, 1657, by me John Cullick, Sec.

Page 155.

Channel, Robert, New London. Invt. £76-10-01. Taken 26 May, 1662, by John Tinker, Obadiah Breuen and John Smith.

Court Record, Page 173—5 June, 1652. Invt. Exhibited by Mr. Tinker. This Court order Lt. Smith, Mr. Breuen and Mr. Tinker to take Care of ye Estate until upon Notice given ye Relatives address unto the Court. What Debts are due from the Estate they are to see discharged.

Chapman, Will. Court Record, Page 49 & 50—2nd March, 1653-4. Whereas, one Will Chapman was complayned of for a Breach of an Order of the Como. Wealth, that noe prson whatsoever, maile or feamale, not being at his or her own disposing, that remaineth under Government of parents, Master, Guardians or such like, shall either make or give entertainment to any motyon or sute in way of marridge with out the knowledge & Consent of those they stand in such relations to, under the severe Sensure of the Court in case of delinqency not attending this order, nor shall any third person or persons intermeadle in making any motyon to any such without the knowledg & Consent of those under whose Government they are, under the same penalty; & it appears to the Court that the said Chapman hath trespessed against the said order in an high nature, going aboute to gaine the affectyone by way of marriage of one Elizabeth Bateman, servant to Capt John Cullick, & hath the same Laid divers unsufferable scandalls & reproaches upon the said Capt & his family and severall others, all which were duly heard & scanned by the said Courte. And it is now ordered, that the said Will Chapman shall be for the which pay for a fine five pounds for Breach of the Said order, & for other misdemeaners he is committed (to) preson for fourteen dayes & then to put in security to before Mr. Webster for the good behavior untill the next quarter Courte at Hartford. And that the sd. Capt Cullick shall use his libberty to give ffamily discipline to his servants, Elizabeth (Bateman) & Will Warren, Thomas Whaples also accessory; and Nich: Olmsted must give security to appear in Court to answer concerning the Business between Will Chapman and Elizabeth Bateman.

Page 176.

Chester, Dorothy, Hartford. Invt. £33-11-08. Taken 27 May, 1662, by Gregory Wolterton, John Barnard & Thomas Bull.

Court Record, Page 174—6 June, 1662: Adms. to Edward Stebbing to administer the Estate and pay the Debts. The remainder to be at his disposal.

Page 8-9-10-11.

Chester, Leonard, Wethersfield. Invt. £1062-01-08. Taken by James Boosey, Sam. Smith. Will dated 22 November, 1637: I, Leonard Chester, of Wethersfield, Gentleman, doe ordain and appoint this my last will & Testament: Imp. I give and bequeath unto my sonne John, all that my howse lott with howses, meadows and other Lands whatsoever, together with that Mill and the appurtenances thereto belonging wch I am in building at the devising of these presents, all wch doe lye, are situate, and have their being in the towne and Libberty of Wethersfield aforesaid, to enter uppon the one halfe Imediately after my decease for and towards his education and maintenance, and upon the other halfe after the decease of

Mary, my Beloved wife, and not before. And if it shall so happen that the said John shall dye without Issue before hee comes to the Age of one and twenty years, that then the said howses, Land and aprtenances thereto, I give and bequeath unto my daughter Mary; and if it shall please God that my daughter Mary shall dye without Issue, that then my will is that the aforesaid howses, Lands, etc. shall be devided amongst the heirs of my Body in Generall; or, for want of Issue, to the Children of my deare uncle Mr. Thomas Hooker, now pastor at Hartford, in Connecticut aforesaid. Item. I give and bequeath unto my daughter Mary £200. Item. I give and bequeath unto my Mother Dorothy Chester £30. And I doe give unto my wife Mary one halfe of my howse lott with howses, meadowes and other Lands whatsoever, together with the mill and the Aprtenances thereto belonging wch I am now building, to have and to holde for her propper use and benefit during the time of her naturall Life, and then to returne to the only use and right of my sonne John, according to the premisses before specified. And I doe appoint & constitute my deare wife Mary my whole and only Executrixe. And I doe appoint Mr. John Plum and Mr. Henry Smith, both of this Towne of Wethersfeild, to bee my ourseers, for wch I doe give unto Mr. Plum: ten shillings to buy him a paire of gloves, and Mr. Smith I give to him thirty shillings. In witness hereunto I have sett my hand and seale the day and yeare Above written.

LEONARD CHESTHER.

In the prsence of us:
Henry Smith.

It is the Last will and testament of Leonard Chesther, Gent., that Mr Haynes and Mr Webster shall take into Consideration the £300 sent over as parte of the portion of his wife since he came to New England, wch was to bee disposed of for her use with her liking, wch being rectified by the two friends above named, then his howsing, Lands, stock and estate to bee disposed of to the benefitt of his Children according as the said Leonard should determine when they conferr with him: And in case hee departe this life before they can visit him, then hee Intreats those two ffriends as his Last will to proportion the estate to his posterity as they judge fitt. And hee makes Mr. Webster and Mr. Newton, of Tonxsis, his overseers.

LEONARD CHESTHER.

In the prsence of
Tho. Hooker, James Boosey, Dorothy Chesther.

Memorandum: Whereas, I have some yeares since drawne up the sum of my thoughts and desires into a writing and Committed it to the keeping of my uncle Thomas Hooker, now deceased, wch writing for present I cannott well come att, and further because in the writing I have not so farr as I remember made any provision for my younger children wch have beene borne since, I doe therefore hereby declare that whatever provision is therein made for my younger Children that were then borne, the same provision I doe appoint to bee made for my younger Children borne since, so that they shall all have portions alike, equal one to another, except my eldest sonne, to whom I have and doe still bequeath a double portion. And whereas, in that my will I have Intreated Mr. John Webster and my Coussin Newton to bee my Executors, I doe hereby make knowne that my desire is to ease them of that trouble and doe Constitute and appoint my Loving wife to be my sole and aloane Executrix. And Lastly, because I have taken no order in that writing for the dispose of what estate I have remaining still in ould England, I doe therefore bequeathe all that estate, whither in Annuity, goods or otherwise, wch either is or shall bee by right appertaining unto mee or mine heirs, and in perticular one Annuity of 30 quarters of Barlye issueing out of the estate of Nicholas Sharpe, deceased, and by his will bequeathed unto mee and mine heirs, for the settling whereof I have sent over a letter of Attornye to my father Wade; all this, with what ever else will bee coming to mee out of ould England, I doe give to my wife during her life, with all the prfitts that shall acrewe therefrom; and after her decease I doe give and bequeath it to my Children, viz., to my eldest sonne a double portion, and to the rest to every one an equal portion. That this is my full minde and finall resolution and will, I doe hereto in testimony hereof sett to my hand & seale this

2 of August, 1648.   LEONARD CHESTHER.
In the presence of us: *Henry Smith,*
Will Smith,   *Thomas Hanchett.*

My desire is to Add something further to my within mentioned will, viz: 1st, In Case that my Annuity in ould England shall not bee sould and so shall fall by Lawe uppon my Eldest sonne, that then whatever I have given to my Eldest sonne by my will, viz., that double portion of goods, shall be translated from him to my other Children to mend their portions; 2nd, In case any of my Children shall proove undutifull and stubborne to their mother, that it shall bee in the power of their mother to take away the one halfe of that portion I have bequeathed to that childe and to give it to such of the rest as shall be more dutifull unto her. These things, though in rude and undigested manner, I desire for the present thus to sett downe, Intending if God spare my Life to reduce all into one Intire writing; this 2 August 1648.   LEONARD CHESTHER.

This Court takeing the Estate of Mr Chesther decd into Consideration on the 21st July, 1651, Judge meete that the Widow should have £300 and the remainder of the Estate to be equally divided amongst the Children. The Eldest to have a double portion, according to the Will. Any Estate that may come from England being also considered with the Estate heere, the wch if it falls to the Eldest sonne, if that amount to £100, hee is to have but a single portion with the other Children.

Page 64.

(From the original copy on file.)

Clarke, Joseph, Windsor. (Died 19 April, 1641. W. R.) Invt. £44-00-00. Taken by Henry Clarke and William Gaylord. Will dated 1st December, 1640: I, Joseph Clarke, of Windsor, being somewhat weake but of prfect memory, doe ordayne this my last will and Testament: First, I bequeath my soule to God, waiting for his salvation through ye alone merit of Jesus Christ, And my Body to Christian Buriall at ye discretion of my Executors. And for my worldly goods, I thus dispose of ym: I bequeath my Estate in Lands and goods to my two Children, in ye discretion of mine Executors, ye wch office I desire ye Church by ye ministers & ye deacons & oversight of ye Elders to undertake; and my desire is yt my house and lott should be Let and farmed at rent for 10 or 12 years, & ye Rent yearly to goe towards ye maintenance of ye Children so long. And if yt will not suffice ym maintenance & ye church see it meete, my desire is yt my lott joyning to ye great River above sequestered meadow bee go to for supply if need require; and after ye sd. ten or 11 years my desire is yt my two children be sett forth in some Godly family for six or seven years or more, in ye Churche's Wisdome, and duringe ye sd. terme my desire is yt ye rent of my house and Land bee resarved by ye deacons for to make portion for my daughter, to be paid unto her at ye age of 21; at wch time also my desire is my house and land bee delivered to my sonne, to whome (in case it bee not otherwise in ye meantime desposed of by ye Church) I bequeath it forever; provided yt in case of sickness or any other disaster my desire is yt ye Church doe dispose of my Estate otherwise as in yts discretion may best Conduce to ye Comfort of my Children.

Witness: *John Warham, Ephraim Huit,*   JOSEPH CLARKE.
John Witchfield, Wm. Hosford, William Gaylord.

Page 122.

Clarke, Joseph, Windsor. Died 2nd May, 1659. Invt. £71-19-02. Taken by Henry Clarke, Matthew Grant & John X Bissell. The next of Kin to ye party is one sister, Mary Clarke, age 21 years.

Court Record, Page 131—1st December, 1659: This Court Grant Adms. to Anthony Howkins in behalf of Mary Clarke. Page 152—7 March, 1660-1: Joseph Bird manifests to the Court his Acceptance and Approbation of the Over-sight and Account of Anthony Howkins respecting the Estate of Mary Clarke.

Page 36-37.

Coale, Jeames, Hartford. Invt. £116-03-04. Taken November, 1652, by Thomas (H) Osmer, John White.

The last Will & Testament of Jeames Coale of Hartford Decd: I, Jeames Coale, of Hartford, uppon the River of Connecticutt, being of perfect memorye and Soundnes of minde, doe according to my duty, knowing the frailty of my Body and uncertainty of my Life, for the preventing of distractions to my selfe while I live and differences in my familye when I am gathered to my fathers, make and ordaine this my Last Will and Testament, and doe dispose of that outward Estate wherewith the Lord hath of his Abundant mercy blessed mee, in mannr following: Imprimis. I give to my deare and well beloved Sonne and daughter, Danyell and Abigail Sullivane, my now dwelling howse in Hartford, with all other houses, orchards, gardens, home lott, with all aptenances thereunto belonging, with one peece of Land being about five Acres more or Less, Lying at penny wise within Wethersfield bounds, As also one parcell of upland being about foure Acres more or less, Lying about the wolfe pound. All wch forementioned Lands and howsing I give to them and their heirs for ever, provided that my sonne Danyell and daughter Abigaille pay yearly to my deare and well beloved wife, Ann Coale, the Just and full sum of three pounds in good Current pay during her Naturall Life. Further my will is, that my wife should have an upper roome at the South end of my now dwelling howse during her widdowhood, with free Libberty of egress and regress without molestation. Further my will is, that she my wife Ann Coale should have the use of their firinge for her owne Comforte in any respect, As also any fruit or herbs in the orchyard or garden for her owne particular Spending, As also the use of the well belonging to the howse. Further, if my wife desires to keepe a Cowe or a hogg or some poultry for her perticular use, Shee providing meate for them, my will is that Shee shall have yard roome for them where my sonne Danyell's Cattle are usually yarded. Item. I give all my Coopers tooles equally to be divided between my well beloved sonne William Edwards and my Loving Coussin Henry Coale. Item. I give unto my deare and well beloved wife Ann Coale all my houshold stuff of every kinde undisposed of, with all my Cattle and Crop of Corne now on the ground, with all my debts owinge to mee, provided that shee payes all my just debts and defray all that charge wch shall be thought necessary by the ourseers of this my will for my Christian Burial. Also, I doe desire and appointe my trusty and well beloved ffriends, Mr. John Webster and William Gibbons, ourseers of this my will. And further, I doe appoint my deare and well beloved wife Ann Coale to be my whole Executrixe of this my last will and testament.

JEAMES COALE.

Witness: *John White,*
Thomas Osmore.

Page 142.

Colfax, William, Wethersfield. Invt. £103-19-06. Taken 20 Sept., 1660, by James Wakely & Samuel Welles.

Court Record, Page 157—6 June, 1661 : Mr. Treat, John Lattimer, William Gutridge, John Ryle are desired & appointed to consider the estate of Widdow Colfax and to Dist. & Settle the portions of ye Relict and ye several Children and make return to ye Court September next. The Widow is not to Marry another before security be given for ye Childrens portions. Report of Dist. on file 31 April, 1680 : To the Mother of the Children, to Jonathan, to Mary, Joseph Bidwell and Mary his wife, give their whole right in the estate of our brother John Colfax, Dec, to our brother Jonathan Colfax ; 9th March, 1680-81, Henry Arnold and wife Elizabeth also resign their right to brother Jonathan Colfax. Dist. by Richard Treat, John Riley & Wm Goodrich.

Witness   by *William House,*
Benjamin Crane, Nathaniel Butler.

Page 59.

Collins, Peter, Pequett, Planter. Invt. £57-08-00. Taken 14 May, 1655, by Richard Smith, John Elderkin, Andrew Lester, Mr. Brewster.

The Will and Testament of peeter Collins plantr of ye Towne of pequott :

Impr I peeter Collins of ye towne doe comitt my soule to god, my Bodie commend I to ye ground. I Constitute John Gager I say to bee my full heire and Executor. I bequeath unto ye prson a forenamed one black cow wth a strake in ye fore head, A Barrow hogg, a sow, a great brass Kettle weighing 8 pound, a feather Bed and a green Coverlitt, allso one sheete ; Also 30 Shillings worth of Tobacco wch is in ye house ; 2nd, I bequeath to Richard poole mye house, home lott, Corne and all belonging to it, all wood cleaft and uncleft, all my Lands except ye land in ye Neck, wch Jacob Waterhouse is to have. I bequeath unto ye aforenamed Richard poole my Brindle cow, allso 30 Shillings worth of Tobacco. 3, I bequeath unto Robbert Burrowes, planter, of pequott, my black cow ; allso, I give unto him one pound 1 shilling wch is due to mee from William Roberts wch was Tho. Stauntons man ; in Like manner I bequeath unto him one third of a Bill of £40 wch Capt James Tonge is indebted to mee. 4, I give unto George Harwood one third of ye afore named Bill ; I say unto George Harwood, planter, of pequott. 5, I bequeath unto Matthew Becworth ye sum of two pound 2 shillings. In Like manner I give unto Tho. Hungerford one pound 10 shillings. 6, I bequeath unto George Tongue one third of ye afore named bill of James Tongue ; allso, to William morton I give a kettle of 5 pound Weight.

Witness our hands ye 7 of May, 1655.   PEETER X COLLINS.
     Richard poole, William Morton.

Page 102-103.

Cross, William, Fairfield. Invt. £94-02-04. Taken 7 September, 1655, by George Hull, Alexander Knowles. Settlement deferred on account of debts to the benefit of the Widow and the orphans. Estate Insolvent.

Court Record, Page 87—May, 1656: Proclamation to the Creditors to present claims at the quarter Court June next, Mr. Ward & Mr. Hill to take the Estate and Distribute as they shall receive orders from the Court. Page 89—5 June, 1656; the Court doth Impower Mr. Ward, Mr. Hill & John Bankes to care for the Estate, to allow the widow for her use, and may sell her, such things as she may wish to purchase from the estate for Account of debts of Cross Estate. Page 102—4 June, 1657: Henry Woolcot and Edward Stebbins to Adms. the Estate. Page 109—3 December, 1657: Distribution to the Creditors allowed by this Court.

Page 126. Will, Page 125-132.

Drake, John, Sen., Windsor. Died 17 August, 1659. Invt. £324-13-00. Taken 14 September, 1659. Will recorded 1659.

First, I bequeath my soule to God that gave it me, and my body to Earthly burial. As for my worldly goods, I thus dispose of them: First, I desire that there may be a Inventory tooke off my State and within twelve months after my decease: I give to my son John £20; and after my wyve's decease, out of the State I have, I give him tenn pounds more; and to my son Job I give my six acres of meaddow that is bounded of the South side with Goodman Phillips, Within twelve moneths after my decease, then, after my wife's decease, I give that six acres forementioned to his sonne Job; and after my wife's decease I give to all of my grand children, viz., three of sonne John, and four of my sonne Job, and one of my daughter Elizabeth Gaylord, three pounds apeece; and too my wife I give all my part off Howsing and Lands that I have in possession ffor to make use of as shee and her ffriends shall think will be fore her best advantage; and my Land that I bought of Goodman Bissell that Lye of the East Side of the great river I give to my sonne Jacob provided that he pay to my sonne John tenne pounds after my wif's decease, ffor to make his porshon £30; the house and my Land that I bought that was Mr Sen Nicholases (Mr. John Saint Nicholas) that lys of the west side of the great river I give to my sonne Jacob, and after my wife's decease he shall pay to the rest of his brothers & sisters sixteene pounds ffor the Land that I have given to my sonne Jacob; my wife is to have the propriety of it for her use while shee live, and after her decease then my sonne Jacob shall have full possession of it with its appurtenances yt appertain thereunto, provided that he pay the formentioned Sums of money to his Brethren, viz., tenne pounds to my sonne John and Sixteene pounds to the rest of his brothers and sisters; too my sonne Jacob I also give him my two tables and a bedsted that he maks use of yt belongs to that end of the House next the Highway in the lower rooms; to my daughter Mary Gayler I give one fetherbed and two blankets and a bolster after my wife's decease; and to my daughter Elizabeth I give one Coverlid after my decease; and to Timothy I give him forty shillings and two good Sutes of Cloths when his time is out; and the rest of Stock shall be equally divided amongst my five Children after my wife's decease.

Witness: *John Bissell,*   JOHN X DRAKE.
         Jacob Drake.

Court Record, Page 131—1 December, 1659. Will proven. Page 132—(Probate Side) 19 December, 1659: The Magistrates of Windsor, wth the Sec. & Thomas fford, Ensign Wilson, Edward Griswold, being mett to settle the difference about ye Estate of John Drake sen., according to ye Courts desires and ordr. After much debate about Job Drake's Demands, at Length the Widow Drake with all ye Children, the Relicts of John Drake sen., came to a mutual Agreement amongst themselves as followeth: Jacob engageth to issue the trouble amongst them to pay £10 out of his owne proper Estate to his Brother Job Drake. The Widow consented to pay him £10, and the rest of the Children consented to pay £10 in porportion to what each had received, and this being paid (£30), it is agreed that all Demands whatsoever respecting these 4 particulars formerly mentioned by Job Drake, viz., his service done for his Father, 2ndly his £20 portion, 3rdly his 2 Journeys to Pascataway, 4th Money lent to his father, last by his Claime to part of ye Home Lott, shall for ye future Cease and be anihilated. It is mutually agreed yt he is to have ye Legacy left upon his Father's Will.

Signed: ELIZ X DRAKE, JOHN GAYLORD,
           JOB DRAKE, JOHN DRAKE, JACOB DRAKE.

Elizabeth Drake, the Relict of John Drake sen., to be Adms.
                              Danll Clarke, Secretr.

Note: On the 20th of November, 1660, John Drake receipts for the sum of £29-00-00, being the full sum due to him and his 3 Children except what is to be paid after ye Death of Widow Drake according to ye Will of John Drake sen.

Ensign, James. Court Record, Page 183—4 September, 1662: This Court doth set the son of William Eares to James Ensign or his assigns as an apprentice until he accomplish ye age of 21 years, and James Ensign is to see him instructed in ye Art of Trade of a Cooper and to give the boy £4 at ye End of this time of service; and if he teach him not a Trade he doth engage to pay £10 in ye Total to ye Boy.

On the 3rd day of March, 1674-5, John Eares appeared and acknowledged he had received full Satisfaction from his Master according to the Order of the Court above specified, and David Ensign showed me a writing at the same time under *John Eares his Hand.*

Witnessed by James Steele and John Shepherd Testifying the same, and desired that it be Certified upon the Record.

Pr *John Allyn, Secretary.*

Field, Zachary. Court Record, Page 110—4 March, 1657: Zachary Field, Atty. to John Smith of Martins Vin Yard per Contra Jonas Weed late of Southampton L. I. Defendant. in an Action of Debt.

Vol. II, Land Records, (this side not paged) Sec. State's office.

Fitch, Samuel.—— Major Robbins and worthy friend being requested by Mrs Fitch to wright to you to Intrust you to order that Tobacco which is due to her, being Executrix to her late husbands Estate, I Will to my son Richard Lord as Attorney to Mrs. Fitch, and what shee receives of you and gives you acquittance of on this Account unto yor selfe shall be sufficient as if it bine done in a more formall way. Wee having not time to wright Richard a letter of Attorney, thos intreating yor favor to ye Family of our decd friend request yor friend to Commend Richard Lord. October last, 1656.

Mr. Samuel Fitch, Debtor   Mr. Samuel Fitch is Creditor.
    £4296-00-00   £4386-00-00

Account Current, errors excepted. Drawn out 6th of June, 1655, by me
Obedience Robbins.

Page 68.

Foote, Nathaniel, Wethersfield. Invt. £244-18-00. Taken 23 September, 1655, by Richard Treat, Samuel Smith & Nathaniel Dickinson. The children: Nathaniel, 7 years; Samuel, 5; Daniel, 4; Elizabeth, 3 years. Court Record, Page 68—7 June, 1655: Adms. granted to the Widow.

Page 4.

Foxe, Christopher, Wethersfield. Died 15 December, 1650. Invt. £16-17-00. Taken 18 December, 1650, by Nathaniel Dickinson & John Nott, Boat Swayne of the Ship Tryall of Wethersfield. An Account rendered by John Sadler of Wethersfield for Charges for 9 weeks and 2 days Care and Expense in the Sickness of Christopher Foxe. This Court gave Sadler power to administer the Estate on the 21st of February, 1650-1.

---

ffynch, Danll. Court Record, Page 100—May, 1657: This Court orders that the Estate wch Danll ffynch left at ffairfeld shall be committed to the keeping or management of his gr. Child Abraham ffynch, hee giving in sufficient security to the Townsmen of ffairfield that the sd. Estate shall be prserved for the use of Danll Fynch his gr. father, or to answer such other just Demands as reason and Justice shall require.

Page 108.

Gaylord, William Jr., Windsor. Died 14 December, 1656. Invt. £423-00-09. Taken by Matthew Grant, Benjamin Newbery, David Wilton & William Haydon. The Legatees: Elizabeth the Widow; The children: Anne, age 11 years & 9 months; Hannah, 10 years; John 8; William, 6 years; Hezekiah, 4 years; Josiah, 2; and Nathaniel, 15 weeks.

My Brother expressed these words unto me & my wife before his decease: that he would that his house & halfe his land should be and remain to two of his Children. Further, that he had £40 with his wife & he would be as good as his word to make it up Four Score at "iter" £80 to her.   JOHN GAYLORD.

Exhibited in Court 5 March, 1656.

Court Record, Page 108 (Vol. III) 2 March, 1673-4. The Overseers move for a Dist. of the Estate of the sd. Gaylord to his Children.

	£ s d
Debts being paid there remains good to be dist.,	383-06-06
To the Widow,	80-00-06
To the Eldest son,	72-06-06
To the Eldest daughter,	33-00-00
To the 2nd daughter,	30-00-00
To the 2nd son,	42-00-00
To the 3rd son,	42-00-00
To the 4th son,	42-00-00
To the 5th son,	42-00-00

This Court appoint John Porter, Jacob Drake and John Gaylord Dist.

Gennings (Jennings) **John.** Court Record, Page 166—5 December, 1661: From this present date John Gennings is by the Court set an Apprentice to Jeremiah Addams during the terme of 7 years; then he is to receive £10 and double Clothing.

Gennings, Joseph. Court Record, Page 166—5 December, 1661: From this present date Joseph Gennings is by this Court set an Apprentice to Richard Treat sen. for 10 years; then the Boy is to be paid £10 and well apparrelled.

Page 82-3-4-5.

Gibbons, William, Hartford. Invt. £1499-14-05. Taken 2 December, 1655, by John White, Andrew Bacon, Nathaniel Ward. Will dated 26 February, 1654-5 :

I, William Gibbins, of Hartford, upon ye River of Connecticutt, yeoman, being of perfect memory and soundness of mind,—make and ordayne this my last will & testament : Imp. I give unto my wife Ursula Gibbons her full thirds of ye proffitts, rents and revenues of all my houses & Lands in Hartford, Wethersfield & Pequett, during her naturall lyfe, except A prsell of swamp bought of Robert Bates, lying in Wethersfield, & a prcell of Land lying in Pennywise, which I bequeath by this my will as followes : As alsoe I give and bequeathe unto my wife Ursula the whole proffits & revenues of ye foresd houses & Landes, viz., the whole of my houses & landes in Wethersfield both of ye East & West side of ye river, untill my daughter Mary Gibbons shall be married or untill shee bee of ye age of eighteen years ; Alsoe the whole of my houses & Landes at Hartford & Pequett, until my daughter Sarah shall bee married or 18 years of age ; (and after this age) my will is that my sd wyfe shall yet have Interest in the free and full use of one of the sellers, the Parlor & ye roomes over the Parlor, for & during her naturall life, as also her thirds of ye orchard & Garden. I give to my daughter Mary Gibbons, at her Marriadge or at 18 years of age, the full & sole propriety in all my Houses & Lands in Weathersfield, both on ye East and west side of ye River, to bee to her and her heirs forever, Except the thirds of ye Revenewes or Rents of yt to her mother during her life & ye prsell of Swampe bought of Robt Bates & the Land at Pennywise, wch sd. thirds given to her Mother shall after her decease be to my sd. daughter Mary & her heirs forever. Item. I give unto my daughter Sarah Gibbons, at her marridge or when shee shall attayne ye age of 18 years, the full & sole Propriety in all my Houses & Lands at Hartford & Pequett, to bee to her & her heirs forever, except the one thirds of ye profitts & revenewes thereof unto my sd. wife Ursula during her naturall lyfe, & ye Use of ye Seller, the parlor, & ye Roomes above ye Parlor, wch after her decease shall bee to my sd. daughter Sarah & her heirs forever. Ite. I give & bequeath unto my daughter Mary one third part & to my daughter Sarah one third & to my wyfe one third of all my Goods, Chattells, debts & other moveables, both within dores & without, my just debts & legesies beeinge discharged. My will is, that the one third part of those foresd goods & debts shall bee to my wyfe's proper use & dispose as her owne propr estate ; And for ye twoe thirds of ye aforesd goods, I give unto my twoe daughters to bee to ym & ye heirs for ever, to bee improved by ye advise of my overseers for ym until they attayne ye foresd age of eighteene years or are maried ; And if Eyther of my sd Daughters depart this lyfe before they bee married or atayne ye age of eighteen years,—then my will is that ye estate given to yt daughter that soe deseaseth shalbee Inioyd by (that) child yt Survives ; & if eyther of ym depart this lyfe after they are Married, & have noe Issue, then ye

one halfe of ye estate given to yt sd daughter shalbee to her husband &
ye other halfe to my survivinge childe.   Item.   My will further is, that
when ye providence of God shall despose of my daughters for marridge,
that then they shall consult wth their mother & my overseers herein. Item.
My will is to give to my brothers Richard, Jon & Thomas Gibbons, in
England, twenty shillings a peece, & to ye Children wch are liveinge at my
decease 10 Shillings apeece.   Item. I give to my sister Hidgcoke £5 wch
shee shal inioy while shee lives & dispose of yt to yt Child shee sees most
deserveing.   I give to the Children of my sister Hidgcocke wch are liveinge at my decease the sum of £15 to be equally divided amongst ym.
Item. I give to my bro. Hidgcocke one sute & Coate of weareinge Apparrell.   Item. I give his son Jno Hidgcocke one prsell of Swampe, about 9
acres, bought of Robt Bates, lieing at Wethersfield, to him & his heirs forever.   Item. I give my Land at Pennywise, nowe in ye Tennoe of Jon
Sadler, towards the Mayntenance of a Lattin scoole at Hartford provided
ye fence be continued in ye same Line & Way of Common fence angle as
yt nowe is; & for ye prsent, until ye Lease I have made to Jno Sadler bee
expired, I give out of ye Rent due from Jno Sadler 50 Shillings yearly.
Item.   I give to my honord friend Mr. Samuel Stone £5, & to Mr. Huett
of Windsor 40 Shillings, & to Mr. Warham, Mr. Newton, Mr. James
Fitch, Mr. Russell & Mr. Stoe, 20 Shillings apeece.   Item. I give to Mr.
Samuel Welles & Mrs Mary Welles £5 apece, & to Mr. John Moudy £3.
Item. I give to my man Isaacke Stiles £3 in case my wyfe & Overseers or
any twoe of ym thinke hime deserveing; and to my man Henry One yeare
of his time; & alsoe I give to ye Artillery in Hartford 40 Shillings; & for
ye time of payment of these foresd. sumes by legacies I leave yt to ye
descreeson of my Overseers, wthin 2, 3 or 4 years.   Item. I give to my
trusty & beloved friends Mr. Samuel ffitch & Richard Lord the sum of
£5 apeece, whom I intreat, appoynt & ordayne to bee Overseers & Supervisors of this my last Will & Testament, intreeatenge them to bee carefull
& faythfull in descharge of ye Trust comitted to ym.   Lastly I doe appoynt
my beeloved wyfe Ursula Gibbons to bee sole Executrix of this my last
Will & Testament, leaveinge & comittinge the Care & Education of my
Children in ye feare of God & all such other ways as may most advantage
ym as they are capable of.   In Witness hereunto I have sette my Hand.
I leave ye Care of my comely cristian burial to my wyfe & Overseers.

Witness: *Jasper Gunne,*   WILLIAM GIBBONS.
         Luke X Hitchcock.

Page 143-4-5.

Gibbs, Widow **Katharine,** Windsor. Invt. £220-07-00. Taken 21
November, 1660-1, by William Gaylord and John Moore. Will dated 12
September, 1660:

In the Name of God, Amen. I, Catharine Gibbs. off Windsor, being sick & Weake off boddy But off perfect Memory, Doe ffor Dyverse Considerations Make & ordayne this my Last Will & Testament In Manner as ffollowing: Imprmis. I Bequeath My sowle unto God yt gave itt, hopeing With him to Inioy Eternall Rest & Pece; & secondly, my Boddy to Convenyent Cristyen Bewryall; & whereas, itt hath Plesed God to Bestow on Mee some part off this Worlds Goods, my Will Concerning yt is yt Itt be disposed off In Manner as ffolloweth, Namely: Ett ye end off ½ yeare affter my decese to enter Possession; I Give & Bequeath unto my Eldest sonne Jacobb my Dwelling Howse, Barne & Orchard, with ye Land Whereon they Stand, & all ye Land Adioyneing thereunto, Wich is my Proper Right By Purchas, With all vnmoveables thereunto belonging, wth ffence or ffences, viz., to him & his heares ffor ever. Provided he has An heir off his owne body Begotten yt lives to ye Age of twenty & one yeares, then the sd. Aeyre to Inioy ye sume affter the ffather's decese; Butt in Case he want such An heire, then affter his decese I give & Bequeath All the Aforesd. vnmoveables wth ffences or Licke Apertyneces unto my second sonne Samuell, & to his Owne Propper yowce; & unto my sonne Beniamin I Give & Grant & Sett over my Lott on ye other syde ye Great River, the which I Purchassed off Gregory Gibbs my son In Law ffor sattisffacktion off ye twenty pounds which his ffather gave att his Decees, viz., to his Owne propper yowce & Acct, only in Case he doth Ethere By ye yeare of ffor Terme off yeare Lett ye sd. Land or yt he sett ye sd. Land to Sale, then my Will is that my son Samuell have the ffirst tender & Refuse off ye same; & my Will ffurther is That in ye ffirst Place all Just Debts Be Payde & Sattisfyed according to ye Spesya, & yt Being Performed I dispose off my Moveables as ffoll: viz., I Give & Bequeath unto my Sonne Jacobb my Greate Chest; & to my daffter in Law his wife my hatts; & unto my sone Beniamin I Give & Bequeath the twoe Gilt Lether Cosyens yt are in ye Abovesd. Chest & whatt Else he hath Bestowed on Mee as ffore Gifft; & unto My sone Jacob's Daffter Mary I Give twenty Shill to be Improved ffor hir Advantage att ye Discresyen off my Exeeckters & to be Payde hir att ye Day of her meryadge or att ye Age off one & Twenty years In Case she Marry nott Before; But In Case she live nott to yt Age, then I Give & Bequeath ye Same unto My yongest sone & Xseckter Beniamin; & Concerneing ye Rest of my Estate my Will is that Affter An Inventory is taken & everything vallewed as equally as may Bee, thatt itt Bee Equally dyvided Between my thre yongest Children, only my Will is yt my sone Samuell's Part Bee in ye Plow & Cart Instruments unless he Refuseitt, & my daffter Sarah's Part Bee in or yt ffore her Part she have ye Refuse off my Aperell & part off howsehold stuff; & ffor ye Exseeketers off this My Last Will & Testament I Mack Choice off, ordayne & Appoynt my twoe sons Samuell & Beniamin, home the Lord dyreckt to Ackt ye up sd. (Amen)

Witness: *John Moore,*   Katharine Gibbs Ls.
    Phillip X (Drake)?

Court Record, Page 145—6 December, 1660: The Will & Invt. of Katharine Gibbs accepted.

Page 127.

Gilbert, Thomas, Wethersfield. Died 5 September, 1659. Invt. £189-07-06. Taken by Thomas Wright, Thomas Curtiss & John Nott.

Court Record, Page 128—6 February, 1663: Order to Dist. the Estate: Debts and Charges being first paid,   169-18-11
There remains,   19-08-07
to be divided to Jonathan, Thomas, Ezekiel and John Gilbert and to Sarah Jenkins. This Court grant Adms. to Jonathan and John Gilbert.

Page 157.

Goit,* John, New London. Invt. £103-00-00. Taken 25 June, 1659, by Hugh Calkin, James Avery, William Nichols, Obadiah Breuen. Will dated 1st August, 1659.

The last Will & Testament of John Goit of New London: Impr. I give unto my wife & my son Joseph the House & Household Stuf wth the Orchard and all Lands above my House, as also all my Great Catle, as also half my Meadows. And they shall enjoy itt to gether as Long as my wife lives, except they both agree to ye Contrary. And also I give to ym my ground on ye other side of ye River, that is, the Lott of 22 acres, as Also half my Land in the Neck. I give unto my 2 daughters Mary and Martha my Farme up Mohegan River, as also 2-3 of the Sheep, as also my other Lott of 30 acres upon the other side of ye River, as also halfe my Meadow, as also the other halfe of my Land in ye Neck; also I give to my 2 sons & 2 daughters 20 Shillings apeice, I mean those absent from mee, in case they bee livinge, to be payd out of the whole. I give to my son Joseph 1-3 of my Sheep; also, after all my Debts bee payd, I give the remaynder to my wife, son and 2 daughters wth mee. Also, I leave to my loving friends Mr. Thompson and James Avery and Wm Nichols to bee my exsequtors to look after ye dispose of my Children, wth my wife; and if anny of the children die before marriage their Estate shall be divided by others then at home.

Witness: *William Douglas,*   JOHN X GOIT.
            Gabriel Harris.

(This Will is entered in the Books of Records Pr me
Inventory recorded 1659.)   *Obadiah Brven, Recorder.*

---

*This name, recorded *Goit,* was probably *Coit.* C. W. M.

Page 48.

Greenhill, Thomas, Hartford. Will dated 16 July, 1653. He gives the Executor power to take a Deed of Lands lately purchased of my Brother John Shepherd and Rebeckah his wife, and may sell any of his Lands to make Payment of Debts which I owe for the purchase of my sister her part in sd. Lands, the remainder of my Lands for the Use of my Mother Rebeckah Addams during her natural life, and after her decease ½ my Lands to the proper use & Estate of her Children, that is to say, to her son John Addams & to her 3 daughters, Hanna, Hester & Sarah, to be divided equally between them. In case of the death of all these children before their mother without Issue, she to inherit their one half, and in case of the death of my sister Rebeckah Shepherds two children, John and Rebeckah Shepherd, before their mother without Issue, she to inherit the remaining half of Lands. All my wearing apparell to my brother John Addams. He desires his Father to defray the Charges for his burrial, and constitutes Mr. William Goodwin and Edward Stebbing Executors,

THOMAS GREENHILL. Ls.

Witness: *Thomas Stanly, James Ensign.*

Court Record, Page 49—2 March, 1653-4: Jeremy Addams objects to sale of land by William Goodwin and Edward Stebbing, Overseers of the Estate of Thomas Greenhill, Decd. This Court Judge that the sale of the home lot in Hartford was legal & Just. Page 83—3 January, 1655, the wife of Jeremy Addams Resigns her right to a parcel of meadow land in the little meadow that was Samuel Greenhill's, to be sowld for the payment of debts. The sd Jeremie Addams did affirm & testifie that there was no need of selling more land, as the debts were all paid.

[Note: For full information as to this case, See Private Controversies, in the Archives of the State Library.]

Vol. II, No. 8 (P. C.): Testimony of Elizabeth Bacon relating to Samuel Greenhill & wife, that Thomas Greenhill & my son Timothy Stanly were of same age; they came over 1634 in the same ship with Samuel Greenhill, his wife & son Thomas, with Mr. Willard, Mr. Pantry, Mr. Crayfoote & my husband Stanly. [Not dated.]

No. 1 of Index, Vol. II, P. C.

Jeremy Addams married with the Widow of Samuel Greenhill. The Children: John, Hannah, Sarah; John, age 33 years 29 May, 1683.

No. 17, Vol. II, P. C.

At a Court of Assistants Held at Hartford 30 May, 1682.

Whereas, Zachary Sanford in Right of his wife hath obtained a Judgement of Court against Sergt. John Shepherd for his Portion of the Estate according to Thomas Greenhills Will: This Court do find by the

Will of Samuel Greenhill that two thirds of Land did belong unto the Children of Jeremiah Addams, and that one third part of that halfe doth belong to Nathaniel Willetts Children, and that one quarter Part doth belong to Zachary Sanford in right of his wife, and upon that part the secretry is to grant Execution upon the aforesd. Judgement. Dated 4 March, 1696.

Note: Vol. II, P. C., has an Index, to which I have referred.

No. 1, Vol. II, P. C.

Power of Attorney from John Shepherd of Cambridge, Cooper, to Mr. Jeremy Addams of Hartford:

Know all men by these presents, that I John Shepherd of Cambridge, Cooper, have assigned, ordained & made, and in my stead and place by these prsents put & constituted Jeremiah Addams of Hartford to be my true and Lawfull attorney for me and two my name & to my use to ask, sue for, require, recover & receive of Mr. William Goodwin & Edward Stebbings of Hartford all & every such debts as are due to mee upon account of Land bought by Thomas Greenhill of Rebecca Shepherd his sister. I say to require, sue for & receive all & every such debts or Summes of money of the said Mr. William Goodwin & Edward Stebbing as sole executors of ye said Thomas Greenhill deceased, giving & granting to my said Attorney my whole power & Authority in and about the prmises, and upon the receipt of any such debts or summes of money to give and seal to Acquittances & discharges for mee, and in my name; & to do, execute & performe as fully & amply in every respect to all intents and constructions & purposes as I myself might or should do if I were personally present, Ratifying, allowing and holding firm & stable all & wtsoever my said Attorney Shall lawfully doe & cause to be done in or about the execution of the prmises by virtue of those presents.

Witness: *Edward Shepherd*   JOHN SHEPHERD Ls.
       John Blackman   REBECCA SHEPHERD.

25 February, 1655.

Court Record, Page 20-22 (Vol. IV)—11 February, 1679: Upon Petition of Nathaniel Willett & Abigail Betts, in behalf of their Children respectively for an Interest belonging to them by Legacy in the last Will of Thomas Greenhill, Decd, when the sd. persons and John Shepherd came and appeared, & their allegations heard and Considered; the sd. Will also was presented; & noe Argument by any so much as tendered to invalidate the same, but contrarialy some what presented for a Court's allowance to practice upon it, which hath been long observed in part, the completing of the Execution not yet being accomplished, much trouble and disturbance hath fallen out betwixt relations for want of Executors who are now all dead, This Court sees no cause to disallow sayd will, & therefore have appointed sayd John Shepherd Administrator with the Will annexed to be a person in Law to see distribution or Execution made accordingly, that so the Estate may be the better preserved & all Controversall matters Issued and prevented. Srgt. John Shepherd appeared in Court and accepted of Administration accordingly.

Colonial Records, Vol. I, Page 360.

Receaved by me, John Shepherd, of my loving Unkel, Gregory Winterton, thirty-four pounds wch he receaved of my Brother Thomas Greenhill for Lands I sold him, for wch I made my Unkel a letter of Attorney. I say receaved by me. August 4th, 1654.   JOHN SHEPHERD.

Greensmith, Nathaniel. Court Record, Page 182—15 October, 1662. At a particular Court held at Hartford 30 December, 1662. The Indictment of Nathaniel Greensmith and of Rebecca his wife for witchcraft: Nathaniel Greensmith, thou art here indicted by the name of Nathaniel Greensmith for not haveing the feare of God before thine eyes; thou hast entertained familiarity with Satan the grand Enemy of God and Mankind, and by his help hast acted things in a preter naturall way beyond human abilities in a naturall course, for which according to ye Law of God and ye established laws of this Commonwealth thou deserveth to die.

The Jury returned that they find ye prisoner at ye Barr, Nathaniel Greensmith, guilty of ye Indictment.

Respecting Rebecca Greensmith, Prisoner at ye Barr, the Jury find her guilty of ye Indictment. The said Rebecca Confesseth in open Court that she is guilty of ye charge laid in agaynst her.

Magistrates:

Mr. Allyn modr,	Mr. Treat,	Danll Clarke, Sec.,
Mr. Willys,	Mr. Woolcot,	Mr. Jo: Allyn.

Jury:

Edw. Griswold, Walter Filor, Ensign Olmsted, Samll Bordman, Goodm Winterton, John Cowles, Samll Marshall, Samll Hale, Nathanll Willet, John Hart, John Wadsworth, Robert Webster.

(See File for Greensmith's Estate as below mentioned:)

Hartford, 11 ffeb. (16)62(3): Respecting the Estate of Nathaniel Greensmith, It is ordered that the Marshall, Mr. Gilbert, James Ensign and Paul Peck shall take care to preserve the estate from Waste and to take in ye account of Debts, and to discharge any just debts, and to pay fourty pounds to ye Treasurer for ye County, and to secure ye rest of ye estate in their hands until March Court next ensueing, when there will be further order taken about ye Remainder of ye Estate. And they are desired and authorized to dispose of the 2 daughters, wth the Advice of ye Assistants in Hartford, & to advice with them about any Expedient in reference to ye premises.   Pr or of ye Assistants: Danll Clarke, Secry.

An Inventory of the Estate of Nathaniel Greensmith, who was executed the 25th of January, 1662, £137-14-01. Other Estate found with the forementioned Estate of Nathaniel Greensmith, with this Exception, viz., that this hereafter mentioned is claimed by Hannah & Sarah Elson. vizt:

£   s   d
44-04-04   JOHN X COWLES,
137-14-01   JONATH: GILBERT,
                                              JAMES STELL.
181-18-05 Total Value.

Note: Part of Inventory at the Prison:

	£ s d		£ s d
Two Blanketts	1-05-00	One Boulster	0-15-00
One Rugg one Blankett	1-15-00	One Bed well filled	2-15-00

Court Record, Page 190—5 March, 1662-3: Daniel Garrett is allowed 6 Shillings a week for keeping Nathaniel Greensmith and his wife, besides their fees, wch is to be paid out of Greensmith's Estate.

Page 86-7.

Gridley, Thomas, Hartford. Invt. £282-12-00. Taken 12 June, 1655, by Nathaniel Ward, Andrew Bacon & James Ensign.

The children: Samuel 8 years of age, Thomas 5, and Mary 3 years. Adms. granted to John Langton, he to pay the Debts and educate the Children.

Court Record, Page 79—December, 1655. Invt. exhibited.

Griffin, Thomas, Estate. Court Record, Page 130—1st December, 1659: John Sadler is appointed to take into his Hands yt Corne yt is part of the Estate of Thomas Griffin now in ye possion of Thomas Coleman, and John Sadler is to be accountable for ye Corne when ye Court takes Ordr for Adms. and to give Security for ye Corne to ye Deputy Gov.

Page 148—7 March, 1660-1: William Wellman complains to this Court his Want of Pay of Thomas Griffin in time of his sickness. This Court order sd. Wellman as Adms. to gather up ye Estate of ye sd. Griffin and to keep an Account of what he doth and present ye Account to ye Comrs at New London, who are to order Wellman his Charges and other Debts to be paid, and what remains Wellman to be accountable for to the County when told thereto.

Page 99-100.

Harris, Walter & his wife, both Deceased at Pequett. Invt. £79-02-03. Taken 14 April, 1656, by Jonathan Brewster, Obadiah Bruen, Wm Meedes and James X Morgan.

The Deposition of Gabriel Harris, Eldest son of Mary Harris, that the above is a true Invt. of all the goods that was left by his Father, Walter Harris, and his Mother, Mary Harris, both Decd. Testified 6 May, 1656, before   JOHN WINTHROPE.

Harrison, Edward. Court Record, Page 5—28 March, 1650: Thomas Whaples affirmed that Edward Harrison, the Winter and Spring before his death, said unto Will: Hill that hee was his Countryman and that hee had no other that hee knew in the Country, and the Chest wch hee had at his howse he did give unto him with all in it if hee dyed a Batchelor in the Country or went a Batchelor out of the Country, and added there was good Lugg in it, or words to that purpose.

John Gilbert, upon Oath before the Governor, affirmed that Edw. Harrison gave unto Stephen Davis £5.

Goodman Hill saith that Edw. Harrison told him that hee had in srgeant ffylers Hand 40 Shillings,   2-00-00
And that Mr. Martyn owed him,   2-10-00
And that Mr. Whiting owed him, before he went to Dillaway,   15-00-00
And that at his Return hee would owe him £5 more,   5-00-00

Page 158.

Hartley, Richard, Sergt., New London. Invt. £276-06-07. Taken 7 August, 1662, by Obadiah Breuen, James Rogers, Samuel Smith, Jo Smith, Jo. Tinker.

Will dated 5 August, 1662: He gives to his wife and his child (a daughter) his Entire Estate. Lieut. Samuel Smith and Ensign James Avery to be Executors & Administrators.

Witness: *Mr. Bulkeley,*
         Obadiah Bruen,
         William Hough.

On File.

Mr. Gershom Buckley, minister, Mr. Obadiah Brewen, Recorder, Mrs Lucresiah Brewster, midwife, and William Hough, Constable, All these being Sworne & examined Say That on Tuesday the 5th of August, 1662, they weare at the house of Peeter Blatchfeild in New London to vissitt Richard Hartley, who there Lay Sick unto death, and being very weake in body yet of meete understanding, he was desired to declare what was his last will & Testament concerning his estate which he should leave, and he declared the same which is above written, which Mr. Brewen aforesaid tooke from his mouth and owned by him in presents of the Rest, namely, that his daughter should have one third Part and his wife should have two third parts of his estate. Then it was asked him whome he would choose for his executors and he Said they were in his minde but he could not express it. Then they named some fewe to him, & when Leiftent Smith was named he chose him, and when Ensigne Avery was named he made choyce of him for another. He was asked about Legasies and he refused to yeald to give any: and further the motion was made for him to Set his hand to ye writing, and he answered in the hearing of William Hough there was no need, there was wittnesses enough. Mr. Buckley allso heard the same words spoken "there was Witnesses enough," but did not minde the party speaking.

Taken upon oathe this 11 of August, 1662.

Before me *Jno Tinker, Asist.*

Harrow, Rich: Court Record, Page 45—1st Tuesday of December, 1653: I doe hereby faithfully promise & heerby binde mee Rich: Harrow to serve Mr. Alcock 4 years after my Arival in New England, as Witt: my Hand the 27th of March, 1650.   RICHARD HARROW.

Note: We arrived at New England about the 15th of April after the date above.

I Tho: Allcott of Hartford doe assigne over Rich: Harrow, with his Consent, to Will: Hill of Hartford for the time hee hath to serve mee from this time. Witness our Hands this 25th January, 1650.

THOMAS OLLCOTT,
RICHARD HARROW.

Page 42-3-4-5-6-7.

Haynes, John, Hartford. Invt. £1400-16-03. Taken 31 June, 1653, by John Cullick, Richard Lord, William Gibbons & Edward Stebbing. Will dated 27 July, 1646: Whereas I, John Haynes of Hartford, upon the River & within the Colony of Connecticut in New England, and by the Good Providence of the Lord called to the Undertaking of a voyage into my native Country of England, and duly weaghing according to my measure the difficulties and Hardness I am liable and exposed to therein, especially in the declining days of mine, when my sun cannot be far from setting, I do make this my last Will & Testament:

Imprimis: I give unto my beloved wife Mabel all that my Mansion House in Hartford together with the Outhouses, Barns, Stables, Orchards & Gardens, with all the Appurtenances, with my Meadow inclosed in the little Meadow, also all my Meadow & Swamp in the South Meadow between my Ox pasture, together with all other Divisions of Lands belonging unto me on this side of the Great River, also 16 acres of Meadow in

Hoccanum. I give the sd. houses & Land during the term of her natural life only, and after her decease I give the sd. houses & Lands afore mentioned to my Eldest son John by my wife Mabel Haynes, and to his heirs forever. I do further give to my wife all that my Houses and Farms on the East side of the Great River commonly called Hoccanum, with all the Lands thereunto belonging (except before excepted), viz., the Close of Upland in ye Close by the Barn, with my Upland Lotts adioining the Meadow I purchased of Nathaniel Ward, and Swamp Ground inclosed, as also the Swamp without the Fence adjoining to Hoccanum that belongs to me, also the Meadow in Hoccanum that now is in the Tenure of James Northam and his partner for a term of years, during her life only. I do moreover give my sd. wife all that my Houses & Farm at Tunxes Sepes, or else Farmington, in the Tenure of Thomas Judd and his Brothers, for the term of her natural life only, and after her decease I give the sd. Farm to my youngest son Joseph. Whereas I am indebted to Mr. Will Tanner of Cophall in England, payable to him by Bill sent into England to my son Mr. Nathaniel Eldred, I do give to my wife all that my house & Land in Windsor in the Tenure of Mr. George Hull, with liberty to make Sale thereof toward the payment of Debts to Mr. Eldred and Mr. Tanner in Case they be not otherwise discharged. And my Will is that my wife possess and injoy the sd. Houseing and Lands during life, and after her decease to be equally divided betwixt my 2 daughters Ruth & Mabel. Also I give to the poor Brethren of the Congregation £5; to Mr. Hopkins, 20 Shillings; to Mr. Hooker, Pastore, £5; to Mr. Stone, £4; to John White, 10 Shillings; to every one of the Children of my first wife, 20 Shillings. I desire Mr. Hopkins, Mr. Hooker, Mr. Stone and Mr. John White to be Overseers to this my Will.

JOHN HAYNES.

In Court 11 July, 1654, mention of a marriage portion to Ruth with Mr. Willis.

Court Record, Page 125—(Vol. III) 5 September, 1672: Mr. Wyllys requests this Court to rule on the Construction of the Will of Mr. Haynes—whether the Estate not willed to particular persons doth belong to all the Children or those only which he had by Mrs. Mabel his last wife. This Court decides in this Case such Estate belongs to the children of Mrs. Mabel Haynes his last wife, so those Grants of Land by the Court made to Mr. Haynes, whether at Pawcatuck or elsewhere, doe only belong to the Children of Mrs. Mabel Haynes.

Page 67.

Hayte, Nicholas, Windsor, Invt. £114-14-09. Taken 30 July, 1655, by Thomas Ford, David Wilton & Matthew Grant. The children: Abigail Foyse, 10½ years of age, daughter of his wife also Decd, Samuel Hayte age 8 years, Jonathan 6, & David 4 years of age.

20th December, 1655: This Court grant Adms. to David Wilton and Matthew Grant; also order Dist. of the Estate. The whole Estate to be equally divided among the four Children at lawful age.

Hemstid, Robert. New London Land Records, Vol. 3, ps 9-10.
The Last Will of Robert Hemstid. September 30th, 1653.

I beeing in pfect memory yet mortall, considering ye uncertenty of my time & nothing more certon than my change, God haveinge blessed me with a portion of these outward thinges, doe dispose of this my state as followeth:

Commiting myselfe unto God,

Imprimis: I leave unto my daughter Marie that peece of land I have upon the neck called Mamacocke in Lew of Twenty pound to be sould or kept for her propper use & benifit.

Ite: I give unto my daughter aforesaid 55 pound starling to be made up out of my vissable estate & to be paid unto her or her assigns and delivered to her or her assigns, with ye Land aforesaid, at ye age of sixteene.

Item: I give unto my daughter Hannah, Therty ackers of upland upon ye east side of ye great River joyning unto & upon ye southward side of Mr. Winthrop's Land, being ye first Lott Laid out. I give unto her Ten pound starling more to be paid & delivered to her or her assigns with ye Land aforesaid at ye age of sixteene.

Item: Of Land Therty Ackers of upland Lying betwixt ye Lotts of Will Bordman & John Stibbins to be disposed of and sould by ye ffeffies in trust for the use of my children if ocasion doe require.

Item: I give unto my sonne Joshua ye rest of my Land after his mother's decease, Therty Ackers of upland upon ye westward side of Nahantick River at a place called Mezsargents head, which I Leave to my wife Joane freely to dispose of ass she sees good for her own pper use, only in case my sonne be capable of improuving land before his mother's decease that then hee shall have that land at Mistick.

Item: All ye land that I Leave to my sonne after his mother's decease but what before is exempted, I Leave to the disposing of Joane my wife dureing her life.

Item: All ye rest of my goods I leave to my wife Joane. In case providence so order that she never marrie my will is that some of ye upland I Leave to my sonne she shall have free Leave to dispose of & alsoe make sale of if the benefit of her or her children shall see call for it.

Item: In case my sonne shall Die before he enioy his land, my will is that Mary, my eldest Daughter, shall have my house Lott for her proper use after her mother's decease, & ye Land at mistick if she die without heires to be divided between the two sisters.

Item: In case any of ye children die, that ye portion or portions of ye Deseased shall be given to ye surviving childe or children.

I leave my wife Joane my executrix, & Obadiah Bruen & John Gadger ffeffies in trust to see with my wife her performance of this my will.

Witness my hand,   ROBERT HEMSTID.

Witnesses heareof:

James Morgan (his marke),
William Meade.

This is the last will of Robert Hemstid, returned to be recorded, Drawed out of his owne will, confirmed with his owne hand by me

Obadiah Bruen,
Recorder.

The age of my three children:
Mary Hempstid was borne
        March 26, 1647.
Joshua Hempstid my sonne was borne
        June 16, 1649.
Hannah Hempstid was borne
        April 4, 1652.
This I Robert Hempstid testifie
        under my hand.

Proved in court upon oath June 13th, 1655.

Court Record, Page 73—13 June, 1655: The last Will of Robert Hempsted, with Inventory, was now exhibited, approved, and was presented to Mr. Obadiah Bruen (for Record?).

Hillier, John, Windsor. Invt. £39-17-11. Taken 24 July, 1655, by Matthew Grant, William Phelps, Robert Howard. Wife Ann; Children: John age 18 years, Mary 16, Timothy 13, James 11, Andrew 9, Simon 7, Sarah 3, Abigail 1 year old.

Court Record, Page 82—20 December, 1655: This Court desire and appoint the Townsmen of Windsor from year to year to take Care of the Childrens Estate until they receive further order from the Court.

Court Record (Vol. 3), Page 132—4 Sept, 1673: Distribution of Estate of John Hillier: To John Fitch his wives part, £5; to John, Eldest son, £6; to Mary, £3; to Timothy, £4-17-11; to James, £5; to Andrew, £5; to Simon, £5; to Sarah, £3; to Abigail, £3. Capt Benjamin Newbery & Deac John Moore appointed to make Distribution.

Page 29-30-31.

Hills, William, Fairfield. Invt. £225-16-10. Taken 16 November, 1649, by Andrew Ward, Simon Hoite and Anthony Wilson. The sum of

Mr. Hills Goods in Windsor inventoried at £111-03-04. Taken 24 September, 1649, by Henry Clarke & Walter ffyler. Will dated 9 September 1649.

The last Will and Testament of Mr. William Hill: Being at present in some weakness of Body yet of Good Mynde and Memory, Commiting my sole to God and my body to A Comly buryall, I do will and bequeath to my beloved wife Sarah the third part of my estate.

I do nexly will unto my eldest daughter Sarah a silver spone.

I do forder will that when the invintary of my estate is made, that my estate shalbe equally devided Amongst my children, only my will is that my Sonn William being my eldest Sonn, for every to parts the rest of my children have he shal have three parts.

Forder I do will if any of my children be taken Away by death before maryage it shal be equally devided Amongst the rest.

Forder it is my will that my sonn William Shal enter upon his portion at his disposall in Maryage.

forder I do will my Beloved wife Sarah to be exsecetar, and over and Above her thirds I do will her power to disspose of five pounds when Shee Seeth Good, this being my last will and testament.

I do Apoint Mr. Jones, Mr. George Hull and Thomas Thornton to be the overseares of this my last will and testament.

WILLIAM X HILL.

To ye honarable Court holden in Hartford, or to whom soever it shal consearne: Mr. William Hill Sending for me on his death bed, I went to him, being far spent when I Cam yet of perfect memory and understanding as I judge, Acquaynted me with his will by word of mouth, which was Thus namly, that his wife shold be exsecutrix and that shee shold have the thirds of what estat he had left, his deats being first paid, and over and above yt his wife shold have five pounds to desspose of; nextly that his Eldest daughter Sarah had her portion, only he would give her a Silver spoone. Nextly that the rest of his estat shold be equally divided amongst five children: William, Joseph, Ignatius, Jeams & Elizabeth; only in the devision his eldest sonn William on the devision shold have one third whitch would be changed in the writing of his will, as his written will can specifie, but upon his wase in writing his fite cam and I conceive his head out of order. To the substance of what is heer writen I dear be desposed, but not derectly to ye very words, as not dearing to trust my memory to fare. By me *Tho. Thornton.*

Court Record, Page 7—15 May, 1650: Mrs. Hill of Fairfield admitted Executrix to the Estate of her deceased Husband. Testimony of Thomas Thornton proven.

Note: The children named in the statement of Thomas Thornton are William, Joseph, Ignatius, Jeams, & Elizabeth & Sarah, the eldest daughter. See Testimony of Thomas Thornton, P. C., mentioning the children: William, Joseph, Jonathan, Sarah and Elizabeth.

Page 123-124.

Hitchcock, Luke, Wethersfield. Invt. £452-00-00. Taken 28 November, 1659, by John Russell Sen, John Hubbard, Thomas Welles. Will dated 17 October 1659: I Luke Hitchcock of Wethersfield, being at present in some weakness of body yet of in soundness of mynde & strength of memory, Considering my mortality and knowing it to be my duty to provide for my ffamily and to settle my estate, that I may leave noe occasion of trouble to them when I am gone, and that I may free myselfe before I dye, I doe therefore leave this testimony upon record as my Last will & Testament: First, I doe professe my fayth & hope to be in the free grace alone of God in Jesus Christ, whos I am & to whom I have for ever given up my Selfe both Soule & body, being fully prsuaded of his unchangable Love & good will both in life & death to me. And for my outward estate I dispose of the same as followeth: ffirst, I doe Therefore bequeath & give unto my wife Elizabeth the full power & dispose of all that estate wch God hathe given mee in howses, Lands, Cattells & goods whatsoever, wth in dores & wthout, provided that in Case she marry agayne that then she betake herselfe to the thirds of my Land & houses, and that she give unto my sonne John the house that I now dwell in wth the out houses thereunto belonging, wth the home Lott, and halfe in quantity of that Lott or prcell of Land wch I lately bought of Mr. John Chester, the homeward side; And to my sonne Luke the other halfe of yt, the Lyne betwixt them running soe as to have both of them the benefit of the water; furthermore to my sonne John that peece of Land Lying in mile meadows wch I bought of William Smith, and my foure acres in Beaver meadow. Alsoe, to my sonne Luke that peece of land in the great meadow, my other peece of Land in myle meadow wth passage thereto throw his Brother's Land; alsoe to give unto my daughter Hannah forty pounds wth her uncle's gift. These portions to be payed to eyther of them at the age of eighteen years or at the deathe of my said wife, wch comes sooner. And my will is that what estate shall be in her hands beyond and above the forsayd portions at the tyme of her marriage that she may devide the same equally amonge my foresayd three children excepting thirds of all my houshold stuff. And further, that Mr John Russell, pastor of or Church, would together wth the church appoint some to see this my will prformed. Heer unto I have subscribed my hand the day & year above written.

LUK HITCHCOKE.

Witness: *Thomas Coleman,*
          Thomas Welles.   Test: *John Russell,* Junior.

Page 105-106.

Holcomb, Thomas, Windsor. Invt. £294-09-08. Taken 1st October, 1657, by Benjamin Newbery, Daniel Clark. Children: Joshua age

17 years, Benajah 13, Nathaniel 9, Abigail 19, and Deborah 6 7-12 years of age. Signed, Matthew Grant.

Adms. granted to the Widow Elizabeth Holcomb. Order of Dist:

	£ s d		£ s d
To the Widow,	42-18-00	To Nathaniel,	28-12-00
To Joshua,	42-18-00	To Abigail,	28-12-00
To Benajah,	33-07-00	To Deborah,	28-12-00

George and Edward Griswold enter a Claime to part of the Estate, but remit the Claim.

James Enno and Elizabeth Holcomb, Widow, were married 5 August, 1658. (W. R.)

On this 15th day of December, 1660, I doe acknowledge to have received of my Father Enno of my wive's portion the whole sum.

SAMUEL BISSELL.

On this 17th day of December, 1660, I doe acknowledge to have received of my Father Enno ye full sum of my portion. Witness my Hand:

JOSHUA HOLCOMB.

Court Record, Page 109—3 December, 1657: Invt. exhibited.

Page 54-5-6-7.

Hopkins, John, Hartford. Invt. £236-08. Taken 14 April, 1654, by John Cullick, John Barnard, James Ensign. Will dated 1st January, 1648-9.

I, John Hopkins of Hartford do make this my last Will and Testament: I make my Wife Jane Hopkins my sole Executrix of my whole estate, out of it she to pay to my daughter Bethiah Hopkins £30. And my will alsoe is that the one halfe of all my Lands & howsing should be my sone Stephen Hopkins to be enjoyed by him and his heyers fforever, when he shall have attayned the adg off twenty two yeares. And my will further is That iff my said wiff should marry again, then the one half off the Estate that she shall then possess, the former portions being paid, shall be paid in Equall proportion to my said Son and daughter or their heyres after the decease of my wiff, these children to be under the control of their Mother. Bethiah until 18 years of age and Stephen until 22 years of age Shall remain with and under the Government of my Said wife until they have attayned their Several ages aforesaid, As also that they shall noe way Contract or Engadg themselves in way of marriage without the knowledge and Consent of my wife aforesaid. I desire Mr. John Cullick & James Ensign to be Overseers.

Witness: *John Cullick,*   JOHN HOPKINS.
William Andrews, James Ensign.

Note: 11 November, 1679. A quit claim or Receipt to Stephen Hopkins from Samuel Stocking and Bethiah Stocking: We have received full satisfaction of Our beloved brother Stephen Hopkins for whatsoever is due unto us by the last will of our Hond Father John Hopkins, etc.

August 27, 1650. (On file.)

Horsford, Will. I Will Horsford do mack this as my Last will and testament: I give to my wife Jane Horsford Halfe my dwelling House, Half my Barne and Halfe my cow house, during the term of her life. I give all so unto my wife that meadowe I bought of Elyas Parckman lying in ye lytell meadow, during her life. All so I give unto my wife one Hoge, Halfe the aplles that growes in the orchard this yeare, 5 bushelles of wheat, 10 bushelles of Indyan Corne. All so Shee is peaceabbly to in Joye the Lands that wear Her owne be fore my maryag. Only half an acker of the orchard which lys by the hie way going in to the medow, wch is specified on wryting, I give to my sonne John Horsford. He I mack my executor and do give unto him all my Lands, Housing, Catell, goods and debtes. What Housing I Have given to my wife during her life yt do give to my sonn John after my wifes life; and all such lands as my wife do in joye during her life whitch was given to my wife at my marryag, specified on wryting, I do give to my sone John and his ayres after my wifes life; and in case my sone dye be fore his mother and Have no children or child either borne or in the wombe to in joye the sayd lands and howsing, I do then give yt to my daughters' children equally to be devided : I do give to my daughters ten pounds apece, to be payd in 2 yeares time. My son is to pay debtes if he takes the exsecutor ship.

WILLIAM HORSFORD.

No Witnesses.

Page 133.

Horsford, William, Windsor. Will dated 6 September, 1654: I do bequeath unto my son John Horsford all my estate in Windsor. I do appoint him to discharge my Bill unto Court for Richard Samwais his children, as also a Bill under my hand to my wife for about £40 if my wife stays in New England, but I hope She will come unto mee in England.

WILLIAM HORSFORD.

Witness: *Walter Fyler, Jane Fyler.*   Recorded 14 July, 1660.

Below is a Statement by William Horsford, once an Inhabitant of Windsor, that he had given and bestowed away all my Housing, Lands, Cattle, Debts, whatsoever due unto me, unto my son John Horsford to be to his use and unto his dispose.

WILLIAM HORSFORD.

Recorded 29 February, 1660-1.

Page 134.

Hull, Mrs. Fairfield. Invt. £29-00-08. Taken 3 January, 1659, by Jehu Burr, Alexander Knowles.

Page 131.

Jackson, William, Seabrook. Invt. £42-00-00. Taken by John Clark, Robert Chapman, William Pratt. Will dated 11 September, 1659: I William Jackson of Seabrook do make this my last Will & Testament. I give unto Mr. James Fitch one Cow, and to William Bement, Mr. Robert Nichols, Robert Bull, James Cornish and Richard Tousland 20 Shillings apeice. All the rest of my Estate I give unto the Church at Seabrook whereunto I belong.

Witness : *William Bachus Jr,*   WILLIAM X JACKSON.
John Clark, James Cornish.

Johnson, Peter. Court Record, Page 65—1st March, 1654-5 : This Court desires Mr. Webster, Mr. Cullick, Mr. Willis and Mr. Tailcoate to examine Mr. Ward's account of Peter Johnson's Estate and to dispose of what is left to the Mother and Children as they shall judge meet.

Page 118-19-20.

Kellogg, Nathaniel, Farmington. Invt. £366-05-00. Taken 21 December 1657, by Edward Stebbing, Thomas Judd, John Minor. Will dated 4 June, 1657.

The last Will & Testament of Nathaniel Kelodg. I Nathaniel kelodg, being weack in body but in good and prfect me mory & understanding, thankes be to All mighty god, do comet my spirit in to the handes of God that gave it and my body to Comly and desent buriall in the plac apoynted thearefore in farmingtonn. Item. I give and bequeathe my wholl esta, Reall and Prsonall, unto my deere and Loving wife Elisebeth kelodg duering the tyme of her Natterall Life, and at the eand thear of I give all my houses and Landes in fermingtun unto my Brother John Kelodge and to my sister Fanne Aallesun and to my sister Rachell Cone, all dwelling in olld England, in that Condition that thay my Houses and Land shall be in at thet tyme, to be equally divided among the thre brother & sisters a fore sayd. And my Will is that thease my Brother & Sisters shall pay to my Cosen Joseph kelodg's three Children £6 Starling, to be equally devided betwixt them equally when thay shal have my houses & Lands : and all so at thet tyme they shall pay £5 to mr Rodger Newton, our pastor. All so I mack my sayd deere & loving wife my solle exsecketrix, & my Will is that She Shold give to my adopted daughter Susan Newton & Rebeckah Meruel such a Convenyant part of my Estate given to my wife as she shall be well a bell to Spare and theare obediant and duty full Carrig shall give ocation of, and my sayd Exiseth itrex Shall bear my funerall Charges and pay my Debtes. And I mack my deere frind Edwerd Stebing supervisor of this my Will and Testament.

Witness: *John Steel,*   NATHANIEL KELLOG.
         Joseph X magatt.

Court Record, Page 123—3 March, 1658-9. Will proven.

Page 15-16.

Kilbourn, Mrs. Frances, Wethersfield. Invt. £349-08-04. Taken 3 December, 1650, by Samuel Smith, Thomas Coleman, Nathaniell Dickinson. Will dated 13 November, 1650.

The last Will & Testament of ffrancis Kilbourne, In ye town of Wethersfield ye 13th November, 1650: Imprs. In lue of fforty shillings she borrowed of Richard Law she hath giuen hime ffive pounds to be payed wthin a yeare or Two. It. I give to my daughter margit, ye wife of Richard Lawe, my ould cloth tow gowne; And to my grand child Jonathan Lawe ffive Shillings. It. I give to my daughter Lidia, ye wife of Robert Howard, ffive pounds as ye ffull of hir portion I promise vppon marriage wth my daughter, to be payed wthin a yeare or 2 after my disseace. I giue to my daughter Meary, ye wiffe of John Root, ffive pounds as ye full of hir portion I promised vppon marrige wth my daughter, to be payed wthin a yeare or too after my desees. It. to my daughter ffrances, ye wife of Thomas Uffoote, Tenne pounds in ffull of his portion promised in marrige with my daughter, wthin two years after my dissese. It. To my gran child Elizabeth Spencer, my outle Black gowne and ? my linse wolse peticote, a black Hatt. It. I giue al ye Rest of my parrell to my three daughters to be divided amongst them, Lidia, Mary & ffrances. It. To my sonn John I giue three shertts, & ye rest of my linning To my 3 daughters equally to be divided to lidia, Mary & ffrances; & I make my sonn John my hole & sole Execitor. The Witnessess yt this is the last Will of Francis Kilbourn is:

Witness: *Samuel Smith &*
Elizabeth his wife, Nathaniel Dickinson.

Court Record, Page 16—5 December, 1651: Will proven & Invt. exhibited, & the Court not being satisfied with the Proof, appoint John Kilbourn Adms. until further Orders. Page 25—1st June, 1651: The Court now approves the Will & confirms John Kilbourn Adms.

Page 154.

Laraby, Greenfield, New London. Invt. £201-03-01. Taken 17 October, 1661, by Thomas Dunke, ffrancis Bushnell, William Lord.

Court Record, Page 164—5 December, 1661: Mr. James Cornish having Married the widow, being unwilling to act without an Order of Court, this (Quarter) Court Order Mr. James Cornish and Mr. Chapman to husband the estate, to Collect and pay debts, and render an account when called for. Page 182—4 September, 1662: Dist. of Estate: To the Eldest son Greenfield Laraby £15-00-00; to John, £12-00-00; to Elizabeth and Sarah to each 20 Nobles. The remainder of ye estate to be to ye Relict.

Page 177-8-9.

Lattimer, John, Wethersfield. Invt. £1657-06-08. Taken 29 April, 1662, by Samuel Boreman, Thomas Hurlbut. Will dated 8 April, 1662.

I John Lattimer of Wethersfield do make this my last Will & Testament: I give to my wife two hundred pounds & also a Room or Rooms in my dwelling house During her natural Life. I give & bequeath to my son John my Dwelling house and barne and all outhouses and halfe my home lott that side next Mr. Chesters which the buildings stand upon; alsoe I give to my son halfe my Great plaine; and also I give to him that tenn acrs of Meadow I bought of Samll Martin and John Kilbourn; and my will is that my sonne John shall possess my houses and Lands which I have given to him when he come to the age of one and twenty years and soner if his mother sees fitt. I give to my son Jonathan when he comes to the age of one and twenty years that house and barne and hom lott which I bought of John Edwards, and alsoe the other halfe of my great plaine; and alsoe I give unto my Sonn Jonathan Six acres of my Lower peace of meadow. I give to my son Bezaleel the house which I bought of Anthony Wright and alsoe all my nine acer pece of plaine; and alsoe I give to my sonn Bezaleel three acres of meadow, which is the remainder of my Lower meadow; and alsoe all that five acres which I bought of Robt. Burroughs. I give to my daughter Rebeckah one hundred and thirty pounds. I give to my daughter Naomi £80. I give to my daughter Abyah £80. I give to my daughter Elishabe £60. And my mind and will is that all the remainder of my estate, if any be, I leave to the Descresion of my beloved wife only, to dispose of it amongst my children. And my will is that all my sons shall receive their portion when they come to the age of twenty and one years, and soner if their mother and Overseers see it good for them. And alsoe my daughters shall receive their portions when they come to the age of eighteen years, and soner if their mother and Overseers see it most Good for them. And my will is that my beloved wife shall be my Executor to Execute my will; and Mr. John Russell, pastor of the

Church of Christ at Hadley, and Mr. Samuel Boreman and Thomas Hurlbut to be Overseers.

Witness: *John Chester,*   JOHN X LATTIMER.
John Betts, Hugh Welles.

Court Record, Page 170—12 May, 1662: Will Proven. This Court grants the Executrix liberty to take her portion out of ye Estate not disposed of to make one third if she sees good.

Lewis, Walter, Wethersfield. Court Record, Page 95—12 June, 1656. The Testimony of Theophilus Munnings, aged 26 years, saith that being at Pequett before the Connecticut Ship which was taken by prince Rupert went forth to Sea, he heard Walter Lewis say that he had given all that he had to Thomas Williams, before Lt. Smith and his wife. Taken upon Oath.   *John Winthrope.*

The Deposition of Thomas Munnings, aged about 26 years, saith that he was in the State of England Service in the War against the Dutch at that (   ) Walter Lewis of Wethersfield was pressed in a Ship of the Same Fleet in the Same Service, the which Ship was called Marmaduke; and being in Fight with the Dutch fleet the sd. Walter had his leg Shott off and dyed about 5 days after, as he was informed by the Seamen of the sd. Marmaduke upon inquiry after this sd. Walter by the Deponent, being his intimate acquaintance, which Caused the Deponent to inquire after him after ye sd. Fight. Taken upon Oath, 6 May, 1656.
                          John Winthrope.

Adms. to Thomas Williams, who gave Bond that if Walter Lewis ever returned, or hath made a Later Will giving his Estate to any other, the sd. Thomas Williams shall answer the Estate in Court.

The Deposition of Lt. Smith and Rebeckah his wife saith that before Walter Lewis went to Sea in the Connecticut Ship which was taken by Prince Robert, the sd. Walter told these deponents yt he did intend to make a Will in Writeing, but now he should have no time. Therefore desired these Deponents to be Witnesses that this was his Will that he gave all the Estate that he had to Thomas Williams of Wethersfield if he never come into the Country again. Taken upon oath before me, 23 June, 1656.
                          John Winthrope.

Page 115-116.

Loomis, Joseph, Windsor. Died 25 November, 1658. Invt. £178-10-00. Taken by Henry Clarke, John Moore.

Court Record, Page 115—2 December, 1658. An Agreement for a Division of the Estate by the Children of Joseph Loomis, Decd, and approved by this Court of Magistrates to be an Equal Division. To Joseph Loomis, to Nicholas Olmsted, to Josiah Hull, to John Loomis, to Thomas Loomis, to Nathaniel Loomis, to Mary Tudor, to Samuel Loomis.

The agreement of the children of Mr. Joseph Loomis respecting the division of the estate of ye father deceased approved by The Court 2 December 1658: We whose names are hereunto subscribed doe by these prsents testify that it is our mutual and joynt agreement to attend an equal division of the estate of Mr. Joseph Loomis, our father, lately deceased, wch said estate being distributed in an equal prption we doe by these prsents engage to set down Satisfied and Contented respecting any future trouble or demands about the fore said estate now pr sented by Inventory to ye Court of Magistrates.
Witness our hand, 2nd December, 1658.

JOSEPH LOOMIS, JOSIAS HULL, THOMAS LOOMIS, MARY TUDOR, NICHOLAS OLMSTED, JOHN LOOMIS, NATH. LOOMIS, SAMLL LOOMIS.

Page 172.

Lord, Richard, Hartford. Died 10 May, 1662. Invt. £3488-11-01. Taken by John Allyn and Jeremie Addams.

Court Record, Page 189—5 September, 1662. Adms. to Mrs. Lord, the Widow, and Richard Lord.

Respecting the estate of Capt. Richard Lord, it being for the present Conceived to amount to £3000, this Court doth Order the Distribution as followeth: To Mrs. Sarah Lord, Relict of ye Sd. Capt Lord, the Summ of £1000; to Mr. Richard Lord his son, £1300; to Sarah Lord his daughter, £700; with a third part of all the Lands in the Naragansett Country and of Land elsewhere that is not already prized in the Inventory. Mrs. Lord hereby engageth to add to the £700 distributed to her daughter, £100 out of her portion to make it £800; and what of estate Mrs. Lord doth take up of her proportion in houseing and Lands, it shall return to the heirs after her decease. Any other estate that she shall be possessed of to be at her own dispose. And what Houseing or Lands doth then return to Mr. Richard or his heirs He or they shall enjoy, paying the value thereof as Mrs. Lord his Mother doth Order.

Page 150.

Lord, Thomas, Wethersfield. Invt. £202-18-00. Taken 5 April, 1662, by Richard Lord & Samuel Boreman. Will dated 28 October 1661. (Thomas Lord brother of Richard Lord):

I Thomas Lord of Wethersfield, being of perfect memory and understanding though weake of body, make this my Last will: And then considering the inability of my elder daughter Dorothy Lord in an ordianry way uncapable of ever carringe for it selfe in this world, seeing that extra-ordinary payns and Care must be taken with it, I, for the incouragement of my Dear and Tender wife to breed up and take the Care of my sd. Daughter, doe freely give my whole Estate during her natural life. I mean my house and Land at Hartford and all that part and portion of Goods and Chattells wch shall appeare to belong to me after the death of my Honoured and beloved Mother, and my house & Lott at Wethersfield, with all my Moveables & Cattell & Debts due either by Booke or Bill, my Just Ingagements being satisfied, trusting she will have a motherly Care of my Sweet Babes; and, if she can, Will dispose part to them that sur-vive; and that She may Sell either of the houses for the supply of her-selfe and children. Moreover I doe Intreat my beloved brother Capt. Richard Lord of Hartford and Mr. Samuel Boreman of Wethersfield to be Supervisors of my will, and to Assist, councill and act for my Loving wife Hannah Lord as her occasion shall require their helpe. Soe I comitt my spirit to God.

Not witnessed. (See File.)   THOMAS LORD.

Court Record, Page 69 (Vol. III)—29 October, 1667: Adms. granted to Gregory Wilterton on the Estate of Thomas Lord, Decd, according to the Will of the Deceased. Gregory Wilterton accepts.

Lord, Mary. Court Record, Page 152—(Vol. III) 2 March, 1675-6: Mary Lord, daughter of Thomas Lord, late Decd, made choice of George Gardner to be her Guardian.

Page 120-21.

Maynard, John, Hartford. Invt. £450-04-00. Taken 24 February, 1657-8, by John Talcott, Edward Stebbing. Will dated 23 January, 1657-8:
I John Maynard of Hartford doe make this my last Will & Testa-ment: Imprs. I give unto my wife Edetha my dwelling house with all my other houses, as also all othr Land lying and being in Hartford, during her life; and After her decease vnto John Day, the youngest son of my wife, unto him and his heirs forever. Also my Will is that John Day, at the age of 21 years or day of marriage, shall receive two kows, too work-ing oxen and one mare, weth one kart and plow, with the taklin thereunto belonging. Also my Will is that Thomas Day, the Eldest son, shall re-ceive £20 Sterling out of my Estate provided he carry well and dutifully to his Mother. I give unto Sarah and Mary Day, my wives daughters, £20 Sterling to each of them out of my Estate, to be paid within two years after my decease, provided that they attend the Counsel of my wif and the supervisors of this my Will. Also I give unto the Rev. Mr. Stone, teacher of the Church of Hartford, 40 Shillings. I make my wife sole

Executrix, and Mr. John Talcott sen. and my Brother Mr. Edward Stebbing and Richard Goodman to be Overseers.

Witness: *John Talcott,*   JOHN MANERD.
Edwrd Stebbing, Richrd Goodman.

Page 81.

Moody, John, Hartford. Invt. £300-14-06. Taken 6 December, 1655, by Gregory Wolterton, John Barnard, Francis Barnard.

The last Will & Testament of John Moody late of Hartford: I doe make my loving wife Sarah Moody sole Executrix, and I doe wil that halfe of all that I have, booth Land and Stuffe (excepting the Howseoldstuffe, which I leave wholly to my wife), I give to my son Samuel Moody for to have it at the age of twenty fower years. I Will also that Elizabeth Pepper shall have five & twenty pound payd her within a year, and a petticote and a wascote & a payer of shooes; and this and all my debts for to be payd out of the whole.

         JOHN MOODY.

23 July, 1655.
Witness: *Gregory Wolterton,*
John Barnard, Francis Barnard.

Court Record, Page 80—December, 1655: Will Proven.

Elizabeth Pepper maketh oath in this Court that about the yeare Ano 1641 Sarah Glover, the Sister of John Glover of Newtowne in New England, being at Mr. John Moodys howse at Hartford, she desired the said Elizabeth to goe with her to John Skinner of Hartford, which the said Elizabeth did. When the said Elizabeth and Sarah were at John Skinners house the said Sarah asked John Skinner for a debt of £13 he owed her brother John Glover, & the said John Skinner answered he had noe money as he was engaged to pay, neither would hee get any for the goods he Brought from England; therefore hee was sorry that he had borrowed it of her brother, & soe went away without any money, but the said Skinner promised to pay the sayd £13 in the best pay he can.

Morrice, John. Invoice of Goods by William Keeny & Samuel Hall.

Court Record, Page 173—June, 1662. Invt. of estate John Morrice & Anthony Sutton was presented and accepted. Adms. to William Keny & Samuel Hall, and what Estate remains is to be delivered to Mr. Hamlin to answer Relations if any appear within one year; if not, he is to account to this Court for that he receives. The Court orders yt Sarah Nettleton shall have a bodkin and pair of Womans Stockings Inventoried in Mr. John Morrice his Estate, She having sent a Venture to Barbadoes by him.

Page 175—13 June, 1662: The Magistrates order that the above named Goods shall be given to Sarah Nettleton, also the Bodkin marked S. N.

Mudge, Widow, Pequett. Court Record, Page 42—2 June 1653: Liberty is granted that the Land belonging to the Widow Mudge at Pequett may be sould for the payment of debts and the bettering of the childrens portions.

Page 153.

Northam, James, Wethersfield. Invt. £278-10-00. Taken 27 February, 1660-1, by John Lattimore, Thomas Hurlbut: My will is that while my wife or Relict continues a widow shee is to have ye whole estate, but if shee marry again Two thirds of the Estate to be to her children. The Widdow doth declare it to be her minde that her eldest son by her first husband should have A lesser share yn any of the rest of the Children, & the Widdow did declare yt it was her husbands minde yt her eldest son by him should have a larger portion yn the rest of the Children, both wch the Court Judgeth equall and ought to be attended.

Page 98. 51-2.

Olcott, Thomas, Hartford. Invt. £1468-08-05. Taken 13 February, 1654, by John Tailcoatt, Edward Stebbing, Richard Lord. Will dated 20 November 1653: In the name of God Amen. I Thomas Olcott of Hartford, being weake in body but through the mercy of God of perfect memory, yett Calling to minde the certainty of Death & the uncertainty of the time thereof, doe make & ordayne my last will & testament. My wife I leave her to the Care of the Church whereof the Lord hath made her a member, & to the Counsell & advice of them in Generall, my over Seers & Mrs. Hooker in pticular; & doe desire their utmost care & indeavor for her good; & I doe ernestly desire her to attend their Counsell & advice to the utmost. The Children which the Lord of his mercy hath given mee I firstly Commite them into the armes of that mercy, & beseech the Lord to make good his ever lasting Covenent that he hath of his rich mercy made with them. And secondly I leave them to the love, Care & faithfull Indeavor of the Church with whom they live & whereof they are members, Intreating them according to the Covenants of the Lord that they will be helpfull to them & watchfull over them for their outward and Spiritual good.

And touching thee worldly goods which the lord hath ben pleased to send me, my will is that after my debts are paid & discharged, that my estate shall bee disposed of as followeth, viz: Unto my deare & loving wife I give unto her the summe of £28 pr year during her life, to be made fare unto her out of my estate partly out of what rents & yearly Annuelltyes are Comming to mee, and prtly so much off my estate to bee putt to it as will prcure, to bee assined to her during her life.   The whole remainder of my estate, except twenty pounds, I give and bequeath unto my children, five or six more or less as it pleased the Lord to leave mee which are sur- viving; to be divided if I have Six Children into seaven equal parts; if five Children, into Six equal pts; or if seaven Children, into eight equal parts.   And I doe give and bequeath unto my Eldest sonn Thomas two Equal parts of the estate soe devided, & unto the each of the rest of my said Children one equal prt. of the state so divided.   And the rest of my Estate not given I give & bequeath as followeth: Unto my deare & ten- der Mother, Mrs. Margaret Charlfount, for her own prticuler use, two pounds; to my deare & much respected sister, Mrs. Mary Hardey, five pounds; to my endeared ffriend & ffaithfull Counseller, Mrs. Hooker, fifty Shillings; to my reverened Teacher, one pounde tenn Shillings; to my Mother Hoare, twenty Shillings; to my Brother Will Wadsworth, one pound; to Brother Will Lewis Seniore, one pounde; to the overseers of this my last will, each of them apeece three pounds.   My desire is that all my said legasyes shall be paid within own yeare after my decease.

I doe make & ordaine my loving wife & my Sonn Thomas Executors of this my will, & I doe desire my deare Bretheren & friends Mr. John Talcott & Edward Stebbin to be overseers hereof, & desire their utmost care & faithfullness herein.   I doe Revoke all other wills by mee made, & doe acknowledge this as my Last will & testament, & in witness hereof have hereunto sett my hand & seall this 20 of November, 1653.

THOMAS OLCOTT.

Witness by us: *Henry Hardye,*
Elizabeth Roberts.

Court Record, Page 55, (Vol. III)—9th October, 1666: Upon re- quest of Mrs. Abigail Olcott and Thomas her son, this Court doth ap- prove Capt. Talcott to be Overseer of the last Will of Mr. Thomas Ol- cott, Decd, instead of Mr. John Talcott, Decd.

(See State Sec. Office. 2 Vol. of Lands):

Mr. Olcott, I pray send mee by my servant 20 pound biskats, and this my noate shall ingage mee to make paymt.   Januar 11th, 1653.

John Barrett.

Recd of Mr Thomas olcott for ye use of my master John Barrett, 20 lbs of Bread.   I say received by me.   Januar 11th, 1653.

Henrick Lucus.

On the 7th of April, 1655, Recd of Mr. Samuell ffitch, as Attorney of Mrs olcott, one day Booke and Debts Booke with some writings yt were transacted by my cousin George Cowning, Decd, For ye use of Mr. Thomas Olcott, decd, wch I promise to be Accountable for to ye widdow olcott or to Any whome Shee shall give power unto.   Witness my Hand ye day and year above written.   ROBERT COWNING.

Recd of Thomas olcott one Bill of Masor George ffawdon for 8 barrells and ½ of Tarr, ye which I am to deliver unto Masor ffawdon upon
ye delivery of 1200 of Tobacco & Caske & a Bill of £200 due from Mr.
Hugh Donne, ye which Tobacco & Caske and Bill I am to returne unto
Thomas Olcott or else ye Bill again.   Also recd of him 10 Bushells of
pease, at 30 lbs. Tobacco & Caske per Bushell, ye which I am to pay within 5 days at Vessell in Nansemyn River.   In Witness hereof I have sett
my Hand this 6th of February, 1653; & for his paines of Recr and bringing ye Tobacco hee is to allow one hundred of Tobacco out of it.

John Wood.

An Inventory of ye Goods of Thomas Olcott, decd, Taken ye 3rd of
March, 1653: Imprimis. 1 Cabbin Bed & Pillow, 1 Blankett, 1 Coverlett,
10 Deere Skinnes, 2 Barrll of Mackerell, 13 Milk Trays & ½ a barrll of
Mackerell, 10 Couple of Dry Fish, 2 pipes of Bread, 1 hhd of Bread, 3 pr
of Stille yards, 1 Hamaccoe.   These pr cells were prised by us,

Tho: Addison,
Robert Ewen, Andrew Wormwood.

In his Chist: 1 old pr of Breeches & 1 Cloake, 1 little Bagg of Ginger
valued 2 shillings, 1 Hatt Brush, 6 little Cals for womans head Rowles,
2 lbs of Marmalett, 2 Cours Shirts & handkerchaises, 1 Pillow Case, 1 pr
old Stockings, 1 Bible, 5 shirts, 2 Bands, 4 Handkerchaifs, 1 old clout, 1
pr of old Sheetes & a Colander, 1 pr of markin fro, 1 old Hatt.   These
goods were vewed by us 6 March, 1653.

Thomas Manninge, Tho: Addison;
Robert Ewen, Hugh Conn, Georg Holmes.

Page 39.

Pantry, John, Hartford. Invt. £1242-01-00. Taken 25 November,
1653, by John Talcott, Edward Stebbing.   Will dated 1st September 1653:
I John Peintre of Hartford, upon the River of Connecticut, being
sick & weak in Body but of perfect memory, Doe mak this my last will
& Testament, this first Day of September in the yeare of our Lord one
Thousand and Six hundred and fifty three.   In manner & form as followeth:

Imprimis.   My will is That my wife Hana shall possess, enjoy, improve and manadge my whoal estat, Consisting in howsing, lands, Cattells
& movables, or what soever doeth properly belong to mee, ffor her own
use and the bringing up of my Children according as I shall Express in
this my will.   My will is that my son John, at the term of twenty years of
age, shall inherit and possess all my howsing and lands Situated and being
in Hartford, of what kind soever, with all immunities and Privileges
thereunto belonging, Toe him and his heires forever, upon the Condition
heer after mentioned: Whereas, by the providence of God my wife is

with child & near the time of her travail, If it be a Man child I give unto
it two hundred Pounds Sterling, to be paid in Corant Estat, at the age of
one and twenty yeares.   If it shall be a daughter I then give unto it one
hundred & twenty pounds, to be paid of Corant Estat, at the age of
eighteen years.   Also I give unto my daughter Hana one hundred and
twenty pounds, to be paid in Corant Estat, at the age of eighteen years.
I appoint my wife sole Executrix. John Talcott & Edward Stebbing to
be overseers.

Witness: *John Pratt,*   JOHN PANTRY.
Thomas Hubbard, James Ensign.

 Court Record (Vol. III)—3 March, 1669-70: John Pantry, a minor
son of Capt. John Pantry, late of Hartford, Decd, chose Capt. John Talcott to be his Guardian.

Page 25.

 Pantry, Margaret, Hartford.   Will dated 12 September, 1651: I,
Margaret Pantry of Hartford, do make this my last Will & Testament:
I bequeath unto my daughter Mary Bryan (Bryant), unto my sister
Brunson her two children by Richard Brunson, John and Abigail Bron-
son, to each of them £6 Sterling, my son John Pantry to be sole Executor:

             MARGARITT X PANTRY.
Witness: *Edward Stebbing & James Ensign.*

Page 22-3-4.

 Pantry, William, Hartford. Invt. £1011-10-00. Taken 29 November, 1649, by John Talcott, William Gibbons & Jeams Ensign. Will not
dated or signed. (In Vol. II).

 I give to my wife Margaret Pantry, with Goods, Rights and Privileges, an Annuity of £15 a year; to his son John Pantry, £240; and to
daughter Mary, £150, wife of Richard Bryan of Milford.

 Memorandum: That whereas, Richard Bryan of Milford hath taken
to wife Mary Pantry, the daughter of William Pantry of Hartford, Deceased, and doth now demand a portion with his wife part of the Estate of
the sd Wyilliam Pantry of his Brother John Pantry, now in possession
of the said Estate: Know all men by these presents, that it is agreed
Between the said Richard on the one parte and John Pantry of Hartford
on the other parte that the said John paying or give Bond to pay £240 or
what of the same remains unpaid, for to be paid to William Gibbins
of Hartford or his Assigns, for the use of the said Richard as his parte of
his father in lawe his estate with his wife as her portion.

Witness: *John Evance,*   JOHN PANTRY.
Peter Prudden, William Tuttle.   RICHARD BRYAN.
      16 November, 1649.

Page 117.

Palmer, William Jr., Wethersfield. Invt. £108-03-06. Taken 10 November, 1658, by Samuel Boreman, John Nott, Thomas Standish.

Court Record, Page 120—2 December, 1658: Adms. to William Palmer. sen.

Persons, Thomas. Court Record, Page 169—6 March, 1661-2: The Court of Magistrates doe order ye Townsmen of Windsor to consider ye Estates of Thomas Persons and Ralph Smith, and to administer ye said Estates in paying Debts and distributing the remainder to ye Relicts as they see Cause.

Pequett Proprietors, a Petition. A Court of Magistrates at Pequett, 13 June, 1655.

Court Record, Page 71—13 June 1655: Record of Division of Land at Pequett, in the Neck, to Several Proprietors. Names of Petitioners to Court: Peter Blachford, Will. Bartlett, Tho. Hungerfoot, Jacob Waterhouse, John Prentice, Andrew Loyden, James Bemus, Matthew Beckwith, William Cumstock, Thomas Bayly, with several others, for themselves and all the rest of the petitionrs and greived persons, doe Ingage themselves to this Court that if they please to heare their Complaints and Judge of them According to their best light and Judgement all the aforesaid greived partyse will Rest satisfied and Contented in the apprehensions and determinations of the said Courte, and doe Ingage themselves that they and every of them Shall never molest or trouble, by sute att Law, Complaint or otherwise, Either The Towne of Pequott or townsmen thereof any time hereafter about anything mentioned in our petition to the Courte att Hartford, or pleaded att this Courte, about any Act or Acts, Covenant or Agreements, of the aforesaid Towne of Pequett, or Townsmen Thereof, in Reference to any Gifts, Grants, devisions or rights of Land in the said Land, or any Rates they have made whereof the aforesaid petitionrs have had just Cause of dissatisfaction and Complaint. The Townsmen also, with Capt. Denison, Mr. Brewster, Will Chesebroake, with several others of the town, present att this Courte, did in like manner Ingage to performe and rest Satisfied in the Judgement of the Courte wherein so ever appears to respect and Concern them or Either of them.

Note: The Courte judges from the testimony of thee Inhabitants that the Land Lathrop bought of John Austin was forfeited to the Towne per Austin before Lathrop bought it.

Samuel Lathrop complains that the Townsmen took from him Land that he bought & paid for.

Page 88.

Phillips, William, Hartford. Invt. £314-04-00. Taken 4 December, 1655, by John Talcott, William Westwood, Edward Stebbing.

Court Record, Page 79—1st December, 1655-6: The Widow Phillips to administer her husband's Estate.

Pickering, John. Will dated 27 August, 1660. (Will on File) :
I John Pickering, late servant of Theodore Atkison, felt Maker in Bostowne, My will is that first Mr. Loueridge be Satisfied for his paynes & Charges in Tending & providing for me in my Sickness & funeral, & then, the rest of my Just debts being Pd., my will is that ye remainder of my estate, both in this Country & England, shall forever belong to my dear Ant. Matson of Bostowne, & her heirs forever, as a Token of my love. I make my friend Mr. Wm. Loueridge of Hartford my Sole Executor, and desire Captain Richard Lord & Marshall Jonathan Gilberd of Hartford to take that pains for me as to see that this my will be duly observed & kept.

                                                            JOHN X PICKERING.
Witness: *John Allyn,*
         Nathaniel Willett.

Page 61.

Pond, Samuel, Windsor. Died 14 March, 1654-5. Invt. £129-02-00. Taken 19 March, 1654-5, by Henry Wolcott Jr., John Moore, Robert Howard, Benedictus Alford sen. Legatees: Wife Sarah, son Isaac 8 years of age, Samuel 6, Nathaniel 3 ¼, Sarah 2 ½ years. This Court order to Dist. to the Mother £40, the rest of the Estate to be equally divided between the 4 Children.

Page 128.

Post, Stephen, Seabrooke. Invt. £442-03-06. Taken ye last of August, 1659, by John Clarke, Thomas Leffingwell, Christopher Huntington.
This According to our best Light is a true Inventory of the Estate of Stephen Post of Seabrook, lately deceased.

Original Signatures   *John Clarke,*
on File. (C. W. M.)   *Thomas Leffingwill,*   Recorded 1659.
                             Christopher Huntington.

Pratt, John, Hartford. Died 15 July, 1655. Invt. £515-02-06. Taken by John Talcott and William Wadsworth. Will dated 11 October, 1654. (On file.)
The last Will & Testament of John Pratt of Hartford: I the sd. John Pratt, having my perfect memory, doe desier to leaue my Soule in the

Everlasting Arms of Jesus Christ, and my temporal Goods to them hereafter mentioned. Imprimis: I give to Elizabeth my wife this Roome which we call the Parlour, with the Bed and Bedding thereunto belonging, wollens, linen, as also her wearing Cloathes, woolen & Linen, together with all other Houshold Improvements comfortable to her outward necessities, & that She shall have the keeping of 1 Cow for her, & necessary firewood Cutt, laid ready for her burning, & five pounds Sterling paid her yearly in Good Country pay; all this to be made Good to her during the time of her natural Lyfe. I give to my son John my now dwelling house with the out houseinge & my homelott with all the appurtenances, to him & his lawfull heirs forever. I give to my son John the 2 meaddow Lotts in the North Meadow which came to me by the Dist. of the Town, with all the Appurtenances thereof, to him & his heirs forever. I give unto my son John that peece of Meaddow I bought of William Edwards, with the Appurtenances, to him & his heirs forever, as also the one halfe of my Upland Lotts lying in the Woods, always provided yt the sd. John Pratt doe make Good the Conditions formerly mentioned to his Mother Elizabeth my wife. My Will is that the sd. House & Househould, with Stock yt is then being, both Corne & Cattle, shall be wholly possest by my son John & his heirs. My Mind is that if my sone John shall dy not haveing any Male Child, then (the) he shall give his Daughter or Daughters £20 apeece at 18 years of age, & in Case a Male Child he shall inherit it at 24 in Casse he survive his father & make good the Conditions to his Sisters. My Will is if my Sone John dy leaveing a wife & Children as above sd. his wife shall inherit till the Children come of age, & shall take her thirds & what hee shall give her by Will. In Casse noe Male Child survive him, then the Inheritance to fall to my son Daniell, making good the Conditions above mentioned. I give to my son Daniel a prcell or prcells of Meadow Land which I bought of William Rescue, with the Upland belonging to it, in ye Necke, wth ye Appurtenances thereof. Alsoe my Will is that within one yeare after my decease my sone John shall pay or cause to be payd to my Son Daniel his heirs or assigns, the full sume of four score pounds in Current Country pay. In Casse my sone Daniell should desire a peece of my Homelott to build & dwell upon, then my Mind is that my sone John should freely grant him one ackre to be laid out where it may best Sute their Conveniences. This is my true Mind & Meaning as my last Will. In Witness I have sett to my Hand the day and year above mentioned.

JOHN PRATT.

Court Record, Page 82—2 October, 1655: Will & Invt. exhibited. Adms. to John Pratt, Eldest son.

Page 161.

Randall, Philip, Windsor. Invt. £113-00-00. Taken 28 May, 1662, by William Gaylord and Humphrey Pinney. Will dated 8 March, 1661-2:

I Philip Randall of Windsor, being aged & full of daies, not knowing how soone the Lord may call for mee out of this life, to prevent trouble doo Leave this as my Last Will & Testament as followeth: my Howse & Land and all the rest of my goods I Leave it all to my wife during her life, and after her decease unto my sonne Abram; also my will is that my sonne shall paye out of it these Legacies: Unto Isack Phellps my grand-child, fiftie shillings; and to Abram Phellps, five pounds; and to Joseph Phellps, fiftie shillings. Also my will is that Joseph shall have a lot of my sonne Abraham which is over ye greate River next above Mr dauisons Land, by vertue of a peece of Land of mine which I gave my sonne in my Lot over ye Great River which he hath exchanged wth Goodman Bissell. Joseph shall have the Lott surrendered up to him at 21 years of age; thus leaveing myselfe & all yt I have, being in the Hands of God to dispose. I set my Hand to this.

In presence of *John Rockwell,*   PHILIP X RANDALL.
              Simon Rockwell.

Page 50.

Richards, Thomas, Hartford. Invt. £38-03-00. Taken by George Steele & Joseph Mygatt. Adms. to the Widow according to the Will. Presented to the Court by Joseph Mygatt, Thomas Selden.

Page 141-2.

Robbins, John, Wethersfield. Invt. £579-18-04. Taken 2 July, 1660, by Richard Treat, Thomas Welles & Samuel Welles.

4 October, 1660: Adms. to Mr. Treat, Mr. Thomas & Mr. Samuel Welles, with Mr. John Chester to preserve the Estate for the Relict. Order to Dist. from the Magistrates, 5 June, 1662:

	£ s d		£ s d
To John Robbins,	150-00-00	To Hannah,	100-00-00
To Joshua,	120-00-00	To Comfort,	100-00-00
To Mary,	109-00-00		

It is granted to Mr. Kimberly, that is to match with Mary Robbins, that he shall keep the young children till they come to age, and the House and Land are bound over, as also the Estate of Mr. Kimberly, both what he hath and his wives portion, for ye discharge of ye 3 young Children who Mr. Kimberly is to educate in reading and writing, and Mr. William Wadsworth and Samuel Boreman to Dist. the Estate.

(Vol. III, New Book). Court Record, Page 62—7 May, 1667: Dist. of John Robbins' Estate, net £509-19-00:

	£ s d
One Holland Sheete,	0-15-00
1 Pillow Beere,	0-04-06
2 Cushions,	0-08-00
2 pewter platters, with the Candle Stick & saucer,	0-11-03
1 Iron Pott,	0-08-00

Received all these things that are writting above.

As Witness my Hand,   JOHN COALT.

Court Record, Page 31—4 March, 1651-2: This Court Confirms the Bargain that John White hath made with John Skinner's Widow for some land that did belong to the sd. John Skinner, Decd., and doe order that the sd. John White shall pay to Joseph Loomis sen., of Windsor.

Page 83—18 January, 1655-6:

	£ s d
The Debts of John Skinner Decd,	60-18-11
There remains to be distributed,	29-17-01
To the Relict,	10-00-00
To Richard on account of Weakness,	11-17-01
To the rest of the Children to each of them,	00-40-00

This Court grant to Owen Tudor, who had married the Relict of John Skinner, a Writing to the Effect that the Widow never was Executrix or Adms. to the Estate of her Deceased Husband.

Page 145—6 December, 1660: John Loomis & John Moore are appointed to husband the Estate yet remaining of John Skinner, and to pay the Legacies as ye come to be due, and to pay out of ye sd. Estate such Debts as appear legally to be due so far as ye Estate will be responsible.

Page 167—6 March, 1661-2: John Loomis and Sergt. Josiah Hull are desired to take Care of and preserve the Estate of John Skinner's Children. Also this Court approve of the placing of Richard Skinner with Robert Reeve from the 1st of November last past for the term of 9 years.

Page 97—(Vol. III) 3 March, 1669: Whereas there was £13 of the Estate of John Skinner, lately deceased, left in the Hands of Owen Tudor to answer a Debt claymed from the Estate of the sd. Skinner for one in England, & no person appearing to demand it this 16 years, upon the Motion of the Children of the sd. Skinner that they might be put in possession of the sd. Estate deposited as aforesd: This Court grant the Desire that John Skinner shall have £6, & Joseph £4 of it, & Richard Skinnner £3, they engaging to be responsible that soe much as they receive shall be forth comeing if demanded.

Page 105—23 November, 1670: It appeareing to this Court that John Loomys hath taken security of Owen Tudor for the payment of £13 of the Estate of John Skinner due to Mr. Glover, the sd. John Loomis is

to see £13 payd according to the Dist., and upon payment to deliver to Owen Tudor the obligation he took of him.
(See John Moody—Elizabeth Pepper's Statement.)

Page 62-3.

Smith, Arthur, Hartford. Invt. £380-02-06. Taken 29 November, 1655, by Thomas Bull, Gregory Wolterton, John Barnard and George Grave.
Court Record, Page 79—1st Thursday in December, 1655: Invt. Exhibited. Page 63—15 June, 1665 (see Vol III, Page 34): Joseph Nash, having married the Widow Relict of Arthur Smith, applys for a Dist. of the Estate of ye sd. Arthur Smith, ordered by the Court:

	£ s d
To John Smith the Farm at Niantick,	80-00-00
To ye 3 daughters to each of them,	35-00-00
To Arthur, at the age of 21 years,	58-00-00
Arthur eventually to have the real estate in Hartford.	

Stead, Thomas. Court Record, Page 38—2 December, 1652: The verdict of us whose names are underwritten, concerning the death of Thomas Steade, servant of Robert Lay of 6-Mile Island, given to the Constable of Hartford, 9th November, 1652: Wee doe finde that the sd. partye, going against his master's Comand, with his master's cannoe, into a place of danger, or that is to the milldam, is guilty of his own death, being drowned.

Andrew Warner, Grego Wilterton, Jes: pr Gunn, Nath: Willett, Tho: Standly, John Bernard, Tho: Selden, Jo: Stedman.

Page 91-2.

Steele, John, Farmington. Invt. £331-00-00. Taken 11 March, 1653, by Thomas Judd, Nathaniel Kellogg.

Page 5-6-7.

Stiles, Henry, Windsor. Invt. £181-07-00. Taken 6 November, 1651, by William Gaylord, William Hayden, Humphrey Pinney.
Court Record, Page 30—1st December, 1651: Adms. to John Styles. Dist. of Estate to Francis Stiles, and to her on Long Island, and to her in England, £26-13-04 apeice, which John Stiles is to pay them; and if that

Brother in England be dead, then his portion shall be equally divided between the surviving Brothers.

[Note: Henry Stiles was killed by the accidental discharge of gun in the hands of Thomas Allyn.]

The Grand Inquest upon the death of Henry Stiles:

Page 29—December, 1651: Indightment of Thomas Allyn: The Jury finds that the peece that was in the Hands of Thomas Allyn going of was the Cause of the Death of Henry Stiles of Windsor. The Inditemt being confessed, you are to Inquire whether you find the fact to bee man slaughter, or Homicide by misadventure, the said Thomas Allyn being Indited for the fact. The Jury finds the same to be Homicide by missadventure.

The Courte Adjudge the said Thomas Allyn to pay to the Country as a fyne £20 for his Sinfull neglect and Careless Carriages in the premises, and that he shall be bound to his good behavior for a 12 month, and that he shall not bear Arms for the same terme.

The Jury:

Edw. Stebbing, John Drake, John White, Humphrey Pinney, Will Gibbins, Steph. Terry, John Moore, Antho, Howkins, Rich. Goodman, Peter Tillton.

Page 163-164.

Styles, John Sen., Windsor. Died 4 June, 1662. Invt. £222-04-00. Taken 6 August, 1662, by William Gaylord & Matthew Grant. Will dated 31 May, 1662:

I John Styles Senior, of Wyndsor, doe make this my Last will & Testament. Imprimis. I give to my wife Rachell all my estate so long as Shee Lives in a widdowhood condition; but if Shee marry, my Estate shall then be divided. My wife shall then have a third part, & ye rest of my Estate shall be equally divided amongst my fower children: to my sone Henry, my sone John, my sone Isace, & my daughter Sary Howard; & also my will is that when my wife dyes ye Estate as Shee Stands possessed of shall be equally divided to my fowre children as aforsayd. And I do desire Jacob Drake, John Gaylord & John Bissell Junior to bee my overseers.

Witness: *John Griffin, John Bancroft.*   JOHN STYLES.

Court Record, Page 179—14 September, 1662: Will & Invt. Exhibited & accepted by the Court of Assistants.

Taintor, Charles. Court Record, Page 131—1st December, 1659: Adms. to his son Michael Taintor.

Page 137.

Talcott, John, Hartford. Invt. £1708-04-04. Taken 4 January, 1660, by William Westwood & John Allyn. Will dated 12 August, 1659:

Being sensabell of my owne mortallity and of the aproaching of my change, not knowing how Sudenly the Lord may put an end to my few dayes in this life, according to my duty I doe make this my last Will and Testament:

Imprimis. I doe give and bequefe my now dwelling house, with all other my houses and yards, home lotts, meadow lotts, both at the upper and lower end meadow both for mowing and ploueing, together with all my upland lotts, improved or not improved, unto Dorethy my loving wife, to improve for her owne proper use during the tarme of her naterall livfe, as allso the use of my hushold Stufe of all kindes, with my Stock of Kattell, for her use. I doe give and bequefe unto my sonn John all that land I bought in Hartford meadow and upland; together with the housing and house lotts I bought of John Stteel and Nathaniel Elly that now my sonn poseseth, unto my sonn for himselve and ayres forever to injoy. I doe alsoe give and bequefe unto my son John my now dwelling house in Hartford, together with my house lott, with all my meadow Land in the North Meadow that come to me by my Lotment from the towne, as alsoe all other that I poses by purchase or chang in Hartford; together with all my upland, improved or not improved, weth all right and priveliges there unto belonging, forever to injoy for himselve and ayers, after the death of my wife; provided that if his sonn John shall contenow to the age of Twenty four years, that then my sonn John shall settell him; or if he departte this Life before he attayne the fore sayd age, then his next eldest sonn that shall attayne the fore sayd age, ether in the house my sonn John now livith in or in the house that now I Live in, and say soe much Land to it for ether of his sonns that shall survive, to his owne proper use that shall posese it, as shall be really judged to be worth twenty pounds per annum, which shall be to him or ayers forever; and allsoe my sonn John shall pay to my use, if it be required towards the discharge of my debts and legeses by my Executrix or her ayers or exeketers, the sum of fifty pounds Sterling of Current pay.

Also I give and doe give and bequefe unto my Sonn Same well all my housing and house Lotts Lying in Wethersfield, both of meadow, swamp and upland, with all my rights thereunto belonging, now in the occupation of John Belden or Enoch Buck or any other, both on the east and west side of the river, forever to injoy, himselve and Ayers; provided that if he marry and leave no issue of his body lawfully begotten when he departt this life, that then his wife shall only posese it during her naterall livfe, and then the land and housing to returne to the eldest sonn then Living of my sonn John, to injoy after my sonn John his death.

Alsoe it is my will that my sonn Same well shall pay or case to be payd unto Dorethy my wife diuering her naterall Livfe, out of the rent of my Land at Wethersfield, ten pounds per annum:

I give unto my Grand Child John Russell, at the age of twenty one years, twenty pounds, to be payd in Current country pay.

I give to my Grand Child John Tallcott, at the age of twenty one years, in Like pay ten pounds.

I give unto my Grand Child Same well Talcott, in like manner ten pounds.

I give unto my Grand Child Elizabeth Tallcott, at the age of eighteen years, ten pounds.

My mynd is that if my kinsman John Skiner and my Kinswoman Sara Stell, or ether of them, shall be living with me in service at my departur this livfe, that they shall have payd each of them soe living with me £10. I give unto my reverend and beloved teacher Mr. Stone £5. I give towards the mayntayning a latin skoll at Hartford, if any be kept here, £5; 'thes four Legeseys to be payd one yere after my death. I do ordayne my loving wife Dorethy my sole Exsecketrige, and doe intreat my loving friend Mr. Richard Lord Senyer and my sonn John to be the Overseers of this my Will, to assist my wife in the full filling of my Will. I doe give unto my overseers 50 Shillings apece, which I hope they accept in Love and answer my request herein. I give unto my sonne John, after my wifes departur this livfe, my fether bed in the parlour Chamber with all the furnetur there unto belonging, as allsoe my "Marter Bok." All my other bokes I give unto my sonne Samewell, as allsoe the beadstead, fether bed, with all the furnetur thereunto belonging, which Standeth in the kitchen Chamber.

To signify that this is my last will and testament, I doe set to my hand the twelfe day of August, one thousand six hundred fifty nine.

JOHN TALLCOTT SENIOR.

Codicil, dated 12th August, 1659: My Will is that if my gr. Child John Russell shall depart this life before he atayne the age of 21 years, that then £20 be payd vnto Jonathan Russell at the fore sayd age; and if Jonathan Russell atayne not the fore sayd age, then it be payd my sonn Russell, witch is an Ishow of all Accompts in reference to my Daughter's portion tow Mr. Russell.

JOHN TALCOTT, SENYER.

Page 95-6.

Thompson, Thomas, Farmington. Died 25 April, 1655. Invt. £549-05-05. Taken 5 December, 1655, by Thomas Judd & John Harte. Will dated April, 1654:

I Thomas Thomson, being in prfect health and memory, doe ordaine this my Last will and Testament as followeth: Imprmis. I give unto my beloved wife, whom I make my executrix, the one halfe of all my Land in ffarmington Bounds, & the one halfe of all my howsing, Barnes & orcharding there uppon, during her natural Life, and all my Goods &

Chatteles, shee paying out such Debts as I owe, & Legacies as I bequeath, as is hereafter expressed; provided all ways & it is my desire, yt my wife shall well educate and bring up my children in Learning, & shee to possess all my Land & Estate untill my two sonnes come to twentie yeares of Age, and then to give them what household stuffe she please, over and above what I bequeath to them. Item. I give unto my two sons, John and Thomas, the other halfe of my Land, Houseing, Barne and Orchard, and the profitts of them, to be equally divided to them & to their heirs, Execer, Admes & Assigns forever. It. I give unto my daughter Beatric my young mare & the Colt she brought, & the pfit of her, & £20 more in Country pay, to be payd her wthin a yeare of the day of her marriage by her Mother or by her two brothers equally between them. It. I give unto my daughter Mary my young mare bought of Richard ffellows, and the pfit of her & £20 more in Country pay, to be paid her wthin a year of the day of her marriage by her Mother or by her two brothers equally between them. It. I give my sone John a young Horse Colt now two year old (Aprl, '54). I give to my son Thomas a young Horse Colt of a yeare old this Spring (Aprl, '54); and after the decease of my wife I give unto my two sonnes John & Tho: all my Lands in Farmingtown Bounds, wth all Houseing, Barnes and Orchards thereupon, to them & theire heirs forever (they paying out to their two sisters £20 apeice in two yeares after), equally to be divided between them. It. I give unto my Children each of them a Byble. I desire my two brothers in England and my Brother Thomas Welles to be Overseers.

By me, THOMAS THOMPSON.

On the 6th of May, 1656, Anthony Howkins, having married the Widow Thompson, is appointed to administer & husband the Estate of Thomas Thompson, he engageing himself & heirs to ye due Execution of ye Will.

Court Record, Page 87—May, 1656: The Court still ruleing on the Will of Thomas Thompson, they finding some points not very clear in Expression.

Page 122—(Vol. IV) 2 September, 1686: This Court being informed that John and Thomas Thompson doe differ about some Lands that were given them by their Father in his last Will. This Court doe order and appoint Capt. John Stanly, Deacon John Langton & Ensign Thomas Heart to lay out to them, the sd. John Thompson and Thomas Thompson, each of them, the just proportion of the Land given them by their Father according to their sd. Fathers Will, & to deliver it to them & cause it to be recorded in their Town Records, & the sd. Thompson to pay them for their pains.

Page 185.

Treat, Matthias, Wethersfield. Died 8 July, 1662. Invt. £178-00-00. Taken 16 September, 1662, by John Nott, Samuel Boreman. The children: Henry age 13 years, Susannah 11, Richard 7, Elizabeth 5, Abigail 3 years, and another expected.

Dist. by Order of the Court: To the Widow, £50; to the Eldest son, £23; to the others, £18 apeice. Anthony Wright, having married the Relict, is appointed Adms.; and Richard Smith sen., Richard Smith Jr., and Thomas Burnham, Overseers to take care that this Dist. be attended to.

Court Record, Page 83—(Vol. III) 4 March, 1668-9: An Order from the Court to the Adms. and Overseers of the Estate to pay to the Eldest daughter, who is of age, her portion of the Estate.

Page 73.

Upson, Thomas, Farmington. Invt. £108-16-06. Taken 6 September, 1655, by Stephen Hart, Thomas Newell, John Cowles & John Hart.

This Writing witnesseth: That I, Steven Upson, acquit & discharge my father-in-law, Edmund Scott, from all Dues, Demands & Debts that were due to me from my sd. father on account of a Legacy due to me by Order of the Court, 7 September, 1671; also what is due to me on my Brother Thomas Upson's Accot as being part of my Father Upson's Estate.

Witness: *Thomas Hart,*   STEVEN X UPSON.
John Wadsworth sen.   20 September, 1680.

John Welton, in right of his wife, acquits his Father Scott on account of Father Upson's Estate, 1st April, 1681.

Samuel Hecocks also discharged his Father Scott on account of Father Upson's Estate, 21 June, 1680.

SAMUEL HICKCOCKS.

Court Record, Page 79—1st Thursday in December, 1655: Invt. exhibited. Adms. granted to the Widow; she desired Thomas Judd and Stephen Hart sen. as Assistants.

Page 114—(Vol. III) 7 September, 1671: Edmund Scott, who had married the Widow, moved this Court for a Dist. of the Estate:

	£ s d		£ s d
To Thomas, Eldest son,	7-00-00	To Mary, eldest daughter,	4-00-00
To Stephen,	5-00-00	To Hanna,	4-00-00

The rest of the Estate to be and belong to Edmund Scott and his heirs in right of his now wife, the Widow of the sd. Upson.

Court Record, Page 140—(Vol. III) 1st April, 1674: Stephen Upson, a minor son of Thomas Upson, made choice of Samuel Wyllys to be his Guardian.

Page 170.

(Inventory on File.)
Varlett, Casper, & Judith his wife, both decd.   Invt.   £205-14-00.
Taken 22 September, 1662.
Court Record, Page 179—11 October, 1662: Invt. exhibited. Adms.
is granted to Nicholas Varlett, who delivered to the Court, upon Oath,
the full Credit of ye Accounts out of Monseur Varlet's Book.
Page 4—(Vol. III) 15 June, 1663: Nicholas Varlet this day in open
Court presented an Account of his Adms. on the Estate of his late Father,
Casper Varlet. The Court ordered that they did free Capt. Varlet and
Mrs. Schreeck of the Bond of Adms.

Page 168-9.

Wakeman, John (late) of New Haven. Invt. £157-16-11. Taken
14 September, 1661, by Richard Lord, William Wadsworth. Will dated
at New Haven, 4 month, 18 day, 1660 (18 June, 1660).
I John Wakeman of New Haven, being weake in body but of sound
understanding and memory, in expectation of my great change, do make
this my last will and testament:

First, I comend my soule into the hands of my Lord Jesus Christ, my
redeemer, trusting to be saved by his merits and intercession, and my body
to be buryed at the discretion of my executors and friends, in hope of a
joyfull resurrection: testifying my thankfullness to God for the free mani-
festation of his grace to me in Christ, and for the liberty and fellowship
vouchsafed me with his people in his ordinances in a congregational way,
which I take to be the way of Christ orderly walked in according to his
rules. But I doe testify against absolute Independence of Churches, and
persecution of any in light or actings, and against compulsion of conscience, to concur with the church without inward satisfaction to conscience, and persecution of such as dissent upon this grounde, which I
take to be an abuse of the power given for edification by Christ, who is
only Lord of the conscience.
As for my outward estate and worldly goods that God hath given
me, which I shall leave, my just debts and funerall charges being satisfied,
my will is that first I give unto my daughter Helina, wife To John Talcott of Hartford, twenty pounds, to be wholy at her owne disposing; and
to her husband, my son-in-law, John Talcott, five pounds and my best
beaver hatt and band; and to ech of their three children five pounds a
piece, namely, unto John, Elizabeth and Samuell, all to be payd within
six months after my decease. It. I give unto my son Samuell Wakeman's
two sons, namely, Samuell and John, ten pounds a piece. It. I give unto
my daughter Kitchell's daughter, Elizabeth, ten pounds. Item. I give
unto my brother-in-law Adam Nicholls of Hartford my cloath cloake and
the suite of the same which was my Cousin John Walker's, and my gray

hatt; and I give unto his wife my sister Anna Nicholls ten pounds, to be wholy at her owne disposing; and to thayr four children twenty shillings a piece, namely, John, Hanna, Sarah and Ebenezer, all which my will is should be payd to them wthin six months after my decease. It. I give unto Hanna Cheeuers five pounds, to be set apart and improved for her, at the end of one Yeare after my decease, as my overseers shall see meet, untill she come to eighteen years of age (which is the tyme agreed upon for her continuence with me or mine), or till the tyme of her marriage, provided she marry wth the consent of my executors and overseers, or wth the consent of any two of them. It. I give to my servant Thomas Huxley my short gun with a rest and my hanger which he useth to train with, upon his good behavior, that is, if he shall carry him selfe honestly and faithfully in his place and service to the satisfaction of my executors and overseers, or with the approbation of any two of them. Then all the rest of my estate, goods, lands, debts whatsoever, I give and bequeath to my son Samuell Wakeman and to my son-in-law and daughter Samuell and Elizabeth Kitchell as followeth, that is, when all my debts and legasyes are discharged (which my mind is should be out of my estate as it ariseth indifferently and at the prises comon in this Jurisdiction). My will is that my son Samuell Wakeman shall have two thirds parte of that my whole estate that remaineth, and my son and daughter Kitchell the other third part equally betwixt them, and my will is that my daughter Elizabeth Kitchell shall have that parte of hers wholy at her owne disposing. And I doe make and appoint my son Samuell Wakeman and my son-in-law Samuell Kitchell to be joyntly executors of this my last will and testament. Allsoe I doe Intreate my beloved friends and bretheren Henry Glover and James Bishop to be overseers of this my will, and for thayr paines herein I give unto ech of them ten shillings. And I further desire my deare and loving sisters, my sister Davis and sister Glover, to asist my executors and overseers with thayr counsell and helpe in prizing, dividing and disposing things equally to mutuall satisfaction according to the true intent of this my will, which I publish with my hand this 18 day of the 4 month 1660 in the presence of

Martha Davis,   JOHN WAKEMAN.
Ellen Glover.

Page 26-7.

Watson, John, Hartford. Invt. £126-01-06. Taken 4 June, 1650, by John White, John Barnard. (Will dated 26 March, 1650.)

I John Watson doe ordayne this my last will & Testament: My debts being paid, my dwelling house and all my moveable goods I give and bequeth to my wife, and the use of my meadow & swamp till my son John Come to Twenty years of age; and my will is that She should bring up my Children; and my will is that my son John shall have my meadowe and swampe at that age afore mentioned. And further it is my will that my wife should paye to my Daughter sara five pound when she is Eighteen years of age, and to my Daughter Mary also five pound at Eighteen years of age. And further it is my will that my son John shall paye to his Mother five pound when he Come to his Land. And it is my will also that if any of my Children departe this life before they Come to the age that is before mentioned, that then the portion of that that dy shall be equally divided between them that are living. And my will is, in Case that my Children Should not be well Educated or not well used, then my overseers despose of them so as they may be brought up in the fear of God, and my wife to paye what shall be thought meete for the bringing of them up. And I ordayne my beloved friends John White & Gregory Wolterton to be overseers of this my will.

Witness: *John Moodie,*   JOHN X WATSON.
         Francis Barnard.

    Court Record, Page 9—6 June, 1650: Will & Invt. Exhibited.

Page 72.

Watts, Richard, Hartford. Invt. £114-17-06. Taken 20 March, 1654, by Richard Butler, Nathaniel Browne and James Ensign.

October the twentieth day, In the year of our Lord one Thousand Six hundred fifty three. I Richard Watts of Hartford, upon the River of Connecticut, beaing weak and ill in my body but in my perfect memory and understanding, Doe make and Ordain this my Last will and Testament in manner and form as ffolloweth:

Imprimis. It is my will that my wiff Elizabeth Watts shall possess and inioy my whole estate during the term of her natural lif. And alsoe I will and give unto my wiff fful power and Authority toe giv & despose at her own will & pleasure Twenty pounds off the estate I leave behind mee. The Resedu of my estate That Shall be remayneng after The death of my wiff It is my will that it be Equally Divided amongst the Children of my Daughter Hubbard & the child of my Daughter Browne, I mean the children now born & that then shall be living. Also I will & give to my Daughter Browne the whole Charge of her board & the board of her child, her husband & servant, ffrom the Time that her husband went ffrom her toward England Toe the Day of my Death, with all other moneys or charges that I have Disbursed ffor her use. That Thes my last Will and Testament be truly & ffaithfully performed, I make & ordayne my wif Elizabeth my Soal Exectrix, And intreat my loving friends Richard Butler and James Ensign to be overseers to this my will.

In Witness hereunto set my mark the day & year first above written.
In the presence of us: *Richard Butler,*   RICHARD X WATTS.
         James Ensign.

    Wee whose names are heer underwritten doe witness that Richard Wats in his last sickness whereof he dyed did express that it was his will that Hana, the Daughter of his Daughter Browne, should have a duble portion off the estate that is to be divided to the children expresst in his will.

Further we witness that it was his will that his son Thomas Wats, after the Death of Elizabeth the wif of the said Richard, should have & inioy as his fforever his three acre upland lott at the Town's End.

Richard Butler.
James Ensign.

Wakeley, Henry, Hartford.   Court Record, Page 7—15 May, 1650: Adms. to the Estate of his wive's other husband. Bond £50, which is left with Mr. Blakeman of Stratford for the payment of £20 to the two children.

Wakeley, James. Court Record, Page 40—1st Thursday in March, 1652-3: James Wakeley proved at this Courte by Samll Steele that the wife of the said James hath in the time of her widdowhood given a bond to Joseph Boosy of £100 forfeiture if shee ever married to James Wakeley.

Page 5—(Vol. III) 8 July, 1663: Ensign Samuel Steele & Alice Wakeley gave an Account of the Dispose & Improvement of the Estate of James Wakeley that was sequestered by order of the Courte. James Wakeley being present again, and this Court was well satisfied and do discharge the sd. Alice and Ensign Steele of the Trust committed to them, and hereby take off the Sequestration that this Court laid upon the Estate.

Page 93.

Webber, Richard, Wethersfield.   Invt. £16-14-07.   Taken 1st June, 1655, by Samuel Smith, Nathaniel Dickinson, with John Riley and John Hurlbut, Constables by appointment of the Governor.   Richard Webber was drowned at the landing place in Wethersfield.

Court Record, Page 68—7 June, 1665: John Ryly and John Hubbard of Wethersfield are appointed by this Court to secure the Estate of Richard Webber, Decd, and to be ready to give an account thereof when called upon, which Service they did accept.

Page 135.

Welles, Thomas, Wethersfield.   Invt. £1069-08-02.   Taken 30 January, 1659-60, by John Cotton & John Deming.   Will dated 7 November, 1659:

I Tho. Welles of Wethersfield, being in health of body but fynding the Symptoms of Mortality uppon me, am called to set in Order that little Estate comitted to me. As I have receaved what I am or have from the devine hand of allmighty God, so I comitte my soull to him, resting uppon his ffree grace and favor manifest through the Lord Jesus, and my body to a comely buriall. My will is that my wife should enjoy the on halfe of my houseing & Orchard & twelve pound pr annum out of my Estate during her life, she keeping the said houseing in Repair, and that the land wch I head of hers should return to her agayne; also I give her the bay mare & two kine, to be Sett forth by my Overseers, and that howsehold stuffe wch remaynes that was formerly hers, and the use of such Implements of household during the tyme she remaynes a wyddowe as my Overseers shall sett forth. Alsoe I give to my grandchild Robert Welles, the sonne of my sonne John diceased, the House & Lott I live uppon, wch I bought of Mr. Plume, & Pennywise to the cross fence on the south side, during his life, and wn he shall have attayned the age of one & twenty years, & after his Decease to his heirs for ever. And wheras ther yet remayneth a little household stuff wch I thought to have divided betwixt my Children, I now conceive yt more convenient that it remayne to my heire Robert Welles, he paying in convenient tyme, as my overseers shall find him able, Twenty pound apiece to my Children, viz., Tho. £20, Samuel £20, My daughter Mary's Children £20, Anne £20, & Sarah £20, & ten pound to my Cossen Robbins' Children. My just debts being first paid, I give my ffarme on the East side of the great River to be divided betwixt my sonne Samuel & my gran child Tho. Welles, sonne to my sonne John deceased; and I give to my sonne Tho. Welles my meadows and swamp in Pennywise on the north side the fence, and also that fower acres of Swamp wch I bought of Nath. Willett, & my upland on the East side the great River by Mr Hopkins ffarme, wth the ffence, having sold that wthhin the fence to Capten Cullick & given Six Rodde in breadth & the whole length to Ed. Andrews. And I desire my Loveing ffriends Mr John Talcoat & Mr Cotton, Techer att Wethersfield, to be overseers of this my will, & give them five pound apeece out of my Estate. And so long as my wife remaynes a widdow Shee may injoy & Improve my whole Estate if my overseers Findye yt meet, they (discharging) out of it my iust debts & takeing in the debts oweing to mee & manteining my heirs, in Lewe of her twelve pounds,—and that shee may keepe the better (words not readable.)

In witness to this my will I have hereunto sett my hand the day & yeare above written.

                                        THO. WELLES.

No witnesses.

The Will of Tho. Welles Esq. within spcified was exhibited and proved and ordered to be recorded 11 April, 1660. The Court doth iudge yt those words the ½ in reference to ye house should have relation to ye orchard likewise. Will Wadsworth and John Deming are appointed by the Court to Assist Mr. John Cotton as Supervisors of ye Will and Adms. to ye Estate of Mr. Thomas Welles Esq., and wt any two of them shall doe shall be accounted Authentick respecting the Execution of the Will of the sd. Esq. deceased. 11 April, 1660.

Daniel Clarke, Secretary.

Court Record, Page 153 (Vol. III) 7 Sept., 1676: Mrs. Welles petitioning this Court for some relief respecting what was allowed her by her husband, This Court order that Mr. Robert Welles doe set her part of her house in repayre according to the order of the General Court, & that what he hath damnyfyed her Barne by parting with the other part of the Barn that did adjoyn to it, he shall repayre, & make up the annuity of Twelve pounds Pr annum that By the will the sayd Mr. Welles is to pay his grand mother. He shall pay to her in wheat, pease & Indian Corn by equall proportion at prise Current. And the orchard Mr. Welles had Layd out to her by Mr. Wadsworth & Mr. Demmon as her part of the orchard, she is to possesse it according to his will, & is not to be molested in it by Mr. Robert Welles; & in case of blasting of wheat, then to pay some in porck.

Page 149.

Whelpsley, Henry. Invt. £280-10-03. Taken by Ephraim Wheeler, Michael Fry, Henry Rowland.

Court Record, Page 173—6 June 1662: This Court orders unto the Relict of Henry Whelpsley the sum of £300 of ye estate of her former husband Treadwell, and what is wanting in that is to be made up out of Whelpsley's estate. Also £20 more as widow to Whelpsley, and this to be effected by Mr. Hill, Cornelius Hull, Michael Fry and Alexander Knowles. And the rest of Whelpsley's estate to be divided amongst his children according to the discretion of those men who are impowered to administer to ye Estate and to dispose of the Children that are not under guardians.

Page 107.

White, William, Fairfield. Invt. £63-01-10. Taken 4 October, 1657, by Andrew Ward, Nathan Gould.

Court Record, Page 109—3 December, 1656: Adms. to Thomas Pell, he to husband the Estate as well as he may for the children, and to report when called for.

Page 92.

Whiting, Giles, Hartford. Invt. £26-15-06. Taken by Bartholemew Barnard, Richard Goodman. Giles Whiting, three days before he died, did in the presence of Edward Stebbing and William Lewis sen. make his last will in words as followeth: I bequeath or commit my soul into the hand of God, and my body to the earth, to be decently and Comely buried. My debts being discharged, I leave the remainder of my Estate to the dispose of my brother William Lewis, to himself and his Children at his discretion.

Page 1-2-3.

Wilcock, John, Hartford. Died 1st October, 1651. Invt. £391-03-00. Taken by John Talcott, Andrew Bacon, John Barnard. Will dated 24th July, 1651:

I John Wilcock of Hartford, upon the River of Connecticut, *payle maker,* being at this present of good memory and perfect senses, doe by this my Last will and Testament give and bequeath to Mary my wife the Sum of twenty pound, to bee paid in Corne, that is to say, forty bushels of wheat, thirty bushells of it in winter wheat and ten bushells in sumer wheat. Also twenty Bushells of Barlye and twenty Bushells of Rye and forty bushells of Indian Corne. Allso it is to be Cleane and Merchantable. Item. I give her my two young Cowes, Allso my best hogg at mattabeseck, Allso two of my best shoates at home; Also I give her my Colt, to be delivered Safe to her uppon May day next ensueing. If the said Colt shall in the meanetime miscarry, Shee shal have Six pounds paid her in stead thereof. Allso I give her my ould howse to dwell in, and that little Closett that is betweene the ould howse and the new howse, during the time of her Life, and my sonne is to keepe it in repairation. Allso I give her one third parte of all my fruite of both the orchards. Allso my will is that Shee should have wood enough for her expense Laid in the yard in Season, fitted for her to Lay on the fire, during the time of her Life. Allso I give her four pounds by the yeare, to bee paid one halfe of it uppon the 25 day of March and the other halfe to bee paid uppon the 29 day of September, during the time shee dwelleth in the howse; but if shee thinks good to leaue the howse and to remove her dwelling, or shall marry, then my will is that shee should allso leave the fruite and the wood, and that she should have six pound paid her by the yeare in manner as aforesaid. Allso I give to my wife the Bedd I Lye upon with all thinges belonging to it as it is furnished, as allso my Linnen except one paire of sheets, as allso my pew, to dispose of as shee pleases. Allso I give to her all my hempe and flaxe, both spun into yarne and unspun, and all that I have growing this yeare, and all my woollen Cloth and stockings that is not otherwise disposed of. Allso my will is that my wife shall give my servant Samuell two suites of Apparrell and all other Convenience according to his Indenture when his time expires. Allso I give her one heive of Bees and all my fowles and all my sugar, honye, spice and Siluer and wamppeage. Allso my will is that, during the time of her widdowhood and dwelling in the howse, shee shall have the use of all my household stuff that is not allready disposed of. Item. I give to my daughter Ann Hall £20 and one remnant of grey cloath and my Long Coate, ten pounds to bee paid the first day of December next, the other ten pounds to be paid uppon the 24th day of June next. Item. I give to my daughter Sarah Biddell my mare and two working stears, Allso a Carte & a plowe with a share and Coulter & a plowe eare, provided that my wife may have the mare for her owne use to ride either to Windsor, to Wethersfield, or to Hartford, or to The Sermon, for the space of two years, and to this end I give my wife my pannell and Bridle. Allso It is my will that my s'onn John Willcock shall provide Stover for the wintering of the two Stears and the mare given to Sarah Biddell. Item. I give to John Biddell's Children forty pounds, to be paid at the death of my wife, equally to be devided amongst so many of Sarah Biddell's Children as then shall be living. Allso I give to Ann Hall twenty pounds more, to be paid at the death of my wife to my daughter Ann Hall, to her Children if shee have any then living; but if shee be dead and leave no Issue, then my will is that ten pounds be paid to John Hall her husband if he be then Living, and the other ten pounds to John Biddell's Children, to be Equally divided amongst them. Ffurther my will is that my wife should at her death give to Sarah Willcock, the daughter of my sonne John Willcock, the sum of five and twenty pounds'. Allso my will is that my maide Elizabeth Wakeman shall serve out the remainder of her Apprenticship with my wife, and that my wife performe all Ingagements to her according to Indentures, and when her time is expired to give her twenty shillings. Item. I give and bequeath to John Willcock, my sonn, my debts and Legacies being paid, all the rest of my goods and Lands unbequeathed, whom of this my prsent Testament I make and ordaine my whole Executor. In Witness whereof I have Sett to my hand and Seale the day and yeare above written. I desire that Andrew Bacon and John Barnard would stand my ffriends and see my will prformed.

Witness: *Andrew Bacon, John Bernard,*   JOHN X WILLCOCK.
            Geo. Grave.

Page 159.

Willey, Isaac, Pequett. Invt. £73-09-06. Taken 1st September, 1662, by Obadiah Bruen, John Smith.

Court Record, Page 178—2 September, 1662: Adms. to the widow. Invt. Exhibited.

Page 97.

Wilson, Robert, Farmington. Invt. £173-07-00. Taken 3 June, 1656, by Edward Stebbing, John Menard. Children: John Wilson, 6 years old; Samuel, 3 years old.

Page 180.

Wolcott, Christopher, Windsor. Died 7 September, 1662. Invt. £372-07-00. Taken 22 September, 1662, by Walter Fyler and Matthew Grant.

Will Nuncupative. As expressed was, that his estate should be divided among his Brothers and Sisters, only that Henry should have something more than the others.

Witness: *Lt. Walter Fyler and William Pitkin.*

Court Record, Page 181—4 December, 1662: Will and Invt. Exhibited. This Court allows Henry Wolcott £18 more than any of the other Legatees, the rest of the estate to be equally divided to the Legatees.

Page 61 (Vol. V) 7 September, 1693: The Estate of Christopher Wolcott Dec. left with his Mother to pay the debts and keep the rest herself, the Lands to be distributed to his brothers and sisters.

Page 79.

Wolcott, Mrs. Elizabeth, Windsor. Will dated 5 July, 1655: I Elizabeth Wolcott doe make and ordain this my last Will and Testament in manner and form following: Imprimis. I will yt my sonn George shall have £5 worth of my part of ye household goods and £5 worth of my cloathes. Allsoe I give unto Simon my Sonne ye bluewish stuff hee bought for me ye last yeare. I give ye rest of my household goods to be equally divided betwixt Christover and Simon, my Sonnes. Allsoe I give ye rest of my cloathes to be equally divided betwixt my two daughters Anne and Mary Allyn. I would intreat Christover to lett Simon to dwell in ye house and to have ye use of halfe of it a while. Allsoe I give my two Cowes to be equally devided among all my Grand Children. Moreover my will is yt whereas I have appointed my part of ye household Goods to be devided betwixt Christover and Simon, except £5 to George, now my Will is yt it shall soe Stand upon yt Condition yt Christover and Simon doe release their parts of ye Household Goods, or else there shall bee soe much taken out of this as their parts of ye rest of ye Goods comes to.

Witness: *John Witchfield.*   Elizabeth X Wolcott.

On the 4th of October (55) ye above written was approved by ye Courte and ordered yt it should bee recorded by ye Secr.

Page 181-2.

Wolcott, George, Wethersfield. Invt. £207-11-05. Taken 12 February, 1662, by Richard Treat and Henry Wolcott.

The 19th of January, 1662, I George Wolcott, weak of Body but of perfect memory, do make & ordayne this my last Will & Testament in manner & forme following: Imprs. My Will is that Elizabeth my wife shall have my Houseing & Land at Wethersfield during the terme of her natural life, she keeping the Houseing & Fences in good repair; also my Will is that my sonne George shall have the sd. Houseing & Lands after the decease of my wife, he paying unto the rest of my Children so much as he shall receive of my psonal Estate by this Will, upon Condition that he carry himself orderly and well, which payment shall be made by £5 per Annum, beginning immediately after the decease of my wife; but if he carry himself disorderly, then my Will is that my sonne John shall have the sd. Houseing & Lands, paying out of it to the rest of my Children as my sonne George should have done, he carrying himselfe orderly & well; and this I leave to be determined betwixt them by my Overseers. Also I give unto Elizabeth my eldest daughter £10 more than unto my youngest daughter. Also I give all the rest of my Estate to be equally divided among all of my Children, George, John, Elizabeth & Mercy. Also my Will is that each of my Children shall receive their several portions as soon as they shall be married or accomplish the age of 21 years. Also my Will is that the benefit of the Improvement of all my Estate, besides my Houseing & Land, shall be for the Use of my Children.

Witness: *John Deming,*   GEORGE WOLCOTT.
       Thomas Atwood.

Also I make my Brother Henry Wolcott Overseer.

Witness: *John Deming,*   GEORGE WOLCOTT.
       Thomas Atwood.

Court Record, Page 182—6 March, 1662-3: Will & Invt. exhibited. Page 130—(Vol. IV) 23 April, 1687: Gabriel Cornish, who married Elizabeth the daughter of George Wolcott Decd, declared in Court that he did not know how he could come at his wive's portion, there being no Adms. now living, and therefore this Court appoint Return Strong & William Hosford to Adms. upon the Estate, and with Mr. Henry Wolcott to divide the Estate to the Children of sd. George Wolcott, and the portion that falls to Mercy Wolcott to be put into the hands of Samuel Butler and Joseph Churchill to improve for her advantage, she being incapable herself. Page 25—(Vol. V) 5 March, 1690-1: Whereas the Estate of George Wolcott hath layen undisposed, this Court, that there may be an Issue to the same, do desire and appoint Mr. John Wolcott of Windsor to administer upon the Estate and to pay to the Children their portions as soon as can be, according to the last Will of sd. Wolcott.

Page 77.

Woolcott, Henry Sen., Windsor. Invt. £764-08-10. Taken 30 June, 1655, by William Gaylord, Thomas Ford, Matthew Grant, John Moore. Will dated 13 May 1655:

I henry Woolcott, sick of body but of prfect memory, doe make and ordaine this my last will and testament in manner and forme as ffollowing: Ffirst, I comend my soule to God my maker, hoping assuredly through ye only merit of Jesus Christ my savior to bee made pr taker of life everlasting, and I comend my Body to ye earth whereof it was made. It. I will yt my wife shall have all my house lott, orchard, garden, hopyard, and my lott in plimouth meadow, during ye tearme of her life. Alsoe I give unto my wife two of my Cowes and halfe of my household goods in my dwelling house. Alsoe I leave my land in England to Henry, my Eldest sonn, without encumbrances. Alsoe I give unto him my two Books of Marters. Alsoe I give to Christopher, my second sonn, my lott in ye great meadow after my death, And my house lott and housing upon it after ye death of my wife, he paying out of it thirtie pounds after my wifes deceased as I shall further appoint. Allsoe I give to George, my third sonn, the five pounds hee owes mee and five pounds more. Allsoe I give to Simon, my youngest sonne, all my land on ye easterly side of the great River and my lott att Arrammetts. Allsoe to the children of Henry, my Eldest sonne, five pounds to Henry ye eldest of ym, and to ye rest of ym fortie shillings a peece. Allsoe I give all ye rest of my goods to bee equally devided amongst all my children. Allsoe I appoint Henry Wolcott, my sonne, to be overseere of this my last will and testament. Allsoe my will is yt Christover, my sonne, shall have my lott in plimouth meadow after ye decease of my wife. Allsoe my will is yt my debts should bee first paid.

October 4, 1655: ye above written being testified to ye Court by mr Henry Wolcott upon oath, and by Mr. Witchfield, to be ye last will and Testament of Mr. Woolcott senior deceased, the Courte approved of ye same and ordered it to be recorded.

John Cullick, Secr.

VOLUME III.

1663 to 1677.

This is the Third Book of the Records
of the Acts of the County Courts and
Courts of Probates in the County of
Hartford, and of Wills and Inventories.

No. 3.

PROBATE RECORDS.

VOLUME III.

1663 to 1677.

Page 79.

Adams, John, Hartford. Died 6 September, 1670. Invt. £74-15-06. Taken 9 November, 1670, by Jonathan Gilbert, Nathan Willett, Siborn Nichols. The children: Rebeckah age 12 years August last, Abigail 11 next February, Sarah 9 March next, Jeremy 6 August last, John 4 September last, Jonathan 2 November last. One yet unborn.

Court Record, Page 103—9 October, 1670: Invt. Exhibited. Adms. to the Widow. John Talcott and Jeremie Addams were desired by the Court to be overseers and to dispose of the Children.

Page 84.

Allyn, Matthew, Windsor. Invt. £466-17-02. Taken 14 February, 1670-1, by Daniel Clarke & Richard Lord. The House and Lands in Windsor not Inventoried because by a Deed of Gift it was made over to Thomas Allyn by Mr. Matthew Allyn at the Marriage of the sd. Thomas Allyn, to be to him & his heirs forever after the death of sd. Mr. Matthew Allyn and Margaret his wife. Prised by Daniel Clarke & Richard Lord. Also a further Invt. of Land & Stock in Kenilworth, valued at £120-00-00, and Land at Ketch prised at £40-00-00.

Will: I Matthew Allyn of the town of Windsor, in the Colony of Connecticut, being at prsent through the tender mercy of God, though weak in body, of good memory & have the use of my understanding as at other times, am desirous to attend the counsell of the prophett in setting my house in order that soe I may with the more Freedom wayte the good pleasure of god whose I am & in whome I doe desire forever to hope, wayte and rejoice; & into the Armes of his mercy I desire to render my soule, & my body to christian Buriall according to the discresion of my children; & for that estate that god hath blest me withall, I doe give & bequeath it as hereafter exprest:

I make my beloved wife my sole executrix of this my Last will & Testament. Imprs: I doe give all the estate that I now stand posest of, both Lands & Cattell & household stuffe, to my deare & well beloved wife margarett Allyn, to be & belong to her during her naturall life, my just debts being first payd; & I desire my sons, John Allyn & Thomas Allyn, & Benjamin Newbery, to improve the same for her comfort; & I command them to be carefull in provideing for her comfortable maintenance as Long as she shall live. And after the decease of my dear & well beloved wife I give unto my beloved sonn John Allyn & his heirs forever, all my Lands & estate lying & being within the Bounds of the towneship of Kenilworth, In the county of New London; I say both the Farme & Stock upon it that is in the hands of my Tennants. I also hereby confirme & ratify to him & his heirs forever all my Land in Hartford that I gave to him as his Marriage portion & which formerly hath bin recorded to him; & after the decease of my wife I give unto my well beloved sonn Thomas Allyn the one halfe of my Farme of Land at Ketch, & neare to Ketch, only out of his halfe I give unto my beloved grand child Matthew Allyn one Hundred Acres of Land whereof twenty Acres shall be meadow; I doe now hereby rattify & confirm the same to him agayn: I likewise give him my tables & stooles that belong to the house, as allso the cupboards.

I doe likewise, after the decease of my beloved wife, give unto my beloved sonn and daughter Benjamen & Mary Newbery & their heirs forever, the one halfe of my Farme of Land at Ketch & near to Ketch, only out of his halfe I give unto my beloved grand child Mary Maudsley & her heirs for ever, fifty Acres of Land whereof Tenn Acres shall be meadow; I give unto Mary Griffin, if she continue her service wth me & my wife till we decease, Forty shillings besides her wages; I give unto John Indian one suit of my cloathes, my sonns to appoynt which; my just debts & Legacies being payd, the remaynder of my estate I give & bequeath to my sonns John & Thomas Allyn & my daughter Mary Newbery, to be equally divided Between them, each of them to have a third part as before, which third parte shall belong to them & their heirs forever.

Finally, I command my children that they be loveing, kind & helpfull one unto another, & that they walke in the fear of God that he may be with them & bless them when I shall be gathered to my Fathers. And that this is my Last Will & Testament, hereby renounceing all former Wills & Testaments that I have made by writeing or word of mouth, & rattifying this, I declare by subscribeing hereto this thirtyeth of January, 1670.

MATTHEW ALLYN.

This was signed & declared to be the last Will & Testament of Mr. Matthew Allyn by himselfe at his house in Windsor the 30th January, 1670.

Witness: *Henry Wolcott sen.,*
Daniel Clarke, Joseph Haynes.

Court Record, Page 107—2 March, 1670-1: Will proven.

Page 91.

Allyn, William, Branton, England, who deceased in his return from Salt Tortudas to Connecticut. Will: I William Allyn of Branton, England, near to Barnstable, County of Devon, being at present at the Island of Salt Tortoodus in the Ship Mary and Elizabeth of Hartford, in New England, my Estate in the Town of Branton I bequeath to my wife Elizabeth during her life, and after her decease this, with all other Estate, to be equally divided to my Children then living, to John, to George, to Joane and Elizabeth. I desire Mr. Giles Hamlin of Middletown and Mr. John Blackleach of Hartford to be Overseers.

Court Record, Page 113—3 June, 1671: An Inventory of the Estate of William Allyn, Boat Swaine of the Ship Mary and Elizabeth, of Hartford, was now exhibited in Court. Mr. John Blackleach, Adms., who is desired to present the sd. Allyn's last Will in Court September next in Case the evidence can be produced who heard him make his Will: Page 114—7 September, 1671: Will proven.

Page 114.

Andrews, Edward. Invt. £265-12-00. Taken 22 September, 1673, by Thomas Bull, Steven Hopkins & Robert Webster.

I, Edward Andrews, Being weak in body yet having good understanding & memorie, doe make this my last will & testament. First, I committ my soule into the hand of Jesus christ, desireing that my body may have comely Buriall. And for the dissposall of that outward estate which God hath given me, my will is that my just debts be first payd, & the remaynder of my whole estate I leave unto my loveing wife for her use & Comfort & to disspose it to my children as Shee and my overseers shall see fitt, as they shall come to age and ability & may consist with her Comfort, only I give to my Brother Josiah Adkins Tenn acres of the Land I bought of Wm. Howlton the North side of it, which shall be to his children which were the children of my Sister. The Ten acres I desire may be layd seven or eight rods wide, & if my Brother see cause he may improve thirty Acres more of my Land Lyeing by that which I give to him & his children, which thirty acres, after the death of my sayd Brother, shall return to my children. My will is that my wife shall be Executrix, & I desire Lt. Thomas Bull & Robert Webster to be overseers.

Witness: *Gershom Bulkeley,*   EDWARD ANDREWS. Ls.
William Goodwine.

Signed: 23 July, 1673.
Court Record, Page 134—25 November, 1673: Will approved.

Page 10.

Arnold, John, Hartford. Invt. £105-10-00. Taken 26 December, 1664, by Thomas Bull & Edward Stebbing. Will dated 22 August, 1664.

I John Arnold of Hartford, uppon the river of Conecticut, being very aged & weak in body & in a dayle expectation of my change from henc, Doe make and Ordain this my last will and testament in manner and fforme as ffolloweth: Imprimis. I give unto my Dear and loveing wife Susana Arnold the sole & ffull use of my now Dwelling hows and howse lott, the barne & all Appurtenances belonging to the aforesaid premises, during the ffull term off her naturall life; alsoe my two kowes. Item. I give my wif to be for her use & at her own dispose all my wearing cloathes, my beds & bedding, with all other my houshold goods, my said wife paying or causeing to be paid such Legacies as I shall heere bequeath unto my Dear and Loving children, viz: I give unto my son Josiah Arnold one cowe and my two acres of Land in the clayboard swamp, after the death of my wife, & my other upland lott neer the townes End. If my son Joseph Arnold Returne to Dwell again in Hartford within two yeares after the date heeroff, I give the one halfe of the said Lott to him and his heirs forever; the other part of it I give to my son Daniell & his heirs forever. Item. I give unto my son Daniell, after the decease off my fore said wife, my now dwelling house, houselott & Barne, with all Appurtenances there unto belonging. My will is that if my son Daniell shall live and be marred & have a child or children, that the fore said premises shall be to him and his heirs for ever; But if he shall mary and dye without issue my will is that his wife shall Enjoy the foresaid premises during her naturall lif, and after her Discease my will is that all those premises I have heerin given to my son Daniell Shall be the estate of my son Joseph Arnold & his heirs for ever. Item. I give unto my dear, loving gr. child Mary Buck ffourty shillings, to be paid at her adge of eighteen yeares or within one full yeare after the decease of my fore said wif. That this my last will & Testament be truly performed, I entreat my loveing brethren Edward Stebbing and Leiftenant Bull to be Overseers hereunto. In witness whereof I have hereunto subscribed my name this two & twentieth day off August, 1664.   JOHN ARNOLD.

Witness hereunto: *James Ensign.*
                 Thomas Bull.

Court Record, Page 26—2 March, 1664-5: Will approved.

Inventory on File.

Atherton, Humphrey, Major. Invt. £283-15-00. Taken 3 April, 1673, by Samuel Wilson, Thomas Mumford & George Crofts. Invt. of what we find in the Narragancett Countrey:

	£	s	d
160 Acres of land upon Boston Neck valued at in this Country pay,	200-00-00		
160 acres of land in Quienesett at	021-00-00		
2 Oxen,	012-00-00		

7 Cowes,	030-00-00
1 old horse, 1 old plow & plow Irons, 1 Chain for a plow,	005-12-00
2 pitch forckes,	000-03-00
2 Bulls, two heifers,	011-00-00
3 earelings, 2 cow calves, & one steere,	004-00-00
	283-15-00

The apprisement of the abouementioned Estate is valued at £283-15-00 at this Country pay of this Colony of Rhode Island & Providence plantation & kings province.

This is a true copy of the original Invt.   Attest: Weston Clarke, Clerk.

Court Record, Page 133—2 September, 1673: This Court grant Adms. on the Estate of Major Atherton unto Jonathan Atherton upon all the Estate that may be found in this Colony; also upon the estate of Mr. Increase Atherton, Late of Dorchester, upon such of his as shall be found in this Colony.   Provided that the Land formerly belonging unto the sayd Major Atherton within this Colony shall be responsible to answer and make good claymes against the estate.   Captain Atherton being the Eldest Brother of Mr. Increase Atherton aforesaid.

Page 141—2 July, 1674: Adms. asks to be discharged from his Bond, as he is to go speedily out of the Country.

Page 143—3 September, 1674: Mr. Hope Atherton & Mr. Timothy Mather informing this Court by their letter to the Governor & Secretary that Capt. Jonathan Atherton, Adms. to the Estate of the Hon. Major Atherton, hath not paid their proportion of the Estate left by their Father in this Colony, & no person appearing to demand & take up the security, this Court see not sufficient ground to release the security.

Page 49.

Backus, William, Norwich. Invt. £102-00-00. Taken 7 June, 1664, by Thomas Leffingwell, John Burchard.

	£ s d
The house & homelot with a prcell of Land lying over the river,	27-10-00
A prcell of Land in the Little Plaine,	05-00-00
A prcell of Land in the Great Plaine,	03-00-00
a prcell of Meadow at Yantick,	02-15-00
another prcell at Boggy Medow,	02-10-00
a prcell of upland medow in the second division,	09-10-00
two oxen,	14-00-00
two cowes & one Calfe,	08-00-00
one steare,	02-00-00
Cart & wheeles & plow & a chaine,	02-00-00
for a beetle & wedges, howes, an axe & a spade & a hatchet,	01-06-00

two sithes & two sickles,	00-08-00
two pease hooks & a Cart rope,	00-05-00
one paire of sheetes,	00-14-00
one paire more of sheetes,	00-11-00
one sheete more,	00-07-00
one sheete more,	00-16-00
one table cloath,	00-04-00
one pillow beare,	00-05-00
one old pillow beare,	00-01-00
a remnant of kersy,	00-08-00
a chest,	00-04-00
a old brass pot,	00-02-00
two firkins, a barrel & a churne,	00-07-00
a tub & a hogshead,	00-06-00
a chest,	00-12-00
one rugg for a bed,	01-10-00
a bed ticking, three blankets, a boulster & a pillow,	04-04-00
fower blankets, one sheete & a boulster,	04-00-00
two spinning wheeles,	00-10-00
two kettles, a pott & skillett,	01-05-00
a fryingpan, a smoothing iron & a skimmer,	00-07-00
one porruger, a lamp & three spoones,	00-05-00
one glass bottle & a stone bottle,	00-02-06
bowels, trayes, dishes, & a basting Ladle,	00-07-06
two siues & a halfe bushell,	00-07-00
a table leafe & a paile,	00-06-00
a gun & a sword,	01-16-00
a chest & trammell,	00-09-06
wearing cloathes,	05-00-00
Cutlers tooles & ivory,	04-00-00

Page 33-4.

Baldwin, Richard, Milford. Invt. £420-15-00 net. Taken 28 September, 1665, by Robert Treat, William Fowler.

Court Record, Page 56—16 October, 1666—The Magistrates Order Dist. to the Relict, £150-00-00; to Silvanus, Eldest son, £70; to each of the other children, £36, at legal age or at their marriage.

Note: This Inventory appears on File, giving the names of the Children which are not found with recorded Invt.: An Inventory of the Goods and Chattells of the late Richard Baldwin of Milford, decd, apprised by us, Robert Treat, William Fowler, this twentie eight day of September, 1665, as followeth: Total Inventory, £420-15-00 (net). The names and ages of the Children: Nathaniel, age 19 years, Sarah 17, Temperance 15, Mary 12, Theophilus 8, Zakaryah 5, Barnabas, ¾ years old. Dist. was ordered the 6th of October, 1666. (Sylvanus?)

Page 22.

Baldwin, Timothy, Milford. Invt. £529-18-06. Taken 6th February, 1664, by Alexander Bryant, George Clarke sen, John Clarke. Will dated 31 January, 1664-5: I Timothy Baldwin of Milford do make this my last Will and Testament: I give to my eldest daughter Mary Smith, the wife of Benjamin Smith, Lands adjoyning Samuel Buckingham and John Lane. Item. I give to my daughter Hannah Baldwin £50. Item. I give to my daughter Sarah Buckingham £50. Item. I give to my son Timothy Baldwin all my houses, Lands and Meadows Lying in Milford that is undisposed of, to enter upon, but two thirds thereof until after the decease of my wife. I give to my three grand children, to each of them, a ewe sheep. Item. I give unto John Mappam, my wive's son, £4 upon this condition, if he be obediant to his mother and carry dutifully towards her. Item. I give unto our Honor Paster, Mr. Newton, £5. I doe give unto my servant Jeremie Andros one sheep when his time is out, to what I have already promised him to be paid by my executrix, in case he carry dutifully to his Dame. I constitute my wife sole executrix, and doe give and bequeath unto her al ye rest of my estate undisposed of, and the Improvement of al my houses, Lands and meadows, till my son Timothy come to ye age of twenty one years. My will is that my son Timothy should be brought up in learning, that he be taught to read and write well. I desire that Mr. Benjamin Fenn, Deacon Clarke, George Clarke Jr. and Samull Coley be overseers.

Witness: *George Clarke, Sen.,*   TIMOTHY BALDWIN, Ls.
George Clarke, Jr.

Exhibited and Proved in ye Court at Milford, 2 March, 1664-5.

Page 104.

Banbury, Justes. (No Inventory.) Will dated 30 November, 1672. The last Will of Justes Banbury: First, I give my Soule to the Lord Jesus Christ, my Redeemer. It. For that Estate that I have to dispose of, I give to my daughter Plumbe my feather bed, to Elizabeth Plumbe my silk Cap, to my daughter Butler my Cloath Gowne & my blew watered one, & to Hanna butler my silkewhood, & Fower payer of shoes, two payre to my daughter plumbe, & two payre to my daughter Butlers children, & each of them a payre of stockings, & to Debora Green my Bedsted, all that to it excepting my bed, & my trunck & my box & all that is in them, my wareming pann, a chamber pott & an iron skillett & my stuffe gowne & my chair, my smoothing iron, my tongs & fire shovel, & Candle Stick; & for the five pound that Joseph Green gave me, I give 20 Shillings of it to Mr. John Whiting, & the rest of it shall be to pay for my Honourable Burial.

Witness: *Gregory Winterten,*   JUSTES X BANBURY.
Jane Winterton.

Court Record, Page 129—6 March, 1672-3: Will proven.

Page 157.

Bartlett, Edward, Windsor. Died at Westfield. Invt. £39-10-00.
Taken 11 April, 1676, by Christopher Crow, Matthew Grant, Jacob Drake.
Will dated 24 February, 1675: I Edward Bartlett of Windsor, being
called forth upon Service for God and the Country, My House in Greenfield, Money due from James Hillier, and all the rest of my Estate, I give
to Benoni Crow, son of Christopher Crow of Symsbury, only my young
bay Horse to Josiah Clarke.

Witness: *Josiah Clarke,*   EDWARD BARTLETT.
Matthew Grant, Jacob Drake.

Court Record, Page 152—12 April, 1676: Will & Invt. Exhibited.
Adms. to Christopher Crow.

(P. C., Vol. I, No. 125.)

Bartlett, Robert, New London. Will of Robert Bartlett of New
London, taken from his own mouth 1st June, 1674:
Robert Bartlett did then express it was his will to give his hous &
house lott & his farme lying up the River to the use of a free schoole to
be kept in the towne, according to what he had declared to Symon Bradstreet, Danill Wetherell & Joshua Raymond, May 27, '74, & desired it
should be so recorded; & did Commit the mannadgement thereof to Edward Palmes, Simon Bradstreet, Daniel Wetherell, Charles Hill, Joshua
Raymond. Edward Palmes, in discourse with the sd. Robert Bartlett,
said: "Robert, I understand you have given the remainder of your estate
to Mr. Rogers & Gabriel Harris." The sd. Robert replied he had not
given away one penny. The sd. Palmes enquired of him what he intended
to doe with the rest of his estate. Robert answered it must be to pay his
debts & burie him, wch he desired should be decently done. Edward
Palmes asked him whome he committed that trust to. Robert replied,
"You five," mentioning the persons above named, and desired that Mr
Rogers & Gabriel Harris should be fully satisfied for what they had done
for him. The sd. Palmes askt him what should be done with the rest of
his estate when his debts were paid & the charge of his funeral satisfied,
if any remained. Robert replied, "I leave it to you." The sd. Palmes
askt, "How would you have it disposed of?" Robert replied, "To some
good use." The sd Palmes asked, "For what good use?" Robert replied,
"Let it goe with the rest."
                    Edward Palmes,
                    Symon Bradstreet,
                    Daniel Witherell.

We whose names are subscribed doe further testify that, being with
Robert Bartlett May 27 ('74), the sd. Robert said he intended his money
given to the setting up of a free schooll which should be for the maintain-

ing of poore children, and that they should be brought up there to learn Latine.

Symon Bradstreet,
Dan Witherell,
Joshua Raymond.

VERA COPIA.

Extracted out of the County records for New London County, & Compared this 11th of March, 1680-81.   Pr me JNO BIRCHARD,
                                                                                Clarke.

Page 118.

Bayse, Elizabeth, Hartford. Invt. £60-14-00. Taken 13 December, 1673, by Stephen Hopkins & George Graue. Will not dated.

I Elizabeth Bayse, being by the Providence of god very wecke but of sound understanding, do make this my last will & testament: I do give to my daughter elizabeth peck my 2 Cushions that was my husband's, in Consideration of her Care & Trouble of mee in my sickness. The rest of my Estate I give to my three daughters, Mary Burr, Lydia Baker and Elizabeth Peck, equally to be divided amongst them.

Witness: George Grave,   ELIZABETH BAYSE, LS.
         Stephen Hopkins.

Court Record, Page 135—15 December, 1673: Will & Invt. exhibited by Samuel Burr and Paul Peck.

Page 94-97.

Basey, John, Hartford, Weaver. Invt. £383-02-06. Taken 29 August, 1671, by Richard Butler, Nicholas Olmsted, George Grave, Jr. Will dated 14 August, 1671.

In the name of God, Amen. I John Baysey of Hartford, in the Colony of Connecticut, in New England—Weaver—being at this present weak in Body but of sound memory and good understanding, considering my own frailty, I have made and ordained this my last will and testament in manner and form following: That is to say, first of all I commit my soul into the hands of Allmighty God, my Creator and preserver, when it shall please him to call for the same out of this transitory Life, and my Body to comely Christian Buriall, in ashured hope of the blessed resurection of the same at the Last day. And as for that portion of worldly goods and Estate that it hath pleased God to Lend mee here for a time, I doe by this my Last will and testament dispose thereof as followeth: First, my will is that all my just debts due from mee to any person or persons whatsoever bee duely discharged and paid out of my personal estate, and that my funeral expenses bee in like manner paid out of my estate.

Item. I give and Bequeath unto my grand son Paul Peck my peice of
upland, being about fower acres, Lying Between Land of Thomas Cattlyn
and Goodman Bacon, as allso my division or part of the upland on the
East side of the great river, to bee his and his heirs for ever after my decease.

Item. I give unto my grandson Joseph Baker my wood Lott, being
about Seventeen acres, Lying between Thomas Bunce his land and Joseph
Eason his Land, to bee his and his heirs for ever after my decease, reserving only to my Beloved wife Elizabeth Basey the use thereof for any fuell
or timber that is there, during the term of her natural Life, and to all my
daughters the use thereof for fuell or timber till such time as it comes to
bee inclosed and otherwise improved.

Item. I give unto my Grandson John Baker my little pasture, beeing
about three acres, Lying neer my son Baker's house, to bee to him and his
heirs for ever after the decease of my daughter Lydia Baker, to whom I
doe give the improvement of it after my decease during her naturall Life.

Item. I give unto my son-in-law John Baker my Loom, with all the
tackling Belonging to it, after my decease.

Item. I give unto my Beloved wife Elizabeth Basey my dwelling
house and House Lott with the Barn and all the Appurtenances, as allso
all my meadow and swamp Land in the South meadow, as allso my
p (   )art of six acres near the towns End, during the term of her natural
Life; and I doe give unto my said wife a third part of all the prese(nt)
corn that shall bee at the time of my decease, and doe except that from being any part in paying any debts or funeral charges. I doe give her one
third part in value of all the moveables, Cattell or other personall estate,
that shall bee Left, to bee at her owne dispose for ever, and shee to have
her choice out of all for that third part.

Item. I give to my eldest daughter Mary Burr my dwelling house,
Barn, house Lott, and all their apurtenances, for ever after the decease of
her mother, and after my said daughter's decease to descend to her child
or children all of them, and so to bee divided that her sons shall have
equal shares therein; and if shee leave any daughter or daughters, then
the division so to bee made that a daughter's part shall bee half so much
as a son's part.

Item. I give unto my daughter Lydia Baker (besides the little pasture mentioned before) one full half of all my meadow and swamp Land
in the South meadow, and shee to have the northermost half, that is to say,
after the decease of her mother, during her Life time, and after her decease to descend to her children surviving her, to bee divided amongst
them in the same proportion as is fore mentioned concerning my daughter
Burr her children.

Item. I give the other halfe of my meadow and swamp Land in the
South meadow to my daughter Elizabeth Peck after the decease of her
mother, and after the decease of my said daughter it shall descend to and
bee divided amongst her children surviving, by the same rule and proportion as is mentioned concerning my daughters aforesaid.

Item. I doe make and constitute my Beloved wife Elizabeth Baysey to bee sole Executrix. I doe desire Mr. Richard Butler and Joseph Easton to bee overseers of this my Last will, and in case of their decease, then my friends George Grave Jr. and Stephen Hopkins to bee overseers in their stead.

Witness: *Steven Hopkins,*　　　　　　　　JOHN BAISIE, Ls.
　　　　(Erased signature　　　　) enior.
　　　　William Pitkin.

Court Record, Page 115—7 September, 1671: Will proven.

Page 191.

Belding, John, Wethersfield. Invt. £911-05-07. Taken 30 August, 1677, by James Treat, John Deming, Samuel Wright. The children: John, age 19 years; Jonathan 16, Joseph 14, Samuel 11, Daniel 7, Ebenezer 4, Sarah 9, Lydia 2, & Margaret 5 months.

Page 12—(Vol. IV)—6 March, 1678-9: This Court being moved to make Dist. of the Estate of John Belding, Decd:

	£	s	d
To the Widow, of Personal Estate,	100-00-00		
To the Eldest son,	148-00-00		
To the five younger sons, to each of them,	80-00-00		
To the three daughters, to each of them,	64-00-00		

And appoint Gershom Bulkeley & Mr. Eleazr Kimberly Dist. and Overseers.

Page 26—21 April, 1680: Report of the Distributors.

Page 102—(Vol. V)—30 March, 1696: Nathaniel Boman, Adms., renders account wherein it appears that £4-04-06 is still due to Lydia Belden, and 10 Shillings to Margaret Belden.

Page 108—15 April, 1696: This Court orders paid to Nathaniel Borman, for his pains as Adms. on the Estate of John Belden, £4-12-00 from Daniel Belden's Estate which lyes in part of his Father's house lott. This Court appoints Mr. John Chester Jr. & Daniel Rose to apprise and lay out to Mr. Borman, and appoints Jonathan Belden to pay his Bill of £8-15-00 in Good Wheat and Indian Corn, in equal proportions, to Mr. Boman.

Dist. File, 1680—Estate of John Belden—To the Widow, to John, to Jonathan, to Joseph, to Samuel, to Daniel, to Ebenezer, by Gershom Bulkeley & Eleazer Kimberly.

Page 46—(Vol. VI)—4 October, 1697: This Court orders Jonathan Belding, Adms., to pay to Lydia Kellogg & Margaret Kellogg from their Father Belding's Estate.

Page 81-82.

Benjamin, Samuel, Hartford. Invt. £98-19-00. Taken by Nathaniel Ruscoe, Stephen Hopkins. Will (Nunc.).

Testimony of Thomas Atwood, age about 60 years, and Thomas Edwards, age about 47 years, given 10 November, 1670: That being with Samuel Benjamin at Hoccanom a little before his death, about 18 September, 1669, we heard him say: "I give unto my loveing wife Mary Benjamin all my whole estate to dispose of at her discretion. I make my brother Caleb Benjamin Overseer."

Witness: *Thomas Atwood,*
          Thomas Edwards.

Court Record, Page 103—9 November, 1670: The Widow engaged to pay to Mary & Abigail, Children of the sd. Samuel Benjamin, £10 a peice at the age of 18 years. Adms. is granted to the Widow.

———————

Page 137-138.

Berding, Nathaniel, Hartford. Died 14 September, 1674. Inventory, £282-15-10. Taken by Paul Peck, George Grave, Caleb Stanly. Will dated 7 January, 1673.

I Nathaniel Berding of Hartford, upon the River of Conecticott, planter, doe in this my last will & testament give unto Abigail my wife the sume of Twenty pownds to be payd her in such pay as may be comfortable for her, not in any horss Flesh. I doe allso give to Abigall my wife Three cowes, both which gifts for her to possesse & Injoy forever. I doe allso hereby give to Abigail my wife the summ of Ten pownds by the yeare, to be payd her fifty shillings in wheat, fifty shillings in pease, fifty shillings in Indian corne, & fifty shillings in porck, all at the countrey price. My will is allso that Abigall my wife shall have the Two old Lower roomes & the Celler & the Leanto for her to Dwell in or to disspose of, all these during the time of her life. I doe allso give to my son-in-law Thomas Spencer, the elder, the sume of £15. I doe allso give unto Samuel Andrews & Elizabeth his wife the sume of £40, to be payd him after the decease of my wife his mother. My parcell of Land at Podunck & my houshold stuffe to be to him for part of that Legacy. I doe allsoe give to Sarah Spencer, to Hanah Spencer, to Mary Spencer, to Martha Spencer, the Fower daughters of Thomas Spencer the elder, the sume of £10 to be equally divided amongst them, that is, to either of them 50 shillings, to be payd to them after my wive's decease. I doe allsoe give to John Andrews 20s. I doe allsoe give to Thomas Andrews 20s. My will is that my debts & these Legacies may be payd out of my moveable estate, that so much as may be of my houseing & other Lands may be kept intire. I have desired Paul Peck, senr, & George Graves to see this my will to be performed, & I doe hereby give to the sayd Paul Peck & George Graves the sume of forty shillings. I doe hereby give the remayning part of my estate to Jarred Spencer, my grandchild, whoe is the son of Thomas Spencer the eldest. I doe allsoe make the sayd Jarred Spencer my Executor. My will allso is that my wife Abigall should have the use of all my houshold stuff, and to choose which 3 cowes she will have.

This is the mark N. B. *of* NATHANIEL X BERDING.

Witness: *George Grave, Thomas Olcott.*

Court Record, Page 144—11 November, 1674: Will proven.

Page 103.

Beswick, George, Wethersfield. Invt. £40-02-06. Taken 4 October, 1672, by Stephen Chester, Jacob Drake.

Court Record, Page 126—5 December, 1672: Invt. exhibited. Ordered £10 to the widoe, the remainder to Creditors. Stephen Chester, Jacob Drake & Josiah Willard apt. by the Court to Dist. to Creditors the rest of the estate.

Debts due from George Beswicks Estate: Walter Grey for rent, Mrs. Wickham, Thomas Edwards, John Waddoms, Mr. Willard, Thomas Williams, Steven Chester, John Curtice, Thomas Harris, Antho. Wright, Goodman Buck, Samuel Smith, John Cherry, Thomas Wickham Jr., Samuel Wright, Jeremie Adams.

Betts, John. Court Record, Page 131—1 April, 1673: John Betts produced a writing in This Court subscribed by Rebeckah Boreman, Mary Wright, Martha Smith and Sarah Butler, which signified that the 13 of March John Betts was married to Abigail Betts, & that the sd John Betts took her in clothes of his own providing to her, Shift & Stareless, being Stript as aforesd by the aforesaid women, *and the sayd John Betts in Court Renounenced all Claymss & Interest to her estate, both Debts and Credits.*

Birge, Jereme. Court Record, Page 85—4 March, 1668-9: Whereas, Jeremie Birge was found dead in the woods under the Bough of a Tree, & Jury panneld & Sworne to view the dead body & to make return what they found, which they accordingly attended and returned by what they sawe & heard, testifyed that the fall of the tree was the only Instrumentall cause of his death by the Lord's ordering providence. *The original verdict was returned under Matthew Grant's hand in the Name of the rest of the Jury, which is on file.*

Page 161.

Bishop, Ann, Guilford, Widow. Invt. £81-09-07. Taken 6 May, 1676, by Andrew Leete & William Johnson. Invt. of Estate in Hartford

taken by James Cornish & Thomas Bunce: By plate in Mr. Steele's Hand
about 18 ounces, which his wife claimes as given to her by her Mother.

This wrighting witnesseth that I Anne Bishop of Guilford, widow,
being weake in body But Sound in mind and memory, Doe make this my
last will and testament in maner and forme following: First, I give unto
my eldest sonne John Bishop the some of five pounds Above his equall
proportion with my other Too children. Item. I give twentie shillings
unto my grand child Elezebeth Hubbard. Item. I give unto Thomas
Smith, who formerly was servant to me, the some of ten shillings. Item.
All the rest of my estate not before nor hereafter willed, & my mind is that
after all my just Debts paid, legacies and all nesesary Charges be payed
and discharged, shall be devided Betwixt my three children, viz., John and
Steuen Bishop and James Steele. And I doe make the saide James Steele,
my sonne-in-law, my full and whole Executor, to doe and performe all
things according to this my will and testament. And I doe give him five
pounds for his pains over and Above his third part of all my Estate, both
here and in England. In witness whereof I have sett to my hand this
twelvth day of June, Ano 1673.   ANNE X BISHOP.
In the presence of
John ffowler,
William Johnson.

John Fowler and William Johnson came before me June 13, 1676,
in the presence of John & Stephen Bishop, & testifyed upon oath that they
heard & saw the said Anne Bishop acknowledge & signe the writeing
above to be her last will and testament.

                                        WILLM LEETE.
Court Record, Page 155—7 September, 1676: Will Proven.

Page 194.

Bissell, John, Windsor. Invt. £520-16-03. Taken 22 October,
1677, by Daniel Clarke, Benjamin Newbery, Return Strong. Will dated
25 September, 1673: I John Bissell of Windsor doe make this my last
Will & Testament: I give to my daughter Mary, the wife of Jacob Drake,
£10; to my daughter Joyce, wife of Samuel Pinney, £30. I give to my son
John £50. The remainder of my estate after my just debts and funeral
charges are paid, with 20 shillings a peice to each of my grand children
naturally descending from my foure sons and two daughters, I bequeath
to my four sons, John, Thomas, Samuel, and Nathaniel. The remaynder
of my estate to be equally divided. I appoint my sons John and Thomas
Bissell to be executors. I desire Deacon John Moore and Daniel Clark to
be supervisors.
Witness: *John Moore sen.,*   JOHN X BISSELL. Ls.
         Daniel Clarke.
Court Record, Page 165—6 December, 1677: Will approved.

Page 98-9.

Blatchford, Peter, Haddam. Died 1st September, 1671. Invt. £239-02-00. Taken by Simon Smith & George Gates & Abraham Dibble. The children: Peter, 4 years of age, Joana 5 years, & Mary 1 ½ years. A Legacy to "Hungerfoots" Children his 2 daughters £8.

Court Record, Page 120—7 March, 1671-2: Invt. exhibited. Adms. is granted to Hannah Blatchford, Widow, and Order Dist. of the Estate: To the Widow £71, to Peter his son £60; and to the daughters £28 apeice. Mr. Nicholas Noyes and George Gates are appointed Overseers.

Page 179.

Boreman, John, Wethersfield. Invt. £88-13-00. Taken 27 February, 1676-7, by James Treat, John Deming, Samuel Wright.

Court Record, Page 161—1st March, 1676-7: Adms. to Samuel Boreman.

Page 179.

Boreman, Joseph, Wethersfield. Invt. £103-05-06. Taken 27 February, 1676-7, by James Treat, Samuel Wright, John Deming.

Court Record, Page 161—1st March, 1676-7: Adms. to Samuel Boreman.

Page 163—18 April, 1677: John & Joseph Boreman, being deceased and having left no will, this Court Order Distribution to be made among the Surviving Brothers and Sisters. Mr. James Treat & Mr. Thomas Catlin are appointed to Dist. the Estate.

See Dist. File: The Estate of the two Brothers deceased is £187-19-06, and being divided into eight parts amounts to £21-16-06, divided as followeth by James Treat and Thomas Catling: To Isacke Boreman, to Samuel Boreman, to Daniel Boreman, to Jonathan Boreman, to Nathaniel Boreman, to John Robbins, to Sarah Boreman, to Martha Boreman, to each £21-15-06.

The Relict's thirds, which was before by Order of the Court appointed, is not included in this Division, date 4 September, 1677.

Page 116-117.

Boreman, Samuel, Wethersfield. Invt. £742-15-00. Taken 2 May, 1673, by the Select Men. The Children of Samuel Boreman & Mary his wife are:

Mary Boreman, b. 14 February, 1644 | Daniel Boreman, b. 4 August, 1658
Samuel Boreman, b. 28 October, 1648 | Jonathan Boreman, b. 4 February, 1660
Joseph Boreman, b. 12 March, 1650 | Nathaniel Boreman, b. 12 April, 1663
John Boreman, b. 12 June, 1653 | Martha Boreman, b. 12 August, 1666
Sarah Boreman, b. 4 March, 1655 |

Court Record, Page 132—12 May, 1673: This Court granted Mrs. Mary Boreman, the Widow of Samuel Boreman, late deceased, Adms.

Page 135—25 November, 1673: An Inventory of the Estate of Mr. Samuel Boreman was exhibited in Court, which was accepted and ordered to be recorded, & Mrs. Mary Boreman is granted Adms. upon the Estate, which by the Court was thus Distributed: To the Relict, £66 of Personal Estate forever, & the Thirds of the profits of the Land during her natural life. To Isaack, besides what he hath received, £38. To Mary, besides some Cattell she claymes, £60. To Samuel, besides some Cattell he claymes, £72. To Joseph, £68. To John, besides a mare, £64. To Sarah, £55. To Daniel, £64. To Jonathan, £64. To Nathaniel, £64. To Martha, £50. The sons to receive their portion at 21 years of age, & the daughters at 18 years of age. Upon the Desire of Mrs. Boreman, Mr. James Treat & Thomas Catlin are appointed and desired to be Overseers of the Children & Estate.

Dist. File: 1st April, 1674, by Josiah Willard, James Treat, John X Riley and Thomas X Catling.

Page 75.

Brooks, Thomas, Haddam. Died 18 October, 1668: Invt. £109-09-00. Taken by Simon Smith & George Gates. The children: Sarah, born December, 1662; Thomas, June, 1664; Marah, June, 1666; Alice, December, 1668.

Court Record, Page 99—11 April, 1670: Adms. is granted to the present Husband of the Widow of sd. Brooks. Order for Dist: To the Widow, £32 and 1-3 of the profits of the Land during life, she maintaining & bringing up the Children & teaching the daughters to read and sew and the son to read and write; to the son £22, to the three daughters to each of them £14.

Page 183.

Buckland, Thomas, Windsor. Died 21 June, 1676. Invt. £36-06-00. Taken by Matthew Grant, John Loomis, Thomas Bissell.

Court Record, Page 158—6 December, 1676: Order to Dist. ½ the Estate to the Widow and ½ to Daughter Hannah (Posthumous). Nathaniel Cooke to be Overseer.

Page 162—18 April, 1677: Nicholas Buckland, for himself and Brother Timothy, having moved the Court to make a settlement of the Estate of their Brother's daughter Hanna Buckland decd, alledging themselves to be the next heirs to that Estate, it being Land: This Court orders that the Estate of Land shall be divided amongst the Children of Thomas Buckland sen. Decd, that are now living: to the sons a double portion, the daughters single portions, paying just Debts that are due from their Brother Thomas Buckland's Estate.

Bull, Thomas. Court Record, Page 83—4 March, 1668: Benjamin Waite Protests against the marriage of Thomas Bull Jr. & Hester Cowles, alias Cole. *The Court orders the Wedding postponed until 7th of April, next, for Benjamin Waite to make good his Clayme.*

Page 155.

Chapman, Edward, Windsor. Invt. £184-10-00. Taken by Deac. Moore, Jacob Drake, Matthew Grant, Return Strong. Exhibited in Court 2 March, 1675.

Elizabeth, the widow. The children: Henry, 12 years of age, Mary 10, Elizabeth 8, Simon 6, Hanna 5, Margaret 3, Sara born last May, now February, 1675.

Court Record, Page 152—2 March, 1675-6: Adms. to Elizabeth Chapman the widow. Thomas Bissell & Return Strong to be Overseers.

Page 161—1st March, 1676-7: Dist., to Elizabeth Chapman the widow, £61; to the eldest son, £30; to the other son, £18; to each of the 5 daughters, £15.

Page 7-8.

Clarke, Joseph, Saybrook. Invt. £143-19-08. Taken 27 August, 1663, by William Bushnell, William Beaumont, William Pratt. Will dated 27 August, 1658, at Milford.

I Being at this Instant Bound upon a voyadge to the west Indes, it being a secret wch the Lord hath Reserved to himselfe wt the event of things shall bee, he haveing his paths in Deep waters, and in whose hand my life and all my comforts Doe remain, not knowing how the Lord may Dispose of mee in the voyage, I leave these few Lynes be hind mee to be attended as my will and last act, viz: I Bequeath and Bestow upon my ffathear Clarke fiftene pounds to purchase a servant; to my Brother John Clarke I give all my wearing cloathes, Linnen and woullen, and hath left at hom and my cloak left at Milford, and he to improve the balance thereof for his eldest son; to my Brother prat's son Samuel, five pounds; to my Brother Huntington's Daughter Sary, five pounds; to Mr. ffitch, foure pounds. Lastly, to my wife, of whom I desire my ffather to take care, I give my house, Land and wt soever ells appertayning to mee, the forementioned Distributions to bee taken out. This I desire may be attended, if it pleases God to deny mee a returne to you againe; and to affairme it to be my act and deed I have sett to my hand the day above written.

JOSEPH CLARKE.

These are the directions ffor ordering of my estate if I returne not home againe, the wch paper I desire may not be opened till nesesety require.

JOSEPH CLARKE.

14 October, 1663: Adms. to Joseph Clark sen. & Joseph Peck to pay the legacies, the rest of the estate to remain to the use of the Relict of the sd. Joseph Clarke.

Page 177.

Colfax, John. Invt. £30-00-00. Taken 1st December, 1676, by Alexander Keeney.

Court Record, Page 159—6 December, 1676: Invt. exhibited. Order that the estate remain with sd. Keeny until further order.

Page 40—(Vol. IV) 20 April, 1681: This Court being moved to come to a Settlement of the Estate of John Colefax Decd, & finding by a Writing under the hands of Henry Arnold & Elizabeth Arnold & Joseph Bidwell & Mary Bidwell that they have past over their Right in the Estate of their Brother sd. John Colefax Decd unto Jonathan Colefax, as by the Writeing on File doth appear, this Court doth confirm the same.

Page 9.

Colles, Tobiah, Saybrook. Died (   ) August, 1664. Invt. £23-18-00. Taken 2 September, 1664, by William Waller & Rennel Marvin. Will dated 12 August, 1664:

The last Will & Testament of Tobiah Colles: I give to John Comstock one Axe and 2 days Work; to Henry Champion 2 days work and one payre of Woosted Stockings; to William Waller 5 Shillings; to Reinold Marvin 2 days work; to Richard Smith 1 days work; to Wolstone Brokeway 1 days work. I do allso give my Cloth Suite & Drawers that be at Wolstone Brockwayes to John Bordon. Also my Sarge Suite and Drawers and my Hatt I doe by this my Will give to Peter Laye, and also my Woosted stockings and Showes I give to Peter Laye. To Abigail Laye, my Chest which is in John Prentice House. My Corne in Timothy Brooks lot, my 2 Steers & my Hogs, & my Land on Black Hall Playne which I bought of William Backhus, all these do I leave with Mr. Laye as his owne. I make John Laye my Executor. My Will is that My Child and its friends shall rest satisfied with that which I have formerly done for it and them in bringing it up.

Witness: *Henry Champion,*   TOBIAH COLLS.
John Comstock, John Bordon.

Court Record, Page 24—10 October, 1664: Will & Invt. exhibited. Adms. to John Laye.

Page 140-1.

Corby, William. Died 10 October, 1674. Invt. £150-13-07. Taken by James Bate and Thomas Shaylor. The children: William, 18 years of age, John 16, Mary 12, Samuel 9, & Hannah 6 years.

THE CREDITORS.

Dr. Thomas Baylett, William Harris, Middletown, Andrew Belcher, Edward Turner, John Trueman, New London, John Handerson, John Spencer, Matthew Joanes, New London, James Bate, Thomas Spencer, Jacob Goffe, A Horse Boat, Richard Piper, Mr. Hamlin, Old Mr. Blackleach for Ropes, Mr. Westall, Nicholas Noyes, Obadiah Abbe, Building Bridge, (Thos.) Dunck, Daniel Braynard, John Bate, Mr. Chapman, John Clarke, William Lewis, Robert Reeve, Mr. Ely, Edward Stolian, Thomas Newell, John Bate, Robert Stone, Jeremie Addams, William Lewis.

Court Record, Page 145—11 November, 1674: Invt. exhibited. Adms. is granted to the Widow, with advice of the Townsmen. *Estate Insolvent.*

Page 43-8.

Crow, John Jr., Fairfield. Invt . £281-11-01. Taken 1st June, 1667, by William Hull, John Burr & Daniel Burr. £17 which was found in a trunk Inventoried by John Hall & Nath: Collins.

An Agreement presented to the Court, 5 February, 1667, for a Settlement of the Estate of John Crow, who died at sea leaving no Will, by William Warren and Elizabeth Warren, John Crow sen., Giles Hamlin & Hester Hamlin. 1-3 part of the Estate to be to Giles Hamlin & Esther his wife and their Children, 2-3 to John Crow sen., to be divided among the other children.

Debts recoverable to the Estate of Mr. John Crow Decd, per his Ledger No. One, 1656:

Arthur Thomas	Bruce James
Benham Mr.	Bull Thomas
Blake Nicholas	Butcher Thomas (Taylor)
Bowden John	Butler William (Farrier)
Brown John	Clinton John
Brown Jo:	Cole Edmund

Cornwall William sen.
Cowley Rode
Crow John sen
Davis William
Dinely John
Dixwell George
Doughty John
Egginton Jeremiah
Ellicott Lt. Thomas
ffanteleroy James
ffanteleroy John
Francis John
Gibbs Francis
Groves Simon
Gwin Paul
Gwynell Richard
Hamlin Giles
Hancock George
Hart Henry
Hill James
Holdip James
Hossey Stephen
Howard John
Hunt Henry
Isaack Thomas
Jackson Christopher
Jackson George
Kemp Daniel
Lamberton Deliverance
Lasal Edward
Leader Richard
Lucena Jacob
Margrets Robert
Mellowes Elisha
Middleton Col. Thomas
Migat Jacob
Morgan Evan
Moseley Henry
Muscamp George
Newman Robert
Newton Thomas
Palmes Edward
Pargite Thomas
Parris John

Partridge John
Perrey Francis
Phillips Nathaniel
Pin Richard
Plumbe John
Price Matthew
Prothers Thomas
Read Gyles
Richolds Thomas
Roots John
Rootsey John
Sanford Peleg
Scot Phillip
Shelley Col. Henry
Sherlock John
Smith Abraham
Souter Henry
Symonds Richard
Thistlewhaite Wm
Torshall Richard
Turpin James
Waldron Col.
Warner Robert
Watson Robert
White John sen.
Wilde Edmond
Wilson William
Win Thomas
Wittin Richard
Wright Edward Jr.

Debts due from the Estate:
Chilley John
Fairchild Thomas
Goodwin William
Hamlin Giles
Lord Richard
Milborne Jacob
Olcot Thomas
Partridge William
Pinchon John Jr.,
Porter James
Pynchon Capt. John
Warren William.

Cullick, Elizabeth. Court Record, Page 63—11 May, 1667: Elizabeth Cullick, daughter of Capt. John Cullick, late Decd, chose Mr. James Richards and Lt. Thomas Bird to be her Guardians.

Page 64.

Denslow, Elizabeth, Windsor. Died 13 August, 1669. Invt. £38-05-00. Taken 30 August, 1669, by Thomas Ford, Matthew Grant & Thomas Dibble. Will dated the 5th of June, 1667.

This is to testify that I Elizabeth Denslow of Windsor doe make this my last Will & Testament: I bequeath unto my grand child Nicholas Buckland all my household stuffe except these things here expressed, which I give unto Sara Buckland my grand child, as the Bed shee now lyes upon and Bowlster & pillow & the new Blankets & materiall suitable to make it a sufficient Lodging, with the Bedstead. Allso, I give unto Sarah Buckland a chist & Box, that By the dore, as also one pewter pott & two pewter Dishes, one of the Biger & one of the lesse. Allso, all my cloathes & lining I Bequeath unto my Daughter Buckland for her to divide Between herselfe & Nicholas & his three sisters that are unmarried. Allso I bequeath unto my grand child Edward Adams his wife my cloake. Item. I will that my grand child Nicholas Buckland shall not require anything for his portion out of his father's estate, the which thing he allso consents unto. Item. I make my grand child Nicholas Buckland my sole executor for all the rest of my estate, onely out of it he shall pay within two years after my death £30, the which I bequeath as followeth, viz: Unto my Daughter Joan Cooke, 20s; unto my grand child Elizabeth Cooke, £3; unto my grand children Samuel Cooke & Noah Cooke, to each of them, 20s to each; to my daughter Buckland 40s; & unto her daughter Hanna Buckland 40s, unto her daughter Temperence Buckland £10, and to her daughter Sarah Buckland £10; In all, £30. Witness: Matthew Grant.

Court Record, Page 90—2 September, 1669: Will Proven.

We whose names are underwritten doe acknowledge we have received of Nicholas Buckland 20 shillings each of us, being given by will of Elizabeth Denslow, late deceased: 25 March, 1673-4. Aaron Cooke, wife Joane Cooke.

4 December, 1671, Received of Nicholas Buckland £10 upon Account of a Legacy given to Temperance Buckland, now the wife of John Ponder, given her by Widdow Denslow, now dec.

John Phelps Received of My Brother Nicholas Buckland, Executor, the Legacy bequeathed to Sarah Buckland, now wife of John Phelps, by the will of Elizabeth Denslow, late dec. 17 June, 1685.

Page 177.

Denslow, Henry. Invt. £215-18-06. Taken 17 August, 1676, by Jacob Drake, Thomas Bissell. Children: Samuel, 17 years of age, and

7 Daughters: Susanna, wife of John Hodges; Mary, wife of Thomas Rowley; Ruth, wife of Thomas Copler. Those unmarried: Abigail, 20 years of age, Deborah 18 (lame and sickly), Hannah 14, Elizabeth 10 years of age.

Court Record, Page 157—11 September, 1676: Adms. to the widow, Lt. Fyler & Ensign Maudsley to be Overseers.

Page 159—6 December, 1676—Order to Dist. Estate: To Samuel £50, to Each of the 7 Daughters £20, including what some have already received, Deborah to have an additional £10 on account of her lameness. The parcell of Land 50 rods by the River, running back 80 rods from the River unto the road westward, which was given by Henry Denslow to the wife of John Hodge & her children, though not recorded, shall be and remain to her and to her children, and the sd. Hodge shall have no power to alienate the sd. Land.

Page 41.

Denslow, Nicholas, Windsor. Invt. £329-02-00. Taken 5 June, 1667, by Matthew Grant, Thomas Ford & Walter Fyler. Will dated 4 March 1666-7.

This is to testify that I Nicholas Denslow of Windsor doe make this my last Will & Testament: Imprimis: I make my wife sole Executrix, and do bequeath to her the Use and Improvement of my Whole Estate during her life, and when she dies I bequeath too Timothy Buckland my gr. Child all my Lott lying at Pine Meadow, both in the Meadow and out of the Meadow adjoining, as will appear upon Record. Item. I doe bequeath to Nicholas Buckland my gr. Child, at the death of my wife, all my Houseing and Homelott and all my Meadow Land in the Great Meadow, either pasture or Plowing, in all the parcels as will appear upon Record. Also I bequeath to him at the time aforesd. the Bedd I lye on and my Furnace Pan and all my Tooles of any sort for Husbandry. Also I give to him my Woodlott. All the rest of my Estate in Cattle of all sorts, Corne or Moveables, within house or without, I leave to the free dispose of my wife, either before or when she dyes, to whome she sees meet, and to receive my Debts due to me or pay out any I doe owe. And I request these my friends to be my Overseers: Mr. Clarke, Capt. Newbery and Lt. Fyler.

Witness: *Matthew, Grant,*   NICHOLAS X DENSLOW.
John Witchfield, George Phillips.

Court Record, Page 96—3 March, 1669-70: Capt. Aaron Cooke moves this Court for a Dist. of the Estate of Nicholas Denslow, late of Windsor, Decd, his wife being Co-heir to the Denslow Estate. No Action.

Page 173.

Dibble, Ebenezer, Windsor, who in Warr with the Indians last December is dead. Inventory £65-05-00. Taken 11 February, 1675-6, by Jacob Drake, Matthew Grant, Thomas Dibble. Estate Insolvent. Relatives, the widow Mary Dibble, daughter Mary age 11 years, son Wakefield 9 years, Ebenezer 5, John 3 years of age.
Court Record, Page 156—11 September, 1676: Invt. Exhibited. Comrs appointed: Matthew Grant, Jacob Drake, Thomas Dibble.

Page 182.

Dix, William, Hartford. Invt. £4-02-05. Taken 1 March, 1676-7, by Nathaniel Stanly, Siborn Nicols, Steven Hosmer.
Court Record, Page 162—1st March, 1676-7: Adms. to Stephen Bracy.

Page 156.

Edwards, John, Corporal. Deceased in December, 1675, Wethersfield. Invt. £164-12-00. Taken 19 December, 1675.

Last Will:

A Deposition of *Benjamin Adams* and *Samuel Williams* that being in the late Service against the enemy in the company of JOHN EDWARDS of Wethersfield, the sayd Edwards, being Mortally wounded, did order that his Estate Should remain to his Mother her life time, and after her decease he willed that his brother Joseph should inherit all the estate. Taken upon oath, 20 January, 1675, before Daniel Witherell, Commissioner.
Court Record, Page 152—12 April, 1676: Will and Invt. exhibited. Adms. to his Mother, widow Tousley.

Page 39.

Edwards, John, Wethersfield. Invt. £400-01-00. Taken 27 December, 1664, by John Chester, William Gutteridg (Goodrich), Samuell Hall, John Deminge. The Legatees: Thomas, eldest son; John, 26 years of age, Esther 23, Ruth 21, Hanna 19, Joseph 16, Lydia [   ] years old.
Court Record, Page 28—2 March, 1664-5: Invt. Exhibited. Dist. Ordered: To the widow £96, to Thomas £30, to John £30, to Joseph £28, to Ruth, Hester and Lydia each £25, to Hanna because of her Impotency £30.
Page 30—9 May, 1665: Adms. to John & Dorothy Edwards, the widow.

Edwards, William. Court Record, Page 77—7 May, 1668: William Edwards, in behalf of his wife, Agnis, Plaintiff; *Contra* Nath: Bearding, Dfnt., in an Action of the Case for Illegall possession of Land belonging to the sd. Edwards, lying on the east side of the Great River, for a Surrender of the sd. Land.

Page 129—6 March, 1672-3: Richard Edwards, as Atty. to his Mother Agnis Edwards, plft.; *contra* Daniel Arnold, in an Action of Debt due upon balance of Accot, with Damage to the value of £6.

Page 136.

Eglestone, Bygatt, Windsor. Invt. £116-03-00. Taken 24 October, 1674, by Old William Trall, Thomas Dibble sen., Matthew Grant. Will dated 13 November, 1673:

I Bigat Egllstone of Windsor, in ye county of Hartford, being aged and weake, doe make this my last will & Testament as followeth: I comit my sould in ye hands of god, and my body to be buryed in seemly maner by my frends. My Estate, which is but Samll, This is my will: My House & Land after my decease I give to my son Beniamin, he being ye staff of my age, on this condition, that he shall maintaine his Moother during her life and pay my Debts. And in case yt my son Joseph should come and demand a portion, his brother shall pay him forty shillings as he is able wth conveniency. Also to my son James & my son Samuel & my son Thomas, And to my Daughters Mary, Sarah & Abigail, to eyther of these three shillings apeece. All ye rest of my estate I give to my son Beniamen, and doo make him my exsequitor.

Witness: *Nath. ffyler,*   BEGET EGLESTON.
     Abraham Randall, John Hosford.

Page 35.

Ellis, James. Invt. £52-13-08. Taken 27 June, 1665, by William Bushnell & Abraham Post. The will Taken according to law by Alexander Chaulker and William Lord, Townsmen of Saybrook, this 27 June, 1665.

The last will and testament of James Ellis, who died in William Prats house the 22 June, 1665:

I James Ellis doe bequeath my goods and estate what I have to William Prat in consideration of my good will that I bore to him above all others, and in Consideration of his great care and cost that he was at wth me in my sickness. These words were spoken in the presence of them who is underwritten, besides other testimonies that doe agree with it. Witness: *John Clarke.* The testimony of *Elizabeth Prat.*

John Clarke & Elizabeth prat have taken there oths that James elise did say that he would bequeath his estate to William prat, only they heard it singly at a different time.

This oath now taken before me, Robert Chapman, this 20 September, 1665.

Court Record, Page 42—10 October, 1665—Will and Invt. exhibited. Adms. to William Pratt.

Page 168.

Elmer, Edward, Hartford. Invt. £471-15-03. Taken 7 June, 1676, by Nathaniel Stanly and John Gilbert in Hartford, and by John Loomis & Jacob Drake in Podunk. Legatees: the Widow; John, age 30 years; Samuel 27, Edward 22, Mary 18, Sarah 12.

Court Record, Page 155—6 and 7 September, 1676: Invt. Exhibited. Adms. to the Widow and her three sons. George Gardner, William Pitkin and Joseph Fitch to be Overseers. Dist: To the Widow, £23; to John, £80; to Samuel, £80; to Edward, £92; to Mary and Sarah Each, £70. By George Gardner, William Pitkin & Joseph Fitch.

Page 41—(Vol. IV) 20 April, 1681: Edward Elmore summoned the Legatees of the Estate of his Father, Edward Elmore, deceased, to appear at this Court to answer his complaint for non-payment of him the sd. Edward Elmore such sums of Money he hath payd for Debts due from the Estate of sd. Elmore, according to their several proportions. The Court having heard their allegations & seen their accots, find them so Litigeous that they see reason to appoint Wm Pitkin and Mr. Thomas Olcott to audite the accots of the Adms. & to find out what were the Debts of the sd. Elmore when he decd, & to what sume it doth amount to, as also what each of the Adms. of the Estate have payd to the payment of Debts, & return the same to the Governor & Magistrates as soon as they may, & then the Court will settle the same according to Rules of Justice. They are allso to bring an Account what the 6 acres of Meadow Lotted to pay Debts was sold for.

Page 32—(Vol. VI) 18 June, 1696: Thomas Long complains that he hath not had that part of his Estate that is due to him in right of his wife from the Estate of Edward Elmer, Decd, but hath been rejected by law of part of the Land that was laid out to him by one of the Adms. on that Estate. This Court do order that the Adms., viz., John and Edward Elmer, do lay out his Land to him the sd. Thomas Long forthwith.

Page 87-8.

Ensign, James, Hartford. Invt. £729-02-09. Taken 23 December, 1670, by James Steele, George Grave Jr.

I James Ensign of Hartford, being at prsent, thorow the wise dispensation of my most mercifull God, weak in body but of sound understanding & memory, waighting for my change, doe therefore declare this to be my Last will & Testament: Whereas, I have formerly given to my son david the swamp Lott Bought of Richard lyman, on the east side of the Great River, & six Acres in the South meadow near the forty Acres, & sixteen Acres of upland Near Rocky hill, & his dwelling house & part of my Home lott which he hath had no Legall assurance of, I doe now give & confirm the same to him and his heirs forever. I doe also confirm to my sonn Joseph Easton & his heirs forever, one Acre & halfe of Land In the Indian Ground, which Land I had of the Widow Watts. I doe give all the rest of my estate of what sorte soever, both goods & chattells, to my beloved wife Sarah Ensign during her Naturall Life, & desire my sonns david ensign & Joseph easton to assist her in the management & improvement thereof, so that she (as much as may) be freed from distractions; & I doe make my beloved wife sarah ensign sole executrix of this my Last will & Testament. After the decease of my wife it is my will that my sonn david, his heirs & assigns, Shall possesse & enjoy my now dwelling house & Home Lott wth all the appurtenances belonging thereto, as allso all my Land In the south meadow, both meadow & swamp, & all the upland I now Stand Seized of or appertains to me & Lying on the south side of the little river In Hartford. I allso give and bequeath to my sonn david & his heires forever, Six acres of Goodman Phillips his swamp Lott on ye east side of the river, & one Third of the Barne standing thereupon, he paying such legacies as I shall appoynt to the value of Fifty pounds.

I give to my son Joseph easton the remaynder of Goodman Phillips his swamp Lott on the east side of the great river, wth two thirds parts of the Barne standing thereupon, he paying such Legacies as I shall appoynt to the value of Thirty pounds.

I give to my daughter Mary Smith, the wife of Samull Smith, what I have Layd out towards the building of their house, & ten Acres of Land Morgagd to Samull Burr, & Twenty pound more to be paid by my executrix & overseers, provided my sayd sonn Samull Smith giving way to have it Bound over so that my sayd daughter shall dispose of it to her children as she sees Cause at her decease. If he refuse that, then I give my sd. sonn & daughter the use of what I have given her as Long as they live, & that at their decease it shall pass to my daughter's children.

I give my Grand Child Ruth Rockwell Thirty pounds; to my Grand children Sarah & Lydia Rockwell five pounds apiece; to my son John Rockwell, as a Token of my Love, forty shillings. I give as a Token of my respect to our Honrd Governor Winthrop, five pound. I give as a Token of my respect to my dear pastor, Mr. Whiting, five pound. I give towards the building of the new meeting house six pounds. I give to John Ayres, to buy him tooles when his time is out, forty shillings. I doe allso desire & Command my Executrix & my two Sons to take care that the Widow Ann Phillips her Last will be duly & faythfully fulfilled. (Not signed.)

The above writing was read to James Ensign the 23 of November,
1670, & owned to be his will; & the reason why he subscribed it not was
because he had a purpose to have added somewhat more.

Attest: John Allyn.
David Ensign,
Joseph Easton.

Inventory exhibited in Court 1st March, 1670-1.

Page 184.

Ensign, Sarah, Hartford, Widow.   Invt. £44-10-00.   Taken 29
May, 1676, by George Grave, John Richards.   Will dated May, 1676:
I Sarah Ensign of Hartford, widow, being sick & weake yet of perfect memorie through the mercy of God, to prevent future trouble doe desire to dispose that small portion of this worlds goods God hath betrusted
me with, in this my Last will & Testament: I give to my beloved daughter Mary Smith an Iron pott & gun, & Blankett I lent her, & a payre of curtains lent her, to be to her & her heirs forever.   I give to my dear daughter
Hanna Easton my Great Table & Forme, & my chest at mr Richards.   I
give to my Grand child Ruth Rockwell one Feather bed & the bedding belonging to it, & my Cow, & cobirons, tongs, & halfe a dozen Napkins, & my
Brass kettle.   I give to my Grand child Sarah Rockwell halfe a dossen of
Napkins, one payre of Sheets & the best rug.   I give to my Grand child
Lydia Rockwell The Trundle bed & beding belonging to it, & halfe a
dozen of Napkins.   I give to Sarah Smith a Small Bible as a token of my
respect to her.   I will that my wollen wareing Cloaths be equally divided
between my daughters Mary, Hanna & Mehetibell, & my Grand children
Sarah, Ruth & Lydia.   I give to my son davids children halfe a dozen of
Napkins & two pewter platters.   The remaynder of my estate I give to my
beloved son David & his heirs for ever, he paying my just debts; & I doe
appoynt him to be executor of this my Last will & testament.   In witness
hereof I have sett to my hand this May, 1676.
To James ensign she gave £5; to Joseph easton, her grand child, 20s
& one of her books; to Ruth, her best hatt & Mr. Hooker's book; to Sarah,
one of Mr. Burroughs' books; & to Mr. Whiting, 20 or 30 shillings if her
estate hold out.
No signature or witnesses.   Exhibited 6 December, 1676.   Proved
and accepted.

attest: *John Allyn.*

---

ffeasey, John.   Court Record, Page 48—1st March, 1665-6:   This
Court desires Marshall Jonathan Gilbert to take into his hands the estate
of John ffeasey, Decd, until he shall receive authority to dispose of the
same.

(Will on File.)

Fenn, Benjamin sen., late of Milford. Invt. £226-00-00. Will dated 14 September, 1672.

The last Will & Testament of Benjamin Fenn: I give to my eldest son Benjamin Fenn my Farm bought of Samuel Backe, late of New Haven, East side of the East River. To my 2nd son Samuel Fenn my house, etc., in Milford. To my youngest son James Fenn my house in New Haven, with the Warehouse and Land belonging to it, East side of the River. And further I give him that farme that the Hond Generall Assembly gave to me to be taken up. I give to my three eldest daughters, Sarah, Mary & Martha, £20 apeice more. I give to my youngest daughter Susanna Fenn that house in Norwalk formerly Joseph Fenn's. My Will is that my gr. child Benjamin Fenn should enter & possess the house at Norwalk at the end of the present lease. (Wife mentioned here.) I give to my son Samuel Fenn my Dwelling house & Houseing with all Appurtenances and Meadows lying or being within the Parish of Chiddington, Maswith, Ivingowing, all of them in Buckingham Shire, which sd. houseing & Lands was given to mee by the Will of the late Agnis Seare, Decd, of the same parish & Shire aforesd, which sd. Houseing & Lands I doe give unto my son Samuel Fenn, to him and his heirs forever, he to pay at stated times £20 to each of his brothers & Sisters. I give all the rest of my Estate to my wife Susannah Fenn, she to be Executrix.

Witness: *Robert Treat,*   BENJAMIN FENN, Ls.
    Ephraim Sanford.

A Copy of Record at New Haven, in the 1st Book of Wills & Invt.
         Test: JAMES BISHOP, CLERK.

Page 174.

Fitch, John, Windsor, who Died 9 May, 1676. Invt. £46-01-00. Taken 1st June, 1676, by Matthew Grant, John Loomis. Will dated 30 August, 1675: I John Fitch of Windsor, being to goe forth and know not that I may return, I give both Land and goods to the Promoting of a School here in Windsor under the direction of the County Court and the Select men of the Towne.

                   JOHN FITCH.

Witness: *John Moore, sen., & John Higley.*

  Note: *With the Invt. is due to the (e)State for his going a Souldier to warre.*

  Court Record, Page 156—11 September, 1676: Will and Invt. exhibited. Adms. to the Select Men of Windsor, with Capt. Newbery and Deacon Moore to Confirm the exchange with Thomas Rowley.

Page 198.

Gaylord, Hezekiah, Windsor, who deceased 12 September, 1677. Invt. £109-14-06. Taken by Henry Wolcott, Jr., Joseph Elsworth. Legatees, the Brothers and Sisters, viz: John Gaylord, William Gaylord, Ann Phelps, Hannah Crandall, Joseph Gaylord & Nathaniel Gaylord, the two last by the Father only.

Court Record, Page 165—6 December, 1677: Adms. to John Gaylord.

Page 26—(Vol. IV) 21 April, 1680: The Estate of Hezekiah Gaylord ordered Distributed as followeth:

	£ s d
Inventory,	109-14-06
Debts,	92-03-11
There remains to be dist.	17-10-07
To the 4 brothers of the Decd £3 apeice,	12-00-00
To the 2 sisters 55 Shillings apeice	5-10-00

Page 106.

Gaylord, Deacon William, Windsor. Died 20 July, 1673. Invt. £296-17-06. Taken by Benjamin Newbery, Henry Wolcott, Jr., & Thomas Stoughton. Will dated 31 January, 1671.

I William Gaylord of Windsor, seriously considering my age, do declare this to be my last Will and Testament: I give unto my sone John Gaylord, his heirs & assigns forever, upon the these Conditions hereafter expressed, all my houseing & Home Lott & orchard as it Lyes, Bounded westerly by the comon high way & Easterly By the meadow, Northerly By the House Lott of Mr. Henry Wolcott & Southerly by the Land of my Daughter Hoskins, provided my sonn John Gaylord freely resigns up his propriety in his owne dwelling house & Barne & orchard & Land, viz., all that is now inclosed with in his fence on the west side of the high way, to my grand sonn John Birge, to be to him and his heirs & assigns forever, imediatly after my decease. But if my sonn John shall refuse to make the exchange, then my will is that my grand sonn John Birge, his heirs & assigns forever, shall possess & injoy my house & Home Lott as it is bounded above. I doe also give unto my beloved sonn John Gaylord & my beloved grandsonn John Birge my meadow Lott in the Great meadow, containing by estimation 16 Acres be it more or less, to be divided between them. I doe give to my Grand Sonn John Birge one parcell of Land I bought of Mr Hanaford, lying on the east side of the great river, being in bredth Tenn rodds, to run the whole Length I purchased. I doe give unto Hezikiah Gaylord, my grand sonn (whoe now lives wth my sonn John) fower rodd in bredth of my Lott over the great River that Lyeth next to the Land I gave his father, there to runn from the great River to the end of the Bounds. I doe give unto my sonn Walter Gaylord of my Lott on the east side of the great River, Ten rod in bredth, to runn ffrom the great River to the end of the Bounds, the Ten rodd to ly next to what I have given Hezekiah my Grand Sonn. I doe give unto my Sonn Samuel Gaylord of my Lott on the east side the great River, Ten rodd in bredth, to runn from the great River to the end of the Bounds. This Tenn rodds to lye next to what I have given to Walter. To my son John I doe give the remaining part of my whole Lott on the east side of the great River, wth the Barne Standing thereon, all that part of my Lott from what I have given to my sonn Samuel to Mr Humphrey Pinneys Lott. And as for my daughter Elizabeth Hoskins, of whose dutifull & Tender respect to me I have had Good Experience & Great Comfort in having by this my will disposed of part of my estate to her sonn John (whoe hath and is a great help in supporting of me in my old age), I am not able to doe for her as otherwise I would, but as a token of my love to her I give her one of my Great Kettles, the brass or Copper one, which she pleaseth. I doe appoint my sonn John Gaylord to be sole executor. And doe desire Capt. Benjamin Newbery & John Allyn of Hartford to be overseers.

Witness: *John Allyn,*   WILLIAM GAYLORD.
   Benjamin Newbery.

  Codicil, dated 14 November, 1672: I give, as a testimony of my Fatherly affection, to my daughter Elizabeth Hoskins, one of my Cowes, which she shall choose, and my brass skillett & a pewter platter & a large pewter bason & the bigger of the Brass milk pans.

Witness: *Daniel Clarke,*   WILLIAM X GAYLORD.
   Benjamin Newbery.

  There was a later Codicil, date 18 December, 1672, in which his daughter Birge is mentioned.

- - - ---

Page 60.

  Gifford, John. Invt. £3-13-00. Taken 3 November, 1668, by John Brunson, William Judd.

  Court Record, Page 81—5 November, 1668: Invt. exhibit, Estate of John Gifford, Decd. Adms. to Mary the Relict, & John and Richard Brunson are desired to assist her. Likewise an Invt. of estate of John Wyott was exhibited. This very small estate of £4 was taken to pay a debt due to the estate of John Wyott, Decd. (from John Gifford).

Page 192.

  Gillett, Jonathan sen., Windsor. Died 23 August, 1677. Invt. £273-10-00. Taken 31 August, 1677, by Matthew Grant, John Loomis, John Moore. Will dated 8 August, 1677:

I Jonathan Gillett sen., of Windsor, do make this my last Will & Testament: Imprimis: My Will is that my wife shall be my sole Executrix, and my son Josiah Gillett to take the Care for ye Improvement of his Mother's Estate for her Use and Benefit that I shall leave her whilst she lives, which she shall have ye Use & Benefit that may be made of the Houseing & Lands of both my Houselotts, my one and that which was my Brother Nathan Gillett's, which are both 9 acres, also at ye upper End of ye 1st Meadow, or that which is Timothy Phelps. All that remains of yt to me, I set out 3 acres to my son John. My Will is that after my decease, as I have expressed, that my son Josias shall take ye Care on him, to be an help and Ayde to his Mother in what shee needs his labor to manage her ocasions, and after her decease he shall injoy for his owne, for himselfe and his heirs forever, my now dwelling house and all the Appurtenances with it, with 5 acres of house Lands & all other parcels of Land, as are expressed to be his Mother's for her use whilst she lives, only excepting the House & 4 acres of ye Houseland to it, which my sonn Jeremy shall posses for his owne after my wifes decease; ye 6 acres in ye 2nd Meadow I set out to him, he is to possess for his one at present.

Thirdly, my Will is that if the Lord should take me and my wife both of us away by Death within this 4 years after ye date hereof, my son Josiah shall pay some legacies, as to his Brother Jonathan Gillett £4 and a gunn, and to his Brother Cornelius Gillett £4, & to my daughter, Peter Browne's wife, £2, and to my daughter, Samuel ffyllyes wife, £2, and to ye two children which I have taken that ware my son Joseph's, Decd, as ye little son Jonathan £5, and ye garle £5. My son Jonathan is to have the other 20 acres of Woodland joining to ye 20 acres expressed to my wife. He is to have his 20 acres next to Thomas Barber, 10 acres of it I give him, ye other 10 he hath bought. Also, Jonathan and Cornelius my sons are to have my 11 acres without ye West Bounds of Windsor, betwixt them, after my decease. And my son John Gillett to have six acres of ye other parcel without ye Bounds at present, and Jeremie to have the remainder of it.

Witness: *Nathaniel Chauncey,*   JONATHAN GILLETT.
        Matthew Grant.

Court Record, Page 164—6 September, 1677: Will exhibited.

Page 177.

Ginnings, Joseph. Invt. £3-14-00. Court Record, Page 159—6 December, 1676: Invt. exhibited by John Belding, to remain with him until further Order.

Page 126.

Goffe, Philip, Wethersfield. Invt. £297-16-09. Taken 2 June, 1674, by John Nott sen., John Kilbourn, Eleazer Kimberly. The children :

Jacob, age 25 years; Rebecca 23, Philip 21, Moses 18, & Aaron, 16 years of age.

Court Record, Page 142—3 September, 1674: Invt. exhibited. Adms. to the Relict & son Jacob. Mr. James Treat, John Waddams to be Overseers.

Page 178.

Goodall, Richard, Middletown. Invt. £74-10-00. Taken 4 December, 1676, by Richard Hall and William Harris.

	£	s	d
To twenty acres of Land bought of Sargt. Cheeny, wth fower acres of pond,	29-00-00		
to twenty acres of Land bought of the towne,	10-00-00		
to sixteen acres of Land bought of George Hubbard,	8-00-00		
to Fower acres & one halfe of pond bought of Alexander Bowe,	3-10-00		
to his part in Mr. Warde's, Ketch,	24-00-00		

74-10-00

There was another parcell of Land recorded to him, but was given to his son John Gill, as is Testified.

Court Record, Page 159—6 December, 1676; Invt. exhibited.

Page 157-8.

Goodrich, John, Jr., Wethersfield. Invt. £81-17-11. Taken 27 March, 1667. Will dated 12 April, 1676: I John Goodrich, the son of John Goodrich sen., of Wethersfield, doe make this my last Will & Testament as follows: And therefore as I doe give up myself to the Lord, so designing that all my Debts may be justly and truly paid out of other Estate, I doe give & bequeath my Land, be it 9 acres more or less, to my loving wife and Child forever. Also, I give my heifer to my sister Mary Goodrich. Also I bequeath my best sute of Clothes to my brother Joseph Goodrich, my father paying the value thereof to such as I am indebted.
Witness: *John Chester,*   JOHN GOODRICH.
     Joseph Edwards.

Memorandum: That on the 27th of June, 1676, John Goodrich & Mary Goodrich his daughter-in-law, did consent and agree in these following articles, first, that the Nine acres of Swamp Land mentioned in sayd Mary's Husband's Will shall be the proper Estate forever of Mary the daughter of the foresd. Mary Goodrich & John deceased, to be delivered to her at 18 years of age or day of marriage, which shall first happen, & in the interim her mother to have the Use of it, & during her Life in Case the Child dye under age, but on the decease of the mother & daughter, the daughter dyeing with out heirs or husband, it to return to John Goodrich & his heirs forever. 2ndly, that all the debts due from John Goodrich, deceased, shall be payd by sayd John Goodrich, & the sayd John Goodrich to receive in consideration thereof all the other Lands left by the deceased, viz, five roods in the playn, Two acres of pastures, and halfe an acre in his Home Lott & the houseing Thereon, for him & his heirs forever; & all the moveable estate whatsoever, excepting a Cow & calfe, & three pounds in cloathes. This we agree to in case the worpll Court that shall have the settlement of the estate see cause to rattify it. As witness our hands the day & year above sayd.

Witness: *Wm. Pitkin,*   JOHN GOODRICH.
      Richard Beckley.   MARY X GOODRICH.

This was approved by the Court, 8 September, 1676.

Attests: *John Allyn, Secretary.*

Court Record, Page 153—8 September, 1676. Will & Invt. exhibited and approved.

Page 175.

Goodrich, Ensign William. Invt. £915-01-06. Taken 14 November, 1676, by John Belden, Samuel Wright, John Robbins. The children: John, age 23, William 17, Ephraim, 14, David 10. The daughters are married.

Court Record, Page 158-9—6 December, 1676: Adms. to the widow. Order to Dist. to the widow £100, Personal, forever; and 1-3 of Realty for life. To John, Eldest son, £230; to William, £150; to Ephraim, £140; to David, £130; to Mrs. Hollister £100 already paid; to Mrs. Welles, wife of Robert Welles, £100; to Mrs. Fitch, wife of Thomas Fitch, £90; to Mrs. Butler, wife of Joseph Butler, £80. Samuel Talcott, Overseer.

I Joseph Butler of Wethersfield have received of Sarah Goodrich, widow, Adms. to the estate of her late husband, Ensign Wm Goodrich, late of Wethersfield, Dec., the full sum of Fower score pounds, which sayd sum is all that was due to me from the estate of my father-in-law, the sayd Ensign William Goodrich, upon account of my wive's portion.

Signed 30 January, 1677.

Witness: *Samull Tallcott,*   JOSEPH BUTLER.
      George Grave.

(Note: *This Receipt follows the Inventory.*)

Page 111-112.

Grave, Deacon George, Hartford. Invt. £278-13-02. Taken 30 September, 1673, by Gregory Wolterton, Thomas Bull. Will dated 17 September, 1673.

I George Grave of Hartford, upon the River of Conecticutt, weaver, doe in this my Last Will & Testament give unto Sarah my wife all my houseing & Barne, orchards, Home Lott, Meadow Land, Swamp Land & upland, & whatever is in my house, for her to make use of during the time of her Life, and after her decease to be disposed of as followeth : I doe also hereby give unto my sonn John Grave one parcell of meadow Land Lying in the south meadow between Mr Richards Land & Mr Whitings Land, which peice of Land is by estimation allmost Three Acres. I doe also hereby give unto my son John Grave one parcell of Swamp Land Lying by the Land called the forty Acres, in the south meadow, Between Mr Goodwins Land and Tho: Catlins Land, which parcell of Land is by estimation Two Acres & a halfe, both which parcells of Land are for him to injoy forever after the death of my wife. I doe also hereby give unto my sonn-in-law Jonathan Deming my Two Cowes, for him to injoy after my decease. I doe also hereby give unto my daughter Mary Dow the sume of Tenn pounds, to be paid to her forty shillings in every yeare until the Ten pounds be discharged, next after my decease. I doe also hereby give unto my daughter Mary Dowe my great Brass pott & pott hooks, & also one feather Bed & Feather Bowlster, & one green Blankett, & one Pillow & two pillow beirs, for her to injoy after my wive's decease. I doe allso hereby give unto my grandaughter Priscilla Markham my least brass pott & pot hooks, & my Iron Kettle, & two of my best platters, a bigger & a lesser. I doe allso hereby give unto priscilla Marcum one Flock bed & one Bowlster, for her to Injoy after the death of my wife. I doe allso hereby give unto my sonn George Grave my house, Barne & Home Lott, orchards & all other of my Lands both meadow, Swamp & upland, Except what is before given away, to him during the time of his life & to his heirs forever, for him to possess after the death of my wife. I doe allso hereby give unto my sonn George Grave (my debts & the Legacies being payd) my Cattell, my household stuffe & what ever els is mine or due to me from any one, for him to possess & injoy forever, after the death of my wife. My will also is that all my Land shall pay their rates, according to their proportion, to the Maintenance of the Ministree at the new meeting house. My will and desire is that my sonn George Grave should take my Estate into his hands & custodie, & the care of my wife, his mother-in-law, & see that shee bee Comfortably provided for during the time of her life, she now not being in a fitt capacittie to help her selfe in this way. Also, if more than ordinary charges should arise by reason of any Long sickness that should attend her, that then the whole estate should share in the Charge that ariseth. Allso my will is that all the Lining that shall remayn after my wifes decease, which is not given before, shall be equally divided between my son George's wife & my daughter Dowe. I doe also hereby make my two sons George Grave & John Grave my Executors of this my last will & Testament. In witness whereof I have hereunto set my hand.

Witness: *John Richards,*   GEORGE GRAVE, SEN.
          Steven Hopkins,

Court Record, Page 134—25 November, 1673 : Will proven.

Page 104.

Griswold, Samuel. Invt. £18-17-11. Taken 26 February, 1672, by James Eno, Benajah Holcomb.

Court Record, Page 129—6 March, 1672-3: Adms. to George Griswold.

Page 121-2.

Hall, John, sen., Middletown. Died 26 May, 1673. Invt. £54-13-07. Taken in June by Robert Warner, Samuel Collins. Will dated 3rd month, 1673:

I John Hall sen. of Middletown, Carpenter, aged about 89 years, do leave what followeth as my last Will & Testament: I give unto my son Richard Hall £10, and I give to his Children a Noble apeice. I give to my son John Hall my Cow and Heifer, to be delivered to him after my decease. I give to the Children of my daughter Wetmore, Decd, 20 Shillings to each; to the Children of my daughter Sarah, Decd, 25 Shillings apeice. I give to my son Thomas Wetmore 5 Shillings. I give 10 Shillings towards the Encouragement of a Reading and Writeing school south side of the Rivulet. I bequeath the Remainder of my Estate to my son Samuel Hall, he to pay all my Just Debts. I request Deacon Stocking and my son John Hall to be helpfull to him as Overseers to see to the Execution of the Premises.

Witness: *Nathaniel Collins,*   JOHN X HALL SEN. Ls.
      William Cheeny.

Court Record, Page 137—5 March, 1673-4: Will proven.

Page 36-7.

Hannis, Richard. Died 20 October, 1666. Invt. £26-08-02. Nuncupative Will. Three days before his death he desired Mr. Giles Hamlin and Jeremie Adams to take charge of his estate until ye next of Kin to him Come or Send for it.

Witness: *Nathaniel Willett, Joseph Smith.*

The Governor and Assistants grant Adms. to Mr. Hamlin and Mr. Adams. Invt. Presented 7 March, 1666, and Adms. granted.

Page 200-1.

Hancox, Thomas (Records of Land in Farmington, Copy). Deed of Purchase dated 1673. Attest, Thomas Bull, Register.

27 June, 1695, & 23 Nov., 1704.

206 PROBATE RECORDS. VOL. III,

Page 29.

Harrison, John, Wethersfield. Invt. £929-06-09. Taken 3 September, 1666, by John Ryley, Josiah Gilbert & Jonathan Gilbert. Will dated 6 August, 1666:

I John Harrison doe make my last Will & Testament. I give to my eldest daughter Rebeckah £60, to Mary my 2nd daughter £40. to Sarah £40. The rest of my Estate I leave to my wife, and with all make her sole Executrix. JOHN HARRISON

Witness: *Jonathan Willoughby, Tho: Wright sen.*
Grissell Willoughby, Margaret Willoughby.

Proven 6 September 1666

The Widow Katharine, Petitioned the Court to settle upon her eldest dau. £210: and to each of the younger daughters £200 because of the Inconsiderate portions left them by their father—Reserveing the House and Lot during life.

Page 13-14-15.

Hollister, John, Wethersfield. Invt. £1642-02-06. Taken 20 April, 1665, by John Chester, Richard Treat, Samuel Boreman, Samuel Welles.

I John Hollister of Wethersfield, being weake in body & of perfect understanding, doe make my last will and testament this third day of April in the year of our Lord one thousand six hundred & sixty five:

Impr. I give to my wife Joana Hollister all my housing and home lot in Wethersfield, and five acres of plaine lying between John Goodrich and Thomas Hollister, and five acres of meddow lying on the north side of the upper high way which I bought of Thomas Parks, & three acres of meddow called Betts Lott lying south of the upper highway, and six acres at the lower end of the meddow lying on the west side of the highway in three several parcells, & two acres that was Samuel Bowrmans yt lys by Rennold's his Lott, and foure acres at the meaddow gate; all this during her life, & after her decease I give my house and Barne & Orchard unto lazarus my fourth son, and unto Stephen that part of the lot beyond the Brooke, and the meddow and plains, equally to be divided between them.

Ite. I give to John Hollister, at the age of 22 years, my whole farme at Naog, for want of heirs to my 2nd son Thomas Hollister, and doe require him to give to his mother every year during her life twenty bushells of apples and two barrells of syder, provided the orchard doe thrive and prosper.

It. I give to Thomas Hollister, at the age of 23 years, all yt prcell of swamp, with Six acres of meddow, all bought of Richard Treat, Jr., and 5 acres of plaine nexe to Thomas Colman, and 6 acres of Upland in my Lot beyond the Brooke, the homeward Side of it, & to his heirs for ever, and for need of issue to the next successively.

Ite. I give to Joseph Hollister, my 3d son, at the age of 23 years, my meddow lot bought of Samuel Hale lying next Mr. Chester, and 10 acres of meddow called Rennolds his lot, and 6 acres of upland lying in my lot beyond the Brooke.

It. I give to my daughter Mary four score pounds.
It. I give to my daughter Sarah three score and ten pounds.
It. I give to my three grand children £5 apeice.
It. The remainder of my estate I give to my wife Joane Hollister, whom I appoint my executrix. I desire Jonathan Willoughby, John Chester, Richard Treat Jr. and Samuel Welles to be my Overseers.

Witness: *Jonathan Willoughby,*   JOHN HOLLISTER. Ls.
John Chester, Samuel Welles.

Court Record, Page 33—1st June, 1665: Will Proven. Page 122— (Vol. IV)—2nd September, 1686: 2 of the Overseers of the Estate having died, Capt. Talcott and John Deming sen. are desired to fill their place.

Page 124.

Hollister, Joseph, Wethersfield. Invt. £154-01-06. Taken 29 August, 1674, by John Nott sen., John Kilbourn, Michael Griswold, Enoch Buck, Eleazer Kimberly.

Court Record, Page 143—3 September, 1674: Adms. to Mrs. Hollister, the personal estate to be divided equally among his Brothers and sister, the Real Estate according to the will of Lt. John Hollister.

Page 25.

Hoskins, Ann, Windsor. Invt. £113-04-00. Taken 1st June, 1663, by William Gaylord, Walter Fyler, Matthew Grant. Ann Hoskins was the Widow of John Hoskins.

The Last will & testament, dated 17 August, 1660, of Ane Hoskins, widow, wife of John Hoskins of Windsor: As for my outward estate, I thus bestow: First, to my sonn Thomas Hoskins I give my part of the housinge & Land which was halfe of all yt was my husband's; this I give to him after my decease, for him to Injoy his life tyme, & after his decease I give it to his sonne John Hoskins. My will is, in case his father dy before he comes to the age of on & twenty years, that the yearly incres of this estate shall be Improved for him & redowne only to him, to be put into his hands at the age of on & twentie years old, booth the housinge, half the orchard & half the Land which was my part he shall wholy have & after yt age for he & his forever; but in case the sayd John shall dy before he Come to this age to poses & injoy this estate, then my will is yt this whole estate yt was mine shall be distributed equally amongst the children of my daughter Wilton's daughter Mary Marshall. Also my feather bead with all his furnituer I give to my sonne Thomas Hoskins, & after his decease I give it to his sonne John Hoskins, all to be kept for him tell the age of on & twenty yeares; & in case he dy before yt age, then this, as the housing & land, be to Mary Marshalls children. Also a brass pot & a brass pan & tow platters & a puding pane & a brasse skellet & bras candle stecke, a puter bason, two poring dishes, two alcemy sponns, a Great Chest & a Cofer, a boxe—all this I give to my sonne Thomas as the other things above. For my overseers I desire John Strong sen. & my son David Wilton.

Witness: *Henry Clarke,*   ANN X HOSKINS.
John Witchfield, Walter Fyler.

Page 32.

Hoskins, Thomas, Windsor. Invt. £450-09-02. Taken 21 September, 1666, by John Moore sen., Matthew Grant, Thomas Stoughton, John Gaylord.

This is the Last wil and testament of Mr. Thomas Hosken of Winsor in conecticut: I do lef my hol estat to my wif elesebeth hoskens for her bringing op of her children, but when my son John Hoskens shal com to ye aig of to and twenti yers, then it is my will that he shal haf half of my estat, and the other half I do lef to his mother elisabeth hoskens. Al so do gif to Joseph (Birge) ten pound, to be paid as his mother shal be abel. Al so tis my will and dasier that good man grant senur and my brother John Gailord be my ofer seers. And her to I do set my hand this present 12 April, 1666.   THOMAS X. HOSKINS.

Witness: *John Gaylord,*
Joseph Gaylord.

Hoskins, John. Court Record, Page 151—5 February, 1675-6: John Hoskins, a minor son of Thomas Hoskins, chose Capt. Daniel Clarke and Capt. Benjamin Newbery to be his Guardians.

Page 134.

Howkins, Anthony, Farmington. Died 28 February, 1673-4. Invt. £332-05-00. Taken by Robert Porter & Thomas Barnes & John Woodruffe. The children: Ruth, age 24 years, John 22, Sarah 16, Elizabeth 14, & Hannah 12 years. Will dated the 26th day of February, 1673-4.

I Anthony Howkins of Farmington, being Stricken in years and finding my sealfe weak in body but of Compitance of understanding for this worke, I give to my wife ann howkins one third parte holl isteat, axseapting my house and homested at Pork brook and the twelfe ackars of Land in the gret madow which I bought of Matthew Webster, which istate I give unto hur during the time of her naturall Life; and it is my will that what of this istate which dos remayne, which is thus given too my wif, I say which is Laft or doe remayne after my wifes departar of her naturall Lif, shall be divided amongst my children which doe survife, that is, amongst John

Howkins, Ruth howkins, sary howkins, Elizabeth howkins, hanna howkins. I give to my son John howkins my house and holle homsted Lying and standing at pork broock which is of The South Side of the hiway which Ledith to harford; allso I give too my son John Howkins the twellfe achars of Land which lyith in the gret madow, which I bought of Matthew Webster. I give and bequeth too my son John howkins a small foulling pes and arapur (rapier), as allso one hors which he hath all rady in posation; allso I give and bequeth too my son John howkins one fifth part of my holle istate which remaynes after my loving wif have resaived hur thurds according to my will; and allso after my sonne John have reasived the house and land, armes and horse formarly axprased & allso I give and bequeath too my son John howkins twellfe ackars of up-land which Lys beyond durty hollf; it is given him and his hayres foraver, he to Com too the injoymant and po sation immediatly after my departar of my Natural life, as after all my just dats ar payd. It. I give to my Son-in-Law John tomson one firelock muscat and a back sord which was his fathers. It. I give too my sune-in-Law John Judd £5-10-00. It. i give to my dautar ruth howkins a cowe which is in the hands of abraham dibull of hadum, and also a fifth part of my istate which doos remayne after my wife have resaived her thirds and John howkins and my just dets are paid, I give too my dautar Sara howkins, I give to my dawter elisabeth howkins, I give too my dawtar hana howkins. I make my wife exsaxritix, and I doe intreat my friends Samuel Wells and John Judd to be Overseers.

Witness: *Samuel Wells,*   (Not signed.)
         Thomas Thompson.

Court Record, Page 139—1st April, 1664: Will and Invt. exhibited. Mrs. Howkins Refuses the executorship. Dist. Ordered according to the will, except that Mrs. Hester Thompson, a daughter of the Decd, is not named in the will, and Mrs. Howkins is given only the use during life. And also it appearing that the Hon. Thomas Welles by his last will gave the said Ann Howkins, his daughter, £20 since her Marriage with Mr. Howkins, This Court doe Order the £20 of the Estate willed Mrs. Howkins be paid to Hester Thompson. Adms. to Mrs. Ann Howkins. Ensign Samuel Steele and John Judd to be Overseers. Sergt. John Stanly & Ensign John Wadsworth, with the Overseers, to distribute the Estate.

Page 219—(Vol. VIII) 1st November, 1714: Capt. Thomas Hart of Farmington now moved this Court to appoint an Adms. on the Estate of Anthony Howkins, Decd. The Court desire to call in John Judd and Robert Booth of Farmington.

Page 225—6 December, 1714: Thomas Hart again presented his Motion that Adms. be committed to some person. Defered until January next.

Page 163.

Howkins, Sergt. John. Invt. £130-04-00. Taken 5 September, 1676, by John X Roote sen., Thomas X Newell sen., & Benjamin Judd. The legatees: Joseph Judd, age 4 years, John Howkins 36, Mary 32, Ruth Howkins 27, Sarah 18, Elizabeth 16, Hannah 14, Elizabeth Judd, 6 years of age. Will dated the 11th of January, 1675-6.

This may informe you and those whome it doth concerne, that if the Providence of God shall soe order it that I fall in the feld and lose my Life or miscarry any other way before I com home, that the small Estat that God hath giuen me shall be disposed as is here mentioned: I giue to my cuzen Joseph Judd my House and Homelott to be possesed by him att 21 yers of age. 2: I bequeath to Joseph Judd my 12 ackers of land in the Great Meadow to be posesed by him att 23 yers of age. 3: The benefit of this house and Land before menshoned I giue the ½ to my Brother John Judd and the other half to my sister Ruth Howkins. 4: As for the rest of my Estate I would haue a true Inuentary taken of it and pay my lawfull Debts out of it, and the rest to be deuid into 6 parts: the one part I giue to my sister mary Judd, the other part I giue to my sister Ruth Howkins, the other part I giue to my sister Sarah Howkins, the other part I giue to my sister Elizabeth Howkins, the other part I giue to my sister Hannah Howkins, the other part I giue to Elizabeth Judd. And if there be a loss to know what account there is between my Mother and I, there is about £3 due to my Mother for my Diat.

JOHN HOWKINS.

This Will was left with his Brother John Judd, not to be shown until it was known whether he lived or noe.

Court Record, Page 155—7 September, 1676: Will & Invt. exhibited. Adms. to John Judd.

Page 9—(Vol. IV) 5 December, 1678: Sarah Howkins, daughter of Anthony Howkins and Sister of John Howkins, Decd, she now being deceased Intestate, her Interest in the Estate of her Father and Brother to be Dist. to her four sisters, Mary Judd, Ruth Heart, Elizabeth Brinsmade & Hannah Howkins, equally.

Page 152.

Hubbard, George Jr., Middletown. Invt. £71-10-07. Taken 1675, by Richard Hall, William Harris.

Court Record, Page 152—2 March, 1675-6: Invt. exhibited. This Court Recommend the Legatees to agree upon a Division and apply for Confirmation of the same.

Page 92.

Hubbard, Thomas, Middletown. Invt. £220-01-00. Taken 5 September, 1671, by Nathaniel Bacon, Richard Hall, Thomas Ranny. Children: Mary, age 14 years, Thomas 10, Ebenezer 7, John 4, George 1½ years of age.

Court Record, Page 115—7 September, 1671: Invt. Exhibited. Estate in Care of Richard Hall and Nathaniel Bacon, to report 1st March next.

Page 2.

Hungerford, Thomas, New London. Invt. £100-05-06. Taken 1st May, 1663, by Obadiah Breuen, Samuel Smith, Robert Royse. The children: Thomas, age 15 years, Sarah 9, Hannah 4 years.

Court Record, Page 6—9 July, 1663: Invt. Exhibited. Isaac Willey and Peter Blatchford to care for the estate.

Page 15—10 May, 1664: Order to Dist. the whole of the estate to the Relict, she to pay to Thomas Hungerford £7; to Sarah £4, to Hannah £4, at (Legal) age.

Page 33.

Janes, Mary, Windsor. Invt. £23-06-00. Taken 16 November, 1666, by Benjamin Newbery, John Moore Sen., Selectmen.

Page 6-7.

Jeffries, Gabriel, Saybrook. Invt. £17-05-06. Taken 28 May, 1664, by the Townsmen of Saybrook: John Westall, John Clarke, Zachari Samford. *He wrought with William Pratt.*

Court Record, Page 22—14 September, 1664: Adms. to John Westall.

Page 90.

Joanes, Richard, Haddam. Invt. £104-00-06. Taken 5 September, 1670, by George Gates, James Bate. The children: Son David, 8 years of age; daughter Elizabeth, 5 years; Mary, 2 years, & Patience, born March, 1670-1.

Court of Assistants, Page 112—18 April, 1671: Adms. to the Relict, Mrs. Elizabeth Joanes. George Gates and James Bate are desired to be Overseers. Order to Dist. to the 3 daughters £4 apeice, to his son £8, to be made out of a peice of Land apprised at £22-10-00. The rest of the Estate to the Relict.

Page 187-8-9.

Kirby, John, Middletown. Invt. £552-05-10. Taken 27 April, 1677, by Nathaniel Bacon, William Cheeny.

The children: Joseph, age 21 years; Mary, the wife of Emanuel Buck, age 32 years; Elizabeth Kirby, Decd, age 23 years; Hannah, wife of Thomas Andrews, age 27 years; Hester, wife of Benajah Stone, 25 years; Sarah, wife of Samuel Hubbard, age 23 years; Bethia Kirby, age 18 years; Susannah, 13 years; Abigail Kirby, age 11 years, & John Kirby Jr., Deceased.   Will dated the 6th day of April, Anno Dom. 1677.

First of all, to the intent that my loveing wife may not be destitute of a Comfortable Subsistence, while She Shall live, I do give and bequeath unto her the possession and use of all my estate (whither houseing, land or other estate) at prsent in my possession, during her naturall life, excepting only what shall afterward be particularly mentioned.   I do also give her liberty, if she see herselfe necessitated so to do, to Sell any such part of my estate as aforesaid for her necessary supply.   I give to my son Joseph & to my daughter Mary, Each of them a portion double to the portion of any of the rest of my Children; and to the rest of my Children, all which are daughters, I do give to each of them a portion equal to one another.   Item. for that parcell of my land wch lyes near to Daniel Harris his farme on the west of Connecticott river, & contains about 300 acres, & another parcell of my land of about 200 acres, Lying about pipe Stave Swamp, on the west side also of Connecticott River, my will is that to which soever of my children or childrens children these parcells of land or any part thereof Shall fall, they shall not at any time be Sold out of the blood; but in Case any of my children or their children see cause to Sell any part, it shall be only from one to another of them, that so these two parcells of land may pertain to some of my children or childrens children to the end of the world.   When the full and final distribution shall be made, then all my estate so distributed (whether formerly received or then to be received by my children or childrens children) shall be prised again at the then present value thereof.   I appoint Capt. John Allyn of Hartford and Deacon Allyn of Middletown & my Son-in-law Emanuel Bucke of Wethersfield Executors.

Witness: *John Wiatt,*   JOHN KIRBY.
Elizabeth Wiatt.

Court Record, Page 164—6 September, 1677: Will proven.

Page 63 (Vol. VII)—March, 1704-5: Whereas, John Kirby, formerly of Middletown, Decd, did by his last Will appoint Col. John Allyn, Deacon Allyn of Middletown, and Emanuel Buck of Wethersfield his Executors, two of which, vizt, Col. Allyn and Deacon Allyn, are Decd, and the other, vizt, Emanuel Buck, not capable of acting by reason of his age and Infirmaties, and the sayd John Kirby did likewise order in his sayd Will that a new apprizall should be made of his Lands after the decease of his wife, Joseph Kerby, sonn of the sd. John Kirby, Decd, prays that Adms. may be granted to him in order to the fulfilling the sd. Will of his Father, Adms. with the Will annexed was granted to Joseph Kirby with an order to exhibit in Court an Invt. of the Land of his sd. Father by the 20th of April next.

Court Record, Page 69—5 September, 1705: Joseph Kirby not having attended the order of this Court as was intended, The parties concerned in sd. Estate, vizt, the Legataries in sd. Will, made application to this Court praying that Alexander Rollo of Middletown may now be appointed, together with sd. Joseph Kirby, to make or cause to be made a new apprisal of the sd. Lands, This Court do appoint the sd. Joseph Kirby and Allex Rollo unto that service, to make return on the first Tuesday of November next. And this Court, considering the difficult circumstances of the sd. work, Do Therefore Order and appoint Thomas Ward, Thomas Stow and John Bacon of Middletown to apprize the sd. Lands presented to them by the sd. Joseph Kirby and Alexander Rollo, according to the direction of sd. Will.

Page 72—7 November, 1705: Lt. Thomas Ward, Thomas Stow and John Bacon, being sworn, did make apprizement of sd. Lands, and under their hands in writing did present to this Court their apprizement thereof, wch this Court accepts. It also appearing to this Court that Mary, one of the daughters of the sd. John Kirby, Decd, hath had of the Estate of her

	£ s d
sd Father,	30-15-00
and that Elizabeth, another daughter, hath had	24-10-00
And Hannah hath had	17-06-00
And Sarah hath had	47-19-06
And Easter hath had	59-10-00
And Bethia hath had	81-00-00
And Susanna hath had	2-10-00
And Abigail hath had	2-05-00
And Joseph hath had	51-18-00

as they and every one of them (except Elizabeth and Bethia, who are deceased) have acknowledged in writing upon Oath, presented now in this Court, which is on file, This Court do therefore, upon Consideration of all the premises, Order and direct Emanuel Buck, alias Enock Buck, the only surviving Executor, to sett out to the several heirs or Legatees of the sd. John Kirby, deceased, or their legal representatives, their several respective remaining parts or portions of their Decd Father John Kirby's Estate, according to his Will. Joseph Kirby prays an appeal may be granted him to the Court of Assistants. To this Alexander Rollo and David Robinson objected against the takeing of his own bond.

Court Record, Page 73—21 November, 1705: Alexander Rollo of Middletown presented to this Court a Letter of Attorney made by Emanuel Buck, alias Enock Buck, of Wethersfield, Executor of the Last Will of John Kirby, formerly of Middletown, Decd, to David Robinson and him sd. Rollo, to impower them as his attorney to make full division and distribution of the said John Kirby's Estate to and amongst his Children according to the sd. Last Will of the sd. Kirby, and in pursuance to an Order of this Court made the 7th of this Instant November, 1705, and also the division and distribution of the said Estate made by them in pursuance and by Vertue of the said power of attorney, with the said Emauuel, alias Enock Buck, his allowance and confirmation thereof, which this Court do accept and allow and do order the same to be recorded and putt upon file. (Not indexed.)

Page 96—16 September, 1707: Joseph Kirby and Alexander Rollo presented to this Court a new apprizement or Invt. of the real Estate of their Father John Kirby, formerly of Middletown, Decd (pursuant to the order and determination of the Court of Assistants held at Hartford the 1st day of May last past), made by a jury of twelve men upon Oath, in Order to have the direction of this Court for another or new Division or Distribution made of the said Estate, And now this Court have again heard all the pleas and allegations of the sd. Joseph Kirby of the one part, and of the said Allexander Rollo and David Robinson (who married two of the daughters of the sd. deceased) on behalf of themselves and the rest of the daughters of the said deceased or their heirs, of the other part, relateing to their claims upon sd. Estate, And upon Consideration thereof Do Find That the sd. Joseph Kirby hath formerly had and received of the said Estate (to be accounted for as part of his portion thereof):
In Moveables, £7-03-00; off the effects of half the Long

	£ s d
meadow Lott sold,	13-10-00
Dwelling house and 4 acres of Land, with 2 acres adjoyning to it,	55-00-00
Barn & 2 ½ acres of Land, part of his Fathers Homestead,	50-00-00
And 350 acres of Land, the East end of the Long lott,	26-10-00
Ten acres of upland, £5; and 5 acres Meadow, Wongunck up lott,	30-00-00
in All	£182-03-00

	£ s d
and is allowed as Adms.	12-15-00
That Mary had received	52-15-00
Elizabeth	32-00-00
Sarah	58-12-06
Easter	74-05-00
Bethia	102-00-00
Susannah	2-10-00
Abigail	2-05-00
Hannah	54-06-00
That the part of the Estate now Invt. by the Jury,	860-14-04
Estate now Indebted to Mary Buck and David Buck her son,	14-16-00
The Jury £7-04-00, to Rollo £13-13-09,	35-12-09
To Land sold, etc.,	37-00-00
Total for Dist.	875-16-04
Out of this already paid to the Children.	561-09-10
There remains undivided the summ of	314-06-06

The Court now Order the Adms. to pay the debts and report to the Court as speedily as may be, when a final Order for Dist. would be made.

Lewis, Wm. Court Record, Page 101—2 September, 1670: Thomas Hancock of Farmington, aged 25 years, & James Bement of sd. Farmington, age 18 years, appeared in Court & upon their oath testified that Mary Whitehead, the known Mother of Mary the wife of Lt. William Lewis of Farmington, in Connecticut, in New England, was, the 2nd of September, 1670, alive, and they had discourse with her in her son William Lewis House.

Page 142.

Lord, Mrs. Dorothy. Invt. £187-17-08. Taken 12 May, 1675, by George Grave, John Shepherd. Will dated 8 February, 1669.

I Dorothy Lord of Hartford do declare this to be my last Will & Testament: First, that all my Just Debts be paid out of my Estate. I do give my now Dwelling house & Barne and my Homelott and my lower Lott in the lower Meadow unto the Children of my son Thomas Lord, Decd, at the age of 18 years. Item: I give unto my daughter Amy Gilbert and her Children 3 acres of Meadow & Swamp land in the upper Lott in the Long Meadow next to that Mrs. Olcott hath now in possession. It. I give unto my son Robert Lord, if he live after my decease so long as to have notice of this my Will, 3 acres in my upper Lott adjoining to that which I have given my daughter Gilbert. It. I give unto my son William Lord 2 acres in my Great Lott in the Long Meadow next adjoining to that which I have given to my son Robert. It. I give unto my son John Lord £10 in Current Pay of the Country. It. Whereas my gr. son Richard Lord hath disbursed several sums of Money or Country pay for the Building of my Chimneys and Shingling my House & repayers about it, I doe for the payment of him, Give, Grant & Confirm unto him & his heirs forever all that my Meadow Lott in the Long Meadow which abutts upon the Great River East, the Little River West, Mr. Westwood's Land North, & Barth Barnard's Land South. I do also give to my sd. gr. son Richard Lord all the remainder of my upper Lott in the Long Meadow which I have not given to my sons Robert and William and my daughter Gilbert and their Children, he paying the Legacies hereafter expressed. To my son John, £10. I give unto my gr. Child Hannah Ingersoll my youngest Cow, and my 3 Cows I give unto my gr. children, Dorothy and Margaret Ingersoll. I give all my Moveable Estate & Cattle to my son William Lord, my gr. son Richard Lord, my daughter Stanton, my daughter Gilbert, and the Children of my daughter Ingersoll, the whole to be divided into five parts, and my daughter Ingersoll's children to have one part and the rest each of them one part. I give unto the wife of Nicholas Clarke 10 Shillings. I Constitute my son William and my gr. son Richard Executors, and desire my friend Mr. John Allyn to be Overseer.

Witness: *John Allyn,*   DOROTHY X LORD.
    Steven Hopkins.

Dorothy Lord doth order the Dispose of her household stuff, after her decease, as followeth: I give to Richard Lord's wife my iron Drippin pan & Great Pewter Pye Plate. Unto Richard Lord Jun. my Great Brass Pott. I give unto Mr. Haynes one payre of my best Sheets & two Napkins & a pewter pye Plate (smaler one) & one pewter Candle Stick. I give unto my daughter Stanton my Great Brass Pann & my great Bible. I give to my son William Lord my Silver Drinking Bowle & my Great Brass Kettle. I give to my daughter Gilbert my lesser Brass Pann & a Brass Scummer & a Brass Chaffing Dish; a great pewter platter to Elizabeth Gilbert, & Two Joynt stooles. I give to my daughter Lord, widow, my bed I ly on & A feather boulster & a brass Skillett. I give to Dorothy Phelps my Coverlid & a feather pillow beere. I give to Margery Ingersoll a white blankett & a pillow. I give to Hanna Kellsey my hood, a scarfe, a Hatt, & a great white Chest, a feather bed & Two Blanketts, a Bowlster & Two pillows, Two payre of sheets, one small pott, one small Brass ketle, one warming pann, & one payre of Curtains & Curtain rods, & one brass Candlestick, & all my Earthern ware. I give to my son Thomas his Chil- dren all the utensills about the fire that are now in my house, & my Table & forme & Chayres. I give to Mary Lord Jun., daughter of my son Thomas, my bedstead. I give to Marjory Ingersoll & her Sister Dorothy, to Each twenty shillings.

Court Record, Page 149—14 May, 1675: Will proven.

Page 160.

Lord, Sarah, Hartford. Will dated 2 August, 1676.

I Sarah Lord of Hartford doe make this my last Will & Testament: For ye Continuance of Love & Peace amongst my Relations, dispose of my Outward Estate as followeth: My Wearing Apparel I doe give unto sundry persons hereafter mentioned. I give unto my daughter Haynes my silk Gown, my Mohaire Petticoat and my red Parragon Petticoat. I give to my daughter Lord my best Broad Cloth Gown and my Red Broad Cloth Petticoat. I give unto Dorothy Ingersoll (alias Phelps) my Coat & Wastcoat of Black Serge. I do give to Hannah Ingersoll (alias Kelsey) my dark Cloth Gown, my Haire Tamy Petticoat, and my green Apron. The rest of my Clothes I give for ye Use of Dorothy Lord Jun. I do give unto my Cousin Priscilla Brackett (alias Renolds) of Boston £10, to be paid at ye End of 5 years next after my Decease. I do give unto my cousin Sarah Brackett (alias Shaw) £10, to be paid at Hartford within 5 years after my Decease. I give unto my Kinsman William Chapman £12, to be remitted him of ye Debt he oweth. I give unto my Cousin Margaret Ingersoll, when she is 18 years of age, one Cow. I do give unto Mary Lord (alias Olmsted) two Eues. I doe give unto Sarah Lord, the daugh- ter of my brother William Lord, 2 Eues. I do give unto Mary Lord, the daughter of my Brother Thomas Lord, at ye age of 18 years, 2 Eues. I do give unto Richard Lord, ye sonne of my Brother Richard Lord, £4, to be paid him at the end of 6 years after my Decease. All which Legacies are to be paid at Hartford out of my Estate. I do give unto my daughter Sarah Haynes and her children ye sume of £180. I give unto my daughter Haines and her Children ye sume of £50 more, in all £230. Lastly, I doe give unto my sonne Richard Lord the whole remaining Estate, both Real & Personal, and appoint him sole Executor, ordering him to discharge all and every of ye Legacies above mentioned, as also to maintain and take ye Care of Dorothy Lord, daughter of my Brother Thomas Lord, Decd, during her natural life, yt she be comfortably and decently provided for. I request my honoured & respective friend Capt. John Allyn and Brother George Graves to be Supervisors.

Witness: *Joseph Haynes,*   SARAH X LORD. LS.
         George Graves.

Court Record, Page 154—7 September, 1676: Will exhibited, and Mr. Richard Lord accepts Executorship.

Page 80.

Loveland, John. Invt. £114-15-08. Taken 2 September, 1670, by Jonathan Gilbert, Nathaniel Willett, Siborn Nichols.

Court Record, Page 103—9 November, 1670: Adms. to the Widow, she to possess the whole Estate.

Page 159.

Luxford, Stephen, Haddam. Died 14 May, 1676. Invt. £24-16-06. Taken by Jarrad Spencer, James Welles & Thomas Spencer.

Court Record, Page 154—7 September, 1676: Adms. to Jarrad Spencer. Order to Dist. the Estate.

	£	s	d
Debts due from the Estate	18	16-08	
Extra Charges added to the above amount in all		24-08-02	

So that there remains in Jarrad Spencer sen. his hands of the Estate Stephen Luxford, £24-08-02 & 2 acres of Swampe Land not prized in the Inventory, which is to remain for the Use of the heirs of Stephen Luxford when they appear, and the Court doth accept of the above and grant to Jarrad Spencer a *Quietus Est.* for his Adms. so far as he hath proceeded as above.

Page 33—(Vol. XII) 7 October, 1735: Whereas, it appears to this Court that there is about 2 acres of Land belonging to the Estate of Stephen Luxford which was never inventoried, this Court grant Adms. on the same unto Thomas Brookes, who recog. £500 with Joseph Fuller of East Haddam.

Page 148.

Marshall, Capt. Samuel, Windsor. Died 19 December, 1675. Invt. £902-15-06. Taken 7 February, 1675-6, by Capt. Newbery, Jacob Drake, John Maudsley, Deacon John Moore & Matthew Grant. The children: Samuel, b. 27 May, 1653; Lydia, b. 18 February, 1655; Thomas, b. 23 April, 1659; David, b. 24 July, 1661; Thomas, 18 February, 1663; Mary, 8 May, 1667; Eliakim, July, 1669; John, April, 1672; Elizabeth, September, 1674.—(W. R.; also see the above named Page 148.)

Will dated 4 September, 1675: Whereas, I Samuel Marshall, of Windsor, am called by the Authority of Connecticut to goe foorthe againe the Indians which are risen up as enemies against the inglish, nott knowing how the Lord will dispose of me, if it be Gods Will that I shall retorne no more, I desire to submit thereto, and therefore doe leave this as my Will: In the ferst playce, I doe give my daughter Lydia Marshall all the Land I bought of Josiah Hull at Hamonosett, to enjoy forever. If she die without Issue, the Estate to be equally divided amongst the rest of my Children, reserving a suitable allowance out of it for my wife. I desire my Brother Capt. Benjamin Newbery, my Kinsman Capt. John Allyn, and my Father Wilton to be Overseers.

Witness: *David Wilton,*   SAMUEL MARSHALL.
     Katharine X Wilton.

Note: *Testimony (attest, John Allyn) that Capt. Samuel Marshall went out with Major Treat and left this Will with his Father David Wilton to keep, Samuel Marshall having died of Wounds December, 1675.*

Court Record, Page 152—2 March, 1675-6: Will & Invt. exhibited. There being no Executor appointed, Adms. was granted to Mary the Relict and Capt. Benjamin Newbery.

Page 26—(Vol. IV) 21 April, 1680: An Account of Adms. was now exhibited:

	£ s d
Inventory	565-00-00
Debts & Charges	63-00-00
Left in the Adms. hands to pay debts	100-00-00
There remains to be divided	437-12-06
To the Widow, of personal Estate,	61-12-06
To Elizabeth, Samuel, Lydia, Thomas, to each	62-13-04
To David, Thomas and Mary, to each of them	62-13-04

And appoint Capt. Newbery, Capt. Clarke, Return Strong & Nathaniel Bissell, Distributors.

Page 123.

Martin, Anthony, Middletown. Died 16 November, 1673. Invt. £184-02-04. Taken 3 December, 1673, by Samuel Collins and Robert

Warner. The children: John Martin, age 11 years, Mary 7, Elizabeth 2 years. Order Dist. of the Estate: To the Widow £15; to John £80; to each of the daughters £40.

Page 163—(Probate Side, Vol. X): An Additional Inventory of Anthony Martin's Estate of Lands on the East side of the Great River, 196 acres, £78-10-00; one parcel in ye last Division, 42 acres and 60 Rods, £8-09-06; one & ½ acres & 8 rods, £1-11-00; total, £88-09-06. Taken 28 March, 1723 by Joseph Rockwell, John Williams & William Ward.

Court Record, Page 12—27 March, 1723: Mary Martin (alias Andrews), a daughter of sd. deceased, sometime of Middletown, Decd, her Children Jonathan Andrews and Mary Andrews of Wallingford and Abigail Andrews of New Haven, by their lawful Attys Matthew Bellamy and Thomas Beach, both of Wallingford, Inform this Court that the sd. Anthony Martin died Intestate and that there never was any perfect Invt. made of his Estate, especially on some divisions of land that have been since his decease laid out in or on his right in Middletown, praying that Adms. may be granted. Thomas Beach appointed Adms.

Court Record, Page 32—6 November, 1723: Thomas Beach of Wallingford, Adms., Exhibits now an Invt. made by a new appraisement at the present value thereof; accepted. The sd. Adms., in behalf of several of the Heirs, viz, Mary Martin and Elizabeth Martin, moved for a Dist. on sd. Estate. Sundry persons appeared before this Court and produced Deeds of Conveyance to them from said Mary Martin and Elizabeth Martin, also from John Martin, son to Anthony Martin, of Ancient Deede. It appears to the Satisfaction of this Court that the Estate of Anthony Martin hath been settled either by Distribution or an Agreement among the Heirs, and conveyed to many other persons. This Court therefore do not Order Dist. From this Judgement Thomas Beach appealed to the Superior Court.

Page 1-2.

Marvin, Reynold, Saybrook. Invt. £806. Taken 28 October, 1662, by John Cornish, William Lord. Will dated 23 May, 1662 (written from his own mouth), And Willed by himself. Unto my son Renold Marvin I give my house and all my Lands. I will that unto Each of my Grand Children there be provided and Given a Bible as soone as they are capable of useing them, and these be provided out of the Executorship. For the moveable Household Goods I doe will that my Son Renold in all particulars have two parts and my daughter Mare one, as followeth, that he may have two feather beds and she one; that he may have two pare of sheets and she one pare as far as they will goe; and so likewise Concerning all moveable goods in the house. Concerning the Cowes and young Cattell my will is that the fore mentioned distribution be attended, Excepting the four Oxen, which I give to my son Renold. Concerning my wives wearing Cloths and linnen belonging to her, I leave it to my daughter Mares dispose. My horses and mares with their Issues I give unto my son Ren-

old, only one horse or mare I give to Mare. Concerning the Sheep and
Swine, I Will that Renold have two parts and Mare one. There is a Debt
of £20 due from John Warner of Farmington, which Debts I give to my
daughter Mare, excepting £5 which I leave with her to be disposed of according to my appointment. I appoint my Son William Waller to be the
Executor of this my Will, to see the performance of it. I appoint that
20 Shillings be allowed out of my Estate for his recompense. That this is
my Act and Deed I do Confirm by subscribing by my Hand.

Witness: *John X Lay senior,*   RENOLD X MARVIN.
          Jeremiah Peck.

   Proven 9 July, 1663.

   Court Record, Page 89—2 September, 1669: *Samuel Collins ptif,
Contra Ensign William Waller, Executor to Mr. Reinold Marvin, Decd,
in account of Goods & Cattell of Mr. Reinold Marvin, which by Will belongs to sd. Collins his wife, etc. Damage £150.*

Page 98.

   Mascall, Thomas, Windsor. Invt. £121-15-06. Taken 13 September,
1671, by William Thrall, Thomas Stoughton.

   Court Record, Page 116—2 November, 1671: Adms. to the Relict.
Order to Distribute to the Widow; To Thomas, born 19 March, 1661, £25;
to Bethiah, b. 6 March, 1660, £15; to Abigail, b. 27 November, 1663, £15.
(See Windsor Records.) Thomas Persons & Jacob Drake to be Overseers.

Page 49.

   Maybee, Nicholas, Windsor. Buried 1 March, 1666-7.—(W. R.)
Invt. £4-12-08. Taken by Bendict Alverd, Wm. Phelps.

   Court Record, Page 70—8 October, 1667: Adms. to James Enno.

Page 102.

   Micaene, John. Died 20 August, 1672. Invt. £14-17-00. Taken by
Benjamin Newbery, John Moore Jr.

   Court Record, Page 124—5 September, 1672: Adms. to Capt. Newbery & Thomas Allyn.

   Miller, Thomas. Court Record, Page 51—9 May, 1666: This Court
considering the Estate of Thomas Miller, Inventoried, and the desire of
his wife, lately deceased, in reference to the wrongs done to her by his
notorious uncleanness, that ye Court would State Some Considerable part

of ye Estate of the said Miller upon her child, the wife of Nathaniel Bacon, doe therefore see just Cause to allow Nathaniel Bacon, husband to Anne Bacon (daughter of ye sd. Thomas and Isabel Miller), all ye wearing Apparell, linin and woolen, wth those other small things mentioned in the Inventory £5-05-00; also the Cow and Calf in Bacons Custody; also ye warming pan and great Bible £5-05-00, to Anne Bacon, in ye old Trunk. And out of ye Estate thirty pounds (£30) more to be paid unto ye said Nathaniel Bacon by the 25th of March next ensueing, in Current Corne, Beef, or Porke, or otherwise to Nathaniel Bacons Content. This being discharged by Thomas Miller, it is to be a final issue of all demands that Nathaniel Bacon may make for charges in Keeping Isabel Miller, or for her burial, or upon any other account for things past. The Lands of Thomas Miller Stand as Security. The pillion is granted to Mary Ward.

Page 195.

Moore, John, Windsor. Invt. £489-04-07. Taken 17 September, 1677, by Benjamin Newbery, Daniel Clarke, Return Strong, Josiah Elsworth. Dictated. Will dated 14 September, 1677: Deacon John Moore being at this prsent his memory & understanding sound though under present sickness, did declare with his own mouth in the prsence of his wife, Robert Hayward & John Moore, Nath. Loomys & John Loomys, that it was his will as followeth: Imprs. He did will to his deare wife the product & improvement of his whole Estate, houseing, Lands & Moveables, so long as She Lives, & fifty pownds to her own dispose to her children or at her discretion at her death; & my will is that the estate that remayns after her death as aforesayd shall be disposed as followeth: to my son John a double portion, & my will is my son shall have all my Land, he paying what his double portion doe not reach to my other children, unto whom, that is, to my four daughters, I doe will the remaynder of my estate in equal proportion.

Witness our hands: *Robert Haywood, John Loomys.*

Court Record, Page 165—6 December, 1677: Adms. to John Moore. Jacob* (John) Drake sen. personally appeared in Court and declared it to be his Will & Desire that the above written Will should stand as the Will of his deceased Father, before Benjamin Newbery, John Moore, Nathaniel Loomis, Thomas Bissell & Nathaniel Bissell. In Court, 6 December, 1677, they did acknowledge that they in their own and their wives behalf did acquiesce in and approve of the Dispose of the Estate of Deacon John Moore as it is expressed by him and written as above.

Attest: *John Allyn, Secretary.*

Court Record, Page 165—6 December, 1677: Adms. granted to John Moore, with the Will annexed.

---

*Jacob Drake seems an error of the Recorder, but was so written.

Note: *The first book of births, marriages and deaths at Windsor is a copy of the original (which original appears only in shreds) and does not contain all the names of the original. Many of the early names were recorded in a Vol. of Lands now preserved in the vault at the office of the Secretary of State.*

Nathaniel Loomis and Elizabeth Moore were married 24 November, 1653. Thomas Bissell and Abigail Moore were married 11 October, 1655. (*Recorded in Vol. of Lands, Sec. States Office*).

(On W. R.): Nathaniel Bissell and Mindwell Moore were Married 25 September, 1662. John Drake and Hannah Moore were Married 30 November, 1648.

Page 62-3.

Morrice, John, Hartford. Invt. £201-12-00. Taken 15 February, 1668-9, by Robert Morrice, Daniel Pratt. Will dated 13 November, 1668.

I John Morrice of Hartford doe make this my last Will & Testament: I do give unto my wife my whole Estate, that is to say, the Improvement and Use of it until my Children come of age to receive their portions, she bringing them up wth the profitts of it. It is my Mind that my wife should have, if she see Cause to accept of it and have Need thereof, Liberty to dwell in my House & have room in the Yard to set her Wood, and hay for a Cow or two, & 1-3 of the Benefit of all my Lands during her natural life. I give unto my son John my Dwelling house and all the West End of my Barn from the floor, and all my House lott so far as the middle of the Floor, & from thence the South Line to run right through my Lott, which sd. South Line shall be the East line of my son John's Homelott. I also give him my old Houselott lying near the Oxpasture by Nathaniel Barding's Houselott, & my Lott in the Soldiers Field which lyeth between Robert Sandford and Goodman Burnham's. I do also give unto my son Joshua the remaining part of my Homelott and the East End of the Barn, wth liberty to make use of the Barn floor, which Barn floor wth ye Barn Doors shall be mayntaned by my two sons, John & Joshua, at their equal charges, they having by my Guift equal liberty to improve them for their own Use. It is also my Will that my sons John & Joshua shall not make Sale of their Proprieties in my sd. Houselott & Barn to any persons without the full Consent of each other. I also give to my son Joshua my Soldiers Field Lott that lyes between Thomas Burnham's and John Church, and 4 acres of Land lying in the Woods near Nathaniel Barding's houselott, and the remainder of my Land in the Woods on the West side of the Great River. I give unto my daughter Mary £20. I make my wife sole Executrix, and desire my loving brother Robert Morrice and my friend Daniel Pratt Overseers.

Witness: *John Allyn,*   JOHN MORRICE. Ls.
      William Wadsworth.

A Codicil bears date 22 November, 1668.

Court Record, Page 85—4 March, 1668-9: Will proven.

Page 60.

Morton, Samuel, Hoccanum. Died 25 September, 1667. Invt. £4-08-00. Taken 21st May, 1668, by Samuel Welles & Hugh Welles.
Court Record, Page 85—4 March, 1668-9: Invt. of the Estate exhibited. Adms. to Thomas Edwards.

Page 66.

Napp, Thomas, Hartford. Invt. £4-17-02. Taken 22 January, 1699-1700, by Nathaniel Ruscoe & Richard Lord. Exhibited in Court 25 January, 1669.
Court Record, Page 89—2 September, 1699: Gregory Wolterton, Ens. Nich: Olmsted, Edward Elmore, John Gilbert, Wm. Warde & George Gates being sworn to make a true verdict upon the death of Thomas Napp, return that they find that he came to the river voluntarily, went into the river and was drowned, being carelessly accessory to his owne death as far as they can understand.
Page 95—25 January, 1699: Bartholemew Barnard appointed Adms. on the sd. Estate.

Page 15.

Orvice (Orvis), George, Farmington. Died 27 April, 1664. Invt. £92-00-00. Taken by John Root, Stephen Hart.
Court Record, Page 33—1st June, 1665: Adms. to the Relict, Stephen Hart and Thomas Barnes to assist. The Debts & Legacies of ye Children of her first husband being discharged, the rest of the Estate to belong to ye Widow to bring up ye younger Children.

Page 172.

Osborne, James, Hartford. Invt. £19-17-09. (Of Lands in Springfield & Hatfield, value not known.) Taken 14 June, 1676, by Nathaniel Stanly and Philip Davis. The children: James, Samuel, Sarah Osborne, Mary Brace & Elizabeth Arnold.
We whose names are underwritten did hear Goodman Osborne say that his Desire and Will was that his wife should have the Use of all his Lands while she lives, and after her decease it should belong to & by his Will be given to his two sons James and Samuel, and sayd he had intended to have given his steere to his son-in-law Daniel Arnold, but his wife was not willing and he would not trouble her, but would give him some of that Debt in Samuel Elmore's hand.
Witness: *Nathaniel Stanly,*
Siborn Nichols, Philip Davis.
Court Record, Page 156—11 September, 1676: Will and Invt. approved.

The Court order that Daniel Arnold shall possess and receive £3 of the Debts in Samuel Elmore's Hand.

Court Record, Page 156—11 September, 1676: Will & Invt. approved.

Page 105.

Pantry, Hannah. Estate Debtor to her Mother Mrs. Welles:

	£ s d
Payd her in Cattle in April & August, 1670,	43-00-00
By Expense of driving them down to Milford, wch was to Elmore, 12 Shillings ; To Messenger, £0-02-06 ; To a horse, 8s ; To Expenses at Highway, £0-00-06,	1-08-06
My son Thomas went to help them with a horse,	10-00
Also 3 August, 1670, pd. Robert Howard for Phissick for her,	1-10-00
By extraordinary attendance & Expenses in that Sickness, in Wine & other things, etc.,	3-00-00
Payd Goodwife Sandford Cure for her, 1672,	0-10-00
By Expenses for her in her last Sickness & in Attendence extraordinary,	03-00-00
By Expenses at the Funeral, Coffin & Grave, etc.,	2-19-00
Of the above written, in Mr. Bryant's hand there is	43-10-00
Her portion was	120-00-00
Her Debt to her Mother besides that in Mr. Bryant's hand,	12-17-06
Remains to be divided in Mr. Bryant and her Mothers hand	107-02-06

Exhibited in Court 1st April, 1673, & Dist. made by the sd. Court.

Court Record, Page 130—1st April, 1673: Order to Dist. the Estate of Mrs. Hannah Pantry, which was £107-02-06, being indebted to her Mother Mrs. Welles for the sum of £12-17-06, this being deducted this Court order the remainder to be divided, 1-3 part to John Pantry, 1-3 to Mary Pantry, and 1-3 to Mrs. Hannah Welles, which Dist. is judged to be consonant with the mind of Mr. John Pantry, Father of the Decd. The full Amount being £35-14-02.

Page 187.

Pierson, John, Middletown. Died July, 1677. Invt. £35-19-00. Taken by Nathaniel Bacon, William Cheeny. He died leaving one son about 3 years of age.

Court Record, Page 164—6 September, 1677: Adms. to the Widow, and Order that the House and Land be reserved for the son after the decease of the Mother, the rest of the Estate to be distributed to the widow and to her heirs. Mr. William Cheeny is desired to act as Overseer.

Page 65.

Phelps, Samuel, Windsor. Invt. £773-15-00. Taken 29 June, 1669, by John Moore, Matthew Grant, Sergt. Benedict Alvord, William Thrall. The legatees: Sarah the Widow, Samuel age 17 years, Sarah 15, Timothy 13, Mary 11, William 9, John 7, Ephraim 6, Abigail 3, Josiah 2 December next.

Court Record, Page 89—2 September, 1669: Invt. exhibited. Adms. to the Relict.

See File: Order to Distribute to the Relict £78 to dispose of as she shall see cause, and one third of the use of Land during life; also the improvement of the whole Estate until the children come of age. To the eldest son £108; to the 2d, £80; to the 3d, £73; to the 4th, 5th & 6th, to each £73; to the three daughters, to each, £48-06-08. William Phelps and George Griswold to be Overseers.

Page 98—3 March, 1669-70: The Widow Phelps desires the Court to appoint Timothy Phelps to assist William Phelps and George Griswold as Joynt Overseers.

Page 70-1-2.

Phillips, Ann, of Hadley & Hartford. Invt. £391-16-09. Taken 13 November, 1669, by Richard Butler & Bartholemew Barnard. Will dated 31 March, 1668-9.

I Ann Phillips of Hadly, in the Massachusets Jurisdiction, Widdow, considering the vncertainty of the term & manner of my death, And that my Estat may be desposed of according to my own mind and Will though at this present I am in health of body and having my perfect memory and Understanding, Doe make and ordain this my last Will and Testament, Wherein I give to my brother John Rogers in England £100, or, if he die, to his son John Rogers, or next, to the Children of my Brother Samuel Young in England. I give to my Brother Samuel Young £100. Special provision is made, if some of them come to live in this Country, of Lands in Northampton and Hartford. I give to Mr. John Hooker, now living in England, £10 if he come to live in this country within 3 years after my decease; if he come not, then what I have given him I give to the eldest son of Mr. Samuel Hooker. Also I give to Mr. Samuel Hooker £10. I give to my Sister Mrs. Wilson £10. I give to Mr. John Russell, pastor of the church at Hadley, £10. I give £5 to the Church at Hadley to buy Potts or Cups for the Communion Table. My will is that all those Legacies I have given to such as live in this Country be payd to each and every one of them within eighteen moneths after my decease, Except the Child or Children of my brother Young if any of them come hither, to whom it is to be paid at their several ages.

My will is that after my decease my Executor or his assigns doe take the first opportunity to Send to my friends in England & give them full and Clear information of this my Last will so far as it Concerns any of them, and continue a yearly sending to them till he shall receive an Answer of or from them, within ten years. If no answer is Come nor order from them in ten years, then my will is that the Legacies I have given them to be disposed off for the reliefe of the honest poore & Encouragement of Schooling in Hartford & Hadley by an equal proportion. I give to my Executor & his heirs all other of my Estate. Item. I give to Samuel Shepherds heir, if living, £5; but if not, I give this £5 to Mr. John Wilson, pastor of the church of Meadfield. Also my will is that my Overseers shall be paid for their pains. I make Mr. James Ensign sole Executor; Mr. Richard Goodman & John White Overseers. ANN X PHILLIPS.

Court Record, Page 111—5 April, 1671: *Upon Motion of David Ensign, this Court having viewed the last Will of Ann Phillips, do declare that the Executor of the Will of sd. Ann Phillips stand obliged to make payment of the Legacies bequeathed to John Rogers & Samuel Young here in Hartford, & that they are not to stand any venture of Transportation.*

Page 180.

Pinney, Nathaniel, Died 7 August, 1676. Invt. £221-18-10. Taken 4 September, 1676, by Jacob Drake, Thomas Bissell, Samuel Pinney, Abraham Phelps & Joseph Griswold. The children: Nathaniel, age 5 years 11 May, 1675; & Sarah, age 3 years 11th October, 1675.

Court Record, Page 156—11 September, 1676: Adms. granted to Sarah the Widow.

Page 161—1st March, 1676-7: Order to Dist. to the Widow £45, to the Son £60, to the daughter £31.

Plumbe, John. Court Record, Page 137—5 March, 1673-4: John Plumbe, as Master of the Ketch, Hartford, Pltf.; Estate of Isaac Grosse, deft.; for expenses, charges and wages due in and upon his voyage to Jamecoe to the sd. Ketch.

Page 151.

Pond, Nathaniel, Windsor. Invt. £66-08-00. Taken 22 January, 1675, by Benedict Alvord, John Moore Jr.

Court Record, Page 152—2 March, 1675-6: Adms. to Nicholas Sension. John Moore Jr. to pay the Debts; and to Samuel Pond, Brother of the Decd, ½ of the Estate, and the other half to Sarah his sister, the wife of Jonathan Hoyte of Guilford.

Page 101.

Richards, Widow. Invt. £24-08-00. Taken 12 June, 1671, by Richard Butler, George Grave Jr. On the 13th of June, 1671, The Estate of

Widow Richards was Dist: To John Richards, to Mary Peck of Milford, to Thomas Richards, & to Obadiah Richards. We whose names are underwritten do jointly agree to this Dist., as also we have attended the Will of the Deceased herein as far as we understand it.

John Richards,
Mary X Peck,
Thomas Richards.

Page 82-3.

Risley, Samuel. Died 8 July, 1670. Invt. £29-04-10. Taken by Nathaniel Willett & Siborn Niccols.

Court Record, Page 102—1st September, 1670: Creditors to mett 2nd Wednesday in November next.

Page 103—9 November, 1670: Invt. exhibited. This Court grant Thomas Edwards Adms. on the Estate to pay the Debts so far as the Estate would go.

Page 104—9 November, 1670: This Court grant Thomas Edward a *Quietus Est.*

Robbins, Samuel. Court Record, Page 7—3 September, 1663: The Court having considered Samuel Robbins' & Mary Browne's offence, doe adjudge them to be married each to the other & pay a fine.

Page 4—29 October, 1663: This Court order that the Marshall Thomas Cadwell deliver all the Estate of Samuel Robbins in his hands that hath been committed to their Care into the Hands of the Townsmen of Hartford to be improved by them for the Use & Relief of Mary Browne as they see Cause. To the publique treasury five pounds, & Samll Robins is to give in forty pound Bond to attend the order of Court & to live wth his wife & not departe & Leav her.

Page 120.

Rockwell, John, Windsor. Died 3 September, 1673. Invt. £186-16-06. Taken by Robert Hayward, Thomas Bissell, Matthew Grant. The children: Sarah age 20 years, Ruth 19, Lydia 17, Hanna 8, Joseph 5, Elizabeth 3 years of age.

Court Record, Page 137—5 March, 1673-4: Invt. exhibited.

Page 140—1st April, 1674: Adms. to the Widow. Order to Distribute to the widow £17-15-00; to Joseph, £48; to Ruth, who had a legacy from her gr. Father Ensign, £10 only; to Sarah, to Lydia, to Hanna, to Elizabeth, £24 to each. Thomas Bissell & Samuel Rockwell to be Overseers.

Page 19-21.

Will on File.

Rockwell, Simon, Windsor. Died 22 June, 1665. Invt. £206-05-06. Taken 27 June, 1665, by Matthew Grant, John Gaylor, William Gaylord.

And near the Evening of the day before his death, Deacon Gaylor, Humphrey Pinne and John Gaylor, being all then with him, seeing him very eill, advised him to declare how his Estate should be dipose of if he should Dey of this Sickness. He desired them to help him by their advice, & they tould him now he should speake freely of himself. Then he thus Exprest himself as followeth: My will is after my death my two Sisters Children shall have my Holle Estate, to every one of them equally, divided among themselves. (Test. in Court 10 July, 1665.)

The Children of Simon Rockwells two Sisters: The Eldest, The wife of Robert Watson, 6 Children: Mary age 14 years, John 12, Samuel 10, Hanna 7, Ebenezer 4, Nathaniel 2 years. The second sister, wife of Sergt. Zachariah Sanford, 4 children: Zachary Sanford, born 1653; Hanna, b. 1656; Ruth, b. 1659; Ezekiel, b. 1663. [*From Saybrook Records, Testimony of Robert Chapman.*]

An agreement: Page 21—6 November, 1665. Dist. Estate of Simon Rockwell between Robert Watson & Zachary Sandford: It is agreed that ye said Watson shall have the Houseing and land, per Invt., £102-02-00, and said Sandford shall have ye moveables, which amounts by Inventory to £104-03-06. And the sd. Watson is to pay the sd. Sandford fourty shillings more as a full division of ye said Estate.

Page 109-10.

Ruscoe, Nathaniel sen., Hartford. Invt. £304-03-00. Taken 18 August, 1673, by John Allyn, Caleb Stanly. Will dated 23 July, 1673, at Haddam.

Nathaniel Rescoe senior being vary sicke and weake, thought good while my Sences ware with me, that in Case the Lord doth take me now away out of the World, my Will and desire is that the Estate which God hath bestowed uppon me should be distributed as followeth: I doe Giue to my Loving wife the ½ of all my hole Estate during her Liufes time, and at her death to retorne it to my son Nathanell; and the other half of my Estate I Giue to my sone Nathanell Rescoe. And I doe Giue to my kinswoman mary Browne one heffer, tooe yeare ould, and vantage. And I doe Giue to Benjamin Newtone one young horse and one pige. Moreover I doe desier the honoured Mr. John Allyn and Caleb Stanly to be helpfull to my wife and son in the managing of their affairs. That this is the Will of Nathaniel Ruscoe senior we doe aphearm.

George Gates,
Henry Cole.

On the 13th of August, 1673, An Agreement of the Legatees tnat Mary Browne and Benjamin Newton to them those small legacies shall be performed, and to Joane Ruscoe, the Relict of the Decd, shall during her life stand seized of the ½ of the Real & Personal Estate, and at her decease shall have liberty by her last Will or otherwise to dispose of £80 ot the Personal Estate in her Hands, and the Remainder to be to Nathaniel Ruscoe.

Witness: *John Allyn,*   Joana X Ruscoe,
        Caleb Stanly.   Nathaniel Ruscoe.

Whereas my Husband & my Hond. Father was by the providence of God seized of his last sickness from Home, & by his Extremitie and want of Assistance made his last will somewhat imperfect, we being Principally Concerned as Legatees to the Decd, have mutually agreed, if the Honoured Court please to confirm our Agreement here, that those Legacies granted to Mary Browne & Benoni Newton shall be performed, & Joanne Ruscoe, Relict, during her natural life shall stand seized of ½ of the Real & Personal Estate of the Deceased, & that at her decease she should have liberty by her Will & Testament or otherwise to dispose of £80 of the Personal Estate in her Hands, The remainder to be to Nath. Ruscoe & his heirs forever. Signed, 18 August, 1673.   Joanne X Ruscoe,
Test: *Caleb Stanly,*   Nath : Ruscoe.
     John Allyn.

Court Record, Page 133—4 September, 1673: A writing was presented in Court as the Last will of Nathaniel Ruscoe, & noe Executor named therein. Letters of Adms. were granted to Joane, the Relict of Nathaniel Ruscoe, and an agreement for a settlement of the Estate was Confirmed by the Court.

Page 130-1-2.

Ryley, John, Wethersfield. Invt. £688-04-00. Taken 11 June, 1674, by John Nott sen., John Kilbourn, Enoch Buck, Eleazer Kimberly. Will dated 13 May, 1674.

Be it known to all men by these prsents, that I Jno Ryley of the Town of Wethersfield do make this my last Will & Testament: I give to my son John Ryley the House & Lott which I bought of John Dickinson, the 4 acres of Land lying at the east lower End of Beaver Meadow wch I had by Exchange of John Betts, The ½ of that Land which I bought of Will Gull, lying in the Plaine, 2 acres of my Plaine at the South Field, wch 2 acres shall be on the north side of it, The ½ of that Land wch shall by Division fall to me on the East side of the Great River. I do give to my son Joseph that House & Homelott which I had by Exchange of Tho: Couch. Item. the other half of ye Land in ye Plaine which I bought of Will: Gull. Item: 2 acres of my Pasture at the South Field, next to his

Brother John. Item: the other half of the Land which by Division shall fall to me on the East side of the Great River. Also, I give to him my gray mare and her Colt, only I do hereby enjoyn him my son Joseph to pay to his sister Mary the sume of £10 in Current pay of the Country 2 years after the Lands shall come into his Hands. Item: I do give to my son Jonathan 3 acres of Land lying at the lower End of ye Meadow between John Damon Jr. and Samuel Boreman. Item: 4 acres in Beaver Meadow between Goodman Churchill & Jonathan Damon. Item: 8 acres at Rocky Hill. Item: my Lott of 50 acres or there abouts in ye Woods or West Division. Further, my Will is, with reference to these my three sons, John, Joseph & Jonathan, that my wife their Mother shall have the thirds of all the yearly products & Increase of such of the Lands bequeathed unto them as are improveable at my Decease, and this she shall have during her life. Item: I do give to my daughter Mary, besides ye £10 above mentioned, £20 more wch my Executor and Adms. shall pay out of my other Estate. Item: I do give to my daughter Grace £20, which shall in like manner be paid by my Executors when she shall come to age. Item: I give to my daughter Sarah £20 when she shall come to age. Item: I do give to my 2 youngest sons, Jacob and Isaac, this house in which I now dwell. Item: 5 acres of Land at the Pond, 5 acres more or less of Meadow Ground within ye Meadow Gate. Item: 4 acres of Land in ye Plaine between Lands of Mr. Robbins & John Dickinson. Item: 4 acres of my Pasture at the South Field, which is the remainder from yt before bequeathed. All which Houseing & Lands shall be equally divided between these my 2 sons, Jacob and Isaac, after the decease of their Mother. I give unto my three older sons my Carpenter Tooles. I appoint my wife sole Executrix. I desire Mr. Bulkeley, my brother John Belding, my Brother Emanuel Buck, and my Cousin Michael Griswold to be Overseers.

Witness: *Gershom Bulkeley,*   JOHN X RYLEY. Ls.
         Michael Griswold.

Court Record, Page 143—3 September, 1674: Will approved.

Page 115-16.

Sadler, John. Invt. £78-18-00. Taken 18 August, 1673. Will dated 8 July, 1673.

I John Sadler doe make & ordain this my last Will & Testament: After my Debts are paid I give my whole Estate to my wife Deborah Sadler, and desire Anthony Wright and Samuel Butler to be helpfull in ordering the business and gathering the debts.   JOHN X SADLER.

Court Record, Page 135—25 November, 1675: Adms. to the Relict.

Note: This Indenture, made the 29 of June, 1643, by and between John Sadler of Wethersfield, uppon Connecticott River, in America, on the one Ptr, and George Willis of Hartford, upon the same River, Gent., on the other parte, Witnesseth: That the said John Sadler, for and in

Consideration that the said George Willis had, before the ensealeing and delivery of the prsents, delivered up Canceled unto the said John Sadler one bill or deed of Morgage bearing date the seaven and twentieth day of March, 1642, of his home and house lott and other lotts to the said home lott belonging, formerly bought of one Edmund Vore of Wethersfield by the said John Sadler, wch was made to one Richard Myles of Uncoway for the payment of Sixteen Pownds ten Shillings Sterling, payable 24 August, 1643, at the House of Nathaniel Foote in Wethersfield. *Extended at 8 per cent. Interest until May next, 28 day.*

Page 166-7-8.

Sandford, Robert Sen. Invt. £414-05-06. Taken 19 June, 1676, by John Gilbert, William Pitkin.

The children: Zachariah Sandford, Eldest son, Elizabeth Colier, Ezekiel Sandford, Mary Campe, Sarah, Robert, Hannah, and Abigail Sandford.

I Robert Sanford sen. doe make this my Last will and Testament as followeth: Item: The house, Ortyard and Lott that was Goodman Phillipps I give to my son Zachariah Sanford and his heirs forever, beeing about two acres of Land (that is, the Ortyard next Phillipps house and the Lot next that Ortyard), to bee his after his mother Decease, hee paying such Legacies out of it as I shall appoint. Item: My other dwelling house in Hartford with the Lot next it, and Harts hill and the (   ) pasture bought of Kellsey, and the barn and Ortyard next Gerrard Spikes lot, and the Land adjoyning to Samuel Olcotts and Specks lotts, I give, after my wives decease, to my son Robt. Sanford and his heirs for ever, hee paying such Legacies out of it as I shall appoint. Item: I give to my daughter Hannah the neck pasture which is next to Caleb Stanlys land, after her mothers decease, the best Kettle and my pistoll, and to Abigail my best skillett. Item: To my Daughter Sarah I give a Great Kettle & a Cowe, after my wive's decease. Item: to Robert Sanford the Land in Soldiers field (   ) and the Land over the Great river in Mr Crows Meadow. Item: My wood Lands I would have them Ly in common for the use of both my son Robert and Zacharyah. During my wives life time I would have her to have the whole of my Estate as it now is myne, and Robt. to Live with her and attend her, and to have my team to help her.

(Not signed.)

Mr. Will Pitkin & Sargt. Tho. Spencer did declare upon oath that they did hear Robt. Sanford declare as his Last will so far as is written.

Court Record, Page 155—7 September, 1676: Will & Invt. exhibited. Adms. granted to the Widow. Page 159—6 December, 1676: Order to Dist. the Estate to the 5 daughters, giving to each of them £20.

Page 125.

Saxton, Widow Sarah, Windsor. She died 13 June, 1674. Invt. £69-19-00. Taken 8 July, 1674, by Matthew Grant, John Moore sen., Nathaniel Cooke. The children: John, born 4 March, 1649-50; Richard, born 1 March, 1654-5; Sara, married, born 26 March, 1647-8; Mary, the wife of George Sanders, born Feb., 1655-6; Patience, born 28 January, 1658-9.

Court Record, Page 143—3d September, 1674: Adms. to John Saxton. Deac. John Moore and Nathaniel Cooke, Overseers. Order to Dist. to John, eldest son, £25; to Richard, £13; to the eldest daughter, £10; to the younger ones, £8-15-00 to each of them.

Scott, Capt. John. Court Record, Page 16—18 May, 1664: *Complaint against, by Mr. Wm Pitkin. Mr. John Scott doth chuse to be tryed by the Bench, & Waves his tryall by a Jury. The Case charging John Cooper with treasonable utrunses against his Magesty the King. This not proven. John Scott himself for his Treasonable words, etc., fined £250. Imprisoned during the pleasure of the Court. Required before his departure to give Bond in £500 for his Good behavior Toward this Government and toward all persons In this Corporation, and not to cause disturbance in this Colony. And this Court doth degrade the said John Scott of his Civil office of Comissioner on Long Island, & disfranchise him of ye priviledge of freedom in this Corporation, & disinable him for giving in Testimonie in any of our Civil Courts.*

24 May 1664: Letter from John Allyn, Secretary, to Mr. Woodhull, with an Incidental mention that the Right Honourable Colonell Nichols hath taken the Government of the Island.

Page 177.

Shadduck, Elias, Windsor. Died 26 May, 1676. Invt. £18-15-00. Taken 12 August, 1676, by Matthew Grant, Thomas Bissell. Legatees: Wife and one Child.

Court Record, Page 156—11 September, 1676: The Small Estate left with the Widow, she to pay debts and funeral charges, Provided they are not more than £12.

Page 76.

Shear, John, Windsor. Died 27 September, 1669. Invt. £147-13-00. Taken 25 October, 1669, by Capt. Newbery, William Trall. Will dated 26 September, 1669.

The last Will & Testament of John Shear, his memory being sound: I giv to my son John Shear my Yoke of Oxen & a young mer a year old, one hog of 2 year old, & two young swine about 2 weeks old. I give also to my loving wife Sarah Sheare all the Estate that she brought to me her husband John Sheare. And as for the Rest of the Estate, I giv to my loving wife Sara Sheare, only she is my sole Executrix. For the true performance of this my Will, I desire my loving friends Timothy Trall and George Griswold, Jacob Gibbs & Robert Hawart, to be my Overseers to this my Will.

Witness: *Rebecca X Owine,*   JOHN X SHEARE.
       Mary Griswold.

Court Record, Page 99—19 April, 1670: Will & Invt. Exhibit approved.

Page 165.

Smith, Jobana, Farmington. Invt. £30-10-09. Taken 1st September, 1676, by John Root sen., Thomas Newell, Benjamin Judd.

Court Record, Page 155—7 September, 1676: Adms. to Jonathan Smith. Order to Dist. the Estate, to be equally divided between the Mother and 5 Brothers and two Sisters of the deceased, and to Samuel, son of Jonathan Smith. This Court appoint Thomas Judd and John Judd to assist the Adms.

Page 113.

Smith, Joseph, Rocky Hill. Invt. £441-07-06. Taken 28 August, 1673, by James Treat, Sergt. John Deming, Emanuel Buck, Townsmen. The children: Lydia, age 19 years, Joseph 13, Jonathan 10, Samuel 7.

Court Record, Page 132—4 September, 1673: Adms. is granted to Lydia, the Relict.

Page 134—25 November, 1673: Order to Dist. to Lydia the Relict £46-06-08 forever, and 1-3 of the profits of the Real Estate during life; to the Eldest son £150, to the two youngest sons £90 to each of them, and £59 to the daughter. This Court appoint Thomas Wright and Jonathan Smith Overseers.

Page 130—(Vol. IV) 3 May, 1687: This Court, upon the Motion of Lydia Harris, Relict to Joseph Smith of Rocky Hill, that there might be a settlement of the Estate of sd. Joseph Smith upon his Children, This Court do appoint Mr. John Buttolph, Mr. John Robbins, with Jonathan Smith, to Dist. the Estate to his wife and Children according to such proportion as the Court hath allotted to each of them in their Dist. of 25 November 1673, & to divide to the sons their proportions in Lands as equally as may be, so far as it will go. You are to take the Eldest son as living.

Page 139-40.

Smith, Thomas, Haddam. Died 2nd November, 1674. Invt. £46-09-08. Taken by Wm Clarke, Symon Smith, James X Wells. Will dated 22 September, 1674.

I Thomas Smith of Haddam do make this my last Will & Testament as followeth: I give my Homelott, Orchard, & Fences about it, to the wife of John Baily, and to her children after her, and also my Freehold on the West side of the River. I give to the wife of Daniel Brainwood all my Household Stuffe & Moveables that by this Will are not otherwise disposed of, and my Hay to Daniel Brainwood. I give my Tobacco to James Welles. I give my Steers to Nicholas Noyes. I give my Cow and my gunn to John Smith. I give my Hogg to John Bailey, sen. I give my turnips equally betwixt James Welles, Daniel Cone, Joseph Stennard and John Bailey. I give what Timothy Spencer oweth me to Daniel Cone. I make John Bailey sen. and Daniel Brainwood my Executors to see this my Will fulfilled and to take Care of my Buryall, on which I would have 40 Shillings expended, 30 Shillings of which I would have John Bailey allow out of what is given to him, & Daniel Brainwood the other 10 Shillings. I would also that James Welles out of the Tobacco I gave him to pay what I owe to John Merrells, which is about 10 Shillings. I give my Wearing Clothes and Bed Clothes to Steuen Luxford. And this is my last Will & Testament, excepting my Debts to be paid as is expressed on the other side of the paper.

Witness: *Nicholas Noyes,*   (Not signed.)
    George Gates.

Court Record, Page 144—11 November, 1674: Daniel Brainard refused the Executorship, & this Court grant Adms. unto John Bailey.

Page 132—(Probate Side, Vol. XII): An Inventory of the Lands of Thomas Smith, late of Haddam, valued at £199-00-00, was apprised 28 December, 1728, by Daniel Clarke, Thomas Brooks & Caleb Cone.

Page 206 (Vol. X)—26 November, 1728: Adms. granted unto John Baily Jr. of Haddam.

Page 210—2 January, 1728-9: John Bailey, Adms. on the Estate in Lands of Thomas Smith, exhibited an Invt. of sd. Estate not before inventoried. Accepted. Also he exhibited an Account of his Adms. of incident Charges of £8-11-06. Upon Motion of the Adms. this Court order that the sd. Estate, after the heirs have refunded to the Adms. the sum aforesd., shall be dist. according to the last Will & Testament of sd. Deceased: To John Bayley; to the heirs of Lydia Spencer, deceased; to Elizabeth Clark, to Benjamin Bayley; to the heirs of Susannah Hubbard; to Nathaniel Bailey and Mary Cornwell, Children of Lydia Bayley Deceased. And appoint Thomas Brooks Jr. Daniel Clark & Caleb Cone Jr. Distributors.

Page 68-9.

Smith, William, Farmington. Invt. £229-00-00. Taken 6 January, 1669-70, by Thomas Barnes, Thomas Orton & John Wadsworth. The children: Jonathan 23 years of age, Jobana 21, Joseph 14, Benjamin 11, William 8, Samuel 5, Susannah 19, Elizabeth and Mehetabell 16. Will dated 14 December, 1669.

I William Smith of ffarmington, being through the visitation of God very weake in Body but of good understanding, doe in the few words following dispose of that little Estate which he hath lent me: Item. I give to my wife 1-3 of my Estate wch shall then be in my house and Homested, the rest of my Estate to be divided in equal portions to my Children. I desire Mr. Anthony Howkins and Brother John Stanly to be Overseers.

That this is the last Will of William Smith of Farmington, though not subscribed by him by reason of bodily weakness, is attested by us.

Samuel Hooker,
John Norton.

Court Record, Page 97—3 March, 1669-70: The last Will and Testament, together with the Inventory of the Estate, of Wm. Smith, of Farmington, was exhibited in Court & ordered to be recorded, & this Court grants Elizabeth Smith, the Relict of the sd. Wm. Smith, power of Adms.; & it being testified by Robert Porter & Jonathan Smith that it was the mind of Wm. Smith, though it be not so fully expressed in his Will, that his Relict should possess the Thirds of his whole Estate, This Court doe order that in the Distribution of the Estate it be accordingly attended.

Page 147.

Stains, Ann. Invt. £27-02-06. Taken by Robert Porter, John Clarke, Samuel Cowles.

Will: This prasant desamber 24, 1670, I an stans or farmingtowne, being stricken in yers, I give to rodger nuton, sun of Mr. rodger nuton of milford, five pounds, two be payed in a cow if worth so much; if not, to be made up in other istat.

It. I give Too willam pixly of north hamton my badd with all the furnyture or bading belonging Too it, which is a flock badd, one grey rodg, twoo blanckets, one boallstar, one pillow, one pil Lou bere, one payre of Shetes, foare cartins, and The Vallyancs belonging To Them.

It. I give to Samuel Coll of farming my bigist ioyrne pot.

It. I give To John cLarck of farmingtoane my skillit. It. I give two elisibath Judd, The daughter of bengiman Judd, my biball. The rest of my istate I bequeath Too Lt. William Lawis, and doo mack him my holl and soull axsackitary, and doo in Tret my twoo frinds Samuel Colls and Samuel Stell too be the oversears.

Witness: *Samuel Stell,*   ANN X STANES.
        Samuel Cowles.

    Court Record, Page 151—26 January, 1675-6: Will and Inventory exhibited. Capt. Lewis nominated Executor, refused to serve. Appointed Adms. with will annexed, to have respect to the Will.

Papers in Custody of William Lewis sen. and Capt. Lewis, on file.

January ye 26, 1675.

    To ye honered Court, Now Sitting at hartford, William Lewis sienor humbly presents these considerations as followeth, representing my Sister Stanes Will, who is Now deceased: First, yt my brother stanes her husband came over into this Country a Servant to Mr. Taps of Milford about ye yeare 1642, and, building of his masters house, resaived a blow with a Laver and broake ye rim of his body, & had a bunch as big as a mans duble fest on his side, & was wholy unfitted for service. And his master, being mutch troubled he could not Labour, my brother, prsaiving yt, tould his master if he would please to dismis him he would go to his brother at hartford and see what he would doe for him, which his master readily acsepted, & so he came to me in sutch a mean habit, being So nearly related to me, I could not Let him go forth to meting til I had first cloathd him from top to toe:

	£	s	d
8 yds. of Carsey to make him large Coate & Sute, yt cost 8 Shillings pr yd, & is			3-04-00
For Lynings of hose & buttens, silke & making,			1-04-00
pr Gloves, stockings, £0-09; pr a hatt, £0-14; & is			1-03-00
pr 4 Shirts at £0-08 apeice, & is			1-12-00
And in this posture continued with me for neare 2 years, and his Dyet for ye time I account			15-00-00
pr the Expenses at his funeral, and coffin & Grave,			02-00-00
			24-03-00

    Respecting my sister Stanes her selfe, I going to England in ye year 1649, found her there in a very mean & low Condition, made her a tender of going to New England & live with me & I would take Care of her, but yt she was not able to do, but I was forced to let her have to cloathe

	£	s	d
herselfe,			5-00-00
as also paying for pasage over ye Sea, pd in New England,			6-00-00
pr a pack and Chest, fraight 30 Shillings, & is			1-10-00
for passage for herself & things from Boston to Hartford			1-10-00
Wood & 2 Bushels of barly Malt,			10-00
			15-01-00

Besides divers other things, as Sugar & Spice and Wine yt I mention not in about, and yet had she herselfe needed this & as mutch more I should endeavoured to supply; but hereby to be inabled to give to other prsons, I am yet to see the reason of, but shall humbly leave It to your honors to consider and determine as God shall guide & rest.

Yours to serve WL by Total £39-04-00.

Page 52-3-4.

Stebbing, Edward, Hartford. Invt. £639-02-00. Taken 19 August, 1668, by Eleazer Holyoke, John Allyn, Thomas Bull & James Ensign. Will dated 24 August, 1663.

I Edward Stebbing do here make my last Will & Testament: First, I give to my wife Frances my houseing & Lands in Hartford, except such Lands as are hereafter mentioned to be sold, which she is to enjoy for the terme of her natural life, as also two best Cows & 3 of the Best Swine, as also ye Use of the Household Stuffe or so much of it as she shall see need to make Use of. Also in ye End of her natural life she shall have liberty to dispose of £40 as she shall see Fit. I give to our beloved son John Chester £40. I give & bequeath, after my wives decease, my Houseing & Land, such of my Lands as shall not be sold to pay my Engagements, I give them to Edward Cadwell, my son Cadwell's Child, and John Wilson, or, if he dye before 21 years of age, I give them to Samuel Wilson. And in Case my gr. child Edward Cadwell dye, then I give the above to the Children of my daughter Cadwell. Also, I give to Samuel Wilson £30. I give to my son Gaylord's Children, Joseph, Benjamin and Joanna, £8 apeice, also Mary Gaylord, whome I do order to be with her gr. Mother. Also, I give to the four children of my daughter Holyoke, 40 Shillings apiece, John's part to be paid at the age of 21 years. Also, I do appoint that John Wilson shall be with his Gr. Mother to help her according to his best skill and ability during her natural life, during which time I desire my Executors that he be instructed in my trade by Caleb Stanly, as it may accord with my wives comfort. I ordain my wife to be my Executrix. I desire the Hon. Mr. Samuel Wyllys, my Brother Eleazer Holyoke, Lieut. Bull and Robert Webster to be Executors. The remainder of my Estate, after the decease of my wife, to be disposed to my daughter Cadwells Children, to John Wilson, and to Mary Gaylord, at the discretion of my Executors. I give to Richard Weller 20 shillings. I give to my Executors 50 shillings apiece.

Witness: *Eleazer Holyoke.* EDWARD STEBBING.

Court Record, Page 79—3 September, 1668: Will proven and Inventory Exhibited.

Page 162—18 April, 1677: Jeremy Diggins, Plntf., *Contra* Thomas Cadwell, Dfnt., in an Action for illegal Detaining a peice of Land in Hartford South Meadow belonging to the sd. Jeremy Diggins in the

Right of Mary his wife, and appointed to him by the Executors of the last Will of Edward Stebbing, Decd.

Page 119.

Stebbing, Mrs. Frances, Hartford. Invt. £82-11-02. Taken 23 December, 1673, by Thomas Bull & Robert Webster.

I ffrances Stebbing, Living in Hartford, in the colony of Conecticot, Widdow, being aged and under many weaknesses of body, but having my perfect memory and Understanding, Doe make and Ordain this my last Will and Testament, wherein I give to my Dear and beloved son Mr. John Chester, now living in or neer unto London in old England, the ffull and Just some of Twenty and four pounds Starling; or, if deceased, to his wife and his two Sons John and Sampson Chester, in equal portion, to be paid in Hartford. I give unto my ffowr grand children, Thomas, William, Matthew and Mary Cadwell, fower pounds a pece, to be paid in Currant Country pay into the hands of my Son Thomas Cadwell. I give to my daughter Cadwell all my wearing apparell, both Woolen and Linen. I Constitute Lt. Thomas Bull and James Ensign Executors. 20th May, 1670.

Witness: *Thomas Bull.* ffRANCES X STEBBING.

Codicil, wherein is given 7 Acres of Land in the South Meadow not before disposed of, it being four score Rod Long and about fourteen Rod and a quarter wide, bequeathed to Thomas, William and Mary Cadwell. And 4 acres more I doe give, two acres of ye said fowre to ye now two youngest children of my son and daughter Matthew and Abigail Cadwell, and the other two acres I leave to the dispose of my two friends in trust, Lt. Bull and Lt. Robert Webster, whom I ordain Executors.

I ffrances Stebbing doe now Rattify the within specified will, dated 20th May, 1670; only the Executors, which I now ordain Lt. Bull and Lt. Robert Webster. And also I now doe bequeath to my daughter Cadwell only my wearing goone, and the rest of my apparell to be divided betwixt ye wife of John Wilson, Mary Day and Mary Cadwell.—12 November, 1673. Also I give to Mr. John Whiting 40s, and my husbands cloak to John Wilson.

Witness: *Eliazer Way,* FFRANCES X STEBBING.
John Wilson.

Court Record, Page 136—20 January, 1673-4: Will exhibited. Proven.

Page 153.

Stedman, Lt. John, Wethersfield. Died December, 1675. Invt. £172-04-08. Taken February, 1675, by Lt. Chester, Ensign Goodrich, John Belden sen., Townsmen. Will dated 11 January, 1675-6.

Lt. John Stedman, the day he went to Springfield pr. the Councils Order, said to Samuel Talcott and William Goodrich, as his will, He gave his Lands to his Son John Stedman Jr., hopeing he would give Something to his other Children. He gave of his Estate other than Lands to his Wife.

Witness: *Samuel Talcott,*
William Goodrich.

Court Record, Page 152—2 March, 1675-6.: Will exhibited. Adms. to the Relict.

Page 11—21 October, 1678: Lt. John Stedman & Elizabeth, wife, being both deceased & Leaving four small children, the Govr & Assistants doe desire & appoynt sargt. John Stedman to take some care & to look after the children that are left by his Father & to dispose of them in such places as they may be well educated, the sd. Stedman to take advice of Major Talcott & Capt. Allyn in the dispose of them.

Page 11-12.

Steele, George, Hartford. Invt. £131-06-10. Taken 21 Dec., 1664, by Thomas Bunce, Samuel Steele. Will dated 24 May, 1663.

I George Steele of Hartford, uppon the river Conecticot, being very aged & under many infirmaties, but haveing the perfect use of my memory and understanding, doe make this my Last will: Imprimis. I give unto my Brother John Steele 50s. Item. I give unto my Daughter Elizabeth Wates my old Mill, my bed with all the furniture belonging to it, Also my vice, my warming pan, frying pan and fier pan, my fier fforks and spitt, my skales and fen and twenty pound of leaden weights, my pek hamer and spincers. Also, I give unto my grandchild Martha Hanison my best chamber pott. Also, I give unto Moses and Micah Mudge ten shillings apeece. Also, I give unto my grandchildren, James and Mary Steele, chests to each one. All other estate not here bequeathed I give unto my son James Steele, whom I make sole Executor, and intreat Thomas Bull and James Ensign to see my will truly performed.

Witness: *Thomas Bull, James Ensign.*   GEORGE STEELE.

Court Record, Page 29—2 March, 1664-5: Will proven.

Page 15-16.

Steele, John sen., Farmington. Invt. £182-06-00. Taken by John Lawton and John Lancton. Will dated 30 January, 1663.

I John Steele of Farmington, being stricken in yeares and weakness, doe see necessary to set on smal occasions in ye world at a stay. I give to my wife Mercy Steele the house wherein I now dwell. I give to my son Samuel Steele a silver Bowle, wch was mine owne, Marked wth three Silver Stamps and an S., all on the upper end of ye bowle. Also, I give unto my son Samuel one half of al my Books, also my gold scales and weights belonging to ym, All which prticulars I give to my son Samuel and his heirs forever. And to avoid other trouble of other Conveyances of house and Land to my son Samuell Steele of what I gave him at his marriage wth Mary Boosy, I here express it that as then I did so here I doe give and bequeath unto my son Samuel Steele a parcel of Land with a tenement standing on it, wch parcel of Land contains by estimation two Acres, abutting on the highway east and River West, and William Judds Land south, and John Steeles Land North; As also a smal parcel of Land on wch his Stilhouse Stands, Containing by estimation nine roods. I give and bequeath unto my two Sons-in-Law, William and Thomas Judd, my now dwelling house and barn, home lott, yards, Garden, orchyard thereto be longing, to be equally devided betwixt the foresaid William and Thomas, to them and their heirs forever, to enter possession imediately after myne and my wives departure out of this natural life. Further, my will is that a few things Should be disposed to my Wife and Children and grand Children: To my Wife, two small Silver Spoones and some small matter of linnen; And to Mary Judd, one peice of Gold; And to Sarah Judd, one peice of Gold; to John Steele, son of *John Steele deceased,* one Silver Spoon; And to Samuel, son of ye said John deceased, one Silver Spoon; and to Benoni Steele, one Silver Spoon; And to Rachel, Daughter of Samuel Steele, one Silver Spoon; to be delivered to them at their marriage by my son Samuel Steele. But my wife and two Daughters shal have theirs imediately after the departure of my natural life. My Sons-in-law, William and Thomas Judd, Executors. Samuel & James Steele to be Overseers.

Witness: *James Steele,*   JOHN STEELE.
           Samuel Steele.

Court Record, Page 34—16 June, 1665: Will proven.

Stevens, Nicholas. Court Record, Page 141—13 August, 1674: There was returned by the Constable of Haddam a verdict concerning the death of one Nicholas Stevens of Rhoad Island:

We whose names are underwritten, being appoynted a Jury to enquire into the cause of the death of Nicholas Stevens of rohd Island, have according to the best of our skill and judgement, viewed his corps & searched to see if there was any wound or any thing that might be a blameable cause of his death, & this we give in our verdict, that we find no wound nor any reason of Jealousy to submit that any man was accessory to his death, but by the overruling providence of the most high & most wise God (who appoynts the time & place of every man's death) was appoynted to period & finish his dayes in this time & place, being drowned in the River.

This Verdict was drawn up & subscribed by the Jury August 6th, 1674, & delivered into the Court the day above written, Together with an Inventory of his Estate signed by Mr Thomas Terry, Mr James Huling & Nicho: Braddock. (On file.)

These engaged to take Care for the Carefull Navigation of the Vessell till she hath accomplish her voyage, & to return the vessell & Estate to the authorities at Rhode Island, The dangers of the seas only excepted.

(P. C. Vol. II, No. 96, Will.   Page 97, Invt.

Stocking, George, Hartford. Invt. [————] Taken 25 May, 1683, by Nathaniel Willett, Thomas Bunce & John Easton.

Will of George Stocking, planter: I do in this my Last Will and Testament give unto Anne my wife all my houseinge, barn, Orchard, home lott, upland, meadow & Swamp land, Cattell, and all my other Estate, for her to use during the time of her natural life, and after my decease to be disposed of as followeth: I doe give to my daughter Lydia Richards, the wife of John Richards, the Sum of £14; & doe also heerby give to my daughter Sarah Olcott, the wife of Samuel Olcott, the sum of £10. I doe also give to the Six Children of Andrew Benton, that is to Andrew Benton Jr., John Benton, Samuel Benton, Joseph Benton, Mary Benton and Dorothy Benton, the sum of £12, to be equally divided among them. I do also give unto Hannah Camp one Mare. My will is that these legacies shall be discharged within one year after my wive's decease. My will also is that if any of my Cattell or other Goods of mine may be Spared, my wife and my Executor, agreeing together aboute it, may sell The same and pay some legacies before given, to whom they shall see meete presently. After my estate is prised, the debts and these legacies being paid, and my desire in this my will being Attended, I doe hereby give the remaining parte of my Estate to my son Samuel Stockinge, both howsinge, Land and whatever else is not given away before, for him to possess and Injoy for ever. I doe also make my son Samuel Stocking Executor. Also, my will is that all my Land shall pay, according to the proportion, to the mayntenance of the Ministry at the new Meeting house in Hartford. I have desired my two friends Gregory Wolterton and Lt. Thomas Bull to see my will performed. In witness whereof I have heare unto set my hand. Dated this 15 day of July, in the year of our Lord God 1673.

Witness: *Gregory Wolterton,*   GEORGE X STOCKING.
         George Grave, sen.

Page 40.

Stoddard, John, Wethersfield. Invt. £407-08-00. Taken 20 December, 1664, by John Chester, William Gutteridge, Samuel Halle, John Deminge, Townsmen. Six children: Mary age 21 years, John 19, Josiah 16, Mercy 12, Elizabeth 8, Nathaniel 4 years of age.

Court Record, Page 27—2 March, 1664-5 : Adms. to Mary the Relict. Dist. Order to the Relict £129 during life, to the eldest son £63, to Josiah £49, to Nathaniel £40, to each dau. £36. John Deming and Samuel Hall, Overseers.

Page 4-6.

Stone, Rev. Samuel. He died 20 July, 1663. Invt. £563-01-00. Taken November, 1663, by John Allyn, William Wadsworth. Will not dated.

Impr. It is my will that Mrs. Elizabeth Stone, my loving wife, shall be my Agent & Sole Executrix, and that wthout any intanglemt or feare ; the legacyes given to her selfe being firstly possessed all & every of them as they follow, & the after legacyes to be made good out of the remayning estate if sufficient; otherwise, a distribution according to that proportion. Yet if there happen any overplus, to be wholy & solely at the dispose to my sd. wife.

Also, I give unto my sd. wife, during the term of her life, halfe my howsing & land within the libertyes of Hartford, & to have the free dispose of the valew of the sd. halfe of my land at the time of her death, by legacy or otherwise ; & also farther it is my will & I doe freely give unto my wife all the household stuff that I had with her when I married her, to be at her full and free dispose as shee shall see cause.

I give to my sonne Samuel Stone, at the time of my decease, the other halfe of my houseing & Lands within the liberties of Hartford aforesd., the other halfe of the houseing at the time of the death of my sd. wife, as also the other halfe of the land, but upon a valuable consideration as before specified. Also, I give unto my son all my books except such as are otherwise disposed of. Provided (that if) my sonne Samuell depart this life before he is married, that then the whole of this my prsent legacy shall return to & be wholly at the dispose of my wife.

Also, unto my daughter Elizabeth I doe give & order to be payd the full sum of £100 in household goods, Chattells & other country pay what my wife can best parte wthall, or in Two or three acres of Land at price currant before the sd. Land be divided betwixt my wife & sonne as aforesayd, & this sayd Legacy to be performed & made good wth in Two yeares after the marriage of my sayd daughter Elizabeth. Provided, that if my sayd daughter shall match or dispose of her selfe in marriage either wth out or Crosse to the minds of her mother & the minde & Consent of my Overseers, then this my Last will concerneing her to stand voyd & she gladly to accept of such summe & quantity or portion as her sayd mother shall freely dispose to her. Or And in case my sayd daughter shall dye & depart this world Before she receive her sayd portion, the whole thereof shall fully returne & belong unto my sayd wife at her dispose.

Also, as a token of my Fatherly Love & respect, I doe give unto my three daughters, Rebecca, Mary & Sarah, forty shillings each of them, to be payd them by my wife in houshold stuffe as it shall be prized in Inventorie.

I desire Mr. Matthew Allyn, my Brother William Wadsworth, Mr. John Allyn & my sonne Joseph Fitch, overseers.

Witness: *Bray Rosseter.*   SAMUEL STONE.

Court Record, Page 12—3 March, 1663-4: Will proven.

Page 78.

Strickland, Thwaite, Hartford. Invt. £55-06-00. Taken 21 June, 1670, by James Ensign, Nathaniel Willett. The children: Elizabeth Andrews, age 23 years, John 21, Joseph 15, Jonathan 13, Ephraim 7 years.

Court Record, Page 101-3—1 September, 1670: Adms. to Nicholas Disbroe.

Page 103—9 November, 1670: Order to Dist: To the Widow £20, & to the five Children to each of them £5.

Page 73-4.

Talcott, Dorothy, Mrs., Hartford. Invt. £275-05-06. Taken 28 February, 1669-70, by John Allyn, Thomas Olcott. Will dated 22 September, 1669.

I Dorothy Talcott, Widdow, of Hartford, doe make my last Will & Testament: I do give and bequeath unto my sonne Samuel Tallcott the arreares of what is unpayd of eight pounds pr annum out of the Rent of Land at Wethersfield, assigned by my deceased Husband to be payd to him during my Natural life. Allsoe, I do give and bequeath to my Son Samll a paire of Holen Pillow beers and a paire of sheets belonging to ye Bed his father gave him, marked with M in Blue. Allsoe, I give him one flock Bed, boulster, and a paire of Blankets Belonging to it, in my Kitchen Chamber, And one Third part of my wearing Cloaths, both woolen and Linnin. Alsoe, I give my son Samll one Third part of my Househould linnin. Alsoe, I give him my Pewter flagon and a Third part of the Pewter belonging to the House, And the Iron Drippin Pan, and the Lest Spitt, And the bigest Iron Pott save one, and the litle Brass Pott, And the lest Trunk, And one of the Chests in the kitchen Chambr, And Three of my great green Cushions. And alsoe I give my son Samll my Silver beer Bowl and Two Silver spoones. I give a Third part of my wearing Cloths to my son Samll, my Turkey Mohaire Coat excepted. The forementioned legacyes, with my debt due to my sonne, John Talcott, or to any other, being first discharged. I do give and bequeath to my sonne John Talcott all other my estate lying and being in Cattelle or kyne, Horse, sheep and swine, as Alsoe all sortes of Corne or graine belonging to me whatsoever. Alsoe I give my Son John my Cloaths, both woolin and linnin, my Turky mohaire Coat, A paire of Holen sheits And a paire of Rought pillow beers belonging to ye bed his ffather gave him, Alsoe my Plate, Pewter and Brass Iron vessels, utensills or Tooles, Armes, ammunisio And whatsoever els apperteynes to me, whether within doores or without (not given expresly to my son Samuel by this my will). I say I give all other my estate to my sonne John Tallcott. I ordain my son John Talcott sole Executor.

Witness: *Jeremy Addams.*   DOROTHY TALCOTT.

Court Record, Page 97—3 March, 1669-70: Will filed by Capt. John Talcott. Also he doth engage to see the Debts duly paid.

Page 3-4.

Tinker, John, New London. Invt. £145-15-00. Taken 22 December, 1662, by Obadiah Bruen & James Rogers. The children: Mary, born 2 July, 1653; John, 14 August, 1665; Amos, 28 October, 1657; Samuel, 1st April, 1659; Roakdey Tinker, 23 February, 1661.

John Smith—Copy.

By a Deed left in the hands of Mr. Buckley, which alsoe is upon Record, he hath upon good, consideration given and made over to his wife his houseing wth one Hundred Ackers of upland, upon the neck of Land called the general neck, towards the Harbours mouth; also one Mare Coult two years old and a yearling heifer bought of Wm Cheesbrook, now by Mrs. Tinker called Blackey; also a farme of two Hundred and Forty acres of upland, and also a parcell of meadow four or six acres if it be to be had, this farme Lying neere to Andrew Lesters farme on the east side of the great River. This farme of 240 acres is by Deed made over by Mr. Tinker to Mr. Richardson for the use of his son John Tinker; also in the same Deed a Cowe wth all her increase made over to Mr. Richardson for the use of Mary Tinker, the daughter of Mr. John Tinker; also a breeding Mare with halfe her increase left Amos Tinker, the Mare being now at Norwoake.

Signed, *Obadiah Breuen, James Rogers, John Smith.* 20 May, 1663.

Court Record (Special) Page 6—9 July, 1663: Invt. exhibited. Mr. Rogers, Mr. Bruen and John Smith to husband the Estate, to pay Debts so far as the Estate proves solvent. *Some action was taken in New London.*

Page 178.

Tore, Jeremy, Boston. Died in Middletown, Conn., 25 October, 1676. Invt. £17-04-00. Taken by Richard Hall & William Harris.

Court Record, Page 159—6 December, 1676: Invt. exhibited of the Estate in Middletown, and to remain in Deacon Hall's Hand until further Order from this Court.

Page 72-3.

Treat, Richard sen., Wethersfield. Invt. £69-10-08. Taken by John Deming, Robert Webster and John Nott. Will dated 13 February, 1668.

The last Will & Testament of Richard Treat sen. of Wethersfield, Colony of Connecticut: Item: I give to my wife Alis Treat, after my decease, all the lands of what kinde soever I stand possessed of, within ye bounds of Wethersfield, and five acres of land lying in the dry swamp, of wch I have improved and pr pared for use, lying next my son James his land. Item. One peece of meddow lying in the great meddow comonly called by the name of send home. Item. The one halfe or eight acres next home of that peece of meddow comonly cald Filbarne. Item. The home lotte by the plaine land side. Item. Ye dwelling howse that I formerly lived in, with Convenient yeard room, and that end of ye barne on ye side the threshing flowre next the dwelling, with one halfe of that lotte belonging to ye said dwelling house lyeing next his son Richards howse & lotte, except my wife & son James shall agree otherwise. Item. All my pasture land fenced in, beyond my Daughter Hollisters lotte. Item. The use of two of my best Cowes, wch shee shall chuse, wch if they shall continue & Stand longer than my loveing wife liveth, they shall be my eldest sone Richard Treats. Item. I give to my wife the Handing bed, bedding, bedsted, wth all the furniture thereto belonging, with the use of so much of the houshold goods during her life time as shee shall judge needfull for her comfort, of what sort soever.

Item. I give and bequeath to my eldest son, Richard Treat, the full possession & Confermation of the farme of Mayog, wth all ye Respective priveledges thereto belonging, with three of my youngest Heifers. Item. I give to my second sonne, Robert Treat, ten pounds. Item. I give to my youngest son, James Treat, besids the lands already made over to him, my Mill & grinding stone, fann, Timber chaine, Stilyeards, and my little bible.

Item. I give to my sonn-in-law, Matthew Camfield, twentie pounds for that wch is remaining of his portion. Item. I give to my daughter Hollister fourtie shillings. Item. To my daughter Johnson ten shillings. Item. My debts being paid, I give to my loveing sons, John Demon and Robert Webster, equally, all the rest of my goods and Chattells whatsoever, except Mr Perkins Book, wch I give to my sonn John Demon, and my great bible to my Daughter Honour Demon, and that money in my Cousen Samuel Welles his hand unto my Cousen Daniel Demong, son of John Demon senir. And my desire is that my son-in-law John Demon, Robert Webster and Richard Treat would be my Overseers for their mutual helpfullness to my wife, & endeavor to see the accomplishment of this my last Will & Testamt. And for the Ratification hereof I have this 13th of ffebruary, 1668, set to my Hand & Seal.

RICHARD TREAT, SEN.

Court Record, Page 97—3 March, 1669-70: Will endorsed & Exhibited in Court, and, with the Invt., approved.

Page 181.

Waddams, John sen., Wethersfield. Invt. £239-05-00. Taken 20 February, 1676-7, by John Belden, Samuel Wright, Selectmen of the Town of Wethersfield.

John Waddams, on his death bed, gave his small Estate to his wife and his son John Waddams, but in her control during life. Dated 19 January, 1676-7.

Witness: *William* X *Morrice,*
Nathaniel X *Graves.*

Court Record, Page 161—1st March, 1676-7: Adms. to the Widow and son John. The Estate to them both; and if John out-live his Mother, the Estate then to be his.

Page 144-5-6.

Wadsworth, William, Hartford. Invt. £1677-10-09. Taken 16 Oct., 1675, by Nicholas Olmsted, Nathaniel Willett. Will dated 16 May, 1675.

Whereas I, William Wadsworth, being weak in Body by the visiting hand of God, but of perfect memory, doe make this my last Will & Testament: I give to my wife Elizabeth Wadsworth £20 a year the term of her life, to be paid, £8 by Samuel Wadsworth, £6 by Joseph Wadsworth, & £6 by Thomas Wadsworth. I give to my son John Wadsworth £10 as a token of my Love. I give to my son Samuel Wadsworth the other part of my Dwelling house, with all the Houseing thereto belonging, and the Land belonging to it. I give unto my son Joseph Wadsworth the house & Land I bought of Daniel Pratt in Hartford. I give unto my son Thomas all my Lands beyond the Great River, and the Barn to be finished out of the Estate, & ¼ part of the Household Stuffe which his Mother have not. I give unto my daughter Stotan £12, to my daughter Ferris £6. I give unto my daughter Ashely 20 Shillings. To my daughter Rebeckah £50 & ¼ part of my Household Stuffe which the Mother have not. I give unto my gr. daughter Long 20 Shillings. I give unto my son Samuel the Corne that is upon the Ground & all the Cattle, And I doe make him my son Samuel Wadsworth my sole Executor to this my Will, and desire Mr. George Gardner and Capt. John Allyn to be Overseers.

Witness: *George Gardner,*   WILLIAM WADSWORTH.
Sarah Howard.

Court Record, Page 151—26 January, 1675-6: Will & Invt. exhibited.

Waite, Benjamin. Court Record, Page 83—4 March, 1669: Thomas Bull, Jr. and Hester Coales (alias Cole). Intention of marriage objected to by Benjamin Waite.

Page 83-4.

Warham, Rev. John, Pastor of the Church at Windsor. Died 1st April, 1670. Invt. £1239-10-00. Taken 30 April, 1670, by Capt. Newbery, Thomas Forde and Samuel Marshall.

At a Court held at Hartford 23 November, 1670, there was considered a paper or papers purporting to be the Last will of Rev. John Warham, which were rejected. And an Order from the Court was Issued that after the decease of Mrs. Warham the Estate shall be equally divided among his three daughters, the wife of Thomas Allyn, The wife of Return Strong, and the wife of Mr. Stodder of Northampton, and these men were appointed Adms. upon the Estate.

Page 98—11 April, 1670: Upon Motion of Thomas Allyn and Mr. Return Strong that the Assistants would take some Care that the Estate of their Father, Rev. Mr. John Warham, might be preserved from Waste, & that Mrs. Warham, Relict, might be comfortably provided for according to her present necessity until they can perfect the Inventory and present it to the Court with all such Writings as may concern the dispose of the Estate, and desire Assistants to appoint Deacon John Moore, Thomas Allyn & Return Strong to take Care that Mrs. Warham be comfortably provided for and the Estate secured in the best way until aforesd. matters be settled.

Page 105—23 November, 1670: Will not proven. The Estate, so much as is left of it, shall pass to the comfortable maintenance of Mrs. Warham during life, & at her decease shall be equally divided to her 3 daughters if they be then living, or their heirs. Also provided that what Estate Mrs. Warham had before marriage with Mr. Warham shall remain at her own dispose. The Court appoint Thomas Allyn, Return Strong, Deacon John Moore & Lt. Walter Fyler Adms.

Page 9—(Vol. VII) 10 March, 1700-1: Capt. Thomas Allyn and Walter Fyler, Adms., now both deceased, and the Adms. is not yet perfected.

Page 26-7-8.

Watts, Elizabeth, Hartford. Invt. £127-02-02. Taken 17 April, 1666, by Richard Butler, Thomas Bull and Gregory Wolterton. Will dated 28 February, 1665-6.

I, Elizabeth Watts, Widow, living in Hartford, upon the Riuer of Conecticut, being ill and weak in body but hauing my perfect memory and Understanding, doe make and ordain this my last Will and Testament in manner and fform as ffolloweth: Imprimis: I giue unto my cosin Mary Smith, Liuing in Banbury, in Oxfordsheir, in old England, £10, to her & her heirs for euer. Also, I giue unto my cosin George Haines (that is blinde) £8. Further, my Will is that whereas my Husband Richard Watts, Decd, in his last Will & Testament did Will & Appoint that that Estate of his that hee left and that should bee remayning at my disease should be diuided to the Children off his daughter Hubbard then born, and to Hannah Browne, in that proportion therein sett down, which Estate did amount to the sum of £26, that these Legacies be truly paid according as his Will doth express. I give to my cousin Daniel Hubbard my part of the mare that is between him and mee. Also, I further give to him a feather bed, a feather Bolster and a feather Pillow, with my Green Rugg, one blankett, a paire of my best sheets, with my bedsted & Curtains, and one of my year-old Steers. Item. I give to my daughter Hubbard my Gown, my Coat & my hood. I give to my daughter Browne my best Stuff petticoat. All other off my wearing Linnen & Wollens my will is that it be equally divided & given to my daughter Hubbard and my daughter Browne & my cousin Mary Ranne. I give to my daughter Hubbard & to my daughter Browne 20s apeece. Also, I give to my Cousin Elizabeth Hubbard my Lest Brass pott. I give to my cousin Hannah Browne my Smugg heifer. I give to my cousin Richard Hubbard my Heifer now with his Father. My other year-old Steier I give to my cousin Nathaniel Browne. I give to widdow Wesley 10s. I give to Thomas Waples 20s; to Widdow Watson 10s; and to her two daughters 5s apeece. I give to Mr. John Whiting, pastor of the Church of Christ heer at hartford, fforty shillings. I give to Hannah Ensign my begger new pewter platter, and to Mary Peck the lesser of them. My will also is that my Maid Elizabeth Taintor have a new cotton suit & all such necessaries as is suitable for one in her condission. Also I give unto Elizabeth Taintor 30s to be committed to the hands of some able friend to be improved for her. My will is that my Executors doe take the first opportunity they can after my decease to give notice to my ffriends in England off these Legacies I have given them and bequeathed to them, Requireing their Order for the Conveyance thereof to them, & upon my Executors attendence thereto to send a full discharge; & my meaning is that my Executors be fully acquitted upon their payment of the Legacies here in New England. I make & ordain Deac. Edward Stebbing & James Ensign Executors, And Lt. Bull to be Overseer.

Witness: *Thomas Bull,*   ELIZABETH X WATTS.
     James Ensign.

Court Record, Page 50—7 May, 1666: Will proven.

Page 52.

Watts, William, in England. Invt. £13-10-00. Taken 2 May, 1668, by Richard Butler, Nicholas Olmsted, Paul Peck, of some Lands in Custody of Thomas Watts, being 3 acres of wood land and half an acre house lott, £11; some tools, 10 shillings; also a legacy from his Mother now in the hands of his brother Thomas Watts, 40 shillings. Per James Ensign.

Court Record, Page 77—7 May, 1668: Invt. exhibited. Adms. to Sergt. Thomas Watts.

Page ?

Webb, Richard. Decd. July last.   Invt.   £234-08-06.   Taken 5 October, 1665, by Richard Olmsted, John Gregory, Walter Hoit.

Court Record, Page—1st November, 1665:   The Widow to be Adms. And whereas, Thomas Butler claims, in the behalf of his wife, a child's portion of the estate, Mr. Campfield and the sd. Thomas hath agreed that the sd. Thomas shall have ten pounds out of the estate sumtimes before Michalmas next, and if not payd until the first of May next, must be other current pay, horse flesh excepted.   Upon this agreement the sd. Thomas acquits the sd. Adms. from any further demands.   *A true copy of the Record.*   WILLIAM HILL, *Clarke.*

Page 170.

Webster, Lieut. Robert.   Invt.   £670-16-08.   Taken 29 June, 1676, by Thomas Bull, James Steele, George Grave.   Will dated 20 May, 1676.

Whereas, I Robert Webster of Hartford doe see Cause to set my house in order and doe declare this to bee my last Will & Testament, I give all to my wife Susannah Webster during her widowhood.   But if my wife change her name, then I give her but one-third part of my estate. the remainder to be equally divided amongst my children, except the Eldest a double portion; to my sons at 21 years of age, and to my daughters at 18 years of age.   I make my wife sole Executrix, and desire Mr. John Coales sen., Andrew Benton sen., and John Blackleach of Hartford to be Overseers.

ROBERT WEBSTER LS.

Witness: *Thomas Stedman, Phineas Wilson.*

Court Record, Page 156—7 Sept., 1676:   Part of Invt. only exhibited. Adms. to the Widow for the present.

Hartford Land Records, Vol. 5—18 March, 1707-8:   Thomas King, John Seymour and Elizabeth Seymour, his wife, all of Hartford, quit claim to Jonathan, Samuel, Robert, William, and the Heirs of John Webster, Dec., all of them sons of the late Robert Webster, Dec.

Page 164-5.

Welles, Capt. Samuel, Wethersfield.   Invt. £1100-00-00.   Taken 15 July, 1675, by Samuel Talcott, John Chester, John Deming.   The children: Samuel, age 16 years, Thomas 14, Sarah 12, Mary 10, Ann 7, Elizabeth 5 years (at date 15 July, 1675).

Court Record, Page 155—7 September, 1676:   Adms. to Mrs. Hannah Welles, the widow.

Page 157—3 November, 1676: Mrs. Welles appeared in Court and relinquished the Adms., not being in a capacity to carry it on. This Court appoint Mr. John Chester and Mrs. Ann Howkins Adms., Mr. Samuel Talcott & John Deming sen., Overseers, desireing Mrs. Howkins to take the family under her care and management. Order for Dist. to the widow 1-3 of the Real Estate according to law, and £50 personal Estate, forever; to Samuel Welles, £380; to Thomas, £230; to Mary, considering her lameness, £140; to Sarah, Ann & Elizabeth, to each £100.

Page 14—(Vol. IV) 24 April, 1679: Mr. Samuel Talcott is desired to assist Capt. John Chester in the Adms. upon Capt. Samuel Welles his Estate.

Page 37—10 March, 1680-1: The Governor and Magistrates did desire & appoynt Capt. John Chester, Mr. Samuel Talcott and Mr. John Deming sen. to dist. the Estate of Capt. Samuel Wells unto his Children according & in such proportion as the Court formerly granted to them.

Page 148—4 March, 1696-7: Whereas is entered 1-3 part of all the Real Estate belonging to Capt. Samuel Wells of Wethersfield, Decd, which Land was set out by the persons above named as the Relict's part of the sd. Estate in the year 1681, The Court order it to be recorded and that the Widow, viz., Mrs. Hannah Allyn (formerly Wells) shall enjoy the sd. 1-3 part of the sd. Estate without Molestation from any person pretending any right hereto during her life.

Page 159—(Vol. VI)—21 July, 1697: *The Lands belonging to the Whorshipfull Capt. John Allyn, Assistant, upon Account of Mrs. Allyn's thirds out of the Lands of Capt. Samuel Welles, decd (as recorded).*

Page 56-8.

Welles, Thomas, The Worshipfull Mr., Hartford. Invt. £1297-11-00. Taken 20 August, 1668, by Eleazer Holyoke, John Allyn, Thomas Bull, James Ensign. The children and ages: Thomas, 11 in Oct., 1668; Ichabod, age 8 years next November; Samuel, age 6, Oct., 1668; Jonathan, 4, Sept., 1668; Joseph, born April, 1667; Rebeckah, 13, May, 1668; Sarah, age 9, April, 1668.

Court Record, Page 79—3 September, 1668: Adms. to Mrs. Hannah Welles, the Relict. Mr. James Richards, James Ensign and Mr. John Allyn are desired, with Consent of Mrs. Welles, to be Overseers. They are desired to advise with Mr. Anthony Howkins and Mr. Samuel Welles in any difficulty that may fall out in the same.

Dist. File: 4 March, 1668-9: Dist. of the Estate of the Worshipfull Thomas Welles of Hartford:

	£ s d
On a Supposition of Estate of	1100-00-00 Net
Subtracting Hanna & Mary Pantry's portions due to them,	240-00-00
And Debts due to persons in the Bay,	50-00-00

From a Total Inventory,   1297-11-00
                                                                 ——————————

There remains for Division,   1007-11-00
To Mrs. Welles, her thirds of the Chattels,   151-00-00
Also a Note,   453-11-00
She to have 1-3 of the profits of Land during life, the
    remainder of Land & Chattels to the Children, Total: 856-11-00
To Eldest son Thomas,   212-00-00
To Samuel & Joseph to each,   120-00-00
To Ichabod,   121-00-00
To Jonathan,   120-00-00
To Rebeckah,   83-11-00
To Sarah,   80-00-00

By John Allyn, James Richards, Thomas Bull and James Ensign. February, 1668.

Page 4—(Vol IV)—10 April, 1678: Upon the Motion of Thomas Welles of Hartford, this Court nominate James Steele, Marshall (George) Grave and Stephen Hosmer, with advice of the Overseers, to assist the Widow in the management of the Estate, and dispose of the Children in the most Just and equal Way.

Will & Invt. on File.

Wellman, William, Kennleworth. Died 5th October, 1672. Invt. £348-18-06. Taken 8 September, 1671, by Henry Farnham & Josias Hull. Additional Invt. of Lands £135-10. Taken 27 May, 1679, by Henry Crane & Samuel Buell, by Order of the Court of Assistants at Hartford. Debts due to sd. Estate, £13-03-03. Sd. Estate is indebted £63-09-09. And he being a Seaman and having trading in many parts of the Country, we fear the Debts will be a great deal more. Debts payde out of the estate by me Elizabeth Joye since the death of my Housband as followeth:

My Brother Samuel Spencer	Mr. Obadiah Wilcockson
Willie Goodman of New London	Edward Parkes
Mrs. Raymond of Saybrook	Mr. Orford
Mr. Chester of New London	John Pratt
Mr. Hill of New London	Mr. Truman
William Stone of Guilford	Mr. Leete
William Beeman of Saybrook	Mr. Lord
Henry Cole of Middletown	Mrs. Cole
John Olmsted of Norwich	Mr. Bryan
John Coking of Norwich	Mrs. Olcott
Henry Gates of Guilford	Mr. Belcher
Mr. Rossiter for Physick	James Tappin
Mr. Condey of New London	Mr. Gilbert
Mr. Collins of Guilford	Daniel Kelsey

Thomas Cooke
James Richards
Robert Reeves
John Mitchell
Abraham Frost
William Kelsey
Edward Griswold
Robert Williams

Thomas Edwards
Mrs. Blackleach
Jeremiah Addams
Thomas Hallibutt
Richard Hallell
My Uncle Spencer
Benjamin Wright

For taking Inventory and carrying it to New London, 10 Shillings.

The children: Mary Wellman, 31 years, Martha 18, Benjamin 17, Elizabeth 14, William 10, Samuel 4, and Rachel one year old, born since her Father made his Will. Will dated 14th March, 1668-9.

Whereas, I William Wellman of Kennleworth, being sick and weake of body but of perfect memory, as my duty is at all time to command and commit my soule to God, as also to set my house in order in reference to my outward estate with which god hath betrusted mee, in token of my love to & care of my wife & Children begotten of my owne body, as my last will & Testament, in the first place I doe Constitute & appoynt my loveing wife Elizabeth Wellman my sole Executrix & to injoy the use of my now prsent dwelling house, outhouses & their appurtenances, with all my land within the plantation & township of Kennleworth aforesd. as they stand severally Recded in the towne records, & for to injoy all with their appurtenances during the time of her natural life, & after her death equally to be divided amongst my three sonns, viz, Benjamin Wellman, William Wellman & Samuel Wellman. Only excepting my sonne Benjamin, who is to receive his pportion of the lands wthin one year after he is of full age, excepting only of the house & home lott, wch is to remain intyre with my sd wife during her life as aforesd; & as a token of my love I doe bequeath unto my Eldest daughter Mary* now living at Norwich, as an addition to what portion shee hath received formerly, the full summe of five pounds to be paid her within two yeares after my decease; and unto my daughter Martha Wellman, now living at New London, I doe bequeath the full summe of twelve pounds to be payd unto her when she hath accomplished the full age of twenty years; & unto my daughter Elizabeth Wellman I doe bequeath the full summe of twenty pounds to be payd unto her when shee hath accomplished the aforesd. full age of twenty years. All the residue of my estate I bequeath unto my wife aforesd & the use of all entire to the end of the terms prfixt, paying forth the legacies to the legatees according to my order & appoyntmt, & towards the education & bringing up of my younger children. To wch sd. last will & Testament,

---

*Note: Thomas Howard and Mary Welman were married in January, 1666. See Caulkins' History of Norwich, Conn., Page 179 (Edition of 1866).

as my sole & free act, I subscribe my name this prsent March 14, 1668-9.
In the presence & WILLI X WELMON.

Witness of us: *Henry ffarnam did*
Edward Griswold, *Take oath this 16 of Septbr,*
Josiah Hull, *1671, that this is the will of*
Henry Farnham. *William Welmon, deceased, before*
me, Josias Hull, Com's.

Page 100.

Whaples, Thomas. Died about 10 December, 1671. Invt. £71-11-06.
Taken 1st January, 1671, by Thomas Bull, Robert Webster, Joseph Nash
and Philip Davis. The children: Rebecca, age 18 years, Hanna 16,
Thomas 15, Joseph 11, Jane 7, Ephraim 6, John 4 years of age.

Court Record, Page 121—7 March, 1671-2: Adms. to the Widow.
Lt. Robert Webster, Lieut. Thomas Bull and Sergt. Joseph Nash to be
Overseers, to assist in the management of the estate and disposal of the
Children.

Page 132-3.

Willard, Mr. Josiah, Wethersfield. Invt. £285-16-00. Taken 23
July, 1674, by John Kilbourn, Enoch Buck & Robert Webster.
The Creditors Cancelled most of the Debts to Mrs. Willard:

Richard Bryant	Jacob Drake	Mr. Lord
Mr. Buckingham	Daniel Emonds	Mr. Miles
Henry Buck	Mr. Gardner	John Nott
Alexander Bryant	Sam: Halls,	Mrs. Olcott
Thomas Crittenden	Thomas Hosmer	Roger Purchas
Nathaniel Cross	Stephen Hosmer	John White
Thomas Catlin	Thomas Lake	Mr. Wilson
Philip Davis		

The Father of the Decd having £25-05-00 in the Homested, is willing
to bestow £20 of it upon the Widow, Mrs. Willard.

Court Record, Page 142—3 September, 1674: Invt. exhibited, And
this Court grant Adms. to Mrs. Willard. The Debts and Creditors to be
presented to this Court at the next session, and Mr. Thomas Hosmer and
her Father and her Brother Mr. Stephen Hosmer, with Mr. Buckley and
Mr. Kimberly, are desired to assist in the Adms.

Page 146—29 December, 1674: A List of Debts and Credits now
exhibited in Court and the Estate found to be insolvent. Then this Court
appoint Mr. Samuel Talcott, Mr. James Treat and Mr. Eli Kimberly to
divide the Estate to the Creditors. Order. Dist.

Page 182-183.

Willcox, John, Middletown. Invt. £409-11-04. Taken 6 June, 1676, by Richard Hall, John Kirby. The children: Sarah Long, age 28 years, Israel 20, Samuel 18, Ephraim 4, Hester 2 years, December, 1675. Mary was born 9 March, 1675-6.

Court Record, Page 155—7 September, 1676: Adms. to the Widow and Deac. John Hall.

Page 161—1st March, 1676-7: Dist. of Estate to the widow according to law ; to the Eldest son, £66; to the 2nd son, £42 ; to the 3d son, £36 ; to the two daughters, £30 to each. Deacon Hall, Ensign White and William Cheny, distributors. Deacons Hall and Stocking, Overseers.

See File: 3 January, 1694-5: The Settlement of the Estate of John Wilcock, deceased, To the Legatees, by us which were appointed by the Court for that service & with the Agreement of the Relicks and all the Legatees, is as follows:

	£ s d
To the Eldest son Israel Wilcox,	66-03-00
To Samuel Wilcox,	48-00-00
To Ephraim Willcock,	36-00-00
To Easter Willcock,	30-00-00
To Mary Willcock,	30-00-00

This is a full Agreement of all the persons concerned, except Ephraim (which was not present), and before thos appointed by the Court, which are:

> NATH: WHITE,
> WILLIAM CHEENY,
> JOHN HALL SENIOR.

In Witness of this Agreement the Relick & the Legatees have set to their Hands:

> JOSEPH HAND SEN. in behalf of ESTHER WILCOCK,
> the wife of JOSEPH HAND JR.   ESTHER X STOW
> SARAH X WILCOCK   SAMUEL WILCOCK
> EPHRAIM WILCOCK   JOSEPH STOW
> MARY X WILCOCK.

March the 16th, 1714: A Dist. of the Half-Mile Lote made by Esther Stow, Adms. of the Estate of John Willcock, to the Children and Legatees, being a peice of Land that was left out of the Inventory, was put in and was divided to them as follows: To Sarah (Israel) Willcock, 15 acres ; To Samuel, Ephraim, Esther and Mary Wilcock, to each of them 7 ½ acres.   Signed: ESTHER X STOW.

Mr. Joseph Rockwell plees to enter upon record to the Children the above written Dist. as it there stands in proportion.
> ESTHER X STOW.

Page 141—(Vol. X) 6 December, 1726: A Dist. of the Estate of John Wilcox, sometime of Middletown, made 13 January, 1694-5, by Nathaniel White, William Cheeny and John Hall, was exhibited by Esther Stow (alias Wilcox), Adms. on sd. Estate, which Dist. some of the heirs appeared in Court and prayed that the same might be accepted, whereupon this Court do receive and accept sd. Dist. Ordered to be filed. Esther Stow (alias Wilcox) moved that she might be discharged in being Adms. This Court, considering her age and Infirmity, do grant her a *Quietus Est.*

Page 142—6 December, 1726: Whereas, it is represented to this Court that there is some Land belonging to the Estate of John Wilcox, decd, which hath been laid out since his decease, and so is not inventoried or Dist., this Court grant Adms. on sd. Estate in Lands unto Francis Wilcox of sd. Middletown and David Ensign Jr. of Hartford, and order that they exhibit an Inventory thereof to this Court as soon as may be, in order to be Dist. to the heirs.

Page 61.

Willcox, Mary, Hartford. Invt. £40-00-04. Taken 1st January, 1668-9, by James Ensign and Paul Peck.

Will: October the ffoureth, in the year of our Lord on thousand six hundred sixty and six, I Mary Wilcock of Hartford, in new England, widdow, Doe mak & Ordain this my last Will and Testament In manner & fform as ffolloweth: Imprimis. I give unto my Cosin Sara Long two pewter platters. Alsoe I give unto my Daughter An Haul forty shillings and my best feather pillow. All other of my Estat that shall remain due to mee by Bill, moovable goods, Cattell, or other houshold goods, Apparell, or any otherwis, my iust debts being paid & all necessary charges about my comly buriall being discharged, I give unto my son-in-Law John Bidwell, whom I make & Ordayn my soal Executor, & intreat my ffriends Deacon Butler & James Ensign to be Overseers unto this my Last will & Testament. In witness whereof I have heer unto sett my mark the day and yeare above written   MARY X WILCOCKS.

That this was distinctly read unto & owned to be understood by the Testator to be her last will & Testament is testified by us.
Richard Butler, James Ensign.

Court Record, Page 69—29 October, 1667: On Motion of Deacon Butler, in behalf of Widow Wilcox, This Court order John to pay to his Mother £6 a year, as on account of weakness she cannot occupy the Old House, Orchards, etc. Will Proven.

Page 92.

Wilcox, Mary, of Middletown. Will dated 3 April, 1671. (No Inventory.)

Mary, the wife of John Wilcox, April the third, being very sick & weak, & as she sayd shee conceived her selfe neer her death yet shee was of sound understanding & memory, shee declared by word of mouth this following to be her Last Will & Testament, viz: She gave to her sonn Samuel Fernsworth Tenn pounds sterling out of her Land in the great Lotts at Dorchester, as a remembrance of her, & the remaynder of the Lott shee gave unto her husband John Willcox. Moreover, she gave unto her sonn Joseph Long the Bill shee had of him for Land he Bought of her; & shee gave her white wascoat & her red Dammy coat to Mary Wilcox; and She gave to Sarah Long her feather Bed & Boulster which is at Hartford In her House all ready, & her Cloath wascoat with the great Silver lace, & a petty Coate Likewise. She did Give & Freely resigne up to her husband John Willcox that part of his Estate which was Mortgaged to her by her sayd Husband, & she desired that that tenn pounds shee gave to her sonn Samuel Fernsworth should be delivered Into the hands of her trusty friend Captain Hopestill Foster of Dorchester, to be kept for him untill he come of age. This above written of her voluntary accord very freely she declared to be her Last will & Testament, the 3 April, 1671.

In the presence of us *John Hall, Ann X Hall.*

John Wilcox owned in Court that he gave his wife Liberty to make her will & dispose of those things mentioned in her will. John and Ann Hall sworn in Court to the truth of what is above written.

Court Record, Page 114—7 September, 1671: The Will of Mary, the late wife of John Wilcox, exhibited and approved.

Page 50-51.

Winchell, Robert. Invt. £61-17-01. Taken 23 January, 1667-8, by Deacon Moore, Capt. Newbery, John Loomis & Matthew Grant. Will Nuncupative, dated 20 January, 1667-8.

We the Underwritten doe witness that, being with Robert Winchell that night in wch he died, desired us to take notice that if he lived not till the next morning, and soe could not have it written, that this was his Will: That before anything was meddled with all his Debts should be payd, and that his two sons Jonathan and David should have ye Lands that is on the North west of the Highway, this being all the Lands he had left, only Jonathan should have the North side and David the South Side. Sister Randall says, "What shall yr daughter have?" He answered, "I have done for her already. And for my eldest son, he is in my Debt; I acquitt him that, yet let them have something." And sayd also, "I desire yt you two and Brother Phelps would be my Overseers." To this we set our Hands.

Memorandum: He expressed yt wt was left of his Estate besides his Debts his 2 sons Jonathan and David should have.

Signed: *Abraham Randall,*
Mary X Randall, Walter ffyler.

Court Record, Page 74—5 March, 1667-8: Invt. Exhibited. Adms. to Jonathan & David Winchell. He had an older son & a daughter.

Page 185-6.

Winthrop, Gov. John, Boston. Invt. in Hartford, £73-01-04. Taken 5 September, 1676, by John Allyn, Joseph Haynes, George Gardner. Will dated 3 April, 1676.

I John Winthrope, of the Colony of Connecticut, in New England, now resident of Boston, being sicke in Body but through Mercy of perfect memory and Understanding, do make this my last Will & Testament: I Will & Bequeath unto my two sons Fitz John & Waitstill, to each of them an equal proportion out of my Estate, which is to be a double portion to each of them (that is, double to what I give to each of my daughters); the rest of my Estate to be equally divided to my 5 daughters, vizt: Elizabeth, Lucy, Margaret, Martha & Anne, only my Will is that in the Computation of my Estate, whereas I have already given to my daughters Elizabeth & Lucy good Farms which they are in possession of, that that may be considered by the Overseers of this my Will hereafter named, and proportionably accounted as part of their portions, abatement to be made out of the present Legacy to them given above accordingly. And I do hereby nominate and appoint my two sons Fitz John & Waitstill and my 5 daughters above named to be Executors & Executrixes of this my last Will & Testament. And I doe request the persons hereafter named to accept the trouble to be overseers of this my Will and to settle all things accordingly, and doe declare that it is my Will that if any question, difficulty or differences arise in or about this my Will, it shall be determined by them or any three of them. The persons are: Of Connecticut, Capt. John Allyn, Mr. William Joanes and Major Robert Treat. Of Boston: Mr. Humphrey Davie, Mr. James Allyn, and my brother Mr. John Richards.

In Witness that this is my last Will & Testament, I have hereunto set my Hands & Seal. Done in Boston this 3 day of April, 1676.
Witness: *Thomas Thatcher sen.,*   JOHN WINTHROP Ls.
          John Blake.

Court Record, Page 154—25 July, 1676: Will proven.
(A Copy on File, & on Record at Hartford, Connecticut.)

Page 66-7-8.

Witchfield, Mrs. Margaret, Windsor. Invt. £280-00-05. Taken 26 August, 1669, by Gregory Stone & Thomas Fox. Will dated 21 April, 1663.

I Margaret Witchfield of Cambridge do see Cause to make, ordain and declare this my last Will & Testament in manner & forme following: I give & bequeath, etc., to my dear Honed Husband, as a token of my Love & duty towards him, my Best peice of plate, to Injoy the same during his Life, & the remaynder of my estate I doe give and Bequeath unto my two daughters, to be equally divided between them, viz, Hannah Goffe & Abiah Goffe. In case of the decease of both without Issue, I doe then give and bequeath the one moyty or half part of my whole estate unto the children of my sister Jane Winship, Deceased; & my will is that Joanne shall have a double portion and that the rest be equal shares; to the reverend Mr. Jonathan Mitchell, whiles he abides in Cambridge, the use of fower Acres of Marsh; also I give him £5; to Mr Samuel Shephard, £5; to Edward & Deborah, the children of samuel Goffe, £5 apeice; to John & Lydia Sprague, the children of John & Lidia Sprague, £5 apeice; to Thomas Faning, £5; To Elizabeth Hayward, my daughter-in-Law, £5; to Hanna Stowers, 10s. Finally, I doe Nominate & ordaine the worpll Captayn Daniel Gookin, Thomas Cheesholme & John Cooper Executors, to whom I give £10 apeice. In case God be pleased to bless my daughters Hanna & Abiah or either them with Issue of their bodies lawfully begotten, that then the Legacies to my sayd daughters shall be and remain to their children after their decease.

Witness: *Thomas Danforth,*   MARGARET WITCHFIELD. Ls.
          Thomas Chesholme,
          Caleb Chesholme.

At a county court held at Cambridge 5 October, 1669, Thomas Danforth and Thomas Chesholme appeared before the Court. Being sworne, doe say that the above named Margarett Witchfield, being of sound mind, Signed, Sealed and published this Instrument to be her Last will, etc. As attest, *Daniel Gookkin, Ass st. Vera Copia* as attests. *Thomas Danforth, Recorder.*

An Invt. of Mrs. Margaret Witchfield, of Windsor, upon Connecticutt River, that was in Cambridge at her decease, which was about the end of the 4 Mo., 1669, £280-00-05. Taken By Gregory Stone and Thomas Fox. Presented in the County Court held at Cambridge 5 October, 1669, as a true Invt. of all the Estate whereof the sayd Margarett Witchfield died Seized in this Jurisdiction.

                                        Tho. Danforth, Recorder.

August 26, 1669.

An Inventory or valuation put upon some estate of Mrs. Margaret Witchfield, late Deceased, which must come to distribution betwixt her two daughters (one the wife of Mr. Henry Wolcott, Jr., the other the wife of John Moore Jr.):

	£ s d
Imprmis. a silver Bowle, a cup & dram cups, 7 spoonss, 3 gold rings, £7-04-00, wearing Clothes £40-18-00,	48-02-00
It. In Parcels, 2 Remnants of New cloth, £23-13-08, In lining for Bedd & Table, £35-13-08,	59-07-04

Ite. In Bedding besides Lining, £28-01-00; In Books, £2-00-
00; In pewter, £4-13-06,   34-14-06
Ite. In Brass, £4-10-00; In Iron for several uses, £3-18-00;
In Truncks, Chests & Boxes, £2-15-00   13-03-00
Ite. In chayres, cushions, wth several particulars,   4-18-00
                                                         ─────────
                                                         158-04-10

Apprized By Capt. Benj Newbery, Matthew Grant, Thom Dibble
sen. In Court, 8 December, 1668.

─────────────

Page 127-8.

Wolterton, Gregory, Hartford. Invt. £585-16-00. Taken 6 August, 1674, by Thomas Bull and Thomas Bunce. Will dated 17 July, 1674.

I Gregory Wolterton of Hartford, upon the river of Conictticote, doe
make this my Last will and testiment, wherein I give unto my wife Jane
Wolterton the some of twenty pound to be payd in moveable goods as is
prised, provided that it be in such as she desire. I doe also give unto
Jane my wife her dwelling, and liberty and use of the newe rooms which
was last bilt, which is next to the garden, but not for to let it away to any
but for to use it for her owne use during the Terme of her life, and for to
use some part of the seller and the (   ) for her Convenientcy, and
liberty for her to set her fire wood in the yard. I doe also give unto her
Six pound, to be payd to her by the yeare by my Executor, during the
Time of her life. I doe also give unto James Wolterton, the son of Matthew Wolterton, that live in Ipsago, in Sufolk, in owld Ingland, ten pounds
if he be living; if not, to his Children, eaquelly devided. I also give unto
Matthew waller, of new london, five pounds. I give also unto Rebecka
Waller ten pounds. I give unto Sara waller five pound. I give unto John
Shepeard sener, the son of Edward Shepard, one peece of Land, by esti-
mation fower acres be it more or les, lying and buting upon benieme har-
bor east, paul peck south, John bidall north, and upon paul peck and John
bidall west; and he is for to pay Twenty shillings to his father Edward
Shepard, Twenty shillings to his sister Debora fairbanks, and Twenty to
his Sister sara Thompson, and twenty shillings to his Sister's aboveseed
Children. I doe heereby give unto hanna lord and to mary lord, the
Daughters of Thomas Lord that is deceased, five pound a peice and the
things that are left in the trunk that was their mothers for to be devided
between them, and Mary foote to have trounke. And also to the Sones
of William Waller deseased, at Lyme (that is to say, to William Waller
ten pound, to John Waller ten pound, to Samuell Waller ten pound, and to
mathew waller ten pound). Mor over I give to wolstone brockwood
seaner ten pound, and to wiliam brockwood his son ten pound. Also I
give to bethia Stoken, the Daughter of Samuell Stoken, five pound. I
give unto Samuel Stoken Seaner forty Shillings, and also unto Steven
hopkines seaner forty shillings. I doe also give unto nathaniell Standly

twenty Shillings; also to mary porter, the wife of John porter, seaner, twenty Shillings; also unto hanna poorter, the wife of Isack Moore, of farmington, twenty shillings. Also I give unto Mr. John whiting, pastor of the Congregation, five pound. Also I give one parcell of land lying in hoccanum, sixe ackers be it more or les, abuting on the great river west, on nathanile baken south, and on the said John bacon north, and upon the Upland East, unto Mr. James Richards and John White forever, and to whom they shall appoint as feoffees in Trust, for the only Use & behoufe for the maintenance of the ministry of the meeting house of the South side of the Riveret, the Church whereof Mr. Whiting is now pastor. Moreover I give unto Elizabeth Andrews, the wife of John Andrews Junior, 40 Shillings. Also I give unto Mr. John Haynes, pastor of the owld Meeting house, 40 Shillings. Also I give unto Dorothy Lord, the daughter of Thomas Lord Decd, 20 Shillings. And moreover I give unto John Merrells, and his heirs forever, booth my houseing & Tan Yard (all that I leave and all my Land that I have not disposed of), whome I or-dayne and appoint Executor to this my last Will & Testament. I doe also desire my loveing friends Mr James Richards and John White senor for to be overseers to this my last Will & Testament. As Witness my Hand & Seal this 17th of July, 1674.

Signed & sealed in presence of   GREGORY WOLTERTON. Ls.
James Richards, John White.

Will proven in Court 26 August, 1674.

Note: *This Will was evidently written and signed by the testator himself (Gregory Wolterton), and the subscribing Witnesses each signed their names in their own Hand.*

Court Record, Page 143—3 September, 1674: Mr. Samuel Collins, in behalfe of the Widow Waller, pretending to make claym to the Estate of Gregory Winterton, & desireing liberty to prosecute the same the 2nd Wednesday in November next, John Merrells engageth not to alienate the Real Estate bequeathed to him by the sd. Wolterton till the sd. Court

Note: *Winthrop Papers, Vol. I, Fifth Series, Page 103—Letter of Elizabeth Stone to Elizabeth Winthrop: "Here is little news stiring, but Goodman Wilterton marrying with Goody Ward of Hadly." Hartford, 24th October,* 1670.

Page 77.

Wright, Thomas sen., Wethersfield. Invt. £101-15-00. Taken 29 April, 1670, by James Treat, Samuel Boreman, John Ryley.

The last Will & Testament of Thomas Wright sen., of Wethersfield, is as followeth: I do give unto my dear wife Margaret, after my decease, all the provisions (that are for Meat and Drink) now in my possession, also the Use of such my Moveables as she shall think needful for her use during her life. My Will is that the Division that I have formerly made of my Land unto my sonns shall stand firme forever, onely in yt my will I give unto my sonn Samuell but halfe my six Acre Lott in ye meadow, together wth foure Acres in ye swamp, which he now enjoyes, all which is in consideration of five Acres of Land which I had purposed to have given him upon the Island. I doe give unto my sonn Joseph halfe my six Acre Lott in ye meadow, that is to say, the north side of ye sd. Lott.

My will is that after all my debts are paid out of my estate, there shall be an equall division made of ye remainder amongst my children. I doe allsoe make my sonn Thomas sole Executor of yt my will, and doe desire my Loving ffriend samuel Hale? senr to be helpfull to him herein. I doe give unto my dear wife Margaret all the Linnen that I have in my possession that was of her owne spining.   THOMAS X WRIGHT.
Witness: *Samll Tallcott, John Deminge, Samuel Hale, Josiah Gilbert.*

Court Record, Page 101—1st September, 1670: Will Exhibited by Thomas Wright Jr. and Samuel Hale. Accepted, only it is ordered that the clause in the Will wherein mention is made of giving to Joseph halfe his six acre lot in the meadow (the north side of the lot) is to be null because it appeard to this Court that part of the lot was, on 6 March, 1688, Sold by the said Thomas Wright to his Son Samuel Wright.

Page 89-199.

Wright, Margaret, Widow, Wethersfield. Invt. £82-19-06. Taken 4 April, 1671, by James Treat, Samuel Wright. Will dated 19 January, 1670.

I Margaret Wright, Widow, being in perfect Memorie although weak in Body, my will is that Estate which I have & shall leave at my death, & all my Lawfull debts being satisfied, & what remains my will is that my Grand Child William Hilier, son of Jobe Hilier deceased, that he shall have a double portion; & my will is that Sarah Hilier, the daughter of Jobe Hilier, should have something more than a single portion, & the other three children of my sonn Jobe Hilier Should have a Single portion a peice; & My will is Margaret Wanton, the Daughter of the wife of my sonn Benjamin Hilier, that she should have forty shillings given her. My will is that the wife of my Son Thomas Wright should have my Cowe, & If it be not Sufficient for her Labour of Love, I leave to the discression of my Overseers to give more. My will is that my Christian brethren Samuel Hale & John Deming Should be my Overseers.
    MARGARET X RIGHT.
Witness: *John Deming, Samuel Hale.*

Codicil: My earnest desire is that my loveing Friend Mr George Gardiner would be pleased to Joyne wth John Deming senr & Samll Hale senr as an overseer of this my Last will and Testament.
    MARGARET X WRIGHT.
Witness: *Samuel Talcott, Thomas Wright.*

Contents of debts payd out of the Estate of Margaret Wright according to the will:

	£ s d
To Thomas Wright for charges,	11-18-09
To Goody Curtice,	1-00-00
To Capt. Thomas,	00-08-00
To Mary North,	01-00-00
To John Deming,	3-14-00
To carrying porck to Hartford,	00-09-00
& for loss of weight,	00-09-00
for loss in cotton yarn,	01-06-00
	20-04-09

The goods in the Inventory Come to £81-19-06. The debts out, there is left £61-16-09. Payd 40s to Benjamin Hilliard's wife. There is to be divided £59-16-09, of which we order £29-00-01 to the three youngest children, & £19-06-08 to the Eldest sonn, & £11-05-00 to Sarah Holanworth, the Eldest daughter. As witness our hands this 22—12—'74. *John Deming, Samuel Hale Sen., George Gardner.*

Received of Mr. John Deming & Samuel Hale sen., for account of Jobe Hillier's youngest Children, The sum of £29. I say received this 27 of February, '78, by me   GEORGE GARDNER.

Mr. John Deming sr: I received yours by my Brother Buttolph, in Answer unto which these are to inform you that I Judge the £29 (you have a receipt of it) what was given by the widow Wright unto Jobe Hilliard's youngest children by his second wife, which was paid unto their mother by order of the court here. Allso I find upon my book an account of 1370 lbs of porck payd my father, which comes to £17-02-06; also an accot of one dd of porck & 33 bush. of Indian Corne payd my Brother Buttolph, which comes to £7-12-06. Pray, sr, send me a coppy of the *widow Wright's will,* & if there be anything behind Let it be payed unto my Brother Buttolph, and I will endeavoar to get a discharge of the children & send it unto you. Not els at prsent, but kind respects to you and yours. I rest yours to serve.   SAMUEL GARDNER JR.
There is still due £6-01-09.

Superscribed: For Mr. John Deming sen., forty-eight bushells of Indian corne upon the accompt of Jobe Hilliard's eldest children. I say received,
    pr me, JOHN BUTTOLPH JR.
The 17 March, 1686.

The above written are true coppys of the original, being examined & compared there with August 24, 1687,
    pr *John Allyn, Secretary.*

Court Record, Page 110—5 April, 1671: Adms. to John Deming and Samuel Hale sen.

Page 59-60.

Wyatt, John, Haddam. Invt. £154-17-10. Taken 7 September, 1668, by Abraham Dibble, Richard Joanes. The children: Mary, age 20 years, married; John 18, Hepzibah 16, Dorcas 13, Sarah 9, Joanna 5, Elizabeth 3, & Israel half a year. Dist: To the Widow, £35; to John, Eldest son, £14; and to the other seven Children, £8 apeice.

Court Record, Page 81—5 November, 1668: Adms. granted to Mary, the Relict, and John & Richard Bronson are desired to assist her.

Page 160—1st March, 1676-7: Order to Dist. the Estate of John Gifford of £4-01-00, taken to pay a Debt due to the Estate of John Wyott.

VOLUME IV.

1677-8 to 1687.

This is the Fourth Book of the Records of the Acts of the County Courts and Courts of Probates in the County of Hartford, and of Wills and Inventories.

No. 4.

No man Wise at all times, nor
Knowing in all things.

PROBATE RECORDS.

VOLUME IV.

1677 to 1687.

Page 167.

Adams, Edward, Windsor, who died 15 August, 1683. Invt. £56-18-02. Taken by Henry Wolcott & Samuel Cross. Daughter, Mary Adams, 12 years of age, 28 August, 1683.

Court Record, Page 80—10 October, 1683: Adms. to the Widow. Order to Dist: to the Widow £31, and to the daughter above named £25 at 18 years of age (born 28 August, 1671—(W. R.) Edward Adams & Elizabeth Buckland were married 25 May, 1660—(W. R.)

Page 127-8-9.

Adams, Jeremy, Hartford. Died 11 August, 1683. Invt. £243-05-06. Taken by Caleb Stanly, Phineas Wilson. Will dated 4 August, 1683.

I Jeremy Adams of Hartford do make this my last Will & Testament: Whereas, I have formerly given to my gr. son Zachary Sandford my Oxpasture Lott in the way to Wethersfield, & put him in possession thereof before Witnesses, I do hereby confirm the same to him & his heirs forever; & the Lott that I have at the Wolfe Pound by Mrs. Webster's I do Will and Bequeath it to my gr. son Zachary, he paying the value of it, as it shall be prized in the Inventory, towards the payment of my Just Debts or to my gr. Children as I shall hereafter expresse; & the remaynder of my Estate, when my Debts are paid, shall be equally divided to my gr. Children, the ½ to my sonn John Adams his Children, and the other halfe to my sonn Willett's Children. And I doe appoint Nath. Willett to be the Executor to this my Will, & Major John Tallcott & Capt. John Allyn to be my Overseers.

Witness: *John Talcott,*   JEREMY X ADDAMS.
John Allyn.

Court Record, Page 72—6 September, 1683: Will proven.
Page 79—18 December, 1683: Whereas, Jeremy Adams his Estate stands Indebted to Mr. Richard Lord in the Full Sum of £117-05-08, for

which there is Mortgaged all that Parcell of Land in Hoccanum Meadow which the sayd Jeremy bought of Widdow Lattimore of Wethersfield, the sd. Mortgage dated 6 December, 1674, I Nathaniel Willett of Hartford, Executor to the Will of Jeremy Adams, not being capacitated to redeem sd. Mortgage, now acknowledge Judgement & the Mortgage is forfeited, and doe Quitt Claim the sayd Land to the Use of Richard Lord.

(Vol. V) Court Record, Page 29—21 April, 1691: Nathaniel Willett, being aged and having lost Jeremy Addams his books and Accounts when his House was burnt, This Court desire and appoint Capt. Jonathan Bull to be Adms. with sayd Nathaniel Willett to the sayd Estate of Jeremy Addams, who are appointed to Issue so far as they are capable as soon as may be and to make Return to this Court.

Adams, Jeremiah. Court Record (Vol. V) Page 125—9 February, 1696-7: I Jeremiah Adams of Huntington, Long Island, son of John Adams and gr. son of Jeremie Adams and Nephew of Thomas Greenhill, make my Brother-in-Law Edward Higby Trustee and Attorney.
Witness: *Mary Udal.*

Page 126-7.

Alvard, Benedict, Windsor. Invt. £229-03-09. Taken 7 May, 1683, by Benjamin Newbery, Daniel Clarke sen. Will dated 30 March, 1683.

I Benedictus Alvard of Windsor do make this my last Will & Testament: After my Just Debts are payd, my wife during her Widowhood shall have the Proffitt, Use & Benefit of my Estate for her Comfortable Livelyhood; but if she marryes, to have £30 of what Estate she shall see Cause to take, to be to her own free Dispose. To my son Jonathan I give 20 Shillings besides what formerly I have given him. To Josias Alvard, my 2nd son, £40 and the Farme that was given me by the Country. To my daughter Elizabeth Drake £5 besides what she hath already received; and a Sheep apeice to each of the Children. To my son Jeremy, after the decease of my wife, all my Houseing and Land in Windsor, together with all other my Moveable Estate in Windsor, and all other Estate that is and shall appear to be due unto me on Books, he paying out of it those Legacies as are before expressed. Also my Will is that my son Jeremy shall be Executor. Further, that my loving wife shall live with my son Jeremy, and that he shall have the Improvement and Management of it, allowing his Mother comfortable mayntenance out of it as long as she lives in this World.

Witness: *Benjamin Newbery,*   BENEDICTUS X ALVARD.
       Daniel Clarke sen.

Court Record, Page 72—6 September, 1683: Will proven.

Page 85-6-7.

Andrews, John sen., Farmington. Invt. £321-19-00. Taken 15 February, 1681-2, by Thomas Porter, Richard Seamor, Tho: Heart. Will dated 9 November, 1681.

I John Andrews, being grown aged, and many weaknesses Attending off me from time to time, And now att this present itt pleases the most High to visit mee with more than ordynarie weakness, yet throw the Good Hand off God upon mee I have at this present thee perfect Use of my Understanding, now I doe think it meet to set that little at stay as I am able that God hath given mee. All my lawfull Debts being discharged, I dispose of my Estate as Followeth: I give and bequeath unto my wife Marie Andrews the new end of my Dwelling House and the Seller under itt ffor her Use and Comfort, (with) the Use off half my Orchard the Frute off it as long as shee liveth; moreover I doe give unto my wife my ffeather bedd with all the ffurniture belonging to it, with liberty to dispose of it as shee pleases. Item. I give to my son Beniamin Andrews my whole House and Barne and Homelott after my wiffs decease. My Mind is that my son Beniamin shall possess, after my decease, half my House and House Lott and Barn upon that Condition that he maintaine his deare mother comfortably so long as her natural life continueth. I give to my son John Andrews my Lott or Devision of Land that abuteth upon Hartford Bounds. I give to my son Abraham Andrews my 20 Acre Lott in the Great Swamp & Joining to his own Lott. I give to my son Daniel Andrews 2 acres of Meadow Land, and I give him my Upland Lott that belongs to my 20 acre Swamp Lott. I give to my son Joseph Andrews my Upland Lott, containing 40 acres, that lyeth near to Middletowne Path. I give to my son Beniamin Andrews all the Division off Upland that belongs to mee that are not yet layd out. Moreover I leave the Rest of my Swine and Corn I have, to discharge my Debts, in my son Beniamin's Hand, as alsoe he shall pay some small legeses, namely:

							£ s d
I give to my grand child						Thomas Barns,	00-20-00
"	"	"	"	"	"	John Andrews,	1-00-00
"	"	"	"	"	"	Abraham Andrews,	1-00-00
"	"	"	"	"	"	John Richards,	1-00-00
"	"	"	"	"	"	Daniel Andrews,	1-00-00
"	"	"	"	"	"	Ezekiel Buck,	1-00-00

Respecting my gr. child Joseph Andrews, my son Joseph Andrews' son, iff he sees meet to lett him continue with my wiffe and my son Beniamin till he is 21 years of age, he shall have then five teen pounds & two sutes off aparill. Iff he sees cause to take him Awey before he is off that age, I doe give him nothing, and he shall pay nothing for ye time I kept him. I give to my daughter Marie Barns my black Heiffer. I give to my daughter Hanny Richards two yearlings. I give to my daughter Rachell Buck, my two year old Red Heifer. My son Benjamin Andrews,

shall be sole Executor. And I desire my loveing friends Capt. John Standly and Isaac Moore to be Overseers with my son Daniel Andrews.
Witness: *Robert Porter,*   JOHN X ANDREWS SEN.
     William Lewis senior.

Court Record, Page 50—2 March, 1681-2: Will Proven.

Page 106.

Atwood, Capt. Thomas (Also called Dr.), Wethersfield. Invt. £148-06-09. Taken 24 October, 1682, by John Kilbourn sen., Thomas Wright. Family: The Widow, Abigail Atwood; Abigail, age 14 years; Andrew Atwood, age 11 years; Jonathan, age 7 years; Josiah, age 4 years.

Court Record, Page 60—13 December, 1682: Invt. Exhibited. Adms. to the Widow. This Court appoynt Capt. Samuel Talcott & Mr. John Robbins to be Overseers, and Order Dist. of the Estate: To the Widow her thirds during life, and to the Children as they come of age or marry.

Page 13-14.

Bacon, Elizabeth, late of Hadley, now of Hartford. Invt. £269-05-00. Taken 23 February, 1678, by Nathaniel Standly, Nathaniel Goodwin and John Marsh. Will dated 30th October, 1671.

I Elizabeth Bacon, late of Hadley, now a resident of Hartford, do make this my last Will & Testament: Whereas my son Caleb Standly, who has taken upon him the Burden & Care of providing for me in my old Age, also left his Brother Isaac's Estate to me, which might have fallen to him (see Records of Court at Springfield, 27 September, 1671), I do give unto my son Caleb Standly all my Houseing and Land in Hadly formerly my Husband Andrew Bacon's, late of Hadley, decd, that fell to me by his last Will, or by the Death of my son Isaac, or by any other ways, to him & his Heirs forever. I appoint my son Caleb Standly to be Executor; and I do appoint him to see that those Legacies given by my late dear Husband to Mr. Russell & Peter Tilton be paid. Other Legatees mentioned: To my daughter Abigail Coles, the wife of Samuel Coles, & to Lois, the wife of Thomas Porter, both of Farmington. My Will is, after my decease a true Inventory of all my Goods, Cattell & Debts be taken, & the Amount I give to my son Caleb Standly, to my daughter Elizabeth Sension, the wife of Mark Sension, my daughter Abigail Coles & my daughter Lois Porter & their Children, to be equally divided among them, that is to say, my son and three daughters; provided that out of my daughter Elizabeth's part £5 to be paid to my gr. child Sarah Sension, daughter of my daughter Elizabeth, & provided that my daughters Abigail & Lois & their Husbands doe legally resign their Rights in the third part of the ½ of my Land at Hadley to my son Caleb

& his Heirs forever (*see Lib: D, fol. 57). If they be not willing soe to doe, then I give them and their Children the third part of half my Land in Hadley, and that which shall be allotted to my daughters Abigail & Lois out of my Moveable Estate shall be and belong to Caleb Standly and his Heirs forever. My son Caleb Stanly to be sole Executor; John Allyn and Nathaniel Stanly Overseers.

Witness: *John Allyn,*   ELIZABETH BACON. Ls.
     Thomas Fitch.

Court Record, Page 12—6 March, 1678-9: The last Will & Testament of Elizabeth Bacon was now exhibited in Court and proven. And whereas, by the sd. Will some part of the Lands in Hadly is Willed to Abigail Cowles, the wife of Samuel Cowles, and to Loeis, the wife of Thomas Porter of Farmington, in attendence to Direction left in the Will of Andrew Bacon late of Hadly, there was exhibited in Court a Deed signed and sealed by Samuel Cowles and Abigail his wife & by Thomas Porter & Loeis his wife, witnessed by John Heart and Benjamin Joanes, and acknowledged 8 Feb: 1678, before Mr. John Wadsworth, Comr, wherein they did fully resign their Right in the sd. Lands before mentioned to Caleb Standly of Hartford, his Heirs and Assigns forever, which is approved by the Court, & by the Desire of Sargt. Caleb Standly here recorded.

Page 118.

Barding, Abigail. Died 20 March, 1682-3. Invt. £19-10-00. A Nuncupative Will exhibited in Court, April, 1683. Testimony of George Graves, aged about 52 years, and Samuel Andrews, aged about 36 years, is that we were with Widdow Abigail Barding about 3 weeks before she dyed, And she did before us declare that her Will was that after her death the sd. Samuel Andrews should have what was due to her from Gerrerd Spencer, and that the sd. Samuel should pay her Debts & Funeral Charges, also that her daughter Hester Spencer should have all her other Goods, excepting som few things she had given away before. Samuel Andrews accepted; only of the above written that he remembers not his gr. Mother's words that he should pay her Debts and Funeral Charges, but owneth that he will do it.   *George Graue,*
                                               Samuel Andrews.

Paul Peck sen., aged about 60 years, testifieth that a day or two before Widdow Barding dyed she tould him that her Will was that Samuel Andrews should have what was due to her from Garred Spencer, & that the rest of her Goods she gave to her Daughter Hester Spencer, except som few small things she had given away before.
                                                 paule Peck sen.

Court Record, Page 68—4 April, 1683: Will proven.

----

*(In the office of Sec. of State of Conn.)

Page 210.

Bell, Robert, Hartford. Died 29 July, 1684. Invt. £28-17-06. Taken by Caleb Stanly, Philip Lewis. The children: John, 6 years of age; Robert 4, and Mary 1¾ years.

Court Record, Page 94—4 September, 1684: Invt. Exhibited in Court by the Relict.

Page 99—5 May, 1684-5: Adms. to Caleb Stanly and Richard Edwards.

Edward King, of Podunk, gave Land, 4 February, 1681, to his son-in-Law Robert Bell and his wife Ruth Bell. (See W. R. of Land, Vol. II, Page 39.)

Page 105—24 March, 1684-5: This Court having considered the Estate of Rob: Bell, do order that £9-10-00 of the Inventory of the Estate be left with the Widow for her Relief, & the rest be disposed to answer the Creditors by proportion as far as it will go. And as to a Tract of Land made over to Robt. Bell by Edward King, it being not expressed that it is past to him, his assigns, Executors or Adms., we are suspicious whether it may be meet to dispose of it to pay Debts least Bell's Heirs recover it out of their Hands.

Page 128—3 March, 1686-7: The Adms. is granted a *Quietus Est.*

Page 187.

Benjamin, Caleb. (Died 8 May, 1684.) Invt. £77-15-06. Taken by Samuel Haile sen., Joseph Hill. The children: Mary, age 13 years, Abigail 11, Sarah 8, John 6, Samuel 5, Martha 3, Caleb ½ years old.

Court Record, Page 93—4 September, 1684: Adms. to Mary, the Relict.

Page 135—(Vol. VII) 7 November, 1709: This Court do order the Clerk to issue forth a Writ to cite Walter Harris sen. of Glastonbury to appear before this Court on the 1st Monday of December next to render an Account of his own and his late wife her Adms. on the Estate of Caleb Benjamin, late of Wethersfield, Decd.

Page 5—(Vol. VIII) 6 February, 1709-10: Walter Harris sen. of Glastonbury now appeared before this Court and exhibited an Account of his own and his late wife's Adms. on the Estate of Caleb Benjamin, late of Wethersfield, Decd:

	£ s d
Paid in Debts	11-05-00
Loss of Horses	8-06-00
And two Cows	7-00-00
And the Court allow Walter Harris	25-00-00
for his wife keeping 2 or 3 of the younger children for	
some years. All which amounts to	51-11-00

Which subtracted from the Moveable Part of sd. Estate,
There remains thereof to be distributed   11-04-06
This Court allow John Benjamin for his Costs   19-09

There remains only to be dist.   10-04-03
1-3 part of this to Walter Harris   3-08-01

And a double portion to John Benjamin, & single portions to each
of the other Children now living. And appoint John Hubbard sen., Benjamin Talcott and Thomas Kimberly, Dist., to divide the Lands & remaining Moveables.

Page 156.

Benton, Andrew, Hartford. Invt. £345-17-09. Taken 4 September,
1683, by James Steele sen., John Merrells. The children: Andrew,
Samuel, Joseph, Mary and Dorothy, by his First wife (a daughter of
George Stocking). By his second wife (Ann Cole): Ebenezer, 9 or
10 years of age, Lydia 7, Hannah, 5 years of age.

Court Record, Page 77—18 December, 1683: Adms. to Joseph Benton. Order to Distribute to the Widow £40; to Andrew, Eldest son, £54;
to Joseph, £34; to Samuel, £34; to Mary, £33; to Dorothy, £33; to Ebenezer, because of his impotency, £49; to Lidia, £33; to Hanna, £33: Stephen Hosmer & John Morrice, Overseers.

Page 236-7.

Benton, Ane, who died 19 April, 1686. Invt. £60-12-06. Taken 14
May, 1686, by Stephen Hosmer, Jacob Wells.

The last Will of Ane Benton, made the twenty-sixth day of march,
one thousand sixe hundred and eighty sixe: Being in sound mind &
perfect memory, and not knowing the day of my death, doe Comit my
soule into the hands of my Redemer, and my body to Comly buryell. I
doe dispose of that estate god has betrusted me with as follows: I give
to my son Ebenezer what of my estate is not hereafter excepted, if he
Lives to nede it. Yn my will is that my dafter Lydia shod have my
litell brass ketell; and my dafter Hannah should have my litell Iron
pote and all my wareing aparell, except won arporne, which I give to
my son Ebenezer. Al the rest, both Lining & wollen, should be divided
between my dafters Lydia and hanah equeilly, and allso my pewter to be
devided betweene them, and my 2 skillets I give ym. I give to Lydia 1
fine pille-bere and 1 paire of sheats and 1 paire of Coten pille beares, and
to my dafter Hanah 1 paire of sheats and the best of the Coten pilleberes;
allso Lydia must be paid the three pounds of what I tooke up in my husbands aparell out of the household stuff; and all these Legaseys to be

paid them, the son at twenty-one years, and the dafters at eightene years
of age.   I desire my loveing brother Nathaniel Cole to be Executor.
Witness: *John Willson,*   ANE X BENTON.
            mathew Grant.

No Court Record found.

Page 253-4.

Bidwell, John sen., Hartford. Invt. £419-10-06. Taken 4 June, 1687,
by William Pitkin, Joseph Olmsted. Will dated 10 February, 1680.

I John Bidwell of Hartford do make this my last Will & Testament:
I doe give to my son John Biddoll, & his heirs forever, my Lott in the
swamp on the east side of the Connecticutt River, being about Two acres
& a half, Lyeing between Thomas Bunce his Land & the Land of Goodman Easton; and allso I doe give & confirme unto him & his heirs forever all my Lands and buildings & appurtenances of them whatsoever,
which Lye or are in the township of Hartford, on the west side of the
Connecticut river.   Also I give unto my son Joseph Bidwell £30 in current pay of this colony, £20 to be payd within two years after my decease,
and £10 to be payd him for the use of his children after my wife's decease.   Also I give to my son Samuel Bidwell £20—£10, to be payd him
two years after my decease, and £10 for the use of his children after my
wife's decease.   Also I give to each of my Two daughters, Sarah House
& Hannah Waddams, £20 apeice.   Also I give to my daughter Mary Meekins the one halfe of my upper Lott in the swamp, Lyeing south of Ozias
Goodwins Land thereby, and the other halfe I give to my grand son
John Meekins, to be to them & their heirs forever, only my will is that my
wife shall have the one halfe of that Lott during her Life, & that John
Meekins shall not have the halfe of that lot unless he live with me or my
wife until he be twenty years of age, If my self or wife do Live soe long.
Also my will is that my wife Sarah Bidwell shall have all my household
goods & stuffe, to be at her dispose forever; & I doe moreover give her
the one halfe part of all my estate whatsoever that is not before disposed
of, both Lands, houseing, Chattells, Cattell, or any other thing whatever it
be, to be For her proper use during her natural Life & no Longer; & If
it shall seem good to my wife at any time to leave that part of the houseing
& Lands & Cattell which I have given her during her Life as before unto
my son Daniel Bidwell, Then I doe give her £8 by the year out of it, the
Lands, houseing & Cattell to be payd her in current pay of the Colony
by my son Daniel Bidwell or who soever enjoyeth the sayd Lands, houses,
Chattells & Cattell.   Also I doe give the other halfe of my whole estate not
before disposed of, both Lands, houseing, Chattells, Cattell, & every other
thing not before disposed of, unto my sayd son Daniel Bidwell & his heires
& assigns forever. Also I doe in like maner give unto him, after the decease
of my wife, the other halfe of my estate which was before given my wife

for and during her natural life. I make my wife Sarah Bidwell and my son Daniel Bidwell Executors, and Mr. John Crow to be Overseer.

JOHN X BIDWELL. LS.

Witness: *William Pitkin, Joseph Olmsted.*

A Codicill, dated 22 August, 1683: I give to my wife Sarah Bidwell, in addition, 2 cowes; to my son John Bidwell 4 acres of Land adjoyning Bartholomew Barnards Land. Son John Bidwell is to pay to Rev. John Whiting 20s, and £20 to my son Joseph Bidwell. And whereas Sarah House & Hannah Waddams were to receive £20 to each, my will is that my daughter House shall have £30, my daughter Waddams £10.

JOHN X BIDWELL. LS.

Witness: *William Pitkin, John Makins.*

Court Record, Page 133—1 September, 1687: Will Proven.

Page 66.

Biggs, William, Middletown. Invt. £139-01-06. Taken 19 August, 1681, by Richard Hall, John Hall Jr. & Samuel Hubbard. The children: William, age 15 years, Mary 14, Thomas 9, Elizabeth 8, Sarah 6, John, 4 years old. Adms. to Mary the Relict. Invt. exhibited 1st September, 1681. Test: *William Leete, Governor.*

Court Record, Page 25 (Vol. V)—6 March, 1690-1: This court appoynt Richard Hall & Mr. Southmayd to Bind out Wm. Biggs, his youngest sonn, to some good place where he may be carefully provided for & Instructed.

Page 57—12 April, 1693: Complaint having been made that there was no Adms. of the Estate, this Court now appoint William Smith & William Taylor Adms., they to report so that Dist. may be made.

Bishop, John. Court Record, Page 11—14 February, 1678: Upon the motion of Sarah, the Widow of John Bishop, late of Wethersfield, deceased, This Court have granted the said Sarah Bishop Adms. upon the estate of the said John Bishop, Dec. Mr. Eli: Kimberly & Mr. Nath: Boweman are desired by the sd. widow to assist her in the premises.

Page 217.

Bissell, John, son of Samuel of Windsor. Invt. £127-02-08. Taken 27 January, 1684-5, by John Loomis, John Moore. The children: Abigail, 3½ years of age; John, 2 years.

Court Record, Page 104—24 March, 1684-5: Adms. to Abigail Bissell, the Widow. Distribution to the Widow £21-13-04, to the son a

double portion, to the daughter a single portion. John Loomis sen. &
John Loomis Jr. to be Overseers.

Page 132.

Blackleach, John sen., Wethersfield. Invt. £373-16-06. Taken 3
September, 1683, by Samuel Talcott, James Treate, Samuel Butler, Selectmen.

Court Record, Page 73—6 September, 1683: The Invt. of Mr. John
Blackleach sen., of Wethersfield, was exhibited in Court, & the Court doe
impower Samuel Butler to Adms. upon the estate till the Estate may be
settled by this Court.

Page 74.—Special Court—29 October, 1683: Mr. John Blackleach
Jr. appeared in Court and made it appear by his Father's Books that his
Father had disbursed upon his Grand Father's account the sum of £225-
09-01, of which sum £69-06-03 was paid as money, all which, pr. order
of the Gen. Court, 13 May, 1675, was ordered to be paid out of sd. Blackleach's Estate in Lands after his decease. This Court appoint Lt. Samuel
Steele & Sargt. Deming to apprize so much of the Lands and Houseings
as may Answer the aforesaid sum, & deliver to Mrs. Blackleach, and when
the debts are paid, the remainder of the Land and Houseing to be distributed amongst Mr. Blackleach his Children (Mr. John Blackleach,
Exercise Hodges, and Mary Jeffries and Benoni Blackleach) if living; to
divide the Land into four parts. And if Benoni be dead, to divide his
part to the 3 surviving Children.

Samuel Butler, Adms.

Note: *The Grandfather was Benjamin Harbert, whose wife (the
mother of Mrs. Elizabeth Blackleach) was Christian Nethercoole. (See
1st Church Catalogue.)*

*See also Mrs. Blackleach's appeal to the Court against the probation
of the will of her mother, on page 46 of this volume.*

Page 192.

Boreman, Mrs. Mary, Wethersfield. Died 3 August, 1684. Invt.
£207-01-02. Taken by Samuel Talcott, James Treat. The children:
Isaac Boreman, Mrs. Mary Robbins, Samuel, Sarah, Daniel, Jonathan,
Nathaniel, & Martha Boreman, and Thomas Robbins.

Court Record, Page 94—25 November, 1684: Invt. Exhibited by
Samuel and Sarah Boreman. Order to Dist. by Samuel Talcott, James
Treat & Samuel Butler.

Record on file: Dist. to Isaac, to Samuel, to Daniel, to Jonathan, to
Nathaniel, to Sarah Boreman, to Martha Robbins, to Thomas Robbins;
by Samuel Talcott, and Samuel Butler.

Page 102—15 May, 1685: The Dist. Report Approved.

Page 12.

Bowe, Alexander, Middletown. Invt. £144-19-09. Taken 12 November, 1678, by Thomas Whetmore, William Harris, Robert Warner. The children: Samuel, age 19 years, Sarah 16, Anna 4, Mary, 2 years of age, one unborn (Rebeckah). Dist. on file, 20 April, 1681.

Court Record, Page 10—5 December, 1678: Rebecca Bowe exhibits the Invt. and a Will of her late Decd Husband, which is imperfect, there being no Executor appointed and some children born since the Will was made. This Court order that the Widow shall possess and enjoy the Estate according to a writing of date 30th October, 1673, made to her before marriage, or the Will, whichever she pleases. Adms. to the Widow. Ensign William Cheeny and Sargt. William Ward, Overseers.

Page 23—4 March, 1679-80. The Widow declines the Adms., which was then granted to William Ward, & William Cheney appointed to assist the sd. William Ward in Adms.

Page 89—2 April, 1684: This Court being informed of the death of the Relict of Alexander Bowe, who hath left 3 young Children (one is with Mr. Collins, one with Ensign William Cheeny, and one with Thomas Ward). This Court appoint Ensign William Ward to make Indentures for the children, to bind them out to their several masters till they be 18 years of age, and the said Ensign Cheeny and William Ward to improve their several portions allotted to them out of their father's estate, to be laid out for their maintenance so long as is needfull.

Page 51—(Vol. V) 23 February, 1692-3: Ensign Ward being deceased (who was Adms. to the Estate of Alexander Bowe, Decd), This Court appoint Lt. Francis Whitmore Adms. with Mr. Cheeny.

Page 104.

Brookes, John, Simsbury. Died 3 September, 1682. Invt. £199-08-09. Taken by John Case, Thomas Barber & Peter Buell. The children: Elizabeth Brookes, aged 19 years; Samuel, age 20 years; Mary 16, Mercy 13, Lydia 10, and Susanna, 7 years of age.

Court Record, Page 58—7 September, 1682: Invt. Exhibited by John Peirce. Adms. to John Peirce & Thomas Barber.

Page 62—13 December, 1682. This Court distributes the Estate of John Brooks as followeth: To the widow, £6 of the personal estate forever, and one third of the real estate during life. The remaynder of the Estate to be divided to the 6 Children of sd. Brookes, so that the eldest son have £10 more than the daughters. This is done because we find that the sayd Brookes, by a writing under his own hand, had so disposed of his estate that his son could not expect a double portion, though he had put no legal stamp upon sd. writing. The children to possess as they come of age. The administrators are to lay out to the widow her £6 in Beding & household goods, and to take care of the payment of the debts,

& to put out the youngest daughter till she be of age; & when the debts are payd, the estate to be distributed.

Page 85—6 March, 1684: The administrator of John Brookes estate being departed, & the estate being in a wasteing state, none to look after it, This Court therefore doe grant Adms. on the Estate to John Higley, whoe accepted of the same in Court.

Page 52.

Brunson, John, Farmington. Died 28 November, 1680. Invt. £312-01-06. The children: Jacob, Isaac, Mary Ellis, John Brunson, Abraham Brunson, Dorcas Hopkins, Sarah Kilbourn.

Court Record, Page 32—2 December, 1680: Invt. now exhibited in Court by Jacob & Isaac Brunson & Dorcas Hopkins. This Court grant Adms. to the Children of the Dec. and appoint Marshall Grave to assist them in the division. There being no will made by the deceased, and finding the sayd John Brunson had in his lifetime allotted to his foure sonns each of them a fifth part of his lands in Farmington, This Court confirms the same to them and to their heires forever; & whereas John had received short of his Brothers £8, it is now considered in the distribution, as also what his daughters have formerly received, and the distributions as followeth:

		£ s d
To Jacob Brunson	Eldest son	72-02-00
To John Brunson		44-17-00
To Isaac Brunson		36-17-00
To Abraham Brunson		36-17-00
To Mary	Eldest daughter	35-16-00
To Dorcas		41-16-00
To Sarah		45-16-00

And this Court orders that there be payd towards the maintenance of the Widdow, yearly, the sum of £10 in good current pay, during the time of her natural life, to be paid by the children in proportion, and more if necessity arise.

Page 179—(Vol. X) 5 March, 1727-8: Whereas it is represented to this Court by George Kilbourn, Thomas Hopkins, John Bracy, Daniel Steele & Hezekiah Hopkins, Heirs by marriage and descent from John Brunson, formerly of Farmington, decd, that there is considerable Estate in Land of the sd. Decd that has not yet been Dist., and necessary to be apprised in order to be Dist. to and among the heirs of sd. John Brunson, This Court grant Adms. on the sd. Real Estate which has not yet been Dist. unto the sd. Thomas Hopkins and John Bracy, and order that they make an Invt. thereof and exhibit the same to this Court as soon as may be, for Dist.

Page 264-5.

Brunson, Richard, Farmington. Invt. £405-08-00. Taken 26 September, 1687, by Thomas Porter, Jonathan Smith & John Norton. Will dated 27 February, 1684.

I Richard Brunson of Farmington do give to my wife during her life half the Use or benefit of my whole Homestead, as also the Lower room of that called the old house & the chamber next above it, & a good Cowe. She having beding & household Implements necessary of her owne, I ad nothing herein, but doe ordain & appoint my son Samuel Bronson my soale executor To my personal and reall estate at the end & Term of my naturall Life, only the Legacies hereafter expressed I doe appoynt him my sayd son Samuel Brunson to pay, viz: That which as abovesayd is bequeathed to my wife he is not to enter upon during her natural Life, & then to take possession of that part of my estate as my whole & soale executor, as also to pay these following Legacies: I having given to my two other sons their portions, I give to my daughter Hannah £4 more, to my daughter Eddy £3 more, to my daughter Abigail 40s more, to my daughter Mary one bed, a new Blanket, one payre of sheets, & to be paid 40s per annum so long as she liveth unmarried, & on her marriage day a good Cowe. What I doe give unto my son Samuel Bronson, my Executor, is as followeth: all my Homelott with houses, out howses, barn, orchyard, garden or gardens, timber wood, underwood, with all the appurtenances thereon or thereunto belonging, excepting that part given to my wife during her Life; then this Instrument standeth good to my son Samuel to possess the whole of my Homelott except that part which is given to my son John Brunson. I give to my son Samuel 5 acres of Pequabock meadow adjoyning John Wadsworth's Land, John Stanly's Land, and on Samuel Gridley's Land, As also 4 acres more or less in Pequabock meadow adjoyning a highway, Moses Ventruss & Thomas Barnes his Land. I also give to my son Samuel Bronson all my other estate, as cattell, horses, neet sheep or swine, with all my Implements of Husbandry, brass or pewter, beding, whatsoever is truly mine, to him and his heirs forever.   RICHARD X BRUNSON. Ls.

Witness: *William Lewis sen., Samuel Lewis.*

Court Record, Page 134—26 October, 1687: Will Proven.

Page 61.

Buckland, Temperance, Windsor. Invt. £90-18-04. Taken 19 August, 1681, by John Loomis sen., John Moore & Thomas Bissell sen. Will dated 21 March, 1680-1.

I Temperance Buckland, Widow, having grown aged & weak, do hereby declare that my Mind and Will is how I would have that portion of the Estate that I now injoy to be disposed of after my decease: Imprimis: I give to my son Nicholas Buckland my now Dwelling house &

Orchard, being my Homelott, 2 acres of Pastureland, & in the Great Meadow 6 acres of Meadowland. This I give to my son Nicholas to be to himself and his heirs or assigns after my decease. Yet this I do desire of him while I live, that he take the best Care he is able for my Comfortable maintenance. I give to my daughter Hannah Buckland all my Household Goods of one Sort & another for her own use and dispose. This is all I have to express, & do witness the Truth of my Will & desire by setting to my Hand.

Witness: *Matthew Grant,*   TEMPERANCE X BUCKLAND, WIDOW.
        John Grant.

Court Record, Page 46—1st November, 1681: Will & Invt. Exhibited. Adms. to Nicholas Buckland.

27 January, 1681-2: Joshua Wyllys gave a receipt for the legacy to his wife, who was Hannah Buckland.

Witness: *Michael Taintor,*   Signed, JOSHUA WYLLYS,
        John Grant.   HANNAH X WYLLYS.

Page 219-20.

Buell, Widow Mary, Windsor. Died 1st September, 1684. Invt. £19-15-06. Taken 11 October, 1684, by James Hilliard & Samuel Barber. Will dated 29 August, 1684.

I Mary Buell, being very weak and nigh to death, but having my natural Understanding, having some smale things to dispose of, my Will is that my Eldest daughter Mary Mills shall have my Westcoate, Coat, & that Hatt which was Sarah's, & 1 white linen apron, & 1 blue Apron which it is woue; & the rest of my Wool & Linen Clothes I give to my daughter Hannah Palmer, & my Hatt, & 1 pewter Platter, & 1 tin pann. I give to my daughter Hepzibah Welles 6 yards of linen Cloth, & I give to my gr. child Mary Palmer Wool Cloth to make her a Coat, & to my gr. Child Sarah Palmer Wool Cloth for a Waste Coat, & the rest of my Wool Cloth is to be divided between my daughters Mary & Hannah, & the rest of my linen cloth is to be diuided between my two daughters Mary and Hannah, & I give to my daughter Hannah 1 blue apron, & that is all that I give to my daughter.   (Will not signed.)

Witness: *James Hillier,*
        Mary X Hillier.

Court Record, Page 105—24 March, 1684-5: Will Proven. Adms. to Peter Buell. Capt. Newbery and John Moore appointed to Distribute the Estate, to be equally divided to the Children of sd. Buell.

Page 72-73.

Bewell (Buell), William, Windsor. Died 16 November, 1681. Invt. £147-12-10. Taken 30 November, 1681, by John Loomys sen., John Moore. Will dated 26 July, 1681.

I William Buell do give to my son Samuel the house and halfe the Homelott, with all the Land, purchased of William Thrall; & to my son Peter halfe the Home lott on the North side, & all the Meadow & the Wood Land that was my owne by guift of the Towne. My Tooles to be equally divided betwixt Samuel & Peter. My son Samuel is to pay out £11, & Peter £6, & this, with the rest of my Goods, to be equally divided between my daughters, only my daughter Mary to have £5 more than either of the others. These two parcells of Land, one by the Gravell hill, the other by the Mill brooke, which I leave to my wife's disposeing If she out lives me, & she is to enjoy all this as long as she lives.

Witness: *Nathaniel Gillett,*   WILLIAM X BUELL.
       Timothy Phelps.
       Job Drake, son of *John Drake, James Hillier.*

Mrs. Mary Bewell, the widdow & relict of Wm. Bewell, Decd., Exhibited Invt. 6th March, 1681-2, before Benjamin Newbery, Commissioner.

6 March, 1681-2: It is mutually agreed By Samuel & peter Bewell, as a final Issue betwixt them, respecting their father's will, as followeth: That all the houseing shall be equally divided betwixt them by an indifferent estimation. Also that peter shall have Liberty to choose which end of the house he will have, both Samuel & peter being bound to give or take according to the estimation that shall then be set upon it. Allso that Peter shall have halfe the Home Lott as it Lyeth on the Northerly side & as expressed in the will, wth the addition of the southerly or other part of the swamp or meadow Lying by the Riverett, which is to extend from the River to the Middle of the Hill or falling ground betwixt the meadow & upland, as allso that all the woodlands & boggy meadow shall be settled upon both of them according to their father's will, which was prsented in Court. Farther, we doe allso agree that the Land Lying in the great meadow shall be equally divided betwixt us both. The aforesaid parcells of Land we agree shall be & remayne to us, our heirs & successors, with all the privaleges thereto belonging; & farther we doe agree that whatsoever of Legacy shall be due by our Father's will, it shall be discharged or payd equally betwixt us; & allso that the Tooles our Father Left us shall be divided according to his will written. For the true performance of what is above written we doe mutually set to our hands.

                          SAMUEL BEWELL,
                          PETER BUELL.

Witness: *Nathan Gillett,*
       George Griswold.

Page 196-7.

Bull, Capt. Thomas, Hartford. Invt. £972-06-00 in Hartford. Taken 24 October, 1684, by Joseph Whiting, Nathaniel Stanly and Stephen Hosmer. £276-05-00 in Saybrook, and £76-00-00 in Joshua's gift of Land. Total, £1322-11-10. Taken 29 February, 1700. Will dated 19 April, 1684.

I Thomas Bull of Hartford, being weake in body Butt in good measure of health and memory, doe make this my last Will and testament: Impr. My will is that all my Just Debts be payd to whom I am Indebted.

It. I give unto my son Thomas Bull of ffarmington That lott att ffower-mile Hill in Hartford Bounds, yt about one Hundred Acres; also I give my sayd son ffifteen pounds of my personal Estate and Two Cows.

Itt. I give unto my son David Bull of Saybrook all That I bought of good Wife Towsland in houseing and Land in Saybrook; And I give unto my said son David £20 out of my personal Estate, and also two of my best Coats for his use.

Itt. I give unto my daughter Ruth Boardman of Cambridge £10, to be paid in 18 Months after my decease.

Itt. I give unto my Daughter Bunts in Hartford £10, to be paid in 18 months after my decease.

Itt. I give unto my Grand Childe Susannah Bunts £5.

Itt. I give unto my daughter Abigail Bull £90 Besides what she hath Received already, to be paid wthin 18 Months after my Decease, of wch sum I doe Appoint my son Joseph Bull to pay £40 out of the best of my household Goods, and I doe apoynt my son Jonathan Bull to pay £50 out of what he shall receive out of my Real and personal Estate, both wch sums to be payd In 18 months after my Decease.

I give unto my son Jonathan Bull Two Acres of my six Acar Lott In the South Meadow In Hartford, and likewise I give him 3 Acars of Meadow out of that 8 Acars that was Capt. Cullett's, Abutting on Goodman Stocking's Lott by the great River's side; alsoe I give him My Two Acar Lott Lying by the Indian ffort by the great River's side. Alsoe I doe give my sayd son Jonathan 6 Acars of my land that I bought of Mr. Hopkins, Lying next Mr. Hooker's Land; Also I give him 3 Acars of Meadow at Hockanum that I bought of Mr Robert Webster, and I give him that Acar of Land that is over against My now Dwelling house that I bought of Thomas Whaples, Deceased; also I give him half that Lott yt I bought of Capt. Cullett of 14 Acars, Abutting on the Land of Steeven Hopkins and Land of Eliezer Way of Hartford; also I give him my Lott and House that I bought of William Warren neare the New Meeting hous In Hartford; also I give him my 18 Acar Lott lying at Rocky Hill, Abutting on the Land of Steven Hopkins; also I doe give unto my son Jonathan Bull the one half of my Land at Nahantick, with half the houseing privileges and apertenances; also I doe give unto my son Jonathan half my Land at Cedar Swamp that I Receved of the Country. And if the lord shall pleas to take my son Jonathan out of this Life before he hath A son, then my will is that All the land he hath Received of me, excepting what is Recorded to him before my death, shall Return to my then surviving Children, to be devided equally amongst them.

Itt. I give unto all my Grand children £20, to be divided equally amongst them.

Itt. I give unto Mr. John Whiting £3, and desire him to be Overseer of this my will.

Itt. I give the Rest of my Estate, both Real and personall, unto my son Joseph Bull, whom I doe Appoynt to be sole Executor of this my Last Will and Testament. And alsoe that my son Joseph doe lett my Daughter Abigail have the use of the Chamber she now Lodgeth In so long as she shall see caus. In witness of the premises I have heare unto sett my hand this 20 August, 1684.   THOMAS BULL.
Witness: *Eliezer Way, Sarah Way.*

A Codicil made about 2 days before the death of Capt. Bull: In consideration that his daughter Bunce had deceased, he gave the £10 devised to her to her daughter Susanna Bunce.

Test: *Abigail Bull & Mr. John Whiting,* upon oath before *John Allyn, Sect.*

25 November, 1684.

Page 139-140.

Bunce, Thomas, Hartford. Invt. £1024-03-00. Taken 3 August, 1683, by James Steele, Nathaniel Stanly, John Easton, in Hartford. £767-03-00. Taken 1683, by Samuel Talcott, John Deming, Wethersfield. A Home Lott & dwelling house, £100; to 9 Acres of meadow Land at the pond, £70; to Land at the wherle pool, £9; to Land in the wett swamp, £6; to 30 acres of Land in the wett swamp, £30; to a Long Lott in the west feild, 22½ acres, £30; to 6 Acres dry swamp, £12; sume, £257; £767-03-00—£1024-03-00. Will not dated.

I Thomas Bunce do give and confirme to John Bunce my sonn & his heirs forever all that my house & Lott & barn with all the appurtenances belonging to it (which I bought of Thomas Gridley) within the Bounds of the Township of Hartford, & my 40 acre Lott which I bought of the aforesayd Gridley which Lyeth near weathersfield Bounds, together with my whole right, title & Interest in the saw Mill that was built by Mr. Gardner, Stephen Hosmer & my selfe, & doe put him in present possession thereof. Moreover I doe give & bequeath unto my sayd sonn John Bunce six acres of Meadow Land in the South meadow on the south side of my Lott Lying by John Wattson's, Thomas Catlin's and Steven Hopkins' Land, as also I give & bequeath to him my Lott Lyeing over against Mr. Webster, which abutts on the Highway east & on John Wattsons Land on the West & on John Richards' Land on the south & on the highway on the North. These two Last parcells of my Land my sayd sonn John Bunce is to possess immediately after the decease of me & my wife Sarah Bunce. Moreover I doe give unto my sayd (sonn) John Bunce out of my moveable estate £10. I doe give unto my daughter Elizabeth White £20. I doe give unto all my grand children to each of them £5. I doe give to my cousin Elizabeth White £5. I doe give to my sister Katharen Clark £10. I doe give to my wife all my moveable estate, both of Cattell & household stuffe, to be to her use & behoofe whilst she shall Live & to dispose of at her decease to our children. I doe give unto her the use and improvement of all my houseing & Land that I stand possessed of at my decease, to be for her comfortable subsistance, she keeping houseing & fences in good repayre; provided, if she marry again she shall have but one halfe of my houseing & Lands. I doe give unto my son Thomas Bunce Jr. & his heirs forever, after the decease of my wife, all my houseing & Lands of what nature & kind soever they be, or wheresoever situated. I doe nominate my sayd sonn Thomas Bunce to be my whole & sole Executor; & to enable him to performe this my Will & to pay such Legacies as I have herein given, I do grant him power to sell any part of my Land at Weathersfield for the end aforesayd, not wth standing any clause or bequest in this my will to the contrary; & that he may have a refuge to repayre unto for advice & councill in all difficulties that may arise in the attendency of this my will, I doe desire my Brethren Ens. Nath. Standly & Steven Hosmore to be my desired overseers to assist him with council & advice as there shall be need.   THOMAS BUNCE.

Witness: *John Allyn, Joseph Whiting.*

A nuncupative Codicil appears upon record, entered upon the testimony of *Thomas Bull and Jonathan Bull* upon oath before John Allyn, Assist, 2 August, 1683, wherein he revokes the Legacy to his cousin Elizabeth White, giveing her nothing, and reduceing the Legacies to his Grand children from £5 to each to 20 shillings to each.

Court Record, Page 73—6 September, 1683: Will Proven.

Page 157.

Burr, Ann, Widow, who died 31 August, 1683. Invt. £09-06-06. Taken 6 December, 1683, by Thomas Butler, Nathaniel Goodwin, also to be Distributors.

Court Record, Page 79—18 December, 1683: Estate to be divided equally to Thomas Burr and Mary Clark, except one Coat which Mary Crow hath.

Page 59-60.

Burr, Benjamin, Hartford. He died 31 March, 1681. Invt. £232-12-06. Taken 15 April, 1681, by Nicholas Olmsted, Caleb Stanly. Will dated 2 June, 1677.

I Benjamin Burr of Hartford do make this my last Will & Testament: I give unto my wife Ann Burr, during her life, excepting only what I appoynt to be payd before her decease. I give unto my son Samuel & his heirs & assigns forever, after my wive's decease, all my Land at Greenfield with all the Buildings thereon, & I doe allso give him whatsoever he hath all ready received from me. Item. I give to my sonn Thomas Burr & his heirs for ever, all my houseing & Land in the Township of Hartford, after my wive's decease; & my teame, that is, two oxen & an Horse, allso all the utensills to the Team belonging, as cart, plow & such like, to be his after my decease; & my will is that he doe with the Teame & utensills all worke for my wife while she Liveth that is to be done with a Teame. Item. I give to my daughter Hannah Burr £10; to my daughter Mary Crow 20s; to my grand child Mary Crow £10. I give £10 to my wife to be at her dispose by her will to such of her children as by their duty & behavior shall in her Judgement best deserve the same. I give to my daughter Hannah £10 more, to be paid by my sonn Thomas Burr after his mother's decease, besides what is above mentioned. Item. My will is that my sonn Thomas shall take care of his mother while they live together in this world, to supply her wants in all respects so farr as the Estate Left to that End will do it. I make my wife Ann Burr & my sonn Thomas Burr Joynt & only Executors.   BENJAMIN X BURR.

Court Record, Page 39—20 April, 1681 : Will Proven.

Page 105.

Burr, Samuel, Hartford. Died 29 September, 1682. Invt. £541-10-11. Taken 5 October, 1682, by Paul Peck sen., Joseph Mygatt, Ciprian Niccolls, George Grave, Joseph Easton. The children: Samuel, 20 years of age; John 12, 5-12; Mary 9, 8-12; Elizabeth, 7 years of age, and Jonathan, 3 years and 8 months.

Court Record, Page 61—13 December, 1682: Adms. to Stephen Hopkins and Thomas Catlin. Order to Dist., With the advice of the Magistrates and Marshall George Grave, to Samuel £160, to John £100, to Jonathan £100, to Mary £80, to Elizabeth £80, as they come of age.

Page 158.

Bushnell, Susannah, Saybrook, who died 18 August, 1683. Invt. £51-18-00. Taken 4 September, 1683, by Nathaniel Chapman and John Bushnell. Will nuncupative. Testified to by Lieut. William Bushnell and Samuell Bushnell. She gave all that she had to her son John Waddams.

Court Record, Page 72—6 September, 1683: Will & Invt. approved. From file: An Inventory of the Estate of Susanah Bushnell:

	£	s	d
her wearing cloaths of woolen	12	06	00
her old Cloath	00	09	00
her bed linnen & wearing linnen & silke & bookes	13	03	00

A feather bed & bed sted one bolster 2 pillow & pillow Coats
   one pare of sheets 3 old Curtains one old ruge 2 old
   blanketts   06-03-00
20 pound in ye hand of Samuel Bushnell   20-00-00

This Inventory taken & apprised by us Select men & apprisers *Nathaniel
Chapman & John X Bushnell* Saybrook September 4th 1683 *The person
presenting the Estate hath acted under oath according to law.
There is no writen will that which shee Left by word of mouth was that
shee gave all that shee had to her son John waddams which testimony we
have reseued from Leftentt William Bushnell & Samuel Bushnell*

Pr Nathaniel Chapman   }
John X Bushnell   } *Townsmen.*

*John Waddams of wethersfeild this 4th of September came to Saybrook
to demand an estate given to him by his mother there is (ordd) & of the
person in law appointed Samuel Bushnell to do the same and haveing
loueingly agree on that accont so that there appeareth no difi-Culty or any
fere of trouble for the futter the said john waddams desireth it may have
its isue at harford Court in 2 resons first it will save hime considerable
Charg to appeare at or County Court 2ly the Condiscon of his family at
present under the afflicting hand I being not willing to deuert the Course
of law settled or the practice of each Courte the going from hath some
times proued troublesome but in this Case as I thinke I do so far under
stand that I do on the former reasons giue countenance as the best way
that the matters be settled at hartford Court unto which Cort I do recommend the isue which is the all at present presentable to your honord members of the Court from your friend and servant dated in Saybrook*

Robt Chapman Assist.

Sept. 4th 1683.

Page 184-5.

Butler, Deac. Richard, Hartford. Died 6 August, 1684. Invt. £564-
15-00. Taken 2 September, 1684, by Paul Peck sen., George Grave. Will
dated 2 April, 1677.

Know all men whom it may concern, that I Richard Butler, being in
bodily health & of sound & perfect memory, doe make & ordain this my
Last will & Testament in Form & maner as followeth: Imprim: I doe
give to my son Thomas Butler my uper Lot in the Long meadow. 2nd I doe
give to my son Samuell all my meadow Land in Weathersfeild meadow. 3,
I doe give to Nathaniel my son my meadow Lot neer the Long meadow
gate. 4, I doe give Joseph Butler My son all my Land in the South
meadow. 5, I doe give to my son Daniel Butler my now dwelling house
wth all appurtenances of building & ground about it, as also I doe give my
son Daniel my Lot comonly called ten acres. 6, I doe give my three daughters, Mary Wright, Elizabeth Olmsted & Hanah Green, twenty shillings

apeice, to be payd out of my moveable estate by my present wife Elizabeth, whom I appoynt my Executor to this my last Will. Allso it is my will that none of these children aforesayd doe possess or enjoy any of these Lands, or ought else mentioned, but with the consent, death, or change of their mother's condition, that is, by marriage againe. But if my wife Elizabeth Butler should change her conditions & marry againe, then my will is that all my aforesd. sonns & daughters doe possess every one his Legacy & my wife only the Thirds; & for the rest of Cattell & household goods I give them all to my wife, provided as afoursayd she continue in widdowhood; but if she marry again, then to take the third of all, as of the house & Land so of Cattell & household Stuffe; & the rest equally to be divided among all my Children aforementioned; & though there may be divers Wills Extant that I have written with my own hand, yet this is my Last & shall stand written wth my owne hand. I appoint my two sons Thomas & Samuel Butler to be Overseers of this my Last will. My will also is that my daughter Mary Wright shall have one feather bed after her mother's decease.

RICHARD BUTLER.

Witness: *Samuel Wright,*
   Samuel Butler.

Court Record, Page 93—4 September, 1684: Will Proven.

Page 246.

Churchill, Josiah, Wethersfield. Invt. £618-12-06. Taken 5 January, 1686-7, by Mr. James Treat, John Buttolph. Will dated 17 November, 1683.

I Josiah Churchill of Wethersfield do make this my last Will & Testament: I give unto my wife Elizabeth Churchill the use of all my Estate, whether Real or Personal, during her natural life, excepting such parcels of Land as shall hereafter be excepted, she paying all my Just Debts. And after her decease my Will is that all my Land & other Estate of mine she shall then stand possessed of, to be divided as follows: I give unto my son Joseph the House & Homelott he now liveth on, with all other Buildings thereon, and one Lott in the Little West Field, containing 10 acres, and another Lott containing 6 acres. I give unto my son Joseph my 50-acre Lott at the West End of Wethersfield Bounds. I do give unto my son Joseph, after the decease of my wife, Elizabeth, 5 acres in the Great Swamp, & 2 acres of Meadow lying toward the lower End of sd. Meadow, & half of my 5-acre Lott at the upper End of the Great Meadow. I give unto my son Benjamin Churchill 6 acres in the Little West Field, also 10 acres more in the West Field. I give unto my son Benjamin, after the decease of my wife, my now Dwelling House & Homelott & other Buildings upon sd. Lott, & 7 acres of Land in the Great Swamp, & 4 acres in Beaver Meadow, & half my 5-acre Lott at the upper End of the Great

Meadow. My Will is that all the rest of my Moveable Estate be equally divided betwixt my daughters Marah Church, Elizabeth Buck, Ann Rice and Sarah Wickham. My Will is that my wife be sole Executrix.
Witness: *Samuel Talcott,*   JOSIAH CHURCHILL. Ls.
          John Deming.
Court Record, Page 128—3 March, 1686-7: Will Proven.

Page 14-15-16.

Clarke, Mary, Farmington. Invt. £273-05-06. Taken 26 February, 1678, by Thomas X Tibbetts sen., Samuel Burwell, Samuel Newton, Elezer Rogers. Invt. at Farmington, £32-16-00. Taken 14 February, 1678, by John Norton, Thomas X Barnes, John Woodruffe. Will dated 28 November, 1677.

I Mary Clarke of Farmingtown do make this my last Will & Testament: I give to my daughter Mary Stevens £16, to my daughter Rebeckah Warner £16, to my daughter Chittingdon £15-15. I give unto my son-in-Law Elnathan Bochford 5 Shillings, to my gr. child Elizabeth Bochford £5. I give unto the Rev. Pastor Newton 5 Shillings. I give unto my brother John Ward of Newark 20 Shillings. I give unto my gr. Child Rebeckah Stevens a pewter platter. I give unto my gr. Child Mary Warner a pewter platter. I give unto my gr. child Abigail Standly a featherbed. I give unto my gr. child Elizabeth Chittingdon a bason. I give unto my gr. child Elizabeth Standly my Chest. I give unto my son-in-law John Standly and my daughter Sarah his wife the ½ of all my Lands in Milford, woodland, earable and Meadow, except my Homestead, to be equally divided. My Will is that my sonn Standly shall have £4-10 by the year paid to him out of the Rent of the Lands at Milford during the Lease of Nathaniel Farrand. I give unto my daughter Abigail Fletcher my House, Barn & Homelott, & the ½ of all my Land in Milford, to be equally divided, that is to say, woodland, Earable Land & Meadow, that is to say, to her & her natural heirs. My Will is that if she dyes without Issue, that the ½ of the aforementioned house & Lands shall return to be equally divided betwixt my 4 daughters. And further I give unto her all my Household Goods that is at Milford that is not divided or disposed of; & if she dye, the forementioned Estate Willed to her shall be divided equally between my four daughters, with this proviso, that my daughter Rebeckah Warner shall have £10 more than any of the rest of my daughters. My Will is that what of my Clothing, Woolen or Lynen, that is at Farmington, that is not disposed of at my decease, that my four daughters, Mary, Rebeckah, Sarah & Hannah, it shall be divided equally amongst them. I appoint my daughter Abigail Fletcher to be my whole and sole Executrix. And I do desire Honoed Major Robert Treate & Mr. Samuel Eales to be Overseers.
Witness: *Robert Porter,*   MARY X CLARKE, Ls.
          John Loomis.
Court Record, Page 12—6 March, 1678-9: Will proven.

Page 48-9.

Clark, Nicholas, Hartford. Died 2nd July, 1680. Invt. £243-02-00. Taken by Nicholas Olmsted and John Gilbert. Will dated 28 January, 1679-80.

I Nicholas Clark of Hartford do make this my last Will & Testament: I give unto my son Thomas Clark my now dwelling House, Barn, and home lott upon which they stand, with the orchard, grass and plowing Land east of the sayd buildings, within the sayd Lott, and Lott within the Long meadow, and two Lotts (one of Two Acres Being upland, and the other being six or seaven of upland) lying on the west side of the brickell swamp, My Lott of Three Acres on the east side of the great River near Mr. Crows habitation, and my lott near John Bidwell (being about eight Acres) on the same east side of the great River, northward of the former, and halfe my fourth Lott being situate near podunk, by estimation being four Acres, to him and his heirs for ever. And by this my Last will and testament I do disalow, disclaime, and declare that my sayd son Thomas nor his heirs for ever shall at any time or times hereafter make any Alienation, change, alteration, deed or deeds, orders of sale, or mortgage of the premises. And I give unto my son Thomas my Cattle, swine, utensells, tooles, apparell, pewter, brass, linnin, and all moveables, within doors and without, with my Just Debts, to him and his heirs for ever. Also, I give and bequeath unto Daniel Clark, son to my son Thomas Clark, that dwelling House that my son Thomas now liveth in, with the Lott that it standeth on, and the lott and orchyard that is next adjoyning to it north, to him and his heirs for ever, and one Lott of four Acres or thereabouts on the east side of the great River, being situate on Nicholas Disbrough south and on Mr Richard Lords North. I give and bequeath unto my son-in-law Alexander Duglass one halfe of my fourth Lott, being situate neer podunk, which lott is by estimation about fouer Acres, to him and his heirs forever, disallowing and forbiding either my grand son Daniel Clark or my son-in-law Duglass, him or them or any of their heires shall not make any Allination, change, Alteration, deed or deeds of sale, or mortgages, upon the premises. And whereas I have given my grandson Daniel the foresayd Legacy, that is, in Case he shall attayne the age of Twenty and foure years, and my son Thomas to improve all the sayd Legacys until then, keeping the House in good repayre, extraordinary Casualtyes excepted. And in case my grandchild Daniel shall not attayne the age of twenty foure yeares, then I give that sayde Legacy to Joseph Clark, my grandchild; and in case he shall not attayne to ye age of twenty four yeares, then do I bequeath it to ye next son Thomas, my grandchild; and if he attaineth not to the fore sayd age, then to the surviving son, to be held upon this tennure aforesayd, as intailed Land, to him, them, and their heires forever. I do allso give and bequeath five pounds, to be payd to my son-in-law Lester of New London out of my Estate by my son, Executor, within one Twelve moneths after my decease. And whatsoever is in this my will and testament omitted or not mentioned, be it in lands, debts, Cattle, swine, or whatsoever estate belongs unto me within the Township of Hartford or Colony of Connecticut, I give to My son Thomas, those legacys aforesayd only excepted, and I make my son Thomas Clark soal Executor of this my last will and testament, and desire my Loveing ffriends Maij. John Talcott and Corp. Thomas Butler to be overseers to my will, and to assist and advise my son Thomas in the fulfilling of the same, and advise him to take their advise in the management thereof.

NICHOLAS X CLARK, Ls.

Witness: *John Talcott, sen., Thomas Butler.*

Court Record, Page 33—2 December, 1680: Will proven.

Page 61-2.

Clarke, William sen., Haddam. Died 22 July, 1681. Invt. £412-18-00. Taken 19 August, 1681, by George Gates, Wm. X Ventrus, Simon Smith, John Spencer, Selectmen. Will dated 30 June, 1681.

I William Clarke of Haddam do make this my last Will & Testament: I give to my wife £4 a year during her natural life. I also give unto her the use of my Dwelling house & the little Orchard, half the Garden so long as she live a Widow. Moreover I give unto my wife a Cow, which my son Thomas shall winter for her during his Mother's life. Also I give unto her half my Household Stuff, & that in her half she be suited with a Bed & Bedding & such things as are most suitable for her, which she shall dispose of at her death to which she please of her Children. I Will unto my son William £25 out of my Estate, which shall be in my Land as it is prised in the Inventory. I do Will unto my son John £20 worth of my Land. I do give by Will unto my son Joseph, notwithstanding anything I have formerly given him, £15 worth of Land, and 1½ acre of the Boggs in the lower Division in the upper Meadow besides the £15. I give by Will unto my daughter Welles & to my daughter Fennoe & to my daughter Spencer £8 to each of them, and to my daughter Hannah £10. All these to be paid out of my Estate as prised with the Inventory. I give unto my son-in-law Daniel Hubbard 5 Shillings, & to my gr. Child Daniel Hubbard I do give 40 acres of Land in my second Division at Machamodus, and a £50 Freehold or Right in the Undivided Lands there as it is laid out to £50 Estate. And it is my Will that he be learned to read & to write. And I declare him to the dispose of my wife so long as she liveth, and then to the dispose of my son Thomas; & in Case my son Hubbard make trouble about him he shall satisfy for his bringing up. At the age of 21 years he shall be free. I give to my son Thomas my Lott I bought of Joseph Arnold in the Home Field, and all my whole Meadow Lott, and my Cow Meadow Lott, and the 6 acres on which my Dwelling house standeth, & the Ort Yards and Houses, at his Mother's decease, or Marriage after my death. My Will also is that my sons William, John &

Joseph have their portions in the Land that are not given away particularly and expressly to Thomas in my Will, and that they agree, by casting Lotts, which allottment shall belong to each of them, not exceeding the value above given to them. I do make my son Thomas Clarke sole Executor.

Witness: *Nicholas Noyes,*   WILLIAM X CLARKE.
George Gates.

Court Record, Page 44—3 September, 1681: Will & Inventory exhibited by Thomas Clarke, Executor. Approved.

Clay, Miles. Court Record, Page 9—5 December, 1678: Whereas, it appears that Miles Clay of Brantry, England, deceased, hath an Estate in the Estate of Zachary Sanford, late of Saybrook, this Court doth grant to John Durant, & John Loomy of Hadly in right of his wife, who are grandchildren to the sd. Clay, administration upon the sd. Estate, they being next of kin & having agreed to accept administration.

Page 3.

Clements, Jasper, Middletown, age about 64 years. Invt. £243-04-00. Taken 7 November, 1677, by William Cheeny, Nathaniel Bacon, John Hall sen. Will dated 13 October, 1677.

The last Will & Testament of Jasper Clements: Imprimis: I give to Eleanor my wife all my Cows & all Cow Kind whatsoever, only a 12 Moneth after my decease to give to John Brown a Cow and a Calf, And Benoni Brown a Cow & a Calf. I give to John & Benoni the new Room & the Sheep House and my Lott at Two Sticks. I give to Nathaniel Brown 17 acres of Swamp in Long Meadow Swamp, & 15 acres of Upland near the south End of the Town. My two great Lotts on the West side of the Great River I give to Nathaniel Brown & John Brown & Benoni Brown, to be divided equally amongst them. I give to Nathaniel Browne two Sheep, & to John Browne 3 Sheep, & Benoni Browne 3 Sheep; and I give to Hanna Lane, the younger, 2 Sheep. I give to my wife all my Household Goods of all sorts, only my Will is that after her decease my great Kettle & my Great Chest shall be my cousin Hanna Lane's. And moreover I give to my wife all other of my Estate which is not herein mentioned, makeing her soale Executrix. I freely give to the Benefit of the Schools in Middletown all my Divisions of Land on the East side of the Great River & which was to have been divided in the year 1674 by the List of 1673, to be disposed of at the Discretion of Mr. Giles Hamlin, Mr. Nathaniel Collins, Mr. William Southmayd, Mr. William Harris, Thomas Allyn & John Hall senior. I do request my trusty friends, William Harris, Thomas Allyn & John Hall, to be Overseers.

Witness: *Thomas Allyn,*   JASPER X CLEMENTS. Ls.
William Harris, John Hall.

Court Record, Page 3—7 March, 1677-8: Will & Invt. Exhibited in Court.

Page 237.

Cole, John sen., Hartford. Invt. £396-18-06. Taken 17 November, 1685, by Ciprian Niccols, Stephen Hosmore. Will dated 4th August, 1683.

The Last Will of John Cole sen is as followeth: That his son John of Farmington should have thirty pound pd him out of his Estate besides wt hee hath had, and should also have his wearing cloathes. Yt his daughter Benton & his daughter Wilson should have five pounds a peice, also pd out of it, & yt his son Job in England should have ten pounds pd if it can be conveyed to him; & yt his Loveing wife should have six pound a year allowed her out of His Estate whille shee Liveth, and a cow, which shall be kept also winter & summer; and she shall have her wood; & ye rest of his Estate shall be divided between his sons Samuel & Nathaniel, excepting ye housing & home Lott, and His will concerning ym is yt his son Samull should have yt home lott, as wide as his own down to the Dich, & yt he should have 20 bushels of apls a year for six year, & ye rest of ye houseing & home Lotts should be to his son Nathaniel, onely his wife shall have two rooms in ye hous while shee Liveth if she se cause to live their, & shee shall have ye dispose of ye houshold stuffe; & hanah yeomons shall have 40 shill; & his will is yt ensighn Nath. Stanly & Stephen Hosmer, his Loveing friends, would se ye performance of this his will.

Witness ye 4th of august, 1683:   JOHN COLE.
Stephen Hosmer, binjeman Grimes.

Court Record, Page 117—4 March, 1685-6: Will Proven. Adms. to Samuel & Nathaniel Coale, with the will annexed.

Page 33.

Cole, Ann, Mrs., Hartford. Died 20 February, 1679-80. Invt. £103-04-06. Taken by Nicholas Olmsted, John Gilbert, Caleb Standly.

Court Record, Page 23—4 March, 1679-80: Invt. Exhibited. By the Testimony of Mr. Samuel Willys, Mr. Jonathan Gilbert & Wm Edwards, Mrs. Ann Cole desired that her son William Edwards & his wife should have the use of her House and Land during life, then to Return to her grandson Richard Edwards and to his heirs forever. Adms. to Richard Edwards. Approved.

Page 221-2-3.

Collins, Nathaniel, Middletown. Died 21 December, 1684. Invt. £679-01-09. Taken by Giles Hamlin, Nathaniel White & William Warde.

The children of the Decd are: Mary, age 18 years, John 16, Susannah 14, Martha 11, Nathaniel 7, and Abigail, 4 years of age.

Court Record, Page 92—4 September, 1684: Mr. John Whiting, Mr. Joseph Whiting, Mr. John King in Right of Mrs. Sarah his wife, and Mr. Nathaniel Collins in Right of Mrs. Mary his wife, are plaintiffs; Corporall Thomas Bissell, Defendant; in an Action of the Case of unlawfull detaining from them their proportion of Land now in your possession, sometime the Land of their Father Mr. William Whiting, Decd, given them by the last Will of their Father.

Page 105—24 March, 1684-5: Adms. granted to Mary Collins. This Court do appoint Mr. Giles Hamlin, Nathaniel White & Deacon John Hall to be Overseers to the sd. Widow & Children, & the Estate is to be dist., to the Relict £57, To John (Eldest son) £147, and the rest of the Children are to have £73 apeice.

Page 64 (Vol. V) 6 December, 1693: This Court appoint Capt. Nathaniel White & Deacon John Hall to Dist. to the Widow & Children of Mr. Nathaniel Collins his Estate according to the Order of the Court as followeth: To the Relict 1-3 part of Real Estate during life, & to John his Double portion, & to each of the rest of the Children their single portions of sd. Estate.

Page 146—(Vol. XIII, Probate Side): We the Subscribers, being the heirs or Legatees of the Estate of our honoured Father, Mr. Nathaniel Collins, and our honoured Mother, Mrs. Mary Collins, both Deceased, being sensible of the necessity of mutual acting something that may prevent all future debates and controversies refering to the Estate above mentioned, we do therefore, in pursuance thereof, all as one thus agree: That we do all of us rest contented in and do hereby acknowledge ourselves full satisfied in what Capt. White and Deacon Hall did in the first Dist. of our Father's Estate made by them do and among us the heirs and Legatees. And also further, we having after our honoured Mother's decease made choice of our Brother Mr. John Hamlin and Capt. White to dist. to and among us our honoured Mother's Estate, do also rest contented in and do hereby acknowledge ourselves satisfied in the Dist. made by the above mentioned Gentlemen, Mr. John Hamlin & Capt. White, And that we do take the several things set out to us by them out of the Moveables of our Mother's Estate without any contention or difference. And we do hereby promise and engage to and with each other we will not at any time after signing of this by any means contend and differ with one an other with respect to the Estate, either in whole or in part, above mentioned, That being completed according to the Dist. entered in our Father's Book. And we do set to our hands & Seals this 5th day of May, 1712.

> JOHN HAMLIN in behalf of his wife.
> MARY HAMLIN alias COLLINS. LS.
> JOHN COLLINS. LS. NATH: COLLINS. LS.
> WILLIAM HAMLIN. LS. THOMAS HURLBUT. LS.

Witness: *Israhiah Wetmore,*
Thomas Anderson.

Page 1-2.

Cornwell, Sargt. William, Middletown. Invt. £251-03-00. Taken by Robert Warner, Richard Hall, John Hall. The children: John, William, Samuel, Jacob & Thomas Cornwell, Sarah Hubbard, Easter Stowe, Elizabeth Hall. Will dated 12 June, 1674.

I William Cornwell of Middletown do make this my last Will & Testament: I give my sone John Cornwell soe much of addition to his present home Lott out of my homelott as may make up his present home lott the full halfe of the whole, the sd. addition to be taken out next to the present divedent line betwixt us. I give allsoe to my sayd sone the on halfe of yt woodland in the south division of Land beyond the mill, lying betweene ye Land of my son William and the Land of William Lucas; the other halfe of the sd. Land to my Daughter Sarah Cornwell. This Land equally to be divided between them. I give moreover to my son John Two Acres of ye meadow & swamp at ye Riverlet at the Western end of that meadow and swamp, to begin next to the Riverlett at the end next unto the Boggy meadow. I give unto my son William Ten Acres of my Land upon the Indian hill at the east end, the whole Bredth of the Lott. More, to my sayd sone one third part of my Land yet to be devided by the List in 1674, on the East side the River; the other two thirds of the abovesayd Land to my sons Samuell and Thomas, equally to be devided among them. I give moreover to my sone Samuel 100 Acres of my Wood Lott at ye Long hill, the remainder to my son Jacob. I give moreover to my son Thomas, beside wt is above sayd, ye remainder of my lott at the Indian Hill, ye Ten Acres as above mentioned Taken out of it. I give to my daughter Esther Willcocke my whole Lott on ye east side of the River Lying against Goodman Colls swamp at ye upper End of the Rocks, with my Lott in the pond. I give to my Daughter Elizabeth Hall one peice of upland Lying in the Boggy meadow quarter between the Land of Deacon Hall and my son Samuel Cornwall. I give to my Loving wife Mary Cornwell my house, homestead, all the buildings, hosehould stufe and movabls wt soever, with ye remainder of my meadow at ye River lot, quietly and peaceably to enjoy ye same, with all the benifits theireof, during ye terme of her widdow hood, and allsoe ye wholl stocke of cattle during ye sayd terme. It is allsoe my meaning herein, and will, yt whille my Daughter Sarah continues in a singlle state, living with & being a help and comfort to her mother, she should have hir maintainance out of the same soe far as hir Mother's comforts will allow. After my wife hir deceas, I will the Above mentioned house, homestead, and meadow Land at ye River lot, & stocke Remaining, to my Sone Jacob Cornwell, he paying all just debts and the charges of my desent funerall out of the same: & allso to his sister Sarah Cornwell·one third part of the valluation of the fore mentioned housing & Lands, as shall be apraised & Inventoryed, In corent pay of the Contry, within twelve months after his possession of the same: In case my wife in the terme above mentioned see caus to chang hir condishon by mariage, It is then my will that my loving wife should have all the houshould stuf what soe ever, and Jacob to allow hir foure pounds sterling per yeare soe long as she live, in good corent pay of ye country, in case shee find need & demand it of him: and that at hir decease my three Daughters shall have the hous hould stufe equally divided among them, only my sone Samuell to have, upon a former promise I made him, one of the featherbeds first taken out & Delivered to him: & the Long table, Joynt stools and bedstead in the new Rome to be Left with or returned to Jacob with the house. I request Deacon Stocking & Deacon Hall to be overseers in order to the Execution of my Will.

WILLIAM X CORNWALL. Ls.

Witness: *Nath. White,*
     Nathaniel Collins.

Court Record, Page 3—8 March, 1677-8: Will proven.

Page 147—(Vol. X) 7 March, 1726-7: Whereas William Cornwall, by his Will on record, did bequeath to his son William one third part of his Land on the East side of the River, to be divided by the list of 1674, the other 2-3 of the aforesd. Lands to his sons Samuel and Thomas to be equally divided between them, and It being represented to this Court by James (Part gone ————————) Gates to sd. Estate by his marriage to Ann Cornwall, daughter to sd. Deceased, that the sd. Lands have not been divided, and praying this Court that it may be done according to the Last Will of sd. William Cornwall, This Court appoint Joseph Frary, Comfort Davis and James Johnson to Distribute and divide the Estate accordingly.

Page 162—1st August, 1727: Report of the Dist.

Page 259-60.

Couch, Thomas, Wethersfield. Invt. £81-11-00. Taken 24 March, 1687, by Mr. James Treat, John Robbins, John Buttolph. The widow, Hanna Couch. Children: Susannah, age 20 years, Simon 18, Rebeccah 15, Hanna 13, Thomas 12, Mary 11, Sara 8, Abigail 6, Martha 3 years. A legacy to the Children from Uncle Simon Couch.

Court Record, Page 133—1st September, 1687: Invt. exhibited. Adms. to the Widow, Hannah Couch. Order for Dist. of the Estate.

Page 116-117.

Cowles, Hanna, Hatfield & Hartford. Died 16 March, 1683. Invt. £107-05-02. Taken by John Marsh, Daniel Clarke. Will dated 27 October, 1680.

I Hanna Cowles, Late of Hatfield, now resident in Hartford, in the Colony of Connecticut, being Stricken in years, doe make this my Last Will and Testament: I doe give unto my son Samuel Cowles £6. I give unto my son John Cowles £6. I give unto my daughter Hannah Standly

Tenn pownds. I give unto my daughter Ester Bull fower pounds. I give to my daughter Elizabeth Lyman £12. I give unto my daughter Mary Dickinson the sum of £10. I give unto the children of my daughter Sarah Goodwin, that shall be surviving at my decease, £6, to be devided equally amongst them. My will & pleasure is that the Legacy of £8 given unto my daughter Goodwin by my husband John Cowles in his Last Will, bearing date 11 December, 1676, be payd by my son John Cowles unto the Children of my daughter Sarah Goodwin, Decd, that shall be living at my decease, equally to be divided amongst them; & this is also my will concerning the rest of those Legacies given by my husband in his Last will unto any other of my daughters, which dispose I thus order, being whole & soale Executrix unto his last Will. I give unto my grand children Hannah & Elizabeth Stanly one payre of sheets. I give unto my three daughters, Ester, Mary & Elizabeth, all my wearing apparell & Lining, to be equally divided amongst them. I give unto my daughter Hannah Standly the value of one fourth part of all my apparell & Linnine given to my Three daughters, out of any other of my Estate that she shall choose before it be divided otherwise, in stead of apparell, & doe also give her the flock bed that I had of my son Stanly, at the price my husband bought it of him, as part of the Ten pownds given her above. I doe also desire my daughter Elizabeth Lyman may have the Feather bed in her Keeping, as part of what is given her in this my Last Will. I appoint my son Samuel Cowles and Caleb Standly to be Executors. I doe give them the remaynder of my Estate, if any should be that is not given away.

Caleb Standly,   HANNAH X COWLES. Ls.
Hannah Standly.

Page 70.

Crow, Christopher, at his farme at Greenfield, in Windsor Bounds. Invt. £109-16-06. Taken 13 December, 1680, by Nicholas Olmsted, John Baker. Children: Samuel, age 21—Jan., 1683; Mary, 18, Oct., 1683; Hanna, 15—Feb., 1683; Martha, 14—May, 1684; Benoni, 12, Jan., 1683; Margaret, 11—April, 1684; Thomas, 5—May, 1684.

Court Record, Page 33—11 December, 1680: Crow had left out of the Colony, and later his wife went, leaving the children and debts. This Court appoint Samuel Burr and Thomas Burr to take an Invt. of the Estate and to dispose of the Children that they may be comfortably provided for.

Page 40—20 April, 1681: Invt. Exhibited. Samuel Burr appointed Adms.

Page 87—6 March, 1684: Adms. of Estate to Josiah Clarke, who appeared to have in hand in Land and other things £73, With something in the hands of Samuel Burr, to Distribute: To the Relict, £10; to The Eldest son £16; to each of the other Children £8 as they come of age.

Page 238-9.

Crow, John sen., Hadly. Died 16 January, 1685. Invt. £118-13-00. Court Record, Page 118—4 March, 1685-6: Invt. exhibited in Court by Daniel and Nathaniel Crow, and they were granted letters of Adms.

Page 121—2 September, 1686: Whereas the County Court in March Last made proclamation that the creditors of Mr. John Crowe's Estate should make up their accots with the Adms., which accounts are now presented to the Court, and this Court doe now order that the Adms. address themselves with all speed as they may to pay those debts that are Justly due From the Estate, & when they have so done to present their accot to the Court in March next, & that what is remayning when there Just charge is payd, shall be divided amongst them.

Page 129 (Vol. III): See Estate of John Crow Jr., when Giles Hamlin presented account of his Adms. upon the Estate of Mr. John Crow, his Brother. Approved and granted a *Quietus Est.*

Page 173-4.

Curtice, Joseph, Wethersfield. Died 31 December, 1683. Invt. £271-09-00. Taken by Samuell Tallcott, John Deming. The children: Joseph, age 9 years; Henry, 7 years; Sarah, 5 years; Thomas, 3 years; David, 1 year old.

6 March, 1683-4: Mercy Curtice personally appeared and gave oath that she had made a due presentment of the Estate of her deceased husband, according to her knowledge. Before Mr. Samuel Tallcott, comr.

Court Record, Page 85—6 March, 1684: Adms. to the Widow, and appoynt the Estate to be distributed: to the Widow, £20 personal Estate & a 3d of the real Estate during her life; to the eldest sonn, £77; to the two other sonns, Thirty Nine pounds a peice; to the Two daughters, Thirty eight pounds a peice; to be payd, the sons' portions at 21 years of age, the daughters' at eighteen years of age, & the rest in reversion after their mother's decease. This Court appoynt Sargt. John Deming & Ebenezer Deming & John Curtice to be overseers to assist the widow in the distribution of the Estate, & ordering & disposeing of the children & their Estate.

Page 71-72.

Curtice, Thomas, Wethersfield. Died 13 November, 1681. Invt. £717-13-09. Taken 9 December, 1681, by Nathaniel Borman, Samuel Butler, William Warner. The children: John, James, Joseph, Samuel & Isaac Curtice, Ruth Kimberly, Elizabeth Stoddor. The distribution followeth:

Page 72—6 March, 1681 (2): The distribution of the Estate of Thomas Curtice of Wethersfield, Joyntly Consented to by all his children

& witnessed by their subscribeing: Imprs. To John Curtice (who hath formerly received in houseing & Land £123), fifty seven pounds. Samuel Curtice haveing all ready received his full portion by deed of gift from his father, the remaynder of the Inventoryed Estate to be equally divided to James Curtice, Joseph, Isaac, Ruth and Elizabeth, to each of them an equal proportion, what Joseph, Ruth & Elizabeth have Formerly received being first added to the sume totall of the Inventory, which doth amount to Thirty seven pownds. And it is further Consented to by the sayd Children, that in consideration of the service that Joseph Curtice & his wife have done for their father during his life, there shall be soe much added to his portion as will make it up £140 with the £4 that he hath formerly received, which addition shall be equally deducted from the portions of the other children according to what they have & shall receive, Samuel excepted.

Signed: *John Curtice, James Curtice, Joseph Curtice, Samll Curtice, Eliezr Kimberly, John Stodder.*

Court Record, Page 52—2 March, 1681-2: Adms. to John Curtice, Joseph, James and Isaac Curtice; & Mr. Kimberly, Lt. James Treat, Mr Steven Chester & Mr Samll Woolcott are appoynted to distribute the sayd estate to the sayd Legatees according to the distribution agreed on & settled by this Court.

Page 179.

Denslow, Mrs. Susannah, Windsor. Died 20 August, 1683. Invt. £60-00-04. Taken by Henry Woolcott, Thomas Stoughton.

Court Record, Page 86—6 March, 1684: Adms. to Samuel Denslow (See Henry Denslow). Dist. after the portions of their Fathers Estate is paid to them, to the son a double portion, to each of the daughters a single portion. Cornett Cossett and Daniel Hayden, Distributors.

Dewey, Israel. Court Record, Page 9—5 December, 1678: Adms. to Capt. Daniel Clarke and Job Drake on the Estate of Israel Dewey, Decd., to pay the debts from his Estate so far as it will go, to perfect the Invt., and report March next.

Page 155.

Disbrowe, Nicholas. Invt. £210-10-01. Taken 31 August, 1683, by Thomas Butler, Zachariah Sandford. The children: Obadiah Spencer's Wife, Samuel Eglestone's Wife, John Kelly's Wife, Robert Flood's Wife.

Court Record, Page 77—18 December, 1683: Adms. to Joseph Strickland to pay debts out of the personal Estate so far and as soon as he can, to render an account, when Distribution will be made.

Douglas, Alexander, Hartford. Died ye 3d October, 1688. Invt. £34-17-00. Taken by Joseph Collyer, Nathaniel Goodwin senr. Will dated 8 September, 1687 (on file).

In the name of God amen. I Alexander Douglas of Hartford, in the Colony of Connecticut, being stricken in years, do soe reason by this my Last Will to make dispose of my Estate: I give unto my daughter Sarah my swamp Lott on the east side of Connecticut River in Hartford, the whole which was given to me by my father Nicholas Clark, to be to her & her heirs forever, as also my warming pan, two payre of Sheets, & one payre of pillow beers, & my best bed & boulster, & my bed rug, & my best chest, & one pewter platter, & so much more of my Estate to be allotted to her as may make her portion as good to the full as any other of my daughters; & the rest of my Estate, of what kind or nature soever it be, to be equally divided between my two other daughters after my Just debts and funeral charges are satisfied. I doe nominate Capt. John Allyn & Lt. Caleb Standly to take care of the children & to dispose of them in the best way they can for their comfort & advantage, and to take care that their Estate may be preserved for them to their best advantage.

Witness: *John Allyn,*   ALEXANDER X DOUGLAS. Ls.
    Caleb Stanly.

Page 16-17.

Driscoll, Florence. Invt. £29-15-00. Taken at Wethersfield. £28-00-06 at Springfield.

Court Record, Page 12—6 March, 1678-9: Invt. Exhibited. Order £15 for the Widow's support, and Adms. to Nathaniel Bissell and John Marsh to Collect & settle debts.

Page 74.

Edwards, Joseph, Wethersfield. Died 10th December, 1681. Invt. £162-19-04. Taken by John Kilbourn, Thomas Wright, William Warner. The children: Sarah, age 10 years; Mary, age 7; Hannah, 5; John, 2; Dorothy, about 4 months old.

Court Record, Page 51—2nd March, 1681-2: Adms. to Sarah the Widow.

Page 109—(Vol. V) 18 June, 1696: This Court being moved to make Dist. of the Estate of Joseph Edwards, of Wethersfield, find his Es-

	£ s d
tate to be	129-00-00
And by Lands of John Edwards given him,	149-00-00
Wch is distributed as follows:	
To the Wido 1-3 of the Moveables, wch is	9-17-00
And 1-3 of the Real Estate, wch amounts to	81-00-00
To the son John,	89-06-08
To the other four Children, to each of them,	44-13-04

They to have part in Hand and the remainder in Reversion after the decease of their Mother. This Court appoint Sergt. John Deming, Mr. Jos: Robbins & William Warner, Distributors.

Dist. File, August, 1697: Estate of Joseph Edwards: To Sarah Edwards, Widow, to John, to Sarah, to Mary, to Dorothy Edwards; by John Deming, William Warner and Joshua Robbins.

Dist. File, 1697: Estate of John Edwards, only son of Joseph Edwards: To his sisters, to Mary Conklin, to Hannah Butler, to Sarah Webster, to Dorothy Curtis; by Robert Welles, Josiah Churchill & Thomas Wright.

Page 105—(Vol. IX) 10 June, 1719: Motion being made to this Court that part of the Estate in Lands of Joseph Edwards, sometime of Wethersfield, Decd, set out and Dist. to the Widow to be improved by her during life, and the sd. Widow being lately decd, sd. Lands may be apprised and Dist. to the heirs of sd. Estate. This Court appoint Jonathan Belding, George Kilbourn and John Rose, of Wethersfield, Apprisers.

Page 106—17 June, 1719: Report of the Apprisers: The amount or value of the Lands is £134-03-03. Report accepted. This Court order Dist. to the heirs of John Edwards, Decd, son of sd. Joseph, £44-18-09, which is his double part; To Sarah Webster, Mary Conklin, Hannah Butler and Dorothy Curtis, daughters of sd. Decd, to each of them £22-09-04. And appoint Roberts Welles, Josiah Churchill & Thomas Wright, of Wethersfield, Distributors.

Page 157.

Edwards, Thomas, Wethersfield. Died 27 July, 1683. Invt. £61-12-00. Taken by Samuel Talcott, James Treat.

Court Record, Page 78—18 December, 1683: Adms. to Samuel Haile. Estate probably Insolvent.

Page 34.

Egleston, James, Windsor. Died 1st December, 1679. Invt. £275-16-06. Taken 24 December, 1679, by Benjamin Newbery, Daniel Clarke, Jonathan Gillett, Mark Kelsey. Legatees: The Relict; John, age 21 March next; Thomas 18, Ester 16, Nathaniel 13, Isaac 10, Abigail 8, Deborah 5, Hanna 3 years of age.

Court Record, Page 17—4 December, 1679: James Egleston being suddenly seized with death, a Jury being sworne to find out the cause and manner of his death, upon oath returned that he was by the providence of God taken with a swond and so dyed.

Page 22—4 March, 1679-80: Adms. to the Widow, and Mr. John Loomis, Jonathan Gillett & Cornelius Gillett are appointed to assist.

Page 26—21 April, 1680: Dist: To the Widow, £35; the eldest son, £45; to six other children, £21 to each; and to the defective child, £36.

Page 27—21 April, 1680: Adms. granted to the Relict and her present husband, James Ennoe. The Overseers to take Security that the Estate of the Children, as they come of age, shall be payd to them.

Record of an Agreement, on File 28 August, 1701, under the Hands & Seals of

JOHN X EGLESTONE, THOMAS EGLESTONE, NATHANIEL EGLESTONE, ISAAC EGLESTONE. Before me, *John Eliot.*

Page 16 (Vol. VII) 4 September, 1701: An Agreement of the sons of James Eglestone, late of Windsor, Decd, respecting a settlement of their Father's Estate, was exhibited in this Court, Accepted, and ordered to be recorded and put on File.

Page 94-5.

Ennoe, James sen., Windsor. Invt. £278-06-01. Taken 19 June, 1682, by Daniel Clarke sen., John Wolcott, Thomas Bissell sen.

Court Record, Page 56—19 July, 1682: Invt. Exhibited by the Widow. James & Hester Ennoe, Adms.

Page 60—13 December, 1682: Capt. Clarke informs this Court that the Children of James Ennoe have an Agreement to settle the Estate of their Father. This Court appoint Lt. John Maudsley, Return Strong and John Moore, Distributors, and to Lay out to the widow Ennoe her jointure of £20.

Farnsworth, Mary. Court Record, Page 69—4 April, 1683: Upon the petition of Mary Farnsworth to this Court (*her husband being departed from her & taken no order for her supply in his absence, but let out his Land & Houseing & Orchard & servant out of her hands*) that this Court would take Care for some suitable provision for her supply, doe order that one halfe the proffits of the sayd Land & Servant be by the Tenant payd to the sayd Mary for her supply during the whole Lease, & that the one third of the Houseing & Lands be secured, after the Lease is out, for the woman's suply during her Life, & that no alienation or dispose be made of it in the meantime.

Page 220-1.

Forward, Samuel. Died 16 October, 1684. Invt. £58-01-00. Taken by Thomas Bissell, Return Strong, Samuel Cross. The children: Samuel, age 13 ½ years; Joseph, age 10 years.

Court Record, Page 105—24 March, 1684-5: Adms. to the Widow. Samuel Cross and Jacob Gibbs, Overseers. Dist. Order the use of 1-3 to the Widow, 2 parts to the Eldest son, and one part to the younger son.

Page 225.

Forward, Mrs. Invt. £5-03-06. Taken 27 June, 1685, by Return Strong, Micah Tayntor.

Court Record, Page 111—3 September, 1685: Invt. accepted in Court, and Jacob Gibbs & Samuel Crosse to Adms. the Estate of Mr & Mrs Forward, & to take care of the Children.

Page 181-2.

Foster, Rev. Isaac, Hartford. Invt. £1507-15-04. Taken 12 February, 1682-3, by William Pitkin, Caleb Stanly.

Court Record, Page 86—6 March, 1683-4: Adms. to Mrs. Mehetabell Foster.

Page 123—27 December, 1686: This Court, being moved to Dist. the Estate of Rev. Isaac Foster, Find by a writing made by the sayd Mr. Foster & Mrs. Mehetabell Russell before marriage, dated 27 January, 1679, recorded, wherein it is agreed that in Case the sayd Foster should decease before the sayd Mrs. Mehetabell, & leave Issue behind him of her the sayd Mrs. Mehetabell, the Estate should descend to her the sayd Mrs. Mehetabell & their Heirs forever; which agreement, though it seems to be contradicted by another writeing made by them and recorded, made after their marriage, yet it doth not alter the force & virtue of the former; & therefore this Court doth Judge the former Writing to give the rule for dividing the Estate, & there being one third part of the Estate of Mrs. Mehetabell Russell that she received by Mr. Daniel Russell's (Her Father's) Last Will at her dispose, & so no more belonging to Mr. Foster, we therefore Distribute his Estate as followeth: £200 to Mrs. Ann Foster, to be paid to her at the age of 18 years (or day of marriage, which shall happen first), and the remainder of the Estate to be to Mrs. Mehetabell Woodbridge & her Heirs forever. Mrs. (Miss) Ann Foster to be payd in good current pay of the country.

Page 175-6.

Fyler, Lt. Walter, Windsor. Died 12 December, 1683. Invt. £629-05-08. Taken by Henry Wolcott, Thomas Bissell sen. Will dated 14 September, 1679.

I Walter Fyler of Windsor do make this my last Will & Testament: As for my Estate, my Will is that my wife shall have the whole of it during her life, to farme out or manage as she please for her own mayntenance, & over and above I give unto her £100 to bestow upon another husband, or to reserve for herself, or to bestow upon whome she please by Will or otherwise. I bestow upon my gr. Child Thomas £20, and upon the other three Children now in being, each of them £5. The rest of my whole Estate I bequeath unto my two sons John and Zerubbabell Fyler, equally to be divided between them, they paying Debts, and also Legacies when the abovesd. four gr. Children come to age. I make my two sons Executors.

Witness: *Return Strong,*   WALTER FYLER.
        Timothy Phelps.

A Codicil, dated 2 November, 1680: It having pleased God to add one yeare more to my Life, I do upon mature thought Establish my above Will with this Alteration, that after their Mother's decease my eldest son John shall have my Homestead, Barne, Garden and Orchard, together with the Press and Mill in the Barne; only my son Zerubbabell in Lands. I give him my wearing Clothes and forgive him at my death whatever he falls in my Debt.

Witness: *Return Strong,*   WALT: FYLER.
        Samuel Cross.

Court Record, Page 83—6 March, 1683: Will & Invt. exhibited by Mrs. Jane Fyler. Proven.

Page 224.

Gardner, Ebenezer, Salem. Invt. of the Estate in Connecticut as Money, £298-00-00. Taken by John Gilbert, Richard Edwards, John Marsh. Will dated 3rd February, 1684.

I Ebenezer Gardner of Salem do make this my last Will & Testament: I give unto my sister Hathorn, for her own use & to be at her own disposal, £100 in Money & all my Household Stuff, except the Pewter & Linen which my wife brought wth her. I give unto my sister Mary Turner £50 in Money. I give unto the four sons of my sister Buttolph, Deceased, £100 in Money each, in equal shares, to be paid them as they come of age. I give unto my brother Bartleme and my sister Swinerton and my sister Willoby and the 3 Children of my sister Pilgrim, Decd, that house & Ground which I had with my wife (excepting the Salt [Marsh] in the South Field) to each an equal share. And my Brother Pilgrim shall have power to make Sale of his Children's quarter part & to keep the Effects in his Hands until they come of age. I give unto my sister Swinerton and unto my sister Willowby my pewter and linen which my wife brought with her, to be equally divided between them. I give unto George Gardner, son of my brother Gardner, my acre of Marsh at Strong Water Brook. I give unto Nathaniel Hathorn, son of my sister Hathorn, all my Salt Marsh in the South Field, which his Father shall have the Use of until he come of age. I give unto Ruth Gidney that £10 in Money I lent her Father, that is now in her Mother's Hands. I give unto Susannah Gardner, daughter of my Unckell Thomas Gardner, £10 in Money; and unto Margaret Gardner, daughter of my Unckell Samuel Gardner, £10 in Money. I give unto the poor honest people in Salem the sume of £50 in or as Money, to be dist. amongst them by my Unckell Samuel Gardner and my daughter Hathorn and my brother Gardner, according to their Discretion. And as for the remainder of my Estate, after my Debts & Legacies are paid, I give the 1-3 part of it unto the 3 Children of my Brother Gardner, George, John & Hannah, to each an equal share. I give unto the 3 Children of my sister Hathorn, John, Nathaniel & Ruth, to each an equal share, which their father may take into his Hands provided he give sufficient security to pay them in Money when they come of age, otherwise to remain in Money in the Hands of my Executors until that time. As for the other third part of my Estate, I give it unto the three Children of my sister Mary Turner, Robert, Habacock and Mercy, to each an equal share, to be paid them when they come of age. I do appoint my brother Samuel Gardner to be my Executor.

Witness: *Daniel Epps, Jr.,*   EBENEZER GARDNER. LS.
   Benjamin Horne.

 Proven 11th May, 1685. Copied from the Records in Salem.

         Benjamin Gerrish, Clericus.
   John Woodbridge, Asst., John Hathorn, Asst.

 Court Record, Page 109—3 September, 1685: A copy of the last Will & Testament of Ebenezer Gardner of Salem was exhibited in Court as it was proven in Salem, together with an Invt. of what Estate he had in this Colony. Lt. Caleb Stanly made Oath that he had made a true presentment of his Estate.

Page 82.

 Gardner, Elizabeth, Hartford. Invt. £381-00-10. Taken 4 January, 1681-2, by Jonathan Gilbert, Phineas Willson, William Burnham. Will dated 16 June, 1681.

 I Elizabeth Gardner of Hartford do make this my last Will & Testament: I give to my son Samuel Stone my feather bed that I Ly upon, & my Green rugg & green curtains, two payre of sheets, halfe a doz of Napkins, halfe doz of Towells, Two pewter dishes (one little one & one great one), Two porringers, one brass ketle that will hold a bout three payles full, one brass skillitt, the table that stands in the studdy, two old green cushions, The bigest Brass candlestick, two earthern blue drinking cupps, & a smale payre of Andirons, & Two Books of Mr. Greenhill's upon "ezekiell"; & it is my will that my son shall have no power to make sale of any of those things above mentioned, but to have the use of them only, for his benefit, as my overseers shall see reason to grant. I give to Elizabeth my daughter all the rest of my houshold stuffe not particularly disposed of in this my will (she giving her engagement to pay to my Grand sonn Samuel Sedgwick sixteen pounds when he shall attayne the age of Twenty one years), & my fower acres of Land in the upper end of the south meadow, & all the rest of my Land not expressly disposed of in this my last Will & Testament, to be to her & her heirs forever. I give to Samuel Sedgwick £16, to be paid by his Mother to him at the age of 21 years; as allso I give to my sd. Grand son Samuel Sedgwick my 6 acres of Land in the 40 acres wth in the sowth mead, with my Long Lott on the east side of the river, & 7 acres of upland Bought of Richard Goodman, being cow pasture, as allso I give him the rest of my 6 acres of Land in the 40 acres from the day of my decease, to be improved for his advantage till he comes of age, as my overseers shall direct. I give to John Robberts, my grand son, the west division Lot in Hartford & my cow pasture Lott neer the blue Hills, to be to him his heirs & assigns forever. I give to my daughters-in-Law, Rebeccah Nash, Mary Fitch & Sarah Butler, to each of them 40 Shillings apeice in silver, If I leave so much; If not, in other pay equivalent; as allso to each of them a suit of my wearing Lining, which I desire them to accept of as a token of my love to them. I give to Rebeccah Butler one acre of Land my husband bought of Nath. Ward, & is now in possession of Mr. John Whitting, to be to her, her heirs & assigns forever, she to possess it at her day of marriage, & her Father to possess it till then. I doe make my Daughter Elizabeth Roberts & my Grand son Samuel Sedgwick Joint Executors of this my last will & Testament. I doe desire Major John Talcott & Capt. John Allyn to be the overseers. And whereas my husband, Mr Samuel Stone, desired in his last will & Testament that my son Samuel Stone should after my decease possess all my Lands, he paying the full value thereof according as I shall dispose thereof, I willingly submit thereto, & therefore doe appoynt my sd. sonn Samuel Stone, If he will hold the Lands I have disposed of as above, that then he doe pay unto each of them I have given Land unto, the full value thereof, which shall be to them, their heirs & assigns forever instead of sd. Land.

ELIZABETH GARDNER.

Witness: *John Allyn,*
Sarah X *Howard.*

Court Record, Page 51—2 March, 1681-2: Will Proven.

Page 28-9-30.

Gardner, George, Hartford. Died 20 August, 1679, at Salem, in the Colony of Massachusetts Bay. Invt. £3001-00-06. Taken (in Hartford) by Nicholas Olmsted, Caleb Standley. Will dated 21 July, 1679.

I George Gardner of Hartford do make this my last Will & Testament: I bequeath to my wife Elizabeth Gardner my Income and my part in the Mills at Salem during her life. I give unto my wife the Rent of the Land I bought of Mr. Fitch, or Use of the Money if he pay for it according to the Contract, the term of her life. Again, I give her the Rent of that land I bought of John Terry during her life, and the two Cows & 2 Calves & 2 Swine at Home, forever, as likewise the Use of what household Stuff in my house is mine, for the term of her life. I give unto my son Samuel Gardner my house & Land in which he now dwelleth at Salem, with all my Upland & Meadow in the South Field, & my part of the Mills after my Mother's decease, & the Farme & Meadow Thomas Gold lives upon, after his mother's decease, & the Houseing & all Appurtenances thereto belonging. I give unto my son Ebenezer all my Houses and Land, with all the Appurtenances thereto belonging, at Hartford & Windsor & Simsbury, after his Mother's decease; likewise I give unto him presently, after my decease, that Land that lyeth by Mr. Babidg, and that acre of Salt Meadow I had of my Father. To my daughter Buttolph I give £300 of my Debts owing me at Connecticut when they are got in, & to my son Buttolph I give £30 he was indebted to me at our last Reckoning, I mean the balance of that Account that was made in the Spring. To my daughter Turner I give the House & Land they now live in, to him & her their natural lives, & then to whome of her children he shall give it after him, provided he give it to one or more of her Children, & £300 of my Debt at Connecticut as it can be got in. To my daughter Hathorne I give £300 of my Debts of Connecticut; but in Case my son Ebenezer doth dye before he be married, then the Estate given to him to be divided equally amongst the rest of my Children; & I likewise give unto my son Ebenezer the Rent of that Farme Thomas Gold liveth on, during his Mother's life, & do give unto my brother Thomas Gardner £20 in provisions. And I do give unto my two cousins, Miriam Hascall and Susannah Hill, £5 each, to be laid out by my sister Grafton. I appoint my sons Samuel and Ebenezer Gardner to be my Executors, and what remaineth after my Debts be paid & Legacies, 2 parts to be to my son Samuel and one part to Ebenezer. And to my servant Arrah I do give him £5 when he hath served my son Samuel 5 years, and then his time to be out. I do intreat my friend Capt. John Allyn to Oversee the performance of this my Will, who liveth at Hartford, to whome I give £5 as a token of my Love, Also I entreat my friend Caleb Standly to oversee the performance of this my Will, who liveth at Connecticut, to whose two daughters I give 50 Shillings apeice. And I do desire my two brothers, Thomas & Samuel Gardner, to oversee the performance of my Will at Salem.

Witness: *Thomas Gardner,*   GEORGE GARDNER.
Samuel Gardner, Joseph Williams.

Attest before *Gen. Daniel Denison* and *Major William Hathorne, Esq.*, 1st September, 1679, by *Hilliar Veren, Clarke.*

This is a true Copy, compared with the originall left on file with the Records of the Court at Salem.

Court Record, Page 18—4 December, 1679: An attested Copy of the last Will of Mr. George Gardner, as it was attested & proven at Salem, & it was also accepted and approved by this Court.

Page 23—4 March, 1679-80: Invt. exhibited in Hartford by Nicholas Olmsted and Caleb Stanly.

Page 111-12-13-14-15.

Gilbert, Jonathan, Hartford. Invt. £2484-17-09. Taken 12 February, 1682, by John Allyn, John Gilbert, William Gibbon. Will dated 10 September, 1674.

I Jonathan Gilbert of Hartford do make my last Will & Testament: I give to my wife Mary Gilbert the use of Homested and Dutch Island, Land I bought of Mr. Callsey, Land exchanged with James Richard, pasture I bought of Andrew Warner, also my wood lott on the west side of Rocky Hill, till my son Samuel attain to 21 years of age, then to be surrendered to him with certain reservations to her during life, then all these to Samuel and his heirs forever, he paying to his brother Ebenezer £30. I give to my son Jonathan Gilbert half the Land at Haddam I bought of James Bates & Thomas Shaylor, or £20 in other Estate, which is his portion with what he had before given him. I give to Thomas Gilbert my House & House lott on the south side of the Rivulet. I give to my son Nathaniel Gilbert my farme at Meridian and £30 more. I give to my daughter Lydia Richison 20 Shillings. I give to my daughter Sarah Belcher 20 Shillings; to my daughter Mary Holton 20 Shillings; to my daughter Hester Gilbert £100; to Rachel Gilbert £100. I give to my son, Ebenezer Gilbert, all that 300 acres of Land I bought of Capt. Daniel Clarke in Farmington, also that purchase of Land I bought of Massecup, comonly Called & known by the name of pagonchaumischaug; also, £50. I desire my wife do remember Hannah Kelly & give her 20s., and more at her discretion if she prove obedient. I give to my grand child, John Rosseter, £10; to my gr. child, Andrew Belcher, £5; to my gr. child, Jonathan Richeson, £5. I make my wife sole Executrix, and desire Capt. John Allyn, my brother John Gilbert, and Sargt. Caleb Standly to be helpful to her, and that she satisfy them for their pains.

JONATHAN GILBERT. Ls.

Witness: *John Talcott, John Gilbert.*

Court Record, Page 65—1st March, 1683: Will Proven.

Page 121.

Gillett, John, Windsor. Invt. £140-14-06. Taken 5 December, 1682, by John Loomis sen., John Moore. Legatees: The Widow, Mercy Gillett, John age 9 years, Thomas 6, Samuel 5, Benjamin 2, Mercy born 30 January last.

Court Record, Page 69—4 April, 1683: Adms. to the Widow, Mercy Gillett, with Jonathan Gillett, Peter Browne, John Barber & Samuel Barber to be Overseers.

Page 96.

Gipson, Roger, Saybrook. Invt. £120-02-00. Taken 6 December, 1680, by John Pratt, Samuel Cogswell, Selectmen of Saybrook.

Martha Allyn did personally appear before me this 7 September, 1682, and gave oath that this is a true Inventory of her former husband Roger Gipson's Estate, Decd. *Giles Hamlin, Commsr.*

The children of Roger Gipson: Samuel age 8 or 9 years, Jonathan 6 or 7, a daughter about 5 years of age, and Roger age one and ½ years.

Court Record, Page 58—7 September, 1682: Adms. to John Tillettson.

Page 69—4 April, 1683: Dist. of the Estate.

Page 241.

Goodfellow, Thomas, Wethersfield. Died 25 November, 1685. Invt. £49-04-06. Taken December, 1685, by Samuel Wolcott & Nathaniel Boreman.

3 March, 1685-6: Mary Goodfellow personally appeared and made oath that she hath presented a true Inventory of her Deceased Husband. Before me, *Samuel Talcott, Assistant.*

Court Record, Page 117—4 March, 1685-6: Adms. to the widow, she to bring up the children. If she can give them anything, it is desired she would.

Page 120.

Goodwin, Ozias, Hartford. Invt. £129-04-00. Taken 3 April, 1683, by Nathaniel Willett, Thomas Butler.

Court Record, Page 69—4 April, 1683: Invt. Exhibited with an agreement of the children for a division of the estate, which was approved by the Court: To William Goodwin sen., £60; to Nathaniel Goodwin, £40; to William Pitkin in right of his wife, £25. Signed and sealed. *Recorded on Page 120 in full with the Inventory, date 6 April, 1683.*

Will & Invt. on File.

Goodrich, John Jr., Wethersfield. Invt. £81-17-11. Taken 24 March, 1676. I John Goodrich, the son of John Goodrich sen., of Wethersfield, in the County of Hartford, in his Majesties Colony at Connecticutt, in New England, being weake in body & expecting my change, but yet having the Use of my Understanding & Reason, do make this my last Will & Testament as followeth: And therefore as I do give up myself to the Lord, so desiring that all my Debts may be justly & truly payd out of other Estate, I do give and bequeath my land (be it nine acres more or less) to my loving wife & child for ever. Also I giue my heifer to my sister Mary Goodrich. Also I bequeath my best suite of clothes to my Brother Joseph Goodrich, my father paying the value thereof to such as I am indebted unto.

Witness: *Jno Chester,*   JOHN X GOODRICH.
       Joseph X Edwards.

Joseph Edwards made Oath, 12 April, 1676, that John Goodrich declared the above written to be his last Will & Testament, before him & Mr. John Chester. As Attest: *John Allyn, Sec.*

Lt. John Chester made Oath, this 19th of April, 1676, that John Goodrich declared the above written to be his last Will & Testament, before him and Jo: Edwards. As Attest: *Samuel Talcott, Commissioner.*

Mary, the Relict of John Goodrich Junr., appeared & made Oath that she made a true presentment of the Estate of her deceased husband to the apprisers, this 6th June, 1676, before the Dept. Governor, Mr. Wyllys, & the Secretary. As Attest: *John Allyn, Secretary.*

Memorandum: That on the 27th of June, 1676, John Goodrich & Mary Goodrich, his daughter-in-law, did consent and Agree in these following Articles: 1st, That the 9 acres of Swamp Land mentioned in sd. Mary's husband's Will shall be the proper Estate forever of Mary, the daughter of the aforesd. Mary Goodrich and John Decd, to be delivered her at 18 years of age or day of marriage, which shall first happen, and in the Interim her Mother should have the Use of it, and during her life in Case her Child die under age; but on the decease of the Mother and daughter, the daughter dying without heir or husband, it to return to John Goodrich and his heirs forever. 2ndly: That all the Debts due from John Goodrich Decd shall be paid by sd. John Goodrich, and the sd. John Goodrich to receive in Consideration thereof all the other Land left by the Decd, viz, 5 Roods in the Plaine, 2 acres of Pasture, & halfe an Acre in the Homelott & the houseing thereon, for him & his heirs forever, & all the Moveable Estate whatsoever, excepting a Cow & a Calfe & £3 in Clothes. This we agree to in case the Worshipfull Court that shall have the Settlement of the Estate see Cause to ratify it.

Witness: *William Pitkin,*   JOHN GOODRICH,
      Richard Beckley.   MARY X GOODRICH.

Approved by the Court, 8 September, 1676.
            Test: *John Allyn Secretary.*

Court Record, Page 60—(Vol. VII) 8 November, 1704: Whereas Daniel Rose, sen., of Wethersfield, made application to this Court for a Settlement of the Estate of John Goodrich Jr., formerly of Wethersfield, Decd, This Court do find that Jonathan Goodrich of sd. Wethersfield, brother of the sd. late John Goodrich Decd, hath obtained a record of the Land or Estate of his Brother John, and also taken possession thereof many years ago. Therefore this Court do not see Cause to give any order respecting the same, but leave the sd. Daniel Rose to proceed as he shall see cause.

Page 35-6. (Will on File.)

Goodrich, John, Wethersfield. Invt. £651-10-00. Taken 6 April, 1680, by Samuel Steele, John Wolcott & Nathaniel Boreman. Will dated 9 June, 1672.

I John Goodrich of Wethersfield do make this my last Will & Testament: Item. I give and bequeath unto my daughter Elizabeth Rose 16 Shillings over & above what I have bestowed upon her already. Item. I give & bequeath unto my son John Goodrich 12 Pence over & above those Lands I have seized in him already. Item. I give unto my daughter Mary Goodrich £50, & to be paid her out of my Household Stuffe and Moveable Goods as they shall then be prised. Item. I give and bequeath unto my daughter Hannah £50, and to be paid her out of my Moveable Goods & Catle as they shall then be prised. Item. I give & bequeath to my two youngest sons, Joseph & Jonathan Goodrich, my Dwelling house, Barn, Homelott, & also all my Land, Meadow & Upland, to be equally improved between them and the profits thereof to be equally divided between them so long as they can or do agree together; but if they difere and do not agree to improve together, then my Will is that my son Joseph shall have my 3 acre Lott in the Meadow and half my Lott in the Great Swamp, the south side, and also my whole Lott in Beaver Meadow, & also that peice of Swamp and Meadow at the rear of the Meadow Gate which Mr. Chester had of me, and also that 4½ acres in the south field, and that acre & ½ in beauer Brook which was sometime John (Tinker's?) Lott, & also half of that 17-acre Lott in the West field & the west side of that Lott. These peices of land I give and bequeath unto my son Joseph. Item. I give unto my son Jonathan all the rest or remainder of my Estate, viz., my Dwelling house, Barn, homelott & whatsoever thereto appurtains, and my Pastar Lott at the West End of the Towne, & also that 5 acres of Meadow I had of Mr. Chester, and also all that 4 acres at the lower Meadow Gate, that I had of Mr. Chester, & also half my Lott in the Great Swamp, the north side, and also half that 17-acre Lott in the little West field. And if it shall happen that my catle & Moveable Estate will not reach to pay my daughters so much as I have bequeathed unto them, my Will is that my two sons, Joseph & Jonathan Goodrich, shall make up the sums in convenient time so as they do not straighten themselves too much. And I do make, ordain & appoint Mr. Gershom Bulkeley and Mr. Samuel Talcott Executors to this my last Will & Testament.

Witness: *Hugh Welles,*   JOHN GOODRICH SEN. LS.
          Mary Goodrich.

The Executors refuse to act.

Court Record, Page 26—21 April, 1680: There was presented to this Court a Will of the sd. Goodrich which had been objected against by the sd. Goodrich his relations, and the Executors refusing to accept of the Executorship laid upon them in the sd. Will, this Court doth now by Proclamation order all those concerned in the Estate of John Goodrich to appear at the Court in September next to make out their respective claims to the Estate, and the Court doth appoint Daniel Rose and Joseph Goodrich to take Care of the Estate that it be reserved and improved.

Page 35 (Pro. Side) 21 April, 1680: Mary, the Relict, Widow of John Goodrich, appeared in Court with the Inventory:

	£ s d
Out of the Estate is paid to the Widow,	50-19-09
In Debts paid and lost Estate,	8-12-00
To Jonathan,	3-16-06
	63-08-03

Page 29—7 September, 1680: Jonathan Goodrich appeared in Court and made choice of Lt. Samuel Steele to be his Guardian. The Court approved of this choice. This Court having considered the Estate of John Goodrich Decd, the Will exhibited in Court being made many years before the decease of sd. Goodrich, & sundry Transactions have passed since the Will was made which hath varied the Estate very much, & the Executors wholly renouncing of the same, this Court do grant Adms. of the Estate unto Lt. Samuel Steele, Daniel Rose and Joseph Goodrich, & order the Dist. to be as followeth:

To Joseph, the Eldest son now living (the eldest son being dead

	£ s d
and compounded with for his portion),	190-00-00
To Jonathan, the next son,	190-00-00
To the three daughters, to each of them,	100-00-00

And the sons are to have their portions in Houseing & Lands, and they to make up the £4 per annum by proportion to their Mother during her natural life out of the Revenue of the Land. Mr. Samuel Talcott, Lt. Samuel Steele and Mr. Eli Kimberly are desired to divide the Estate to the Legatees. Mr. Read is to receive £50 out of the Estate, Mr. Rose £15, and Mr. Maynard £8.

Page 35—(Vol. VII) 11 November, 1702: This Court, upon Application of Sergt. Crafts in behalf of Jonathan Goodrich, son of John Goodrich, formerly of Wethersfield Decd, do order that the Clerk grant a Writ or Citation requireing Mr. Daniel Rose, one of the Adms. on the sd. John Goodrich his Estate, to appear at the Court to be holden the 1st Tuesday in March next, to render an Account of his Adms. on the sd. Estate, the foresd. John (Jonathan) Goodrich complaining that he hath not received his full part of the Estate according to the Dist. of Court, 2 September, 1680.

Page 40—2 March, 1702-3: Adms. granted further time to finish his Adms.

Page 43—7 April, 1703: Mr. Daniel Rose appeared in Court according to Citation and gave an Account thereof to the Court's Satisfaction.

Page 60—8 November, 1704: Whereas Moses Crafts, Atty. to Jonathan Goodrich, cited Daniel Rose to appear and render an Account of his Adms. on the Estate of John Goodrich Decd, the sd. Rose now appeared in Court and made it appear by Record that he had already rendered an Account to the Satisfaction of the Court, and that therefore he is not requireable to render further Account.

Page 219.

Grant, John, Windsor. Invt. £424-00-00. Taken 2 September,
1684, by John Loomis sen., Samuel Cross, Nicholas Buckland. Legatees:
The Widow, John age 13 years, Josiah 2, Mary 11, Elizabeth 7 ½, Abigail
5 years of age.
   Court Record, Page 104—24 March, 1684-5: Adms. to the Widow.
John Loomis, Samuel Grant and Samuel Cross to be Overseers.

Page 88.

Grant, Matthew, Windsor. Invt. £118-18-06. Taken 10 January,
1681-2, by Thomas Dible sen., John Loomis. Will dated 9 December,
1681.
   I Matthew Grant of Windsor, beinge aged and under present weakness, yet of Competency of understandinge, doe by this declare my Last
Will concerning the dispose of my Estate as followeth: 1st, I doe declare
that my son Samuel, my eldest son, is already satisfied with the portion I
made over to him in Lands already recorded to him, and that is my will
concerning him. 2dly, Concerninge my son Tahan, my will is that he shall
have as a legassy, payd to hime in Country paye by my son John, the full
some of five pounds, and this to bee payd two yeers after my decease. Alsoe I doe appoynt hime to gather upp all the debts oweinge to me in this
towne or elsewhere, and my will is hee my son Tahan shall have them for
his owne. 3dly, my will is that my son John, with whome I have lived some
time, I doe give to hime all my meadow land in the great meadow; also I
give to hime my pasture land lyeinge belowe the hill agaynst Thomas
Dibles home lott and my owne. Alsoe, I doe give hime, the sayd John, my
home lott and orchard with the ould houseinge which I built before hee
came to dwell in itt. Alsoe I doe give to hime my wood lott lyeing in the
quarter lotts. Alsoe I give to my son John all the rest of my estate except-
inge my wearinge cloathes. My son John shall paye to my son Tahan five
pounds as is already expressed in my will concerninge hime, at the time
and manner afforesayd, and alsoe unto my Daughter Humphreys five
pounds in Country pay, two yeers after my decease. Alsoe my will is and
I doe give my Daughter Humphrey as a Legassy five pownds, to bee payde
in country paye two yeers after my decease. Alsoe I doe make my son
John sole Executor of this my last Will & Testament. As Witness my
Hand:
Witness: *John Loomys senr,*   MATTHEW GRANT. Ls.
         Thomas X *Dibble.*
   Court Record, Page 51—2 March, 1681-2: Will proven.

Page 67.

Grant, Peter. Hartford. Invt. £50-13-06. Taken 5 October, 1681,
by Philip Davis & Thomas Bunce Jr. The children of Peter and Mary

Grant: Mary Goodfellow, age 18 years; Sara 17, Ruth 15, Thomas 13, John 10, Rachell Grant, age 5 years.

Court Record, Page 46—1st November, 1681: Adms. to the Widow, Mary Grant. The House and Lands to the two sons after the Decease of their Mother.

Page 41—(Vol. V) 13 April, 1692: Whereas there was a house and Land by the Court formerly setled upon the two sons of peter grant, they being deceased, the daughters of peter Grant appeared in Court & made Clayme to the sayd house & Land, & desired the Court to setle a distribution of the Estate upon them the sayd daughters of peter Grant, viz, Mary Baker, Sarah Wheeler, Ruth Grant & Rachell Grant, The Court saw reason to make an equal division on the estate to the sayd daughters, either by Samuel Wheeler agreeing with them what their proportions shall be, & in case they disagree, then deacon Hosmore & Bevill Waters to divide.

Page 102.

Graves, Nathaniel, Wethersfield. Died 29 September, 1682. Invt. £439-02-08. Taken 30 October, 1682, by John Kilbourn, Thomas Wright, William Warner. Legatees: Martha Graves (Widow), Sarah Bradfield, age 26 years, Mary Graves 24, Rebeckah 22, Martha 15, Abigail 13 years.

Court Record, Page 60—13 December, 1682: Adms. to the Relict, Mrs. Martha Graves. Mr. John Robbins, Sergt. William Warner, Overseers. Order to Dist: To the Widow, £99 of Personal Estate, & the remainder to the 5 daughters.

Page 221.

Gray, Walter, Hartford. Invt. £2-19-06. Taken 31 January, 1684-5, by John Wadsworth, John Gilbert.

Court Record, Page 105—24 March, 1684-5: Adms. to Lt. Joseph Wadsworth & John Gilbert. Estate divided amongst the Creditors.

Page 64.

Griffin, John, Simsbury. Invt. £184-18-00. Taken 23 August, 1681, by John Case and Samuel Willcoxson. The children: John 25 years, Thomas 23, Ephraim 12, Nathaniel 9, Hannah 31, Mary 27, Sarah 26, Abigail 21, Ruth 16, and Mindwell 19.

Court Record, Page 44—1st September, 1681: Invt. exhibited. This Court grant Adms. on the Estate to Hannah Griffin, the Widow, & her two sons, John & Thomas Griffin.

Page 69—(Vol V) 4 April, 1694: An Account of the Wastage of John Griffin's Estate being brought into this Court, amounting to £21-09-00, by the Account appears a clear Estate of £125-05-09, which this Court

Dist: To the Eldest son a double portion, viz, £22-15-06; and equal portions, viz, £11-07-09, to each of the other nine Children. And whereas the Town of Simsbury granted to the Widow of sd. John Griffin a peice of Upland of about 4 acres near John Terrie's Land, and 12 acres under the Mountain, which, by the sd. Widow's mind declared, and consent of the Rest of the Children, the sd. Land should belong equally to Ephraim and Nathaniel Griffin, This Court doth approve thereof, and doe order Mr. John Higley, John Slater & Peter Bewill to make a Partition of the Estate accordingly.

Page 193-4.

Grihms, Henry, Hartford. Invt. £745-00-00. Taken 1684, by Stephen Hosmer, Bevell Waters. The children: Benjamin age 22 years, John 19, Joseph 17, Mary 16, Sarah 13, Elizabeth 10, Susanna 7, Rebecckah 4 years of age.

Page 235.

Grihms, Mary. Invt. £65-15-06. Taken by Nathaniel Willett & Stephen Hosmore. Will dated 27 July, 1685.

Mary Grihms her Will was that if her son Benjamin bring up her youngest daughter, he should have Two Cowes towards it of her Estate, & the rest she hath to dispose of should be divided among her three sons, save that her daughters should have each of them a pewter platter apeice, & that her napkins should be divided among her daughters. Her will also was that her Brother Benj: should have her second daughter & her brother Joseph her third daughter & John Watson her fourth daughter, and they were to learn them well to read, & mayntayne them well, & so have them untill they were growne to age.
Witness: *Stephen Hosmore,*
   Benjamin Grihms.

Page 205-6-7-8-9-10.

Griswold, Michael, Wethersfield. Died 26 September, 1684. Invt. £628-01-00. Taken by Samuel Talcott, Samuel Butler, Timothy Hide. Will dated 10th September, 1678.

I Michael Griswold of Wethersfield do make my last Will & Testament: I give unto my wife Anne Griswold all my houses & Lands, whether upland or meadow or Swamp Land (The Land only excepted that my son Thomas Griswold hath in possession), & also all my household stuffe, all my Implements For Husbandry, & all my Cattell, Horses & swine, together with all such goods, Chattells & debts whatsoever to me in any wise or right belonging, to possesse & enjoy all my sayd Houses, Land & Estate as afoarsayd, with all the proffitts & benefits thereof, to the only proper benefit & behoofe of my sayd wife during her natural life, & after her de-

cease to be disposed of as hereafter expressed. I give to my son Thomas Griswould 1 ½ acres of upland where his house standeth, & his Barn, also 3 roods of Land in the Great meadow, bounded West on Land of Lt. John Hollister; also I give to my son Thomas 1-4 part of my Lot in the dry swamp of 11 acres, bounded west on Land of Enoch Buck, south on Land of Samuel Talcott. I give to my son Thomas 2 ½ acres of my meadow Lott called or known by the name Send Home. Also I give him ½ of my Lott at the whirl pooles which I had of Sergt. John Kilborn, & one ½ of my Land by Beavour brooke wch was given me by the Towne of Wethersfield. Also I give him halfe of my 50-acre Lott that Lyeth next to farmington Bounds. All the Land aforesayd, & every part and parcell thereof, I give & bequeath to my sayd son Thomas Griswold to be to him and his heirs forever, Imediately after my decease or the decease of my wife, which shall Last happen. Item. I give to my son Isaac Griswold halfe that Home Lott which I bought of Luke Hitchcock, also 2 ½ acres of Land In Beavour meadow which I purchased of Jehu Burr, And also halfe that Lott in the great meadow which I purchased of Wm Hills. Also I give to my son Jacob Griswold halfe the Home Lott I bought of Luke Hitchcock, Also one halfe of the meadow Lott I bought of Wm Hills. I give to my son Michael Griswold my now dwelling house, barn & all my Home Lott. I give to my Fower sonns above named all my divisions of Land on the east side of the great river, to be equally divided between them. Item. I give and bequeath to my daughter Hester Bradly 20s, & to her children, Ann, Abigail & Mary & Hester, to each of them 20s, which Legacies I appoint my son Thomas to pay to my daughter Hester, and to her Children. I give to my daughter Abigail Lattin 20s, and to her daughter Ann Lattin £5. I appoint my son Michael to pay the sd. sum of six pounds to my daughter Abigail & her child. I give to my daughter Sarah Hill £10, & doe appoynt my two sonns Isaac & Jacob to pay the same, each paying £5. All the Legacies to be paid to my daughters & their children within five years after my decease or the decease of my wife, which shall last happen. I give to my son-in-Law, Obadiah Willcox, one shilling. MICHAELL GRISWOLD. Ls.
Witness: *Gershom Bulkeley, Eliazer Kimberlye.*

(The property was by this will to pass by entail, but in a codicil this part was revoked.)

Codicil, dated 22 September, 1684: My will is that all & every of my sons shall have & enjoy all and every their portion in houses & Lands without entailement, haveing full power to sell & alienate any part or all of their severall portions to any person or persons as they shall see good.

MICHAEL X GRISWOLD

Witness: *John Buttolph, Eleazur Kimberly.*

Will Proven 18 December, 1684. *John Allyn, Secretry.*

Page 107.

Hall, Edward, Wethersfield. Died 26 August, 1682. Invt. £7-08-00. Taken 20 September, 1682, by John Kilbourn, Thomas Wright. Anna Hall, the Widow; Hanna Hall, her Child Mary, 2 years old.

Halloway, John, Court Record, Page 72—(Vol. III)—20 January, 1667: *Mary Halloway, wife of John Halloway, seeks separation from her husband. Have been married fower yeares and some moneths.*

Page 201. (Will on File.)

Halloway, John, Hartford. Died 18 October, 1684. Invt. £46-06-00. Taken by Ciprian Nichols, John Skiner, Philip Lewes. Will dated 14 February, 1680.

I John Halloway of Hartford do make this my last Will and Testament: I having no relations to dispose of it to, It is my will that all my just debts & funeral charges be discharged & honestly payd, and that the remainder of my estate in Houseing & Lands shall be & belong to the use of the ministry of the first Church of Christ in Hartford forever as parsonage Land, as also all other of my Estate which I shall stand possessed of at my decease that I shall not have otherwise disposed of. I do give & bequeath the same for the use aforesayd that it may be so improved for the ease of my brethren & the Comfort of a faithful Labourer in God's Harvest in this place. I doe constitute & appoint my loveing friends, Capt. John Allyn & Sergt Caleb Stanly, to be the Executors of this my Last will & Testament, who I desire to take care that my Estate be settled according to this My Will.   JOHN X HALLAWAY. Ls.

Witness: *John Allyn, Caleb Stanly.*

Court Record, Page 95—25 November, 1684: Estate of John Halloway. Adms. to Lt. Caleb Stanly. By direction of Major Talcott & Capt. Allyn, nobody living with John Halloway, the Selectmen took an Inventory of what Estate they could find.

Page 128—3d March, 1686-7: Adms. report accepted & granted a *Quietus Est.*

Harbert, Christian. Court Record, Page 129—3 March, 1686-7: Will now Exhibited by Capt. Whiting, made with her husband's Consent. Approved.

Mrs. & Mr. John Blackleach appeal to the Court of Assistants.

Note: Mrs. Elizabeth Blackleach was daughter of Benjamin Harbert and Christian Nethercoole his wife. (See 1st Ch. Rec. for the marriage, and Private Controversies for the *Appeal.*) See also Page 46 of this volume.

Page 92-3-4-5-(See File—Will with Invt.)

Haughton, Richard, Beverly, Mass., who died at Wethersfield 23 May, 1682.   Invt. £493-09-03.   Taken by Ciprian Nichols, Caleb Stanly & Phineas Wilson.

Know all Men by these presents, that I Richard Haughton of Beverly, by the providence of God being at Wethersfield and detained by sickness, not knowing how God by his providence may dispose of me, being weake in body though of perfect Memory & understanding, doe request and appoint my beloved friends Mr. Nathaniel Standly and Mr. William Pitkin, both of Hartford, to take care of and manage all my concerns in this Colony, & more especially that of the Vessell Building at Middletown, to carry it on; also to receive all my debts, and to pay all due from me; & my two friends, Mr. Nathaniel Standly and Mr. William Pitkin, I appoint Administrators to ye Estate in my hands or belonging to me in this Colony.   Also I request Mr. Jno ffoster of Boston to supply these men wth Goods and to assist them yt the Vessel may be carried on.   This being my Last desire & Will as to my affairs here, as Witness my hand this 12th of May, 1682.   RICHARD X HAUGHTON.
Witness: *John Kilbourn, Will. Gibbon, Timothy Hide.*

Invt. of the Estate of Mr. Richard Horton, who died in Wethersfield 23 May, 1682, taken by John Kilbourn, William Warner, £493-09-03.   His Estate at Wethersfield, £4-08-00.

BILLS:

Richard Hawton is Debtor to John Honeywell, to Diett a fortnight and lodging for his nurs when sick, 10 shillings; to his diett, attendence and all things in the house during his sickness, being 3 weeks to his burial, £2-14-00; to sider expended at his funeral, 6 shillings; total, £6-10-00.

Mr. Richard Horton Dr. to Thomas Atwood, by 24 days of myself & wife tending him, sitting up 5 nights, myself and wife 2 nights, He Being exceeding trublesum & Noysum, I count well worth ye phisick and Cordial Constantly Administered to him in ye Time, £08-00-00.

THOMAS ATWOOD.

An Invt. taken 27 May, 1682, apprised in good country pay, £224-02-01, by Ciprian Niccols, Caleb Standly, Phineas Wilson.

County Court Record, Page 56—21 June, 1682: Mr. John Harris appeared in Court and presented a letter of Adms. granted by the Hon. Simon Bradstreet, Esq., Gov. of Mass., to Capt. John Hull Esq., Assistant to Mary Haughton, the Relict, Widow of Richard Haughton deceased, to Adms. upon the Estate of Haughton aforesaid, asserting that she had put in security to Exhibit a true Inventory of the said Estate.   Attested under the seals of the office.

Pr.   Isaac Addington, Cler.

Page 22-3-4-5.

Haynes, Mr. Joseph, late Rev. Teacher of the 1st Church in Hartford. Invt. £2280-17-00. Exhibited in Court 4 December, 1679. Will dated 26 February, 1676.

I Joseph Haynes of Hartford, in the Colony of Connecticott, perceiving the Shaddows of the Evening to bee uppon mee, beeing weak in body but (   ) true and good memory, Doe in the fear of God and in Obedience to wholsom Rules of Righteousnes for the Setting of my house in order, make this my Last Will and disposition: In the first place, as the main matter, I do desire utterly to renounce myself and to have all my dependence uppon the sovereign mercy of God and the alone precious righteousness of the son of God, hopeing that though my sins have been before him, yet he will gratiously behold mee in the face of his Anointed. So also in the second place, I do thus dispose of what God hath gratiously given mee in manner and form as followeth: Whereas, by an ingagement made to my Loveing wife Sarah Haynes sometimes before our marriage, I did promise to make her a joynture of my Lands at Farmingtown, as also to give her three hundred pounds or the third part of my Estate, I doe by this my Will Joynture my said Loveing wife in all the rents and proffitts of the said Lands at Farmingtown during her natural life, as also my Will is that shee bee paid Three hundred pounds out of my other Estate, which three hundred pounds shall bee paid within two years after my decease, or within one year if my wife desire it. Also I do give unto my said Wife the use and all the benefitts of my whole Estate till my children come in age to receive their several portions, for the bringing upp and Education of my children. And I do make my said Wife Sole Executrix of this my Last will and Testament. Also my Will and mind is that when my son John Haynes hath Attained to the age of 23 years, or bee married, that my mansion house at Hartford, with the Barnes, out houses, homested garden and yards, together with all my little meadow before my house, as also all my Grass Ground and plow Land in the South meadow, together with my oxpasture which is inclosed, both pasture Land and plow Land, and my wood lott not farr off the oxpasture, as also all my right in that Land in the woods that Lately hath been laid out as is to bee seen in the town book, with all the rights and priviledges whatsoever to any of those Lands beforementioned do any wayes belong, to remain to him and his heirs for ever. Allso I give him all my books and manuscripts that any wayes concern Learneing, only my mind is that if my wife shall remain in her Widdowhood, that the Parlor and the Studdy shall bee for her dwelling, and all needful use of the Celler and Kitchen. My will further is that after the decease of my wife that my whole farme at ffarmingtowne with my pasture thereunto belonging, in the occupation of Thomas Nowell, together with all other priviledges of Land, divided or undivided, in the Precincts of that towne, bee divided equally between my two daughters Mabell Haynes and Sarah Haynes, to them and their heirs forever. Also I give all my undivided Lands and grants of Court to bee equally divided amongst my Children and their heirs forever. My mind also is that if my wife bee now with Child and that the Lord in mercy give the Life of it, that the £180 that was given by my mother Lord to my wife and her children as is thereby exprest in her Will, should bee to that child. I do also give to that child all my part of that Land that is in the hands of John Babcock, in narragansett, near Pacatuck. Also, if that redundant £40 mentioned in my mother Lord's Will do come, I do give that to this Child. And if by virtue of my mother Lord's will my other children doe receive or recover any part of the mony given by my said mother, then they shall each of them allow to this Child as much out of their portions each of them as they have out of the said mony bequeathed by my mother. My mind is that the £30 in mony of myne in the Hands of my Brother Mr. James Russell, and £20 in mony now in the house, be left in the hands of my wife, by her to be improved towards the bringing upp my son John in Learning (mainly abroad). I give unto my (only) sister Mrs. Ruth Willys £5, and to all her children 20s apeice. Also I give to each of the children of my sister Mrs. Mabel Russell 20s apeice. I give to my cousin Richard Lord, son of my Brother Richard Lord, fourty shillings. I desire that my honoured and my intimate friends, my Brother Mr. Samuel Willys, My Brother Mr. Richard Lord, and the Reverend Mr. Gershom Bulkeley, to be Supervisors of this my Last will & Testament, and doe order them thirty shillings apeice for their care and Love.

For the Establishing of all which I have hereunto put my hand and seal this 26 February, 1676.   Jos. HAYNES. Ls.
Witness: *Samuel Willis,*
    Richard Lord, William Pitkin.

Court Record, Page 18—4 December, 1679: Will & Invt. exhibited in Court.

Note: £3 *of the Inventory, in the hands of Timothy Hide, sent to Barbadoes.*

Page 186-7.

Hayward, Robert, Windsor. Invt. £96-02-00. Taken 28 August, 1684, by Daniel Clarke sen., Job Drake sen., John Moore.

Lydia Haward, the Relict, aged 70 years or thereabouts, & James Miles, aged 35, Testify that to their knowledge Robert Hayward in his life time gave unto Ephraim his son that parcell of Land that sometime belonged to the sayd Robert Hayward, Lying in a Meadow called Mr. Phelps his Meadow, & owned it a little before his death. And Widow Hayward farther sayth that her son Ephraim had the possession of the Sayd Land before her husband's death. They both, and Job Drake sen., doe testify that Robert Hayward freely gave Edward King's Mortgage to his son Ephraim, only Ephraim was not to turn King out of dores while he lived, he the sd. King duly discharging the rates.

Lydia Hayward & James Miles personally appeared & gave oath to the above written Testimonies before *Benjamin Newbery, Comr,* 3 Sept., 1684.

Court Record, Page 93—4 September, 1684: Invt. Exhibited. Adms. to Lydia, the Relict, & Ephraim Hayward, the sonn of sayd Robert Hayward.

Page 149.

Heart, Elisha, Windsor. Invt. £24-14-08. Taken 9 October, 1683, at Windsor, by Samuel Grant & John Porter Jr.; 4 December, 1683, by Joseph Pomeroy Eleazer Wilcox, by us at Westfield.

Court Record, Page 76—6 December, 1683: Adms. to Edward Neale, Thomas Loveland. Dist. by Order of Court to Said Heart's eight Sisters, to each an equal portion.

Page 119.

Heart, Steven, Deacon, sen., Farmington. Invt. £340-04-00. Taken 31 March, 1682-3, by Thomas Heart, John Heart. Will dated 16 March, 1682-3.

I Stephen Heart of Farmington do make this my last Will & Testament: For the settleing of this my Estate, my Will is as followeth: That my Farme which I formerly have given to my three sons, John Heart, Steven Heart & Thomas Heart, the ½ of my Farme to John, ¼ to Steven, the other quarter to Thomas. I give to my gr. son Thomas Porter & to my son-in-law John Cole my plowing Land & Meadow & Swamp which was sometime part of Andrew Warner's Farme, & abutts on my son Steven Heart's Land on the North. I do give it to them to be equally (divided) betwixt them, the ingagement of my wife being fulfilled. I give to my sons Steven and Thomas Heart that 10 acres of Land which I bought of Andrew Warner, that lyes in the Farme Meadow, to be equally divided betwixt them. I give to my sons Steven and Thomas Heart and to my daughters Sarah Porter and Mary Lee, my Swamp Lott in the Great Swamp and all the rest of my Upland Divisions, divided or undivided, to be equally divided betwixt them. I give to my gr. child Dorothy Porter £10. I give to my gr. child John Lee £3. I give to my gr. child John Heart, my eldest son's son, £3. I do give to my beloved wife a little Kettle that holds about a peck, as also a colt which I gave her, which was recorded to her. And as to all the rest of my Estate, within dores and without, all dues & Debts (except 1-3 part of all my Linen, & a Cow, & £10 given to my wife, as also £5 of Annuity during her natural life in case she survive me, as may appear by a former Instrument), And as for the rest as abovesd., I give to my sons, Steven and Thomas Heart, and my beloved daughters, Sarah Porter and Mary Lee, and my son-in-law, John Cole, whom I make my Executors.

Witness: *John Wadsworth sen.,*   STEVEN HEART.
     Robert Porter.

Court Record, Page 69—4 April, 1683: Will proven. Mrs. Margaret Heart, Ensign Thomas Heart, Sarah Porter and Mary Lee personally appeared and made oath to the Inventory.

Page 143-4-5.

Hills, William sen., Hartford. Died July, 1683. Invt. £274-00-02. Taken August, 1683, by Bevel Waters, Nath. Willett, Townsmen. Will dated 21 February, 1680-1.

I William Hills sen., of Hoccanum, within the Township of Hartford, doe make this to be my Last Will & Testament: And in the first place, after my death, I desire my Executors & Overseers to take care for a decent Burial, & my desire is that due care be taken for payment of all my just debts. Imprimis. My will is that my wife Mary Hills & my son Jonathan Hills be Joynt Executors of this my will. My will is that my wife shall have the use of the one halfe of my housen & Lands that I now live in and upon, & the halfe of all my stock, catle & moveables during her naturall life, which sayd Lands are 8 acres on the east side of my dwelling house & about 18 acres of the west side of my sayd house. I give to my wife the use of one halfe of 17 rods wide of unimproved Lands Lying on the east end of the foresayd 8 acres which runneth to the east end of the 3 mile Lotts, during her Life. I give and bequeath, & my will is, that my sonn Jonathan Hills shall have the other full halfe of the foresayd housen and Lottments with their appurtenances, & my will is that after my wive's Decease I doe give the whole and full of that Land left in her hand to my son Jonathan Hills & to his heirs forever, with all catle, Stock & moveables, to have and to hold forever. And Whereas I have one Lott of Twenty-five rods broad abutting on the widdow Andrews house lott on the West, running to the end of the 3 mile Lotts east, abutting on the country Highway on the south, & on the widdow Andrews Lott North, that she bought of Deacon Wm. Holton, One Third part of said Lott being taken off which I have sould to Mr. William Pitkin, the other Two parts thereof Left and remaining in my hands I give and bequeath Two Thirds thereof to my Daughter Mary Hills and her heirs for ever, and the other Third of ye foresayd Two parts I give and bequeath to my Daughter Hanna Kilbern, to her and her heirs forever. And Whereas there is a consederable part of that Land I bought of Thomas Hosmore of Hartford, Lyeing in & within the south division, wch I have not yet taken up, I doe give that sayd Land (about six score acres, abutting on Benjamin Hills & Joseph Hills there Lotts on the west, & abutting on James Curtice on the south, & on my Land on the North, running east to the end of the 3 mile Lotts), my will is, & I bequeath, the sayd Land & all of it to my sonn William Hills, to my son John Hills, to my son Joseph Hills, & to my son Benjamin Hills, to my daughter Sarah Ward, & to my daughter Susannah Kilbourn, to be divided by an equal proportion to each child, & their heirs forever; & at the death of my sonn William Hills the proportion given to him I give and bequeath to my grand sonn, the eldest sonn of my son William, whoe is of the same name to him, and to his heirs forever. Farther, my will is, that within one yeare after the death of my wife, Mary Hills, that my son Jonathan Hills shall pay out of the Estate the just & full sume of Ten pounds to my daughter Mary Hills. And my will is that all my Land given to my children shall forever & att all times hereafter contribute & pay a Just proportion of all rates, dues & Leases required toward the Mayntenance of the ministry of that particular Church within the Township of Hartford which my overseers of this my will & Testament shall by their Joynt act in writeing under their hands agree upon. I doe desire Major John Talcott, Mr. Jonathan Gilbert & Corporal Gilbert to be my overseers with full power to fill vacancies in case of the death of any of them. Farther I doe desire & will that the revenues of the Lands in Farm-ington that I have right unto by & in right of my wife, that it be duly demanded & received for the help of my wife, & desire my overseers with my Executors to take care about the same, which is the final conclusion of this my Last Will & Testament.   *Pr me* WILLIAM HILL., SEN., LS.

Witness: *John Hill,*
       Thomas Kilbourn,
       John Gilbert.

Court Record, Page 76—6 December, 1683: Will Proven.

Page 247.

Hilton, John, Middletown. Invt. £39-00-00. Taken 17 January, 1686-7, by Richard Hall, John Hurlbut. The children: John age 11 years, Richard 7, Ebenezer 8 months, Mary Hilton 14 years.

Court Record, Page 127—3d March, 1686-7: This Court leaves the Estate with the Widow, she to receive and pay the debts. Richard Hall & John Hall Jr. appointed to assist the Adms.

Page 163-4.

Hosford, John, Windsor. Died 7 August, 1683. Invt. £1203-17-04. Taken 14 November, 1683, by Jacob Gibbs, Samuel Cross. The children: William, b. 25 Oct., 1658; John, 16 Octo., 1660; Timothy, 20 Oct. 1662; Ester, 27 May, 1664; Sarah, 27 Sept. 1666; Samuel, 2nd June, 1669; Nathaniel, 19 August, 1671; Mary, 12 April, 1674; Obadiah, 28 Sept. 1677. (W. R.). Attest:

Henry Wolcott, Register.

Court Record, Page 81—10 December, 1683: Invt. of the Estate of Mr. John Hosford was exhibited in Court. Adms. to the Widow and the son William. Timothy Thrall, Abraham Phelps and Samuel Cross to be Overseers to assist the Widow & her son in the Adms. and dispose of the Children. Order to dist. the Estate as followeth:

	£ s d
To the Widow, of Personal Estate (& 1-3 of the Real Estate),	85-00-00
To William Hosford, the eldest son,	225-10-00
To John Hosford,	121-15-00
To Timothy Hosford,	121-15-00
To Esther Hosford,	100-00-00
To Sarah Hosford,	100-00-00
To Samuel Hosford,	114-00-00
To Nathaniel Hosford,	114-00-00
To Mary Hosford,	100-00-00
To Obadiah Hosford,	132-00-00

Note: *John Hosford sen., who died 7 August, 1683, married, 5 November, 1657, Phillipi Thrall. She died May, 1698.* (W. R.)
Record of Agreement, on File 1701, between the Children of John Hosford:

Signed: DEBORAH HOSFORD, LS.   JOSEPH PHELPS, LS.
ohn Eliot, *Justice of Peace.* TIMOTHY HOSFORD, LS.   NATHANIEL HOSFORD, LS.
SAMUEL HOSFORD, LS.   JOSIAH X OWEN JR., LS.
ESTHER PHELPS, LS.   OBADIAH HOSFORD, LS.

Page 11—(Vol. VII) 8 April, 1701: Mr. John Eliot did exhibit in this Court an Agreement, under the Hands and Seals of the Children of John Hosford sen., formerly of Windsor, Decd, and their legal Representatives, respecting the Settlement of that Estate, which the Court accepts and ordered to be kept on File.

Will on File.

Hosford, William, Wyndsor. Died 29 May, 1688 (W. R.) Will dated 28 May, 1688: I William Hosford of Windsor do make this my last Will and Testament. My will is yt my much Honrd Mother, who is weake of Body, shall have the Benefit & improvement of my whole Estate during her natural life, excepting Tenne pounds which I doe allowe to be in the hands of my executor; ffive pounds of the Tenne pounds I give freely to my Executor; ye other ffive pounds my will is that my said Executor Lay it out or improve it for and toward the cureing of my Lo Broyr Obadiah Hosford, who is exercised wth weakness. After the decease of my honord mother, all of my Estate which remains to be equally divided amongst my Brothers and sisters and my Neice Sarah Phelps, daughter of my sister Sarah, who married Joseph Phelps, the sonne of Timothy Phelps, of Wyndsor. I appoint my Brother John Hosford Executor. I desire Benjamin Newbery sen., Timothy Thrall & Sergt. Timothy Phelps to be Overseers.   WILLIAM HOSFORD, LS.
Witness: *Benja: Newbery, Justice,*
Timothy Phelps.   7 Dec., 1688.

Page 255-263.

Hosmer, Thomas, Hartford. Invt. £1036-00-00. Taken 14 July, 1687, by Ciprian Niccolls, Jacob White. Will dated 27 February, 1685. I Thomas Hosmer of Hartford do make this my last Will & Testament: I give to my wife £5. I give unto my gr. son Thomas Hosmore 1-3 part of all my Land in Hartford except what is otherwise disposed of, also £20 to stock sd. Land; but if he die before 21 years of age, to be divided equally betwixt my son Stephen's sons. I give to my son Buckingham £150. I give unto my daughter Hunt £125. I give unto my daughter Hannah Malby £18, which is the Reversion due to me of the Estate of Josiah Willard of Wethersfield. I give unto my son-in-law Malby £5. I give unto my 3 gr. Children, Thomas Buckingham, Thomas Hunt & Hannah Hosmore, £5 apeice; & to the rest of my gr. children 40 Shillings apeice. If any of my Children shall bring up any of their Children to learning so as to make them fit for publique Service, to each such gr. child I bequeath £10 apeice, to be paid them at the age of 21 years. I give £5 towards a free School in Hartford when there is any such settled effectually. I give to the Poor 40 Shillings, as my Executors shall see fit. I give my Books to be equally divided betwixt my son Buckingham and my son Stephen. I give to the Rev. Mr. John Whiting £5. I give to my daughter Hunt and to my daughter Buckingham 20 Shillings apeice in money. I give to my son Buckingham in money 40 Shillings. I give to the Rev. Mr. Samuel Hooker 40 Shillings. I give unto my son Stephen Hosmore 3 acres of my Meadow Land lying next Mr. Hooker's in Hartford South Meadow, & my now Dwelling House & Barne & Yard & Orchard, whom also I appoint sole Executor. I give to my daughter Hannah Malby 40 Shillings in Money, & in case she live to be a Widow & in Want, I do bequeath her £20 more to be paid her as she needs it. I do give unto the Children of my Kinsman Thomas Selden 40 Shillings.
Witness: *John Wilson,*   THOMAS HOSMORE. LS.
Nathaniel Cole, Ichabod Welles.

Court Record, Page 133—1st September, 1687: Will proven.

Page 47.

Howkins, Mrs. Anna, Farmington. Invt. £119-13-04. Court Record, Page 31—2nd December, 1680: Exhibited an Invt. Adms. to John Thompson; Samuel Gridley and Capt. John Standly to be Overseers. The children: John Thompson, Thomas Thompson, Beatrice Parker, Mary Hally, Hester Gridley, Elizabeth Brinsmade, Hanna Howkins. Distribution: To John Thompson, Eldest son, £12-18-04; Thomas Thompson, £6-09-02 (to this John allowed 40s from his portion); to Beatrice Parker, £4; to Mary Hally, £4; to Hester Gridley, being neglected in her father's Will, £16-05-10; to Hanna Howkins, £4; to Elizabeth Brinsmade (£4).

Page 227a-227b.

Hubbard, George, Middletown. He died 16 March, 1684-5. Invt. £243-10-00. Taken 13 May, 1685, by Giles Hamlin, Nathaniel White, William Warde. Legatees: the Widow, son Joseph age 42 years, Daniel 41, Samuel 37, Nathaniel 33, Richard 30, Mary (the wife of Thomas Ranny) 44, Elizabeth (the wife of Thomas Wetmore) 25 years of age. Will dated 2 May, 1681.

I George Hubbard of Middletown, being about 80 years of age, yet in comfortable health of bodie and having the use of my understanding as formerly, do make this my last Will & Testament:

Imprimis: I give to my Eldest son Joseph Hubbard, besids what I have formerly given him, one Acre of my meadow At a place called pasen chauge on the East sid the Great River, to ly on the North sid the Cricke which Runs through my Land. It. I give to my son Danill Hubard, besids what I gave him formaly, two Acres of Swompe at the west end of my Long meadow swompe Next the bogie meadow. It. I give to my son Samuel, besides what I formerly gave him, the on halfe of my halfe mile Lott on the East sid the great River, divided by the List in 1673. It. I give to my son Nathaniel Hubard my peice of bogie meadow, being about on acre & quarter, Lying Next Mr. Giles Hamlins meadow; more over I give to my sayd son Nathaniel all that my meadow on the South sid of the Crick at pason chag on the East sid the Great River; more over I give to my sayd son the one halfe of my Leaven acre Lott at the South End of the towne; I give allso to my sayd son the on Halfe of my Great Lott at the Long Swamp, as allso the on halfe of my great Lott in the westermost Rang of Lotts. It. I give to my daughter Elizabeth Hubard All the Rest of my Land on the East sid the Great River, besides what is formerly Desposed of, both which is Layd out & which is Lotted for by the List of Estate in the yeare 1673, only my half mille Lott excepted; It. I give to my Daughter Mary Rany fourty shillings out of my Estate, but on further consideration instead of that fourty shillings I give my sayd daughter the on halfe of my halfe Mille Lott on the East sid the Great River, devided by the List in 1673. It. I give to my son Richard Hubard my hous I now Dwell in & my barne and all other buildings, with my home Lott they stand on; as also my Long meadow Land & the Rest of my Long meadow swampe besids that I have given to my son Danill, hee allowing my son Daniel a Lamas highway to goe to the Swampe I give him if need Require; more over I give to my sayd son the other halfe of my Leaven Acre Lott at the south end of the towne, as allso the other halfe of my Great Lott at the Long Swampe, & Likewise the other halfe of my great Lott in the Westermost Rang of Lotts. Moreover it is my meaning herein, and my will is, that my sayd son Richard shall be my solle Executor, Injoyning him to provid Comfortably for his mother During her widow hood, And to pay all my Just Debts for my Desent Buriall; more over I give to my Loving wife Elizabeth Hubard all my housould Goods During her Natural Life, and after her Deseas my will is that my houshould Goods be equally Devided between Nathaniel And Richard & Elizabeth, Except the Great

Kettle, which I will to my son Richard. And farther it is my will that my Loving wife shall have the South end of my hous To Dwell in by her self if shee see caus, & rome in the seler for her nesesary use During her widow hood. More over on farther Consideration my will is that my wife Shall have halfe my hom Lott & halfe my orchard during her widow hud, as also on Cowe, And soe to provid for her selfe, & that my son Richard shall pay her three pownds pr year of Corent pay of the Country During her natural Life.

GEORGE X HUBARD, senior.

Upon farther Consideration I see cause to give the whole eleven acres of Land over the two Sticks brooke by the fulling mill to my Son Nathaniel.

GEORGE X HUBARD, SENIOR.

Signed in presents of us:

Sar. Samuel X *Ward.* I Request my Loving brethren
John Hall senior, Robert Warner & Deacon John Hall
Ebenezer Hubbard. to be the over seers to the per-
formance of my will. 27 February, 1683-4.

Court Record, Page 112—3d September, 1685: Will Proven.

Page 248.

Hubbard, Joseph, Middletown. Invt. £139-11-00. Taken December, 1686, by Nathaniel White, Robert Warner. The children: Joseph age 15 years, Robert 13, George 11, John 8, Elizabeth 3 years of age.

There is also a Legacy by Capt. Watts his Will to Joseph Hubbard.

Court Record, Page 127—3d March, 1686-7: Adms. to the Widow. Order to Dist. the Estate and appoint Lieut. Nathaniel White, Robert Porter (now Dec) & Robert Warner Overseers to assist the Widow in the management of the Estate.

Page 139—4 March, 1696-7: It appears that two of the Distributors above named Deceased. The Court appoint at the desire of Robert Hubbard, one of the Children, Ensign John Hall and Sergt. Thomas Warde, with Capt. White, to distribute the Estate according to the former Order of the Court.

Page 102—(Vol. VII) 2 February, 1704-5: Robert, George & Elizabeth Hubbard of Middletown, children of Joseph Hubbard, being all of lawful age, Exhibited in this Court an Agreement in writing under their hands & seals, made for the division & settlement of the Estate of the sd. Joseph Hubbard, and all acknowledged the same before this Court to be their free act and deed. This agreement on File, made with the consent and approbation of their Mother: Robert Hubbard is to have the whole Homestade and Twenty acres of Land out of the East side of that Lott upon which his brother George hath built and upon which he doth now dwell. George Hubbard is to have the remainder of the Lott upon which he now lives, being about 75 acres. And John Hubbard is to have about

17½ acres where he now lives, and the meadow Lott at wongonk, and the one acre of Land at passon chauge. And Elizabeth Hubbard, their sister, having already received £6-10-00 in pay, is to have £13-10-00 more in Country pay, to be paid betwixt George and John Hubbard within three years after the date hereof. And the above Robert doth by this Instrument take the care of their mother, and doth bind him, his heirs, Executors and administrators, to provide for her and give unto her a comfortable subsistance of food and rayment during her natural life, and other necessaries that she shall want. In witness whereof the said Robert, George, John and Elizabeth Hubbard, And Mary, their Mother, have unto this Agreement set their hands and seals this 3d day of June, 1704.

ROBERT HUBBARD Ls.
GORG HUBARD Ls.
JOHN HUBARD Ls.
ELIZABETH X HUBARD Ls.

Witnesses present:
John Hamlin,
George Stocking.

acknowledged 3 December, 1707, *before me, John Hamlin, Assistant.*

Page 68.

Hutchins, John. Died September, 1681. Invt. £38-18-00. Taken 30 September, 1681, by Nathaniel Bowman, Samuel Butler, William Warner. Children: Sarah age 4 years, Ann 1½ years.

Court Record, Page 47—1st November, 1681: Adms. to the Widow.

Page 191.

Jellicoe, Thomas, Middletown. Invt. £21-13-09. Taken 4 August, 1684, by Richard Hall, William Warde, John Warner.

Court Record, Page 92—4 September, 1684: Adms. to the Widow, Mary Jellicoe.

Page 235.

Kelsey, John, Windsor. Invt. £10-16-06. Taken 22 July, 1685, by John Loomis, John Moore.

Court Record, Page 112—3 September, 1685: Adms. to Thomas Kelsey.

Page 56.

Kenee, Alexander, Wethersfield. Invt. £80-06-00. Taken 1st October, 1680, by Nathaniel Boreman, John Wolcott. Legatees: The Relict, son Alexander age 18 years, Thomas 16, Sarah 16, Joseph 14, Lydiah 11, Ebenezer 8, Richard 6 years.

Court Record, Page 32—2 December, 1680: Adms. to the Relict.

Page 40—20 April, 1681: The Estate to be left with the Widow until the children come of age, for their bringing up, there being but £52-11-08 left after Debts were paid, and no Estate in Land.

Page 122.

Keeny, Alice, Wethersfield. Died 23 February, 1682-3: Invt. £50-14-06. Taken 5 March, 1682-3, by Samuel Talcott, James Treat, Samuel Martin, Thomas Bruer, Husband to Sarah the daughter of Mrs. Alice Keeny.

Court Record, Page 70—4 April, 1683: Invt. Exhibited, with an account of the debts, which Jonathan Colfax did engage to see paid; also to pay to the five youngest children ten shillings apiece, the Eldest son and daughter having (had) from the Estate, and this to be the distribution. Jonathan Colfax to Adms. the Estate.

Page 154.

Langton, John Jr. Invt. £85-17-09. Taken in Farmington, 3rd December, 1683, by John Heart & Thomas Heart. John Langton left a son John Langton about 13 moneths old.

An Appriesment of some Houseing & Lands belonging to John Langton Jr., Decd., taken in Northampton according to a desire of Deacon Langton, by us whose names are underwritten:

	£	s	d
Imprimis: By 10 acres of Land, part plowing & part Mowing, lying in the Great Meadow,	50-00-00		
More, 2 acres & 60 Rods now in the possession of the Widow or Relict of George Langton,	12-05-00		
By an House & half the Homelott,	35-00-00		
By Half a Homelott bought of Goodman Weller,	3-00-00		
More, £8 due to him from Salmon of Northampton, given him by (his wife) Mary Langton's Father,	8-00-00		
	£108-05-00		

Joseph Hawley,
John Bridgman.

Court Record, Page 77—18 December, 1683: Adms. of the Estate to Deacon John Langton. And appoint Mr. Wadsworth and Lt. John Standly to be the Overseers. And the Estate is by this Court given to John Langton, son of the decd, at the age of 21 years; & if he die before that age, to be equally divided amongst Deacon Langton's children then surviving.

Inventory on File.

Lattimer, Bezeliel, Wethersfield.   Invt. £42-17-00.   Taken 31 May, 1688, by Jno Wells, Jno Chester.   Legatees: Jona: 6¾ years old, and Bethsheba 3 months old.   ,

Court Record, Page 66—(Vol. VI) 17 January, 1688: Whereas Saint Tryon complains that her husband William Tryon hath fraudently conveyed away from her a Writing made between them before marriage, where by she is greatly injured and prays relief from this Court, she producing two Evidences that there was a writing made but not signed until after marriage, viz, the next morning, this Court do order that the sd. William Tryon shall have the Improvement of the Estate of Bezaleel Lattimore, Decd, provided he maintain the two Children of the sd. Lattimore; or only 1-3 part thereof (which is his wive's part of the sd. Estate), and the two children with their part of the Estate be put into their Guardians Hands, viz, Thomas Wickham and Ebenezer Deming; and that he shall have the Improvement of four acres of Land purchased by her after the decease of her husband Lattimore, the right to remain in her to dispose at her death, the sd. Tryon consenting to the same.

Page 67—17 January, 1698-9: Upon the request of Saint Tryon, this Court appoint Cornet Thomas Wickham and Ebenezer Deming to be Guardians to Jonathan and Bathsheba Lattimore, Children of Bezaleel Lattimore, late of Wethersfield, Decd.

Page 46—(Vol. VIII) 7 January, 1711-12: Whereas the Court of Probate did grant Adms. upon the Estate of Bezaleel Lattimore, late of Wethersfield, Decd, to Saint Lattimore, Widow of sd. Decd, and the sd. Saint Lattimore neglecting in her life time to finish her Adms., and she being now dead, this Court grant Adms. to Josiah Atwood, son- in-law to the sd. Decd, on the remaining unadministered Estate of sd. Bezaleel Lattimore, Decd.

Page 69—(Vol. IX) 1st July, 1718: This Court order the Dist. of a parcel of Land in Wethersfield granted by the Town, being the 110th Draught drawn by Saint Lattimore, late of Wethersfield, Decd, as followeth:

To the heirs of Jonathan Lattimer, Decd, son of the aforesd. Bezaleel Lattimer, Decd, 2-3 part thereof. To Bathshua Atwood, wife of Josiah Atwood, of sd. Wethersfield, and daughter of the aforesd. Bezzaleel Lattimer, 1-3 part thereof. And whereas the sd. Saint Lattimer in the time of her Widowhood bought 4 acres of Land of Samuel Bowman of Wethersfield and died intestate, this Court order a Dist. of sd. 4 acres, To the Heirs of Jonathan Lattimer a double part, and to the other two children of the sd. Saint Lattimer, Decd, to Bathshua Atwood and Abial Tryon, to each a single share. And appoint David Goodrich, Nathaniel Burnham sen. & Joshua Robbins distributors.

Page 23—(Vol. X) 2 July, 1723: Report of the Dist. by Nathaniel Burnham and Jonathan Burnham.

Page 123-4.

Leete, William, Esq., late Governor of the Colony of Connecticut. Invt. £1040-05-01. Taken 1st May, 1683, In Hartford, & 8 May in Guilford, by Thomas Macock and Stephen Bradley. Will dated 2 April, 1683.

I William Leete Esq. of Guilford do make my last Will & Testament: I doe bequeath unto my Loving wife Mary Leete the use of the Hall Chamber in my house at Guilford, Well furnished with necessaries for her use of beding, linen & chairs, if shee please to dwell there. She is to have free ingress and Egress without molestation, and likewise she shall have Rent of half the houseing and Land at the Island, & of the Church, Houseing & Land at New Haven, & £6 a year more out of my Estate during the terme of her natural Life. Nextly, my will is that my lame daughter Graciana shall have the rest of my houseing and land in the whole Home Lott at the Towne, both the use & fee simple of it; & of what household stuff I Left there is to be for her maintenance comfortably, which if my son John shall undertake & performe during her life, the Inheritance shall be his after her decease, I having a respect to Gracianas comfort during her lifetime in that also, then to John & his heirs forever. I give to my daughter Ann £100. As for my other children, viz, Andrew, William & Abigail, although I had upon their marriages given them their portions as I was able, yet I give my two sonns Andrew & William my farme at Cause sen. Chaug & what Harmon Garrett gave me about Stoneington, halfe unto Andrew & halfe to William. My Land at Clabord hill I give to Andrew, & what I bought at Homonoscitt of John Meggs to William; & unto Abigail my daughter Woodbridge I give Ten pounds in household Stuff or Stock. I make my three sons, John, Andrew & William, my Executors. Unto this I sett my hand & seale, being well known both (to) the Court & many others.   WILLIAM LEETE, GOVR.
of his Maties Colony of Connecticut. Ls.

I desire my loveing friend Mr. Joseph Eliott to be overseer, to set all things right betwixt my wife & children in case any difference should arise.

Hartford, 2 April, 1683: I doe allow £15 out of my Estate towards makeing my farme at the Island Tenantable; & it is my will that if any part of the rents assigned for my wive's Comfortable Mayntenance fayle, my three sons shall make it up by equal portions to her.

WM. LEETE, GOVR. OF HIS MATIES COLONY OF CONNECTICUT. Ls.

Court Record, Page 71—16 May, 1683: Will & Invt. Exhibited by William & Mrs. Mary Leete. Will Proven.

Page 46.

Lewes, Joseph, Simsbury. Invt. £33-18-00. Taken by John Case, Samuel Willcoxson.

Court Record, Page 29—2 September, 1680: Adms. to Elizabeth Lewes, the Relict. John Case is desired to assist the Widow.

Lewes, Mary, Farmington. Court Record, Page 148—4 March, 1696-7: A Petition, as her husband has escaped out of the Colony, that the Estate being small may be secured for her subsistence. Order the Estate of James Lewes, what is left of it, be secured for her by the Townsmen of Farmington and Improved for her Maintenance.

Page 152-3-4.

Lewes, William sen. (the aged), Farmington. Invt. £280-co-oo of Estate of William Lewes sen., Decd., at Farmington, sometime living in Hadley. Lands in Hadley and Hatfield apprized by Aaron Cooke sen., Samuel Porter sen., 3d December, 1683.

4 Dec., Capt. William Lewes made oath that this is a true Inventory of his Father William Lewes Estate at Hadley & Hatfield, to the best of his knowledge. Will dated 30 August, 1683.

I William Lewis, being stricken in years, do think it meet to set in order the Estate which God hath graciously given me. Item. I give to my grand child Ezekiel Lewes all my Estate at Hadly, also all the Land on Hatfield side, he paying his brother Nathaniel the Just sum of six score pounds when he comes to the age of 21 years. If Ezekiel die, Nathaniel to possess it. If both die, then to my grand child Abigail Lewes and her heirs forever. I give to Abigail one piece of Land at Hartford, four acres within the meadow gate that leads to the neck, bounded on the Highway west, Bartholomew Barnard South, Richard Goodman East, & John Allyn north. Also I give to Abigail Lewes one parcell of Land toward the south end of the Long meadow, north on Bartholomew Barnard, east on the Great River, on my own Land south, and the Rivulet west, by Estimation one half acre. I give to my grand daughter with this provision: In case my grand child Philip Lewes will pay to my gr. child Abigail Lewes £40 in Current pay of the Country in sixteen years, that is to say, £2-10 per year to my overseers before the middle of January as Rent, then and thereafter to be to Abigail & to her heirs forever. I give to my grand child Ebenezer Lewes the Smith's tools that I bought of John Holloway. I make my son William Lewes Executor. I desire Lt. Samuel Steele of Wethersfield and Samuel Patrick of Hadly to be Overseers.   WILLIAM LEWES.

Witness: *Robert Porter, Thomas X Newell sen.*

Court Record, Page 77—18 December, 1683: Will and Invt. Exhibited.

Vol. IV., P. C., No. 143.

No. 144, Statement of *James Steele sen:* This may Satisfi this honored Court, or whom els it may consarn, that I being occasionally at Capt. Laweses hous sum time be fore old Mr Lawes died, sd. Mr Lawes falling in to sum discors with me about his gransone philip Lawes at Hart ford,

amongst other discours he sd. that sd philip owed him a considerable sum for rent. I do not remember the particular quntyty how much, but I know it was a great delle, and hee desired me to tell sd. philip that he must provid to pay him. I tould him he had best to wrighte to him, and so he did and sent the letter by myself and prayd me to deliver it to his gran son and so I did. Capt. Lawes red the leter to his father in my hering. I doe not remember the particklers of the sd. leter, but the substance of it was respecting what we had bin speking of respecting philip Lawes above sd.   JAMES STEELE, SEN.
Hartford, March 7—'90-'91.

Page 261.

Loomis, Joseph, sen., Windsor. Died 26 June, 1687. Invt. £281-14-08. Taken 12 July, 1687, by Henry Wolcott, John Wolcott, John Loomis. The children: Joseph age 38 yr., John 36, Mary 34, Hannah 25, Matthew 23, Stephen 20, James 17, Nathaniel 14, Isaac 9 years of age.

Court Record, Page 132—1st September, 1687: Invt. Exhibited.

Page 134—26 October, 1687: An Inventory of the Estate of Joseph Loomis, formerly Exhibited in Court, was now considered, & this Court appoynt Joseph his son and Matthew Loomis Adms. Order to Dist., and appoint John Loomis & John Moore distributors.

Page 6—(Vol. VIII) 6 February, 1709-10: Joseph Loomis, son of Joseph Loomis sen., formerly of Windsor, Decd., in Court shows that he and his Brother Matthew Loomis, now Decd., have paid the Debts and delivered the Portions of the Estate to his Brothers and Sisters, and is granted a *Quietus Est.*

Page 242-3-4-5.

Lord, Richard, Sometime of Hartford. Invt. £5832-11-11. Taken 25 June, 1686, by John Allyn & William Pitkin.

Special Court, Page 113—20 February, 1685: Mrs. Mary Lord informing this Court that she hath by a Letter from one Robert Goffe, master of a vessel lately cast away at Monomay, & other ways, been acquainted with the death of Mr. Richard Lord her husband, & a considerable Estate Lost or in great Hazard to be lost that was in the vessell except speedy course be taken to recover & preserve the same, & desireing this court would be pleased to Impower some person or persons for that and all other occasions to administer to ye Estate of the sd. Mr Richard Lord deceased, as the case may require, This Court having considered the sayd Mrs. Lord's motion doe see cause to grant her desire therein, & doe appoynt Mrs. Mary Lord, the relict of the sayd Mr. Richard Lord, & her son Richard Lord, his son, to be administrators to the Estate of sd. Mr. Lord; & in regard Richard Lord her son is not yet of age, the soale power of Adms. is granted to her the sayd Mrs. Mary Lord for the present until her son be of age, or till there be further order taken in the case either by a will ap-

pearing of Mr. Richard Lords deceased and an Executor therein nomin-
ated & appoynted, or the Court shall see Just reason to give other order
therein.

Page 121—2 September, 1686: Inventory Exhibited in Court.

Page 122—21 October, 1686: Upon request of Mrs. Mary Hooker,
Administratrix of the Estate of Mr. Richard Lord of Hartford, deceased,
this Court doe grant Adms. upon the Estate of Mr. Richard Lord, Decd.,
to Mr. Thomas Hooker her present husband. Mr. Richard Lord Jr. appeared in Court & made choice of Capt. John Allyn & Mr. William Pitkin
to be his guardians, sd. Richard Lord being of full age according to Law
to choose guardian, viz, above 16 years.

Page 122-123—27 December, 1686: Dist. by the Court to Mrs. Mary
Hooker £900 of Personal Estate forever and one third part of the real Estate during Life, & the whole of the Estate to be under her management,
she Mayntaining her son Richard suitably & according to his degree untill
he shall be Twenty one years of age, or his day of marriage, which shall
first happen.

Page 51—(Vol. V) 8 February, 1693: Doctor Thomas Hooker,
Adms. to the Estate of Mr. Richard Lord Decd., in behalf of his wife Mary
Hooker, Relict of the Deceased, appeared in Court with Richard Lord,
son of sd. Deceased, and gave an Account of his Adms. Accepted to the
full Satisfaction of Mr. Lord, when the Court released sd. Doctor Hooker
& Mrs. Mary Hooker from their Adms. & committed the Care of the Estate to Mr. Richard Lord.

Page 150.

Maccoy, Hugh, Wethersfield. Died 31 July, 1683. Invt. £100-13-06.
Taken by Samuel Talcott, James Treat.

Court Record, Page 76—6 December, 1683: Adms. to Capt. Samuel
Talcott to pay the debts and keep the rest for further Order of the Court.

Page 87—6 March, 1684: Alice Maccoy having made it appear to this
Court that before Marriage Hugh Maccoy hath past over the whole of his
Estate to said Alice, Capt. Talcott having given up the Adms., this Court
grant letters of Adms. to Nathaniel Bowman In behalf of sd. Alice and for
her use, he paying to the Treasurey of the County £15 for what expenses
they have been at in hearing of these several Courts, he paying debts.

Page 102—(Vol. V) 30th March, 1696: Mr. Nathaniel Boman gave
an Account of his Adms. on the Estate of Hugh Maccoy, by which it did
appear unto the Court that he hath paid all the Debts due from the Estate
of Hugh Maccoy and that there remains of the Estate £50 in Land wch
is to be disposed as the County Court shall determine. The Court grant
unto Mr. Nathaniel Bowman a *Quietus Est*. The Land being left in Mr.
John Maccoy's Hands at 20 Shillings per Annum rent, to be disposed of
as the County Court shall order.

Page 137-138.

Marshall, Widow Mary. Invt. £130-07-11. Taken 3 September, 1683, by Benjamin Newbery, Daniel Clarke sen., Henry Wolcott. The children: Samuel, Lydia, David, Thomas, Eliakim, John, Elizabeth.

Court Record, Page 73—6 September, 1683: Adms. to Capt. Newbery, Return Strong, Nathaniel Bissell.

Page 79—18 December, 1683: The Widow Mary Marshall Dying Intestate, this Court Order to Distribute to the Children: to the Eldest son a double portion, & to the other 6 equal portions ; also to secure the portions of the younger children until they come of age. Capt. Benjamin Newbery, Return Strong, Nathaniel Bissell & Henry Wolcott, Distributors.

Page 149.

Martin, Samuel, Wethersfield. Died 15 September, 1683. Invt. £25-15-06. Taken by Samuel Talcott, James Treat. The Estate to the Widow, Phebe Martin.

Court Record, Page 76—6 December, 1683: Adms. to the Widow to pay the debts, and the remainder of Estate to be as her own Estate.

Page 51.

Miller, Thomas, Middletown. Invt. £486-04-00. Taken 10 September, 1680, by Thomas Wettmore, James Tappine, Richard Hall & William Cheeny. The children: Thomas age 14 years, Samuel 12, Joseph 10, Benjamin 8, Margaret 4, Sarah one year old. Will dated 11 August, 1680.

The last Will & Testament of Thomas Miller of Middletown, in the County of Hartford, being something about 70 years of age, not knowing the day of my death, is as followeth: After my committing of my Spirit to God who gave it, & my Body to a decent Burial, I do dispose of that portion of worldly Goods as followeth: Imprimis: My Will is that my Estate shall be divided equally amongst all my sons after my wives decease, they paying my daughters out of it half so much apeice as any of their portions, my wife injoying the Use of my House & Lands & Stock for her Life time. The other Lands which are not fit for Improvement at present, nor under fence, may be divided to them as part of their portions as they come to age. As respecting my daughter Bacon, I have already paid her her full portion before her death, & therefore do not see Cause to do anything now to my son-in-law Nathaniel Bacon, & making my loving wife Sarah Miller sole Executrix.

Witness: *William Cheeny,*   THOMAS X MILLER SEN.
       John Hall.

Court Record, Page 32—2 December, 1680: Will exhibited by the Relict and proven.

Page 192—(Vol. X) 7 May, 1728: Whereas Thomas Miller, formerly of Middletown, in & by his last Will & Testament did appoint his wife Sarah executrix and/impowered her to set out of his Estate to the Children their portion in sd. Will, and the sd. Executrix being lately deceased, not having fully dist. sd. Estate according to the sd. Will, this Court do appoint & impower Messrs. Samuel Hall, Solomon Adkins & Samuel Frary, of Middletown, or any two of them, to Dist. the Estate of sd. Decd. not before proportioned to & amongst the Heirs of the sd. Decd.

Dist. on File: 10 December, 1728: To the Heirs of Thomas Miller (eldest son), to Samuel Miller, to the Heirs of Joseph Miller, to Benjamin Miller (4th son), to John Miller (youngest son), and to Isaac Johnson in Right of his wife Margaret Miller, to George Hubbard in Right of his wife Mehetabell Miller, to Smith Johnson in Right of his wife Sarah Miller. By Samuel Frary, Solom Adkins & William Rockwell.

George Hubbard, who married Mehetabell, one of the daughters of the deceased, desired an Appeal from the Judgement of this Court in accepting the aforesd. Dist., to the Superior Court. Granted.

Page 210—2 January, 1728-9: Report of the Dist.

Page 130.

Mills, Simon. Died 6 July, 1683. Invt. £168-07-00. The children: Eldest daughter Mary Humphries age 20 years, Hannah Mills 18, Sarah 13, Abigail 11, Elizabeth 9, Prudence 7 (Decd), John Mills age 14 years, and Simon 5 years of age.

Court Record, Page 72—6 September, 1683: Adms. to the Relict and Peter Buell.

Page 78—18 December, 1683: This Court having granted Adms. to the Widow of Simon Mills and Peter Buell on the Estate of Simon Mills, do divide the Estate as followeth:

	£ s d
To the Relict, of Personal Estate & 1-3 of the Real,	16-00-00
To the Eldest son John Mills,	22-00-00
To the rest of the Children, to each,	11-00-00

The sons to receive their portions in Land as they come of age, the rest in Reversion after their Mother's decease. This Court appoint John Case and Samuel Willcox to be Overseers.

Dist. File, 24 July, 1691: Upon an Order of the Court made 18 December, 1683:

	£ s d
To the Eldest son John Mills,	22-00-00
To Samuel Humphrey, husband to Mary the Eldest daughter,	13-16-03
To Simon Drake, husband to Hannah,	13-17-00
To Sarah Mills,	12-02-00
To Elizabeth Mills,	13-00-00

Page 188—(Vol. VIII) 5 April, 1714: This Court orders the Estate of Simon Mills, late of Simsbury, Decd., shall be dist. and divided to the Children & heirs of the sd. Decd by the Rule and Proportion according to an Order or Decree of the County Court holden at Hartford 18 December, Anno Dom 1683; and for that End do now order and appoint Mr. Joseph Case, Mr. Joseph Phelps and John Slater, of Simsbury, to divide the sd. Estate accordingly, and make return thereof to this Court on or before the 1st Monday of June next.

A Settlement by Arbitration of the Estate of Simon Mills of Simsbury, who died 1683, made this 25th March, 1719. (Vol. IX, Page   ):

Know all Men by these presents: That we the Undersigned do acknowledge ourselves firmly bound unto each other in the sum of £100 current money or Bills of Credit, and to the true performance hereof we do bind ourselves and each of our heirs firmly by these presents, in Witness whereof we have set to our Hand to stand to, abide by, and in all things stand to the final end and Judgement of Deacon Cornish, Samuel Case & Joseph Case, of Simsbury, Arbitrators indifferently chosen, elected and named by each party to complete and make a final Dist. of the Estate of Simon Mills of Simsbury Decd., and to judge, order, arbitrate and determine all differences that has, shall or may arise concerning the premises relateing to the sd. Estate, according to Justice and Ecquitty, provided the sd. Arbitrators doe bring in their reward under their hands & Seals at, on or before the 6th day of April next ensueing the date hereof. Then this Obligation is to be void & of non effect, otherwise to stand and remain in full force & virtue. In Witness whereof we have set to our Hands & Seals the date abovesd.

SAMLL HUMPHRIS SEN. LS.   SAMUEL TULLER LS.
SIMON X MILLS LS.   THOMAS ELLSWORTH LS.
JOHN MILLS LS.   DANIEL LOOMIS LS.
JOSEPH MILLS LS.   THOMAS HORSKINS LS.
BENJAMIN MILLS LS.   HANNAH X LOOMIS LS.
Witness: *James Hilliyer Jr.,*
        Jacob Tuller.

Page 132-133.

Mitchell, John, Hartford. Died 28 July, 1683. Invt. £132-01-09. Taken by Caleb Standly, Zechariah Sandford. The children: Mary age 28 years, John 25, Sarah 21, Margaret 19, Mabell 17, Miriam Mitchell 15, The Relict Mrs. Mary Mitchell.

Court Record, Page 73—6 September, 1683: Adms. to John Mitchell.

Page 77—18 December, 1683: Distribution: To the Widow Mary Mitchell, 6 acres of Land in the neck which John Mitchell had of Thomas Huxley for Land that was the Widows, and £10; to John Mitchell, £24-17-00; and to the five daughters £12-08-00 to each. Lieut Caleb Standly & Thomas Olcott distributors. Mrs. Mary Mitchell did in Court accept of the Distribution.

Page 223.

Mitchell, Sarah, Hartford. Invt. £27-02-03. Taken 23 January, 1684, by William Gibbons & Mary X Gilbert. The brothers and sisters: John, Mary, Margaret, Mabel & Miriam.

Court Record, Page 104—24 March, 1684-5: Adms. to John Mitchell. Lieut. Standly & Mr. Thomas Olcott to Dist. the Estate equally to John Mitchell and to his four Sisters.

Page 194-5.

Morrice, Robert, Hartford. Died 19 November, 1684. Invt. £63-08-03. Taken 21 November, 1684, by Thomas Olcott, Caleb Standly. Robert Morrice's Estate is in debt to several persons:

	£	s	d
To Dr. Williams,	3	07	00
To John Andrews wife for Washing & 15 days nursing,	1	13	00
For his Funeral, To 3 gallons of Wine, in Money,		12	00
To Samll Spencer, for Rum, Money,		03	06
To Wm Goodwin for a Graue,		06	00
To Joseph Strickland for a Coffin,		10	00
To John Willson for Cyder,		10	00
To Lt. Caleb Standly,			
To Mrs. Gilbert,		02	06
To John Easton,		00	06

Will dated 7 June 1684. I Robert Morrice of Hartford, in New England, being in Good health and memory, do make this my last Will & Testament: Item. I give unto Hannah Standly, the wife of Caleb Standly, my Book called "The Saints' Everlasting Rest," of Mr. Baxter's Works. I give to Hanah Pitkin, daughter of Caleb Standly, my Book called the "Godly Man's Heart." To Elizabeth Standly, their other daughter, my Book called "Abram's Intercession for Soddom." I give 10 Shillings to John Andrews. To John Willson, my Executor, I give 40 Shillings. To Samuel Spencer, my Overseer, 20 Shillings. To John Tiliston, my Kinsman, to Jeremy Diggins & Thomas Andrews, I give all my Wearing Apparrel, equally to be divided between them. To Mary Diggins, daughter of the sd. Jeremy Diggins, I give all my Silver Money be it more or less, also my Bed & all my Bedding, & my Book called "Heaven upon Earth"; also I give her my Great Bible, my Trunk wth smale things in it, my spice Box, and Mr. Marshall's Book. To young Jeremy Diggins I give my Book called "God's All Sufficiency." To Elizabeth Diggins I give my liudry cupbord. Also I give to young Jeremy Diggins my Siluer Hattband & Siluer Buttons. The wife of John Willson & the wife of Samuel Spencer I give each of them 5 Shillings. It is my Will that the Residue of my Estate be equally diuided between the three forenamed children of Jeremy

Diggins. I appoint John Willson my Executor, & Samuel Spencer my Overseer.

Witness: *Lydia* X *Willson,*   Robert X Morrice. Ls.
          William Pitkin.

Court Record, Page 94—25 November, 1684: Will exhibited by John Willson, Executor. Lt. Caleb Standly having done many services for Robert Morrice, as all his family, having baked his bread for a number of years, this Court allows him out of the Estate four pounds for it.

Page 141-2.

Moses, John, Windsor. Died 14 October, 1683. Invt. £575-01-00. Taken by Henry Wolcott, Timothy Phelps sen., Daniel Birge. The children: John age 28 years, Timothy 14, Mary 22, Sarah 19, Margaret 17, Martha 12, Mindwell 7 years.

Court Record, Page 75—6 December, 1683: Invt. Exhibited.

Page 79—18 December, 1683: Adms. to the Widow and son John. Order to Distribute: To the Widow, £64 of personal Estate forever, and one third of the Real during Life; to the Eldest son, £124; to Timothy, £66; to Mary, Eldest daughter, because of her weakness, £70; to the others £60 to each at lawful age. John Moore and Return Strong to be Overseers.

Page 84—6 March, 1684: Whereas this Court hath been informed that in John Moses' Inventory there is a parcell of Land bought of Sarah Linsley, 13 acres, valued at £13, which is Judged worth £60, that parcell of Land is by these appointed to distribute the estate to be Valued in proportion as the other Land, & what overpluss it makes is to help beare what the Estate is fallen short since the Inventory was taken.

File Record, 12 February, 1683: An accott of the Widdow's part of the Moveables Layd out to her. Inventory of the Estate of Mary Moses, deceased. Taken 23 September, 1689, £62-12-00, by John Moore.

Estate of John Moses, Simsbury, 1690-1—To the constable of Simsbury to serve and return: In their Maties Name you are required to warne John Moses of your Town to appear at the Court to be holden at Hartford the first Thursday in March next, to Answer Samuel Farnsworth in Right of his wife, as he is Administrator to the Estate of John Moses deceased, in action of the case for his neglecting to make payment to sayd Farnsworth the sume of Seventy pounds due to him in the right of his wife as her proportion of her father's Estate allotted to her by the Court, wth necessary costs & charges. Hereof fayle not. Dated at Hartford, Feb. 10, 1690-1.   *John Allyn, Secretary.*

February the 11th, 1690.

Then this warrant was served upon John Moses by me,
John Robearts, Constable for Simsbury.

Received of John Moses, as Administrator to ye Estate of John Moses deceased, in Right of my wife Mary, the daughter of the said deceased, as part of her portion ordered and distributed to her out of the Estate of the said John Moses deceased, the sum of seventeen pounds seven shillings and six pence. I say received the 16th of January, 1690, pr. me,

Signed and sealed   SAMUEL FARNSWORTH.
in presence of:
Samuel Clarke sen.,
Timothy Phelps sen.

Page 241.

Mygatt, Widow Ann, Hartford. Will dated 28 December, 1681. I Ann Mygatt, Widow of Joseph Mygatt, do make this my last Will & Testament: I give to my daughter Mary Deming all my Woolen Apparrell excepting my Broad Cloth Coat, which I give unto my gr. daughter Sarah Mygatt. I give to my daughter Mary Deming my Bed whereon I lye & all its furniture thereunto belonging. And further, my Will is that my wearing Linen be equally divided between my daughter Mary Deming & my gr. daughter Sarah Mygatt; & my Will is that the remainder of my Estate be equally divided between my daughter Mary Deming and my gr. son Joseph Mygatt, excepting my Chest.
Witness: *Paul Peck sen.,*   ANN X MYGATT.
          George Grave.

Court Record, Page 115—4 March, 1685-6: Will proven. Order to Dist. Persons concerned in the Dist. agreed to it in Court.

Page 55-6.

Mygatt, Deacon Joseph, Hartford. Died 7 December, 1680. Invt. £368-11-06. Taken 10 December, 1680, by Thomas Bull sen., Paul Peck sen., George Grave. Will dated 27 November, 1676.
I Joseph Mygatt of Hartford do make this my last Will & Testament: Whereas, in a Writing bearing date 27 November, 1654, I have already engaged the manner of a dispose of my Estate after my Death, I do now for the substance thereof fully consent thereunto, only some things mentioned needing some explication I thought good to mention, 1st, that I have already paid the marriage portion for my son Jacob as is expressed in the Agreement, & have built a house for him of more value than was promised, & have truly fulfilled that first particularly. 2nd, Whereas it is mentioned in the Agreement with Mrs. Susannah Fitch, & the Trustees in behalf of her Brother, that the Estate by her should be let out to procure a farm, that it might have been so but they conceived that it might be more advantageous to adventure the Money abroad, being at that time in a way of Trade, the which with their desire I consented too,—these things being

confiscated, I do dispose of my whole Estate as is there mentioned, only my Mind is that in Case the £12 be not paid to my wife (as is expressed), that so much of my Lands be sold (that may best be spared) as may enable the true performance of the yearly Annuity willed to her during her natural life. I give unto Joseph Deming, my gr. son, all my Wearing apparrel. I appoint my gr. child Joseph Mygatt to be my Executor. I desire my friend Paul Peck sen. and my son John Deming to be Overseers.

Witness: *Jos: Haines,*   Jo: MYGATT. Ls.
        Paul Peck.

Court Record, Page 33—29 December, 1680: Will proven, and approved so far as consistent with a former writing.

Page 7-8.

Nash, Joseph, Sergt., Hartford. Invt. £419-13-10. Taken 3 September, 1678, by Thomas Bull, Thomas Bunce, Nathaniel Stanly. Will dated 19 January, 1675-6.

I Joseph Nash of Hartford do declare my last Will & Testament: My Will is that my just Debts be paid, & that being done, with my Funeral Charges & Necessary expenses defrayed, the remainder of my Estate I give to my wife Margaret & Sarah my only Child in such proportion & manner as is hereafter in this my Will expressed. I give to Margaret my wife 1-3 part of all my Moveable Estate both Goods & Cattle, And I give to Sarah my daughter 2-3 parts of all my Moveable Estate both Goods & Cattle: & for as much as our daughters that have been disposed of already have had the best of the Moveables, my Will is that my sd. daughter Sarah shall have in her part of the sd. Moveables the best featherbed & Boulster & two Pillows, the best Coverlet & Curtains & Furniture of the sd. Bed, & also my great Copper Kettle, also one great pewter Dish or platter (which is the bigest). These particulars first excepted, my wife to choose in the rest of the Moveables half her third part, & then the Residue to be divided according to proportion both in Quantity & Quality upon the Advice of my Overseers. I do give unto my sd. daughter Sarah my House, Houses, & all my Lands, with all Rights & Privileges belonging to them, to her & her heirs in full Right & Title, only the following caution to be observed: that for the support & Relief of my wife, my Will is, that there shall be yearly paid unto her my sd. wife, or to her Order, in Hartford, the sum of £4 during the term of her natural life; and also, if my wife for her better support in her widowed condition shall make choice to keep the sd. Houseing & Lands in her hands, then my Will is that while she remains my Widow she shall injoy the sd. Houseing & Lands, and that my wife pay or caused to be paid unto my sd. daughter Sarah, yearly, in Hartford, £7, and shall keep and maintain Houseing & Fences in Good repair, Also discharge all Dues both civil & ecclesiasticall. And further it is my Will, that my Lands should pay to the Ministry at the New Meeting House. My

Will is that if my daughter Sarah die without Issue, that my Houses & Lands shall pass to my eldest brother, Capt. John Nash, and his heirs forever. I appoint my brother Capt. John Nash, of New Haven, Executor, and appoint Robert Webster and Andrew Benton to be Overseers.

Witness: *John Whiting,*   JOSEPH NASH. Ls.
        John White.

Court Record, Page 8—17 October, 1678: Will proven.

Page 100.

Nichols, Adam, Hartford. Died 25 August, 1682. Invt. £8-05-00. Taken by John Marsh & Caleb Standly.

Adam Nichols is in Debt, besides what his Estate hath paid for his maintenance before his Death at Goodman Peck's, about £6-00-00. Goodwife Peck also gave Accot of fower Napkins Addam Nichols gave to his daughter Hester Ellis, and one Bellmetle skillett, when his daughter was last at sd. Peck's, and left one Napkin at Haddam when he went down to visit his son and daughter, & half a sheet and one Napkin more was disposed of for his Buryall linen.

Court Record, Page 58—7 September, 1682: Invt. exhibited. Adms. granted to Caleb Stanly and John Marsh, with advice to render the Estate to his son and daughter provided they give security for the Debts due from sd. Estate. (See Will of John Wakeman on page 158 of this volume.)

Page 103.

North, John, Wethersfield. Died 6 August, 1682. Invt. £133-07-00. Taken 5 September, 1682, by John Kilbourn & Thomas Wright, Selectmen. The children: John age 10 years, Mary 8, Susannah 6 years. The Widow, Susannah North.

Court Record, Page 61—13 December, 1682: Invt. Exhibited. Adms. to Susannah North, Widow. Robert Francis & Joseph Churchill appointed as Overseers to assist the Widow in the management of affairs, with Order for Distribution of the Estate.

Page 103.

North, Samuel. Invt. £188-05-06. Taken by Thomas Heart, Thomas Porter, Richard Seamore, Selectmen. The children: John age 13 years, Samuel 10, Thomas 8, Hanna 4 years.

Court Record, Page 60—13 December, 1682: Adms. to the Widow. Order to Dist: To the Widow £20 and 1-3 use of Real Estate, to Eldest son a double Portion, to the rest of the Children single Portions. John

Norton sen. is appointed to assist the Widow in the best manner he may.

Page 73 (Vol. V) 6 September, 1694: Whereas, there was a complaint made by John Norton sen. & John Norton Jr. that the Children of Samuel North had not received of John Rue their portions distributed or allotted to them out of their father North's Estate, & sewed sayd Rue for security of what was still to be payd of the sayd Children's portions, This Court doe order the sayd John Rue to pay the remaynder of Tho. North's portion forthwith unto the sayd Thomas North besides what he is to receive in Land, & to give John Norton sen. sufficient security for the portion that is allotted out unto Hanna North by the Court, as sayd John Norton Jun. is guardian unto the sayd Hanna North. All which being don, to be the finall acquittance of the sayd John Rue respecting Samuel North's Children their Estates or portions.

Page 75-76.

Nott, John, Wethersfield. Died 25 January, 1681. Invt. £533-15-10. Taken by John Kilbourn, Thomas Wright, William Warner. Will dated 10 February, 1679.

I John Nott of Wethersfield, aged and infirm, but of perfect understanding & Memory, being desirous to settle things in order, doe make and ordain this my Last Will and Testament in manner and form following: Item. I give and bequeath to my wife Ann Nott Convenient and necessary house roome In my dwelling house where I now live, & also £6 pr annum to be payd to her yearly out of the proffits & rents of my estate, & also the free use of so much of my household goods as she shall have need of to enjoy the sayd comfortable houseroom, together with the yearly payment of £6 pr yeare, & also the free use of my household stuffe as aforesayd for & during the full terme & time of her natural Life. I give and bequeath to my sayd wife a good milch Cow, to take her choyse of all the Cowes I have. Item. I give to my daughter Elizabeth Reeves £30, to be paid to her out of my moveable Estate. I doe also give to my sayd daughter the one halfe of my houshold Stuffe, to be delivered to her after the decease of my wife. I give to my daughter Hanna Hale Tenn shillings. Item. I give & bequeath to my son John Nott all my houses & Lands that I have here in Wethersfield or els where, together with all my goods, Chattells & debts, that is to say, all whatsoever which I now have or shall have & stand possessed of or have good & Lawful right to at the time of my decease, the legacies only excepted before given to my wife & to my two daughters, & my sayd sonn paying to my wife out of the proffitts of my estate the yearly Rent of £6 pr yeare, year by yeare, for and during the full term of her natural Life. I ordain my son John Nott sole Executor of this my Last Will & Testament.   JOHN NOTT.

Witness: *Eleazer Kimberly, Ruth X Kimberly.*

Proven 27 February, 1681. before me, *John Chester, Comissioner. John Nott, Elizabeth Reeve, Hanna Haell.*

Ann Nott appeared and made oath to the Invt.
Court Record, Page 51—2 March, 1681-2: Will Presented in Court.

P. C., Vol. IV, No. 1-2-3.

Olmsted, John, Norwich. Invt. £973-05-06. Taken by Solomon Tracy, Samuel Lothrop. Exhibited in Court 22 September, 1686.

Will: I John Olmsted of Norwich, being about 60 years of age, make my Wife Elizabeth sole Executrix, my Servants to have their liberty at the death of my Wife, but my Negro Servant Tony not only to have his liberty but to have ten acres of Land in some Convenient place.

JOHN OLMSTED.

Witness: *Christopher Huntington,*
Thomas Adgate.

Proven 20 September, 1689.

Will of Elizabeth Holmsted, 15 October, 1689, Relict of John Holmsted, says her husband gave her all his Estate to despose of as she saw fit. For Love and affection for the two sons of her husband's Brother, Richard Olmsted of Norwalk, viz, Lieutenant James Holmsted and Ensign John Holmsted, I have given to each of them an Allottment at the new plantation Lying at the Northwest of Norwich, Each Allottment Contayning by Estimation about a Thousand acres of Land, with all Rights, Etc., by deed of gift to them. I give to Sargt. Richard Baskett (written now Richard Bushnell), my Kinsman, a Tract of Land on the East side of the little Rivulet at Wequetequock adjoining that of Daniel Tracy. I also give him 4 acres of Land at Yantick, by that of William Hide west, Thomas Post north and east. I also give him 10 acres of Land at Wequetequock; also Land east side of the Shoetucket River at Wequanack, on said River east, the Highway north, and upon Land of Thomas Leffingwell and Richard Wallis. My will is that £50 be paid for the relief of the poor of Norwich, per advice of Rev. James Fitch, sen. I give to my brother Adgate's three children, viz., Sarah, Rebeckah & Thomas, £6 to each. To my brother's eldest daughter, Abigail, a parcel of Land over the River which her husband bought of John Arnold. To Tony (the Negro), Ten acres was given: 3 acres in the little plain, 3 acres in the Great plain, and 4 acres at Wequetequock. To Hannah (the Indian Maide) and to the nine Children of my brother & sister Nuell of Farmington, 5 Shillings apiece. I give to the Rev. James Fitch sen. £10. The Residue of my Estate to my Kinsman and Executor, Samuel Lothrop.

ELIZABETH X OLMSTED.

Witness: *John Post, John Burchard.*

It appears that James Olmsted and Samuel Newell asked for a review.

Page 198-9-200.

Olmsted, Capt. Nicholas, Hartford. Died 31 August, 1684. Invt. £421-08-00. Taken by Caleb Stanly, John Marsh. Will dated 20th August, 1683.

I Nicholas Olmsted of Hartford do make this my last Will & Testament: I give to my wife £5 a year during her Widowhood, and £4 a year if she marry, during her natural life, to be paid her yearly by my sons, Samuel 40 Shillings and Joseph 40 Shillings and Thomas 20 Shillings. I give to my son Samuel Olmsted my Dwelling house in Hartford after my decease, only the Use of some part of it to his Mother. I give unto my son Samuel ½ of my Barne, and all that part of my Homelott not given to my son Thomas. I give the other half of the Barne to my son Thomas, and I give my Barn Yard equally to my sons Samuel & my son Thomas, with my Well in the same. I give to my son Thomas that part of my Homelott next Mr. Haynes' and Mr. Hooker's Homelott, to be divided from my son Samuel's part of my Homelott as followeth: From the Barne to the Highway to be divided by the fence that fenceth in the Barn yard, and above the Barn from the middle of the Barn Floor up to Jeremy Addams's Homelott. The remainder of my Homelott I give to my son Samuel, and to his heirs, forever. I give unto my son Thomas my Meadow lott in the Long Meadow lying between Deacon Butler's and Lt. Joseph Wadsworth's Land. I give unto my son Thomas my Upland Lott in the West Division in Hartford. I give unto my son Joseph Olmsted & his heirs all that Division of Upland, & the Swamp Land belonging to the same, upon which he hath built his house on the east side of the Great River. I give unto my son Joseph all my Meadow Land on the east side of the Great River, he paying 20 Shillings unto his sister Gates, and 40 Shillings per Annum to his Mother. I give my Farme of Land lying in the Woods, adjoining to Jeremy Addams's land in the Road to New London, unto my son Samuel and my son Thomas, to be equally divided between them. I give to my daughter Sarah Gates 20 Shillings. I give all my Right & Title to that Land purchased of Joshua, son of Uncas, by the town of Hartford, on the East side the Great River, to my son Samuel Butler and my daughter Rebeckah Bigelow and my daughter Mabel Butler, to be equally divided between them. I give to my son Samuel, my son Joseph and my son Thomas all my Right in a parcell of Land given by Joshua, son of Uncas, in his last Will, to be divided amongst several persons in Hartford. I give to my daughter Bigelow 40 Shillings. I make my son Thomas Olmsted my sole Executor, and appoint Mr. William Pitkin and Caleb Standly Overseers.

Witness: *Caleb Standly,*   Nicholas Olmsted.
        Timothy Cowles.

Court Record, Page 95—25 November, 1684: Will & Invt. Exhibited.

Osborn, David. Court Record, Page 14—24 April, 1679: An Inventory of what was the Estate of David Osborn was presented in Court, which did amount to £7-02-00; & according to the desire of the Widow (his relict) & Brother, The Court orders it to be delivered to sargt John Kilbourn to discharge his funeral Charges & other charges due from him, & the rest to goe onward for his dyat with him.

Page 249-50.

Osborn, John sen., Windsor. Died 27 October, 1686. Invt. £315-17-06. Taken 25 November, 1686, by Henry Wolcott, Jacob Drake, Daniel Hayden. Will dated 14 October, 1686.

I John Osborn sen. of Windsor do make this my last Will & Testament: I give to my wife Ann Osborn my personal and real Estate during her natural life, except that parcell of Land only that I now improve at Namerick which I give to my son John, Within a year and a day after my decease. I give to my son Samuel my now dwelling house and Lands adjoyning, after mine and my wive's decease, he paying to his brothers and sisters such legacies as hereinafter shall be expressed. I give to my son Nathaniel that part of my house lott west side of Connecticut River, east of the Town Street, bounded North by John Gaylord Jr., south by Robert Watson, East by Isaac Pinney's Meadow, after the decease of my wife and myself. I give to my gr. son Daniel Prior my Wood lott above Namerick, bounded south by Jacob Drake, and £10. My son Samuel to pay his four sisters, Mary, Hanna, Ester & Sarah, £10 to Each. Samuel to pay my gr. child Hana Shadduck £5 in case she abide with my wife until 18 years of age or till my wives decease. I constitute my wife Ann sole Executrix, and desire Jacob Drake, Daniel Hayden & Nathaniel Gaylord to be Overseers.   JOHN X OSBORN SEN.
Witness: *Jacob Drake, Mary Drake.*

Court Record, Page 128—3 March, 1686-7: Will Proven.

Page 173.

Owen, Daniel, Windsor. Died 1st March, 1682-3. Invt. £18-06-06. Taken by Jacob Drake, Josiah Elsworth.

On the 26th day of February, 1683, Mary (Bissell) Owen, the Widow & Relict of Daniel Owen, made oath to the Inventory.

Court Record, Page 85—6 March, 1683-4: Adms. to Cornet John Bissell to pay the debts, and the rest of the Estate to the Widow.

Page 240.

Parents, John, Haddam. Died 8 July, 1686. Invt. £84-10-01. Taken by George Gates and Simon Smith. Will dated 27 April, 1686.

I John Parents of Haddam do make this my last Will & Testament: It is my Will that my daughter Mary shall abide with Mr. Nathaniel Chapman until she comes of age or marry, & that my daughter Elizabeth shall be disposed of by my Trustees as they shall think fit or convenient for her comfort. My whole Estate to be divided to these two daughters. Should both die, to fall to the Trustees equally. I doe appoint William Ventrus, Joseph Arnol sen. and James Wells sen. to be the Trustees.

JOHN PARENTS.

Witness: *Thomas Brooks, Moses X Ventrus, Alexander Rollo.*

Court Record, Page 120—2nd September, 1680: Will Proven.

Page 80.

Payne, John, Middletown. Died in the year 1681. Invt. £82-03-00. Taken February, 1681, by Richard Hall, Samuel Hubbard, John Savage. The children: Jobe age 4 years, Patience 3, Abigail one year.

Court Record, Page 50—2 March, 1681-2: Adms. to the Widow. Richard Hall & Deac. Samuel Stocking to be Overseers.

Page 107.

Payne, Widow Hannah, Wethersfield. Died 25 September, 1682. Invt. £6-16-10. Taken 29 September, 1682, by John Kilbourn, Thomas Wright. The children: Hannah age 20 years, Thomas 9 years.

Court Record, Page 79—18 December, 1683: This Court grant to Hannah Payne to Possess her mother's Estate, she agreeing to pay the debts.

Page 258-9.

Persons, Joseph, Simsbury. Invt. £124-17-00. Taken 2 May, 1687, by Joshua Holcomb, John Higley, Samuel Willcox, Selectmen. He died 15 April, 1687, leaving one daughter, Mehetabell, about 4 years of age.

Court Record, Page 133—1st September, 1687: Adms. to the Relict. Joshua Holcomb to be Overseer.

Page 70—(Vol. V) 12 April, 1694: Order all the Land of sd. Persons to be and belong to his daughter Mehetabell.

Page 65.

Persons, Thomas, Windsor. Died 14 December, 1680. Invt. £20-00-00. Taken by Henry Wolcott & John Bissell.

Thomas Bissell appeared & testifyed upon oath in Court, September 18th, 1681: The Inventory within written was a presentment of the Estate of Thomas Persons deceased, & if more come to light he will count it to be added. The sd. Thomas Bissell is Admitted Adms. of the sd. Estate, to receive and pay all just Debts according to proportion, & the Estate with amount unto.

Attests: WILLIAM LEETE, *Governor.*

The following is Thomas Bissell's Account of Thomas Persons's Estate, 3 September, 1685: The Invt. £16-14-11, I returned indebted as followeth:

To Goodman Howard, To Thomas Eglestone, To John Williams,
To Nath: Bissell, To Joshua Welles, To Thomas Bissell,
To Goody Marshall, To William Smith, To Nath: Cook,
To Lt. ffyler, To Ephraim French, To Goodman Dible,
To Joseph Persons, To Thomas Burnham, To Capt. Allin.
To Lt. Lord, To Goodman Stevens,

Signed, *Thomas Bissell, senr.*

Inventory on File:

Phelps, Joseph, Simsbury. Invt. £84-09-06. Taken 5 March, 1683-4, by John Terry, Joshua Holcomb & John Case. The children: Joseph 17 years of age, Hannah 15, William 13 years, Sarah 11 years, and Timothy 4 years of age.

Court Record, Page 87—6 March, 1684: An Invt. of the Estate of Joseph Phelps was exhibited in Court, proven & ordered to be recorded. And this Court grants Adms. to the Widow, £6 of the Personal Estate & 1-3 of the Real Estate during her natural life, and to the Eldest son £22, and to the rest of the Children £11 apeice. And Timothy Phelps, Thomas Barber and John Terry are desired to be Overseers.

See File: The Petition of Mary Phelps, Relict to Joseph Phelps, of Symsbury, To the Honourable County Court now sitting at Hartford, Humbly showeth: That your poor Petitioner, when shee married to Joseph Phelps, was a widow, And was left by her former husband in somewhat a comfortable Condition. And after shee was married to this man, carried a considerable Estate with her to the value of £40 or £50, but since his decease is left in a very helpless Condition; having but £6 allowed In Moveable estate, with the third of the Land for life, which will not yield above 20 Shillings per Annum, which is but a very small matter to maintain me, having a young child left By Joseph Phelps, my deceased husband, to be brought up out of it. Having therefore heard of the Readyness of this Court to hear the cry & to help the fatherless and the Widow, made me Bold humbly to move your honours that some more of the Estate may be settled upon me for the Bringing up of the Child. However, if the matter be difficult, that at least you would be pleased to order that I might have that mare and Cow that is left and was part of my own Estate which I carried with me when I married my late husband. Hoping your honours will take the matter into serious Consideration, I shal not farther enlarge, but, begging Gods presence with you, rest your humble Petitioner.

Northapt, 28 August, 1684. MARY PHELPS.

Page 77.

Phelps, William sen., Windsor. Invt. £472-19-06. Taken the last day of February, 1681, by John Wolcott, Thomas Stoughton, John Bissell. Will nuncupative.

10 February, 1681: His Will was that his brother Timothy should have all his Estate to dispose of & to be sole Executor; that his brother Timothy should have his choice for his third out of all his Outlands. Witness: *John Loomis sen., Benedict Alvord.*

Court Record, Page 51—2 March, 1681-2: This Court having considered the Claims presented by the Widow Phelps & her Attorney, find that by Virtue of a Jointure agreement the whole personal Estate, together with his houseing and two thirds of all his outlands, are the proper Estate of the Widow, and advise that the Out Lands be indifferently divided, two-thirds to the Widow according to Joynture, and one third to Timothy Phelps, the debts to be paid by each in proportion.

Page 10-11.

Phillips, George, Windsor. Invt. £174-17-00. On the 12th day of July, 1678, The Townsmen of Windsor Met in the Room where George Phillips was found dead on the 9th of July before, to take the Inventory. Those were John Loomis, Jacob Drake, Thomas Bissell, Matthew Grant.

Now we copy it out of the Town booke to present it to the County Court which will be (held) on the 5 of September, the first Thursday in the moneth: To begin with, Houseing & Lands: By agreement between George Phillips & Israel Dewey, Israel hath Builded a New end to George's old house, & took down his old chimney of wood & clay & set up a new stone chimney, & we have not Taken to Inventory the new, but only the old house without the chimney, with the Barne & the houseland, which Matthew Grant measured & find it one acre three-quarters of an acre, & we value it at £55-00-00.

Court Record, Page 10—5 December, 1678: Mr. Gardner, in behalf of John Saunders (alias Phillips); Mr. Pitkin, in behalf of John Grummin of Fairfield. Appoint Mr. Gardner and John Grummin Adms. Also allot to Mr. Thomas Judd £4, Thomas Loomis £5, Thomas Porter £3, to Robert Porter £3. They appear in some way related to him (the sd. Decd). The remainder of Estate to be divided between John Saunders and John Grummin in right of his wife, who are the next of kin to the said Phillips, one his brother's son, the other his sister's daughter. John Saunders to have two thirds, and John Grummin one third.

Page 164-5-6.

Pinney, Humphrey, Windsor. Died 20 August, 1683. Invt. £780-05-00. Taken by Henry Wolcott, John Bissell & Daniel Hayden. Will dated 3 June, 1682.

The last Will & Testament of Humphrey Pinney of Windsor: Imprimis: I do hereby declare and my Will is, that my wife Mary Pinney is by me appointed Executrix. I give to my wife Mary Pinney my Houseing & Lands during her natural life, & after her decease my son Samuel to have 1-3 part of my Lott on the East side of the Great River. It is to be understood that that 2 acres that he hath now in possession is to help make up the third part of the Lott that Samuel is to have, & is to have on the South side of the Lott next to Samuel Gaylord. I give to my son John Pinney the other 2-3 of my Lott on the East side of the Great River. Also my Will is that my sons Samuel Pinney & John Pinney shall pay to my gr. child Sarah Pinney, daughter of Nathaniel Pinney, £5, that is to say, Samuel Pinney and John Pinney to pay 50 Shillings apeice. My Will is that my Houseing and all the rest of my Lands I give to my son Isaac. Also my Will is that my son Isaac Pinney shall pay to my gr. Child Nathaniel Pinney, son of Nathaniel Pinney Decd. £10. Also I give to my three daughters, Mary, Sarah & Abigail, 5 Shillings apeice. Also my Will is that what Estate I have in Old England, my wife shall have 1-2 of it and my son Isaac the other half of it. Also my Will is that all the rest of my Moveable Estate, without dore and within, I give to my well beloved wife to dispose of as she see cause. Also my Will is that my son John & my son Isaac shall not sell, alienate or mortgage all nor any of the abovesd. Lands until they are of the age of 50 years, except it be to their own brothers.

Witness: *Abraham Randall,*　　　　HUMPHREY X PINNEY.
　　　　Cornelius Hall.

Court Record, Page 81—10 December, 1683: Will proven.

Page 188-9-190.

Pinney, Mrs. Mary, Windsor. Died 18 August, 1684. Invt. £356-02-06. Taken 4 September, 1684, by Henry Wolcott, John Bissell, Timothy Thrall sen. Will dated 12 September, 1683.

In reference to that Estate which my husband hath left me, I Mary Pinney of Windsor do make my last Will & Testament: I give to my son Samuel, £5; to his daughter Mary, 40 Shillings. I give unto my son Isaac £5. I give to my daughter Mary Phelps, £5; to my daughter Sarah Phelps £20. I give £3 apiece to the Children of my daughter Abigail, to Mary, Abigail and John. The rest of my Estate, both in New England and Old England, I give to my son John, whom I appoint my sole Executor. If my daughter Sarah Phelps should die leaving no Issue, the legacy given to her shall be returned to my Executor.

Witness: *Benjamin Newbery, Daniel Clark sen.*   MARY PINNEY.

Court Record, Page 93—Will Exhibited 4 September 1681. Page 94—25 November, 1684: Approved.

Page 4.

Piper, Mr. Richard,   Haddam. Died 3 April, 1678. Invt. £204-03-00. Taken by James Bates, George Gates. Will dated March, 1677-8.

I Richard Piper of Haddam do make this my last Will & Testament: I give to Sarah Gates Jr., a one year old Heifer. I give to Susannah Ventrus my Bible. I give to John Ventrus my Tenant sawe, a shave & froe; To John Ackly a mare; To Samuel Ackly a mare & colt, and all my Rights of Land East side the Great River; to John Kinard my house lot that was Abraham Dible's, also land that lies by John Bates and Edward Parfell's, and all my Land on the West side of the River. And my will is that John Kinard Come and occupy the Land foure years, or else it shall return to the Executor. I give to Edward Parfell all my Land & other Estate not disposed of in this my Will, and appoint him my Executor.

Witness: *George Gates, Thomas Spencer.*   RICHARD PIPER.

The Estate Indebted to Tho. Dunk of Saybrook, John Chappell of Lyme, Mr. Hamlin of Middletown, John Baley, John Hollibut, to Good man Tappine, to John Blake, Goodman Rogers of New London, Goodman Harris of Middletown, Goodman Ventrus, Mr. Chapman, Jonathan Gilbert, Mr. Wilson, Ensign Spencer, John Wyott, John Allyn & Major Talcott. Total, £16-05-03.

Court Record, Page 5—10 April, 1678: Will Proven.

Page 11.

Porter, David,   of London. Died 4 June, 1678. Invt. £20-04-00. Taken by John Marsh & Caleb Standly.

Court Record, Page 10—5 December, 1678: Adms. to Mrs. Abigail Olcott to pay Just debts and hold the remainder until his Mother or brother shall order the disposal of it, they being next of kin. He came to his death by drowning it appears: As by a pint of Liquor to those who dived for him, By a quart to those who brought him home, By 2 quarts wine and a gallon of syder to the Jury of Inquest, By 8 gallons of wine &

3 quarts for his funerall, By a Barill of syder for ditto, By a Coffin 2 shillings, by a winding sheet 18 shillings; to pay Goodwin for a grave, 5 Shillings.

Page 242.

Powell, John, Windsor. Invt. of Aparell, £3-09-00. Taken 5 March, 1685-6, by Job Drake sen., John Moore.

Court Record, Page 118—4 March, 1685-6: Adms. to John Moore to pay the debts and return the Overplus if any to the County Treasury.

Will on file.

Pratt, John. In the name of God amen. I John pratt sen. of Hartford, being grown in years & at prsent labouring under some weakness of body, am willing to setle my Temporal affaires, that when I am gathered to my fathers peace may be continued in my family, doe therefore make & declare this to be my last will & Testament, hereby disannulling & makeing voyd all former wills & Testaments by me made, whither they were made by word or writing: And first, it is my will that all my just & honest debts be duly & Truely payd out of my Estate; & for the remaynder of my Estate I doe order & dispose of the same in Maner & forme followeing: That is to say, my houseing & Lands given to me by my Honoured Father to be and remayne according as he hath disposed of them by his Last Will & Testament, allways provided that the possessor of them make good the conditions expressed in his will, viz, that my dear & well beloved wife stand quietly seized & posest of the one Third part thereof to her own proper use & behoofe during the whole Terme of her naturall Life; & for her Third part it is my desire she may take the Middle Lott in the Long meadow which is Bounded North on Samuel Burr's Land & South on Land of Steven Kellsy's; but if the possesor of them agree not to that, then the Honord Court to assign & set out to her her Thirds according to Law & custom in that case. It is my will, also, that the possessor of the Land aforesayd doe, according to my sayd father's will, pay unto each of my daughters that shall be liveing at my decease the Sume of Twenty pownds apeice; & for the remaynder of my estate, it is my will that it be disposed, & I doe hereby dispose of it, as followeth: First, I doe leave my whole Estate with my wife to enable her to bring up my children in the feare of the Lord, so long as she bears my name; but in case she should by the providence of God change her name, then it is my will that she shall enjoy the Thirds of my Lands above mentioned & Twenty pounds out of my Estate, she leaving the remainder of my estate to be disposed to my children as Followeth: To my son John, beside what he Receives of my Estate by my Father's will, I give unto him Twenty shillings; to my sons Joseph & Jonathan I give & bequeath my now dwelling house & barne, wth the Nine acres of Land upon which it stand,

tween them, & the same to be their heirs & assigns for ever; & for the remaynder of my personall Estate, it is my will that it be equally divided be-
& Thirteen acres of land in the neck of Land, to be equally divided between my five daughters & two younger sonns, & delivered to them as
they come of age, if my wife can spare it, or els to be delivered to them
when my sayd wife shall change her name, or at her decease; & If any
of my children dye before they be of age, their portion shall be equally
divided amongst my surviving children; & I doe hereby constitute my
Loveing wife to be Executor to this my Last will & Testament; & that
she may (have) a refuge to repayre unto for advice & help in dispose of
the Estate or children, I doe desire my dear Brother Daniel prat & Capt.
John Allyn to be my overseers of my Estate. In Witness hereof, & for
confirmation of the premises, I have hereunto set my hand, April 9th,
1687. JOHN PRATT.

John Pratt senr. signed & declared The above Written to be his Last
Will & Testament, he being of good & sownd understanding when he did
the same. In presence of us:
(The names of Witnesses Evidently cut off.)

Court Record, Page 19—31 July, 1690: This Court appoint Deacon
Stephen Hosmore & Joseph Easton to lay out to the Widdow of John
Pratt deceased, now the wife of John Sadd, her thirds of the houseing &
Land according to the order of the general Court.

Page 51—(Vol. V) 15 February, 1692-3: Upon the motion of John
Pratt, he being of age to receive his Portion given him by his Father
John Pratt, & the desire of his mother hepsibah sad, executrix to the estate of sayd John Pratt, that the sayd Joseph prat might have his proportion of the houseing & Land set out to him that was given him by his
Father, This Court doe appoynt Sargt. John Marsh & Robt. Sandford to
make an equal division of the houseing & Lands given, between the sayd
Joseph pratt & his brother Jonathan pratt, according to the Tenoure of
their father's Last will & Testament, that so the sayd Joseph pratt may
have the possession of his part given unto him.

16 February, 1692-3: We whose names are underwritten, being desired by the Court to divide the Land of John pratt, deceased, betwixt
Joseph pratt & Jonathan pratt, which was given them by their father, we
have accordingly divided it as to quantity according to the best of our
skill.
John Marsh,
Robert Sandford.

The above is a True Coppy of the return, as is attested Feb. 23,
1692-3. *Pr. John Allyn.*

Page 218.

Randall, William, Hartford. Died December, 1684. Invt. £18-08-06.
Taken 24 February, 1684-5, by Philip Davis, John Merrells. Will dated
7 April, 1684.

The last Will & Testament of William Randall is as followeth : I give to my wive's eldest son, Thomas Grant, Two Axes & a stubbing How & a broad Howe & Two augers. I give to John Grant, my wive's youngest son, a peire of Betlrings, Two wedges & Two axes, a bridle & Saddle (a Musket & Sword If they can be redeemed from Joseph Andrews). The rest of my household Stuffe I give to my wive's youngest daughter, Rachel Grant, vizt, an Iron Pott, Trammells, Spit, Slice & Tongs, a Bed & Coverlett, a Table, Pewter platter & Bowell, a frying pan, & two Chests, with other Smale things, which I give to the sd. Rachel grant at her Mother's decease or upon her own marriage.

Witness: *Stephen Hosmer,*   WILLIAM X RANDALL.
      Noah Cooke.

Court Record, Page 104—24 March, 1684-5 : Will proved and approved by the Court & ordered to be recorded, & this Court grant Adms. on the Estate to Widow Randall with the Will annexed, & what Estate is not by Will disposed is to be to the sd. Widow Randall.

Will on File.

Randolph, Mary, Hartford. Will dated 2nd July, 1687. I Mary Randolph of Hartford do make this my last Will & Testament: I give unto my son John Grant my house, orchard & Land, provided he pay all my Just debts. I give to my daughter Sarah Wheeler a Tramell & Pr of Tongs, a fire slice, box Iron & heaters, 2 wedges, a lace Handkerchief and two earthern platters. I give to my daughter Rachell Grant all my beding with Blankets & Bedsteads & all belonging to them, & a brass Kettle, a brass Skylitt, & a great Iron pott, a pewter platter, cup and Bason, & 3 Earthern platters, & 2 Chests with locks to them, & a Table, platter, dishes, & all other things wch I have belonging to womans imployment, all my wearing apparell, woolen & linnen; & yt this is my Last Will concerning ye disposall of ye little Estate wch God hath given me, I signify by setting to my hand this second of July, 1687.

                             MARY X RANDOLPH. Ls.

Witness: *Stephen Hosmer, Priscilla X Gillett.*

Mary Randolph, her son John Grant being deceased, shee giveth her House, orchard & Land yt shee had given to him, unto her son and daughter Samll & Sarah Wheeler, this seventh of November, 1687, they paying her debts.

Witness: *Stephen Hosmer,*   Proven 8 March, 1687-8.
      Sarah X Waters.   *John Allyn, Judge.*

Page 57-8.

Reeve, Robert, Hartford. Invt. £692-09-06. Taken 11 February, 1680-1, by Nathaniel Standly, George Grave, John Skinner. The children: Sarah age 19 years, 25 December, 1682; Mary 17, 31 July, 1682; Elizabeth, 14 in December, 1682; Hannah, 12 in October, 1682; Nathaniel, 10 in October, 1682; Robert, 7 in April, 1682; Ann, 7 in April, 1682; Abraham, 5 in September, 1682; Mehetabell, 3 in March, 1682-3.   Will dated 23 December, 1680.

I Robert Reeve of Hartford do make this my last Will & Testament: I give to Elizabeth, my well beloved wife, £30 of my personal Estate, to be to her and to her Heirs forever; and a third of my real Estate during her life; & I haveing received but little of my Father Nott, who hath a good Estate, I hope he will remember her and my children and doe something for them.   It is my will the improvement of my Estate to be to my wife for the bringing up of my Children, till they come of age.   I appoynt my Wife Elizabeth to be my Executrix, & my friends Capt. John Allyn, Ensign Stanly, and my Brother John Skinner, to be Overseers.   Furthermore I give toward the building of Mr. Foster's house forty Shillings.

ROBERT REEVE.

Witness: *John Allyn, Nathaniel Stanly.*

Court Record, Page 37—3d March, 1680-1:   Will Proven.

Page 62—13 December, 1682:   This Court appoint Capt. Allyn, Nathaniel Stanly and John Skinner to Dist. the Estate according to the Will.

Page 66—1st March, 1683:   This Court consider the Overseers' action.   Though the Estate be distributed it shall not be alienated.

Page 82—10 January, 1683:   This Court appoint Richard Edwards & Texell Ensworth to Adms. on the Estate of Robert Reeve deceased. And all persons that have any of the sd. Estate in their possession or under their Improvement are hereby ordered to deliver the same wth the Improvement and Profits thereof unto the sd. Children or to those that have power to receive in their Right.   Whereas two of the children of the sd. Robert Reeve died before they came of age to possess their Estate, this Court orders their portions shall be divided amongst the Survivors according to their Father's Will.   And whereas two of the Overseers to the Will of the sd. Robert Reeve, who were also the Dist. of the sd. Estate, are dead, viz, Col. Allyn & John Skinner, This Court see Cause to appoint Sergt. Thomas Bunce and Sergt. John Marsh to Dist. the Estate.   The Estate that did belong to the two Children that are deceased, viz, Nathaniel and Ann, to the surviving children.   And the Court desire those persons to attend that work and make return thereof to this Court.

Page 109.

Reinolds, John, Wethersfield. Died 15 November, 1682. Invt. £120-19-06.   Taken 12 December, 1682, by John Kilbourn sen., Thomas Wright.   The children: Keziah, age 16 years 16th Jan. next; Anne 14, 24 Feb. next; Rebina 11, 11 Dec. next; John 9, 29 June next; Jonathan 6 years, 2 February next.

Court Record, Page 60—13 December, 1682: Adms. to the Widow, Mary Reinolds. *A Legal Distribution to be made.*

Page 42-3-4-5.

Richards, James, Hartford. Died. 11 June, 1680. Invt. £7931-01-00. Taken by Nathaniel Standly & James Steele. Will dated 9 June, 1680.

I, James Richards of Hartford do make this my last Will & Testament: I give to my wife Sarah Richards one third part of the proffits, Rents, and Revenues of all my Lands, both in Old England and New, during her natural life, and £300. I give to my Hond. Mother-in-law, Mrs. Ursula Gibbons, £30 per Annum during her life (this was in lieu of what Mr. William Gibbons had given her in a composition of accounts), and £200, to be at her own dispose. I give to my son Thomas Richards, his heirs and assigns, all my Land in Old England, & Buildings, the deed thereof in the hand of Mr. Ralph Ingram, London, linen draper. I give to my daughter Sarah, having paid her marriage portion, now give her £100 sterling. I give to my daughter Mary Richards all my farm at Nawbuck and £300. I give to my daughter Jerusha Richards all my Lands in Wethersfield and £300. I give to my daughter Elizabeth Richards all my Houseing and Lands in and about New London, also other Estate to the value of £450. I give to an unborn child of my wife, if it live, £700. To my Nephew Thomas Bradford I give 10 acres of Land at Rocky Hill. To my brother John Richards, Esq., my Biggest silver Tankard and my Watch. I give to the South Church in Hartford £10 in plate for the use of the Sacrament. I give to the lattin Schoole in Hartford £50. I give to the Rev. John Whiting, my Pastor, £15. I give to the poor in Hartford £20. I give to Mercy Bradford, my Kinswoman, £10. I appoint my wife Sarah Richards and my son Thomas Richards Joynt Executors; also appoint Capt. John Allyn & Brother John Richards, of Boston, Overseers.

JAMES RICHARDS.

Witness: *John Allyn, Samuel Hooker.*

Court Record, Page 28—2nd September, 1680: Will Proven.

Page 170-1 (Probate Side): An Account of the Disposition of the Personal Estate of the late James Richards of Hartford, Esq., to the Legatees hereunder named, 29 September, 1691:

	£ s d
Capt. Benjamin Davis & his late wife,	431-12-05
To Mr. Benjamin Alford & his wife Mary,	431-12-05
To Mr. Gurdon Saltonstall & Jerusha his wife,	431-12-05
To Mr. Thomas Richards,	181-12-05
To Mr. John Davie & Elizabeth his wife,	581-12-05
To Mrs. Ann Richard Decd.,	700-00-00
To Mrs. Ursula Gibbons Decd.,	200-00-00
To Mrs. Sarah Richards, Relict of Mr. James Richards,	100-00-00

This Accompt above stated agreed uppon between Mrs. Sarah Davie, Executrix to the Estate of Mr. James Richards of Hartford, in the Colony of Connecticut, and the Children & Legatees of the sd. James & Sarah. In Witness whereof they have hereunto set their Hands the 8th day of October, 1691 Anno *R:Rs & Reg: Gul: & Mar: Ang: &c. Tertio.*
Benja Davis, Thomas Richards, Benjamin Alford, Gurdon Saltonstall, John Davie, Sarah Davie.
A Copy of the Original on File, pr me, *Caleb Stanly, Test:*

Court Record, Page 90—3 March, 1706-7: An Account of the Division of the Personal Estate of James Richards, Esq., late of Hartford Decd., under the Hands of Sarah Richards, Relict of the sd. Decd, Thomas Richards, Benjamin Davis, Benjamin Alford, Gurdon Saltonstall & John Davie, bearing date of 8 October, 1691, was exhibited in this Court and ordered to be put on File.

Page 98.

Robinson, Samuel, Hartford. Died 30 August, 1682. Invt. £55-09-00. Taken by Caleb Standly, Nathaniel Goodwin. The children: Sarah, age 17 years 1st June, 1682; Samuel, 14—22 December, 1682; Mary, 10 —9 August, 1682; John, 6—7 June, 1682; Hannah, 3—3d July, 1682. Record given by their Mother.
Court Record, Page 58—7 September, 1682: Adms. to the Widow, Mary Robinson. Samuel Spencer & Nathaniel Goodwin to be Overseers.

Page 182-3.

Roote, John sen., Farmington. Invt. £819-07-00. Taken August, 1684, by Thomas Porter, John Heart, John Woodruff. Will dated 22 April, 1684.
I John Roote sen. of the town of Farmingtown do make this my last Will & Testament: I give to my wife Mary Roote a Constant Comfortable maintenance to be paid to her by my Executors during her Widowhood, and £20. But in Case she marry again, I give her £20 more, and then the Constant maintenance to cease. I doe solemnly charge my sons Joseph & Caleb, as long as the care of their Mother shall be incumbent upon them, to carry very dutifull and tenderly towards her & see from time to time that she want nothing for her comfortable support, and I hope that the Overseers of this my Will will have an eye to this care. To each of my sons which are already married, 20 shillings; & to my gr. Children 5 Shillings. I give to my daughter Mary, the wife of Isaac Brunson, £15. I do confirm to my son Steven Roote the 20 acres of Land, which I engaged upon his Marriage with his Wife that now is. I give to my son Joseph both my Looms with all the Tackling. To my sons Caleb & Joseph I give the

remainder of my Estate. My sons Caleb & Joseph to be Executors, and Mr. Hooker and Caleb Standly to be Overseers.

Witness: *Samuel Hooker & Thomas Hooker.*   JOHN X ROOTE SEN.

Court Record (not found) 4 September, 1684: Joseph Roote gave oath to the Inventory.   *Test: Samuel Talcott.*

Page 17-18.

Rowlandson, Rev. Joseph, late Pastor of the Church at Wethersfield. Died 24 November, 1678. Invt. at Lancaster, £129-00-00. Taken by Ralph Houghton, Roger Sumner. Invt. at Wethersfield, £290-16-00. Taken by Samuel Talcott, John Deming sen., John Deming Jr. Mrs. Mary Rowlandson, the Widow. Children: Joseph age 17 years, Mary age 13 years.

Court Record, Page 14—24 April, 1679: Adms. to the Widow Mary. The Rev. Joseph Haynes, Mr. Gershom Bulkeley & Mr. Samuel Talcott are desired to assist the Administratrix.

Page 97.

Sandford, Ann, Hartford. Will dated 12 July, 1682: I Ann Sandford of Hartford do make this my last Will & Testament: Whereas my husband's Estate was settled by the Honoured Court, 6 December, 1676, & several portions allotted to my Children after my decease, it is my Will what the Court allotted my son Zachary to be to him & the Kirbine that was his father's, and that my son Robert make up the rest of his portion to him. Also, that my son Robert pay my son Ezekiel his portion; also to my daughters that are married. And it is my Will that my son Robert do make their portions to them according to sd. Order of Court; & to my daughter Hannah I do Will that besides that what her Father did give her that she shall have a Bed & Boulster, & Pillow, & two pare of Sheets, & a pare of Blanketts, & a Curtain that belong to the Bedd, & a little Kettle, & the bigest pewter Platter, & a linen Wheele, & the Nobed And Iron, & a Cow, all these things so far as they will go to make good the proportion alloted to her by the honoured Court. I give to my daughter Abigail the Bed I lye on, with the Furniture, with other Household Goods & one Cow to make up her portion. And whereas my daughters Hannah & Abigail have been tender of me all along, and abode with me hitherto, I give to each of them a new Coverlid, & I give them my young mare. And whereas my son Robert hath also abode with me and carried on my occasions & provided for me this seven years past, I do leave the remainder of my Estate with him to enable him to pay my Just Debts & Legacies. I do also make him soale Executor. I do give my Prentice boy John Ar-

nold unto my son Robert, he to fulfill his Indenture at the Expiration of
time; and I do give him the sd. John a good new Bible.

Witness: *John Allyn,*   Ann X Sandford. Ls.
     Samuel Spencer.

Court Record, Page 58—7 September, 1682: Will proven.

Page 257-8.

Sandford, Nathaniel, Sometime of Hartford. Invt. £1100-16-00.
Taken 16 June, 1687, by Caleb Standly, Jacob White, Bevell Waters,
Thomas Marshall. As it was presented by Susannah Sandford, relict of
the sd. deceased, with her claim to the same by virtue of a deed of guift
from her deceased Husband, dated 22 February, 1677, under which respects only she presented the sayd Estate to the apprisers, as she declared
to us before we Inventoried the same.

Court Record, Page 133—1st September, 1687. Invt. Exhibited and
accepted. The following petition was also presented by Phineas Willson,
claiming certain of the above property in right of his wife (daughter of
Nathaniel Sandford), in opposition to the claim of the Widow Sandford
made by virtue of the above-mentioned "deed of gift:"

THE PETITION.

May it Please this Honoured Court: That I may not be esteemed as one that despiseth his Birthright or doth slight that which
God, the Law of Nature and the Law of nations hath given to me, I
crave the patience of this Honored Court to heare mee a word or two.

1st, In right of my Wife I am the only heire of my father Sanford,
both by the Law of God and the Law of man. Where there is noe Son,
but a daughter, the daughter is Heire (as in the case of Zelophehads
daughters) hath been determined by God himselfe—Numbers, 36: 2d.
And the practice of this honoured Court hath been answerable thereto.
And the Law of the Colony, wch is soe well known I need not recite it,
doth alsoe Order the same (fol. 36).

2ly, I being his heire in right of my wife, I ought to possess his Estate: the Conclusion necessarily follows the premises. And I doe not
doubt but that the justice of this Honoured Court will put me in possession of that Estate my father hath Left, which I onely Crave. And that
he hath Left an Estate, I neede not take paines to prove it. His Inventory
now Exhibited in Court will declare the same. A little to Cleare this, I
shall make it appear (1) that my father Sanford dyed possessed of an
Estate in Lands, & (2) that this Land in Right of my Wife belongs to me.

1st. That my father dyed possessed of Lands Is proved (1) by the
Inventory, (2nd) by the Records in the towne booke, and (3rd) by the
Deeds of Lands in my Fathers hand, which if the honoured Court doe

desire to see they may Comand. (2ly). That this Land belongs to mee in right of my Wife, What is first above written doth sufficiently prove, and therefore I need say noe more to itt. As for the Deeds my Mother presents to this honoured Court whereby Shee doth labour to disinherit my Wife, and mee in her right, I thanke her for her Love, and her Attorney for the Exercise of his Witts therein, although it be to little purpose, ffor I presume this Honoured Court is more just than to be taken with such Chaffy trash as The Attorney hath shakt out of his bag, thereby to be Led to take away our just Right. As to the Lands, what Lands are passed over to my mother by the Deed are there described, where they Lye and what they are, by their abutments and alsoe the number of Acres, precisely 26 Acres (be it more or Less), which is only that within those Abutments and noe more, as by the said Deed will appear.

2ly. My father had noe more Land to pass over to her or any other Person, and therefore hee was uncapable of Passing over any more to her at that time. And what itt hath pleased God, by his blessing upon my fathers Industry, to add to his Estate since, I humbly Conceive my Mother must produce another Deede of guift for, before shee Can Lay any Lawfull Claim to itt, ffor hee that pays mony before hee hath itt ought to be examined how hee Came by itt, and hee that gives Land before hee getts itt Cannott then perfect his deed of guift.

3ly. My father hee himselfe knew he had past over noe more to her, or else hee would not have made Sale of such a Considerable tract of Land to Mr Watson as hee hath done since this deed of guift.

4ly. Those expressions in the Deed that are soe Comprehensive, mentioning all his Estate or Substance, quick or dead, moveable or immoveable, in whatt place they shall or may be found, they are predicated upon his personall Estate onely, as may appear by the said Deed. Also, my mother well knows, if shee please to declare itt to this honoured Court, that my father in her hearing often said that hee would make my son Nathaniel his heire or Possessor of all his Lands, which hee would not have done had hee past away all his Lands (as my mother would have itt by this Deed) before. It is well knowne my father had a great Love for mother, as hee ought, and was willing to please her as far as hee might, but never had any purpose or thought expresst to disinherit his Daughter.

I shall say noe more. The Justice of my Case will Speak for itts selfe. I Leave it with this honoured Court to give a Righteous Judgment upon ye Case, and I shall Waite for itt. Onely I desire to remind the honoured Court of this, that my mother by the Deed is Cutt of from all Claims of thirds to my father's Estate by the Law title Dower, for shee is otherwise provided for by the Deed. I might insist that the Deed doth give my mother what household Goods and Stock was there in being when the Deede was made, and that what hath been raysed since belongs to mee; but I doe att Present Leave all to this honoured Court's Consideration, and doubt not but a Righteous and just Issue will be granted.

Your most humble servt,

PHINEAS WILLSON.

September 1st, 1687.

Page 134—14 October, 1687: Mrs. Susannah Buttolph presenting to This Court an agreement made between Mr. Wilson and herself for the distribution of the Estate of Nathaniel Sandford, which, bearing date 6 September, 1687, is Signed & sealed by the sayd Sandford and Wilson & acknowledged before John Allyn, Assistant, the same day, This Court approves of the sayd agreement to be the Distribution of the sayd Nathaniel Sandford's Estate.

(This agreement not found.)   John Allyn, Assistant.

Page 228-9.

Savage, John, Sergt., Middletown. Died 6 March, 1684-5. Invt. £480-15-06. Taken 12 May, 1685, by Giles Hamlin, Nathaniel White, William Warde. Legatees—John Savage, 33 years of age; William 17, Nathaniel 14, Elizabeth 30, Sarah 28, Mary 27, Abigail 19, Rachel 12, Hannah 9 years. Will dated 22 November, 1684.

I John Savage of Middletown, in the County of Hartford, do make this my last Will & Testament. I give to my wife Elizabeth Savage my Dwelling House & Homelott with all the Houses thereon, with all my Household Goods & all my Stock of Cattle & Swine of all sorts, during her natural life; also my Long Meadow Lott the use of it her lifetime, & all the Land I bought of Anthony Martin adjoining to my Homelott & to that which was Anthony Martin's Homelott & to that which I gave to my son John by a Deed of Guift, that is, for her lifetime; by this last I mean all that was my own Swamp as well as that I bought, & all the Meadow which was William Blumfield's saving a small peice which I formerly gave to my son John, & all my Wongunck Meadow on the South side of the little Brook, all those during her natural life, & one peice of Upland adjoining to Isaac Willcox's Land, being about 7 acres, to have it for her Use till my son William come of age to inherit it; provided, & it is herein intended, that in Case my wife should see Cause to change her Condition by marriage, that then neither my Stock of Cattle or Household Goods shall be disposed of to any but my Children. She hath the larger part of the Estate in her hands. My wife Elizabeth to be Executrix and request my son John to be of assistance to her in it. I request my friends and brethren Nathaniel White and Samuel Hall sen. to be Overseers.

Witness: *Nathaniel White,*   JOHN SAVIDGE.
         Samuel Hall.

Court Record, Page 112—3 September, 1685: Will proven.

Page 21.

Scott, John. Invt. £29-02-01. Taken 11 August, 1679, by Samuel Steele, John Wolcott.

Court Record, Page 15—4 September, 1679: Adms. to Edward Scott, Lt. Samuel Steele to assist.

Page 9-10.

Smith, Elizabeth, Farmington. Invt. £143-04-03. Taken 4 December, 1678, by Thomas Porter sen., John Thompson. The age of the orphans as followeth: Jonathan, age 23 years, Jobana 21, Joseph 14, Benjamin 11, William 8, Samuel 5, Susannah 19, Elizabeth & Mehetabell, 16 years of age in 1669. Will dated 15 November, 1676.

I Elizabeth Smith of Farmington do dispose of that little Estate that God hath graciously given me. My Will is that my son Jonathan shall have the Use & Benefit of my House & Homestead, Barn, Orchard, Lott & those things that are thereon, not accounted as Moveables, until my youngest son Samuel Smith is of the age of 21 years, & then Samuel to have ½ of the whole, that is, of the House & Homestead above specified; & that the other half shall be my son Jonathan's and my son William's, equally proportioned. I give to my son Jonathan my Right of Land in the Great Swamp toward Middletown. I give to his son Samuel, my gr. Child, a little peice of Land in the Great Meadow. I give to my son Joseph my Horse & one of my Working Oxen. To my son Benjamin I give a 4-acre Lott given me by the Town, and the other of my working oxen. I give to my son William Smith a sword that was his Father's. I give to Samuel that Gunn which I have, & to Jonathan that Pike that was his Father's. To my daughter Mehetabell I give all my Household Stuffe, Bedding & Apparrel, as also that which was her sister Elizabeth's, of all sorts, as also my Flax & half a peice of fine Cloth; & the rest of that Cloth I give enough of it to my daughter Susannah to make an Apron, and the remainder shall be divided for the Use of my 4 younger sons. To my daughter-in-law Rachel Smith I give a Child's Blankett which she hath already in possession. As for my daughter Susannah, although I can freely pass by her offenses done to myself, yet I cannot but testify against her in some of her unworthy carriages towards me for some while back; but still I have a motherly tender affection towards her and freely give her that Cow commonly called White Face. As for what is left, my Will is that out of it my Just & Lawfull Debts be duly paid and discharged, and after my daughter Mehetabell hath her Legacy out (left her by her Father's Will) it shall be divided amongst all my Children equally. My desire is that my youngest son Samuel should be with his Brother Jonathan until he be 21 years of age, his brother carrying well to him and teaching him to read & write and to learn him some trade, except there appear just Grounds to the Contrary. As for my sons Benjamin & William, I would have them also settled and placed under good Government to learn some useful trades. I desire my son Jonathan should be Adms, also that Lt. Samuel Steele & John Judd be Overseers.

Witness: *John Thompson,* ELIZABETH X SMITH.
   John North sen.

In a Codicil she mentions the Decease of William, & gives his Legacy to her daughter Mehetabel, & the Sword to her son Samuel.
Witness: *Jonathan Smith,*   ELIZABETH X SMITH.
            Rebecca Bird.

Court Record, Page 9—5 December, 1678: Will & Invt. Exhibited and approved. This Court grants & Orders that the Estate of Elizabeth and William Smith shall be divided in equal proportions among the surviving brothers and sisters.

Page 211.

Smith, John, Wethersfield. Died 17 December, 1683. Invt. £18-08-00. Taken by Samuel Talcott & John Deming Jr.
Court Record, Page 92—3 September, 1684: Adms. granted to Mary Smith, the Relict. of sd. Decd.

Page 260.

Smith, Joseph, Wethersfield. Invt. £200-10-09. Taken 13 June, 1687, by John Buttolph & John Robbins. The surviving heirs are Mary Smith, widow, and one son ¾ of a year old, name Joseph.
Court Record, Page 100—5 March 1695-6. This Court grants Adms. on the Estate of Joseph Smith, son of Joseph Smith of Rocky Hill, unto Jonathan Smith his Uncle, who is to bring in an Invt. of the Estate the 2nd Monday in April next.
Page 33—(Vol. IX) 4 June, 1717: Upon the Motion of Samuel Smith that Adms. should be granted on the Estate of Joseph Smith, late of Wethersfield, decd, this Court order that those concerned in sd. Estate be notifyd to appear at this Court on the 1st Tuesday of July next, that they may, if they see meet, object why Letters of Adms. should not be granted on sd. Estate. The persons concerned are Samuel Smith and Lydia Cole of Wethersfield.
Page 42—3 September, 1717: Persuant to a Motion, May 8th last, by Samuel Smith, that Adms. should be granted on the Estate of Joseph Smith, sometime of Wethersfield, Decd, this Court are of the opinion that Adms. should be granted. Therefore order the Clerk to notify those concerned on sd. Estate (Jonathan Smith, Daniel Smith and Lydia Cole of Wethersfield) to appear before this Court on the 1st Tuesday of October next, one or more of them, as the Court shall think meet, to take Letters of Adms. on sd. Estate.

Smith, Richard. Court Record, Page 101—6 March, 1684-5: Whereas, Richard Smith of Hartford hath presented to this Court a paper under his hand wherein he hath declared him selfe Non solvent, & Tenders that

he will deliver up his Estate to be disposed of in the best way to satisfy
his Creditors in proportion as the Estate will hold, the sayd Smith takeing his oath that he is Non solvent, & delivering his Estate up to Lieutenant Caleb Stanly & George Grave (the whole of his Estate upon his
oath), who are by this Court appoynted to receive it, & proclamation is to
be made in Court that all the Creditors of Richard Smith shall make up
their accounts & Lay their claims to the Estate sometime between this &
the 20th of May next, & report the first Wednesday in June next. The sayd
Stanly & Grave are to make distribution of the Estate amongst the Creditors by proportion, according as the Estate will hold; & those actions now
entered in Court against sayd Richard Smith are to fall & be no farther
prosecuted, & Court charges to be abated; & the sayd Lt. Stanly & Marshall Grave are to return an account of their acting so as it may (be) kept
upon files. Proclamation was accordingly made in Court.

Page 12—(Vol. V) 6 March, 1689-90: Proclamation was made in
the Court that all Creditors to the Estate of Richard Smith should make
up their Accounts with Mr. Joseph Whiting betwixt this and September
next, for then the Court purposeth to make a Dist. of his Estate to the
Creditors. And the Court grants Adms. upon the Estate to sd. Whiting,
who is to take the best Care he can to preserve the Estate for the Creditors, who is to be accountable for what he receives & no farther, and to be
satisfied for his pains about it.

Page 225.

Spencer, Jarrad, Ensign, Haddam. Invt. £124-12-00 of Estate
not disposed of by Will. Taken 29 June, 1685, by Joseph Arnot & Alexander Rollo. Will dated 17 September, 1683.

The last Will of Ensign Jarrad Spencer of Haddam: I give unto my
son William the Land which I bought of Steven Luxford's Estate. How
I come by it the Court Record will show. I give unto my son William
1-3 part of 48 acres lying by that wch was commonly called Welles his
Brook. I give to my son Nathaniel my now Dwelling house wth the Lott
that was the Houselott, with an Addition lying by the side of it, granted
by the Committe. I give unto my daughter Rebeckah that Houselott I
bought of Thomas Smith. Likewise I give unto my daughter Rebeckah
1-3 part of the Lott by Welles his Brook. I give unto my son Thomas 40
acres on Matchamodus Side. I give unto my son Thomas his son, Jarrad
Spencer by name, my Rapier. I give unto my son Timothy Spencer the
remainder of that 6 score acre lott whereof his 2 brothers had their shares.
The other 6 score thereof I dispose of as followeth: To Grace Spencer,
the daughter of my son John Spencer, 40 acres; to Alice Brooks, the
daughter of my daughter Brooks, 40 acres; to Grace Spencer, the daughter of my son Samuel Spencer, I give the other 40 acres. I give unto Jarred Cone, the son of my daughter Cone, my Carbine. A pewter Flagon
and Urim Bason I give to the Church at Haddam, if there be one within

five years. It is my Will that my son John Spencer his Children and my son-in-law Daniel Cone his Children have an equal proportion of my Estate with my other Children. It is my Will that however my Estate falls out for portions to my Children, that my daughter Ruth Clarke's portion shall be £15, which was my Covenant with her father at her marriage, which £15 she hath received some part thereof, as my Books will testify; & to son Joseph Clarke I give him 40 acres of land at Matchemodus. It is the humble request of Jarrad Spencer that the honoured Major John Talcott and Capt. John Allyn would be pleased to oversee this his Will. I appoint my two sons Daniel Brainard and William Spencer Adms. to the Estate.

Witness: *John James,*   JARRAD SPENCER.
Joseph Arnot.

Court Record, Page 111—3 September, 1685: Adms. to Daniel Braynard and William Spencer, with the Will annexed.

Page 99-100.

Spencer, John, Haddam. Died 3 August, 1682. Invt. £267-00-06. Taken 7 August, 1682, by George Gates, Joseph Arnold. The children: Rebeckah 16 years of age, Jarrard 14 years, Benjamin 11 years, Lydia 10 years, and Grace 6 years. Will nuncupative. He declared it as his Will that his Eldest son Jerrard Spencer and his Eldest daughter Rebeckah should be at the disposal of his Brother-in-law Daniel Braynard and his own sister Hannah the Wife of Daniel Braynard. That his son Benjamin should be with Nicholas Noyse of Haddam till 21 years of age. That his Father Howard should have his daughter Lydia. That his brother-in-law John Kennoe & his Sister Rebeckah Kennoe should have his youngest daughter Grace Spencer. He declared his Will that Thomas Brooks, whom his sister Brooks had committed to his Care when at the age of 4 years and whom he had brought up to the age of 18 years, should show all respect to his Mother, now the wife of Thomas Shaylor; but the two years time which he was to have lived with his Uncle he now gave to himself; also gave him 20 shillings, and desired his Overseers to take Care of him because he was too young to be wholly set free. He gave £30 to each of his sons and £20 to each of his daughters, left money to buy books for them, and desired they all should be well clothed with linen and Woolen. He gave to Good wife Smith, for Kindness and attendance, 20 shillings; also to his sister Shaylor. He desired Nicholas Noyes, George Gates, Daniel Braynard, Daniel Cone & Thomas Spencer might be Overseers.

Witness: *George Gates, Thomas Spencer.*

Court Record, Page 58—7 September, 1682: Adms., With Will annexed, to Daniel Braynard, Thomas Spencer.

Page 51—(Vol. V) 8 February, 1693: Grace Spencer, daughter of John Spencer, late of Haddam decd., chose her Uncle Nathaniel Spencer to be her Guardian.

Page 262.

Spencer, Sergt. Thomas, Hartford. Died 11 September, 1687. Invt. £139-19-00. Taken by Caleb Standly and Aaron Cooke. Will dated 9 September, 1686.

I Sergt. Thomas Spencer of Hartford, being very aged, do declare this my last Will & Testament: I give to my Eldest son Obadiah Spencer my Houseing and Lands in Hartford, all my Lands east side and west side of the Connecticut River within the bounds of the Town of Hartford, to be to him and to his Heirs forever, immediately after my decease, he paying such legacies as I shall appoint by this Will. I give to my son Thomas £15, of which he hath £5, and Obadiah shall pay him £10 more. I give to my son Samuel (he having received a good portion from his Uncle) my wearing apparrell. I give to my son Jarred my shop and Tools & £12, all of which are in his hands. The rest of my moveable Estate I give to my five daughters, Sarah, Elizabeth, Hanna, Mary and Martha, to be equally divided to them by their brother Jarrad. I do make my son Obadiah Spencer my Executor. I desire Capt. Allyn, Lieut. Caleb Standly and my Cousin Samuel Spencer to be Overseers.

Witness: *John Allyn, Hanna Allyn.*   Thomas X Spencer.

Court Record, Page 134—26 October, 1687: Will aproved.

Page 202.

Stedman, Samuel. Invt. £04-00-00. Taken 23 November, 1684. A gunn & sword at Samuel Butlers, a Chest and things in it, a box of old lasts, pincers, etc., his shop to be taken off the Land.

Court Record, Page 95—25 November, 1684: Adms. to Sargt. John Stedman.

Page 231-2-3-4.

Steele, Lt. Samuel, sometime of Farmington, now of Wethersfield. Invt. £725-07-10. Taken 14 August, 1685, by Samuel Talcott, Robert Welles, John Robbins. Invt. in Farmington, £457-05-00. Taken by John Judd & John Woodruffe. Total, £1182-12-10. Will dated 10 June, 1685.

I Samuel Steele of Wethersfield, being very aged, do make this my last Will & Testament: I give to my wife, if she survive me, £80, to be to her proper Estate, also £12 per annum and her firewood brought home ready cut & fit for use, to be paid her during her natural life. If she should marry again, the £80 being paid and four of the £12 per annum being paid,

the rest of the £12, with firewood, etc., shall cease. I give to my daughter Hannah Steele £40. I give to my two sons James and Ebenezer my Houseing and Lands in Wethersfield and Farmington, to one the whole in Wethersfield, the other the whole in Farmington, James takeing his choice; also to these two my share in the saw Mill, in equal proportion. I give to my four daughters £20 to each. I appoint my wife and two sons James and Ebenezer Executors, and request my Kinsman Mr. John Wadsworth of Farmington & Capt. Samuel Talcott of Wethersfield to be Overseers.   SAMUEL STEELE.
Witness: *John Wadsworth, Samuel Hooker, Sen.*

5 July, 1685: A codicil provides for the building of a new barn at Farmington, at the expense of the two Brothers, before Distribution of the Estate.   SAMUEL STEELE.
Attested by *Mr. John Wadsworth* & *Mrs. Mary Steele:* That Lt. Samuel Steele left it within the discretion of the Overseers to alter the length of the Barn.—8 September, 1685.
Witness: *Eleazer Kimberly, John Welles.*
Court Record, Page 83—6 March, 1684: Mary Steele and Sarah Standly, daughters of James Boozey, late of Wethersfield, only and Proper Heirs (to certain Lands) given to them by their Father's will, unlawfully detained by Emanuel Buck, a suit in Court to recover. [*See James Boosey, on pages 48 and 98 of this volume.*]
Court Record, Page 112—3 September, 1685: Will Proven. John Wadsworth & Samuel Talcott appointed to Dist. the Estate, *and they decide that The Barn shall be forty-two feet in length and no more.*

Page 180.

Stiles, John, Windsor. Died 14 December, 1683. Invt. £96-15-00. Taken 10 March, 1683-4, by John Bissell, Daniel Hayden. Rachel Stiles, mother to John, made Oath to the Invt.
Court Record, Page 86—6 March, 1683-4: Dist: To the Eldest son a double portion (John Stiles, son of John Stiles, appeared in Court and chose Daniel Heyden to be his Guardian); To Thomas, Sarah, & Hannah, Equal portions. Ephraim being in his father's life time disposed to John Steward, he having engaged to give him a portion at his decease, we grant him only £5 out of his Father's Estate. Adms. to Henry Stiles, Cornet Bissell, Daniel Heyden.

Page 136.

Stocking, George. He died 25 May, 1683. Invt. £257-09-00. Taken by Nath. Willett, Tho. Bunce, John Easton. Invt. in Middletown taken 8 June, 1683, by Nath: White & John Warner.

Court Record, Page 73—6 September, 1683: An Inventory of the Estate of George Stocking was exhibited in Court. Adms. to Samuel Stocking.

Page 78—18 December, 1683: This Court haveing viewed that presented as the Last Will & Testament of George Stocking in the circumstances of it, together with what George Stocking hath declared to George Stocking & Capt. Allyn, & his declaration of his will in part contradicting, doe Judge that the will presented is of no value, & therefore the Court distribute the Estate as followeth: To Samuel Stocking, £100; to Hannah Benton's children, £41; to the wife of John Richards, £41; to the wife of Samuel Olcott, £41; & to John Stocking, who hath lived with George Stocking, his grandfather, for some years, the remainder of the Estate, being £34, we distributed to John Stocking; and desire & appoint Marshall George Grave & Thomas Bunce to make this Distribution. (See Will, Vol. III.)

Page 168-9.

Stocking, Deacon Samuel sen., Middletown. Died 30 December, 1683. Invt. £648-08-08. Taken by Giles Hamlin, William Ward. The children: Samuel 27 years of age, John 23, George 19, Ebenezer 17, Steven 10, Daniel 6 years old, Bethia Stow 25, Lydia Stocking 21 years. Will dated 13 November, 1683.

I Samuel Stocking of Middletown do leave this my last Will & Testament: I give unto my loveing wife Bethia Stocking my whole Homestead lying on the both sides of the Highway with all ye Buildings thereon thereunto belonging, with my whole Lott in the Long Meadow, with my Lott at Pistol Poynt, & half of my Meadow lying on the other side of the Brook, that part of it that lyeth next to the Great River, with all my Meadow Lands at Wongunk, together with all my Stock & Moveables; these I give my wife during her Widowhood, and upon marrying again I Will to her £4 yearly to be raised out of that Estate which I have agreed to my son Daniel Stocking. I give to my son Samuel Stocking my whole Allottment upon the Hill between the Land of Lt. White and Israel Willcox, only excepting 6 acres adjoining to the Land of Lt. White, which I give to my daughter Bethia. Moreover I give to my son Samuel the remaining half of the Meadow over the Brook, with 10 acres of the Swamp adjoining to it. I give him my whole Allottment at the Cold Spring on the west side of the Way to Hartford. I give to him, sd. son Samuel, the whole of my Lott at Pipe Stave Swamp, with the half of my Allottment next unto Wethersfield Bounds, with the halfe of my Lott at Pistol Poynt, upon his Mother's decease. I give unto my son John Stocking the whole of the Land and Buildings at my Father Stocking's decease bequeathed me by his last Will, within the Bounds of Hartford. I give unto my daughter Lydia my Lott lying next unto Thomas Ranny's, and butting upon ye Commons West and Dead Swamp East, with a good Milk Cow, to be delivered her within 12 months after my decease. I give to my sons

George & Ebenezer all my Lands on the East side of the Great River, to be equally divided between them, excepting the ½ of my Great Lott next unto Haddam Bounds. I give to my son Steven my whole Lott upon the Hill, bounded upon ye Lands of Thomas Rannie North, the Commons East, West & South, with my whole Allottment in Boggy Meadow, with all my Meadow & Upland in the farther Neck, giving the Improvement of the Boggy Meadow unto my son Samuel till the abovesd. child is of age to inherit. I give to my son Samuell (*Daniel, see original paper on File*) my whole Homestead lying on both sides of the Highway, with my Lott in the Long Meadow, with half my Lott at Pistoll poynt, with ½ of my Lott lying on the West side of the way as you goe to Hartford, adjoining to the Land of Anthony Martin on the North, the Land of Thomas Ranny South, the Highway & Commons West. This I say I give to my son Daniel, that is to say, the West end of it, the other halfe of sd. Lott to be to my son Samuel. These aforementioned parcells of Land as specified I give to him my sd. son Daniel & his heirs forever, with the other halfe of my Lott next Weathersfield Bounds. I give to our Pastor, Rev. Nathaniel Collins, £3, my son Samuel to be sole Executor. After the decease or marriage of my wife, my Estate to be equally divided amongst my children. I desire Mr. Nath. White & John Savage sen. to be Overseers.

Witness: *Nath: White,*   SAMUEL STOCKING SEN.
      John Savage sen.

A Codicil, without Change of the above, signed 25 December, 1683.

Court Record, Page 85—6 March, 1684: Will proven.

Page 161.

Stone, Samuel, Hartford. Died 9 October, 1683. Invt. £29-08-00. Taken 2 November, 1683, by Nathaniel Willett, Nathaniel Goodwin, Bevil X Waters.

Court Record, Page 82—10 January, 1683: Adms. to Thomas Butler.

Page 212-13.

Stoughton, Thomas, Windsor. [*Son of Thomas Stoughton senior (Thomas the Elder, or Ancient Stoughton). See page 1, also Peter Baret's Letter on page 44, and also page 64, of this volume.*] Died 15 September, 1684. Invt. £941-08-00. Taken by Timothy Thrall, Daniel Hayden, Abraham Phelps.

Court Record, Page 103—24 March, 1684-5: Adms. to the Widow, Mrs. Mary Stoughton, and appoint Return Strong and Timothy Thrall, with advice of Capt. Newbery, to Distribute the Estate: To the Widow £100, to her and her heirs forever; To John Stoughton £199, to Thomas £136, to Samuel £126, to Israel £126, to Elizabeth £116, to Rebeckah £116. Mr. Wadsworth, Abraham Phelps and John Loomis to be Overseers.

Page 174-5.

Stow, Thomas sen., Middletown. Invt. £42-05-06. Taken 23 February 1683-4, by Giles Hamlin, John Hall sen., John Warner. Legatees: John Stow sen., Nathaniel Stow, Thomas Stow, Samuel Biddoll. Will dated 26 January, 1680-1.

The last Will & Testament of Thomas Stow sen., Middletown: Imprimis. I give to my son John Stow one parcell of Land in Middletown on the West side of the West River, both that within and that without the fence, which is mine. More over I give to my sayd son my great Kettle after my decease. More over I give him the one halfe of my great Lott at the Streits Hill. I give to my son Nathaniel, besides my house, Home Lott in the Boggy meadow Quarter which I made sure to him by a former Contract, that is, to him & to my sonn Thomas & Samuel Biddoll, the other halfe of my great Lott at the Streight Hills, & my halfe mile Lott on the east side of the great river, to be divided equally amongst them. Moreover I give to my son Nathaniel all my household Goods after my decease, peaceably to enjoy, with all my part in the Cattell & Swine; & that (this) is my will & full Intent, I witness by setting to my hand.

THOMAS STOWE. SEN.

Test: *John Hall,*
    Josias X Adkins.
Proven 6th March, 1683-4.

Page 181.

Talcott, John, Hartford. Invt. £453-02-00. Taken 10 March, 1683, by Thomas Olcott, Philip Lewis. The Inventory is as followeth:

	£	s	d
Mr. John Talcott's Wearing Apparrel,		13-05-00	
In Books,		1-05-00	
In Amunition £15-02-00, In two Cowes £08-00-00,		23-02-00.	
By Lands adjacent to the Homelott,		80-00-00	
By his Lott about the Middle of the Long Meadow, formerly Steele's, 22 acres,		200-00-00	
By the Houseing and Homelott,		150-00-00	
Total:		453-02-00	

Court Record, Page 95—25 December, 1684: This Court grants Adms. on the Estate of Mr. John Talcott to Major John Talcott, and order to Dist. his Estate as followeth: To Joseph Talcott his houseing and Lands, he being the next Heir to Mr. John Talcott, and it also being correspondent to the Guift of Mr. John Talcott sen. Decd. who gave it (to) his gr. child Mr. John Talcott Decd; & that the remainder of his Estate be equally divided amongst the rest of the Children of Major John Talcott.

Page 27-8.

Thrall, William, Windsor. Died 3 August, 1679. Invt. £158-09-06. Taken by Christopher Sanders, Jacob Drake. Will dated 11 December, 1678.

I William Thrall of Windsor do give and bequeath my Outward Estate, my House Barn & all my Lands of one sort or other, Upland or Meadow, to my son Timothy Thrall, to be his & his heirs forever, yt with this Proviso, that upon his possession thereof he stand bound to discharge the Legacies as followeth: First: that he pay to Daughter Phillip(i) Hosford the sum of £45, to be paid within 3 years after my decease. Second: that he pay to Samuel Cross, & also to her that was Mary Cross, both which live with me, 5 Shillings apeice. Third: That he pay to Mr. Benjamin Woodbridge 20 Shillings. It is my Will & I do give to my gr. child Sarah Hosford the little House I have begun to build on John Hosford's Land. For my Household Goods, what is in the possession of my son Timothy Thrall I do bestow on him, & what part of my Household Goods is in the possession of John Shepherd I do give to my daughter Phillipi Thrall. A Cow of mine in John Hosford's Hands I do give to Daughter Phillip(i) Hosford, & the Cattle or Stock in my son Timothy Thrall's Hands I give to him. I ordain my son Timothy Thrall Executor. Also I desire Mr. Benjamin Woodbridge and Abraham Phelps to be my Overseers.

Witness: *Job Drake,* WILLIAM X THRALL.
Mary Woodbridge.

Court Record, Page 18—4 December, 1679: Will & Invt. proven.

Page 234.

Tomlinson, Thomas. Died 27 March, 1685. Invt. £68-09-07. Taken 22 April, 1685, by John Gilbert, Philip Davis. The children of Thomas and Elizabeth Tomlinson: Sara Bishop age 20 years, Mary Tomlinson 18, Ruth 15, Phebe 12, Elizabeth 10, Hannah 6, Thankful 1 year old.

Court Record, Page 112—3 September, 1685: Adms. to the Widow (Elizabeth), she to bring up the Children. No Distribution.

Page 69.

Treat, Henry. Invt. £126-05-07. Taken 5 September, 1681, by William Burnham, Philip Davis, Thomas Kilbourn.

Court Record, Page 45—1 September, 1681: Adms. to Ensign Standly, Philip Davis and William Burnham, & to dispose of the children to best Advantage.

Dist. on File: 8 April, 1696: Estate of Henry Treat. Philip Davis & William Burnham, Adms. To his son and to his daughter, by William Burnham, Benjamin Churchill.

Note: *There was among the Debts paid: To William Warren and his wife, for Keeping the Children of Nathaniel Crow; to Widow Mary Smith, for keeping the Children of John Smith and Widow Smith.*

In Court, 5 June, 1710, a part of the Estate not yet distributed.

On 4 April, 1709—(*Another paper*)—Distributed to Matthias Treat from the Estate of his Father Henry Treat, and to Sarah Treat, the wife of David Forbes.

Page 13—(Vol. VIII) 5 June, 1710: William Burnham, Adms. on the Estate of Henry Treat, exhibited an Account:

	£ s d
Paid in Debts and Charges,	55-15-01
Delivered to Matthias Treat,	15-06-09
To Sarah Forbes, wife of David Forbes,	8-01-04
Total,	79-03-02
Total Inventory,	86-05-07
There remains to be dist.,	7-02-05
To Matthias Treat,	5-00-03
To Sarah Forbes,	2-02-02

The Court grants unto William Burnham, Adms., a *Quietus Est.*

Page 161-2.

Vore, Richard, Windsor. Invt. £81-15-00. Taken 11 December, 1683, by John Loomis sen. and John Moore. Will dated 1st July, 1683.

The last Will of Richard Vore of Windsor: I make my wife Ann Vore to be sole Executrix of my Estate, & my Will is that during her natural life she shall possess & injoy my Houseing & Lands lying & Cituate in the Township of Windsor, as also my Goods, Household Goods & other Estate, more particularly my House & Homelott on the north side of the Rivulett, wth Orchard, Fences, Yards, or what else belongs thereto, as also my Land lying in a place called the Neck, counted 3 acres. Secondly: My Will is that after the Death of my wife (if she shall survive me) my daughter Abigail, now wife of Timothy Buckland, if she be living, shall enjoy my House & Homelott, yt provided my Will is that neither my daughter nor her husband shall have any power to alienate or dispose of the same or any part thereof, but shall keep & preserve Intire; yet they may enjoy the Benefit & Profit thereof so long as my daughter shall live, & after her decease it shall belong to her Children, if any living; if not, the sd. Homested shall belong to my other daughters or their Children. Thirdly: I give to my daughter Cooke, the wife of Nathaniel Cooke, 5 Shillings in addition to what I have already given her, also the Land lying in the Neck, after the death of my wife. Fourth: I give Thomas Alvard, son to my daughter Mary Alvard deceased, 5 Shillings, Fifthly: I give to the eldest child of my daughter Sarah Persons, Decd, who was wife to

Benjamin Persons of Springfield, 5 Shillings. Sixthly: My Will is that my Household Goods & Chattells of all sorts not disposed of which I have by Will left to my wife for her Use, she hath hereby full power to dispose of them, as she shall see Cause, amongst my Children. I request Capt. Benjamin Newbery, John Moore & John Loomis sen. to be Overseers.

Witness: *Samuel Mather,*   RICHARD VORE.
        John Loomis sen.

Court Record, Page 81—10 December, 1683: Will proven.

Page 77.

Wadsworth, Elizabeth. Invt. £51-10-06. Taken by Nathaniel Stanly, William Burnham.

On the 6th day of March, 1681-2: This Writeing witnesseth an Agreement made with Samuel Wadsworth & Joseph Wadsworth & Thomas Wadsworth & Elizabeth Terry & Jonathan Ashley & Rebeckah Wadsworth concerning an Estate of our Mother, decd, as followeth:

	£ s d		£ s d
Samuel must have	7-10-00	Elizabeth Terry is to have	3-15-00
& for the Funeral	5-00-00	Jonathan Ashley is to have	4-10-00
Joseph is to have	3-15-00	Rebeckah is to have	20-00-00
Thomas is to have	3-15-00	John Wadsworth is to have	3-00-00

As Witness our Hands:

Samuel Wadsworth, Joseph Wadsworth,

Thomas Wadsworth, Jonathan Ashley.

Page 109.

Wadsworth, Samuel, Hartford. Invt. £1108-04-01. Taken 17 September, 1682, by Richard Edwards, Jarrad Spencer. Will dated 16 August, 1682.

I Samuel Wadsworth of Hartford, being sick & weak but of good understanding & memory, doe make this my Last will & Testament, & thereby doe setle & dispose of that Temporal estate God hath given me as Followeth: To my beloved Brother Joseph Wadsworth I give & bequeath my Lott in the Long meadow between Major Tallcotts Lott & Captn Allyn, to be to him & his heires forever. I give unto my Brother Thomas my house & Homelott & halfe my ox pasture & halfe my souldiers feild & all my Timber & Shingles for my New building. I give unto my sister Sarah Ashley halfe my souldiers feild & halfe my ox pasture, to be as equally divided as may be. I give to my sister Rebeckah Wadsworth my six acres of Land in the south meadow & Three Cowes. I give to my cousin Wm. Wadsworth £5 as a token of my Love. I give to my Sister

Elizabeth Terry £20 a year for the Three next years ensueing, to be payd by Joseph, Thomas & my sister Ashley yearly. I give my household stuff to my sister Terry & my sister Ashley, to be equally divided between them. I give unto my beloved Brother, Mr John Wadsworth, £10. Unto my cousin Elizabeth Terry £20 I give her. I doe make my beloved Brothers Joseph & Thomas Wadsworth & Brother Ashley Joynt Executors of this my Last will and Testament. In Witness whereof & for Confirmation hereof I have set my hand. I give unto my brother Thomas my man servant during his time he is Bound to me. I give unto my cousin that lives with me a new suit of searg, & the rest of the searg I give to my sister Rebeckah. I give to my Brother Joseph my best suit, & my money I gave to my Brother Joseph formerly, & so now doe dispose of it to him. As Witness my hand.   SAMUEL WADSWORTH.

Signed & declared in presence of us:
John Tallcott sen,
John Allyn, Sarah Haward.

Court Record, Page 61—13 December, 1682: Will proven.

Page 131.

Wakeley, Alice, Wethersfield. Invt. £348-19-04. Taken 6 September, 1683, by Samuel Talcott, Eleazer Kimberly.

Court Record, Page 73—6 September, 1683: Adms. to Lt. Samuel Steele & Ensign Nathaniel Standly.

Page 67.

Walkeley, Richard, Haddam. Died 6 August, 1681. Invt. £164-13-00. Taken by George Gates, Simon Smith, John Spencer, Selectmen.

Court Record, Page 46—1st November, 1681: Adms. to the Widow. Order to Dist: To the Widow, £17-13-00; to the Eldest son, £70; to the youngest, £40; to the daughter, £30. George Gates & Simon Smith to be Overseers.

Page 177.

Warde, John, Middletown. Invt. £446-18-00. Taken 22 February, 1683-4, by Giles Hamlin, William Warde. The children: John Warde age 18 years, Andrew 16, Ester 14, Mary 11, William 9, Samuel 4, & one she goeth with.

Court Record, Page 87—6 March, 1684: Adms. to the Widow and Dist: To the Widow, £64; to the eldest son, £103, £10 of which was given him by his grand Mother; to Each of the other Children, £46-10-00. This Court do appoint William Harris, the Father of the Relict, wth Mr.

Hamlin, to assist the widow & dispose of the children and distribute the Estate.

Page 211-212.

Warham, Mrs. Abigail, Windsor. Died 18 May, 1684. Invt. £126-14-06. Taken by Henry Wolcott, Thomas Bissell, Return Strong. Will nuncupative. We the underwritten, being present wth Mrs Warham, who spent her last days in our family, she discourseing with us respecting her Estate, declared that she had formerly given her cousin Miles Marwine such a multitude that if she had Thousands she would not give him a penny. She did not know whether she had anything to give away. Disowned that she had any Will, and sayd further that her cousin Miles Marwin desired that she would make over her Estate to him. She did not know but that she might live to need and expend it all. This she had said before. Mary, the wife of Captain Newbery, and Abigail the daughter, both affirm that Mrs. Warham said to them, when she was of good understanding and sound memory, concerning her Estate, that if there was anything left when the Court had the consideration thereof, she had thought little Miles Marwin should have somewhat, and the other that lived wth her so long; & as for her moveables that were brought into our house, Return Strong, Mary Newbery & Abigail do Testify she freely gave them to us & said they should not be taken from us. The above was by her declared to us sometime last March.

(Signed) 4 September, 1684. *Benjamin Newbery, Mary* X *Newbery, Abigail* X *Newbery, Return Strong.*

In Court, 10 March, 1684-5: The children of Miles Marwin were Elizabeth (she lived longest wth Mrs Warham), John Marwin, Abigail, Thomas, Samuel & Miles Marwin.

County Court Record, Page 102—5 March, 1684-5: Plea of Mr. Edwards in behalf of Miles Marwin set aside (reference to Court of Assistants 9 May, 1671). Adms. to Capt. Newbery & Return Strong, with Order to Distribute: To Miles Marwin Jr., 1-3 of the Estate: to Elizabeth, 2-3 of one third; and to John, Thomas, Samuel, & Abigail Marwin, the remainder. Miles Marwin Jr. to possess the Lands if he desire it, he paying to his brothers and sisters as the Administrator may appoint.

Page 81.

Warner, Andrew, Middletown. Invt. £329-05-03. Taken 20 February, 1681-2, by William Warde, Samuel Stocking, John Hall. Legatees: Andrew Warner age 19 years, John 11, Joseph 9, Abigail 21, Mary 17, Hanna 13, Rebeckah 6 years.

Court Record, Page 50—2nd March, 1681-2: Adms. to the Widow. John Warner and Robert Warner, Overseers.

Page 89—2 April, 1684: The personal Estate all to pay the debts; to the Widow the use of one-third of the Real Estate during life; to the Eldest son, £86; to the other 4 Children, £43 to each.

Page 32.

Warner, Daniel, Farmington. Invt. £51-07-00. Taken at Farmington by John Norton & John Woodruffe. Invt. £68-13-06 at Mattatuck. Taken by Samuel Hitchcock, Isaac Bronson, 1679. The children: Daniel age 12 years, John 8, Abigail 6, Samuel 4, Thomas 2 years of age.

Court Record, Page 18—4 December, 1679: Adms. to Sarah, the Relict. John Langton to be Overseer. William Higginson owes this Estate £11-00-00.

Page 26-7.

Warner, John, Farmington. Invt. £123-03-00. Taken 1679, by John Norton and John Woodruffe. Will dated 14 March, 1678-9.

I John Warner of Farmington, in the County of Hartford, do think it meet to make this settlement of my Estate. I do give unto my son John Warner ¼ part of my farm at Crane Hall, and the ¼ part of my Meadow Lott called Moore's Corner; also the fourth part of the Lands on the Forte Hill. I give unto my son Daniel Warner ¼ part of the same Land. I give unto my son Thomas Warner ¼ part, half the house & Homelott with these Considerations, that he shall see meet to come with his family to settle in it within the space of eight years after the date hereof; but if my son Thomas shall not come within the time specified, then he shall sell it to my son-in-law William Higgison at a reasonable price. I give unto my son-in-law William Higgison ¼ part of my Farme at Crane Hall, ¼ part of my Meadow Lott called Moore's Corner, ¼ part of my Land at Forte Hill, as also ½ of my now dwelling house & Homelott & Barne thereon, all which the sd. William Higgison is to enjoy after the departure of the natural life of me John Warner & Margaret my wife; also my Lott called the Great Swamp, also ¼ part of all my Divisions of Land belonging to me in town, with my 4-acre Lott, & also the Grant of that Tract of Land given me by the Country as a Pequott Soldier, to come into the present possession of these Lands. I also give to my daughter Sarah Higgison my best Kettle. I do give unto my wife ¼ part of my Farme called Crane Hall, & the fourth part of my Land called Moore's Corner, and the ½ of the House & Homested, with all the Moveables & Personal Estate that is mine, the use & Improvement of them during the time of her natural life. I give unto my four sons the remainder of my Estate, to be equally divided amongst them, viz, John Warner, Daniel Warner, Thomas Warner and William Higginson, after the decease of the natural life of me John Warner and Margaret Warner my wife. I appoint my four sons Executors, & entreat my loving friends William Lewis sen. & Lt. Steele to be my Overseers.

Witness: *William Lewis,*   JOHN X WARNER SEN.
         Samuel Steele.

Court Record, Page 18—4 December, 1679: Will proven.

Page 68—(Vol. XIII) 23 June, 1740: Ephraim Warner, son of John Warner & gr. son of John Warner sen., the 1st of the name in Farmington, Decd., in behalf of himself and as he is attorney to the Heirs of Daniel Warner, son of the sd. John Warner sen., of sd. Farmington, deceased, showing that by one Residuary Legacy in the Will of sd. John Warner sen. all the remainder of the Estate was given to his 4 sons, viz, John, Daniel, and Thomas Warner and William Higginson, after his & his wife Margaret's decease, there hath been no division of sd. Legacy, and the Executors being deceased, this Court appoint Capt. Isaac Cowles, Giles Hooker and Gershom Lewis to Dist. sd. Legacy or Estate to the Heirs of the sd. John Warner or their Legal Representatives, viz, John, Daniel and Thomas Warner and William Higginson.

Page 131.

Watson, Margaret, Hartford. Died March, 1682-3. Invt. £54-13-00. Taken May, 1683, by John Coale, Stephen Hosmer.

The last Will & Testament of Margaret Watson, who deceased March last past, did declare her Mind & Will as followeth concerning her Estate, & how she would have it disposed of, as she did declare it to Sarah Watson & John Merrells sen: She bequeathd to her daughter Sarah Merrells her red cloth Petticoat. She gave her searge Petticoat & her Penny stone Petticoat to her daughter Mary Seamore. She gave to her gr. child Sarah Merrells 1 Pillow beere & one sheet & a white apron. She gave to her gr. child Susannah Merrells 1 Sheet & 1 Pillow beere. She gave to her gr. child Mary Seamor 1 Sheet & 1 blankett & her green apron. She gave to her gr. Child Margaret Seamor 1 Sheet & 1 blankett & a Neck Handkercheire. She gave to her gr. Child John Watson 1 great pewter Platter & a Porringer. She did desire that her daughters, Sarah Merrells & Mary Seamor, should have £5 paid to each of them, that was bequeathed to them by their Father's Will. Also she did desire that the now wife of her son John Watson may have the use of the House & Homested if it should please God that my son John should die before her, for her lifetime.   SARAH X WATSON.

Court Record, Page 73—6 September, 1683: Adms. to John Watson with the Will annexed. *He in Court allows to John Seamor & his heirs forever the Land he possesseth, which was part of the Home lott of his Mother Watson.*

Page 214-15-16-17.

Watts, Elizabeth, Hartford. Died 25 February, 1684: Invt. £332-19-00. Taken 4 March, 1684-5, by Joseph Wadsworth, Philip Davis, John Merrells.

The Last Will and Testament of Elizabeth Watts, *Widdow of Capt. Thomas Watts,* is as followeth:

I Elizabeth Watts, being week in body but sound in mind and memory, doo account it my duty to mak a settlement and dispose of that which is under my Care. Whereas my late dere husband by his Last Will Left an Estate in my hand to dispose of as God should derect me, as may more fully apeer by the sd. will of my sd deer husband, I doe therefore dispos of the sd. Estate as hereafter followeth: Impr. I will and bequeath to my brother James Steele (clothes & personal Estate). 2ly, I will and bequeath to my brother Steele's fower daughters, viz, Elizabeth Steele, Mary Hall, Sarah Steele and Rachell Steele, thre score pounds; and to my litel cousen James Hall my bigest wine Cups. 3ly, I will and bequeath to my littel Cousen Thomas Steele the best beed in the Chamber, my husband's bibell, and the great Silver Cup, and my husband's platt buttons, and his Raper and beelt, to be kept till he com of age. 4ly, I will and bequeath to my Cousen Samuel Hubart the beed and furnitur to it, in the paller. I will and bequeath to my Cousen Benony Browne my husband's Cloake and raper that was my brother Brown's. I will and bequeath to my Cousen Martha Henderson the beed that is in the garret Chamber, the rug that is on Cousen Steel's beed; also I give her the third bigest platter and one of the best of the platters that goe about the hous, and two porengers that are used about the hous, and a quart skellett, and a great skellett without a frame; also I give her my Cloth sarg sutt and my sarg Coatt I usaly were, and my seniston peeticoatt and mow hare pety coatt and six napkins, also my saf gard and riding hood when my Cousen beety brings them hom. I will & bequeath to my Cousen Elizabeth Steele a dosen of Napkins marked M. S. I will and bequeath to my Sister Willett a pece of new Sarg bought for a peetyCoatt, and a Sutt of my best Wering lining, and a holon arpen with a pece down the sid, a paire of Cotten Gloves that ware my huspan, and two of his bands. I will and bequeath to my litle Cousen Samuel hubert my little Silver dram Cup and two Silver Spoons. I give to my Cousin James Steele's wife a sutt of wearing lining. I will and bequeath to my cousen Lanes daughter Beety a yard of new holan of that which is in the Chest, my wearing Linen to my Cousen Marcy Steele, Samuel Hubarts wife, Martha Henderson, Elizabeth Steele & Betty Steele. I appoint My Cousens Samuel Steele and Samuel Hubert to be Soule Executors, and my brother James Steele & Nathaniel Stanly to be Overseers.

Witness: *Richard Hakes,*   ELIZABETH WATTS.
   William Davenport. (Last) date 14 February, 1684.
                                    Proven 14 March, 1684-5.

Page 146-7.

Watts, Capt. Thomas,   Hartford.   Invt. £1383-02-10.   Taken 22 October, 1683, by Nathaniel Standly, John Easton. Will dated 6 August, 1683.

I Thomas Watts of Hartford do make this my last Will & Testament: I give to my wife Elizabeth Watts my personal Estate forever, and my Real Estate to her during her natural life, and after her decease I give it to my brother's son Samuel Hubbard, whom I have brought up from a child; my Homested, 3 acres of Land in the Indian field, one acre by the River side, 5½ acres in meadow which I bought of Nathaniel Warde, 20 acres of upland adjoyning Mr. Joseph Mygatt, 10 acres at the four-mile hill, all which I give to the said Samuel Hubbard and to his heirs forever, to come into possession within a year after my wife's decease. I give to my Kinsman Samuel Steele Jr. 5 acres of Land I bought of Nathaniel Warde, 3 acres I bought of John Arnol(d), all lying in a place called Ward's field, adjoyning James Steele sen, Noah Cooke & John Merrells, all which I give to the sd. Samuel Steele & his heirs forever, to be in possession within one yeare after the decease of my wife. I give to the other six of my sister Hubbard's Children, to Joseph, to Daniel, to Nathaniel, to Richard, to Mary Rannie, to Elizabeth Hubbard, I give to them £100, to be paid to them within one year and a day's departure of my wive's Natural Life. I give to my brother Brown's Children, to Nathaniel, to John, to Benony Brown, to Hannah Lane (the wife of Isaac Lane), I give and bequeath to these four Children of my Brother Brown all my Lands Lying in the bounds of Middletown, and £38 more, to be paid out of my other Estate. I give to my Brother James Steele's two sons, James & John Steele, £50 (to James £30, and John Steele £20). I give to Mr. John Whiting £20. I give to the poor of the new church in Hartford £20. I give to Martha Hannison, to her own proper use, 7½ acres of Land called by the name of Pesiponck; also £20 in other of my Estate. I give to Samuel Steele sen., my Kinsman, £10. All the remainder of my Estate I give to my wife Elizabeth Watts, and do make her sole Executrix; and I Intreat James Steele sen. and Ensign Nathaniel Standly to be Overseers.   THOMAS WATTS.
Witness: *James Steele sen., Samuel Steele sen.*

County Court Record, Page 76—6 Dec. 1683: Will Proven.
Page 129—3 March, 1686-7: This Court appoint to lay out to the Legatees of Capt. Watts' will their several portions of Land according to the Order of the General Court at their last session, and to Meet and bound it according to said Order. And this Court appoint Marshall Grave, Steven Hosmer and Thomas Bunce distributors.

Page 251-2.

Way, Eleazer, Hartford. Invt. £867-03-11. Taken 9 August, 1687, by Richard Edwards, Daniel Taylor.

Court Record, Page 133—1 September, 1687: Adms. to the Relict. Page 225—(Pro. Side, Vol. V)—A Dist. of Mr. Eleazer Way's Estate: Be it known to all whome it may concerne; that we whose names are underwritten have by these presents firmly and fully for ourselves and for our Heirs forever agreed and have settled and divided the Estate of Eleazer Way, Decd, as followeth: To Mary Way, the widow, the Use of Land valued at £202-10-00 during life, and her share of the Moveables to her satisfaction. To Ebenezer Way a double share of the Estate. And the remainder of sd. Land to be divided equally between the three daughters or Legatees, that is, to Ichabod Welles in behalf of his wife Sarah, & to Joseph Welles in behalf of his wife Elizabeth, & to Lydia Way, or to their heirs. To Ebenezer Way a double share of the whole Estate when the Widow's thirds is taken out. The Debts to be paid out of the Estate in proportion to the shares which should yet appear to be legally due.

Signed:

MARY WAY, Ls.   JOSEPH WELLES, Ls.
EBENEZER WAY, Ls.   LYDIA WAY, Ls.
ICHABOD WELLES, Ls.

Witness: *Edward Allyn,*
William Warren.

On the 6th of February, 1695-6, Mary Way & Ebenezer Way, Ichabod Welles & Joseph Welles in behalf of their wives, & Lydia Way, all of them personally appeared in Hartford & acknowledged the abovesd. Agreement to be their free voluntary act before

Me: Nathaniel Stanly, Assistant.

Exhibited in Court and confirmed, 5th March, 1695-6.

Page 158-9.

Welles, Mrs. Elizabeth, Wethersfield. Invt. £328-12-06. Taken 3d September, 1683, by Samuel Talcott, James Treat, Samuel Butler. Will dated 28 March, 1678.

My Estate I dispose of as followeth: I will that all those debts I ow in right or conscience to any man or men be well & Truly contented & payd out of my Estate in the first place. My fourteen acres of Land in the great meadow & Thirty acres in the West field I give unto my son Robert foote & to his heirs forever, prohibiting him the sale of the same, he paying for these Lands forty five pounds, to be payd: to the Children of my Daughter Sarah Judson Deceased, Nine pounds; & to my foure daughters, viz: my daughter Churchill, my daughter Goodrich, my Daughter Barnard, & my Daughter Smith, to each of them Nine pounds a piece. I give vnto my son Nathaniel Foote, eldest son, & his Brother, Eleven pounds; & to their children: To Daniel forty shillings, & To Elizabeth fower pownds, which Legacies, both the eleven pownd, forty shillings, & fower pounds, shall be payd out of The money Nathaniel

Graves owes Me By Bill. I give & bequeath unto my Grand son John Studder halfe my Great Lott which Lyes at the further Bownds of the Towne, & the other halfe of the sayd Lott I give vnto my grand sons Joseph & Benjamin Churchill & their heirs forever. The remainder of my Estate (when a Legacie is pd. to my overseers out of it) shall be divided into five parts; one part I give to my daughter Judson's Children, to be to them & their heirs forever; & to my daughter Churchill & her children one fifth part, & to my daughter Goodrich & the children one-fifth part, & to my daughter Barnard and her children one-fifth part, & to my daughter Smith & her Children one fifth part. It is my will that what I give my fouer daughters shall be wholly at their dispose, to dispose among their children as they see good. I do nominate & appoynt my wel beloved Captain John Allin to be Executor; & my beloved Brother Mr John Deming sen. & my Grand sonn Henry Buck to be the desired overseers of this my will; & as a token of my respect to them I give them thirty shillings a piece out of my Estate; & for the confirmation of the premises I have hereunto set my hand this 28 day of March, 1678.

Memorandum: It is my will that the nine pownds apiece I give my foure daughters' heirs, & the fifth part of my Estate I give them, shall be divided among the children of each of them, the one halfe of it imediately after my decease.   ELIZABETH X WELLS.

This signed & declared by Mrs. Elizabeth Welles in presence of us:
Joseph Rowlandson,
John Deming.

Memorandum: I give to my grand son Nathll ffoott, the Eldest son of my sonn Nathll, the one halfe of my fourteen acres of meadow, & one halfe of my thirty acres of upland lying in the West field, wth liberty of takeing the first choice, he paying one halfe of the Legacys wch were to be paid my sonn Robt had he lived to possess ye sd. Land. My will is that that part of ye eleven pounds wch I formerly willed to sd. Nathaniel, grand son, & his Brother, wch belonged to him by will, shall be equally distributed between my four daughters above mentioned. And for the confirmation of the prmisis I have hereunto set my hand this 16th day of August, 1682. *Memorandum: All rents of Land due to me I will to be divided equally amongst my fower formentioned daughters and their heirs.*   ELIZABETH X WELLS.
Witnessed by us:
Samuel Talcott,
John Deming.

Mrs. Elizabeth Welles's Will, 1683:

Dist. of Estate on the reverse side of the paper as follows:

	£	s	d
To Samll Foote	5	10	00
To Elizabeth ffoote.	4	00	00
To Lift. Smith	1	07	06

To ffrancis Barnard   1-07-06
To Josiah Churchill   1-07-06
To Lift. Tracy   1-07-06
To Danll ffoott   2-00-00
                                                    _____
                                                           £17-00-00

Page 134.

Welles, Mrs. Hannah, Hartford. Died 9 August, 1683. Invt. £495-02-09. Taken by Ciprian Niccolls, Caleb Standly, Steven Hosmer.

Court Record, Page 73—6 September, 1683: Adms. to Ichabod Wells, and appoint Ciprian Niccolls, Steven Hosmer & Sergt. Standly to assist in distribution. After the debts are paid and former legacies, the remainder to John Pantry a double share, and to all the rest of Mr. Welles' Children equal portions. Mrs. Bidwell and Mrs. Micks to receive each a gold ring that their Mother gave them before her sickness, though not delivered. And the younger sons to be clothed out of the Estate before Dist.

Dist. File: Estate of Mrs. Hannah Welles, 8 December, 1683: To John Pantry by his Mother, to James Judson by his Wife, To Thomas, to Samuel, to John Bidwell, to Nathaniel Meekes, to Jonathan Welles, to Joseph, to Ichabod Welles. By Caleb Stanly, Ciprian Nickols, Stephan Hosmer, Ichabod Welles, upon account of Mrs. Allyn's thirds out of the lands of Capt. Samuel Welles, Decd, now wife of Lt. Col. John Allyn.

Page 77—18 December, 1683: Adms. account of Dist.: To the 7 Children. Ichabod to enjoy 3 acres of Jonathan's Land in the South Meadow till Jonathan is of age, and £187 of Joseph's Estate to remain in Ichabod's Hands till Joseph comes of age.

Page 18.

Welles, Hugh, Wethersfield. Invt. £317-14-03. Taken 12 June, 1679, by James Treat, Thomas Hollister. Will dated 20th November, 1678.

I Hugh Welles in the town of Wethersfield do make and ordain this my last Will & Testament: I give to my wife Mary Welles 1-3 part of my Houseing & Land, with ½ of my Household Stuff during her natural life. I give to my son John Welles all my Wearing Apparrel, all my military Arms, ½ of my Household Stuff, all my Carpenter's Tools and all other Tooles & Implements whatsoever, also my Stock of Cattle, Horses and Cows, one Cow only excepted. I give to my son John 2-3 of all my Houseing and Lands, ½ acre of Land (bounded upon the Green or Common, adjoining to the Lands of William Goodrich & Anthony Wright) only excepted, and also the immediate reversion & remainder of my Houseing & Lands before given to my wife Mary during her natural life, which sd. Reversion is not to include any part of that half acre of Land before excepted, all which sd. Houseing & Lands & Reversion of Houseing & Lands I give to my sd. son John to be to him & his heirs successively forever, after my decease. I give to my daughter Mary Robinson £5. I give to my daughter Rebeckah £5, and to my daughter Sarah Bishop an half of acre of Land before particularly mentioned, to be to her & to her daughter now living. Also I Will my sd. daughter Bishop £5. I give to my gr. Child Thomas Robinson, the son of Thomas Robinson, £5. I give to my gr. child Will Robinson, the son of Thomas Robinson aforesd., £1. I give to my gr. Child Mary Robinson 10 Shillings. I give to my gr. Child Samuel Latham, the son of my daughter Rebeckah, £3. I give to my gr. Child Sarah Latham £2. I give unto my gr. Child Sarah Bishop £3, and also the half acre of Land, to be possessed after the decease of her father and Mother. I give to my Cousin Will Savage, the son of John Savage of Middletown, £1. I give the rest of my Cousins, the Children of John Savage, to each 1 Shilling apeice. And my Will is that all the Legacies shall be paid by my son John or his heirs. And my Will is that if my son John Welles should die without Issue, the Land, etc., given to him shall be to the use of my gr. child Thomas Robinson the Entail, or next to Will Robinson, or next to Samuel Latham, etc. I constitute my son John Welles my Executor, and Mr. Gershom Bulkeley and Eleazer Kimberly, Overseers.

Witness: *Samuel Wright,*   HUGH WELLES. Ls.
          Eleazer Kimberly.

Court Record, Page 14—24 April, 1679: Will proven. The Estate of Mr. Welles being considerably in Debt, this Court doth Order that if the Executor doe see need to part with any Land to pay the Debts, that he doe take the Houselott as it is prised in the Inventory & pay so much of the Debts out of his own proper Estate as the House lott is prised in the Inventory, & he so doing, the entayle of the sd House & Lott is hereby cut off.

Page 89-90.

Whitemore, Thomas sen., Middletown. Invt. £468-02-03. Taken 7 January, 1681-2, by Nathaniel White, Robert Warner, John Savage. Legatees: John 36 years of age, Thomas 29, Samuel 26, Israhiah 25, Beriah 23, Nathaniel 20, Joseph 18, Josiah 13, Benjamin 7, Elizabeth 32, Mary 31, Hannah 28, Sarah 17, Mehetabell 13, Abigail 3, Hannah one year old. Will dated 20 July, 1681.

The last Will of Thomas Whetmore sen., aged 66 years, is as followeth: I give to my son John Whetmore part of my Lott in the Boggy Meadow Quarter, that is, 20 Rods wide lying on the south side of that lott, going as far East as my Land goeth; moreover I give to my son John ¾ of my Great Lott that lyeth West from the Town, to take the whole Bredth half the length, beginning at the farther end, and likewise half the

Bredth of the other half next the Town, and to take it on the North side. And my Will is that my son Beriah shall have the other half of that half next to the Town. Moreover it is my Will that my sd. son John shall have all my proportions or Interest in the Three Mile Lott on the East side of the Great River, that is, the farther Three Miles on that side Eastward. I give to my son Thomas Whetmore half my Long Meadow Lott, lying on the North Side; moreover I give to my sd. son Thomas half my Lott at Caugenchawke, and the other half I give to my daughter Hannah Stow. I give to my son Samuel Whetmore a parcell of Land on the North side of the Small River which I bought of Goodman Savage, being about 10 acres lying on the West End of Goodman Savage's Lott, only reserveing 4 acres of that Land for my daughter if she survive. I give to my sd. son my Round Meadow Lott, being near 6 acres, only reserving and willing 1-3 part of it for my daughter Abigail if she survive, or else to remain to Samuel. I give to my son Israhiah Whetmore my Upland Lott on the East side of the Great River, being about 22 acres lying in the Half Mile Lotts against the Town, as also a peice of Meadow at Wongunk joining to his brother John; also 4 acres in the Pond on the East side of the Great River between Ensign Cheeny & Mr. Nathaniel Collins; moreover I give my sd. son one parcell of Land in the last Half Mile Division on the East side of the Great River. I give to my son Beriah Whetmore that peice of Meadow at Wongunk called the Platt Meadow; I give to my sd. son one acre of my Homelott next to the Great River, on the Condition that he come to settle upon it; if not, he shall not have it. I give to my son Nathaniel Whetmore half my Land in the Boggy Meadow Quarter and that which lyeth without the Fence as it now standeth, and the other half to my son Joseph Whetmore. I give to my daughter Sarah Whetmore and my son Josiah Whetmore & my daughter Mehetabel my Great Lott at Streights Hill, to be divided equally among them. I give to Katharine, my loving wife, the rest of my Homelott, with all the Houseing thereon, during her natural life; also the ½ of my Long Meadow on the South side, & a parcel of Land which I have at Passenchauge on the East side of the Great River. I give to my wife my Fields Lott during her natural life or until Benjamin fulfills the age of 21 years, then it shall be settled on him as his. Moreover, as I have received of my wife Katharine £20 of her Estate, £6 whereof I have already paid her, yet notwithstanding I appoint and my Will is that £20 be paid to her out of my Estate in Household Stuffe & Stock. I give to my daughters Sarah & Mehetabell & Abigail & Hannah Jr. £6 apeice, and to this my youngest daughter Hannah one peice of Land of 20 acres lying near the Streights on the West side of the Great River. I give to Thomas & Joseph all my Carpenter Tools. I appoint my wife and son John sole Executors.

Witness: *Deacon Samuel Stocking,*   THOMAS WHETMORE SEN. Ls.
John Hall sen.

Court Record, Page 50—2 March, 1681-2: Will proven.

Dist. File: We whose names are here under written, the proper Children now living and representatives of such as are deceased, of Thomas Whetmore senior of Middletown, decd, have unanimously Consented and agreed that the Estate of Benjamin Whetmore, decd, our Brother, both Personal and Real, shall be divided and distributed in manner following, that is to say: That Abigail Whetmore, now wife of Samuel Bishop, and Hannah Whetmore, shall each of them have a double portion of the sd. Estate, and the remainder shall be equally divided amongst the (proper) Children of sd. Thomas Whetmore and their Representatives. As Witness our Hands and Seals, 6 March, 1699-1700.

SAMUEL BISHOP,	SAMUEL WETTMORE, Ls.
HANNAH WHETMORE,	ISRAHIAH WETTMORE, Ls
ELIZABETH WHETMORE,	BERIAH WETTMORE, Ls,
ELIZABETH ADKINS,	NATHANIEL WETTMORE, Ls.
MARY STOW,	JOSEPH WETTMORE, Ls.
NATHANIEL STOW,	JOSIAH WETTMORE. Ls.

Mary, Widow of Jno Wetmore, & Elizabeth Wetmore, humbly request the honoured Court to appoint Israhiah Wettmore, Beriah Wettmore, and John Bacon, Andrew Bacon & Alexander Rollo, Distributors.

Court Record, Page 10—(Vol. VII) 8 April, 1701: Israhiah Wetmore of Middletown presented to this Court an Account of his Adms. & Dist. of the Estate of Benjamin Whitmore, late of Middletown, Decd, as also an Agreement under the Hands of the Brethren & Sisters of the sd. Benjamin manifesting their Satisfaction respecting the Disposal of the sd Estate, which the Court accepts. Ordered recorded and kept on File. Also this Court grant him a *Quietus Est.*

Page 150-1.

Whitcombe, Job, Wethersfield. Died 8 November, 1683. Invt. £27-17-00. Taken by Samuel Talcott & James Treat. The children: Mary Whitcombe 12 years of age, Job 9, Jemima 6, John 4 years old, Will dated 27 October, 1680.

I Job Whitcombe, being in perfect memory, do ordain, constitute and appoint this Writing to be my last Will & Testament: I do give unto my wife Mary Whitcombe all my Estate, either in House or Land or other things to be at her Dispose for her own good and the Good of my Children, excepting what Legacies are hereafter expressed, which by my Will are given to my Children; and if any of the sd. Estate shall remain in her hands at the day of her decease, or if she marry, then the sd. Estate to be equally divided amongst my 4 children when they shall come to age, that is, when my two sons attain the age of 21 years, and my two daughters the age of 18 years. I give unto my son Job my Musket and Back Sword and Belt, at the age of 16 years. I do give unto my son John my Fowling peice, Rapier & Belt, when he shall attain the age of 16 years. I do give unto my daughter Mary my warming pan, after my wive's decease. I do give to my daughter Jemima my Iron Kettle, after the decease of my wife Mary. My Desire is that all my Children be disposed of where they may have suitable education. My Desire also is that my brethren Jonathan & Josiah be Overseers to this my Will.

Witness: *Samuel Talcott,*　　　　　　Job Whitcombe. Ls.
　　　　Mary X Whitcombe.

Court Record, Page 76—Will Proven & Invt. Exhibit approved.—6 December, 1683.

Whiting, William. Court Record, Page 92—4 September, 1684: Mr. John Whiting, Joseph Whiting, John King in right of Sarah his Wife, Mr. Nathaniel Collins in right of Mary his wife, Plaintiff; Capt. Thomas Bissell Defendent. For unlawful detention of Lands, their Proportion, sometime the Land of their Father, Mr. William Whiting, Decd. Nonsuited.

Page 171.

White, Elder John, Hartford. Invt. £190-09-00. Taken 23 January, 1683-4, by Nathaniel Standly, Steven Hosmer, Thomas Bunce. Will dated 17 December, 1683.

I Mr. John White of Hartford do make this my last Will & Testament: I give unto my son Nathaniel £30 and my best broad Cloath Coate, & also give him My iron bound chest in my Chamber, & my Cobirons in my parlour, & that part of my oxpasture which lyeth on the Left hand of the way as we go to Wethersfield, bounded upon the highway, next Henry Grime's Land North, Mr. Nickolls his Land South, the South Meadow East. I give to my son Daniel White £20. I give to my son Jacob White that part of my ox pasture in Hartford which lyeth on the right hand of the way Leading to Wethersfield, bounded East by the highway, by Jonathan Bygelow his Land south, by Henry Grimes his Land North, & Lt. Webster's Land West. I impower my Executor to give to my daughter Hixton according to his discretion as he shall see her need calls for. Whereas I intended to give a parcel of meadow Land in Great Ponsett to Stephen Taylor, yet now being forced to pay a great summe of money for the Redemption of his house & home lott, now see cause to dispose of that Land for the payment of that debt, and shall leave to my Executor with the advice of the Overseers to give either to him or the rest of my daughter Hixton's Children. I give to my grand child Stephen Taylor things at Nathaniel White's, at Hadly. I give to Sarah White, the daughter of my son Nathaniel White, £5. I give to Mr. John Whiting, my honoured Pastor, £5 in silver. The remainder of my estate shall be divided among my Grand Children (viz.): Jonathan Gilbert, son of my daughter Mary, my son Nathaniel's Children, my son John's Children, my son Daniel's

Children, & my daughter Sarah's Children. I appoint my son Nathaniel White to be sole Executor, & Ensign Nathaniel Stanly and Stephen Hosmer to be Overseers.   JOHN X WHITE SEN. LS.

Witness: *Caleb Watson, Mrs. Mary Watson.*

Court Record, Page 85—6 March, 1684: Will Proven.

Page 145-146.

Williams, Amos, Wethersfield. Died 20 August, 1683. Invt. £217-15-00. Taken by Samuel Talcott, James Treat. The children: Amos age 13 years, Samuel & Elizabeth 6, Susannah 3 years.

Court Record, Page 76—6 December, 1683: Invt. exhibited.

Page 10—(Vol. VI) 3 January, 1697-8: Lt. Thomas Hollister moving this Court that some suitable persons be appointed to Dist. the Estate of Amos Williams, late of Wethersfield Decd, he the sd. Hollister having married the Relict of sd. Williams, this Court appoint Nathaniel Foote, William Burnham and Jonathan Boreman to Dist. the Estate according to an Order of Court made 18 December, 1683.

Dist. File: 1701: To Amos, to Samuel, to Susannah, to Elizabeth Williams alias Hollister. By William Boardman, Nathaniel Foote & Jonathan Boardman.

Page 24—(Vol. VII) 1 January, 1701-2: Whereas the Court did formerly appoint some persons to Dist. the Estate of Amos Williams, late of Wethersfield Decd, to the Widow and Children, they have proceeded therein so far as at present they can, there being £80-18-06 wanting of the Estate. The Distributors having made Return thereof under their hands, viz, William Burnham, Nathaniel Foote & Jonathan Boreman, it being moved to this Court how the remaining part should be paid or made up, the Court are of opinion that the persons to whom the sd. Estate was committed in Trust, their Executors or Adms., should make it good.

Page 218.

Williams, David, Windsor. Died 7 September, 1684. Invt. £8-01-00. Taken by Thomas Bissell, Return Strong.

Court Record, Page 104—24 March, 1684-5: Adms. to John Owen and Thomas Bissell, to pay the debts, and the remainder of the Estate to be in hands of John Owen until further Order from this Court.

Page 5-6.

Wilton, Lt. David, of Northampton. Died 5 February, 1677-8. Inventory £101-11-09. Taken 2 March, 1677-8, by Benjamin Newbery, Daniel Clarke. Will dated 25 December, 1677.

I Lt. David Wilton of Northampton, in the Colony of Mass. Bay, do make this my last Will & Testament: I give to my gr. child Samuel Marshall half my Property at Northampton, & the other half by reversion after the decease of his wife and daughters. If Mr. Joseph Hawley, who hath married Lydia my gr. child & is now living at Northampton, see cause to settle there and build an house, I give him Land which lyeth between Elder John Strong's Home lott and my own, provided he build on it and live there four years, then it shall be to him and his wife and their heirs forever; or els it shall be to Samuel Marshall. I do give to my Wife Katharine Wilton the other halfe of Property at Northampton, also the house in Windsor which was formerly belonging to my son Samuel Marshall Decd, also £75 due to me in Boston, in the hands of Mr. John Pynchon to pay for said House & to the Creditors of the sd. Samuel Marshall Decd., all which I desire my wife to have and enjoy during her natural life, provided she pay or cause to be paid Certain legacies herein named. And before a division is made my wife shall have free liberty to take out £50 to give to whom she shall please of the sd. Estate, excepting the sd. Samuel Marshall his portion. I give to the College in Cambridge £10. I give to my daughter Mary Marshall, Widow, £10. To my Brother Nicholas Wilton my best Clothes. To my sister, Joan Wilton, £1. I give to John Taylor sen., £3. I give to the Church in Northampton my silver Bowl. I give unto my wife all the rest of my Estate, both Moveables & Immoveables, to possess during her natural life, unless any of my gr. Children shall come to age or marry, that she shall see Cause to give them their portion. I do also give unto my wife my part of the Saw Mill in Northampton during her natural life. Whereas Mary Marshall is my real & native heire, if she shall outlive & survive my wife she shall have the Estate which I left to my wife, to possess the same during her life, but it shall remain to her own children, namely, the part of the Saw Mill and the 9 acres of Land in Munham Lott to Samuel Marshall, after her deceas, the rest to be equally divided to her Children. To my gr. son Thomas Marshall, who now lives with me, if he continue with my wife until he come to 21 years of age, to have £12 more added to his portion. I appoint my wife to be sole Executrix, and desire Capt. John Allyn of Hartford, with Rev. Mr. Solomon Stoddard, Lt. William Clarke & Medad Pomeroy, to be the Overseers.

Witness: *Joseph Persons,* DAVID WILTON. Ls.
Joseph Hawley, James Cornish.

Page 129.

Wilton, Nicholas, Windsor. Died 3 August, 1683. Invt. £42-11-00. Taken by Henry Wolcott, Nathaniel Bissell, Samuel Cross. The children: David & John Wilton.

Court Record, Page 78—18 December, 1683: Adms. to the Towns-men, & to dispose of the boys until they come of age. David to have a double share and John a single share, to be secured to them by the Adms.

Page 202.

Wolcott, Hannah. Dist. 24 November, 1684: Whereas the Estate of our Sister Mrs. Hannah Wolcott hath hitherto been unsettled by reason of our Sister Sarah Price's Claim to the Estate by virtue of a promise from the decease, but being prevented from perfecting her Will, now Capt. Benj. Newbery & our brother Josiah Wolcott being empowered in behalf of our sister Price to Compound and settle the Estate, it is mutually agreed that our brother-in-law James Russell esq., in his kindness to our deceased sister, and of her kindness toward Mary the only daughter of our sister Russell, Deceased, we do agree that the sd. Russell shall have £40 as money of the Estate, & that our sister Price have one halfe of the re-mainder of her whole Estate, the other halfe to be equally divided among the Brethren.

(Signed) BENJ. NEWBERY, HENRY WOLCOTT, JOHN WOLCOTT, SAMUEL WOLCOTT, JOSIAH WOLCOTT.

Approved by this Court 25 November, 1684.
Capt. Benjamin Newbery in behalf of Mr. John Price, & Mr. James Russell, with Mr. Henry Wolcott, Mr. John, Mr. Samuel, & Mr. Josiah Wolcott: A mutual agreement to distribute the Estate of Mrs. Hannah Wolcott aforesaid. (See Court Record, Page 95—25 November, 1684.) Approved.

Page 37-8.

Wolcott, Henry, sen., Windsor. Invt. £2743-12-00; in Wethersfield, £1234-04-00; total £3977-16-00. Taken 19 & 24 July, 1680, by Capt. Benjamin Newbery, John Loomis sen., Thomas Bissell *(Windsor)*; by Nathaniel Boreman & Samuel Steele *(Wethersfield)*. Will dated 21 September, 1670.
I Henry Wolcott sen. of Windsor do make this my last Will & Testament: I give to my wife, besides the £10 per annum which was granted her before our marriage out of my Land at Tollon Mill, all my Houseing & Lands in Windsor during her life. I give her the use of half my Land at Wethersfield until my son Samuel shall be 21 years of age. I give to my son Henry all my Book accounts, my ring that I seal with, my best sword, Pistols & Brass gun. I give to my son John all my Houseing and Lands in Windsor, after the decease of my wife, the use of half my Land in Wethersfield during the life of my wife. I give him all my Houseing and Lands in Tollon, now or late in the improvement of John Dart, during the natural life of my sons John Wolcott, Samuel Wolcott and Josiah Wolcott,

he paying £5 per annum to my Executor for the use of the rest of my children until their portions hereafter mentioned are all paid. I give to my son Samuel half my Land at Wethersfield, at the age of 21 years, also my Land at Wellington called Longforth, 11 acres, during the life of my sons John, Samuel & Josiah Wolcott, he paying £10 per annum to my Executrix for the use of it for the use of the rest of my Children until their portions are all paid. I also give to my son Josiah Wolcott half my Land at Wethersfield, after the decease of my wife. I give him my Land in Tollon which is now in the possession of John Wolcott, after the termination of the Estate that was granted by my Uncle Christopher Wolcott unto John Wolcott sen., long since deceased, at the age of 21 years, during the natural lives of any of my three sons John, Samuel and Josiah Wolcott, he paying £10 per annum to my Executrix for the use of the rest of my Children until their portions are all paid to them. I give to my daughters Sarah, Mary & Hannah Wolcott, to each £250 Sterling. I will that my wife shall have the improvement of the portion of each of my Children until they come of age or marry. I give to Ambrose Fowler £2, to Nathaniel Cooke 40s, to Rebeckah Kellsy 40s. My will is that the rest of my Estate shall be equally divided amongst all of my Children: Henry, John, Samuel, Josiah, Sarah, Mary & Hannah Wolcott.

HENRY WOLCOTT. LS.

Witness: *Joseph Haines, Nathaniel Collins.*

My wife to be Executrix, and my brother-in-law Capt. Benjamin Newbery and my son Henry Wolcott to be Overseers.

A Codicil, dated 2 October, 1671: By my Last Will & Testament, dated 21 September, 1670, I did give unto my three younger sons, John Wolcott, Samuel Wolcott & Josiah Wolcott, my three Tenements in England during the time of their natural lives, viz, my Land in Tolland which is in the occupation of John Dart & John Wolcott, & my Land in Wellington Called Longforth, which is in the occupation of Hugh Wolcott. I will that if my Eldest son Henry Wolcott desires to have the Lands in England, He shall pay unto my Executrix for the use of the rest of my Children the sum of £300 in Current New England Money, to be paid in six years after my decease, by £50 per annum. HENRY WOLCOTT. LS.

Witness: *Jos. Haines, Nathaniel Collins.*

Court Record, Page 106—23 April, 1685: Mrs. Sarah Wolcott, the Executrix, being deceased, this Court doe appoint Mr. Josiah Wolcott, with the assistance of Capt. John Allyn, to finish the Administration on the Estate of Henry Wolcott according to the settlement of the Court.

Page 203.

Wolcott, Sarah, Windsor. Died 16 July, 1684. Invt. £191-03-06. Taken 19 December, 1684, by Benjamin Newbery, Return Strong & John Moore. An Agreement to divide the Estate into Parts, Mr. Henry Wolcott to have two parts, Mr. Josiah Wolcott to have two parts, and Mr. John Wolcott, Mr. Samuel Wolcott and Mrs. Sarah Price each to have one part. Confirmed by the Court. Mr. Henry Wolcott, Adms.

Page 101.

Woodruff, Matthew sen., Farmington. Invt. £252-05-00. Taken by Thomas Hart, Thomas Porter, Richard Seymore. Will Nuncupative.

6 September, 1682: To his son Samuel is bequeathed a large portion of the Estate upon condition that he maintain his Mother. He gives to sons John & Matthew lands, & to his daughter Hannah Seamore £5, to be paid to her by her brother John. Proven 14 December, 1682, upon Testimony of *Robert Porter* that this was declared to be the Last Will of MATTHEW WOODRUFF.

Court Record, Page 60—13 December, 1682: Adms. to Samuel Woodruff with the Will annexed. One daughter not being mentioned in the Will, this Court order paid to her what the rest of the daughters have had, and the remainder of the Estate to be distributed according to the Will.

Page 31.

Wright, Anthony, Wethersfield. Invt. £216-09-03. Taken 23 October, 1679, by Samuel Steele, John Woolcott.

Court Record, Page 18—4 December, 1679: Adms. to Mary Wright, the Widow.

Page 151-2.

Wright, Thomas, Wethersfield. Died 24 August, 1683. Invt. £673-00-00. Taken by Samuel Talcott & James Treat. The children: Thomas Wright age 23 years, Mary 18, Hannah 13, Lydia 11 years of age.

Court Record, Page 76—6 December, 1683: Adms. to Thomas Wright. Order to Distribute the Estate: To Thomas a double portion, to the three sisters to each a single portion. Samuel Wright and Samuel Butler to be Overseers.

Page 107.

Wyard, Robert. Died 11 September, 1682. Invt. £180-02-00. Taken by Nathaniel Willett, Philip Davis, Ciprian Niccols.

Court Record, Page 65—1st March, 1682-3: List of Creditors and account of debts exhibited.

VOLUME V.

1687 to 1695.

This is the Fifth Book of the
Records of the Acts of the County
Courts and Courts of Probates
in the County of Hartford,
and of Wills and Inventories.

No. 5.

PROBATE RECORDS.

VOLUME V.

1687 to 1695.

Page 213.

Ackley, Nicholas, Haddam. Died 29 April, 1695. Invt. £188-11-00. Taken 8 May, 1695, by John Scovel, John Bate, Alexander Rooly (Rollo). The children—5 Sons: John, Thomas, Nathaniel, James, Samuel; and 5 daughters: Hanna, Elizabeth, Sarah, Mary & Lydia.

Court Record, Page 89—5 September, 1695: Adms. to John Ackley.

Page 97—20 March, 1696: An Agreement between the Widow & Children of Nicholas Ackley, which this Court approve.

Dist. on File: To the Mother-in-law £12 and her own Estate that she brought to the House; the Eldest son a double share, and each of the others a single share. Signed:

Witness: *John Chapman,*   MIRIAM ACKLEY,   JAMES ACKLEY,
       Abel Shaylor.   THOMAS ACKLEY,   ELIZABETH X SHALOR,
                   NATHANIEL ACKLEY,   HANNA X PURPLE,
                   JOHN ACKLEY,   MARY X BEPPIN,
                   SAMUEL ACKLEY,   SARAH SPENCER,
                   LYDIA ROBINSON, wife of THOMAS ROBINSON.

Page 89.

Adkins, Josiah, Middletown. Invt. £67-10-00. Taken 1st January, 1690-1, by Nathaniel Stowe, John Hall, sen., Samuel Hall. The legatees: Solomon Adkins age 12 years, Josiah 10, Benjamin 8, Ephraim 5, Sarah 16, Abigail 14, Elizabeth 3 years old. Will dated 1st September, 1690.

I Josiah Adkins of Middletown do leave this as my last Will & Testament: I give to my wife Elizabeth Adkins my House, Houselott & Stock, for her life time, and to be at her dispose at her death, only willing her not to dispose of it but to my Children then surviving. I give to my 4 sons, Solomon, Josiah, Benjamin & Ephraim, my Boggy Meadow & Swamp, equally to be divided between them. My Will is that after my wife's decease all Moveables in the House shall be equally divided amongst my 3

394 PROBATE RECORDS. VOL. V,

daughters, Sarah, Abigail and Elizabeth. I give to my other 3 Children,
to whom I have formerly given according to my ability, that is, to Thomas,
Samuel & Elizabeth Gilman, 10 Shillings apeice. I request my Brother
Nathaniel Stowe & Mr. Thomas Warde to be Overseers.
Witness: *Daniel Hurlbut,* JOSIAH X ADKINS. Ls.
  John Hall sen.

Court Record, Page 23—5 March, 1690-1: Will exhibited. Adms.
to the Widow Elizabeth, with the Will annexed.

Page 194-5.

Adkins, Thomas, Hartford. Died 23 October, 1694. Invt. £182-
15-00. Taken 13 December, 1694, by Joseph Olmsted, William Pitkin.
The children: Mary age 22 years, Thomas 21, William 19, Jane 16,
Josiah 9, Sarah 12, Benoni 4 years. Will dated 23 October, 1694.
  The last Will & Testament of Thomas Adkins is as followeth: That
my wife shall live in my house as long as she is a Widow if she please,
& improve my Estate, with my son Thomas, for the Good of the Family.
Also my Will is that what Estate my wife brought with her shall return
to her again. Also that all my homestead, with the Grass Land in the
Swamp, be equally divided between my son Thomas & my son Josiah.
Also that my son Thomas shall have my house & shall have my Share of
Team & Tackling. Also that my son William shall have a lott at the
farther End of my Land. Also that my brother Gabriel shall have my
little boy Benoni & bring him up till he come of age, if he please; and if
he take him before he is able to earn his living then he shall have some
of my Estate to help to bring him up. I give to my daughter Jane the
Bedd that I lye on, with the Furniture thereto belonging. I give to my
daughter Mary a black Heifer. I give to my son Benoni a lott of 10 acres
abutting on the Country Road and so eastward. My wife & my son
Thomas to be my Executors. (Not signed.)
Witness: *John Williams,*
  Gabriel Williams.

Court Record, Page 77—19 December, 1694: Adms. to the Relict
& son Thomas. The Inventory of Mrs. Elizabeth Adkins was taken 11
November, 1700, and mentions the above named children. (See Vol. VI.)
  Page 82—7 March, 1694-5: This Court being desired to make Dist.
of the Estate of Thomas Adkins, doe find the Estate to amount to £150-
02-07. Order to Dist. 1-3 of the Personal Estate to the Widow and 1-3
of the Real during her life. To the Eldest son a double portion, and to
the rest equal portions, and what they have already received or is given to
them to be a part of their portion allotted to them by Distribution. And
appoint Deacon Joseph Olmsted and Capt. Joseph Fitch Dist. to divide
the Estate to the Legatees, and appoint Thomas Adkins Adms., and the
Relict is released.

Page 59-60.

Invt. in Vol. VI.

Alderman, William, Farmington. Invt. £42-09-06. Taken 25 August, 1697, by John Hart & Daniel Andrews sen. Invt. of Land in Simsbury, £53-00-00. Taken 13 April, 1698, by John Higley, Samuel Wilcoxson, John Moses & John Slater sen. The children: Thomas age 14 years, William 12, John 3, Joseph 1, Mary 17, Sarah 6 years.

Court Record, Page 134—2 September, 1697: Adms. Granted to the Widow of William Alderman, late of Farmington, Decd.

Page 30—(Vol. VI) 14 April, 1698: Invt. exhibited by Mary the Relict, who appeared in Court and was given full power to Adms. on the Estate.

Page 56—1st September, 1698: It appears that the Estate of William Alderman is non solvent. The Court orders the Creditors to bring in their Accounts to the Clerk of the Court.

Page 227-8.

Allyn, Col. John, Hartford. Invt. £1806-13-10. Taken 12 November, 1696, by Cyprian Nickols, Thomas Bunce & Joseph Easton.

Note: Items from the Inventory of Col. John Allyn:

	£ s d
Two Negroes: A Man and Woman, in Cash,	45-00-00
A Bill due from Robert Lane,	145-00-00
A Tankard,	8-00-00
A Candle Cup,	3-06-00
A Salt Seller,	3-09-06
A Dram Cup,	10-06
A large Spoon,	13-06
A Ditto (broken),	8-00
	8-00
In Cash & Plate,	206-15-06

Court Record, Page 121-2-3—18 November, 1696: Adms. to Joseph Whiting, William Whiting & Aaron Cooke. They are to report to this Court March next. And further, this Court do appoint Sergt. Thomas Bunce & Mr. William Pitkin to Dist. the Estate as follows:

	£ s d
To the Relict 1-3 part of the Real Estate during life,	406-00-02
The Real Estate in all amounts to	1220-05-00
To Each of the five children,	162-14-00
To the Relict in Moveables,	46-00-02
To each of the Children in Moveables,	46-00-02
To the Relict, Plate & Money,	24-02-09 ½
To Each of the Children, in Cash & Plate,	24-02-09 ½

The 1-3 to the Relict in Real Estate, to be divided to the Children after her decease.

Record on File: 23 November, 1696: To the Widow of Col. John Allyn, To William Whiting, To William Southmayd, To Aaron Cooke, To Elizabeth Allyn; by Thomas Bunce & William Pitkin.

Page 146—(Vol. IV) 4 March, 1696-7: Report of the Dist. of the Estate of Col. John Allyn, per Sergt. Thomas Bunce and William Pitkin.

Allyn, Benjamin. Court Record, Page 153—(Vol. IV) 16 April, 1697: Benjamin Allyn, son of John Allyn, late of Windsor, decd, did appear before Mr. John Moore, Commissioner, and made Choice of Lt. Return Strong to be his Guardian.

Page 58-9.

Allyn, Martha, Middletown. Died 19 May, 1690. Invt. £58-03-09. Taken 23 March, 1690, by John Hall sen. & Samuel Collins. Will dated 30 April, 1690.

I Martha Allyn of Middletown, in the Colony of Connecticut, do leave this as my last Will & Testament: I give to my son Samuel those things belonging to a man's work. To my daughter Martha, all my Household Goods. To my cousin Obadiah Allyn, a pot which was Obadiah Allyn's Mother's. I request my son John Tilleson & my Cousin Obadiah Allyn to take Care of my Children, and that they may be Overseers of my Estate. And further, I request our faithfull Pastor Mr. Noadiah Russell to be one of my Overseers.

Witness: *John Hall sen,*   MARTHA X ALLYN.
       William Southmayd.

Court Record, Page 14—27 May, 1690: Will & Invt. exhibited. There being no Executor appointed, Adms. is granted to John Tilliston with the Will annexed.

Page 222-3.

Allyn, Capt. Thomas, Windsor. Died 14 February, 1695-6. Invt. £1174-13-09. Taken 27 February, 1695, by Return Strong Sen. and John Porter.

Court Record, Page 101—5 March, 1695-6. At a County Court: An Invt. of the Estate of Capt. Thomas Allyn of Windsor was now Exhibited, wherein It appears that Matthew Allyn, the Eldest son, had received of his Portion before Marriage, of his Father in a house and Lands with an Engagement to pay at a late date £100 in addition, which in Value and amount was a full double portion of his Father's Estate. The Court Order

Dist. to the 4 other sons and the 4 daughters, Children of the sd. Thomas Allyn and Brothers & Sisters to the sd. Eldest son Matthew Allyn.

The Court appoint Mr. Return Strong and Daniel Hayden, wth Col. Allyn, to Distribute the Estate among the Children in equal Portions, Reserving Cloth and yarn so much as may be necessary for present clothing before the division, then all to receive (not excluding Matthew). Samuel Allyn and Matthew Allyn to be Adms.—8 April, 1696.

Dist. File: 5 June, 1702: By Agreement of Legatees: To Matthew, Thomas, John (Dec.), Samuel, Benjamin Allyn and Abigail Bissell (Jane, Sarah and Hester not Mentioned in the Agreement, but 4 daughters were subjects of the Order of the Court as above said).

Page 32—(Vol. VII) 8 September, 1702: The Adms. on the Estate of Capt. Thomas Allyn cited to appear with their Account.

Page 40—2 March, 1702-3: Report by Capt. Matthew Allyn and Samuel Allyn, Adms. on the Estate of their Father Capt. Thomas Allyn decd. This Court appoint Lt. Return Strong, Lt. Daniel Heydon and Alexander Allyn to Dist. to such of the Children (Matthew excepted) as will pay their rateable part of debts due of £61-13-08, for which there is not Personal property sufficient to pay. There remains yet considerable Land undivided.

Page 62—19 December, 1704: Whereas, there was an Order of the General Court of the 11th May, 1704 (respecting the Dist. of the Estate of Capt. Thomas Allyn which was partly made by the County Court and afterwards by Order of the General Court, which Dist. interfere by setting Land to Matthew Allyn which was before set out to his Brethren) directed to this Court to inquire into that matter and to make such Orders concerning a new Dist. of the Land formerly Dist. which have interfered as aforesd., as also concerning the remainder of the Lands belonging to sd. Estate of Capt. Thomas Allyn which is not yet Dist., and pursuant thereunto, Matthew Allyn, Thomas Allyn, John Allyn, Samuel Allyn, Benjamin Allyn, and Abigail Bissell, Widow, of sd. Windsor, Children of the late Thomas Allyn, being summoned, appeared before this Court. Whereupon this Court do now order a new Dist.

Page 65—6 March, 1704-5: There was exhibited in this Court an Agreement made by the Children of Capt. Thomas Allyn, under their Hands & Seals, respecting the final Settlement of the Estate of their Father, which this Court accepts & approve, and order to be kept on File. Matthew Allyn for himself, & Samuel Allyn for himself and his sister Jane Decd, personally appeared in this Court and acknowledged the sd. Agreement to be their Act and Deed.

Page 66—5 April, 1705: Dist. exhibited and rejected by the Court, which now appoints Richard Lord, Aaron Cooke and Caleb Stanley Jr. to dist. the Estate with regard to an Agreement of the Heirs. And whereas, Ebenezer Gilbert of Hartford, who married Esther, one of sd. Children, hath complained to this Court that his Charge was £48 in the 1st Dist. of sd. Estate, which he cannot understand how it was paid to him, This Court do therefore order the sd. Lord & Dist. to examine and inquire into that matter.

Page 68—26 April, 1705: Matthew Allyn having paid Debts from his Personal Estate amounting to the sum of £34-04-09, is directed to make Application to the General Court to sell Land to reimburse himself.

Page 93—7 May, 1707: Matthew Allyn, Adms. on his Father's Estate, now exhibits a Distribution of the remaining part of sd. Estate by Thomas Stoughton, Job Drake and Nathaniel Loomis. Per Order of 13 February, 1705-6. (See Order of Court, 1696.)

Will not Recorded—See File.

Allyn, Thomas, Middletown. Invt. £946-10-00. I Thomas Allyn of Middletown, in the Colony of Connecticut, do make my last Will & Testament: Imprs. I give to my beloved wife martha Allyn, for the terme of her life, my now dwelling house, home lott, orchard and barne. Also I give to my wife, for terme of her life abovesd., my heather lott in the large meadow near the reveret, buttinge upon the great river east, the reveret west, Mr. Giles Hamlings land South, Ensign William Wards land north. I give also to my wife, during her life, two acres of plowland in my lott bounded upon the great river east, upon John hamlins West, upon Widow Wetmore, Samuel hoale senior and John bacon north, upon John Hulbut and the Widow adams south. Also to my wife, during her widow hood, all the household Stuff which was my proper Estate before I married this my wife, and that which Shee brought with her, to be and remain her own forever. I give also to my wife, during her widow hood, my team, two oxen and a hors, and two cowes. Imprs. I give to Obadiah Alline Junior my Lott at wongoge, to him and his aires for ever, buttinge upon the Creek South, and agst. Widow hubards land west, Nathaniel bacons and I. Wetmore's land north. I give also to Obadiah Junior, abovesd., my upland lott att Wongoge, Containing 29 acres more or less, to him and his airs for ever. I give to my Kinsman obadiah Alline Senior my Lott on the east sid the great river, Cont. two hundred acres more or less, to him and his aires forever. I give also to these sons of my Kinsman Obadiah alline Senior (Thomas Alline, Samuel alline and John alline) my division of Land at Coking Choaged, to them and their aires for Ever, to be equally divided to them at the discretion of my over seers in Case they agree not. I give to my wives sonn Samll Gibson six acres of meadow lyinge in the longe meadow, buttinge upon a high way and the great river east, Thomas rany north, Samll hoult Senior South, the land comonly Called the heather nek west. I give also to Samll Gibson three acres of Swampe Joyneing to the meadow given as abovesd, to him and his aires for ever. My will is that his mother shall have the improvement of the meadows and Swamp abovsd. till Samll Gibson comes to the age of twenty one years; and in case he dy before he comes to that age, the meadow and Swampe abovesd. to returne to his brother Roger Gibson upon the same terms. I give also to Samll Gibson nineteen acres of river meadow and Swampe, his mother to improve it as abovesd; and in Case of his death before he comes of age, then to return to his brother Roger Gibson, to him and his aires for ever, and my wife to improve as abovesd. till he coms of age of twenty one years. My will is that these lands which I have given to the son of my Kinsman obadiah Alline that their father shall have the improvement of them until they come to the age of twenty one years; and if one dy before he Come of age, then the Lands to be equally divided to the survivinge brothers; and if they all dy be-before they come of age, then the Lands to return to their father obadiah Alline senior, my Kinsman, and his aeres forever. I doe give and be-queath to my beloved wife Martha Alline my now dwelling house, home lott, barne and orchard, to her and her son roger and his aeres forever, provided my wife pay unto my Kinsman obadiah Alline Senior, or to his acct. or order, the full and Just sum of thirty pounds, in Cattell or any provision pay, within the terme of ten years after my decease, out of what I have willed to her for terme of life and for ever. I give also to my Kinsman obadiah Alline Senior all the Land and meadow which I have given to my wife during her natural life, that is to say, six acres of Meadow and Swamp and two acres of plow land, to him and his aeres for ever, to have and possess imediately after the decease of my wife. I give also to my wives daughter Martha Gibson ten pounds, to bee paid by the Legatees Equally When Shee comes to the age of Eighteen years. I appoynt my Kinsman Obadiah Alline Senior Executor and adminis-trator to this my Last will. I appoint my beloved wife Martha Alline Executrix and administratrix of this my Last will. I request my Loveing friends (and appoint them) Robert warner and Samll Collins Senior my overseers. This is my Last will and Testament, as witness my hand the 15 October, in the year of our Lord 1688, in the fourth year of the reign of our soverine James, by the Grace of God King of England.

Witness: *Robert Warner,*   THOMAS ALLINE. Ls.
          Samll Collins.

Court Record, 5 Feb., 1688. Held at Hartford by John Allyn, Judge; Humphrey Davy, Mr. Jno Wadsworth, Justices. Obadiah Allyn & Mar-tha Allyn accepted of their being Executors according to the Will, which was Proved by the oath of *Mr. Samll Collins & Robt. Warner.*

Page 173.

Andrus (Andarus), Abraham, Waterbury. Died 3d May, 1693. Invt. £177-17-00. Taken 5 September, 1693, by Thomas Judd, John Welton. The children: Sarah, Abraham, Mary, Benjamin, Robert, & one unborn.

Court Record, Page 61—7 September, 1693: Adms. to the Widow, Sarah Andrews, & the Court doe order the widow to improve the Estate for her best advantage. She being with child by the sayd Andrews, the Court doe not distribute the Estate till she is delivered, and till the debts are payd or ordered to be paid. (Name omitted) & Thomas Porter to be Overseers.

Page 83—20 March, 1694-5: Upon request of Sarah Andrews of Waterbury, Widow of Abraham Andrews, for a distribution of her Decd husbands Estate, she having given account of a House and Home lott sold to her Brother Robert Porter, This Court order a Distribution.

Page 61.

Andrews, John, Hartford. Died 6 June, 1690. Invt. £99-09-00. Taken 24 June, 1690, by George Grave, Joseph Mygatt. The children: Samuel, age 20 years, Jan., 1689-90; Mary, 8 years. February, 1689-90.

Court Record, Page 15—26 June, 1690: Adms. to the Widow, & Order to Distribute the Estate.

Page 91.

Andrews, Thomas, Middletown. Invt. £56-09-06. Taken 3 March, 1690-1, by William Cheeny, Samuel Collins, Daniel Markham. The children: Thomas, John, Samuel, Hannah, Elizabeth, Sarah, & Abigail Andrews.

Court Record, Page 24—5 March, 1690-1: Adms. to the Widow. David Sage & Isaac Johnson to be Overseers.

Page 64—6 December, 1693: The Children request a Settlement of their Father's Estate, the mother having married and moved fro the Jurisdiction of this Court. Thomas Andrews appt. Adms. to pay the Childrens portion as they come of age.

Page 125.

Arnold, Daniel. Invt. £52-11-00. Taken 25 March, 1692, by Joseph Easton, Ichabod Welles, Selectmen. Will Nuncupative. The Testimony of John Mason, aged about 40 years, and his wife Hannah, about 37 years of age, and Elizabeth Arnold, aged about 45 years: Each of them doe Testify and say that Daniel Arnold did give to each of his Children fower pounds out of the fifty pounds John Mason is to pay for the Land he bought of the sayd Arnold. This we did hear him say in his last sickness.

Court Record, Page 40—13 April, 1692: Adms. to John Mason With will annexed.

Page 60—(Vol. VI) 4 November, 1698: John Mason having Died, Adms. was now granted to Nathaniel Arnold, son of Daniel Arnold Deceased.

Page 132.

Arnold, Joseph, Haddam. Died 22 October, 1691. Invt. £151-10-00. Taken 2 March, 1691-2, by Daniel Braynard, Timothy Spencer. The children: John age 29 years, Joseph 26, Samuel 23, Josiah 21, Susannah 16, Jonathan 12, Elizabeth 9.

Court Record, Page 44—21 July, 1692: Adms. to the Widow, with Joseph and Josiah Arnold.

Page 53—30 March, 1693: An agreement by the Children to settle their Father's Estate: John, Joseph & Jonathan to receive £11 each. Samuel has his portion by a Deed of Gift of Land from his Father at Machamoodus. Josiah to have £118 out of this, to pay £10 apiece to his two sisters and to pay all the debts. There being no provision for the wife, although she be married this Court confirms the Agreement with the caution that if the woman see Cause she shall have her thirds of the profits during life, the agreement to the Contrary notwithstanding.

Baker, Joseph. Court Record, Page 28—8 April, 1691: Whereas Joseph Baker, by the last Will of John Basey of Hartford, had a parcell of Land given him of 17 acres valued in the Inventory at £10, and the sd. Joseph Baker being Deceased, we, upon Motion of John Baker, the Father of sd. Joseph Baker, Dist. the sd. Estate equally between the Brothers of sd. Joseph Baker that are now living.

Page 128.

Baker, Joseph, Windsor. Died 11 December, 1691. Invt. £179-11-04. Taken by Samuel Baker, Job Drake. Will dated 5 October, 1691.

I Joseph Baker of Windsor, in the Colony of Connecticut, doe make this my last Will & Testament: I give to my son Joseph Baker, when he shall come to the age of 21 years, ¼ part of my Estate. I give unto my daughter Lydia, when she come to the age of 18 years, ¼ part of my Estate. My Will is that my wife Hannah Baker shall have the use of all my Estate until my Children come of age. Also, to have the use of my House & ½ of my Estate during her life. Also, to spend the Estate, so far as she shall need, ¼ part. I give to my wife, to dispose of as shee see Good, the other ¼ part. I desire my Brother Samuel and my neighbor Job Drake to be Overseers.   JOSEPH BAKER.

Witness: *Samuel Baker,*
Job Drake.

Court Record, Page 41—13 April, 1692: Adms., with the will annexed, to the Widow and Samuel Baker. Will proven.

Page 53-4.

Barnes, Thomas sen., Farmington. A Deed of Guift made by Thomas Barnes sen. (which is to stand as his last Will), dated 9 June,

1688: This may certify to all Concerned: That I Thomas Barnes sen., of Farmington, for & in Consideration of the natural Love & Good Affection to my wife & Children hereafter mentioned, & for other good Causes moving, have given and granted as followeth: To my beloved wife Mary Barnes I give the Use & Improvement of halfe my Homelott, Dwelling house, Orchard, Barn & Yard lying and being in the Township of Farmington; as also the Use & Improvement of halfe my Land in Paquabuck Meadow & Con chee. The Use of the Lands and houseing above mentioned I give to my sd. wife during the term of her natural life. The particulars above mentioned, according to the Tennour expressed, I give to my wife provided she shall pay or cause to be paid the ½ of my Just Debts. To my son Thomas Barnes I give the ½ of my Homelott, Dwelling house, Orchard, Barn & Yard lying and being within the Township of Farmington; also half my Land in Pawquabuck Meadow & Conshee, with half my Quick Stock & halfe my Household Stuffe; the other halfe I give to him after my wife's decease. To my son Ebenezer I give ½ the Lands in Pawquabuck Meadow and Conshee after his Mother's decease; also, my 4 acre Lott lying at Rattlesnake Hill, & ½ of the rest of my Woodland or Outlands lying in the Farmington Bounds, at the age of 21 years. The other halfe of these last mentioned Woodland or Outlands I give to my son Thomas Barnes. To my Children which are already gone from me and disposed in marriage, I have formerly given according to my Ability, with which I expect they shall acquiesse.
Witness: *John Stanly sen.,*   THOMAS X BARNES.
   John Hooker.

John Hooker of Farmington made Oath on the 7th of February, 1689-90, before William Lewes, Comms., that the Instrument was the free Act and Deed of Thomas Barnes sen., Decd.

Court Record, Page 11—6 March, 1689-90: Will approved by the Court.

Page 151-2.

Barnes, Thomas sen., Middletown. The Last Will and Testament of Thomas barnes senior, Dwelling in Middletown, in the County of Hartford and Collony of Connecticutt, Is as follows:

Imprimis. I give to my Eldest son John barnes fourty acres of upland which I bought of Mr. Mose & Thomas Wheeler, Lying together. More over I give to my said son that Land on which his hous standeth, bought of old Goodman Wheeler, and I give him allso a part of that Land I bought of old Goodman Loe.

It. I give to my son Thomas Barnes that parcell of upland where hee hath built his hous, to lye on the south sid, from the Crooked tree where Mr. brecot & I parted, to the Great Chesnut tree, & so by the bogie meadow sid till they com At the old Lines. I give him a peice of land I bought of loe & Els, that Is, from the front Line to the meadow; the one halfe of that I give to Thomas, and the other halfe to my son Daniell.

It. I give to my son Danill Barnes all that upland on the north sid of my son Thomas as far as my Land goeth.

It. I give to my Daughter mercy Jacobs twenty acres of upland, that is, that Land on which their hous standeth, that is, to her and her younger son, to them & to their heirs for ever.

Ite. I give to my Daughter martha twenty shillings, my son Thomas to pay her it after my Deseas.

It. I give to my Daughter Elizabeth twenty shillings, my son Danill to pay it her after my Deseas.

It. I give to my youngest son, maibe Barns, all my Land in Middletown, after my wivs Deseas (all but the hous & home lott). At my Deseas the hous and home lott I will to my loveing wife During her naturall Life. More over I give my said wife two Cows, and my will is that my son maybe shall Look after and provid for the keeping thos two cows which I give my wife. My will is my wife shall have all my mouabls During her naturall life.

It. I give to my Daughter abigaill three pounds, and my son maibe to pay it her after my Deseas.

It. I give allso to my louing wife all my bees and sheep, if there be any Remaining. My will is that after my wiues Deseas all my utensills belonging to the hous shall bee my son maibes, and what Cattell shall be remaining after my Deseas I give to my said son maibe. Farther, my will is, that as I have Done according to my abillety for my sons John and Thomas and Danill, soe I expect, and it is my will, that John and Thomas shall pay to their mother five bushells of wheat a year, yearly, During the time of her widowhood, and Danill five bushells of wheat yearly During the same time.   THOMAS BARNES.

Signed in the presence of
Daniel Harris Juner,
John Hall Senior.

ffebruary 25, 1683-'84.

John Hall sen., being infirm in body & not able to come up to the Court, appeared before me and gave oath yt the above, as he was a witness, that Thomas Barnes, the siner hereof, was, to the best of his Judgement, of a sound understanding. October ye 6th, 1692.
P. John Hamlin, Commisior.

Court Record, Page 60—7 September, 1693: The Last Will and Testament of Thomas Barns, of Middletown, was exhibited in Court, proved, and ordered to be recorded.

Beckley, John, Wethersfield. Court Record, Page 106—8 April, 1696: An Inventory of the Estate of John Beckley was exhibited in Court.

Page 108—8 April, 1696: Order for Distribution: To the Widow, 1-3 part of the Real Estate during Life; To the eldest son a double portion, and to the other Children single portions. And appoint Ebenezer Deming and Benjamin Churchill of Wethersfield Distributors.

Dist. File, 11 January, 1699: Estate of John Beckley. To the Widow, to ye Eldest son, to Robert Webster, to Samuel Spencer, to Matthew Cadwell, to ye youngest daughter. By John Deming & Benjamin Churchill.

Page 72-3.

Beckley, Sergt. Richard, Wethersfield. Died 5 August, 1690. Invt. £383-05-00. Taken 2nd September, 1690, by Samuel Butler & Nathaniel Bowman. Will dated 15 May, 1689.

I Richard Beckley of Wethersfield doe make this my last Will & Testament: Imprimis: I give to my wife Frances convenient Rooms in my Dwelling house, also as much of my Household Stuff and other Moveables as she shall want during her natural life. Also, I give unto my sd. wife 1 Bible, the best Bed & Bedstead in the house with all the Furniture thereunto belonging, to her & her heirs & assigns forever. Also I doe order & Will that my son Nathaniel Beckley shall maintain his Mother, my sd. wife, honourably and comfortably all the days of her natural life, out of the Estate I have hereafter by this my Will given to him. I give to my son John Beckley, my eldest son, all the Lands of mine in his possession and Improvement that his houseing standeth upon, and also so much Land out of my Farm as will make up the Rest 100 acres. Also I give to my sd. son John 2 Barrells of Cyder a year out of the fruit of my Orchard, & to have it as soon as my Orchard will yield 4 barrells a year. I give to my 2nd. son, Benjamin Beckley, all the Lands in his possession of mine which his house now standeth upon, & also all the Land that my young orchard is upon on the West side of the River, with the sd. Orchard. Also I give to my sd. son Benjamin ½ of my Grass Land, and so much more of Land out of my Farm as will make up that I give him 100 acres. Also I order that my son Nathaniel Beckley shall help my sd. son Benjamin to build and finish a Barn for the proper use & Estate of my sd. son Benjamin. I give to my son Nathaniel Beckley, my 1st. son, my Dwelling house, Barn, Outhouses, Orchards, Yards & Convenient Passages, also ½ of my Mowable Grass Land. I give to my eldest daughter Sarah £8, to Mary £6, to Hannah £6, and to my gr. child Richard Beckley, the son of my son John Beckley, 10 acres of Land and one Musket. I make my son Nathaniel Beckley sole Executor.

Witness: *Nathaniel Bowman,*   RICHARD BECKLEY, Ls.
        John Welles.

Court Record, Page 18—4 September, 1690: Will approved.

Dist. File: 12 November, 1701: To Benjamin, to Nathaniel, to Richard (grandson).

By William Warner, Thomas Welles & Jonathan Belding.

Page 134-5-6.

Bidwell, John, Hartford. Died 3rd July, 1692. Invt. £1081-06-00. Taken 25 August, 1692, by Stephen Hosmer & Joseph Mygatt.

Court Record, Page 44—28 July, 1692: Adms. to Sarah, the Relict of John Bidwell, decd.

Page 45—1st September, 1692: Invt. of the Estate of John Bidwell exhibited in Court by the Relict. There being no Accot of his Debts & Credits given into the Court, this Court orders the Relict, who is Adms. to the Estate, to bring in an Accot thereof to this Court at their Adjournment, when Dist. may be granted on the Estate. This Court appoint Mr. Ichabod Welles, Daniel Bidwell & Joseph Mygatt to be Assistants to the Widow and Overseers to the Children.

Page 133.

Bidwell, Joseph, Wethersfield. Invt. £254-04-00. Taken 17 June, 1692, by Samuel Hall Jr., Joseph Hill, Thomas Fitch. The children: Amy 14, 2d Oct., 1692; Joseph 12, Benjamin 9, Ephraim 6, Lydia 3 years of age, Mary 4 months old. Will dated 2 June, 1692.

I Joseph Bidwell of Wethersfield doe make this my last Will & Testament: My will is that my wife have my entire Estate for her maintanence and the bringing up of my Children. If she marry, then to make an equal division to all my Children of all my Estate which is left at her Marriage, excepting her thirds. My wife to be sole Executrix. I desire Deac. Samuel Butler and my brother Jonathan Colefox to be Overseers.

JOSEPH X BIDWELL.

Witness: *Sarah House,* wife of *William House,*
    Elizabeth Arnold, Wife of *Henry Arnold.*

Court Record, Page 44—2 July, 1662: Will approved.

Page 184.

Bissell, Jacob, Simsbury. Died 1st August, 1694. Invt. £166-16-09. Taken 23 August, 1694, by Peter Buell, Nathaniel Holcomb, Jeremiah Gillett, John Slater, sen. Legatees: Mary, the Relict, and son Jacob, born 8 June last, 1694.

Court Record, Page 71—6 September, 1694: Adms. to (Mrs.) Mary (Bissell), and appoint Jonathan Gillett and James Ennoe to assist.

Page 30 (Vol. VI)—13 April, 1699: Order to Dist. to the Widow 1-3 part, and to Jacob Bissell, the son, 2-3. By John Higley & John Slater, who report 5 September, 1698. (See also Page 53, Court Record: *This Order was reversed by the Court of Assistants.*)

Page 24 (Vol. VIII) 4 December, 1710: Peter Buel and his Wife Cited to appear and give account of Adms. on Estate of Jacob Bissell.

Page 30—3 April, 1711: Peter Buel of Simsbury and Mary his wife (late Mary Bissell, Widow), Adms. on Estate of Jacob Bissell, sometime of Simsbury Decd, being summoned to appear before the Court to render account of the Adms. on that Estate, appeared and by copies of record showed that they had several years before fully Adms. on the same, and rendered their account thereof to the County Court or Court of Probate in this County; and that the remaining part of the Estate was distributed and divided according to law between Mary the Widow and Jacob Bissell, a minor, only son and heir of the sd. Decd. Peter Buel now informs this Court that the said Jacob Bissell, the son (who was a minor about 16 years of age), is also lately deceased Intestate and without Issue. For himself and his wife Mary, and also for and in behalf of the children borne of her, he Claimed all the Estate of Jacob Bissell, the son deceased, and prayeth the Court to so decide. John Pettebone, Jr., in behalf of Mary his Wife, and Stephen Pettebone, in behalf of Deborah his Wife, sisters of Jacob Bissell, the Father, and John Bissell, son of John Bissell, one of the Brothers of Jacob Bissell, the Father Decd, and their Children Representing them, appeared before this Court and Claimed the same estate, as being next of kin to both the said Jacob Bissells, the Father and the son, and heirs of the sd. Jacob Bissell, the Father, who was the last possessor thereof, and exhibited their pleas and reasons to show their sd. right, and prayed that an order of the Court may be made settling the same on them. The Court ordered the Estate to Peter Buel his Wife Mary, and their Children. The other parties appealed to the Court of Assistants, who reversed the decision, giving the Intestate Estate to the Brothers and Sisters of Jacob Bissell, The Father, deceased.

Page 90—6 October, 1712; An Order of Court was Issued to Distribute to Uncles and Aunts according to a Decree of the Superior Court, 16 Sept., 1712.

Distribution as per File, 21st October, 1712: To James Eno, sen., in right of his Wife Abigail Bissell; To John Pettebone, in right of his Wife Mary Bissell; To Joshua Bissell, To Heirs of John Bissell; To Stephen Pettebone, in right of his Wife Deborah Bissell; To Nathaniel Phelps, in right of his Wife Hannah Bissell; To Elizabeth Root, of Westfield; to John Bissell, to Abigail Baker, to a daughter of Samuel Bissell named Mary, to Each Uncle, Aunt and Cusson. By John Higley, James Cornish, Joseph Phelps.

- - - - - - -

Inventory on File.

Bissell, Lt. John, Windsor. Died at New York, 1688. Invt. £49-10-00. Taken by Jacob Drake & Abraham Phelps. Exhibited in Court at Hartford, 7 March, 1688-9.

- - - - - - -

Inventory on File.

Exhibited in Court, 15 March, 1693-4.
Bissell, John, Lt., Windsor. Invt. £301-04-00. Taken 7 November, 1688, by Samuel Mason & Nathaniel Bissell.

(See W. R. for the following items):

John Bissell & Isabell Mason were married 17 June, 1658.

Mary, daughter of John Bissell Jr., born	*22 February, 1658-9.*
John, son, " " " " "	*4 May, 1661.*
Daniel, son, " " " " "	*22 September, 1663.*
Dorothy, dau. " " " " "	*10 August, 1665.*
Josiah, son, " " " " "	*10 October, 1670.*
Hezekiah, son, " " " " "	*30 April, 1673.*
Ann, daughter, " " " " "	*28 April, 1675.*
Jeremiah, son, " " " " "	*22 June, 1677.*

Court Record, Page 15—30 May, 1690: Whereas, there has not been a Dist. of the Estate of Cornet John Bissell, this Court now appoint Capt. Samuel Mason and Nathaniel Bissell to Dist. the Estate of John Bissell sen. of Windsor, and John Bissell Junr., all valued as Money.

On the 15th of March, 1693-4 (see File for Dist.):

	£ s d
To the Relict:	63-10-00
To Daniel Bissell,	42-08-06
To Josiah Bissell,	42-08-06
To Jeremiah Bissell,	42-08-06
To Samuel Bissell,	42-08-06
To Dorothy Stoughton,	42-08-06
To Ann Bissell,	42-08-06

Page 30—16 May, 1691: Whereas, the County Court held at Hartford 26 June, 1690, ordered Capt. Samuel Mason and Mr. Nathaniel Bissell to Distribute the Estate of Cornet John Bissell to the Legatees according to the Dist. the Court made at the aforesd. Court, Capt. Mason his occasions being such he cannot attend, the Court now see Reason to appoint Mr. John Moore and Mr. Daniel Heydon to Dist. the Estate according to the sd. Order of Court, they taking the advice of sd. Capt. Mason and Mr. Nathaniel Bissell therein.

Page 168.

Bissell, John Jr., Windsor. Invt. £64-18-06. Taken 12 April, 1693, by Daniel Heydon sen. & Samuel Pinney sen.

Court Record, Page 67—15 March, 1693-4: This Court having received a Copy of the Dist. of the Estate of Lt. John Bissell, sen., of Windsor, and John Bissell, son, they do approve and confirm the same, and appoint Daniel Bissell & Lt. Daniel Heydon & Job Drake, son of John Drake, to perfect what is to be done in the Dist. or payment thereof.

Page 70—4 April, 1694: Complaint being made by the persons concerned in the Estate of John Bissell Decd, that in the last Settlemt of sd. Estate, Josiah and Hezekiah Bissell being put to the old Houseing prised at £20 Money, will have their portions much worse than the other children, and Capt. Samuel Mason having been acquainted with it and returned his concurrence, the Court see Cause to alter the Dist., viz., that the sd. houseing all of it shall stand in the reversion part of the Estate and be dividable amongst all the Children after their Mother's decease, and that the ¼ part of the Lott on the East side before stated as part of the Reversion part shall, after their Mother's Decease, belong wholly to sd. Josiah and Hezekiah, to be equally divided between them, which is valued at £16-10 Money; & that £3-10 Money out of John Bissell's Jr. his Estate be paid to the sd. 2 sons, that is, 35 shillings to each, to make up £20, the value of their former parts of sd. houseing; and that the sd. 2 sons have the benefit of the Houseing in the Interim if they will keep it in good repair as they find it; and also that they have the present benefit of the Upland part of the Aliottment over the River.

Dist. File, 1693-4: To the Estate of John Bissell sen. and John Bissell Jr., to the Relict, to Daniel, to Josiah, to Hezekiah, to Jeremiah, to Samuel, and to Dorothy Stoughton & to Ann Bissell.

Page 32.

Bissell, Joseph, Windsor. Invt. £195-04-00. Taken 29 October, 1689, by John Maudsley, John Moore.

County Court, Page 6, at Windsor, 11 November, 1689: Adms. to the Widow & her Father Strong, with Mr. John Moore.

Page 77—5 December, 1694: Order to Dist. to the Widow, to the Eldest son a double portion, and the remainder of the Estate, the houseing and Lands, to return to the two sons after their Mother's decease. This Court appoint John Fyler & Return Strong Distributors.

Dist: Page 143—(Vol. IV) 4 March, 1696-7: Mr. John Moore in Court renounced his Adms. on the Estate of Joseph Bissell of Windsor Decd, he declaring to the Court that he never did act in that Capacity. The Court see Cause to grant him a *Quietus Est.*

Page 13—(Vol. VII) 17 April, 1701: Upon the prayer of Lt. Strong, the Court appoint Lt. Daniel Heydon, Lt. Samuel Cross and Sergt. Benajah Holcomb to Dist. the Estate of Joseph Bissell, late of Windsor Decd, according to an Order of Court formerly made respecting the same, and make return September next at the County Court.

Page 12—(Vol. VII) 17 April, 1701: This Court do appoint Lt. Return Strong Guardian to Joseph and Benoni Bissell, minor children of Joseph Bissell Decd, son of Thomas Bissell aforesd.

Page 28—(Vol. VIII) 5 February, 1710-11: Return Strong of Windsor, late Guardian to Joseph Bissell of Windsor, cited to appear before the Court with an Account of his Guardianship.

Page 32—2 April, 1711: Return Strong cited to appear and render an Account of Guardianship to his gr. son Joseph Bissell of Windsor. Capt. Higley and his wife, who was Mother to Joseph Bissell, also cited to appear.

Page 27-8-9-30-1.

Bissell, Thomas sen., Windsor. Invt. £864-10-00. Taken 16 October, 1689, by Samuel Grant sen. & Return Strong. Will dated 24 August, 1688.

The last Will & Testament of Thomas Bissell sen. is as followeth: First. My will is that my wife have for her use, and the use of my children under age, My now dwelling house & Homested, and my lot above scantic, & my lot of 16 rod that lyeth betwixt Brother Nathaniel's land, & also about twelve rods Broad next to Goodman Taylor's throughout the three miles, this to have the improvement of till they that I shall give it too Come of age, & then when my youngest sons come of age it shall be at her liberty to have the improvement of one third of the Land I now dispose of on the East side of the River on the South side of Scantic, or Ten pounds the year, to be payd by those that possess my lands on the East side of the River. Also I give my wife one Hundred pounds of my moveable Estate for her proper use. I give to my son Thomas half of my farm that I had of my Father Moore. I give to my son John my House & lott on the west side of the River by goodman Randall's, & 2 acres I bought of John Stoughton, & 2½ acres I bought of John Stiles, my Wood lot by John Owen, £20 of my moveable Estate, and 1-3 of my land at Symsbury. I give to my son Joseph, beside what he hath in the Saw Mill & what I must pay to John Higley for his House, My lot by Plymouth Meadow, 1-3 of land at Simsbury, and the half of my Division Land on the west side of the Great River. I give to my son Benjamin my lot I bought of Goodman Taylor, ¼ of my Division Land on the East side of the Great River, and an equal share of halfe my farm I had of Father Moore, with his Brothers Ephraim & Isack, & one third at Simsbury with John & Joseph. I give to my two sons Ephraim & Isack my now Dwelling House & Homested & that 8 rod broad I bought of My Brother Samuel, & that 8 rods I bought of my father that Joyns to it, & that part of my lot that lyes in the Woods on the North side of Thomas Barn(s) on the East side of the Country Road to the end of the three miles, & a halfe of my devision Land on the East side of the Great River, & a equal share of halfe my farm I had of father Moore, with their Brother Benjamin, and this to be equally divided betwixt them. I give to my daughter Abigail £30 more. I give to John Stoughton, my son, 40 shillings beside what he hath received with his wife Elizabeth; and his two sons, John and William, that were the sons of my daughter Elizabeth, shall have £10 apiece. I give to my daughter Sarah £80. My Wife & my son Thomas to be Executors.

Witness: *Henry Wolcott,*   THOMAS BISSELL, sen.
Return Strong, Samuel Bissell.

A Codicil, dated 26 July, 1689—I nominate Mr. Henry Wolcott, Capt. Return Strong, My Brother Nathaniel Bissell, & John Mason to be Overseers.   THOMAS BISSELL, sen.

Witness: *Henry Wolcott,*
Return Strong, Samuel Bissell.

Court Record, Page 5—11 November, 1689: Will proven.

Page 12 (Vol. VII)—17 April, 1701: Ephraim Bissell, a minor son of Thomas Bissell, made choice of Mr. John Moore to be his Guardian. Isaac Bissell, a minor, made choice of Deacon Job Drake for his Guardian.

Page 99-100.

Blake, John, Middletown. Invt. £230-12-06. Taken 19 January, 1690, by Richard Hall, William Sumner. The children: Mercy age 17 years, Sarah 16, Mary 14, Elizabeth 12, Abigail 10, John 8, Jonathan 6, Stephen 4, Richard Blake 11 months.

Court Record, Page 25—5 March, 1690-1: Adms. to the Widow, and appoint Richard Hall & John Hall, her Father & Brother, to assist in the Administration.

Dist. File: 6 April, 1705: An Agreement to Dist. the Estate to Sarah Blake (Widow), to John, to Jonathan, to Stephen, to Samuel Roberts and Mercy his wife, to John Roberts and Sarah his wife, to Mary Johnson (now widow), to Joseph Johnson and Elizabeth his wife, to Thomas Bibbins and Abigail his wife.

Page 15 (Vol. XI)—3 March, 1729-30: John Blake of Middletown Died Intestate, and that part of his Real Estate set out to the Widow Sarah Blake hath never been dist. to her, and ought to be anew apprised before a just Dist. can be made. This Court appoint Richard Blake, of Middletown, Adms.

Page 108.

Blancher, Richard, Hartford. Died 19 April, 1691. Invt. £181-11-08. Will dated 19 March, 1691-2.

I Richard Blancher of Hartford doe order this to be my last Will: I do Will & bequeathe my House & Lands in Hartford to my son William, to be possessed by him at the age of 21 years, which will be 4 years complete from the 10th of June next ensueing the date of these presents. In default of Issue, I will the Estate to Mr. Timothy Woodbridge & his heirs, etc. I do desire Mr. Timothy Woodbridge to take care of my son William for his Education till he come to the full age of 21 years. I appoint Mr. Timothy Woodbridge & Mr. Joseph Easton sen. to be my Executors.

Witness: *Rebeckah Bowman,*   RICHARD X BLANCHER, Ls.
          Mary Hall.

An Addition was made to this Will, 17 April, 1691: (His son William was found to be one year older than he thought he was.) "And doe leave my son William Blancher with Mr. Timothy Woodbridge of Hartford & Joseph Easton of the same town, as overseers to take full care of him for 3 years; to let him have one year Schooling, then to put him out to some honest man to learn a trade (what trade, yourselves and my son William shall think best)."

Witness: *Joseph Smith,*   RICHARD X BLANCHER.
    Thomas Bowman.

Page 163—Will on File.

Bowen, Daniel, Wethersfield. Died .5 September, 1693. Invt. £139-06-08. Taken by George Buttolph, Jonathan Colefax & Nicholas Morecock. The Nuncupative Will of Daniel Bowen is as followeth:

Sarah Butler, aged fifty years or thereaboutts, and Sarah Benjamin, Aged eighteen years or thereabouts, testifyeth as followeth: That on or about the forth day of September Last past, We being att the house of Mr. Nathaniel Bowman in Wethersfield, in their Majesties Colony of Connecticut, There tending Mr. Daniel Bowen in his Last Sickness, who Deceased on or about the fifth day of September abovesd., the sd. Daniel Bowen being very weak In Body Butt Better Composed In his mind than some Time he had Been In that his Sickness, Then Sarah Butler afforesayd Asked sayd Daniel Bowen Whether he Desired Mrs. Irenia Hubburtt should Be sent for. His (sd. Bowen's) Answer was that he did not Desire she should Be sentt for. Sarah Butler then sayd to him shee feared he would not gett over or Recover of his Sickness. He sayd he hoped that he should get over it. Then Sarah Butler Asked him what hee would doe with his Estate. He Answered he had not much, But then he sayd, Danll Bowen Did Declare, That his Mother And Relations should have his Estate if he did nott Recover. Sarah Benjamin doth not Remember the words "sending for Mrs. Irenia Hubburtt," but the rest she remembers, & they were both prsent when they heard the discourse above sayd; & she then sayd, Sarah Butler sayth, that the Occasion of her propounding these Questions to sayd Bowen was because she heard of severall Claymes to his Estate.

Mrs. Sarah Butler & Sarah Benjamin personally appeared in Court at Hartford, 7 April, 1694, & made Oath to the above written, & they also Testify that they judge he was of Good understanding & memory, his discourse being rationall. As attests: JOHN ALLYN, *Clarke.*

Court Record, Page 62—7 September, 1693: Invt. Exhibited by James Petty, of Southold, L. I., Adms. to Nathaniel Foote, he having given Bond with two Sureties, Lt. Joseph Wadsworth & Cornett Samuel Talcott.

Page 74—14 September, 1694: Nathaniel Foote appeared in Court and gave account of his administration. Evidence having been presented that Josiah Bowen was brother to Daniel, this Court grant Adms. to Josiah Bowen of the estate which was to go to his Mother, Brother & Sisters, as he said in his last sickness in presence of Sarah Butler & Sarah Benjamin, and allowed by the Court as his Last Will.

On File:

The testimony of Jacob Conklin, ae 25 years, James Blinn, ae 20 years, Jonathan Hall, ae 17 years, and Mary Edward, ae 19 years, doe declare that about 17 days past, we being all on bord the sloop Adventure together, near the town of Haddam, Daniel Bowen, lately deceased, being on bord sd. vessell with us, the said Bowen not being well but of sound understanding, and he discourseing of Mrs. Irene Hubbard of Southold, we heard sd. Daniel declare he had such a grate affection for her that in Case he should dye all the estate that he had in the world shee should have it. To these statements they made Oath, as written and signed by them, before

John Allyn, Clerk of Court.

Testimony was offered by James Petty, ae 34 years, and John Homan, ae 22 years, that Daniel Bowen was heard to say, in presence of Wm. Man & Thomas Young of New London, that if he died within a year and a day Edward Mahune should have all his Estate. All being together at plum gut. Sworn in Court.

Attest: *John Allyn, Clerk.*

Inventory, taken 5 September, 1693. £139-06-08. Sloop Sea flower at Southold, L. I. By George Buttolph, Jonathan Colfax and Nicholas Morecock.

Comrs. Carr, Magistrate or assistant, one of their Majesties Justices of peace in Theire Collony of Rhode Island and prouidence plantations, in New England: To all to whome These presents shall Come, Greeting: Know Yee That on The day of the date heerof Before mee personally appeared Joseph Robbinson of the Island Bermudas, aged about twenty years, & upon soleman Oath taken before mee did declare, testifie & depose that he did well know and was acquainted with Benjamin Bowen of Deuonshire Treibe, in the Island of Bermudas aforesd., decd., and also Daniel Bowen, marriner, & Josiah Bowen (heirs right), the two reputed sons of the sd. Benjamin Bowen & so owned & acknowledged by him, & that the sd. Josia Bowen (who likewise appeared together with the Deponent at the time of making this affidavit and in my presence hath under-writt this certificate) is the reputed next brother of the sd. Daniel Bowen, said to be lately dead at Wethersfield, in theire majesties Collony of Connecticot, in New England aforesd., whether the sd. Josia Bowen is now intended to look after the Concerns left by his sd. Brother. Giuen under my hand in Newport, in The Collony aforesd., the first of February, 1693-4.

Caleb Carr, Assistant.

Joseph Robinson,
Josia Bowen.

Page 137.

Brace, Stephen, Hartford. Invt. £322-06-06. Taken 31 August, 1692, by Stephen Hosmer, Jacob White Will dated 2nd May, 1692.

The last Will of Stephen Brace of Hartford is as followeth: I give unto my eldest daughter Elishabah £20 in Cattle & Sheep and other very good pay. I give unto my other 3 daughters, Phebe, Elizabeth and Ann, £5 apiece. I give to my son Stephen my House, Barn & Homelott when he comes to age, only my wife shall have the disposing of my house, which is new built, while she liveth, unless she see Cause to marry again, and my daughter Elishabah shall have liberty of a room in my old House to dwell in for this 10 year if she marry not before. I give to my son Stephen all my Lands in the Meadow and half my Land at Rocky Hill & my Land at Pattacunk. I give to my son John the other half of my Land at Rocky Hill and £10 more, to be paid him when he is of age. I give to my son Henry £10, who I desire may be put out to learn a Trade. The rest of my Estate, after my just Debts are paid, I give to my wife to dispose of as she seeth Cause. Also, I give her the Use of 1-3 part of the Lands while she remaineth a Widow. I appoint my wife Executrix, desiring that my son Stephen may be joined with her when he cometh to be of age.

Witness: *Jacob White,*   STEPHEN BRACE, Ls.
Stephen Hosmer, Nathll Smith.

Court Record, Page 46—1st September, 1692: Will proven.

Inventory on File.

Browne, Benoni, Hartford. Died 8 May, 1688. Invt. £32-12-09. Taken 9 June, 1688, by Cyprian Nichols & Jonathan Bull.

Nathaniel Willett and Isaac Lane appeared before the Court of Pleas and made oath that they made a true presentment of the Estate of the Deceased.

Test: Joseph Whiting, Clerk.

Page 127-8.

Browne, Peter sen., Windsor. Invt. £408-15-06. Taken 23 March, 1691, by John Moore, Cornelius Gillett, John Fyler. Will dated 17 August, 1689.

I Peter Browne sen. of Windsor doe make this my last Will & Testament: I give unto my wife Mary the Use of my whole Estate during Widowhood. If she marry, I give the Use of 1-3 part of my Real Estate to her during life, and £10 of my Moveable Estate. I give to my son Peter my Dwelling house & the Barn & the land whereon it stands. Item. I give to my three sons, John, Jonathan and Cornelius, the remainder of that Land whereon my Barn stands, from that I have given to Peter to the foot of the Hill, for places for them to build upon, John to lye next to his brother, Peter and Jonathan next to the Hill. I do hereby injoin my four sons, Peter, John, Jonathan & Cornelius, to provide yearly so much for their sister Mary as will comfortably winter her a Cow, and bring it home to my Barn and secure it, so long as she remains unmarried. I give to my daughter Mary the use of the new lower room so long as she remains unmarried, and then to return to Peter; also I give her a yerling heifer and a small brass Kettle & a small Iron Pott, a pair of Trammells, the bigest peuter Platter and a pewter basin. Also I give to my two daughters which are married 20 Shillings apeice, and to the other 6 daughters, Mary, Hepsibah, Esther, Isabell, Deborah & Sarah, I give the rest of my Moveables, to be equally divided among them. I appoint my wife and sons, Peter and John, sole Executors.

Witness: *John Fyler,*   PETER BROWNE.
    John Moore.

Court Record, Page 41—13 April, 1692: Will proven.

Page 184-5.

Brunson, Elizabeth, Farmington. Invt. £69-14-08. Taken 26 April, 1694, by Thomas Porter & Samuel Hooker. Will dated 6 April, 1694.
The last Will & Testament of Elizabeth Brunson: I give to my son Samuel Orvis my Lott in Paquabuck Meadow, which Lott lyeth between Capt. John Stanly's Land & Samuel Gridley's, and a Chest & a Anchor or small Cask. I give to my son Roger Orvis one acre of Land in my Lott in Pequabuck Meadow, and one Cow. I give unto my daughter Mary, the wife of Samuel Scott, a brass Morter and Pestal, and 2 Hatts, and a small Chaire, & a young Steer. I give to my son David Carpenter a great Bible, and to his daughter Mary I give a silver Bodkin, and to his daughter Elizabeth I give my white worked Sampler. I give to my daughter Mary Hinman a desk, and a sermon Booke I give to her son Joseph Heacox. I give to my daughter Elizabeth Hill my Bed & Boulster & Pillow which came from England, with Sheets & one Pillow Beere & a black Apron. I give to my gr. Child Mary, the wife of Thomas Barnes, a silk Scarfe in her possession already, with my old Clothes and Hose & Shoes and an Iron Pott & a Trunke. I give to my gr. Child Experience Chapell a heifer, a box, a skillett, pinte Pott and a Basin & Porringer. I give to Martha Orvis a brass Pan, and to Deborah Orvis a pewter Plate, and to my gr. Child Samuel Orvis my rope Hooks, and to my gr. Child Martha Scott a brass Candlestick and painted Box. I give to Hannah Hough, my gr. Child, a brass Box with pott hooks, when she comes of age. I give to my daughter Elizabeth Hill and Mary, the wife of Samuel Scott, and Mary Barnes and Experience Chapell all my Lining. I make Thomas Barnes my sole Executor, & Sergt. Thomas Porter & Sergt. John Hart to be Overseers.

Witness: *Thomas Porter,*   ELIZABETH X BRUNSON.
    John Wadsworth.

A Codicil dated 14 April, 1694.

The following joint receipt and acknowledgment also appears:
Know all Men by these presents: That we the Underwritten, the Children and Legatees of the Widow Elizabeth Brunson of Farmington, late Decd, have received of Thomas Barnes, Executor, whatsoever was willed to us by the aforesd. Elizabeth, and doe hereby bind ourselves and heirs to rest satisfied with what we have received, and do hereby discharge the sd. Thomas and his heirs forever.

Signed:

SAMUEL X ORVIS,

Witness: *Roger Orvis,*   ROGER X ORVIS,
　　　　Moses Ventruss,   ELIZABETH X HILL,
　　　　Nathaniel Wadsworth.   MARIE X SCOTT,
　　　　　　　　　　　　　EXPERIENCE X CHAPPELL.

Court Record, Page 71—6 September, 1694: Will proven. Invt. exhibited and approved by the Court.

Page 226.

Brunson, John, Waterbury. Invt. £150-06-06. Taken 17 November, 1696, by Isaac Brunson, Tho. Judd the Smith, Timothy Standly. The children: John aged 26 years, Ebenezer 19, William 14, Moses 10, Sarah 24, Dorothy 21, Grace 7 years.

Court Record, Page 121—18 November, 1696: Adms. to the Widow and Isaac Bronson, to pay the debts & report.

Page 33—(Vol. VIII) 4 April, 1711: John Brunson, a minor about 14 years of age, grand son of John Brunson formerly of Wethersfield, chose John Hopkins of Waterbury to be his gardian.

Page 36-7.

Buckland, Timothy, Windsor. Died 31 May, 1689. Invt. £167-08-00. Taken November, 1689, by Timothy Thrall, Zerubbabell Fyler. The children: Thomas age 24 years, Abigail 22, Mary 19, Hannah 13, Elizabeth 10, Esther 6.

Court Record, Page 7—11 November, 1689: Adms. to the Widow & son Thomas. Dist: To the Widow, £11; to each of the five daughters, £10. The Remainder to Thomas Buckland. He to pay his Sisters' portions as they come to 18 years of age.

Page 64—(Vol. VII) 6 March, 1704-5: An Agreement in Writing made for the Settlement and Dist. of the Estate of Timothy Buckland, late of Windsor Decd, between the Widow & Children of the sd. Decd, under their Hands & Seals, was exhibited in this Court, accepted and allowed.

Page 91—(Probate Side, Vol. X): We whose names are underwritten, being desired by Thomas Buckland of Windsor to apprise an old house and about 2 acres & ½ of Homested, being under Oath, have apprised the house at £4 and the Lands at £7 per acre; all, both House and Land, £21-10-00.   All which House and Land belonged to his Father Timothy Buckland of Windsor decd, as he informed us, and was left out of the Inventory.   Apprised by us March 9th, 1722-3, as Money.

Israel Stoughton, John Gaylord.

Page 22—2 July, 1722-3:   Thomas Buckland, Adms, exhibited an Addition to the Invt. of £21-10-00.   Ordered recorded and kept on File.

Page 27—6 August, 1723:   This Court now order that the sd. Estate above mentioned be distributed as followeth: To Thomas Buckland, Abigail Hosford, Mary Buckland, Hannah Gillett and Elizabeth Burleson, the Children, in equal parts.   And appoint Israel Stoughton, John Gaylord and Samuel Strong, Dist.

See Dist. per File: 24 May, 1725:   To the Widow Abigail Buckland, to Thomas, to Hannah Gillett, to Abigail Horsford, to Mary Buckland, to Elizabeth Burleson wife of Fearnot Burleson, to Nathan Gillett & Timothy Horsford.   By Thomas Sikes & John Gaylord.

Page 112.

Buckland, William, Hartford.   Died 13 May, 1691.   Invt. £64-05-03.   Taken 1st September, 1691, by John Wilson & Roger Pitkin.

Court Record, Page 41—13 April, 1692:   Estate Insolvent.

Page 179-180.

Bunce, Sarah, Hartford.   Died January, 1693-4.   Invt. £49-12-06.   Taken by James Steele, Joseph Mygatt.

The Last will of Sarah Bunce, Late wife unto Thomas Bunce senr of Hartford Deceased: I give & Bequeath unto my grand child sarah meekins fifteen pound, of wch a feather bed & furniture & a great Brass Kettle shall be part.   It. I give unto my grand child John meekins five pound & a chest.   It. I give unto my grand child Thomas Meekins fourty shillings & a chest.   It. I give unto my grand child Mehetabell meekins Twenty shillings.   It. I give unto my son John Bunce his two eldest Children Twenty shillings a peice.   It. I give unto my sons Thomas Bunce & John Bunce ye rest of yt Estate wch my husband left me to dispose of, to be divided equally between them, whom I make overseers unto this my will; & yt this is my Last will & Testament, I declare by setting to my hand & seal this nineteenth of august, one thousand Six hundred & Eighty nine.   SARAH X BUNCE. LS.
                                                                                senr

In presence of
Stephen Hosmer,
Richard Burnham.
Court Record not found.

Will & Invt. recorded in Vol. XI, Page 1 *(Ante)*.

Bird, Joseph, of Farmington. Invt. £230-15-08. Taken 13 January, 1695-6:

	£ s d
Houseing And Homestead,	50-00-00
5 acres of land at the Slipe,	22-10-00
By 8 acres of Land in the Great Meadow,	36-00-00
By a lot at the Mountain, 11; by 2 ½ acres of Land, 2; by Cattle, Horses, Sheep & Swine, £40-10,	43-18-00
By Household Goods, £12-01-04; By Corn, Flax, Wool, Beds, £4-15-01,	16-17-02
By Beds & Bedding, £11-07; by lining, £4-13,	16-00-00
by Pewter & Bras, £2-07-00; To Iron Pots & Tramels, £2-04,	4-11-00
by Linen Cloth, feathers & Silk grass,	3-13-06
by loom and gears & yarn, £2-01	2-01-00
by Cart, wheels, and other things belonging to it,	6-07-06
by Wearing Clothes, arms & amunition,	10-17-06
By Divisions of land in the Town bounds, Divided & undivided,	10-00-00
	£230-15-08

Apprized by *John Judd sen.,*
Thomas Porter, John Thompson sen.

The Children of the Decd are as follows: Samuel age 29 years, Joseph 27, Thomas 25, Nathaniel 23, James 18, Mary 35, (Marcy, see original Invt. on file) wife of Jonathan Smith, Elizabeth 33, Ruth 20, Mindwell 15 years of age. Will dated 13 February, 1695-6.

The last Will & Testament of Joseph Bird sen. of Farmington, as followeth: I give & bequeath unto my beloved wife My dwelling house & homested and all things pertaining thereto, for the term or time of her life, she to have the profits and Incomes of the same for her own proper use and benefit for the time aforesaid. I also give her one Cow and Six Sheep, also half my household Stuff, beding and linen & all other things that are ordinarily used in the house, as also ten pounds of Sheeps Wool; & I give ten pounds of flax. The house and Cow, Sheep, household Stuff, Wool & flax I give and bequeath to my wife for her own proper Estate to use and dispose of as she pleaseth. The remainder of my Estate I do will it to my Children by an equal proportion to each of them, with this Expectation, that my son Samuel with what he hath had shall have £5 more than his brethren and sisters, and that my son Joseph & my daughter Elizabeth shall have 15s apeice more than their younger brethren & Sisters. My sons' part of my Estate they shall have it out of my Lands: Further, my Desire is that my son James & my daughter Mindwell should dwell with their Mother until they are of age, and also that my wife should be administrator to my Estate, and desire that my son-in-Law Jonathan Smith and my son Samuel Bird should assist & help in the case.

JOSEPH BIRD senr.

Witness: *John Wadsworth,*
Jonathan Smith.

Note of Recorder: This should have been Recorded in the Book of Probate Records (Vol. not stated).

Court Record, Page 105 (Vol. V) 8 April, 1696: Will & Invt. Exhibited.

Dist. File, 3 March, 1718-19: To the Widow, to Samuel Burd, to Joseph, to Thomas, to Nathaniel, to James, to Jonathan Smith in Right of his wife, to Elizabeth Burd, to Ruth Burd, and to Mindwell Burd. By Jonathan Smith as Overseer, and John Hooker sen. & Isaac Cowles as distributors.

A 2nd Dist., per File, 2 March, 1730: To the Widow, to Samuel Burd, to Joseph Burd, to Thomas, to Nathaniel, to James, to Mary, to Elizabeth, to Ruth, and to Mindwell Burd. By Joseph Hawley, Isaac Cowles & Daniel Judd.

Page 87-8.

Burnham, Thomas, Hartford. Died 24 June, 1688. Invt. £69-06-06. Taken 11 October, 1688, by Nathaniel Stanly & George Grave. Will Nuncupative.

Testimony of Caleb Stanly, that Mr. Thomas Burnham a short time before he died sent for Col. John Allyn and himself and asked John Allyn to write his Will, which he did write according to his desire, which he gave to his wife Ann Burnham to keep. He gave to his daughter Rebeckah Burnham his House & Home lott, & His wife Ann Burnham to be Executrix. He gave to his three sons, Thomas, John and Samuel, his plowing Land in Podunk Meadow, to be equally divided among them. He gave a parcell of Land Eastward of Edward Kings Land neer Podunck Brook unto William Morton his Wife. Also he gave Land in possession of Samuel Gains that he bought of Richard Risley unto the wife of Samuel Gains during her life, and afterward to one of her sons. He gave to Thomas Gains, his grand son, all his right in the Land he had in Partnership wth Mr. Lord at the saw Mill. He gave his daughter Morton £10, and to his daughter Moorcocke £10, and some small Legacies to his sons Richard & William Burnham.

In Court, 26 January, 1690: Rebeckah now the wife of William Man.

Court Record, Page 15—26 June, 1690: Upon complaint of Wm Man that his wive's father Thomas Burnham's Will and Testament was neglected to be Exhibited in Court & the Inventory of his Estate, and that thereby he the sayd Man was like to be dispossessed of what his Father gave to his Wife, the Governor and Assistants appointed the Court this day to meet and settle it. Result: the Will could not be found, and the Inventory that was taken after the decease of sd. Thomas Burnham, with the Testimony of Caleb Stanly to the General provisions of the Will, were accepted by the Court.

John Allyn, Assistant (upon his office oath),
John Allyn, Secretary.

To the Honourd Court of Assistants now sitting In Hartford: Whereas the Last will & Testament of Mr Thomas Burnham Deceased Is by som (as is supposed suriptissous (   ) or means Taken or Removed out of ye Custody of ye Relict & Executrix of said Will, by which Removal or Concealment of said Will ye Just & Legall Settlement of ye Estate of ye Deceased According to his said Will hath been obstructed, therefore that Justice & Right may bee Done And ye said Will proved According to Law, I Humbly crave yt ye several psons be sumoned to Appear att This Court to be Examined Concerning said Will uppon there Oath.

To the Marshall, to serve upon Mrs Burnam :

Mrs. Ann Burnam, these are to acquaint you that Mr. Wm Man Makes Complaint that to his great damage you doe neglect the duty of your place, as you are made executrix by the Last will & Testament of your late deceased Husband, in not Exhibiting his sayd will Into the court & proveing the same together with the Inventory of his Estate ; & it being known that your deceased husband did make, declare, signe & seale his Last will & Testament, & Left it in your keeping, the Assistants of this county have ordered that Thursday, the 26th of this Moneth, there shall be a speciall county court held at Hartford to prove the sayd will of Thomas Burnam Deceased, & the Inventory of his estate to be Exhibited, where you are to appear to make oath that you have made a True prsentment of the Estate of the deceased to the apprizers If you are capable ; If not, Mr Wm pitkin is desired to repyayre to you to give you your oath, & you are therefore required in their Maties Name to deliver your sayd husbands will to the Marshall to bring it to me that it may by me be preserved & presented to the court afoarsayd to be proved, or your selfe appear & present it to the court the 26th of this month as above, & of soe doeing you may not fayle. Dated in Hartford, June 19, 1690.

P. John Allyn, Assist.

24 June 1690.

Honred Sor, Mr Ayllin : Thes ffew Lines are to Lett you understand my Ssorrowffull Condishon. I have bene weke and Lame a long time, and Now did begin to be som what beter be ffor my son Will man did make so much trobell by ye athority in Sending up ye marshall, and by Souerving Warnts on all my Children, by which mens greved me very much, as I have declared to ye marshall when he was at my house. Thear ffor my earnest desir is that you would Not Let any thing goe fforward in a way off Setling my estate whillst I Can Spak with you my Sellffe, and then I hop I shall do it to all my Childrens' Satisffaxshon. Ye writin which my son Will man took, I know not what was in it, for I never heard it read. My son Will man asked me to se ye writing. I told him he mit. So when he had it he took it and put it in his pocit with out my Leveffe.

off an X Burnham.

(On file.)

Page 130.

Butler, Daniel, Sargt., Hartford. He Died 28 March, 1692. Invt. £391-01-00. Taken 11 April, 1692, by James Steele sen. & Joseph Easton.

Court Record, Page 42—13 April, 1692: Adms. to the Widow, Deac. Joseph Olmsted and Deacon Samuel Butler to be Overseers. Order to Dist. to the Children as they come of age, (no names given.) The names and ages of the Children of Daniel Butler, from original Inventory on File: Sarah was born 28 September, 1680; Mabel was born 12 August, 1684; Elizabeth was born 22 November, 1686; Mary was born 7 November, 1689; Hannah was born 17 November, 1691.

Vol. VII, Court Record, Page 60—8 November, 1704: Estate of Daniel Butler, Hartford: Mabell Tainter (formerly Mabell Butler) Widow, Relict of Daniel Butler Decd, Exhibits account of Adms. Allowed. Also allowed £71-13-11 for loss and for bringing up the children. Order to Dist. according to an Order of this Court, 13 April, 1692.

(Record of distribution on File, date 6 April, 1705: To Mabell Taintor, formerly wife of Daniel Butler, to Mabel, to Elizabeth, to Mary, to Hannah Butler.) Mary chose Joseph Olmsted for her Guardian; Hannah Chose Roger Pitkin for her guardian. Thomas Bunce, Capt. Roger Pitkin and Deacon Joseph Olmsted, distributors.

Page 120.

Butler, Elizabeth. 11 September, 1691. Invt. £101-04-06. Taken by Samuel Butler & Daniel Butler.

Court Record, Page 34—3d December, 1691: Adms. to Samuel & Daniel Butler. Dist. to her children: Nathaniel, Joseph, Daniel, Samuel Butler, Elizabeth Olmsted, Abigail Butler. Daniel Butler, though a Legatee, made Oath with Mary Butler to the Nuncupative Will of the Decd, that the Estate should be divided equally among her children, and it appearing by the Testimony of Mary Butler that Elizabeth Butler, decd, nere her death did declare that it was her minde that after her death her goods should be equally divided unto her five children, Nathaniel, Joseph, Daniel and Samuel Butler and Elizabeth Olmsted; and Daniel Butler, although he be a legatee, yet affirmed that he heard his Mother say & declare the same as is Testified by Mary Butler, which this Court accepts as the last Will of sayd Elizabeth Butler; onely whereas there is a debt of about Thirteen & fourteen pounds sayd to be due from Thomas Butler, Adms. to his Father's Estate, and upon his own proper accot, which debt, this Court, with consent of Samuel Butler, Daniel Butler and Joseph Olmsted, doe remit to the sayd Thomas Butler & to his Brethren & Sisters, onely Thomas Butler to have a double portion of it.

Page 155-6.

Butler, Ensign Samuel, Wethersfield. Died 30 December, 1692. Invt. £579-07-00. Taken 25 February, 1692-3, by John Wiard, Joseph Churchill. Will dated 30 December, 1692.

I Samuel Butler of Wethersfield doe make this my last Will & Testament: I Will to Samuel Butler, my eldest son, my Dwelling house & Homelott, with all other Buildings, with the Appurtenances, and also all my Land lying at the upper End of the Great Meadow, and my best Bed but one, with the Furniture, and my Sadle, and also my Great Iron Pott and Trammell, he paying the Legacies of £5 to my daughter Mary Hopkins and £10 to my daughter Dorothy. Item. I give to my son James Butler my Lott in the Little West Field, 28 acres more or less, and my 2-acre lott at the lower End of the Great Meadow, also my Gunn and Sword. I give to my son Jonathan my 50-acre Lott in ye Woods, and all my Interest in the Purchased Land in Hartford on the East side of the River. I give to my son George my 10-acre Lott in the Little West Field, also 8 acres more or less in the Wet Swamp. I give to my daughter Elizabeth Emmons my proportion of Land in the Indian Purchase on the East side of the Great River in Wethersfield, besides what I have given her already, and also 1 of my bigest pewter Platters. I give to my daughter Mary Hopkins £5, to be paid by my son Samuel as abovesd., and one of my bigest pewter platters. I give to my daughter Sarah Butler one of my bigest platters. I give to my daughter Dorothy £10, to be paid by my son Samuel as abovesd., and my best Bed with all the Furniture, and my Chest. I give her the 2 bigest Kettles, and also one of the Bigest pewter Dishes. I make my son Samuel Butler Executor, and Benjamin Churchill & Thomas Wickham my Overseers.

Witness: *Benjamin Churchill,*　　SAMUEL BUTLER, Ls.
John Welles, Joseph Wright.

Court Record, Page 52—2 March, 1692-3: Will proven.

Buttolph, George. Court Record, Page 108—13 May, 1696: An Inventory of the Estate of George Buttolph was exhibited in Court. (Estate, £204-03-06.) This Court grants Adms. to the Widow & Relict, and appoint Mr. Henry Buck and John Buttolph to assist her.

Page 117—8 September, 1696: This Court coming to a Dist. of the Estate of George Buttolph, Decd.

	£ s d
The Whole Estate amounting to	204-03-06
The Widow's part,	43-06-08
	160-16-10
The Debts,	131-15-00
There remains	29-01-00
To the Eldest son,	14-13-04
To the other 2 Children, to each of them,	7-06-08

Page 153-4.

Buttolph, Lt. John, Wethersfield. Died 14 January, 1692-3. Invt. £1042-03-02. Taken by Robert Welles, John Chester Jr., Joshua Robbins, Benjamin Gilbert. pr Land at norwitch new uilleg a bout 3000 or 4000 acres. pr Stock of Horses & Cattle there (yet unknown). Will nuncupative, dated 13 January, 1692.

Lt. John Buttolph, being very sicke, did desire us whose Names are underwritten to take notice what his minde was concerning his Estate: That after his debts and Funeral Charges being paid, his eldest son John Buttolph shall have a double portion of all his Estate, the rest of his Estate to be equally divided amongst the rest of his children. It was his Will that his daughter Abigail shall have the best feather bed with all the furniture to it, the rest of her portion to be in pewter and Brass and Iron; and if that will not amount to her part, then it shall be made up out of the Land at norwiche that I had with her Mother. I doe declare that the worshipll Capt. Mason and my eldest son John Buttolph shall be the Executors. And I desire that these two men shall take care also of my three youngest children, Jonathan, Abigall and James. And my Will is that my eldest son John shall have the first choice of my Estate after my Debts are paid. I also declare that my son George his wife Elizabeth Buttolph shall have £10 in such Goods as she shall choose, for her own proper Estate besides her husband's portion, for her loving, careful paines in attending of me in my sickness. I also desire my son John Buttolph shall have my great Seal Skin Trunk.

Witness: *Nathaniel Bowman,*
Obadiah Dickinson, William Burnham.

Will proven 6 March, 1692-3.

Court Record, Page 52—2 March, 1692-3: Will exhibited. Inventory ordered forthwith.

Page 53—2 March, 1692-3: David Buttolph made Oath that he had made a true presentment of the Estate of his Decd Father.

Page 190.

Cadwell, Thomas, Hartford. Died 9 October, 1694. Invt. £693-18-00 Taken 8 November, 1694, by Joseph Wadsworth, Zachary Sandford, John Marsh. Will dated 11 February, 1691.

I Thomas Cadwell of Hartford doe make this my last Will & Testament: I give unto my wife Elizabeth my entire Estate for her use during life, except what I have already conveyed to my son Thomas & to my daughter Mary Dickins, which she hath already exchanged with Mr. William Gibbins at Podunk that piece of Land in the South Meadow which was formerly my Father Stebbins'. I give unto my son Edward my Lott in the Landing Place lying between Mrs. Abigail Olcott & Nath: Stanly's Lott. The reason why I give my son Edward (he being my Eldest son) no more, is because of that good Estate his Grand Father Steb-bings gave him which came to him in right of my wife his Mother, who was the only child living of his said Grand Father when he deceased. I give to my son Thomas, besides that part of my Home lot which he is already possessed of, all my lott in the long meadow called Grant's lott, containing about 4 acres, Lyeing between Lt. Col. Talcott & John Daye's Lotts, all wayes provided the sayd Thomas relinquish his Clayme to one acre & one Rood of Land in the south meadow, that his sister Mary Dick-ins may not be molested or troubled In that Land in the south meadow that was formerly given to her. Also I give unto him the one halfe of my Grass lott at the Lower end of the Long meadow Lyeing between Mr Lord's & Thomas Olmstead's Lotts. Also my wood Lott in the ox pas-ture Lying between Lt. Col. Allyn's Land North and John Skiner de-ceased his Lott south, & this he is to receive at the decease of me and my wife Elizabeth, he paying his proportion of Legacies to his sisters. I give to my son Samuel the one half of my Dwelling house, Barn, Yards & Home-Lott. I give my son Matthew the other half of my Dwelling house, Barn, Yards & Homelott. I give unto my daughter Mary Dickins £4 in addition to what I had formerly given to her. To my daughter Abi-gail, to Elizabeth, to Hanna, to Mehetabell, to each £20, all to be paid after the decease of me & my wife. My wife Elizabeth to be sole Executrix, and desire Mr. Nathaniel Stanly and Capt. Caleb Stanly to be Overseers.

Witness: *John Pantry,*   THOMAS CADWELL, Ls.
    Thomas Olcott.

Court Record, Page 77—14 November, 1694: Will proven.

Page 75.

Carrington, John, Waterbury. Invt. £120-12-11 (and wife both Deceased). Taken 30 June, 1690, by Abraham Andrews sen., Benjamin Barnes, Thomas Judd the Smith. Children: John, age 23 years, Mary 18, Hannah 15, Clark 12, Elizabeth 8, Ebenezer 3 years.

Court Record, Page 18—4 Sept., 1690: Adms. to John Carrington, Benjamin Barnes & Thomas Judd the Smith, to be Overseers.

Page 24—5 March, 1690-1: The Overseers impowered to dispose of the three youngest children to such places and employments as they Judge best for the children. To take care of their portions and not be overruled by John Carrington the Administrator.

Page 38—3 March, 1691-2: Dist: To Eldest son, £23; to the rest of the children, to each, £12.

Page 136.

Carrington, John Jr., Waterbury. Invt. £64-13-02. Taken 31 August, 1692, by Thomas Judd sen., Thomas Judd Jr. Also an Invt. of

£3-19-00, of Cooper's Tools, Timber & Clothes, taken at Farmington by Thomas Judd & John Hooker. Brothers & Sisters of the Deceased: Clarke, Ebenezer, Mary, Hanah & Elizabeth Carrington.

Court Record, Page 45—1st September, 1692: Invt. Exhibited. Adms. to Benjamin Barnes and Thomas Judd the Smith, they to pay the debts & Legacies which was made or due from his Father's Estate, the remainder to be divided equally between his Brothers & Sisters.

Page 56—12 April, 1693: Adms. account of debts of John Carrington Jr.'s Estate, £57-15-02.

Page 81—7 March, 1694-5, relates to sale of Land to pay the debts. This Court appoint Isaac Brunson & Timothy Stanly to advise with the Adms.

Page 181-2.

Case, Richard, Hartford. Died 30 March, 1694. Invt. £203-02-06. Taken 2nd April, 1694, by William Pitkin, Obadiah X Wood. Will dated 8 September, 1690.

I Richard Case of Hartford doe make this my last Will & Testament: My Will is that my wife Elizabeth Case shall have my whole Estate, with Houseing & Lands and all Moveables, for her Use & Benefit and to bring up my children, during the time of her natural life. And I give to her and her heirs forever that small lott layd out on the East side of the Great River as her father Purchass his allottment. Also, after the Death of my wife, I give to my son Richard Case the older part of my Dwelling house, and the old or first planted Orchard, and that peice of Land where the passage is on the Common Way upon the Hill to the house. Also to my son John Case I give the other part of my Orchard, Homelott & House, with the Chimney part therein. Also, after her mother's decease, I give to my daughter Mary Case that 10 acres of upland that lyeth next Eastward from that hereby given to John Case, and the 1-3 of all my Moveables. Also the rest of my Land I give equally to my sd. three Children, their heirs and Assigns forever. I ordain my sd. wife and my Kinsman Mr. Thomas Olcott to be Executors.

Witness: *William Pitkin,* RICHARD X CASE. LS.
      Thomas Olcott.

Court Record, Page 69—4 April, 1694: Will proven & Inventory exhibited. This Court appoint Mr. Thomas Olcott and William Pitkin Jr. to be Overseers.

Page 118.

Church, John, Hartford. Invt. £510-16-02. Taken 9th November, 1691, by John Wilson, Samuel Olcott, Thomas Olcott. The children: Richard, John, Samuel, Joseph age 15 years, Deliverence 12 years, Sara Knight, Mary Standish, Ruth Church, Ann Church age 18 years, & Elizabeth Church 17 years of age.

Court Record, Page 33—2 December, 1691 : Invt. of the Estate of John Church sen. of Hartford was exhibited in Court, and the sd. John Church sen. having deceased and left no Will or disposal of his Estate, this Court do, with the Consent of his Eldest son Richard, grant Adms. on the Estate to John & Samuel Church, his sons, and do distribute the Estate as followeth : To Richard his Eldest son £40 & his west Division Lott, which he accepts as his full portion.   To John his 2nd son, who hath long lived with his Father & hath been a great help in gaining his Estate, the ½ of his Neck Lott, and his Swamp Lott in Windsor, and his Lott near the Blue Hills, part whereof is fenced in already.   To Samuel, the ½ of the Homested, both of Lands and Buildings, and ½ of a Swamp Lott on the East side of the Great River, & the ½ of the Soldiers Field & Lott adjoining.   To Joseph Church, the ½ of the Neck Lott and 2 Lotts on the Southward of John Church his Woodlott.   To Deliverence Church, the other halfe of the Homested & Buildings, & ½ the Swamp Lott on the East side of the Great River, and the Lott in the Pine Field, and the other half of the Lott in the Soldiers Field and Lott adjoining. To the daughters, each of them £28 apeice, to be distributed to them by Ensign Zach. Sandford and Sargt. Nath : Goodwin, and delivered them by the Adms., who are to take Care for the payment of all Just Debts, and for the Disposal of the 2 younger sons to some good trades.   Joseph Church and Deliverence Church chose Deacon John Wilson and Samuel Spencer to be their Guardians.

Dist. File, 1691 : Estate of John Church sen. to Sarah his wife. The children being of age to act for themselves, mutually agree for Division. John Church, Samuel, Ann and Elizabeth Church. Witness : Samuel Spencer, Samuel Olcott. Another paper has the names Richard Church, Sara Knight, Ruth Church, Ann Church, Elizabeth Church, and Mary Standish, wife of Thomas Standish. By Zachariah Sandford, Nathaniel Goodwin sen. On another paper : To Samuel Church, to Deliverence Church, to John Church ; by Zachariah Sandford, Nathaniel Goodwin sen. (Note : *All appears to have been written with the same Ink and by the same hand as the original agreement 1691.*)

Page 81.

Clarke, Nathaniel, Windsor. Will dated 29 April, 1690 : Whereas I, Nathaniel Clarke of Windsor, am by the providence of God called forth to goe out against the common enemie for his Maties service and the defence of the Country, & considering the Perrel & Hazard of such an undertakeing, & being now of good understanding & memory, I count it my duty to settle that Estate God hath bestowed upon me : My Estate, both of houseing and Lands, that by deed of guift is past over to me by my honoured father Capt. Daniel Clarke, and all other Estate that I shall leave behind me, I give to my brother Daniel Clarke, he paying £3 to each of my sisters, Elizabeth, Mary & Sarah, daughters of my Father &

Mother. I give to my Brothers Josiah Clarke & John Clarke the sum of 5 Shillings apeice. I give to my Brother Samuel Clarke 1 parcel of Land in Windsor Bounds containing about 33 acres, in a place called Pipe Stav, and 1 parcel of Meadow Land at or near a place called Wash Brook, he paying to my 3 sisters above mentioned the sum of £2 apeice. I appoint my Brother Daniel Clarke to be my Executor.

Witness : *Caleb Stanly,*   NATHANIEL CLARKE. LS.
          Roger Pitkin.

Court Record, Page 19—4 September, 1690: Will proven.

Page 216.

Clarke, Thomas, Hartford. Invt. £456-15-09. Taken 8 November, 1695, by Thomas X Burr, Aaron Cooke & Nathaniel Goodwin. His children: John, Daniel, Joseph, Thomas, all of age, & the Eldest daughter Mary, 20 years of age, Ann 18, Elizabeth 16, and Sarah 10.

Court Record, Page 91—11 November, 1695: Invt. of the Estate of Thomas Clarke was exhibited in Court. Adms. to the Widow. The Court dist. the Estate as followeth: To Daniel Clarke, 3 acres of Land by Mr. Crow's on the East side of the River, and 2 acres of the Dugley's Swamp on the East side of the River, and 3 acres in the Long Meadow. To Joseph Clarke, the Lott on the Brick Hill Swamp, about 8 acres and ½, the Lott on the East side of the River by Bidwell's Pasture. To the Widow, of Personal Estate, £55-05-05. To Thomas Clarke, halfe the Lott adjoining to Mr. Bidwell's Pasture, & 15 acres of 4-Mile Hill, and the Upland Lott there on the East side. To John Clarke, the house & Homested on the East side of the Highway, he paying £30 out of it to his youngest sister Sarah, and to the other 3 daughters, Mary, Ann & Elizabeth, £30 apeice. And it is agreed between the sons and the Widow that she shall possess the whole of the Land till she shall marry again, and after that she shall possess 1-3 of the Land during her naturall life.

Page 4-5.

Coale, John sen., Farmington. Invt. £341-09-09. Taken 2 November, 1689, by Thomas Bull, Thomas Porter, Jacob Brunson. The children: John Coale, age 24 years, Samuel 13, Nathaniel 11, & Rachel (Coale) Smith, 21 years. Will dated 12 September, 1689.

The last Will & Testament of John Coale sen. is as followeth: I John Coale sen. do give unto my son John Coale ½ of my Estate, excepting Household Stuff, and the Use of the other half of my Land until my other 2 sons attain unto 21 years of age. This I do give unto my son John Cole upon these Conditions: that my beloved wife Rachell be comfortably & well maintained by him the sd. John Coale, with one end of my house as she shall choose, with all other things suitable for her ranck & Condition. Moreover I leave all my household stuffe to my wife, to be dispose by her unto my Children after her Decease. I give my daughter Rachel Smith £20, to be paid by my son John, whóme I appoynt Executor. I leave in John Coale's hands the other half of my Stock & Moveable Estate out of Doors, until the other sons come of age. I give to my son Samuel ¼ part of my House & Homested, as also ¼ part of all my Land, at the age of 21 years. I do give the other ¼ part of my Homested and Land unto my son Nathaniel. I doe give unto my sons Samuel and Nathaniel ½ of the Moveable Estate, excepting household stuffe, to be paid to them at the age of 21 years, also excepting the ½ of £20, which £20 I doe give to my daughter Rachel Smith, to be paid to her out of the Stocks by my son John, whome I appoint my Executor. I give unto my daughter Rachel Smith a Chest now standing in the Chamber, made by her Grand Father Coale. I desire Thomas Hart & Thomas Porter to be Overseers.

Witness: *Samuel Coale,*   JOHN COALE SEN.
     Nathaniel Coale.

(This Will taken from his own mouth this 12 September, 1689.)

Court Record, Page 4—6 November, 1689: Will & Invt. Exhibited and Proven.

Page 17—(Vol. VIII) 3 July, 1710: This Court now order, by Summons, Capt. Thomas Hart, Lt. Samuel Wadsworth & Sergt. Thomas Porter to appear and be sworn to make Dist. of part of the Estate of John Coale according to an Order of Court 3 May, 1708.

Page 18—4 September, 1710: A Distribution of part of the Estate of John Coale Sen., formerly of Farmington Decd, pursuant to an Order of this Court of 3 May, 1708, was now exhibited by the distributors (who were sworn before this Court faithfully to Distribute the same), approved and ordered on file.

Dist. on file: To John, to Samuel, & to Nathaniel Cole.

Page 112.

Coaltman, John. 1st September 1691. To the Honoured Court: Whereas, there was formerly an Inventory of the moveable Estate of John Coaltman, late of Wethersfield, Deceased, taken, and the land that belonged to the Estate of the said John Coaltman left out, it being then practiced and a custome not to mention land in Inventories, but since the Lawes provided otherwise, and that the orphans may know where to seek their owne in time to come, it is by the relict of the said John Coaltman desired that the land should also be Inventoried, which is as followeth as the Law requires: The House, Orchard & three and a half acres of the Home lott on the north side, and three and half acres on the south side the Home lot, & two acres in the Great Meadow. Invt. £110-00-00. Apprised by John Chester & James Treat.

Court Record, Page 154—(Vol. IV) 14 April, 1697: Mary Sherman, formerly Widow, Relict of sd. Coaltman, Adms. & Moves for a Dist. This Court Joyn Mr. John Denison to the Adms. in the Dist. to the Widow and 3 daughters (not named).

Page 158-9.

Cockshott, James, Machamoodas. Died 11 January, 1692-3. Invt. £36-16-00. Taken by George Gates & Alexander Rollo. The Estate is Indebted to the following persons: John Clark of Saybrook, to Daniel Braynard sen., John Bate, Edward Turner, John Bayley sen., George Gates, Joseph Goss, James Cole, Francis Whitmore, Edward Wale or Wate of Lyme. to Doct. Butler, to Samuel Arnol, to Jonathan Tillyson, to Halyburt of Middletown, to Mr. Sumner, to Thomas Lord, to John Arnol of Haddam, to Thomas Shaylor, to John Schovel, to Thomas Clark, John Ackle and William Robords.

Court Record, Page 53—2 March, 1692-3: Invt. Exhibited.

Page 62—7 September, 1693: An account of debts now presented of the Estate of James Cockshott of Haddam. This Court orders one third to the Widow, and the rest proportionally to the Creditors.

Page 188-9.

Cole, Samuel, Hartford. Died 16 March, 1693-4. Invt. £425-00-00. Taken 29 May, 1694, by Ciprian Nichols & Jacob White. Will dated 15 March, 1693-4.

I Samuel Cole of Hartford doe make this my last Will & Testament: I give to my wife Mary all the Use of my Estate until my Children attain their ages, sons to 21 years and daughters 18 years of age. I give to my wife 1-3 part of all my Moveable Estate, & 2 rooms in my Dwelling house, which she shall choose, during her Widowhood, & 1-3 part of all my Lands during her natural life. I give to my son Samuel Cole a house & Barn & Homelott. I give to my son Ichabod my Land at the Ox pasture, bounding upon Goodman Davis North and Benjamin Grimes South. I give to my other 2 sons, John & Jonathan, all my Land at Poke Hill, to be equally divided between them. My Will is that my 3 daughters, that is, Elizabeth, Dorothy & Hannah, shall have £20 apeice out of my other Estate. My Will is that if there be any Estate left it shall be equally divided between my Children. I appoint my loving wife sole Executrix, and when my son Samuel shall attain the age of 21 years I appoint him to be joint Executor with his Mother. I desire my loving brother Nathaniel Cole and Samuel Kellogg to be my Overseers.

Witness: *Caleb Watson,* 　　　　　　　　　　　　(Not signed.)
　　　　　Mary X Seamore.

Note: He said, "I leave it with my Executor & Overseers, according to their best discretion, to put my sons out to trades that may be most suitable."

Court Record, Page 31—3 September, 1691: Will proven.

Page 42—(Vol. VII) 7 April, 1703: Whereas, Samuel Cole did in his last Will appoint Mary his Relict and Samuel his son Executors, Samuel having refused the Trust, Mary Cole is appointed sole Executrix.

Page 28—(Vol. VIII) 5 March, 1710-11: The Court order and appoint Ichabod Wells, Samuel Kellogg & Thomas Hosmer to make Division of 2 certain peices of Land lying at or near Poke Hill in Hartford, late belonging to Samuel Cole of Hartford, Decd, and by him given in his last will to his two sons John and Jonathan Cole, to be equally divided between them.

Page 223-4.

Coliyer, Elizabeth. Invt. £155-12-04. Taken 21 February, 1695-6, by Aaron Cooke, Timothy Phelps. Will dated 27 December, 1695.

I Elizabeth Coliyer of Hartford doe make this my last Will & Testament: I give unto my son Joseph Coliyer £5, and unto my two sons Abell and John Coliyer all the Tackling which belongs on to the team, everything as though particularly named, to be equally divided between them. And to each of them I also give a horse Colt. I do give unto my daughter Mary Phelps of Simsbury 40 Shillings. I do give unto all those of my Children who have wrought for me in Spinning or otherwise, for procuring divers peices of cloth not now come home from the Weavers, I say I give unto them all the Cloth not now come home equally, excepting unto those who have done most at the work or procuration of it I give more than an equal part, as shall be judged convenient by my Overseers. I give and bequeath unto all my Children who now live at home all that provision which is now laid out for my family Use, and not to be divided if they can agree to live together upon it. I do also give and grant unto my two sons Abell and John Coliyer full and free liberty of the Use of my Team so long as they can improve them beneficially to pay my Debts. I desire the honourable John Allyn and my Brother Ensign Zachary Sandford and my brother Robert Sandford to be Overseers and to Administer on my Estate.

Witness: *Caleb Stanly Jr.,*   ELIZABETH X COLIER. Ls.
Elizabeth X Goodwin.

Court Record, Page 99—5 March, 1695-6: Will & Invt. exhibited and approved.

Page 220.

Collins, Samuel, Middletown. Invt. £216-10-06. Taken 1st February, 1695-6, by Daniel Markham sen., Samuel Bidwell, William Sumner. The children: Edward, Martha, Samuel, Sibbell, Mary, Abigail, all of age.

Court Record, Page 97—5 March, 1695-6: Adms. to Mrs. Mary Collins. Mr. John Hamlin, Daniel Marcum and William Sumner to be Overseers.

Court Record, Page 84 (Vol. VIII) July, 1712: Mrs. Mary Collins of Middletown petitioned this Court for permission to sell some of the land which belonged to her husband Samuel Collins, late of Middletown, Decd, to pay some debts.

Page 86: Permission to sell to the value of £42-18-00, due to Estate of Mr. Richard Bryan.

Page 215—4 October, 1714: The Widow now deceased and Adms. not finished. Adms. to Sergt. William Ward of Middletown.

Page 119.

Colyer, Joseph, Hartford. Died 16 November, 1691. Invt. £220-06-00. Taken by John Wilson and Samuel Olcott. The children: Joseph, age 23 years, Mary Phelps 22, Sara Colyer 18, Elizabeth 16, Abel 14, John 12, Abigail 9, Susannah 7, Ann 4 ½ years of age.

Court Record, Page 34—2 December, 1691: Adms. to Widow Elizabeth Colyer. By the wish of her husband, the whole Estate to go to her during life. Court Order, then, the moveables to be to the daughters and the Houseing & Lands to the sons. Ensign Sandford and Robert Sandford are recommended as advisers.

Page 149—(Vol. IV) 14 April, 1697: John Collier, son of Joseph Collier, chose Zachary Sandford to be his Guardian.

Page 10—(Vol. VI) 3 January, 1697: Lt. Zachary Sandford moving this Court to appoint Mr. Richard Lord and Aaron Cooke to Dist. the Land of Joseph Collier unto his sons according to an Order of the Court made formerly.

Page 208.

Corbe, Samuel, Haddam. Died 10 April, 1694. Invt. £60-17-07. Taken 25 April, 1694, by Shubael Rowley, Thomas X Robinson. The legatees: The Relict, daughter Mary 17 Months Old, a posthumous son Samuel 3 months Old.

Court Record, Page 87—16 May, 1695: Adms. to the Widow. Shubael Rowley & Thomas Crippin to be Overseers.

Page 47—(Vol. IX, Probate Side): An Agreement between the surviving heirs for the Settlement of the Estate of Samuel Corby, late of East Haddam, deceased:

These may signify to the Honoured Court of Probate to be held at Hartford, that We whose names are hereunto subscribed have agreed to divide the Estate of Samuel Corby of East Haddam, who departed this life the 10th day of April, 1694, as followeth: First, the Widow Mary Corby, Relict of sd. Samuel Corby, hath received £10 as her part, and the rest of her thirds she gives in equall proportion to her two Children, namely, Samuel and Mary Corby. Secondly, that Samuel, the only son of sd. Samuel Corby, shall have all the Land that did belong to his honoured Father at his decease, he paying to his sister Mary Corby £1-10-11. Thirdly, that Mary, the daughter of Samuel Corby, shall have the rest of the moveable Estate that did or doth belong to the sd. Estate. And Whereas the above said Samuel Corby is not of lawfull age to act for himself, he hath made choice of his Uncle Thomas Crippen to be his Guardian, who doth consent to the above sd. Agreement. As Witness our hands,

Witnesses present:

Thomas Gates,
Daniel Braynard.

MARY X CORBY, WIDOW,
SAMUEL X CORBY,
MARY X CORBY,
THOMAS X CRIPPEN, Guardian.

Page 117.

Cornwall, William, Middletown. Invt. £415-17-00. Taken by William Southmayd, Francis Wetmore. The children: William, age 20 years, Jacob 18, Ebenezer 2, Experience 9 years. Will Nuncupative.

The Dying words of William Cornwall sen. were as followeth:

"I give to my Eldest son William and my youngest son Ebenezer all my lands at home, to be equally divided between them, Ebenezer not to have his part before his Mother's death. To my son Jacob I give all my land at the upper lott. To my daughter Experience I give my house and lott at Towne, and fower cowes, at my wive's decease, if she hath them." This was sworn to in Court by Sergt. John Hall and the relict of William Cornwall, 9 October, 1691.

Court Record, Page 33—9 October, 1691: Adms. to the Widow with Will annexed.

Page 42—13 April, 1692: A son was born after the death of the Father, for which no provision was made in the Will, which the Court Considered and made order to the Legatees to pay £70 in the proportion which they have received, to the young son.

Page 264—(Probate Side, Vol. IX): An Agreement dated 3 May, 1718, to inform the Court as followeth:

The Agreement of us, Children of William Cornwall, viz., William, Jacob, Experience and Arthur her husband, as to the divideing of the Estate left to them by their Father William Cornwall, late of Middletown, Deceased. In the first place, which is left according to the Will, and what was not disposed by Will, left to the Relict of William Cornwall, Deceased, and the part of the Estate belonging to that child which is deceased, viz, Ebenezer:

	£ s d
To William, the Eldest son,	87-03-04
To Jacob, the second son,	83-19-00
To Arthur, and Experience his wife,	64-07-04

Witnesses: *Ephraim Goodrich,*   Signed: WILLIAM CORNWALL. Ls
        Samuel Hall.   JACOB CORNWALL, Ls.
                                ARTHUR BEVINS. Ls

Acknowledged in Court, 6th May, 1718, to be their voluntary Act and Deed.

Test: Hez: Wyllys, Clerk.

Page 113-14.

Cowles, Samuel, Farmington. Died 17 April, 1691. Invt. £503-14-08. Taken by Thomas Porter & John Heart. Will dated 15 April, 1691.

I Samuel Cowles doe make this my last Will & Testament: The Land I have already given to my eldest son Samuel I doe hereby ratify & confirm unto him, and with other Lands I doe give to my son Samuel a double portion of all my Lands, either divided or undivided, in Farmington, with the rest of my sons at my Decease. I give to my wife Abigail Cowles the benefit of the Middle part of my homelott, with all my houseing & Barnes, & a third part of all my other Lands in Farmington, during her natural life; & the Use of all my household Goods, she paying my daughter Elizabeth £20 at 18 years of age. I give all my houseing & Land, layd out or not layd out, unto my other six sons, Timothy, John, Nathaniel, Isaac, Joseph & Caleb, to be equally divided amongst them at 21 years of age, onely reserveing my wive's thirds & part of the Homelott, to be divided after my decease amongst all my sons. My Will is that the younger sons' Land shall be in my wive's improvement until they be of age to receive their portions in Land; or, in Case of her decease, in my son Samuel's Improvement, with whom I leave the special Care of my young Children. Having given to my daughters that are married £20 to each, and ordered £20 to be paid to my daughter Elizabeth, I give unto my four daughters, after the decease of their Mother, all my Household Goods, to be equally divided amongst them. I appoint my wife Abigail Cowles and my son Samuel Cowles to be Executors, & Brother Thomas Bull and Brother Thomas Porter to be Overseers.

Witness: *Caleb Stanly,*   SAMUEL COWLES, SEN. Ls.
        Sarah Stanly.

Court Record, Page 31—3rd September, 1691: Will proven.

Page 165-6.

Crane, Benjamin sen., Wethersfield. Died 31 May, 1691. Invt. £526-12-00. Taken 13 February, 1692, by Henry Crane, Jonathan Deming & Nathaniel Foote. The children: The Widow, Benjamin Crane, Jonathan, Joseph, Jo:, Abram, Jacob, Israel, Elisol, and Mary Crane.

Note: The House & Homested, that is, with all the Buildings, The Tan House excepted, that belongs to John, which he claims in his own Right, which is recorded to him with the Land he stands possessed of in his own Right.

Court Record, Page 61—7 September, 1693: Adms. to the Relict. Mr. James Treat to be Overseer.

Page 67—13 March, 1693-4: Order to Dist., Mr. James Treat, Lt. Henry Crane, and Nathaniel Foote to be Distributors.

Page 177.

Crane, Benjamin Jr., Wethersfield. Invt. £55-03-06, personal estate. Taken 9th November, 1693, by John Welles, Daniel Bowman.

Page 78—(Vol. VI): Inventory of Real Estate, £216-00-00. Taken 4 March, 1698-9, by Jonathan Boreman & Jonathan Belding.

On the 5th day of March, 1697-8, Mrs. Martha Terry, formerly Martha Crane, Widow of Benjamin Crane Jr., Decd., personally appeared before Capt. John Hamlin and my self (Caleb Stanly) at Hartford, and presented the Invt. of Houseing & Lands at Hartford above apprised, to be added to the former Inventory of her former Husband Benjamin Crane, Decd.

Court Record, Page 65—(Vol. V) 3 January, 1693-4: Invt. presented by Martha, Widow, Adms.

Page 34—(Vol. VI) 13 April, 1699: This Court being moved by Samuel Terry of Enfield, who married Martha the Widow of Benjamin Crane of Wethersfield, Decd, for a distribution of the Estate of sd. Crane, Order 1-3 part of the personal Estate to the Widow forever, and 1-3 part of the Real Estate during life; and to Isaac Crane, the child, 2-3 of the Moveable and 2-3 of the Real Estate to him and to his heirs forever. This Court grant to Samuel Terry Adms. in right of his Wife, and Order that Samuel Terry shall have the use and benefit of two-thirds of the Houseing and Lands for the bringing up of the child till he come of age.

Page 10—(Vol. VIII) 1st May, 1710: Isaac Crane, a minor 17 years of age, son of Benjamin Crane Jr., late of Wethersfield, Decd, chose Jonathan Boreman of Wethersfield to be his Guardian.

Page 36—2 July, 1711: This Court order that the Clerk, upon the request of Lt. Jonathan Boreman, Guardian of Isaac Crane, son of Benjamin Crane Jr., late of Wethersfield, Decd, shall Issue forth a writ to cite Samuel Terry of Enfield and Martha his wife, Adms. on the Estate of sd. Benjamin Crane, Decd, to appear in Court and render account of their Adms.

Page 89—6 October, 1712: This Court orders that Samuel Terry, Adms. on the Estate of Benjamin Crane Jr., Decd, do render to this Court an Account of his Adms. on or before the 1st Monday of March next ensueing.

Page 117—2 March, 1712-13: Samuel Terry of Enfield and his wife Martha Terry, Adms., exhibit now an account of their Adms., whereby it appears that they have paid in Debts and Charges (including what has been by them expended in bringing up and subsisting Isaac Crane, only Child of the sd. Benjamin Crane, Decd, and also what is spent for the necessary support of the family & Reparing the Buildings and Fences) amounting to the sum of £195-08-01, including what was by this Court formerly allowed, and that there is due and paid into the sd. Estate for the Rents and Profits of houseing and Lands, the sum of £57-00-00. This Court having examined the Account (and also heard and Considered the several Objections against the same by William Warner Jr., of Wethersfield, and others) do approve and allow the sd. Account. William Warner (who is one of the legal Representatives of the sd. Decd) appealed from this Resolve and order of this Court to the Superior Court.

Page 140—4 May, 1713: Samuel Terry of Enfield and Martha his wife, Adms. on the Estate of Benjamin Crane Jr., are granted a *Quietus Est.*

Page 206-7.

Crane, John, Wethersfield. Died 21 October, 1694. Invt. £417-06-04. Taken by John Chester Jr. & William Warner. The Tan yard (the Reversion of it) belongs to the Estate, but the Rent is due to the Widow Crane sen. during her life. Legatees: The Widow, & Josiah Crane, age 13 months, 22 April, 1695.

Court Record, Page 75—2 November, 1694: Adms. to the Widow. This Court appoint Mr. John Chester Jr., Nathaniel Butler and John Wyott to be Assistants.

Page 100—5 March, 1695-6: Dist. according to law. Mr. Jno. Chester and Ens. Wyott, Distributors.

Page 67—(Vol. VII) 5 April, 1705: Samuel Walker, Adms., renders Account of Debts paid and received.

Page 121—7 February, 1708-9: Exhibits a further Account of more Debts due from the Estate.

Page 10—(Vol. VIII) 3 April, 1710: This Court do order that the Clerk do issue forth a Writ to require Samuel Walker of Wethersfield, but now residing at Strattford, with his wife, Adms. to the Estate of John Crane of Wethersfield Decd, to appear before this Court & render Account of their Adms. on the Estate on the 1st Monday of July next, or sooner if they can.

Page 14—5 June, 1710: Samuel Walker & Abigail his wife, Adms. on the Estate of John Crane, Tanner, of Wethersfield Decd, exhibited now in this Court a full acct. of their Adms., whereby it appears that all the debts due from the Estate have been paid and the sd. Abigail's third part of the moveables taken out. There still remains in the hands of the Adms. the sum of £285-09-09 for the use of the son and heir of the sd. John Crane, Decd. Approved.

(See file), Page 248—4 April, 1715: Samuel Walker of Wethersfield, Adms., exhibited now in this Court a receipt under the hand of Josiah Crane (now of full age), only child of the sd. John Crane Decd, whereby it appears that sd. Josiah Crane hath received of sd. Samuel Walker his full share of his father's Estate as assigned him by Order of this Court 5 June, 1710. Thereupon this Court do grant to Samuel Walker and Abigail his wife, Adms., a *Quietus Est.* And do discharge Isaac Ryly of Wethersfield from his obligation as Guardian to the sd. Isaac [*Josiah*] Crane while in his Minority.

Page 131—4 July, 1709: Josiah Crane, a minor 15 years of age, chose Capt. James Steele to be his Guardian.

Page 162-3.

Crow, Daniel, Hartford. Died 12 August, 1693. Invt. £330-14-00. Taken 25 August, 1693, by Joseph Olmsted, Roger Pitkin & William Pitkin, Jr.

Court Record, Page 61—7 September, 1693: Adms. to the Widow. No children. Distribution to brothers and sisters, the widow to have the use of 1-3 of the real estate during life, and all of the personal, she to pay the debts.

Page 214.

Crow, Nathaniel, Hartford. Died 30 July, 1695. Invt. £507-02-10. Taken 7 September, 1695, by Joseph Olmsted sen., William Pitkin. Legatees: The relict Mrs. Deborah Crow, Elizabeth age 10 years, John Crow 8 years, Deborah 2 years & 3 months.

Court Record, Page 90—5 September, 1695: Adms. to the widow, with Mr. William Pitkin & Deac. Olmsted to be overseers. Order of Dist: 1-3 part of the personal Estate to the Relict forever, and the use of 1-3 of the real estate during life. To the eldest son a double portion at 21 years of age, and single portions to the daughters at 18 years of age.

Page 121—(Vol. VII) 7 February, 1708-9: Deborah Crow, a minor daughter of Nathaniel Crow, late of Hartford Decd, chose Thomas Olcott to be her Guardian.

Court Record, Page 3 (Vol. VIII) 6 February, 1709-10: Andrew Warner, late of Hartford, now of Windham, and Deborah his wife, Adms. on the Estate of Nathaniel Crow, late of Hartford deceased, now presented an account of their Adms: Paid out £48-08-11, and there has been spent, wasted or lost of the Moveables, £48-12-10. The whole of the moveable part of the estate was Invt. at £121-02-10. Of this there remains for Dist. £24-01-01. One third part, vizt, £8-00-04, being the proper right of Andrew Warner and Deborah his wife; and other £8-00-04 the right of Daniel Dickinson, who married Elizabeth, one of the daughters of the sd. Decd; and other £8-00-04, the residue, the right of Deborah Crow, one other daughter of the sd. Decd. The said Andrew & Deborah Warner have already distributed and paid out the same to them. This Court allow and approve, and now discharge the said Andrew & Deborah Warner, Adms., and grant a *Quietus Est.* And whereas, the County Court held at Hartford September 5th, 1695, did order and direct the way and manner of the distribution of the Estate of the said Nathaniel Crow deceased, and therein (amongst other things) did order that John Crow, the eldest and only sonn of the said deceased, should have and receive his whole portion thereof out of the houseing and lands at inventory price: The real part of said estate is £386-00-00, which with the £24-01-01 of moveables amounts to £410-01-01 in the whole. This Court do now order and decree 1-3 part of the houseing and lands to and for the use of the sd. Andrew Warner and Deborah his wife, relict of the said deceased, for the term of her life. To John Crow, the only son, the sum of £201-00-04; and to Daniel Dickinson and his children by his late wife Elizabeth aforenamed, the sum or valluc of £92-09-10; and to Deborah Crow £92-09-10; all at inventory price. And this Court appoint Capt. Roger Pitkin, Deacon Joseph Olmsted and Daniel Bidwell, senior, distributors. The estate now distributed to John Crow, to the Children of Daniel Dickinson in right of his wife Elizabeth, and to Deborah Crow, youngest daughter of said deceased, by Capt. Roger Pitkin, Deac. Joseph Olmstead & Daniel Bidwell.

Page 217—4 October, 1714: Daniel Dickinson now exhibits in Court a Dist. of the Estate of Nathaniel Crow, late Decd, per Order of Court, 6 February, 1709-10.

Page 121-2.

Curtice, James, Wethersfield. Died 5 September, 1690. Invt. £125-16-03. Taken 15 September, 1690, by Joseph Bull & Jonathan Bull. Legatees: The Widow, & Daughter Abigail, age 5 years—26 August, 1693.

Court Record, Page 37—18 January, 1691-2: Invt. Exhibited by the Relict. Adms. to Andrew Robe, who had married the Widow.

Page 57—12 April, 1693: Dist. ordered: To the Widow, one-third of the personal estate, £15-04-11, and one-third of the real estate during life; and two-thirds to the daughter, £31-09-10, of personal Estate, and 2-3 of the Real Estate when she comes of age or Marriage, and the whole at her Mother's decease.

Page 5.

Davis, Philip, Hartford. Invt. £375-13-02. Taken 22 October, 1689, by Ciprian Nichols and Stephen Hosmer.

Court Record, Page 4—6 November, 1689: Adms. to the widow. Capt. Stanly & Mr. Nichols to be overseers. Dist: To the Widow; to the son of the eldest daughter, £30; to Hannah, the daughter of the sayd Philip Davis, the remainder of the Estate.

Page 84-5-6.

Davie, Humphrey, Esq. Died 18 February, 1688. Invt. £277-09-09. Taken 13 August, 1689, by John Allyn and James Steele. There is a bed & bedstead, silk Curtains & valents, Boulster, pillows, rug, blankets, brass Andirons, brass fire shovel, Tongs & bellows, which my Mother Mrs. Sarah Davie refused to have prised because she said my Father Mr. Humphrey Davie gave them to her At Boston. The newer dwelling house, & an house which air made over by my father Mr. Humphrey Davie to my Mother Mrs. Sarah Davie for her security for four Hundred pounds which my father was obliged to give her, & also for security of Mr. James Richards's children's portions. There is a small dwelling house with about 2 acres & a half of Land to it, at Boston, nigh Beacon Hill. There is part of a powder Mill at Dorchester, & a small orchard at Rumney Marsh. There are some moveables left at Boston, and land at Eastward, not yet known.

Court Record, Page 5—6 November, 1689: Invt. exhibited by John Davie. Proclamation to creditors to appear before this Court the 1st Thursday of September next.

Page 21—5 September, 1690: John Davie, having formerly appeared in Septr Court, now appeared on the 28th of November, 1690, & requested a *Quietus Est.,* he having finished his Adms.

Page 38.

Denslow, John, Windsor. Died 10 September, 1689. Invt. £62-12 06. Taken 10 November, 1689, by Timothy Thrall and Abraham Phelps.

Court Record, Page 7—11 November, 1689: Adms. to John, eldest son, two of the children being lame or decrepit. Dist. deferred.

Page 18—31 July, 1690: Distribution to John, the eldest son, the houses and lands, he having paid £26-00-03, and is to pay to the other four children of John Denslow, as they come of age, £5-10 to each.

Denslow, Joseph. Court Record, Page 24—5 March, 1690-1: Joseph Denslow being deceased and his relations refuseing to accept of the Adms. this Court grants Adms. on the estate to Mr. Alexander Allyn, he taking and presenting to the Court an inventory of the estate of sd. Denslow to September Court next, and to secure what estate he can find in his hands till the Court shall grant Dist. of the Estate.

Page 55—12 April, 1693: Mr. Alexander Allyn being made Adms. to the estate of Joseph Denslow of Windsor Decd, presented an Accot of his estate by inventory, and of his dispose thereof, which is approved and accepted by the Court, and grant him a *Quietus Est.;* and do order Mr. Allyn to have 10 shillings more than Mr. Markham for his pains in this affair.

Page 132.

Dibble, Mehetabell. Died June, 1692. Invt. £14-11-00. Taken 26 July, 1692, by Thomas Huxley, Samuel Benton and Joseph Mygatt.

Court Record, Page 44—28 July, 1692: Invt. Exhibited by Mrs. Bidwell; Adms. to Samuel Benton, who is to pay the debts and distribute the remainder to her brothers & sisters.

Page 73.

Dow, Samuel. Died 2 June, 1690. Invt. £21-15-00. Taken 24 October, 1690, by George Grave sen. and Thomas Olcott.

Court Record, Page 19—5 November, 1690: Invt. Exhibited.

Page 20-21.

Drake, Job sen., Windsor. Invt. £583-04-00. Taken 28 October, 1689, by John Maudsley & John Moore. Will dated 14 September, 1689.

The last Will & Testament of Job Drake sen. of Windsor: I give unto my wife the Use of my Dwelling house & Barn, Orchard & Home-lott, except that which I give unto my son Job, with my Pasture I bought of Goodman Bissell, the Land in the Little Meadow & the 10 acres of Land I had of my Brother Christopher, & the Inclosed Lands in the Wood, & that which lyeth against the Door of my Dwelling house, & £40 of my Household Goods. I give unto my son Job 6 acres of Land that I had of my Father Drake. I give to him & his heirs forever my Dwelling house, Barn, Orchard & Homelott, with all my Land within the Township of Windsor, excepting such parcels as I shall otherwise dispose of, provided that he record to his son Job that house and that part of the Homelott, with his Barn, which he now injoyeth, with his lowest Lott toward Poduncke, at 21 years of age. I give to my daughter Elizabeth the 4 acres of Land in the Great Meadow that I bought of Goodman Thrall, at my wife's decease. I give to Ephraim Colton 40 Shillings and a small Rapier. I have given to my gr. Child Israel Dewey 2 young Steers, as also a Chest marked E. D. To my gr. Child Susannah Packer, my Land at Greenfield, & the product of 14 acres I sold to Nathan, or the Land if he pay not for it, according to his Bill or Bonds. I give to Joseph Dewey £4 of my Estate, to be paid to him when my son Job possesseth the rest of my Lands. I give to my gr. Child Mary Drake that which is due to me from my Father Drake's Estate, also from my Brother Jacob's Estate, also £4. I give to my gr. son, Joseph Dewey, Land over the River above John Osborne's, which was my Father Drake's. I give to my gr. Child, Job Colton, £5 in a young beast, and a gunn. I give to Elizabeth, my son Job's wife, 50 Shillings in some good thing. The remainder of my Estate to be divided amongst my Children, that is, to Job, Abigail, Elizabeth and Esther. I ordain my son Job Drake to be sole Executor, & desire John Moore and Thomas Griswold to be Supervisors.

Witness: *John Richard,*   JOB DRAKE SEN.
   James Glen.

Court Record, Page 5—11 November, 1689: Will proven.

Page 22-3-4.

Drake, Jacob, Windsor. Invt. £551-14-09. Taken 25 September, 1689, by Daniel Clarke sen., John Moore. Will dated 2 August, 1689.

The last Will & Testament of Jacob Drake: I give to Mary my wife the Use of all my Real and Personal Estate during her natural life, and at her death to dispose of £100 of my Personal Estate to whom she pleaseth. I give unto Nathaniel Gaylord's two Children, Hezekiah & Nathaniel, my Lott beyond Rocky Hill, about 26 acres; & unto Nathaniel Gaylord I give 2 acres of Land next adjoining to his Meadow Land on the South side. I give unto Jacob Drake, son of Job Drake, all my Houseing and Homested, with Land that was my Father Drake's and that which was purchased of Mr. Saint Niccolases Overseers. I give to John Elderkin the Lott over the Great River that is commonly called Fellows Lott, he paying his sister Bashua £10, and Abigail Due's 3 Children, Israel, Mary & Joseph, £10 apeice. I give to my Cousin John Gaylord, son of Sargt Gaylord, a Lott on the East side of the River called Hoskins Lott, bounded North by John Birge, south by Land of Thomas Bissell. I give to my Brother Job Drake half the Lott that was my Father Drake's lying above Namerick, the other half I give to Nathaniel Gaylord. I give to Thomas Deble the Lott that I purchased of Prior, at the age of 21 years. I give to Joseph Elderkin 3½ acres in the Great Meadow, bounded south by Nicholas Buckland, North by Abram Phelps. I give to Joseph Drake, son of John Drake, 2 acres of Land in the Great Meadow, South Samuel Marshall's, North Nathaniel Winchell's. I give to Nathaniel Gaylord 15 acres upon the Pine Meadow Playne, which I bought of Humphrey Pinney. I appoint my wife and Cousin Job Drake Jr. to be Adms. on the Estate, and desire my Brother Drake, Abraham Phelps, Nathaniel Gaylord, and my Cousin Job Drake to be Overseers.

Witness: *Abraham Phelps,*   JACOB DRAKE.
   Job Drake sen.

Court Record, Page 6—11 November, 1689: Will Proven.

Page 26—5 March, 1690-1: A Report to this Court that the Estate will not hold out to pay all the debts and Legacies, the Court orders to first pay the debts and distribute to the Legatees *(Pro Rata.)*

Page 25.

Drake, John, Simsbury. Died 9 July, 1689. Invt. £393-15-00. Taken 30 October, 1689, by John Higley, Thomas Barber and Peter Buell. The children: Mary, age 15 years, Hanna 11, John, 1 year old.

Court Record, Page 6—11 November, 1689: Adms. to Mary Drake, the Widow; John Higley and Thomas Barber to be Overseers.

Page 60—7 September, 1693: Adms. on Estate of Mary Drake, now deceased, to Mary Drake & Mr. John Higley, who is chosen and allowed to be Guardian to the youngest daughter. (A legal distribution follows.)

Page 107—(Vol. VII) 5 April, 1708: John Drake, a minor about 19 years of age, now residing in Danbury, son of John Drake, chose Deacon Job Drake of Windsor to be his Guardian.

Page 186—(Vol. VIII) 5 April, 1714: A Dist. made on the Estate of John Drake of Simsbury, made by John Higley pursuant to a Decree of the Court of Assistants holden at Hartford 26th May, 1691, was now exhibited in Court by Capt. John Higley of Simsbury, which Dist. this Court accepts, and grant John Higley, Adms., a *Quietus Est.*

Page 24.

Drake, John sen., Windsor. Invt. £223-02-02. Taken 31 October, 1689, by John Moore. Will dated 12 September, 1689.

I John Drake sen. of Windsor doe make this my last Will for the disposal of my Estate: I give to my son Job 20 Shillings besides what I have already given him. I give to my son Enoch Drake that Lott in the Great Meadow which was Mr. Huit's, about 3 ½ acres. I give to my son Simon my House & Homelott & Barn & my Woodlott upon the Mill Brook, being about 15 acres. I give to my son Joseph the remainder of my Lands on the East side of the Great River. I give to my 3 daughters, Lydia, Elizabeth and Mindwell, the remainder of my Land which is undisposed of in the Lott going to Hartford, known by the name of Clay Bridge. Also, I give to my daughter Mary the Woodlott, being about 15 acres, lying by my brother Job's Pasture. I give to my son John's three children £20, that is, to his son John £10, and the two daughters £5 apeice. It is my Will and I doe hereby give to my daughter Ruth and my son Simon Drake that Land which I bought of Mr. Howkins and Capt. Marshall, being about 5 acres, upon the Condition as followeth, viz., that they pay to my son John's three Children the £20 I have given them, as they come to be of age; and what the Land comes to more at £8 per acre shall be paid to all my daughters equally. Also my Will is that my 40 acres of Woodland which was granted me by the Town shall be to him or them of my Children which will give most for it, & the price of it to be equally divided amongst all my Children. I appoint my son Job Drake and my son-in-law Samuel Barber to be Executors.

Witness: *John Moore, sen.,*   JOHN DRAKE.
       John Haile.

Court Record, Page 6—11 November, 1689: Will proven.

Page 26.

Drake, Mrs. Mary, Wife of Jacob Drake. Will dated 8 September, 1689.

The last Will & Testament of Mary Drake, wife of Jacob Drake Jr., Decd.: I give, after my Just debts are paid, the rest of that Hundred Pounds which my loveing Husband gave me by Will, I give one half to my Brothers Samuel Bissell and Nathaniel Bissell, the other half to Samuel Pinney, my brother-in-law, & to my Kinsman Nathaniel Gaylord. And for my apparell, I give equally to my sister Joyce Pinney and my kinswoman Abigail Gaylord. That share of Estate which is due of my Mother Drake I give one half to Thomas Dibble and the other half to Sarah Hutchins, my Maid. My Brother Samuel Bissell and Nathaniel Gaylord Each to pay to Mary Trumble 10 Shillings.   MARY DRAKE.

Witness: *Thomas Elsworth,*
       Dorothy X *Colt.*

Court Record, Page 6—11 November, 1689: Will Approved.

Page 8—13 December, 1689: This Court appoint Samuel Bissell, Nathaniel Bissell, Samuel Pinney & Nathaniel Gaylord Adms. with Will annexed.

Page 172.

Drake, Mary, Relict of John of Simsbury. Died 7 August, 1693. Invt. £388-09-00. Taken 23 August, 1693, by John Higley, Samuel Willcoxson and Peter Buell. The children: John, 5 years of age, Mary 19, Hannah 15. Invt. presented in Court 7 Sept., 1693, by Mary Drake, the daughter, John Slater sen. and Thomas Barber.

Page 104.

Durant, George, Middletown. Invt. £120-07-00. Taken 23 February, 1690-1, by Samuel Collins and William Sumner.

Court Record, Page 25—5 March, 1690-1: Invt. Exhibited and approved. Edward Durant, son of the deceased, personally appeared with an affidavit of the Correctness of Invt. *(See Invt. side, Page 104.)*

On File, not on Record.

Easton, Joseph sen., Died 14 August, 1688. Invt. £20-04-01. Taken 1st September, 1688, by George Graue & Jonathan Bull.

Will this Twenth day of January, 1687: I, Joseph Easton, seart, of Hartford, in his Maigst Territory or Dominion of Newengland, Being weake in Body but of perfect memory & Remembrance, praised be God, do make and ordain this my last Will and Testament in maner and form as followeth: First, I Bequeath my soul into the hand of God my maker, hopeing for acceptence of him only in and by Jesus Christ my only Saviour; and as for my Body, to be Buried in Christian Burial at the discretion of my Executor hereafter named. My will is that all my just debts be truly paid to whom I am Indebted. I give unto my son Joseph Easton fourty shillings Beside what land or other goods I have formerly given him. Item. I give unto my son-in-law John Skiner fourty shillings beside what he has already received of me. Item. I give to my son-in-law Robert Sherly ten pounds, which, with the other Legacies above named, is to be paid to the several Legatees above named within twelve months after my decease. Item. I give to my four Children, to say, John Easton, Joseph Easton, Mary Skiner, and Sarah Sherly, all my Houseall goods that do appear to be properly myne or belonging to me att my decease, to be equally divided among them, excepting what I have particularly given to them in my will · & as to goods bought since my son John married, they are already his. I do give to my son John Easton my Arms, or that is to say, three guns, two swords & two belts; also my great Bible and a Divinity Book of Mr. Thomas Goodwin's works, to him and to his heirs forever. Also, I do give unto my said son John Easton all the Rest of my Houses, Leases, Lands, Tenements, and goods whatsoever, all my Rights, titles, properties in or belonging to me in Hartford or Elswhere, to him my said son John Easton and his heirs for ever. Also, I doe ordain and appoint that my son John Easton shall have the first choice of my Housall goods that is to be divided Between my fouer Children above mentioned. I do also appoint my son Joseph Easton to pay his proportion of the Charges of the proveing and approveing of this my Will, & of the Inventory, in proportion to what he do have or has formerly had of my Estate. I do appoint my son John Easton sole Executor, and Hond John Allyn, Esq., Lt. Joseph Whiting and Ensign Nathaniel Stanly to be Overseers.

                                                    JOSEPH EASTON.

Witness: *Thomas Bunce,*
         Jonathan Bull.

Page 93.

Eglestone, Samuel sen., Middletown. Invt. £105-15-09. Taken by Samuel Collins, William Sumner & Daniel Marcum. The children now living: Samuel age 28, Sarah 21, Susannah 17, Nicholas 14, Mercy 12, Mary 9, Ebenezer 6 years of age. Guardians and Overseers made choice of are: For Sarah & Nicholas, Ensign Samuel Collins; the others, Susannah, Mary and Ebenezer, request Deacon Daniel Marcum to be their Guardian, and they all jointly request Ensign Samuel Collins and Deacon Daniel Marcum to be their Overseers.   *Samuel Collins, William Sumner, Daniel Marcum.*

December 20, 1686: Land recorded to Samuel Eglestone Jr., dwelling in Middletown, in the County of Hartford, the Land lying in the same town: One parcel given him by his father Samuel Eglestone, lying in the West Field, containing 8 acres & 2-3 of an acre, abutting on the Swamp East, on undivided Land West, on John Stone's Land North, and Benajah Stone's Land South; & ½ of his Meadow at Maramarsh, beginning southwest on that Meadow which his Father bought of William Harris, which was formerly William Smith's half of all the Meadow, ½ of the Upland belonging to the sd. Eglestone at the Farm; all these Lands the sd. Eglestone giveth to his sd. son Samuel, and this for his son Samuel's portion of Estate, not being engaged to give his son any more portion. As Witness his Hand,   SAMUEL EGLESTONE SEN.

Pr me John Hall, Recorder.

Endorsed: I doe hereby acknowledge to have received full satisfaction as for my portion of my father's Estate according to the Tenor of the Record within written: Witness my hands 6 March, 1690-1.
Witness: *Samuel Collins,*   SAMUEL EGLESTONE.
Caleb Stanly.

Court Record, Page 24—5 March, 1690-1: Adms. to Samuel Eglestone & Deacon Daniel Marcum. This Court allows the Overseers as above.

Page 34-5-6.

Elsworth, Sergt. Josiah, Windsor. Died 20 August, 1689 (W.R.) Invt. £655-00-00. Taken 17 October, 1689, by Abraham Phelps, Benajah Holcomb, & James Ennoe. The children: Josiah, born 5 November, 1655; Elizabeth, 11 November, 1657; Mary, 7 May, 1660 (W. R.); Martha, 7 December, 1662; Thomas, 2 September, 1665; Jonathan, 28 June, 1669; John, 7 October, 1671; Job, 13 April, 1674; & Benjamin, 13 years, January Next, 1676. Will dated 11 August, 1689.

I Sergt. Josiah Elsworth of Windsor doe make this my last Will & Testament: I give to my wife, after my decease, the whole Use & Profits of my Estate during Widowhood, and one year more if she should marry, and afterward £50 in Current Country pay out of the Moveable Estate that may best suit her, only with this proviso, that if God should in his providence, in the Juncture of time, dispose of my daughter Martha in marriage, then out of the Moveable Estate to pay her a portion according to what her elder sisters already have received. Item. I give to my eldest son Josiah my now dwelling house, Barn, Orchards, Outland, & Meadow on the East side of the Common Street down to the River, he resigning to me what Land he doth improve on the East side of the Great River when he shall come to enjoy this abovesd., he also paying to his 3 sisters £30 in Country pay, to each an equal proportion, sometime within two years after possession. I give unto my two sons Thomas and Jonathan the whole of my Lott on the West side of the Common Street over against my Dwelling house, and all my Lott adjoining to Pine Meadow, by them to be equally divided; also 1 Farme on my Lott over the Great River upon Scantick Brook, on either side my Lott which they shall choose, three score Rod in Breadth and 8 score Rod in length. I give to my 3 youngest sons, John, Jobe, and Benjamin, all the rest of my Lands not yet disposed of over the Great River, each of them paying to their 3 sisters, Elizabeth, Mary, and Martha, £10 apeice in Country pay within two years after they come to a free Enjoyment of the Lands. All the rest of my Moveable Estate, after my wife's marriage or decese, I give and bequeath to my six sons & 3 daughters, to be equally divided amongst them. I desire my son Josiah and my son Nathaniel Loomis to assist my beloved wife in the Adms. and Distribution of my Estate.

Witness: *Timothy Thrall,*   JOSIAH ELSWORTH. Ls.
       John Gaylord.

Court Record, Page 7—11 November, 1689: Will proven.

Page 48-9.

Evans, Nicholas, Simsbury. Died 29 August, 1689. Invt. £110-10-00. Taken 3 March, 1689-90, by John Higley and Joshua Holcomb. The children: Mercy age 16 years, Samuel 14, Nicholas 12, Hannah 10, Joseph 8, Thomas 5, Abigail 3, Benonie 17 weeks.

Court Record, Page 10—6 March, 1689-90: Adms. to the Widow, and appoynt Mr. John Higley, Benajah Holcomb & John Williams to be Overseers.

Page 17—(Vol. VII) 4 September, 1701: Robert Westland of Windsor, and his wife Mary, formerly wife of Nicholas Evans late of Simsbury Decd, moves this Court for a Dist. of sd. Estate. Mary the Widow, now wife of Robert Westland, was Adms. This Court appoint Capt. Higley, Ensign Samuel Humphries and Sergt. Willcoxson Distributors.

Page 58.

Flood, Robert, Wethersfield. Died 16 December, 1689. Invt. £117-14-00. Taken 6 February, 1689-90, by John Chester Jr. & Samuel Butler. The children: Robert age 16 years, Abigail 14, John 12, Thomas 9, Mary 7, George 4 years of age.

Court Record, 6 March, 1689-90, Page 11—Adms. to the Widow. Capt. John Chester and Ensign John Chester to be Overseers.

Page 87—2 May, 1695: Matthew Barnes, who married Abigail Flood, was this day called to account for their Adms., which this Court accepted & Order Distribution: To the eldest son, £15-02-08; to each of the other five children, £7-11-04.

Page 149-50-51.

Forbes, James, Hartford. Died 27 March, 1692. Invt. £344-11-05. Taken 16 December, 1692, by Joseph Olmsted and Roger Pitkin.

11 January, 1692-3, an Agreement of the Heirs for a settlement and Division of the Estate: To the Widow Katharen Forbes, to David Forbes in Land, to James Forbes in Land, to William Roberts in right of his wife Dorothy, land to equal £20, to Mary Forbes £20, to Sarah Forbes £20, to James Forbes, the Eldest son, he paying all the Debts due from the Estate & Portions aforesaid. All the remainder of the Estate to the sons & William Roberts, to them & their Heirs forever.
Witness: *Joseph Olmsted,*
Roger Pitkin.

John Forbes, Dorothy Roberts, Mary Forbes, David Forbes and Sarah Forbes, being all of age, to receive their portions; and James Forbes will be 16 on the 14th of May next.

Court Record, Page 50—11 January, 1692-3: Invt. & Agreement Exhibited in Court and confirmed. Adms. to John Forbes; and Deac. Olmsted and Roger Pitkin to make Distribution according to this Agreement.

Page 73-4.

Fyler, Mrs. Jane, Relict of Lt. Walter Fyler of Windsor Decd. She Died 11 September, 1690. Invt. £122-05-08. Taken 10 November, 1690, by Henry Wolcott & Atherton Mather. Will dated 22 June, 1687.

The last Will & Testament of Mrs. Jane Fyler of Windsor is as followeth: My Will is that my son John Fyler shall have of that my Estate my husband willed me to my free dispose, £30. My son Zerubbabell Fyler shall have £20, my son Zerubbabell's son Thomas £10, and Zerubbabell £10, and his daughter Jane shall have out of the same Estate all the Beds & Bedding in the Kitchen Chamber & Pilion & Pilion Cloth and a little Brass Skillett. And his other 3 Children to each of them I give the sum of £5. And my Will is that my daughter-in-law, Zerubbabell's wife Experience, shall have all my Wearing Clothes, Woolen & Linen. I appoint my two sons John & Zerubbabell Fyler my Executors; and John Loomis sen. and Nathaniel Loomis sen. my Overseers.
Witness: *Samuel Mather,*   JANE X FYLER. Ls.
Joseph Loomis.

A Codicil, dated 17 May, 1689.
Court Record, Page 19—5 November, 1690: Will & Inventory exhibited. Adms. to Zerubbabell Fyler, John Fyler refuseing the executorship.

Page 110.

Gaylord, Benjamin, & his Widow. Invt. £21-11-00. Taken 5 February, 1690-1, by John Porter, William Williams.
Court Record, Page 26—5 March, 1691-2: Adms. to John Porter to dispose of the Estate & of the Children to the best advantage.

Page 26-7.

Gaylord, Sergt. John, Windsor. Died 13 July, 1689. Invt. £293-01-00. Taken by Henry Wolcott, John Birge. The children: John Gaylord, Widow Mary Loomis, & Elizabeth Gaylord.
Court Record, Page 6—11 November, 1689: Adms. to John Gaylord. Dist: The Land to the Eldest son, the Personal Estate equally to the two daughters.

Page 66.

Gaylord, Samuel sen., Hatfield (Mass.) Died September, 1689. Invt. £239-08-01. Taken 25 October, 1689, by Deacon Church, Jos. Belknap, Samll Partrigg. Will dated 22 September, 1689.
I Samuel Gaylord sen. of Hatfield, in the County of Hampshire, in the colony of Mass., doe make this my last Will & Testament: I give to my son Samuel Gaylord my house and Homested in Windsor on the West side of the River, & half my Allottment on the East side of the River in Windsor, accordingly as I formerly made it over to him by a Deed, Bounded on the North side by Samuel Pinney, he to pay my son Griswold £6 and then to have the whole of the Lotts besides what my son Elsworth hath. I give to my daughter Griswold, so much of the Land of sd. Lott on the East side of the River. To my daughter, the wife of Josiah Elsworth, Land on the East side of the River; also I give her, as abovesd., ½ of what Estate will appear to be my Estate in Hatfield, after my decease and the decease of my wife. I give to my daughter Sarah, the wife of John Alexander, ½ of my residuary Estate in Hatfield. I give to my daughter Abigail, the wife of Joseph Wascoat of Stamford, if she be living to receive it, £5. I ordain my wife Mary, and Mr. Samuel Partrigg, to be joynt & sole Executors.
Witness: *Thomas Nash,*   SAMUEL X GAYLORD.
            Samuel Sedgewick.

Court Record, Page 18—4 September, 1690: Will Proven.

Page 35—3 December, 1691 : Adms. to Mrs. Mary Gaylord (Widow) with will annexed.

Page 69—4 April, 1694: Mary Gaylord, of Windsor, Exhibits account of her Administration of the Estate of her Decd husband, Samuel Gaylord. She desired to be released from further Adms., and also to claim her thirds & to renounce all other Claims by Virtue of her husband's will. Whereupon this Court appoint Lt. Abraham Phelps & Samuel Pinney to lay out to the Widow Gaylord the thirds of her husband's Estate.

Dist. File, 8 April, 1696: Estate Samuel Gaylord sen. An Agreement signed by Richard Hubbell and wife Elizabeth, Joseph Griswold and wife Mary, Joseph Wescott and wife Abigail, Josiah Elsworth and wife Martha, John Alexander and wife Sarah, Samuel Gaylord Jr. Deceased.

<hr>

Page 78.

Gaylord, Samuel, Windsor. Died 19 August, 1690. Invt. £121-00-02. Taken 3rd March, 1690-1, by Timothy Thrall and Abraham Phelps. Due to him as a soldier to Albany, £0-12-02. Debts & Legacy due to the Widow of Joseph Griswold, £6, per will of Samuel Griswold Decd. Legacy due to wife of Joseph Wascoat, £5. Total, £27-10-00. Will dated 7 June, 1690.

This Writing testifieth that I, Samuel Gaylord, of Windsor, in the County of Hartford, in the Colony of Connecticut, in Consideration of my present Call being going out to War, do leave this my Will as followeth : That in Case the providence of God so ordereth that I Come not home again, I Will to my wife Mary Gaylord all my Right & Title, both of Houseing and Lands, in the Township of Windsor, as or else where, during the time of her natural life ; as also I give to my wife all my Moveable Estate. And after my Wive's death I Will the whole Right of Houseing and Lands to be equally divided between Samuel Hubbell, the son of Richard Hubbell which he hath by my sister Elizabeth Gaylord, and Samuel Alexander, the son of my sister Sarah, the wife of John Alexander, if I return not again, to be and remain to them and to their heirs forever.

Witness: *Joseph Gaylord,*   SAMUEL X GAYLORD.
          Thomas Judd Jr.

Proven in Court, 6 November, 1690.

<hr>

Page 82-3-4.

Gilbert, Corp. John. Invt. £417-19-10. Taken 13 January, 1690-1, by Joseph Wadsworth and Thomas Olcott. He died 29 December, 1690. Will dated 1st August, 1690.

I John Gilbert of Hartford do make this my last Will & Testament: I give unto my wife the Lott in the long meadow, 3 acres given us by our Mother Lord; also £10 and the use of my Homested during life. I give to my son Thomas Land in the long meadow I bought of John Black-leach. I give to my son Joseph My Homested, with all the appurtenances, to enjoy one-half at my decease, and the whole after the decease of my Wife; also my little pasture I bought of Mr. Richard Edwards; also Woodland I bought of Daniel Garrett. I give to my son James my Lott in the Pine Field (about 4 ½ acres) which I bought with my house. I give to my daughter Dorothy Palmer, in addition to what I have already given her, the sum of £10, within 2 years after my decease. I appoint my wife and my son Thomas Gilbert Executors.

                                                    JOHN GILBERT. Ls.
Witness: *Thomas Olcott,*
         William Goodwin.

Court Record, Page 22—15 January, 1690-1: Will Proven.

See Ante-Nuptial Agreement on File:

An Agreement by and between Josiah Gilbert and Mary Ward, Widow, in the year of 1681: The Condishens hereof: That whear The within bounden Josiah Gilbert shall by the Grace of God marry and take to wife one mary Ward, widow, if the said Josiah, af tar the said marriage had and solomised, hapen to dey before The said mary, That Then The said Jos: shall leaue The said mary tow roomes in the west end of the Dwelling house now in being, with one-Third part of his barn and out housing, fold, yards, and with all freedom Conuenience Therein; as allso one-Third part of his orchard, one The South side, and foure akers of land, tow akers of it abounding one The great Riuer east, and a deuiding fence north, and The orchard west; and The other Tow akers one the south of Diuedent brook, whare The said Mary shall make choyce with Conuenient ways for Transportation; and forty shillings yearly in Corent pay of This Contory, to be paid att The said house by The asins of the said Josiah G: to The said M: or hir asins, aftar The deth of Jo: to be imployed and Disposed to the proper use of The said mary W: During hir life; and if aftar hir Widowhood, to Return The housing unto The eares or asins of the said Jo: It is further granted, That The said mary W: shall, aftar mared solomised, bring The improvement of hir premeses according to Law now in hir possesion in to the free use of the said Joshua G: with Thirty tow pounds of hir Joynter portion, and The other Thirty Tow is for hir att hir Time before his Deth to Declare and make hir Will, deuise and giue att hir plesur, To what parson or parsons and unto what use or porpos as shee will att hir plasure, and allso do permit hir excetors To prove, declare and proforme hir will without intersaption. In Conformation hereof,
We sat to our hands october ye 18.

Witness: *Daniel Harris,*   JOH. GILBERT,
         Isaac Johnson.   MARY WARD.

Wethersfield, ye 2nd March, 1695-6. We whose names are hereunto subscribed, haveing an Interest in & to ye Estate of Josiah Gilbert, late of Wethersfield, Decd., by right of our wives, who were all of them ye Daughters of ye sd. Josiah Gilbert, & haueing as yett not obtained a diuision of ye sd. Estate whereof our Honed father, ye sd. Josiah Gilbert, dyed Intestate, which Estate hath now of a long time bene undeiuded as to an absolute settlement of ye same, where of we whose names are under written have sustained much Damage by Reason ye same is not Deuided as it ought to haue been, & being sencible yt ye sd. Estate is in a suffering Condition for want of Settlement, & ye Right heirs being sufferes thereby: Therefore, we whose names are hereunto subscribed Doe Desire our Respected vncle ffrancis Whitmore of Middletown to Make Complaint in our behalfes to ye County Court at Hartford, & Inform ye Honed Magestrates of ye Condition of ye prsons & ye Condition of ye Estate In order to a Just & Equall Distribution, that Soe euery one may Know, haue & Injoye what of right ought to be theire owne. In witness that this is our Desire, & yt we haue Imployed ye sd. ffrancis Whitmer about ye pemises, we haue hereunto subscribed our names ye Day & year aboue written.

JONATHAN X DEMING SEN.,
JOHN RILEY,
JACOB WILLIAMS,
SIMON WILLARD.

Court Record, Page 97—5 March, 1695-6: Mr. Francis Whetmore, in behalfe of Wido Gilbert, moued this Court to grant an Order that Josiah Gilbert's Estate be Inventoried. This Court appoint Mr. John Chester Jr. and Lt. Wm Warner to take an Inventory and cause it to be presented to this Court. Inventory also on File: Personal Estate, £121-01-06, taken att Money prise, 29 September, 1688, by John Robins, Lt. William Warner & Sergt. Jno. Wells. Inventory of Real Estate, £271-10-00, Taken ye 17 March, 1695-6, per appoyntment of the Court, & apprised as Country pay, per William Warner & John Chester Junr. An Estate in Land at Bantry not known what quantity so as to prize itt. The Children of Josiah Gilbert (with the Inventory):

Benjamin,	Eldest	son	Eliz: Demong,	Eldest	daughter
Josiah,	2nd	son	Lydia Ryley,	2nd	"
Eleazer,	3rd	son	Sarah Williams,	3rd	"
Moses,	4th	son	Mary Willard,	4th	"
Caleb,	5th	son	Amy Gilbert,	youngest	"
John,	youngest	son			

Page 106—8 April, 1696: Jacob Williams made oath that he made a true presentment of the houseing and Lands of his father-in-Law, Josiah Gilbert Decd., unto the Apprisers. Invt. accepted in Court.

Page 108—23 April, 1696: Adms. to Josiah Gilbert, the second son of the Decd. And this Court order the Adms. to deliver up the Estate to the Wido what becomes due to her by her Joynture. The Children of sd. Mr. Gilbert are desired to agree about the Dist. of the Estate, and they are to be mindfull of the youngest son.

Page 158—(Vol. IV) 18 June, 1696: This Court having been desired to make a Dist. of the Estate of Mr. Josiah Gilbert, do find:

	£ s d
His Inventory in Real Estate in Pay,	271-10-07
And in Moveable Estate in Money,	121-01-06
In Pay,	242-03-00
The Total is,	513-13-00

Which was ordered to be dist. as followeth: In the first place, wt the Widow is not paid of her Joynture, it be in the 1st place paid to the Widow, and her Annuity set out to her, and that the remainder of the Estate be divided to the Children. What is behind of her Joynture this day is to be paid by Benjamin, he having given his word to the Court he would do it, and he having the Improvement of the Lands hitherto.

Page 117—(Vol. V) 3 September, 1696: Lt. Thomas Hollister having refused to Act as Distributor, this Court appoint Joseph Mygatt Distributor.

Page 144—(Vol. VI) 4 March, 1696-7: Lt. John Chester & Lt. Hollister having refused Dist., this Court appoint Capt. Joseph Wadsworth with Mr. Joseph Mygatt, Dist. See File for Estate that Mary Ward carred to Josiah Gilbert's house when married to him, in January, 1687-8. Accot as followeth: February, 1687-8:

	£ s d
Cowes,	12-00-00
One Horse bought of her father,	05-00-00
8 Swine,	14-00-00
20 Bushells of Ind: Corne,	01-05-00
payd Ensign Ward for Jos: Gilbert, 35 Shillings,	01-15-00
To Hay sold to Ensign Ward and Jno Black, 25s,	01-05-00
To Cash 4s, or in pay 8s,	00-08-00

The sumers work of 2 boyes, 1 of 14 years old, ye other capable of earning his victualls *(returned home before winter, having no recompence)*. The Summer work of Mary, about 16 years old.
The Use of the Cowes the summer (   ) at winter.
The Charge of bringing vp Jno, son of ye sd. Josiah, from March, last week, 1689, to the present April, 1696-7 (7 years).

An Account of what was returned to ye sd. Mary Ward after her husband's Decease:

	£ s d
2 Cowes,	08-00-00
By her husband's contract of marriage she is to have 40s annually, wch now, the last of August, is 7 years,	14-00-00
Of which she hath received 46s of Benjamin Gilbert,	2-06-00

There is still due, August, 1695,	11-14-00

Also sd. Benjamin witholds 2 ackers of ye best of ye Land
Granted by contract of marriage, whereby those that
have leased ye Land do withold 20s per year for 6 years

	£	s	d
now last August,		6-00-00	
So due to ye Widdow, August, 1695, on Joynture acctt,	£17-14-00		

Page 150—(Vol. IX) 2 May, 1721 : Upon Motion of Capt. Ephraim
Goodrich that the Lands of Josiah Gilbert sen., sometime of Wethersfield
Decd, may be dist., this Court cite Lt. Jonathan Belding, John Reignolds,
Daniel Williams and Thomas Deming to appear to object, if they see
Cause, why Dist. should not be made.

Page 157—1st September, 1721 : Upon the Motion (as per File) of
Capt. Ephraim Goodrich that the Lands of Mr. Josiah Gilbert may be
dist., and John Reignolds also moving this Court for a Dist. of the Lands
given by Mr. Josiah Gilbert to his wife for her Improvement during life
(she being lately decd), this Court order that the Matter be deferred.

5th December, 1721 : Withdrawn by Capt. Goodrich and John Reignolds.

Page 174—5 September, 1722 : It appears to the Satisfaction of this
Court that Dist. had been formerly made, and therefore do not see Cause
to order any Distribution.

Page 8—(Vol X) 5 March, 1722-3 : Upon Motion of John Rey-
nolds, one of the purchasers of part of the Estate, for an Order of Court
to set out the Widow's thirds of Land, a Writ was Issued to cite the heirs
and purchasers, viz., Capt. Ephraim Goodrich, Widow Lucy Edwards,
Jonathan Belding, David Williams and Thomas Deming. The one objection was from Ephraim Goodrich, whose plea was not considered
sufficient, and he appealed to the Superior Court.

Page 10-11—22 March, 1722-3 : The Heirs move this Court to set out
a highway mentioned in the Dist. of this Estate ; also to set out to the Heirs
the Land on the Westerly side of Highway ; also to set out in severallty
the Widow's third or Joynture ; and all to be done as nigh as possible according to the former Distribution on file. The Court appoint Ebenezer
Belding and Jonathan Burnham.

Page 16—23 April, 1722-3 : A Return was made to this Court of the
setting out a Highway mentioned in a former Distribution of the Estate
of Josiah Gilbert, sometime of Wethersfield Decd., and also the setting
out to and amongst the Heirs and Assigns of sd. Gilbert The Upland on
the West side of the sd. Highway, and also the setting out in severallty
to the sd. Heirs and Assigns the Widow's thirds or Joynture, according
to the Order of this Court, March 22d last, which this Court do allow and
approve, and ordered to be kept upon File, or recorded if the severall
parties see Cause to pay for the doeing thereof.

Page 159. (Will on File).

Gillett, Jeremiah, Windsor. Invt. £56-12-00. Taken 19 March, 1692-3, by Job Drake Jr., James Enno and Joseph Phelps Jr. Will dated 17 December, 1692.

I Jeremiah Gillett of Windsor doe make this my last Will & Testament: I give to my wife all my whole Estate for her Use & Improvement during the time of her natural life, as also my house & Homested, the Land being 3 acres more or less, bounding East on Josiah Gillet, north the Highway, West Jonathan Gillett, South against the Mill Brooke. I give my Marsh Land at Simsbury (the sd. Land given me by his last Will) I give to my wife as her proper Right, to sell or dispose of to whom she will. I give my daughter Deborah, at the day of her marriage, my Woodland, which is 10 acres more or less. I give my Homested, that Land being 5 acres more or less, to my daughter Deborah after her Mother's Decease. My Will is my wife shall give my daughter, after her marriage, 20 shillings per year, to be paid in Apples or Syder, or in Both. I constitute my wife to be sole Executrix.

Witness: *John Fyler,*   JEREMIAH GILLETT. Ls.
    Benjamin Bartlett.

Court Record, Page 56—12 April, 1693: A Will was exhibited in Court and was not allowed. Some Testimony was offered by Timothy Phelps sen., age 54 years, Joseph Loomis, age 41 years, son of John Loomis, Peter Brown, age 25 years, & Joseph Skiner. Order to Dist. the Estate to the Widow Deborah and the daughter. Adms. was granted to James Eno & Deborah the Relict.

Page 62—7 September, 1693: It appears the daughter had died. This Court now Order her part of Jeremiah Gillett's Estate to be divided among the uncles and aunts, her father's brothers and sisters. Lt. Return Strong and Mr. John Porter appointed Distributors.

Page 36—(Vol. VI) 13 April, 1698: Whereas, there have been differences between Jonathan Gillett of Windsor in behalf of himself and his brothers & sisters on the one part, and Samuel Adams of the same Windsor on behalf of his wife Deborah, as she was Adms. to the Estate of Jeremiah Gillett, her late Husband, on the other part, respecting the division of the estate of the sd. Jeremiah Gillett, which was ordered by the Court to him sd. Jonathan Gillett, and set out to him and them, his brothers and sisters, by Lt. Returne Strong and Mr. John Porter, by the Order of sd. Court, as by the Records of the Court may fully appear. And that the sd. Difference may be put to an End and fully issued, they the sd. Gillett and the sd. Adams have mutually and full agreed, and do by these presents fully and absolutely agree in manner and form following: (——————————) And for Confirmation hereof, and every part of this Agreement, we have hereunto set our Hands this 30th day of April, 1695.

Witness: *Daniel Clarke sen.,*   JONATHAN GILLETT,   PETER BROWN,
    Joseph Mygatt.   CORNELIUS GILLETT,   SAMUEL X ADAMS,
                    JOSIAH GILLETT,   DEBORAH X ADAMS.
                    SAMUEL FFILLEY,

Page 1-2.

Goodwin, William sen., Hartford. Died 15 October, 1689. Invt. £196-19-06. Taken 5 November, 1689, by John Marsh & Zachariah Sandford. Will dated 25 June, 1689.

I William Goodwin sen. of Hartford do make this my last Will & Testament: I give to my wife Susannah Goodwin that part of my Homelott & House, or Houseing upon it, not given to my son Nathaniel, during the term of her natural life; and also I give her liberty to make Sale of the Same for her maintenance if need so require, to be offered first to my son Nathaniel Goodwin or his heirs before it be disposed to any others. Also, I give to my wife all my Moveable Estate that I stand possessed of at my decease, unless it be one Cow, she paying my just Debts & Legacy given to my daughter Susannah Goodwin at my decease. Also, I give to my wife 20 Shillings per year, to be paid by my son William Goodwin or his heirs during the term of her natural life; and 20 Shillings per year more, to be paid her yearly by my son Nathaniel Goodwin or his heirs for the Improvement of my 2 acres of Meadow Land east side of the Great River in Hartford. I give unto my son William Goodwin the house & Homelott that was formerly my Uncle John Morrises, he paying 20 Shillings per year to his Mother (if she do see Cause to demand it) during her natural life. I give to my son William Goodwin all my Upland on the East side of the Connecticut River which abbutteth upon Sergt. Nathaniel Goodwin's Land South, and upon Richard Gilman's Land North. I give unto my son Nathaniel Goodwin the remaining part of my House & Homelott in Hartford not already given unto him, after my decease, or the decease of my wife (if she hath not need to sell it for her maintenance). Also, I give unto my son Nathaniel Goodwin 2 acres of Meadow Land on the East side of the Connecticut River, he paying 20 Shillings per year to his Mother during her life, and paying £5 unto his sister Susannah Pratt within one year after the decease of his Mother. I also give unto my daughter Susannah Pratt one Cow. I hereby make my wife Susannah Goodwin sole Executrix.

Witness: *Nathaniel Goodwin,*   WILLIAM GOODWIN. Ls.
    Caleb Stanly.

Court Record, Page 3—6 November, 1689: Will proven.

Page 161-2.

Gozard, Nicholas, Windsor. Invt. £206-10-00. Taken 23 August, 1693, in Windsor, by Abraham Phelps and Job Drake; in Simsbury, by John Higley, Samll Wilcoks and Joseph Owen. The legatees: The Widow, Elizabeth; son Nathaniel, age 16 years; John, age 11 years; Elizabeth, age 21 years.

Court Record, Page 61—7 September, 1693: Adms. to the Widow, and appoint John Slater & Ebenezer Hill to be Overseers.

Page 211.

Grant, John, Windsor. Died 19 July, 1695. Invt. £223-16-00. Taken 13 August, 1695, by Job Drake sen. & Thomas Stoughton. Legatees: The Widow, Elizabeth; son John, 4 ½ years of age; Elizabeth, 3 years.

Court Record, Page 89—5 September, 1695: Adms. to the Widow; Mr. Job Drake sen. and Thomas Stoughton to be Overseers.

Page 107—(Vol. VII) 5 April, 1708: John Grant and Elizabeth Grant, children of John Grant late of Windsor, chose their Father-in-law Joshua Willis Jr. and Samuel Rockwell to be joynt Guardians to each of them. This the Court allow and approve.

Page 110—3 May, 1708: Samuel Rockwell objects, and Mr. Willis did not give Bond, and their Uncle Matthew Grant was chose, who gave Bond alone as Guardian.

Page 111—14 May, 1708: Joshua Willis Jr., Adms. in right of his late wife Decd, presented to this Court an Account of his and his late wife's Adms. on that Estate, which the Court accepts. Order to Dist. the Estate: To John, the Eldest son, £9-11-08; and to Elizabeth Grant, the daughter, £4-15-10. And appoint Capt. Thomas Stoughton and Deacon Job Drake Jr. Distributors.

Page 159-60.

Grant, Tahan Jr., Windsor. Died 21 April, 1693. Invt. £92-12-06. Taken 2 May, 1693, by Samuel Grant sen., and Job Drake sen. Legatees: The Relict, & Hanna, his daughter, age 3 years; son Thomas, 9 months old.

Court Record, Page 57—8 May, 1693: On motion of Nathaniel Bissell, This Court grant Adms. to the Relict and Nathaniel Bissell, the Father-in-law of the Decd.

Page 59—7 September, 1693: Invt. Exhibited, and Job Drake, son of John Drake, with Thomas Bissell, to be Overseers.

Page 137—(Vol. VII) 5 December, 1709: Thomas Grant, a minor 17 years of age, son of Tahan Grant of Windsor, chose Matthew Grant of Windsor to be his Guardian.

Page 160-1.

Grant, Tahan sen., Windsor. Invt. £300-08-00. Taken by Samuel Grant sen., Return Strong sen. and Samuel Cross. The legatees: Hannah, the Widow. Children not married: Thomas, 22 years; Hannah, 25; Joseph, 20; Sarah, 18; Mary, 15 years of age.

Court Record, Page 61—7 September, 1693: Adms. to the Widow; and Thomas Grant, Samuel Cross & Samuel Grant appointed Overseers.

Page 145.

Grave, George, Marshal, Hartford. Died 3 December, 1692. Invt. £623-16-00. Taken 22 December, 1692, by John Easton and Joseph Mygatt. Will dated 29 October, 1686.

I George Grave of Hartford Doe make & ordaine This as my Last Will and Testament: Imprimis. I Doe Give to my Wife Elizabeth one Rome In my Now Dwelling House, wch shee shall Chuse, to Have the ffull & free use of it so Long as shee Lives. Farther, I Give unto Her, as Her owne for ever, My Best Bed with all The Furniture Thereunto Belonging; also all Hir wearing aparrell; also all The Lining wee Now Have, as sheetes, Table Cloaths and Napkins; & also a porage pott, one small brass kettle, one skillet, one warming pan, twoe pewter platters, one Bason, & one payr of fyer Tongs. Also I give unto Hir, During Hir Naturall Life, Eleven pownds pr Annum, To Bee payd Hir In good Currant pay of this Collony, yearly, by my Executors out of the Rents off my Lands & other Estate: Item. I Give to my sonn John Grave the one Half of my Great pasture Near Rockey Hill, I mean That Half That I have formerly put Him Into possession off; But In Case my sonn John Doe not Like that Half, then Hee shall Have Liberty to Divide the whole pasture equally, & His Brother Georg shall Have Liberty to Choose wch part he will. Also, I Give to my sonn John, at the south end off my Home Lott, so much as with what I put Him In possession of fformerly will make it up one Acre. Also, I Give unto Him six Acres of my ten-Acreer Lott In the south meadow, wch is to Bee Equally Divided for quality Betweene His Brother Georg & Hee. Farther, I Give unto my sonn John the one-Half off my Lands In the west Devision and The one-Half In the east Devision, In Hartford Bownds, to Bee equally Devided Betweene His Brother Georg and Hee. Item. I Give to my sonn Georg my Now Dwelling House & Barne, with all the Rest of my Home Lott not Disposed of to John. Also, I Give unto him my Little pasture on the west syde of my Home Lott wch I purchased of Jonathan Bull. Also, the one-Half of the Great pasture near Rockey Hill. Also, ffour Acrees off my Ten-Acreer Lott In the south meadow. Also the one-half of my Lands In the West & East Divisions In Hartford Bounds. Also, Whereas George Grave my son Hath Ingaged to take off & Discharge a Debt that is Due from me to Thomas Catlyn of aboute £20, I Doe Therefore, for That & other Considerations, Give unto my sonn Georg Grave my whole Team, (viz.), my Cart, Horss, my twoe workin oxen, my Cart & wheeles, my plow & Harrow, with all other utensills Belonging to The Teame; also, my two young steres. Item. I Give unto my Daughter Elizabeth the sum of £30—£4 to Bee payd at my Decease In my Great Brass Kettle, The Rest to Bee payd at my Wife's Decease. Item. I Give to my Daughter Sarah £30—£4 to Bee payd at my Decease In my Black cow, The Rest to Bee payd at the Decease of my Wife. Item. I Give unto my Daughter Mercy £30—£4 to Bee payd at my Decease In my Red Cow. All the Rest of my Estate I Give to my two Executors Joyntly for the payment of my Just Debts and

Legacies. I appoint my two Sonns, John Grave & Georg Grave, Joyntly to Be Executors.

The signature torn off; allso the signatures of the Witnesses. But the Widow and Children agreed to accept the cancelled will as valid, and signed the agreement as written below the will, 5 December, 1692.

> ELIZABETH X GRAVE,
> JOHN GRAVE,
> GEORGE GRAVE,
> ELIZABETH X MITCHELL,
> SARAH X LOOMIS,
> MERCY X GRAVE.

Page 169-70.

Haile (Halle), Samuel sen., Glastonbury. Died 9 November, 1693. Invt. £100 of Personal Estate. Taken 13 November, 1693, by Eleazer Kimberly & Joseph Hills. Will dated 26 December, 1692.

I Samuel Halle sen. of Glastonbury do make this my last Will & Testament: Whereas, I have formerly given my sons Samuel, John, Thomas & Ebenezer Considerable portions in Lands, I do therefore now give unto my beloved son Samuel Halle my Muskit and my two Horse Brands To him & to his heirs forever. I give to my son John the best pair of my wearing shoes that I shall have at my decease. I give to my son Ebenezer all my right and Title to 3 score acres of Land granted to me by the General Court for my service in the Pequot War, also my great Bible and all the rest of my books, except one I gave to my daughter-in-law Naomi. I give to my son Thomas my great iron Pot, Grindstone, Peas Hook, and all my Casks & Barls that have been used to hold Corn. I give to my daughters Marrie, Rebeccah, and Dorothie, to Each of them, one of my Great Pewter platters, and to my daughter Rebeccah my three-pint Pewter Pot. I give to my Grand Children John Halle and Thomas Halle, the sons of my son John Halle, all my Interest in the tract of land lying on the East side of the Town of Glassonbery and being six mild in length and five in breadth, to be to them and their Heirs forever. I give to my gr. Child Abigail Benjamin all of my Bedsteds, Beds & Bedding, and all the Linnen that I shall leave at my decease; also, one Cow & one mare, and my great Brass Kettle, fire pan, Tongs, Trammell, Frying pan & Warming pan, 1 pewter platter, and Bason with my name on it.
I appoint my sons Samuel Halle and Thomas Halle Executors.

Witness: *Eleazer Kimberly,*　　　　　SAMUEL X HALLE SEN. Ls.
　　　　　Samuel Emmons.

Court Record, Page 63—6 December, 1693: Will proven.

Vol. IV, P. C., No. 117.

Hall, Francis, Stratford. Will dated 6 May, 1686: I ffrancis Hall of stratford, in ye Colloney of Conecticott, being yet of sound Mind & not knowing ye day of my death, being aged and Crazie, make this my last Will in maner & form following: It. I giue unto my wife al yt was left her by her last husband, John Blakeman of Stratford, decd, except what is disposed off already, which was not done without her Consent. Shee is to possess all lands and houseing during her natural life, & then to be to ye heirs of ye aforementioned John Blakeman, it being agreeing to ye Condishons shee made with mee at Marriage. Concerning my son Isaac, I giue to him & his wife & al my grand Children one shilling apeice, & haue & shall hereafter leaue further order about Isaac. I giue unto my son Samuel Hall & his heirs all yt part of my farm lands & tenements whatsoever, situate in ye Township of ffairfield, which I have already given by Deed. I make him my only heir, he to pay Debts, Legacies & Funeral Expenses; and if my son Samuel can have comfortable assurance from his Brother Isaack Hall yt he will for ye future live in peace and renounce all Causes of after contention from themselves & their heirs forever, then yt my son Samuel Hall make over to him and his heirs forever soe much of ye land as ye said Samuel see Cause. It. Concerning my three daughters, vizt, mary, elizabeth & rebeckah, I have already ingaged my son Samuel, when I made him a deed of guift of ye part of my farm, to giue unto my daughter mary 40 Shillings by ye yeare during her natural life, & to ye other two sisters £10 apeice, to be paid unto them as they haue ociasion for it. I giue unto my daughter Hannah a horse or mare & a heifer or steere. It. Besides what is abouesaid, I giue to my wife a warming pan & my written books yt are legable, al yt are written in Carracters; shee may dispose as shee please. Since I begun this my Will I did agree with my son Isaac, as is exprest in my day booke, page *152:* will more fully appeare, yt he should possess two years gratiss without paying for ye time, but his patience not holding out soo long, he began againe to be troublesome & broke ye peace, giuing some bad & threatning words very unComfortable to mee, though I used ye best words I could to him for peace my life time; but it's from ye good pleasure of him who doth all things well, & unto his hands I leaue him. I desire Mr. Chancey, Mr. Pittman, Mr. sherman Junr. and Josiah nicolls to be Ouerseers to advise my son Samuel, who is my heire and Executor. *I subscribe my name with my owne hand, legable & in carrecters.*   FFRANCIS HALL.

Witness: *John Blakeman,*
       Thomas Broddgate.

Stratford, 9th July, 1689: Francis Hall presented this as his Last Will, & acknowledged it to be his Will and Testament. Before me, *Joseph Hawley, Commissioner.*

Page 204-5.

Hall, John sen., Middletown. Invt. £345-01-00. Taken 14 February, 1694-5, by John Hamlin, John Hall & Israhiah Wetmore. Will dated 23 May, 1691.

I John Hall sen. of Middletown doe leave this underwritten as my last Will & Testament: I give to my wife Mary Hall the whole of my Estate, both House & Goods, Land & Chattells, during her natural life, with power to alienate any part if she stand in need. I give to my wive's son Ebenezer Hubbard my house & Barn & Homelott, and my Meadow & Farme and Upland against the Towne over the Great River, excepting 2 acres, which I give to my kinsman John Hall, my brother Richard Hall's gr. Child. I give my sd. son-in-law Ebenezer Hubbard all my other Outlands that his Mother doth not for her need dispose of, he to pay out of my Estate, after his Mother's decease, £3 of Current pay of the Country to the Church of Middletown, and to my kinsman John Hall, my brother Samuel's son, 20 Shillings. The rest of my Estate to be and remain to Ebenezer Hubbard and to his heirs forever. I appoint my loving wife Sarah (*Mary* in original Will on File) sole Executrix, and her son Ebenezer to be my Executor after my wife's decease.

Witness: *Nathaniel Browne,*   JOHN HALL SEN. LS.
          Richard Hubbard.

(Note: *Sarah Hall was the Widow of Thomas Hubbard.*)

Court Record, Page 80—7 March, 1694-5 : Will proven.

Page 143-4.

Hall, John, Wethersfield. Invt. £247-04-07. Taken 23 November, 1692, by Nathaniel Boeman and Obadiah Dickinson. Legatees: Rebinah, The Widow ; and Elizabeth, 9 months old.

Court Record, Page 48—7 December, 1692: Adms. to the Widow Rebinah Hall, she to have the Improvement of the whole Estate until the daughter comes of age, *then a legal division.*

Page 104-5.

Hall, Richard, Middletown. Invt. £432-11-00. Taken 2 April, 1691, by William Cheeny, Deacon John Hall & Samuel Hall. Will dated 11 January, 1690-1.

The last Will and Testament of Richard Hall, being about 71 years of age: I doe leave this as my last Will & Testament: I give to my wife Mary Hall £6 per Year during her natural life, as also so much room in my house as may be comfortable for her, and all my household Stuffe, and one Cow, ingaging my son John Hall to pay to my wife the £6 per year for her Use, and he my sd. son to have in his Hands, till his mother decease, all the Land that are now improved, both Homelott and Long Meadow. I appoint my sd. son to provide winter meat for her Cow. I Will to my wife for her lifetime so much of the Garden as I now make Use of, and half the Orchard. I give to my eldest son John Hall my House I now live in, after my decease, reserveing comfortable room therein for my wife during her natural life. Also, I give unto my sd. son all my Lands that lyeth at home, except 3 acres at the West End, which I give to my son Samuel after my wive's decease. Moreover, I give to my sd. son my Long Meadow Lott, he paying to his Mother £6 per Year while she liveth, and winter meat for one Cow. Also, my Upper Lott at Wongunck and Lower Lott at Wongunck, and my Half-Mile Lott; also half my 15 acres I live on. I give unto my son Samuel Hall the house which is at the West End of my Lott, which was built for my son John, and 3 acres of my Lott at that End. Moreover, I give to my son all the Land in the New Field, from the East End of the Fence as it now standeth, and all that without the fence but 30 acres that is of that Lott. I give to my daughter Mary my Lott in the Westermost range of Lotts, being 230 acres, as in the Deed of Gift expressed. I give to my daughter Jane 30 acres of Land in the Boggy Meadow Quarter. I give to my daughter Sarah Blake 7 ½ acres in my Wood Lott near the Town. I give to my daughter Anne £10. I make my son John sole Executor.

Witness: *John Hall,*   RICHARD HALL. Ls.
      Samuel Stow sen.

Court Record, Page 27—8 April, 1691: Will proven.

Page 75-6.

Hall, Samuel sen., Middletown. Died 14 March, 1690-1. Invt. £324-10-06. Taken 5 November, 1691, by Nathaniel White & David Sage. Will dated 13 March, 1690-1.

The last Will & Testament of Samuel Hall sen. Imprimis: I give to my Eldest son Samuel my Dwelling house & Barne & Homelott, all but 2 acres, which I reserve for my son Thomas, & all my Meadow in the Long Meadow & Swamp, in the Boggy Meadow Swamp, and my small Upland Lott next to the Plaine; & my Will is that my sd. son shall provide for and comfortably maintain his Mother during her Widowhood, and then Samuel to pay his Mother £2-10 during her natural life. I give my sd. son part of my Meadow & Upland over the Great River. I give to my son John my house & Lott in the Towne on the South side, and my Land in the Field, and my 2 Lotts by the Town side which were laid for Wood-lotts; & my Will is that my sd. son John shall pay his Mother 30 Shillings per year during her natural life. I give to my son Thomas 2 acres of my Homelott which I live on, and the rest of my Meadow and Upland on the East side of the Great River. Farther, It is my Will that my wife Elizabeth shall have half my Household Goods and one Cow as hers during her natural life. I give the other half to my son Samuel. I appoint my son Samuel Hall sole Executor.

Witness: *John Hall sen.,*   SAMUEL HALL. Ls.
        John Savidge.

Court Record, Page 19—5 November, 1690: Will proven.

Page 55.

Hamlin, Giles sen., Middletown. Died 1st September, 1689. Invt. £2249-18-06. Taken by John Allyn, Nathaniel White, William Southmayd and John Hamlin. Will dated 30 August, 1689.

I Giles Hamlin of Middletown doe constitute & ordain this my Last will & Testament in maner following: To my son John Hamlin all that Land that he now possesseth, viz, the Home lot which I bought of Abram Smith & one parcell of meadow in the Long meadow which was formerly Henry Coales. Allso, I give to my son John one-halfe of my Lott at Goose's delight, one halfe of my Lott by Lucas's, one-halfe of my Two wood Lotts neer the Towne, my division of Land neer Capt. Harris's, halfe of my out division of Land upon the Straights Hill, halfe my halfe-Mile Lott, halfe of the swamp I bought of hopewell, & halfe of my upland & pond Lyeing on the east side the great River, as allso £30 of Money which I promised to Lay out with him in part of a vessell, as allso one Silver platter, one great silver spoon, as allso one Cowe & one breeding mare, as allso one silver Hatband, the bigest of the Two. All this I give to him & his heirs forever. To my son Wm I give my house & Hom stead with all the Buildings upon it, allso my Land on the west side of the High way Lyeing between Richd Hall's & John Hamlin's, as allso my Lot next towards Turner's which I bought of Thomas Miller, allso my Meadow & Swamp in Long meadow, as allso that parcell of meadow on the South side the Rivulett, & allso my wet meadow & my out division of Land in the boggy meadow quarter, halfe of my Lott at Goose's delight, halfe my Lot by Lucas's, halfe of my Two wood Lotts neer the Towne, halfe of my out division upon the Straights Hill, halfe my swamp I bought of Hopewell, halfe of my upland & pond Lyeing on the east side the great river, as allso one silver spoon & silver Tumbler, as allso one silver Hat band. All this I give to him & his heires forever. To my sons Giles & Richard Hamlin I give all my Lands at Hartford together with my Interest in the Mills, they payeing to their Mother £14 pr year in curant pay of the country during the time of her naturall Life. As also to Giles two silver spoons (one guilt one & the other of the great ones), & a silver wine cup. To Richard, one silver spoon & silver dram cup. And this I give to them & to their heirs forever. To my Loveing Wife hester Hamlin I give what rooms in my now dwelling house, with convenient selleridg for her use, as she shall choose, with the use of what moveables she shall see cause to make use of; also the Improvement of what stock she shall apprehend may be for her advantage, during the time of her widdowhood. To my daughter Mary I give £100 in money, & a proportion of household stuffe as my daughter Mabell hath had, as allso silver spoons & silver plate, as allso my servant Joan in case she shall need her and my Wife can spare her, & allso Two cowes. This I give to her & her heires forever. To my daughter Mabell I give £50 in money besides what she hath already had, & one silver spoone, & allso one silver porringer & goblet between Mary & Mabell as they shall agree. This I give to her and her heires for ever. To Samuel Hooker I give that Cow he had of me. To young John Hamlin & young Samuel Hooker I give to each of them one of the small silver spoons; & after my Just debts being discharged & my Legacies payd, my will is that the remaynder of my estate be equally divided between my sons. My Wife Ester and my son John Hamlin to be Joynt Executors: & I doe request my much Honord friend Col. John Allyn of Hartford and Liuetenent Nathll White of Middletown to be overseers, & for their paines to be allowed £5 apeice. I give my two gr. sons John & Giles Southmayd, I give each of them an ew sheep; and to my two grand sons John Hamlin & Samuel Hooker I give each of them an ew sheep.

GILES HAMLIN SEN. LS.

Witness: *Nath White senr,*
Noadiah Russell.

Court Record, Page 12—6 March, 1689-90: Will proven.

Page 90-1.

Haywart, Ephraim, Windsor. Invt. £142-02-00. Taken 12 November, 1690, per Timothy Phelps sen. Will dated 29 October, 1690.

I Ephraim Haywart of Windsor do ordain this my last Will & Testament: I will that, my just debts and funeral expenses being paid, which I desire should be done out of the Mortgages that at present are in the occupation of Edward King at Podunk one of them, the other in the possession & occupation of John Millington, if any thing remain It shall return to the benefit of my two Children, Benjamin and Mary. To Benjamin 2-3 out of my Real Estate, and 1-3 to Mary out of my personal Estate. I ordain Mr. John Moore and my kinsman Mr. Job Drake my Executors, & Desire them to befriend me and my Children. For supervisors of my Will I desire My Uncle Capt. Daniel Clarke & my Brother-in-law Mr. Return Strong; & these friends I desire to dispose of my Children: Mary to the age of 18 years, and Benjamin till 21 years of age. I desire my son may be placed with a carpenter to learn the trade.

EPHRAIM HAWART.

Witness: *Daniel Clarke,*
Thomas Marshall.

Legatees, a son 4 years of age and a daughter 2 years of age.

Court Record, Page 23—5 March, 1690-1: Will & Invt. Exhibited. John Moore & Job Drake to make up accounts. Estate Insolvent.

Page 31—3 September, 1691: Adms. to Rev. Solomon Stodder, Mr. John Moore & Return Strong, they to Distribute to the Creditors in Just proportion.

Page 56—12 April, 1693: This Court appoint Mr. John Moore and Mr. Return Strong to take care of the Estate and to dispose of the Children at discretion.

Page 36—(Vol. VII) 15 December, 1702: Benjamin Howard, a minor son of Ephraim Howard, late of Windsor decd., chose his Uncle Return Strong to be his Guardian.

Page 76—(Vol. IX) 6 August, 1718: William Mitchelson of Windsor informing this Court that Adms. was granted 10 August, 1691, to Solomon Stoddard, John Moore and Return Strong on the Estate of Ephraim Howard, this Court not finding any Record that the Adms. rendered Account of their Adms., or of any Dist. returned, This Court grant Adms. to William Mitchelson.

Page 206.

Heacox, Sargt. Samuel, Waterbury. Invt. £434-00-00. Taken 5 March, 1694-5, by Timothy Stanly, John Hopkins and Thomas Judd the Smith. Some Estate was situated in Farmington. Invt. £10. Taken by John Stanly Jr. & Samuel Wadsworth. The children: Samuel, age 26 years, William 22, Thomas 20, Joseph 17, Steven 11, Benjamin 9, Ebenezer 2, Hannah 24, Mary 14, Elizabeth 12, Mercy, 6 years of age.

Court Record, Page 80—7 March, 1694-5: Adms. to the Widow and her son Samuel; Timothy Stanly, Isack Brunson & Steven Upson to be Overseers. The deceased having expressed his will that there be an equal distribution of his Estate, This Court so Order.

Dist. File, 6 March, 1704-5: Dist. of the Estate of Samuel Hitchcock of Waterbury as followeth: To Samuel, to William, to Thomas, to Joseph, to Stephen, to Benjamin, to Ebenezer, and to the four daughters as above named. By Timothy Stanly, Stephen Upson & Isaac Brunson.

Court Record, Page 66 (Vol. VII) 5 April, 1705: A Dist. of the Estate of Samuel Hitchcock, late of Waterbury Decd., under the Hands of Timothy Stanly, Stephen Upson & Isaac Brunson, was exhibited in this Court, viz, of his Real Estate, which Dist. this Court accepts and order to be kept on File. The four daughters having given discharges to Samuel, the Adms., this Court order the sd. Adms. to render an Account of his Adms. to this Court in September next.

Page 66 (Vol. VII) 5 April, 1705: Benjamin Hitchcock, a minor son of Samuel Hitchcock, chose John Hopkins to be his Guardian; and Stephen Hitchcock chose Timothy Stanly for his Guardian. And this Court appoint Thomas Hitchcock to be Guardian unto Ebenezer Hitchcock.

Page 93—5 May, 1707: Ebenezer Hitchcock, being now 14 years of age, made choice of his Brother William Hitchcock to be his Guardian.

Page 178.

Heart, Margaret, Farmington. Invt. £54-14-06. Taken 12 January, 1693, by Thomas Porter Jr. and John Heart. Will dated 18 February, 1691-2.

This Indenture, made the eightenth day of fabarnary, In the year of our Lord one thouson six hundered and ninty one & too, Wittneseth: That I, margeret harte, of farminton, in the colliny of conecticute and County of harford, being aged & weake of body, do think it meet for to settle that Little estate that God hath given unto me, which is as follows: I doe by these preasents give, grante, bestoe, bequeath, allynate, pasouer for ever to my three well beloved children in maner & forme: Iteme. First, I giue to my eldest son John Smith one pauter candlesticke, one pot posnete, one brase Ladle and one cushon. This I giue as a tocon of my loue, and ad no farder, to my eldest son, upon the consideration of that he hath reseued a duble porsion alrady. Iteme. Secondly, I giue to my son arthur smith one wool bead, and a feather boulster, and one pillow, & too good bead blankits, and a couer Lide, and one pauter dish, and too paire of sheets. And I giue to my son arther's too daughters, ech of them, a paire of sheets. Iteme. Thurdly, I giue to my daughter Elizabeth Thomson my great bras cattle, and my bible, and my wareing cloths; only I would have my son arther's wife have a sute of lining of mine and one paticote; the rest of lineing I giue to my daughter elezibeth when that which I otherwise is disposed of which I have and shall order heare and apointe pote. Item. Fourthly, I giue to Elizabeth Thomson, my granchild, one table with a draue in it, & a mudleing brase cattle, and a coper skillite, and a cushon stoole, and a paire of sheets, and a table cloth, and six napkines, and too touels, and one porringer. Item. I giue to Thomas Thomson, my gran child, a cowe which is in his father's hand which I have not reseued anything for it. Furder, I give to Thomas a porringer. Itime. I giue to my gran child an Thomson a father bead and flock boulster, and a strawe bead & stad to, with too feather pillows and bouster, two blankits and a wroge, and too pair of sheets, to pair pillow bers, too touels, six fine napkines, too cosers, too porringers, and sixteen chars, and my curtines and valantes belonging to the bead, and a iron pote I giue to Elezibeth Thomson my gran child. Furder mor I giue to margret orton a paire of curtins with vallante, my gran childe. Furder more I doe desier and hearby impour Thomas Thomson my son, after my deseas, to call in my deetts and desier him to pay my deets, and under this consideration I giue vnto my son Thomas Thomson all the rest of my Estate which is not hear pertickulerly mentioned. In testimony that this wrighting is my acte and deed, and that I doe heare by these prssant giue, grant, bequeath, allignate, pasouer and bestoe for euer, at the end and tarme of my naturall Life, the things aboue mentioned to the pasons aboue mentioned, I doe set to my hand the day and yeare aboue sayd, and seale.

Witness: *Samuel Newell,* MARGRETT HART. Ls.
Thomas bird. Proven 1st March, 1693-4.

Court Record, Page 67—1st March, 1693-4: Adms. to Thomas Thompson with the Will annexed.

Page 12-13.

Heart, Stephen, Farmington. Invt. £633-14-06. Taken 1689, by Isaac Moore & Thomas Heart & John Heart. The children: Stephen age 27 years, Thomas 23, John 20, Samuel 17, Sarah 14, Ann 11, Mary 7 years.

A QUIT CLAIM, DATED 7 NOVEMBER, 1689:

Be it known unto all Men by these prsents: That I, Stephen Heart of Farmington, in New England, for and in Consideration of my natural Love to my Brothers & Sisters, Children of my father Stephen Heart, lately deceased, and for other good Causes mee hereunto moving, have remised, released & quitted Claim, and doe by these presents remise, release & quitt all Claim, freely, fully and forever, to my Brothers and Sisters aforesd., which I have or ought to have unto, in or upon any part of the Estate of my sd. Father Decd, whether Real or Personal, more than an equal part thereof with each of the sd. Children of my sd. Father, & doe forgoe & forsake hereby all Right to a double portion of the sd. Estate, only reserveing to myself a single portion thereof; always provided, and it is hereby provided and reserved as a principal Condition & Provisoe of this Release of Claim to all above a single portion of my sd. Father's Estate, that none of my sd. Brothers or sisters, or any, by or from them, doe ever hereafter make claim to any part of the Lands at a place called Nod, given by my gr. father Stephen Heart Decd, & now in my possession, as also that I doe reserve the half of the Crop that grew on the sd. Land at Nod this present year and relinquish all Right in the other half of the sd. Crop.

Witness: *Caleb Stanly,* STEPHEN HEART. Ls.
Joseph Fitch, Thomas Heart.

Court Record, Page 4—6 November, 1689: Adms. to the Widow. An Inventory of the Estate of Sargt. Stephen Heart was Exhibited in Court, and the Eldest son is to have the Land at Nod and halfe the Corn there. The Widow to have one-third of the personal Estate forever, that at Nod Excepted, and the use of one-third of the Real Estate, that at Nod Excepted, to be to her during her Natural life. And the remainder of the Estate to be equally divided among all the Children of the deceased. And Ensign Thomas Heart & John Heart & Thomas Porter, son of

Thomas Porter, are appointed Overseers to assist the Widow in the settlement of the Estate.   The Resignation of the heir is the ground of this
Distribution, which is also upon record.

Page 51—(Vol. VIII) 4 February, 1711-12:   The Court cites the
sons of Sergt. Stephen Hart to appear and take Adms. on their Father's
Estate, themselves or any of them; or, if they decline, they may signify
the same to this Court, that Adms. may be granted to some one else.

Page 53—5 February, 1711-12:   This Court grant Letters of Adms.
on the Estate of Sergt. Stephen Hart unto Samuel Judd of Farmington.

Page 75—5 May, 1712:   Upon the Motion of Samuel Judd, Adms.,
this Court do order that (seeing the Adms. who were formerly appointed on that Estate are now dead, not having finished their Adms.
thereon) the persons who were appointed to be Overseers of the sd. Estate
be cited to appear before this Court on the 1st Monday of June next, to
render an Account of their Proceedings relating to that Estate.

Page 216—4 October, 1714:   Capt. Thomas Hart of Farmington
presented to this Court a Dist. made on the Estate of Sergt. Stephen Hart,
and moved for a Confirmation thereof.   Deferred until the 1st Monday of
November next.

Page 220—1st November, 1714:   A Dist. made on the Estate of
Sergt. Stephen Hart, and on his son Samuel Hart, deceased, being laid
before this Court by Capt. Thomas Hart of Farmington, on the 1st Monday of October last past, now moved for a Confirmation thereof, which
Dist. was made by the sd. Thomas Hart and John Hart sen. of Farmington.   And Thomas Hart, John Hart & Samuel Judd, sons of the sd Decd,
appeared before this Court and declared that they were well satisfied and
contented with the sd. Dist.   Ordered to be kept on File.

Record: 21 July, 1712:   To Stephen, Thomas, John, Samuel, Sarah
Hart (alias Tuttle), Anna Hart (alias Judd), and Mary Hart.   (From
File.)

Page 245—7 March, 1714-15:   Mr. Thomas Hart now moved this
Court that the Land set out for defraying the Charge of the Dist., viz, 26
acres at Misery Meadow, might be set out to him, he paying the sd
Charge.   *This Court don't see Cause to reverse their former Decree.*

Page 252—2 May, 1715:   Upon Motion of Capt. Thomas Hart, this
Court order Samuel Judd of Farmington to pay the £5 ordered him to pay
to the Executors of Samuel Hart's Estate, and Dist. of the Estate of Sergt.
Stephen Hart, both of Farmington decd.

Will on File.

Hendy, Jonathan, Wethersfield.   Will dated 18 May, 1688.   We the
Underwritten doe by these presents declare whome it may Concerne that
on the 14th day of this instant May Jonathan Hendy of Wethersfield, in
the County of Hartford, being weake in Body & neer unto death, yet of
perfect memory & good Understanding, did farther dispose of the Worldly

Estate and in our prsents and heering make this nuncupatory will as his last Testament: *Videl:* That all his just Debts being first payd, out of the remainder he did bequeath £10 to his Mother & £5 to his sister Hannah Belden, and all the rest of his Estate to his Brother Richard Hendy. And he did nominate and appoint Benjamin Churchill of Wethersfield to be the Executor of this his last Will & Testament. In Witness whereof, we have hereunto set our hands.   *Benjamin Churchill,*
                                                               John Wiard.

Will on File.

Hennyson, John, Hartford. Will dated 17 May, 1687. I John Hannyson of Hartford, Husbandman, doe make and ordain this my last Will & Testament: Item. I give to my wife Martha Hannyson all my Real & Personal Estate now in my hands and possession or any way belonging or appertaining to me, to have and to hold the same during her natural life, or otherwise to be disposed of by her to my Children how or when she shall see Cause before her decease, wth the Consent and Approbation of my Overseers. And if my sd. wife shall keep the Approbation ye aforesd. Estate during her life, that then, at her decease, no bargain, sale or Instrument whatsoever shall alienate ye same from my Childn. My Will is that all my Just Debts be paid (to whome I am indebted) *by my wife,* who I hereby make and constitute my sole Executrix, & desire Ensign Jonathan Bull and Samuel Steele may be Overseers.
Witness: *William Whiting,*   JOHN HANISSON. Ls.
         Benoni Brown.

Page 133.

Hill, John, Hartford. Invt. £45-10-06. Taken 20 August, 1692, by Thomas Kilbourn and Samuel Welles. Nuncupative Will, dated 1st September, 1692. The Testamony of Jonathan Hill, aged 28 years, and Dorothy Hill, aged 25 years, is as followeth: That when our Brother John Hill lay sick of the sickness whereof he dyed, we did hear him say that when his debts were paid his wife should enjoy all the Estate during her natural life; and what was left after her decease should be divided equally between his two daughters. Sworn in Court, 1st September, 1692, before
Witness: *Jonathan Hill,*   JOHN ALLYN.
         Dorothy Hill.

Court Record, Page 45: Adms. to the Relict with the will annexed. Will approved.

Page 168-179.

Hills, William, Hocanum. Invt. £119-18-06. Taken 8 December, 1693, by Siborn Nickols, James Steele sen., Tho. Dick r so. The children:

Ebenezer, age 17 years, John 14, Joseph 10, Mary 26, files 24 (Phillis), Hannah 21, Esther 12. Will Nuncupative.

The Testimony of *Thomas Kilbourn*, age 38 years, and *Richard Risley*, age 45 years (is) as followeth: That sometime about Michalmas, 1692, being desired by William Hills of Hocanum to take notice of what he sayd, in order to his disposeing of his Estate, he being in a weake Condition: Imprimis. His daughter Phillis should have one Cowe & one young beast; & he said something about sheep, & some bedding, & the boy Hossington to be at her dispose till he come to full age; & to his daughters Mary and Hannah Twenty shillings to each of them; & then his honest debts to be payd, & then what did remayne to be equally for use and bringing up, & to be equally divided among them. Farther, one swine was Phillis, one ....

Court Record, Page 66—1st March, 1693-4: Adms. to the Widow. Richard Risley and Sergt. Kilbourn to be Overseers.

Page 107—8 April, 1696: Order to Dist: To the Widow, her thirds. To the Eldest son a double portion. To the others, to Each a single portion. Sergt. Thos Kilbourn and Jonathan Hills, Distributors.

Page 97-8.

Holcomb, Joshua, Simsbury. Died 1st December, 1690. Invt. £474-08-00. Taken 25 December, 1690, by John Higley and Samuel Willcox (Selectmen) and Benajah Holcomb and Nathaniel Holcomb (brothers). Legatees—Ruth Holcomb, the Relict; dau. Ruth, age 26 years; Thomas 24, Sarah 22, Elizabeth 20, Joshua 18, Deborah 16, Mary 14, Mindwell 12, Hannah 10, Moses 4 years.

Court Record, Page 25—5 March, 1690-1: Adms. to the Widow, Ruth Holcomb. Mr. John Higley and Benajah Holcomb, Overseers.

Page 61—7 September, 1693: Order to Dist: To the Widow, £35-13-04 & thirds. To the Eldest son, £73-04-04. To the 2nd son, Joshua, £53-00-00. To each of the others, £34-10-00.

Report of Dist. on file, 1694-5: To the Widow, to Thomas, to Ruth, to Sarah, to Elizabeth, to Deborah, to Mary, to Moses, to Hannah, to Mindwell. By John Higley, George Griswold & Benajah Holcomb, Distributors.

Hollister, Joan, Wethersfield, Decd. Court Record, Page 75—2 November, 1694: This Court appoint Lt. Stephen Hollister Adms. on the Estate of Joan Hollister, there being no Inventory taken of the same.

Page 144.

Hollstead, Henry, Hartford. Died 16 June, 1692. Invt. £10-19-05. Taken by Daniel Bidwell & Roger Pitkin. Will dated 14 June, 1692.

The last Will & Testament of Henry Hollstead, Decd. I comit my Soule to the Mercy of God, hoping to be saved through fayth in Jesus Christ; my Body to decent christian Buryall; & as for that little portion of the World God hath given me my Will is that my Master John Meekins sen. should have the whole dispose of it, that is, as follows: To pay my Funeral Charges: 2nd, to pay himself his just Dues. 3rd, to pay all my Just Debts so far as my Estate will goe, and to call in and demand all that is due or owing to me from any person or persons, upon Book or otherwise. And my Will is if any of my Estate be left when my Funeral Charges are paid, and my Just Debts, that then the rest of my Estate I freely give to my kind and loving master John Meekins sen. for his owne, to have forever; & my Will is that my sd. Master take forthwith unto his custody & keeping whatever I have or doth belong to me; & my Will is that John Meekins Jr. should have my Bible and Mary Meekins my Iron Pott & Sarah Meekins my Iron Kettle. I being in good Understanding but weake in Body, have hereunto set my Hand.

Witness: *Roger Pitkin,*   HENRY X HOLSTEED.
        Thomas X Trill.

Court Record, Page 48—7 December, 1692: Will & Invt. exhibited. John Meekins to pay debts and take the remainder for himself.

Page 98.

Hooker, William, Farmington. Invt. £364-11-06. Taken 1689, by Thomas Porter Jr. & John Heart. Will dated 8th August, 1689.

I William Hooker of Farmington, being weake in Body but composed in Minde, do dispose of my Estate: I give to my wife Susannah the 1-2 of my Estate, both Personal and Real, forever, except my house, which I give to my brother Thomas Hooker, and my Great Bible, which I give to my Honoured Mother. The rest of my Estate, Personal and Real, I give to my daughter Susannah and her heirs forever, the whole to be under the Improvement of my wife for the *Eudication* of my daughter till she shall come to the age of 18 years, or be disposed of in marriage. In Case of her death, her Estate to be returned to my Natural Relations, James, Roger, Nathaniel & Daniel Hooker, my Brothers, and my two sisters, Mary & Sarah Hooker.

Witness: *John Hooker,*   WILLIAM HOOKER. Ls.
        Stephen Roote.

Here is part of the Inventory of William Hooker:

	£ s d
Brass Kettles, £15-13-00; More Brass Skillets, Warming pans, Mortarpestle, Candle Sticks, Scimer, Ladle,	21-13-00
Pewter Platters of divers sorts & sizes,	15-09-00
One brass Pot & Skillett, £0-20; Two payre of Andirons, Tongs, fire pen, chafen dish, £3-00,	4-00-00

3 dozen & eight Porringers,	4-05-00
Ten pewter Tanckers, £2-08; Five Chamber pots, £1-04,	3-12-00
5 dozen of pewter spoons, £0-15; 1-2 doz. accumy spoons, £1-08	2-03-00
Plate, £1-00-04,	1-01-04

Court Record, Page 25—5 March, 1690-1: The last Will & Testament of William Hooker was exhibited in Court and proven.

Page 39—(Vol. VI) 13 April, 1698: This Court appoint John Hooker to be Guardian to Susannah, daughter of William Hooker Decd.

Page 53—1st September, 1698: This Court do appoint Capt. Thomas Hart of Farmington and Ensign Thomas Bunce of Hartford to make Division of the Estate of Mr. William Hooker, Decd, which was by his last Will given as followeth: 1-2 of his whole Estate, both Real & Personal, to the Relict, and the other 1-2 to his daughter Susannah. And according to the intent of the Testator the Division was made, Mr. John Blackleach, who married the Relict, being dead, and his wife also, they having had the Estate above mentioned in their possession and Improvement.

Page 15—(Vol. VII) 30 June, 1701: This Indenture, made this 7th day of October, in the year of our Lord One thousand six hundred Ninety and Eight, in the 10th year of the Reign of King William of England, *fidei de fensor,* between John Hooker of ffarmington, in the County of Hartford, within his sd. Majty's King William his Colony of Connecticott in New England, as Guardian to Susannah Hooker, daughter of William Hooker, late of said ffarmington deceased, on the one party, and John Olcott of the Town of Hartford, within the above mentioned Colony of Connecticott, as Guardian to John Blackleach, sonn of John Blackleach, late also of said ffarmington deceased, on the other party, Witnesseth: That they the said John Hooker and John Olcott, as Guardians to their respective Wards abovenamed, have mutually agreed, & do by these presents mutually agree and covenant each with the other, that the Estate of the above named William Hooker Decd which he stood possessed of, either in his own right or in right of his wife Susannah (after wife of the above named John Blackleach decd) at the time of his decease, both real and personal, whether in Old England or in New England, and also all the rents, debts and dues what so ever to the said Estate belonging, shall be divided equally in value betwixt them the said Susannah Hooker, daughter of Willm Hooker above named deced, and John Blackleach above named, also deced.

And secondly: That whereas, part of the said Estate of the above said Willm Hooker decd, vizt, Lands, goods, etc., at the Towne of Milford, within the above said Colony of Connecticott, hath been and is, since the sd. Hooker's decease, sold and alienated by him the above named John Blackleach decsed, they have agreed that the same so alienated, or the value thereof according as it hath been apprized and Inventoried, or shall be apprized by indifferent persons, shall be esteemed and accounted part of the Moiety of the said Estate, to be distributed & set out to him the said John Olcott as Guardian, for the use of his respective Ward, vizt, John Blackleach.

And thirdly: That all The houseing and Lands within the Township of ffarmington above sd., belonging to the Estate of the said Willm Hooker deced, shall be set out to him the said John Hooker, Guardian as aforesaid, for the use of his respective Ward, vizt, Susannah Hooker, as part of her Moiety of said Estate, to be to her distributed as aforesaid, and that there shall be allowed and set out to said John Olcott, for the use of his Ward above named, so much as is the apprized value of the Moiety, or halfe part of said houseing and Lands, out of some other part of the said Estate.

And fourthly: That all the Estate of the said Willm Hooker deced, when so euer and what so euer it be, shall be distributed and set out equally in value as above said and according to Inventory price, or, in want of That, by apprizall as above sd. (haveing respect to the third and fourth particular of this their agreement above written), by Serj. Thomas Porter and Ensign John Hart of ffarmington aforesaid, which being done, it shall be and remain to the only proper use and behoof of them the said Susan: Hooker and John Blackleach foreuer.

Witness: *Richard Blackleach,*   JOHN HOOKER. Ls.
         Caleb Stanly Jr.

Page 16-17-18.

Hopkins, Stephen, Hartford. Invt. £591-09-06. Taken 6 November, 1689, by James Steele sen. and Joseph Mygatt. Will dated 28 September, 1689.

I Stephen Hopkins sen. of Hartford do declare this to be my last Will & Testament: My Just Debts being paid out of my Estate, I give all the remainder of my Moveable Estate, except what I do hereafter give unto my wife Dorcas during her life, and at her decease my Will is that she bestow it upon my Children as she shall see Meet. I give her the Use of the new End of my now dwelling house, half the Celler, half the Barn, half my Orchard, and half the Garden, during her life. I give unto my wife the Use of my Share in the Mills during her natural life, & the Use of ½ of my Lott by Hannison's during life. I give unto my son John Hopkins, besides what I have already given him, my Lott in the Last Division in Hartford, about 50 acres; also 5 Shillings out of my Estate. I do give unto my son Stephen Hopkins, besides what I have already given him, my two parcels of Land in the Meadow called Indian Land, after my wifes decease; also give him 5 Shillings; also give him the Use of 2 acres in my Meadow Division until my son Joseph Comes of age. I also give unto my sd. son Stephen my Lott on the East side of the Connecticut River forever. I give unto my son Ebenezer Hopkins my now dwelling house, Barn & Outhouses & Homelott, to have the same as soon as he comes of age, all except what my wife is to have so long as she lives, and at her decease the whole to be his forever. I give unto my son Joseph Hopkins the ½ of my Lott by Hannison's as soon as he comes of age, the other half at my wife's decease, & 5 shillings. I give unto my daughter Dorcas Webster 40 Shillings besides what I have already given her. I give to my daughter Mary Hopkins £15 out of my Estate when she comes of age. My Will also is that at my wife's decease my sons Stephen, Ebenezer & Joseph do pay unto my daughter Mary 40 Shillings apeice. And my Will also is that at my wife's decease my Right in the Mill shall be equally divided among my Children. I appoint my wife & four sons, John, Stephen, Ebenezer & Joseph, Executors; and desire my friends John Easton and Joseph Mygatt to be Overseers.

Witness: *James Steele sen.,*   STEPHEN HOPKINS, Ls.
          John Easton.

Court Record, Page 5—6 November, 1689: Will proven.

Page 177-8.

Hosford, Jane. Will dated 23 July, 1655. This is the last Will & Testament of Jane Hosford, the wife of Mr. William Hosford: I being going after my husband unto old England, and not knowing when God may take me out of this Life, do dispose of my goods as followeth: Imprimis: I do bequeath, and it is my Will, that after my decease the Church of Wyndsor, of which I am now a member, shall have and forever enjoy that peice of Meadow Land which belongeth unto me, Called Hoyt's Meadow, for the Use of a pastor or Teacher of the Church, as the Church shall see most Need, and, when one dead, to goe successively to another always. Item. Concerning the rest of my Estate, in the Hands of whosoever it is left or may be found, I bequeath unto my sister Elizabeth Wildish and her Children, which I suppose live in Rochester in Kent, to be equally divided among them.

Witness: *Jo: Warham,*   *Signum:*   JANE X HOSFORD.
John Russell, Walter Fyler.

Entered in the Public Records, 25 January, 1677, Lib. D, Fol: 20.
                                    Per *John Allyn, Secretary.*

John Russell personally appeared on the 31st day of October, 1692, and acknowledged his signature.
                    Before *Henry Wolcott, Commissioner.*

A General Court held at Hartford 10th of May, 1694: Capt. Daniel Clarke, as Attorney for the Church of Christ, of Windsor, desired this Court that they would declare their approbation of Mrs. Jane Hosford's Will and Testament. Approved. Mr. Henry Wolcott, Adms., with the Will annexed.

Page 174-5-6.

Hosmer, Stephen sen., & Deacon. Died 4 November, 1693. Invt. £1820-11-00. Taken 2 January, 1693-4, by John Wilson, Thomas Bunce

& Cyprain Nichols. The children: Hannah Post, age 23 years, Dorothy 20, Thomas 18, Stephen & Hester (twins) 14, Mary 9, Deborah 7, Clement, 3 years of age. Will dated 2 November 1693.

I Stephen Hosmer of Hartford do think meet to make my last Will & Testament: I give to my wife 1-3 part of the Rent of my Land at Hartford during life, and the use of 2 rooms in my house during Widowhood, and I give her £50 of Household Stuff to be at her dispose. *I also give her my coper Stell and worm, and desire her to Stell it out of the house, especially if she see itt be like to bee a snare or temptation to her son Thomas.* I also appoint her sole Executrix until my son Thomas cometh of age. I give to my eldest daughter Hannah Post £120, part of which I have already paid. I give to the rest of my daughters, Dorithe, Hester, Mary, Deborah and Clemont, £100 to each of them. I give to my son Stephen my Lott on the West side of the Wethersfield Highway, by Samuel Wheeler's, & 6 acres of my Land in the Meadow, half my Land in the 40 acres (when his brother Thomas hath had a third part which his gr. father gave him); also I give him one peice of Land at my Saw Mill, on the south side of the Mill, West and North on the West North River, and South on Mr. Hooker's Land; also, if he settle his abode in this towne, I give him 1½ acre of Land in my Homelott to build upon (on the south side next Goodman Whaples); and if he desire to be brought up to Learning, I give him £20 in Money towards it. The rest of the Charge about it shall come out of his land, which his Brother Thomas shall have liberty firstly to redeem. The rest of my Estate I give to my son Thomas, whome I make my Executor with his Mother during Widowhood; and if she marry, to be sole Executor.

Witness: *Samuel Willis,*   STEPHEN HOSMORE, Ls.
Timothy Woodbridge, John Haynes.

Court Record, Page 65—22 January, 1693-4: The Inventory, together with the last Will & Testament, of Deacon Stephen Hosmore was exhibited in Court, proven and ordered to be recorded. This Court having considered the last Will of Mr. Stephen Hosmor, they do find in their Judgement Deacon Hosmore's Will is towards his wife too hard. And having discoursed with Thomas, the Eldest son of sd. Hosmore, who is now 18 years of age, he expressed himself willing to ad to his mother's Estate so much as may make her part of the Moveable Estate £100 *besides the Stell,* which this Court allows and approves of, and confirms the Will, with this Addition, that the son Thomas hath consenteth to. By the Desire of the Widow, Mr. Nichols & Deacon Wilson to be Overseers.

Page 63.

Hurlbut, John, Middletown. Died 30 August, 1690. Invt. £374-15-06. Taken by Nathaniel White, John Hamlin and John Hall sen. Legatees: John, born 8 Dec., 1671; Thomas, b. 20 Oct., 1674; Sara, b. 5 Nov.,

1676; Mary, b. 17 Nov., 1678; Marcy, b. 17 February, 1680; Ebenezer, b. 17 January, 1682; Margaret, b. Feb., 1684-5; David, b. 11 August, 1688; one child about 3 months old, since March, 1690-1.

Court Record, Page 17—4 September, 1690: Adms. to the Widow, with advice of Capt. Nathaniel White in her administration.

See File: *Under this date, 6th May, 1698, appears upon a broken and part-missing paper an Agreement for the Settlement of the Estate, signed by the Underwritten Legatees:*

Witness: *Ebenezer Deming sen.,*	MARY X HURLBUT,
John Hamling, Ellexander Rollo,	MARY X HURLBUT,
and *Andrew Warner.*	NATHANIEL CHURCHILL,
	MARCY X HURLBUT,
	JOHN HURLBUT,
	MARGRIT HURLBUT,
	THOMAS HURLBUT,
	EBENEZER HURLBUT,
	SARY X HURLBUT,
	DAVID HURLBUT.
	MEHETABEL X HURLBUT,

Page 91—(Vol. XI) 11 May, 1733: An Agreement for the Settlement of the Estate of John Hurlbutt of Middletown, Decd, made Anno Dom. 1698, was now exhibited in Court with the Hands of the heirs affixed thereto, and under the hands of Mr. John Hamlin and Ebenezer Deming, Distributors.

Page 53.

Hurlbut, Thomas. Died September, 1689. Invt. £57-19-02. Taken 6 March, 1689-90, by Robert Welles and Samuel Butler. The Widow, Elizabeth Hurlbut; son Timothy, age 9 years; Nathaniel, 7; Ebenezer, 4 years.

Court Record, Page 11—6 March, 1689-90: Adms. to Stephen Hurlbut. Est. Insolvent.

Page 68.

Joanes, Francis, Middletown. Invt. £41-07-08. Taken 2 September, 1690, by Wm. Sumner & John Blake.

Court Record, Page 18—4 September, 1690: Adms. to Edward Durant and John Blake.

Page 129.

Judd, Benjamin & Wife. Invt. £292-13-07. Taken by Thomas Porter & John Thompson sen. The children: Benjamin, age 21 years, Nathaniel 8, Jonathan 3, Mary 16, Sarah 14, Hannah 11, Easter, 6 years old.

Court Record, Page 39—3d March, 1691-2: Whereas, the Administrator of the Estate of Benjamin Judd is Decd, Adms. is granted to Benjamin Judd his son & to John Judd, who, with William Lewes, are to take Care for the dispose of the children.

Page 41—13 April, 1692: Invt. now Exhibited of the Estate of Benjamin & Mary Judd. Dist: To Eldest son, £70; to the other two, to each, £35; to the four daughters, to each, £32-18-00; £10 left with the Adms. to bring up the youngest child till he is fit to put out to service.

Page 139—(Vol. IV) 4 March, 1696-7: Whereas, at a County Court held by adjournment, 13 April, 1692, Adms. was granted to John & Benjamin Judd upon the Estate of Benjamin & Mary Judd of Farmington, the Adms. request that William Lewes be joyned with them in the distribution: This Court do ad him to them to do that work, and do fully impower them to put out the youngest son to good service.

Page 7.

Judd, Benjamin. Invt. £267-03-00. Taken 1689, by John Norton & John Judd. Legatees: Benjamin Judd, age 18 years, Mary 14, Sara 12, Hannah 8, Nathaniel 6, Hester 3, Jonathan, one year old.

Court Record, Page 3—6 November, 1689: Adms. to the Widow (Mary Judd).

Page 24—(Vol. VII) 7 March, 1701-2: Hester Judd, a minor daughter of Benjamin Judd, late of Farmington Decd, chose Joseph Webster to be her Guardian.

Page 40.

Judd, Philip, Waterbury. Invt. £329-10-00. Taken 2 November, 1689, by Isaac Brunson, Joseph Gaylor & Thomas Judd the Smith. Land at Farmington, £90-00-00. Taken by William Judd & John Judd. The children: Philip, age 8 years, Hannah 5, William 2, Benjamin, 3 months old.

Court Record, Page 7—11 November, 1689: Adms. to the Widow, and appoint William Judd, Ensign Thomas Judd & Thomas Judd Jr. to assist.

Page 25—5 March, 1690-1: Whereas, the late Wife of Philip Judd is removed from Mattatock or Watterbury, & it is to be feared that the Estate and Children may suffer thereby, This Court grant administration to Ensign Thomas Judd & Thomas Judd the Smith.

Page 35—3 December, 1691: Adms. account on the Estate of Philip Judd: They found expended of the Estate by loss of Cattle and the bringing up of the Children, £44-05-06; and they find the Estate indebted to £174-11-04, Account whereof is on File.

Page 42—(Vol. VII) 7 April, 1703: Deacon Thomas Judd of Waterbury renders an Account of his Adms. on the Estate of Philip Judd.

Page 49—5 November, 1703: Deacon Thomas Judd, Adms., renders an Account:

	£ s d
Inventory,	329-10-00
Debts due from the Estate,	138-17-09

There remains,	190-12-07
Loss upon the Estate,	46-13-06

There remains to be Dist. among the wife & Children,   143-19-01

And this Court appoint Lt. Timothy Stanly & Sergt. Isaac Bronson, of Waterbury, and Mr. John Wadsworth, of Farmington, Distributors.

William Judd, a minor son of Philip Judd, chose Lt. John Stanly to be his Guardian. Recog. £50.

Page 50—5 November, 1703: Benjamin Judd, a minor, chose John Hopkins to be his Guardian.

Page 67—5 April, 1703-4: Jonathan Judd made choice of Samuel Webster for his Guardian.

Dist. File: 11 May, 1704: To the Widow, to Philip Judd, to John Stanly Jr. (Guardian to William Judd), to John Hopkins (Guardian to Benjamin Judd), and to Hannah Judd. By Timothy Stanly & John Wadsworth.

Page 79.

Judd, Sergt. William, Farmington. Invt. £694-06-06. Taken by Thomas Porter and John Judd. The children: Thomas, age 27 years, John 23, Samuel 17, Daniel 15, Mary Jones 32, Rachell 20, Elizabeth 12.

Court Record, Page 20—5 November, 1690: Adms. to the Widow and John Judd.

Dist. File: 27 December, 1690: Pursuant to an Act of the General Assembly, 5 November, 1690:

	£ s d		£ s d
To the Widow,	223-00-02	To Daniel,	64-00-00
To Thomas Judd,	128-00-00	To Mary Jones,	64-13-00
To John,	65-00-00	To Rachel,	64-01-07
To Samuel,	65-00-00	To Elizabeth,	64-00-00

A 2nd Dist. by Agreement, 7 April, 1719, of that part of the Estate that was settled upon our Mother.

Signed,   DANIEL JUDD,   SAMUEL JUDD,
THOMAS JUDD,   ELIZABETH X JUDD.

Also set out to the heirs of John Judd, Decd, his three Children: William, Eunice and Rhoda Judd.

Test: *Hez: Wyllys, Clerk.*

Page 22—(Vol. VIII) 6 November, 1710: Report of the Dist. by Mary Judd, Widow, and John Judd sen., Adms.

Page 317—(Probate Side, Vol. IX): An Agreement of Heirs to divide that part of the Estate which was settled upon our honoured Mother for her Dowry during life, that this be to Thomas Judd, our Eldest Brother; to the heirs of John Judd, son of William Judd Decd; to Samuel Judd, to Daniel Judd, to Elizabeth Judd.

Signed and Sealed, 7 April, 1719:

THOMAS JUDD, LS, SAMUEL JUDD, LS.
DANIEL JUDD, LS.

Page 101—7 April, 1719: Agreement acknowledged in Court. Accepted, ordered recorded & filed.

Page 12—(Vol. XI) 1729-30: Thomas Judd, Eldest son of William Judd, late of Farmington Decd, together with Daniel Judd, another of the heirs to the sd. Decd William Judd, showing to this Court that there were several parcells of Land of their sd. Father that was set out to them, sd. Thomas & Daniel Judd, together with their Brother Samuel Judd, who is now decd, and they tenants in Common and the surviving party, viz, Thomas & Daniel, moved that this Court, pursuant to a law of this Colony intitled "An Act to Inable Guardians to Divide Lands," Would appoint some suitable persons to divide sd. Lands between and amongst the sd. Thomas Judd, Daniel Judd and William's sd. minors, the guardians to sd. minors joining in this Motion: Whereupon this Court do appoint John Porter and Deacon John Hart of Farmingtown, with Abigaill Judd, Guardian and Mother to one of sd. minors, to make a Division of sd. Lands between sd. surviving parties and the sd. minors, children to Samuel Judd deceased, and that the sd. Division be not delayed. Daniel Judd also showing to this Court that the sd. Samuel Judd Decd and the sd. Daniel Judd have bought of John Root's heirs severall parcells or Lotts of Land in the Township of Farmingtown, in which Lands the sd. Daniel Judd and the orphant Children of Samuel Judd Decd ly as tenants in Common, and the sd. Daniel Judd moves to this Court that pursuant to the aforesd. Law this Court would appoint some meet persons, with the Assistance of the Guardians of sd. minors, to divide sd. Lands between the sd. minors and the sd. Daniel Judd: This Court do therefore appoint John Porter and Deacon John Hart of Farmingtown, together with the Assistance of the Widow Abigail Judd, Guardian and Mother to one of the sd. minors, to make a just and equal division of what Lands have been so bought of the sd. John Root Jr. his heirs by Samuel & Daniel Judd, between sd. Daniel Judd and sd. minor of Samuel Judd Decd.

Page 16—3 March, 1730: An Agreement for the distribution of several peices of Land divided amongst the heirs of William Judd of Farmington Decd, viz, Thomas Judd, John Porter, Daniel Judd, John Hart, William Judd, and Abigail Judd, all of Farmingtown, exhibited in Court, Accepted, and ordered on File.

Page 2-3.

Kennoe, John, Haddam. Invt. £49-08-06. Taken 5 February, 1687-8, by James Welles, John Bate & Alexander Rowle. Will *Nuncupative,* dated 3 June, 1687-8:

These are to certify all whome it may concerne, that I, John Kennoe, of Haddam, bestowe & give my three-acre lott unto my wife and son, as also my House, Moveables and Homested, unto the above-sd. persons, with the 6 acres in the Little Meadow, as also the 26 acres lying by John Bate, with my Right in the Undivided Land belonging unto me. I farther give and bestow on the above mentioned persons my horse and Cattle, Great & Smale, & likewise my swine. And unto Grace Spencer, living with me, I give 40 Shillings in Country Pay.

Witness: *John James.*   JOHN KENNER.

The age of the Children: John Kennoe, 6 years old, & Elizabeth, 2 years.

Court Record, Page 3—24 October, 1689: An Inventory of the Estate of John Kenner was exhibited in Court, and the Court finding no Will made by John Kennoe which can be proven, made Dist. of the Estate: To the Widow, 1-3 part of the Lands during her natural life, & £12 of Personal Estate. And to the son, the whole of the Lands, 2-3 when he comes of age, and 1-3 after his Mother's decease, & £6 in Inventoried Estate; & to the daughter, £13 of the Personal Estate when she comes of age.

Page 18—4 September, 1690: The Adms. refuse to act, and this Court appoint Thomas Shaylor Adms.

Page 64—6 December, 1693: Thomas Shaylor has recd of the Estate £12-08-09. This Court leave it with the said Shaylor, He paying the Interest to the Widow of the said Kennae, now the Wife of John Tanner. And the said Thomas Shaylor, with Alexander Rowley, bind themselves in the sum of £20 in money to pay the sayd money to the Child when it comes of age, and to pay Interest at the rate of £6 per Hundred as it becomes due.

Thomas Shaylor, Alexander Rowley.

Note: *The son received his portion in Lands, the Daughter in Money.*

Page 91—(Vol. VII) 3 March, 1706-7: The County Court at Hartford, 6 December, 1693, did order that Thomas Shaylor of Haddam, who then had the Custody of £12-08-09 as Money of the Estate of John Kenner Decd, should still have and keep the same until Elizabeth, daughter of the sd. John Kenner, is 18 years of age. And now the sd. Thomas Shaylor presents a receipt to the Court and discharge of both Principal and Interest, under the hand of the sd. Widow and Elizabeth her daughter, now of age. This Court fully discharge Alexander Rollo and Thomas Shaylor.

Page 10-11.

Langton, Deac. John, Farmington. Invt. £304-03-09. Taken 1689, by Thomas Porter Jr. and John Heart. Will dated 22 July, 1689.

I, John Langton, inhabitant of ffarmington, upon Connecticut, in New England, being through the mercy of God well Composed in minde but weake in body and uncertaine of departure, doe dispose of my outtward Estate in manner following: Imprimis. My will Is that my Just debts shall bee payed by my Executor, wch being discharged, I give to my beloved Wife one-halfe of my Estate, personal and Real, during her natural Life, except what I shall in this my will give to my daughter Elizabeth Langton and my grand son John Langton. Unto my daughter Elizabeth Langton and her heires I give and bequeath The summe of Sixty pounds, To bee payd by my Executor at Three payments, in wheat, Indian Corne and Porke, by equal proportion, at price currant with the merchant. Unto the sayd Elizabeth my daughter I doe also give the one-halfe of my household goods, and halfe my homelot in farmington on which my mansion house now standeth, with halfe ye orchard adjacent to It, and one acre of mowing Land, in Eighty acres, wch shee shall choose, and one acre of plowing Land in my Lot bought of John Coales, where shee shall see cause to take It. Moreover I give to her one acre of mowing Land and one acre of plowing Land Lyeing in ye Slipe, wch shee choose. Unto these Lands above mentioned my will is that my Executor shall allow her Liberty of passage. I doe also give unto my daughter Elizabeth Langton the leanto In the house in which I dwell in, the whole Length of it with the cellar underneath, & Liberty of fire in the other roome below. These above mentioned Legacis I give to my daughter Elizabeth Langton & her heirs forever. To my Grand son John Langton I give ten pownds & my division of upland Lyeing in farmington against Wethersfeild. And whereas I gave my son John, now deceased, a portion of Land in Northampton, the same gift I doe now confirm to John Langton my grandson. I also gave to my son Samuel Langton about four acres of Land in Northampton, which gift I now Confirm to ye said Samuel's Heires. Moreover my will is that my Executor make good the inheritance of my son John's Estate, Left in my hands, unto my grand son John Langton. To my son Joseph Langton and his heires (which Joseph I Constitute sole Executor to This my Last will) I give the one-halfe of my Land in farmington (except what is before mentioned to my daughter Elizabeth and grandson), to be entered upon by him at my decease, the other halfe at ye decease of my wife, as also my dwelling house (except what I before excepted) and what remaineth of my Estate Is not predisposed in this my Last Will and Testament. I request my ffrinds Mr Samuel Hooker sen. and Capt. John Standly to be overseers to this my Will, in Confirmation of wch I have sett to my hand and Seale, July 22-'89.

Witness: *John Hooker,*   JOHN LANGTON, Ls.
    Thomas Standly.

Thomas Standly made oath that this instrument above written was Deacon Langton's act & deed, August 6, 1689, before me.

John Stanly, Comr.

Court Record, Page 5—6 November, 1689: This Court doe leave wth Capt. Stanly & Samuel Cowles, as Overseers, the child of John Langton. The Child and his Estate to be disposed of for his bringing up, and we are willing the Boy's Aunt should keep the Boy and have the benefit of his Estate towards it.

Page 10—6 March, 1689-90: The grandson not being able to care for himself, This Court do assign Capt. John Stanly & Samuel Cowles to be guardians to the sayd child & his Estate.

Page 21—5 November, 1690: Whereas, it appears the Boy John Langton had died, this Court grant Letters of Adms. to his Aunt Elizabeth Langton, and order the whole Estate to her as next of kin to the deceased.

Page 47—7 December, 1692: Elizabeth Langton is now the wife of Luke Hayes.

Large, John, Haddam. Court Record, Page 26—5 March, 1690-1: Invt. Exhibited. Adms. on the Estate of John Large to Edward Shipman, Father-in-law of sd. deceased, with the Relict.

Page 86.

Lathrop, Benjamin. Found aboard the Sloop Adventure, belonging to Benjamin Lathrop, Decd, 9 June, 1690: Invt. £38-07-08. Taken by John Smith & William Whiting.

Court Record, Page 22—13 June, 1690: Invt. of the Estate of Benjamin Lathrop on board the Sloop presented by Malatye Lathrop. Adms. to Mr. Richard Edwards.

Page 80.

Lee, John, Farmington. Invt. £359-01-08. Taken 30 October, 1690, by John Heart and Thomas Porter. The children: John Lee, age 31 years, Stephen 22, Thomas 19, David 16, Mary Upson 26, Tabithy Lee, 13 years of age.

Court Record, Page 20—5 November, 1690: Adms. to the Widow and Thomas Porter, weaver. Ensign Thomas Heart & John Heart to be Overseers. Thomas Heart and Thomas Porter to Distribute per order of the Court.

Page 193-4.

Lewes, John, Farmington. Invt. £157-06-02. Taken 20 October, 1694, by John Stanly Jr. and Samuel Newell. Legatees: His Brothers and sisters—Philip Lewis, Samuel, William, Ebenezer and James Lewis, Hanna Marsh, Sarah Boltwood, Felix Selden.

Court Record, Page 77—14 November, 1694: William Lewis made oath that he had made a true presentment of the Estate of the decd, which this Court accepts and orders recorded. And this Court grants Adms. unto Samuel & William Lewis, and order to Dist. the Estate to the Brethren & Sisters, both by Father & Mother; & this Court appoint Sergt. Samuel Wadsworth & Sergt. Samuel Hooker, Dist.

Page 194—(Vol. VIII) 3 May, 1714: Benjamin and Jonathan Judd moved the Court for a new Dist., they being interested and not considered in a former Dist. The Court order William Lewis to appear in Court and show cause why this motion should not be granted.

Page 203—22 May, 1714: Benjamin & Jonathan Judd now presented their former Motion for a new Dist., but this Court do not see Cause to make any Alteration, whereupon Jonathan Judd appealed to the Superior Court.

Page 65.

Lewis, Capt. William, Farmington. Invt. £1025-19-00. Taken 28 August, 1690, by Thomas Bull and Thomas Porter. The children: Philip, Samuel, William, Ebenezer, John, James, Ezekiel, Nathaniel, Mary Judd, Sarah Boltwood, Hannah Marsh, Felix Selden, & Abigail Lewes.

Court Record, Page 18—4 September, 1690: Invt. Exhibited by the Relict and John Lewis.

Page 20—5 November, 1690: Adms. to Philip and William Lewis, Mrs. Lewis having an Interest in the Estate by Joynture. This Court appoint Deacon Hosmore. The Widow and Children choose, the one Bevel Waters, the others John Thompson, to make an equal division as they can to the Widow.

Dist. on File, 7 June, 1707: To Samuel, to William, to John and James (both deceased), to Mary Judd, to Sarah Boltwood, to Hannah Marsh, to Felix Selden. By John Wadsworth, Samuel Newell sen.

Page 26—6 March, 1690-1: Distribution of the Estate of Capt. William Lewis, The Joynture being already settled: To Philip, the Eldest son, a double portion, and to the rest of the Children a single portion. This Court appoint Deac. Stephen Hosmer & Thomas Bunce to Dist. the Estate to them & Mrs. Lewis's Joynture in Land and Negroes, the reversion thereof to be accotd part of the three youngest children's portions in the Dist., that is to say, to the value of £100 Money.

Page 26—5 March, 1690-1: Nathaniel Lewis, a minor son of Capt. William Lewis, chose Capt. John Stanly to be his Guardian.

Page 27—6 March, 1690-1: By request of the sons of Capt. William Lewis, John Lewis was Joyned to Philip & Wm Lewis as Adms. to the Estate of Capt. William Lewis.

Dist. Estate of Capt. Wm Lewis, late of Farmington, 1st October, 1691: To Philip, to Ezekiel, to Nathaniel, to Samuel, to Ebenezer, to John, to James, to Mary, to Sarah, to Hannah, to Felix, & to Abigail.

Private Controversies, Vol. 4, No. 145:

William Lewis sen., Farmington. From the Will, 16 July, 1689: I give to my loveing wife 1-3 of my Lands during her Life. I do give to my son Philip a full confirmation of the living he liveth upon at Hartford, according to the tenure of my Hond Father's Will. I give to Samuel Lewis, I give to William Lewis that Land I bought of Isaac More, vnlest that already sold to Thomas Orton, which lyeth in Barrett's. I give to John, to James, to Ebenezer Lewis.

P. C., Vol. 4, No. 150:

To the Honoured Ajourned Court sittin in Hartford, 8 April, 1691: I understand that in the Distribution of my Honoured Husband Capt. William Lewis Decd his Estate, made by the County Court 8 March, 1690, your Worships have seen meete to dispose of my Estate or that part of it, viz, the Hundred pound Sterlinge expressed in the Jointure made to my Honoured Father Ezekiel Cheever for the only use of me my heirs and Asigns, by which act of Distribution I doe apprehend that either myself or the three youngest Children of the fore said Capt. William Lewis is, or each of us, wronged. Therefore, having this opportunity, I doe see meet by my petition to move the Honoured Court to Consider the Case and to act and do in it accordinge as the Rules of Equity, Law & Reason Doth require. In Case my prayer be not Considered & my Expectation answered herein, I Doe Declare my self Justly Agrieved & Dissatisfied, & doe purpose in my own intention to make my Application to the Court of Assistants for relief according as the Law Doth Direct.

7 April, 1691.   Your Humble petitioner, MARY LEWIS.

Court Record, Page 112 (Vol. VII) 7 June, 1707-8: This Court do order and appoint Samuel Newell and John Wadsworth of Farmington to divide and actually set out upon the ground all the Lands of or belonging to the Estate of Capt. William Lewis, late of Farmington Decd, valued in the Inventory at £40, unto and among the Children of the said William Lewis Decd, or their legal Representatives, according to the intent, meaning and direction of the distribution made of the Estate of the sd. William Lewis and his son John Lewis deceased, together, and report to this Court.

Page 12—(Vol. VIII) 1st May, 1710: Report of the Dist.

Page 69—(Vol. IX) 1st July, 1718: James Lewis of Jamaica, Long Island, appeals from a Decree of the Court, 17 March, 1709-10, allowing a Dist. of the Estate of William Lewis of Farmington.

Page 75—5 August, 1719: William and Nathaniel Lewis were cited into Court to object, if they see Cause, why the sd. James Lewis might not have an Appeal from the Judgement of the Court of Probate held at Hartford 17 March, 1708-10, receiving and allowing a certain Dist. This Court having heard and considering the Pleas of the Parties, do not see Cause to grant the sd. James Lewis Liberty of an Appeal. Order that he pay Costs.

Page 77—27 August, 1718: James Lewis appeals to the Superior Court to have the Dist. nullified and a new apprisal by a Jury of 12 Men. Appeal barred by the Court.

Page 40.

Loomis, Thomas, Windsor. Invt. £377-01-06. Taken 1st November, 1689, by John Moore and Joseph Loomis. The children: Thomas, b. 17 March, 1655-6; Hannah, b. 8 Feb., 1657-8; Mary, b. 16 Jan., 1659-60; Elizabeth, b. 21 Jan., 1663-4; Ruth, b. 16 Oct., 1665; Sarah, b. 1st Feb., 1667-8; Mabell, b. 27 Oct., 1672; Mindwell, b. Aug., 1676; Benjamin, b. 20 May, 1679.

Court Record, Page 7—11 November, 1689: Adms. to Thomas Loomis.

Page 12—6 March, 1689-90: Dist: To Eldest son, £130; to the youngest son, £65; to the Lame daughter Sarah, £50; to Each of the other daughters, £24 (a part before received by the Married daughters). William Judd, Michael Tayntor & John Lee sign as having received. Again Hana had £8, Mary £7-01-08, and Elizabeth £11-03-00.

Page 64—14 December, 1693: The Brothers-in-Law of Thomas Loomys of Windsor having appeared before the Court of Assistants, October Last, & Desireing This Court to Settle the Father of sayd Loomys his Estate, they being dissatisfied with the Dist. of the County Court: The Court of Assistants turning it Back to the Consideration of the County Court, who, having Laboured in it, The sayd Tho. Loomys, John Lee in behalf of his Wife, & Michael Tayntor, agreed in Court that Benjamin Loomys his portion should be as the former Court ordered, £65, & Wakefield Dible's wife's portion £50, & that Thomas Loomys should add to the portions of his six sisters now surviving Fower pounds Ten shillings apeice to each of them, to be paid as soon as he can conveniently, in corn, porck or Neat Cattell; & the Court appoynts Thomas Loomys to be Administrator to his Father's Estate.

Page 16—(Vol. VII) 4 September, 1701: This Court being desired to appoint Dist. to the Estate of Thomas Loomis, formerly of Windsor Decd, This Court do therefore appoint Mr. John Moore, Capt. Thomas Stoughton and Deacon Job Drake to Dist. the sd. Estate, or Benjamin's part of it, according to an Order of Court made 14 December, 1693, and make return thereof to this Court.

Page 28—2 March, 1701-2: There was presented to this Court a Dist. of the Estate of Thomas Loomis Decd, under the Hands of Capt. Stoughton and Deacon Drake, which this Court do not see cause to accept, and order the Dist. to be sent for before the Court of Probates some time, to render their reasons to this Court of their Proceedings therein.

Page 61.

Lucas, William, Middletown. Invt. £71-05-00. Taken 30 June, 1690, by William Sumner, Isack Johnson and Daniel Marcum. The children: William age 23, John 21, Mary 18, Thomas 14, Samuel 11 years of age.

Court Record, Page 18—4 September, 1690: Adms. to William Lucas, the son. Isack Johnson and John Blake to be Overseers.

Agreement on File: An Agreement, dated 26 May, 1704, betwixt William, John, Thomas & Samuel Lucas, sons of William Lucas of Middletown Decd, concerning the Dist. of their sd. Father's Estate: William Lucas, the Eldest Brother, is to have all the Land and other Estate belonging to their sd. Father, excepting what is after divided and what proper portion doth fall to their sister Mary, now wife of John Scovill. And John Lucas doth hereby accept of 7 acres of Land to be laid out to him in that Lottment of Land whereon his Brother William's house stands on. And Thomas and Samuel Lucas do accept of as their portion the remainder of that Lottment of Land of which their Brother hath sold 7 acres to Joseph Starr, and a Lottment of Land on the East Side of the Great River, containing about 104 acres, which Sale of the above 7 acres of Land by William to Joseph Starr, the above John, Thomas & Samuel Lucas do approve of, and do hereby declare the Deed to be valid and effectual. And they do also bind and ingage themselves, joyntly and each for his own part, firmly to adhear and stand to this Agreement and Dist. of their Father's Estate.

Witness: *Richard Goodale,*   WILLIAM X LUCAS. Ls.
      Alexander Rollo.   JOHN X LUCAS. Ls.
                          SAMUEL LUCAS. Ls.

On the 5th day of April, 1726, John Lucas being decd, William, Thomas & Samuel Lucas now appeared before the Court and acknowledged the same to be their free Act & Deed. Signed:

                          WILLIAM X LUCAS,
Witness: *Isaac DeMedina,*   THOMAS X LUCAS,
      Abraham Kilbourn.   SAMUEL X LUCAS.

Page 126—(Vol. X) 5 April, 1726: Agreement accepted.

Page 186.

Marshall, David, Windsor. Invt. £263-17-00. Taken 7 July, 1694, by Timothy Phelps sen. and James Ennos. Will dated 22 June, 1694.

I David Marshall of Windsor doe make this my last Will & Testament: I give to my little son David Marshall, at the age of 21 years, ½ of my houseing & Homested, and the whole after my wife's decease. Also, I give unto my son my Swamp or Meadow Land lying by Hoyt's Meadow. Also my Great Lott, 65 Rods in Breadth, & to take his part on the westerly

side next to George Griswold's Land, and the length to run the whole
length of the sd. Lott, excepting only 4 or 5 acres, which I have exchanged
with Benajah Holcomb for the Land where my house now stands, to be
to him forever; only the sd. David Marshall is hereby bound to pay unto
his two sisters £5 apeice in Country pay within 2 years after he comes to
be possessed of the premises. I give unto my wife Abigail Marshall, after
just Debts & all Expenses are paid, the Use & Benefit of my whole Estate,
Personal or Real, until my Children come to age, and half of all the Moveable Estate to be at her own dispose forever; and also half the house &
homested during her natural life, & 1-3 part of the benefit of the Real Estate. I give unto my two daughters Abigail and Hannah Marshall, to be
equally divided betwixt them, all my other Land not herein disposed otherwise, and also half of my Moveable Estate. It is my Will that my wife
Abigail Marshall shall be sole Executrix, and that my brethren Thomas
Marshall & William Phelps, with Benajah Holcomb sen., shall be Overseers.

Witness: *Daniel Griswold,*   DAVID MARSHALL. LS.
    John Griswold.

Note: *In the Inventory mention is made of "Brads & Sparables."*

Page 147-8-9.

Marshall, Thomas, Hartford. Invt. £286-11-03. Taken 29 December, 1692, by Bevell Waters & John Catlin. The children: John, 21 years,
24 February next; Thomas, 16 last October, 1692; Elizabeth, 14, October,
1692; Benjamin, 8, February next. The Eldest daughter of age, and married to Stodder.

The last Will & Testament of Thomas Marshall of Hartford: *(Nuncupative):* We underwritten, being together at the house of Thomas
Marshall, lately deceased, in the time of his last sickness, about the 3rd of
this moneth, and he being then of sound understanding, declared in presence of us this following to be his last Will: Imprimis: That he gave
to his eldest son John that part of his Lott that lyeth on the East side of
the Road that leadeth from Hartford to Wethersfield, with the half of his
Barn (the north End), with 14 Rods of Land adjoining to it to make a
Cow Yard, & a Loome with what belongs to it. This he to possess when he
is of age. Item. After all his Just Debts were discharged, he gave the
Remainder of his Estate, Real & Personal (all except another Loom,
which he gave to his son Thomas to possess it when he comes of age), to
his wife to be possessed by her during her Widowhood. After her decease
his son Thomas should have the ½ of the Homelott and the Dwelling
house, and that his son Benjamin should have his other half of the Homelott, it being the ½ of that part of his Lott that lyeth on the West side of
the Road leading from Wethersfield to Hartford; & that the Household
Stuffe should be equally divided to his 2 daughters Mary & Elizabeth,

saving that Elizabeth should have the Great Kettle above her halfe; also that Elizabeth should have £10 of the Stock and Mary £5. He further declared that it was his mind that his youngest son Benjamin should, if he see Cause, have that parcel of Land which he bought of Susannah Sandford, which was confirmed by Susannah Sandford and Phineas Wilson to him to build upon.

Witness: *Mary X Catlin,*   (Not signed.)
Sarah X Waters, Mary X Campe.

And all appeared 30th December, 1692, and made Oath to the above-written.

Before me, John Allyn, Assistant.

Court Record, Page 50—3 January, 1692-3: Adms. to the Widow. John Catlin and Bevell Waters to be Overseers.

Page 51—11 January, 1692: Invt. exhibited by the two sons, John & Thomas. The Widow being deceased, Adms. is granted to Capt. Niccols & Bevell Waters & John Catlin.

Dist. on File, 10 April, 1696: To John, to Thomas, to Benjamin, to Mary Stoddard, to Elizabeth Marshall, Thomas' Estate in John Catlin's Hand, Elizabeth & Benjamin's Estate in the Hands of Bevell Waters. John Marshall & Nathaniel Gladden's part of the Estate was delivered to themselves.

Page 21—(Vol. VII) 13 November, 1701: John Catlin sen. presented to this Court a Dist. of the Estate of Thomas Marshall sen., late of Hartford, under the Hands of the sd. Catlin & Capt. Ciprian Nicols, who made oath to the truth of the several articles and deliveries thereof, except one, that is, £7 delivered to John Marshall. Mr. Bevil Waters not being present, it could not be completed.

Page 33—8 September, 1702: Mr. Bevil Waters and John Catlin, Adms. on the Estate of Thomas Marshall Decd, being cited to appear before this Court to render an Account of their Adms. on that Estate, the Court do not see Cause to accept their Account.

Page 181.

Mather, Katharine, Windsor. Invt. £39-07-06. Taken 20 February, 1693-4, by Return Strong sen. & John Fyler.

Court Record, Page 66—1st March, 1693-4: Adms. to Samuel & Atherton Mather.

Page 68-9.

Maudsley, Capt. John, Windsor. Invt. £228-02-08. Taken 1st September, 1690, by John Moore sen. and Timothy Phelps. Capt. John Maudsley's Estate in Westfield: Inventoried at £543-06-00. Taken 1st September, 1690, by Josiah Dewey, Nathaniel Weller & John Richards. Will dated 17 August, 1690.

I John Maudsley of Windsor doe make & declare this my last Will & Testament: I give to my wife Mary all my Right and Interest in the Grist Mill at Windsor, also 50 acres of Land at Ketch, she to dispose of the Mill and Land to any of my Children as she shall see cause. Also I give her ½ of all my Houseing and Lands and Moveable Estate of all sorts during her life. I give to my son Benjamin all my Houseing and Land in Windsor except what I have already given to my wife. This I give him in Case my wife see cause after my decease to live at Westfield. I give to my other sons and daughters all the rest of my Estate, my sons to have £10 apeice more than my daughters, and to have their portions in Lands. Also I make and appoint my wife and son Benjamin Executors. And I desire the Rev. Mr. Samuel Mather, Henry Wolcott, Ensign Josiah Dewey & Nathaniel Weller to be my Overseers.

Witness: *Samuel Mather,*					JOHN MAUDSLEY.
Henry Wolcott, Atherton Mather.

Court Record, Page 18—4 September, 1690: Will proven.

Page 44—1st September, 1692: Benjamin Maudsley Renounces being Executor on his Father's Estate.

Page 82—7 March, 1694: Whereas, Benjamin Maudsley Renounces being Executor, Now Mary Phelps, the Relict of said Capt. Maudsley, being unable to perform the service, presents her son Joseph Maudsley & her son Isack Phelps as Adms., which the Court impower to act to preserve the Estate and to pay the Legatees their Portion as they come of age.

Will on File.

Merrells, John. In the Name & Fear of the Eternal God, Father, Son & Holy Spirit, to Him Be Given all Glory now and for ever more, Amen. I John Merrells of Hartford, In New England, Being now, through the Gratious providence of God towards mee, In good Health of Body, And Having the Right use of my understanding & Reason, thought good to manifest to those persons it may conserne what my minde and will is conserning the dispose of those (things) that God hath given mee liberty to dispose off: My Will is that my loveing wife shold Have Half my Dwelling House with Half my Home Lott & the priviledges there unto Belonging so Long as shee shall Remain a Widow; and if shee [   ] This Estate [   ] to my Children when they come of age to receive Their portions. And if it so Returne, my Will is that my wife shold Have six pounds pr year out of my Estate, to Bee payd Hir yearly by my Children during Her Natural Life. Also I give unto my sayd wife thirty pounds, to Bee payd out of my moveable Estate, to be Hirs for Ever and at her owne dispose. Farther, my Will is that the Rest of my Estate Bee disposed of as is Hereafter expressed, That is to say, my whole Estate undisposed off as abovesaid Being Divided into so many parts and one part More than I shall have Children surviving mee at my Decease, my Will is That my daughter Sarah, Carrying well to Her

mother and pleaseing Hir In matching, shold have £5 more than equal
share of my Estate [   ] Also my will is [   ]
eldest [   ] Nathaniel proceed, And Learn the Trade off
a Taner, and is likely to Improve the sayd Trade well, that Hee the sd.
Nathaniel shall Have twoe parts of my Estate, it Being Divided as above
sayd.   Otherwise my Will is that hee shall Have But an Equal share with
the Rest of my Children that shall survive mee, the whole Estate Being
Divided into Equal parts according to the Number of my Children surviving mee.   Also my Will is that my sonn Nathaniel, Attending the Conditions abovesayd so that he Receives a Double portion, that Hee shall Have
half my Homestead & half the Tan yard, with all the appurtenances thereto belonging, as part of His portion.   Or if it comes to more than his
share as is before expressed, that Hee shal pay so much to the Rest of my
Children as it Comes to more than His part of my Estate.   My Will is that
iff either of my other sonns will Learn my trade of a Taner and is Likely
to Improve it Well, that that sonn that so Does shall Have the other Half
of the Tanyard with half the fats & Houseing and other Conveniences
thereunto Belonging; also the other half of my Homestead which is Left
with my wife During her Widdow hood, or shee Resigning it upon the
Conditions above sayd, I say that that son shall Have that Half of the
Homestead after his Mother [   ] And the half of the
Tanyard I ffreely give to that sonn that shall Learn the Trade as He is
Likely to Improve it well and upon the condition above expressed.   That
half of the Tanyard is not to bee putt in with that I Call my Estate to Bee
Devided amongst my Children surviving mee as abovesayd.   Also I Give
to the Rest of my Children surviving mee, each of them, an equal share of
my Estate divided as abovesayd.   Also my will is that None of my Lands
nor Tanyards that I shall Dye possessed off shall Bee Allienated to any
other Prson that is not of my posteritie for ever, in Case any of the same
(viz.) of my sonns will purchase of thore who are minded to Dispose of
theire parts, and Give so much as it is worth at the time of sale.   And I
Doe apoynt & Constitute my Loveing wife Sarah Merrills to Bee my
Executrix to this my Last will & Testament, and my Trusty & well be
Loved ffrinds and Brethren ensine Nathaniell Stanly & Thomas Bunce and
John Seamor & John Watson to Bee helpfull to my [   ]
Have sett to [   ]
Hand this 11 day of Aprill, 1684.   JOHN MERRELLS.
Signed in presence off us :
Steven Hopkins,
Thomas Olcott.   *Filed 1712.*

Page 131.

Mecumpas, Mary. This may informe whome it may concern : That
the Indian Woman called Mary Mecumpas doth declare that shee hath
not nor will not give her young Girle she had by mingoe, Thomas Olm-

sted's Negroe, to any english man, but doth give her unto an Indian woman that is her cousin, called Sarah; & allso she sayth she giveth unto her daughter 2 acres & halfe of Land now improved by Robt. Shurley when the time is out that he hath hyred it, which is 2 years more. 27 September, 1692.

As witness: *Siborn Niccols,*
   Stephen Hosmore, and by their desire recorded.

Page 210-11.

Mitchell, John, Hartford. Died at Barbadoes 1st June, 1695. Invt. £88-11-06. Taken 10 August, 1695, by Thomas Olcott sen. & Daniel Clark, Smith.

Court Record, Page 88—13 August, 1695: Adms. to the Widow. Thomas Olcott & Jonathan Loomis to be Overseers.

Page 138.

Moore, Martin, Hartford. Died 5 September, 1692. Invt. £66-05-02. Taken by Joseph Bull and Joseph Mygatt.

Court Record, Page 47—12 October, 1692: Adms. to David Ensign.

Page 207-8.

Moore, Philip sen., Hartford. A free Negro. Died 12 April, 1695. Invt. £99-11-06. Taken 16 April, 1695, by Richard Risley and Thomas Kilbourn. Will dated 27 November, 1693.

I Philip Moore sen. of Hartford doe make this my last Will & Testament: I give unto my wife Ruth Moore the free Use & Improvement of all my Personal & Real Estate during her life. I give to my son Phillip Moore 10 Shillings & the Improvement of the Estate I have given his Children, after the death of his Mother, until they come of age. To my daughter Susannah Sesions & her Children, my Land at Hoccanum. I give liberty to my son Cato or his wife or Children to build upon one acre of Land or plant an orchard upon it as soon as their time is out with Mr. Woodbridge, if they see cause so to do. I give unto my daughter Susannah my dwelling house and an acre of my Homelott on the West side of the Highway at Hoccanum, the whole Breadth of my sd. Lott, only adding what may be needful to the Breadth of the Highway betwixt Henry Arnold's Land and mine so far as my daughter's acre will extend. I give unto my son Philip Moore's children the remainder of my Homelott upon the West side of the Highway at Hoccanum, and all the remainder of my Woodlott on the East side of the Highway beyond that I sold to Henry

Arnold. I give unto my wife all my Moveable Estate. I constitute my wife Ruth Moore sole Executrix.

Witness: *Caleb Stanly sen.,*   PHILIP X MOORE. Ls.
Caleb Stanly Jr., Sarah Stanly.

Philip Moore being a free negro, signed, sealed and declared this Writing to be his last Will & Testament.

Court Record, Page 86—18 April, 1695: Will approved.

Page 32-3.

Moses, Mary. Invt. £62-12-00. Taken 23 September, 1689, by John Moore. Nuncupative Will, dated 9 September, 1689. Mary Moses' last Will was that her son John should have 2 Barrells of Syder, and that Timothy should have the Cyder Mill & Press, & the rest of the Estate should be equally divided amongst the rest of her Children.

Witness: *George Norton,*   (Not signed.)
George Drake Jr.

Court Record, Page 7—11 November, 1689: Will & Invt. exhibited. This Court appoint Timothy Phelps & Josiah Gillett to Dist. the Estate.

Page 38-9.

Newbery, Benjamin, Major Windsor. Invt. £563-18-00. Taken 8 October, 1689, by John Moore and John Loomis.

Court Record, Page 6—11 November, 1689: Adms. to Benjamin Newbery, Eldest and only son. This Court Order all the lands that Major Newbery died possessed of to be the proper Estate of Benjamin Newbery his son and proper Heir, except the two miles in Length woodland of Miles Humphrey's land that was, which we allott to Thomas Newbery's sons, & Order to the daughters of Major Newbery £44 to each with what they have already received. What is due to Ephraim Hayward's Wife is to be secured for his two Children when they Come of age. (See Page 90, Vol. V, Pro. Rec.)

Page 110.

Newbery, Thomas, Windsor. Died 30 April, 1688. Invt. £49-07-00. Taken 28 May, 1688, by Lt. Allyn and Return Strong. 19 June, 1688, the real estate was entered by Ensign Benjamin Newbery, No. A, Fol. 140, on the Margin (Vol. VI): Invt. Real Estate, £280-00-00. The children: Hanna, the Eldest, age 8 years; Thomas 6, Joseph 4 ½, Benjamin one year old.

Court Record, Page 25—5 March, 1690-1: Thomas Newbery his Estate being distributed formerly, this Court now came to a Consideration of the same and find the

	£	s	d
Personal Estate, with a third advance, comes to	74	00	06
Debts being paid,	45	05	02
The Woman's thirds is	9	13	06
There remains of Personal Estate,	289	01	10
To the other three Children, apeice,	57	16	04

Adms. is granted to Return Strong. John Wolcott and Col. Allyn to be Overseers.

Dist. File. 8 March, 1705-6: Estate of Thomas Newbery. An Agreement of Heirs: To Hannah Newbery, now wife of Henry Wolcott Jr., to Joseph Newbery, and to Benjamin Newbery, yet a minor.

Page 47-8.

Newell, Joseph, Farmington. Invt. £57-09-00. Taken 14 November, 1689, by Jonathan Smith & John Thompson. Will dated 2 November, 1689.

The last Will & Testament of Joseph Newell of Farmington: I Joseph Newell do give to my Brother John my House & Lott with all the Privileges thereon, he paying £5 to his five sisters, 20 Shillings apeice, namely, Rebeckah, Mary, Sarah, Esther & Hannah. Item. I give my Mare & Colt to my brother Thomas Newell. Item. I give to my brother John my Cloth Jacket, and my Baranett Jacket to my Brother Thomas, and my haire Camletts Coats to my brother Samuel. And I give my Cloth Coat to Joseph Woodford. I give to my brother John my old Cloak. I give to my brother Thomas my big Gunn. Item. I give to Esther Woodford my Chest. I give my other Gunn to my brother John Stanly's son Samuel. Item. I give to my Brother Thomas North my Cutlash. Item. The rest of my Estate I give to my dear Mother (she discharging my Debts), namely, a peice of Serge for a paire of Breeches, with divers other things, & some linen, Corne & Flax.

Witness: *John Thompson sen.,*   JOSEPH X NEWELL.
        Mary X Woodford.

Note: *The Widow Newell personally appeared December, 1689, and made Oath to the Inventory of the Estate of her son Joseph Newell, before*
William Lewes.

Court Record, Page 10—6 March, 1689-90: Will & Invt. exhibited. Adms. to Widow Newell, his Mother, with the Will annexed.

Page 13-14.

Newell, Thomas, Farmington. Invt. £449-17-06. Taken 7 November, 1689, by John Stanly and Samuel Cowles. The children:[h] John

Newell 42 years, Thomas 39, Samuel 28, Rebeckah Woodford 46, Mary Bascom 44, Hester Stanly 37, Sarah Smith 34, & Hannah North 31.

Whereas, Thomas Newell of Farmington, lately deceased, died without any Will, it is mutually agreed between the Widow of the sd. Newell & all the Children that were present at the County Court when the Dist. of Thomas Newell's Estate was made: The Widow & Relict of the sd. Thomas Newell reserveth the full dispose of her thirds of all the Moveable Estate for her maintenance. It is also agreed by the Widow & Children that Rebeckah Woodford, gr. Child of the forementioned Thomas Newell, that hath lived several years with her gr. Father & Mother, shall have £10 in Moveable Estate given her out of her gr. Father's Estate before any other Dist. be made. We have given into the Worshipfull Court the several sums that each of the Children have already received, as near as we can, intreating them to make an equal Dist. of the forementioned Estate according to our Agreement. Unto all which we have set to our Hands & Seals this 8th of November, 1689.

Witness: *George Grave,*   REBECKAH NEWELL, Ls.
     Caleb Stanly.   JOHN NEWELL, Ls.
                    SAMUEL NEWELL,
                    RICHARD NEWELL,
                    JOHN STANLY, Ls.
                    THOMAS NORTH, Ls.
                    REBECKAH WOODFORD, Ls.
                    (a grand Child.)

An Account of the Several sums that the Children of Mr. Thomas Newell have already received out of their Father's Estate before he deceased:

	£ s d		£ s d
To Samuel Newell, Deed of Gift.			
		To Mary Bascom,	40-00-00
To the Eldest son John,	34-00-00	To Hester Stanly,	28-00-00
To Thomas Newell,	65-00-00	To Sarah Smith,	40-00-00
To Rebeckah Woodford,	30-00-00	To Hannah Smith,	28-00-00

Court Record, Page 5—6 November, 1689: Adms. to the Widow and Samuel Newell. John Stanly and Samuel Cowles to be Overseers.

Page 126.

North, John sen., Invt. £224-11-00. Taken 12 February, 1691-2, by John Thompson sen. and John Orton. Legatees or Children: Joseph & Mary Searles & Sarah Woodruff.

Court Record, Page 39—3 March, 1691-2: Adms. to Thomas North. This Court Distribute the Estate as followeth:

	£ s d		£ s d
To Thomas North,	69-16-00	To Mary Searles,	27-18-00
To Joseph North,	24-18-00	To Sarah Woodruff's	
		Children	31-08-00

(Sarah Woodruff was alive at her Father's Decease.)
Ensign Thomas Heart and Mr. Thomas Bull to Dist. to the Legatees.

Page 164.

Olcott, Abigail. Died 26 May, 1693. Invt. £229-03-06. Taken July, 1693, by John Wilson and John Marsh sen. Will dated 12 January, 1691-2.

The last Will & Testament of Abigail Olcott of Hartford: Having formerly given my son Thomas a peice of Gold, I give my son John a 10-Shillings peice of Gold, and to my son Samuel and daughter Elizabeth Hide I give my bigest peice of Gold, to be divided between them. I also give to my daughter Hide my two black gowns and my mohaire petticoat and my silk Cloak & my wearing linen & a dozen of Holland Napkins. And to my daughter-in-law Sarah I give my Cloth Gown and Cloth Petticoats and serge Cloak. It is my Will that £50 I gave to my gr. Children Thomas and Mary by a former writing shall be paid out of such Debts as are due to me. And the rest of my Estate, both Personal & Real, I give and bequeath the same to my sons Thomas, Samuel and John, and my daughter Elizabeth Hide, to be equally divided between them, excepting my son John to have a double share. I appoint my sons Thomas & John Olcott to be Executors, and Col. John Allyn and Doctor Thomas Hooker to be Overseers.

Witness: *John Allyn,*   ABIGAIL OLCOTT. Ls.
          Richard Edwards.

Court Record, Page 62—7 September, 1693: Will proven.

Page 12—(Vol. VII) 11 March, 1700-1: Mr. Thomas Olcott sen. of Hartford moves this Court to provide Forr Remidie for him against those wrongs done to him by his Brother Mr. John Olcott, Co-Executor with him in his Mother's Will, who doth delay the Estate in his hands greatly to the prejudice of the Complainant. The Court order the Clerk to grant a Writ to the sd. Mr. Thomas Olcott to summons his sd. Brother to appear at the Court of Probates to be held on the 17th day of this Instant, there to answer his Complaint in the Case aforesd.

Page 221.

Orton, John, Farmington. Invt. £486-09-03. Taken 24 January, 1695-6, by John Judd, John Heart and Joseph North. JOHN MOORE *Testifies that John Orton, at two several times, told him and showed him a* *writing in which he desired that his wife Mary should have all that she brought from her Father Tudor's Estate in addition to all she would have from his Estate, and that it should be at her own disposal.* (See this Note appended to the Inventory:) Sworn in Court 6 March, 1685-6.

Court Record, Page 97—5 March, 1695-6: Adms. to the Relict and Thomas Orton.

Page 107—8 April, 1696: The *Nuncupative* Will to the wife allowed by the Court. Deacon Thomas Bull, Mr. John Wadsworth & Jonathan Smith to Distribute the Estate.

Dist. File: 13 June, 1696: To the Widow Mary Orton, to Thomas Orton, to John & Samuel Orton, to Marget Orton or her Guardian Samuel Newell, to Mary Orton. By Thomas Bull & John Wadsworth.

Page 39—(Vol. VII) 2 March, 1702-3: This Court do appoint Mr. John Hooker and Mr. John Stanly, both of Farmington, to be Overseers to John and Samuel Orton, sons of John Orton, late of the sd. Town Decd.

Page 14—(Vol. VIII): Thomas Orton and John Thompson of Farmington, sons of John Orton, late of Farmington, made Application to this Court for an Order for perfecting the Dist. of the Estate of the Decd which was begun and in a general manner performed by Deacon Thomas Bull and John Wadsworth, and also for a Division of that part of the Estate which was allotted for Mary Orton, one of the daughters of the Decd who died before she came of age. This Court do order that part of the Estate ordered for the sd. Mary shall be equally divided between the rest of the Children of John Orton Decd, and John Wadsworth, William Lewis and John Orton 2nd are by this Court appointed to divide and dist. the same accordingly, and also to perfect the aforesd Dist. according to the Order of the County Court 8 April, 1696, and actually to divide the Lands belonging to the sd. Estate and mark out the Divisions for the Ground.

Page 18—4 September, 1710: John Wadsworth and William Lewis appeared before this Court and were sworn truly and faithfully to dist. the sd. Estate.

Dist. File, 4 September, 1710: To Thomas Orton, to John Orton, to Samuel Orton, to John Thompson in Right of his wife Margaret. That portion which was formerly dist. to Mary to be now divided amongst the others equally by John Orton, William Lewis & John Wadsworth. This Dist. is, by the Desire of John Thompson, entered at Large in Farmington, 1st Book of Records, Page 201-2—26 October, 1710, pr me

JOHN HOOKER, REGISTER.

Page 21—(Vol. VIII) 6 November, 1710: Report of Dist. of that Estate which was allotted to Mary, one of the Daughters, to be put on File.

Page 6.

Osborn, Widow Ann, Windsor. Died 28 August. 1689. (W. R.) Invt. £91-01-00. Taken 31 October, 1689, by Samuel Grant and Isaac

Morgan. The Legatees: John Osborn, age 43 years, Nathaniel Osborn 36, Mary Owen, Samuel Osborn 26, Hester Owen 22, Sarah Wright 20, Hannah Egleston 24.

Court Record, Page 4—6 November, 1689: Invt. Exhibited of Mrs. Ann Osborn's Estate. Adms. to John & Samuel Osborn. Nathaniel Bissell & Job Drake, son of John Drake, to Distribute the Estate.

Note: *John Osband & Ann Oldage m. 19 May, 1645.*—(W. R.)

Page 217.

Peck, Paul, Hartford. Died 23 December, 1695. Invt. £536-05-00. Taken 6 January, 1695-6, by Ciprian Niccols & Joseph Easton. Will dated 25 June, 1695.

I Paul Peck sen. of Hartford doe make this my last Will & Testament: I give to my eldest son Paul Peck the Lott wherein his Dwelling house now standeth, and my Lott called Springfield, containing 3 acres; also the ½ of my Island in the South Meadow in Hartford; he the sd. Paul Peck paying such Legacies as herein after shall be appointed him. I give to my grand son Paul Peck, son of my son Paul Peck, all my right, Title and Interest in and to that land on the East side of the Connecticut River lying five miles in Length from the east end westerly, which was purchased by the Towne of Hartford of Joshua an Indian, Unncas his son, to be unto him my said grand son Paul Peck & his heirs forever. I give and bequeath unto my grand son Samuel Peck, who now liveth with me, my now dwelling house & the northermost end of my barne, with all the yards, gardens & Orchards thereunto belonging, and all the remainder of my Home Lot not otherwise disposed of In this my Last Will, viz, from the North side of the threshing floor eastward to the Highway & Westward to the rear of my lott, to the North bounds of my sayd Home lott, at my decease and the decease of my wife his grand Mother, he paying five pounds in Current country pay to my son-in-law Joseph Benton within two years after he cometh to the possession of the sayd house & Home lott, & ten pounds to my grand daughter Ruth beach, at fower payments, within fower years after he cometh to possession of my Homested. I give to my son Joseph Peck, and to his Heirs forever, that parcell of Land which was sometime Robert Bartlett's Land, situate or Lying on the north of Land given to my son-in-law John Shepherd & my grand son Samuel Peck, & Eastward of Lands belonging to John Shepherd, John Bigelow & Samuel Steele, & on John Shepherd's & Samuel Peck's Land Sowth, & on Land sometime John Hannison's west, and on Sergt. John Shepherd & Samuel Burr their land North. I give to my son-in-law John Shepherd that lot on which his Dwelling House now standeth. I give and bequeath to my loveing wife Martha Peck £7-10-00, to be paid her yearly by my sons. I give to my 4 daughters, viz, Martha Cornwall, Mary Andrews, Elizabeth Howe of Wallingford, & Sarah Clarke, £20 to each. I ordain my two sons, Paul Peck and Joseph Peck, and my son-in-law John Shep-

herd, to be my Executors, and I desire Capt. Ciprian Niccols & Joseph Easton to be Overseers.   PAUL PECK. Ls.
Witness: *Caleb Stanly,*
    John Richards sen.

  Court Record, Page 94—15 January, 1695-6: Will proven.

Page 64.

  Peering, Samuel, Windsor. Invt. £6-14-00. Taken 30 August, 1690, by John Wolcott and Timothy Phelps.
  Court Record, Page 17—4 September, 1690: Adms. to Samuel Cross, he to pay the debts and account to the Court, there being no other heir to it that is known.

Page 136.

  Peirse, Edward, Simsbury. Died 17 August, 1692. Invt. £4-16-00. Taken 31 August, 1692, by Samuel Willcoxson sen. and Peter Buell.
  Court Record, Page 66—1st March, 1693-4: Adms. to Samuel Williams. Peter Buell to pay the debts if the Estate will hold out.

Page 81.

  Peters, Arthur, Wethersfield. Died 30 October, 1690. Invt. £54-01-06. Taken by Samuel Hale Jr., Samuel Welles and Richard Treate Jr. Will dated 7 October, 1690.
  I Arthur Peters of Wethersfield do ordain this my last Will & Testament: I give to my truly & well beloved friend Ephraim Goodrich all my Estate, Whether in Lands or otherways, in any manner belonging to me, he paying all my just and lawfull debts.   ARTHUR X PETERS.
Witness: *Joseph Butler,*
    Rebeccah Bowman.

  Court Record, Page 21—28 November, 1690: Will Proven. Adms. to Ephraim Goodrich with Will annexed, he engageing to pay all of Arthur Peters' Just debts.

Page 212.

  Phelps, Joseph, Windsor. Invt. £473-05-06. Taken 2 September, 1695, by Abraham Phelps sen., John Porter and John Drake sen. The legatees: Hester Phelps, the Relict; Mary Phelps, age 20 years; Sarah Phelps, age 18 years; Joseph 16 years, Hannah Phelps 14, Mindwell 12, Hester 3, Abigail 2, Benoni 10 weeks.

Court Record, Page 89—5 September, 1695: Adms. to the Widow. Lieut. Abraham Phelps & John Porter to be Overseers.

Page 100—5 March, 1695-6: Order to Dist. by Mr. Porter, Abraham Phelps and Job Drake sen.

Page 24—(Vol. VII) 7 March, 1701-2: Deacon Job Drake presented a Dist. of the Estate of Joseph Phelps, late of Windsor decd.

Dist. File: To the Widow Hester Phelps, to Joseph, to Benoni, to Sarah, to Hannah, to Mindwell.

Page 121.

Phillips, George, Middletown. Invt. £30-18-00. Taken 11 January, 1691-2, by John Hamlin and Francis Whitmore.

Court Record, Page 37—14 January, 1691-2: Adms. to John Thompson of Middletown. This Court judge it meet to allow the widow a bed and furniture for herselfe and another for the children, which amounted in the Inventory at six pounds; a pot to dress her victuals, & a kettle, & a Tubb to wash her Clothes in & brue her beer, & a dish & spoon to eat her victualls with, & the rest to be reserved in the Adms. hand till the Creditors shall be appoynted to receive it.

Page 46—1st September, 1692: This Court made proclamation that all the Creditors to the Estate of George Phillips, deceased, should appeare at Middletown, at the house of Mr. John Thompson, on the 1st Wednesday of October next, by themselves or attourneys, to receive their dues from sayd Phillips his Estate so far as it will reach by proportion; & this Court doe nominate & appoint Mr. John Hamlin & Mr. Wm. Southmayd to make Dist. of the Estate amongst the Creditors by equall proportion as the Estate will beare.

Page 200.

Pitkin, William, Hartford. Died 15 December, 1694. Invt. £703-19-06. Taken 10 June, 1696, by Joseph Olmsted, Nathaniel Goodwin sen. & Daniel Bidwell. The children: George Pitkin, 20 years September next; Elizabeth Pitkin, 18 next October; Ozias, 16 years September. (Age of the 3 youngest Children.) Will dated 27 September, 1694.

I William Pitkin sen. of Hartford do make this my last Will & Testament: I give to my brother Roger Pitkin and to my sister Martha Clarke and to my Cousin Roger Pitkin to each of them 10 Shillings. Item. I give to my beloved brother Capt. Caleb Stanly & my brother Nathaniel Goodwin 5 shillings to each. And to each of my grand children now living that shall attain the age of 12 years, I give a new bible. To my beloved wife I give the one-half of the rest of my moveable or personal Estate, given to be hers forever, and one-third of all my houscing and Lands for her life only. I give to my daughter Hannah Cowles 10 acres of upland, to her and her heirs, including her now husband. To my daughter Elizabeth Pitkin and to my two sons Roger & William Pitkin I give the half of the Land given me by Joshua Uncas his son & the Land given me by Owaneco, Equally to divide. I give them all my Books & Manuscripts. I give to my two sons John and Nathaniel Pitkin and their heirs all my Meadow or Swamp Land northward of John Day's Lott up to the four acres given to my son William. To my two sons George and Nathaniel Pitkin my Dwelling house, Barn, Outhouses, and all the Land they stand on that are adjacent to them, as orchards, Gardens and Yards, and a pasture, Plow Land and Bush Lott. I make my wife Hannah Pitkin & my two sons John & Nathaniel Executors, my two sons Roger Pitkin and William Pitkin to be Overseers.

Witness: *Joseph Olmsted,*　　　　　　　WILLIAM PITKIN. Ls.
Daniel Bidwell.

Note: *See page 54-55 (Vol. VIII): Invt. of Capt. Daniel Clarke.* Court Record, Page 79—30 January, 1694-5: Will proven.

Page 57.

Porter, Daniel sen., Farmington. A Deed of Gift in lieu of a Will, dated 15 August, 1688:

To all Christian People to whome it may concerne: Know ye that I Daniel Porter sen. of Farmington, in the County of Hartford, in New England, for and in Consideration of my natural Love & Affection to my beloved wife & Children, & for other good Cause thereunto me moving, have given, granted, assigned, set over & confirmed, and do by these presents give, grant, assign, set over & confirm, fully, wholy, clearly, & unto them in manner as followeth: Item. I give unto my wife Mary Porter all my Household Goods & one Cow, the use of the longer rooms in my Dwelling house and a comfortable maintenance here provided for her by my sons John and Samuel Porter, during her Widowhood. I give my daughter Anna my heifer with a Calf, also some other Cow, to be wintered and summered for her by my sons John & Samuel Porter during the time of her single state; also a peice of Land, unless my sons see Cause to pay her the sum of £10. I give to my son Daniel Porter my Woodlott lying against Wethersfield Bounds. Unto my sons Daniel and Richard Porter I give my Farme lying part in Wallingford, butting upon Farmington on the North, 60 acres of it to Daniel Porter & 40 acres to Richard Porter. To my son Nehemiah Porter I give my 20 acres of Land in the Great Swamp, also my Division of Land adjacent to the Great Swamp. I give to my son John Porter the Land which I bought of Thomas Richeson, both Swamp & Upland. I give to my daughter my Lands lyeing in or by the Great Swamp which I received by an Exchange for other Lands with Joseph Woodford, all which parcels of Land aforementioned lyeing within the Township of Farmington except the forementioned Farme. To my sons John & Samuel Porter I doe give my Dwelling house & Outhouses, Barn, Orchard & Homelott in Farmington, and also my Lands in Farmington Meadow, and all my Land at the Long Swamp, and all my Pasture Land lying in the Mill Swamp, also all my Land at the Great Pond; & also I give unto my sons John & Samuel Porter all my Personal Estate except what was given before to my wife and my daughter Anna, as all my Cattle, Horses, Sheep & Swine, as also all my Tools & all the Implements belonging to my teame and Husbandry, the forementioned John & Samuel Porter receiveing and paying all my Just Debts and providing for their Mother according to what is before mentioned. The remainder of my Land lying in the Township of Farmingtown I give to my Children, Daniel, Nehemiah, Richard, John, Samuel & Anne Porter.

Witness: *John Stanly sen.,*   DANIEL X PORTER. LS.
    John Hooker.

Court Record, Page 14—9 April, 1690: The son of Daniel Porter, Bonesetter, of Farmington, presented a Deed of Gift whereby his Father disposed of his Estate. Approved as his Will & Deed.

Page 100-1-2-3.

Porter, John sen., Windsor. Died 2 August, 1688. Invt. £993-02-04. Taken 19 September, 1688, by John Moore sen. and Return Strong.

Whereas, our Honoured Father John Porter of Windsor Died Intestate and did not make any legal settlement of his Estate, He did inform us of some things of his purposes. We therefore, his Children, John Porter, James Porter, Nathaniel Porter, Samuel Porter, Samuel Grant sen. as guardian to Hezekiah Porter, and Thomas Bissell as guardian to Joseph Porter, in compliance with what we know to be the mind of our Father deceased, have for ourselves, our heirs, Executors & Administrators, Mutually and unanimously agreed to make Distribution of our Father's Estate as followeth. Signed by above named parties, by Enoch Drake in behalf of his Wife Sarah, and Thomas Loomis in behalf of his Wife Hanah, and Rebeckah and Ruth Porter, all signed and sealed. Entered and Recorded in Windsor, 2 Book of Records of Land, Page 241-242. Acknowledged 12 January, 1688-9, before John Allyn, one of the Council of his Majistie's Territory of New England.

Witnessed by *John Allyn.*
     Thomas Allyn.

Court Record, Page 11—6 March, 1689-90: Joseph Porter's Guardian being deceased, this Court appoint John Moore to be Guardian & to take Care of all his Concernments.

Page 25—5 March, 1690-1: Agreement exhibited and approved, and Adms. granted to John Porter.

Note: (W. R.)—*Nathaniel Loomis & Ruth Porter married 28 November, 1689; Timothy Loomis & Rebeckah Porter married 20 March, 1689-90; Thomas Loomis & Hannah Porter married 17 December, 1682.*

Page 11.

Porter, Robert. Invt. £253-00-01. Taken 19 September, 1689, by John Hart and Thomas Hart; in Farmington by John Stanly, Thomas Judd, Thomas Smith and Benjamin Barnes. The children: Thomas, Mary, Elizabeth, Sarah and Annah.

Court Record, Page 3—6 November, 1689: Invt. Exhibited. Adms. to Thomas Porter, son of the deceased. Dist: To the Widow one-third; the Adms. to pay to Mary Hubbard £5; to Abraham Andrews his Wife, £9; to Ann Browne, £31; to his second sister, Elizabeth Andrews, 5 Shillings, she having received her full portion; and the remainder to Thomas Porter forever.

Page 56—12 April, 1693: Thomas Porter in Court presented discharges From Thomas Andrews and Wife, Mary Hubbard, Abraham Andrews and his Wife, & John Browne, of all Claims against the Estate of Robert Porter Decd.

Page 196.

Porter, Samuel, Windsor. Invt. £210-00-00. Taken 19 December, 1694, by Timothy Phelps sen. and Thomas Stoughton. The next of kin: The Brothers & Sisters, John Porter, James Porter, Nathaniel, Hezekiah, Joseph Porter, Sarah Drake, Hannah Loomys, Rebeckah Loomys, Ruth Loomys.

Court Record, Page 78—25 December, 1694: Adms. to James & Nathaniel Porter. Daniel Heyden & Return Strong to distribute the Estate.

Page 106.

Pratt, Daniel, Hartford. Invt. £762-10-06. Taken 29 April, 1691, by John Wilson and Joseph Easton. Will dated 19 April, 1690.

Whereas, I Daniel Pratt am at prsent under weakness of body & know not how soon the Lord may put an end to my days, now being of good understanding & memory, I desire to set my house in order & to bestow & dispose of that Estate God hath betrusted me with by this my Last Will, that peace may be continued among my children I shall be Layd in the dust: I give and bequeath my house & Land where at present I dwell, both in the meadow & the upland, in Hartford & Windsor Bownds, wth all other my Buildings & orchards & garden therein being, as also my pasture on the right hand of the Road as you go from hence to Hartford (lying over against Col. Tallcot's Lot in the neck), my whole lot, wth in fence & out of fence, I give to my sonn Daniel & the heirs of his body lawfully begotten for ever; & for want of such heirs, the same to return to my daughters or their children. My said son Daniel paying to my daughters such legacies as I shall in this my Will appoint him. My personal Estate that I do not bestow upon my children I desire it be not

Inventoried, but leave it with my son Daniel & Enable him to pay debts and legacies. I doe give unto my seven daughters Thirty five pounds appeice. Some of them have received considerable already: to my daughter Hannah £29; to my daughter Goodwin I have already given her £33-10; and to my daughter Mary Sandford I have already given her £35-05. I make my son Daniel sole Executor, and to advise with Col. Allyn & Ensign Stanly.   DANIEL PRATT.

Witness: *John Allyn.*

Court Record, Page 30—31 April, 1691: Will Proven.

Will on File. (Not found on Record.)

Pratt, John sen. Will dated 1687. In the name of God I John Pratt of Hartford, being grown in years & at prsent Labouring under some weakness of body, am willing to set my Temporal affayres, that when I am gathered to my fathers peace may be continued in my family, Doe therefore make this my Last Will & Testament: My houseing & Lands given to me by my Honoured Father to be and remain according as he hath disposed of them by his Will, always provided that the possessor of them make good the Conditions expressed in his will, viz, that my wife stand quietly seized of one-third part thereof to her own proper use during her life. It is my Will also that the possessor of the Lands doe, according to my Father's Will, pay unto each of my daughters that shall survive me the sume of Twenty pounds apeice. And for the remainder of my Estate, it is my Will that it be left wholly with my wife to enable her to bring up my Children, so long as she bears my name; but if she marry she shall enjoy the thirds of my Lands above mentioned & Twenty pounds out of my Estate. The remainder of my Estate to be disposed to my Children: To my son John, besides what he receives of my Estate by my Father's will, 20 shillings; To my sons Joseph & Jonathan I give my now dwelling house & Barne, wth the Nine acres of Land upon which it stands, & the thirteen acres of Land in the neck, to be equally divided between them. And for the remainder of my personal Estate, it is my will that it be equally divided between my five daughters & Two younger sons, and delivered to them as they come of age if my wife can spare it, or Else at her Marriage or decease. I doe hereby Constitute my loveing Wife to be Executrix, and desire My Brother Daniell Pratt & Capt. John Allyn to be Overseers.   JOHN PRATT SENIOR.

Witness's names cut off.   9 April, 1687.

Court Record, Page 19—4 September, 1690: This Court appoynt Deacon Stephen Osmer & Joseph Easton to lay out to the Widow of John Pratt deceased, now the wife of John Sad, her thirds of the houseing and Lands according to the order of the General Court.

Page 51—15 February, 1692-3: Upon the motion of John Pratt that Joseph Pratt, he being of age to receive his portion given him by his Father John Pratt, & at the desire of his mother Hepsibah Sad, Executrix to the Estate of the sd. John Pratt, that the said Joseph Pratt might have his proportion of the Houseing and Lands set out to him that was given to him by his Father, The Court appoint Sergt. John Marsh & Robert Sandford to make an Equal division (according to the Will) between the sd. Joseph Pratt and his brother John Pratt.

Page 70-1.

Randall, Abraham, Windsor. Died 22 August, 1690. Invt. £140-05-00. Taken 31 August, 1690, by Timothy Thrall & Daniel Heiden. Will dated 7 June, 1689.

I Abraham Randall of Windsor doe make this my last Will & Testament: First, I comit my Soule unto the Hands of God, & my Body to be buried as near my first wife as conveniently may be. I haveing taken my Cousin Abraham Phelps from a Child to be my adopted son, living with me many years till his marriage, doe make him my heir and Executor, hopeing that he will faithfully perform this my Will. I give to my wife £4 per year, to be paid to her yearly according as I have given her in a writing; also, as an Addition to my first promise to her, my best Bed with other Household Stuffe. I give to my Cousin Isaac Phelps of Westfield 20 Shillings; also to my Cousin Joseph Phelps of this town 20 Shillings. The rest of my Estate I give to my Cousin Abraham Phelps sen.

Witness: *Timothy Thrall sen.,*　　ABRAHAM RANDALL. Ls.
John X Denslow.

Court Record, Page 18—4 September, 1690: Will proven.

Windsor Records:

Abraham Randall & Mary (Phelps) married 1st December, 1640; Abraham Randall & Elizabeth Kerbe of Middletown were married 27 October, 1681. Elizabeth Randolph was living at Wethersfield, 1697, who was sometime the wife of John Kirby of Middletown.

Page 10.

Rixs, Thomas, Wethersfield. He died 21 May, 1690. Invt. £36-00-00. Taken by John Chester and Benjamin Churchill.

Roberts, John. Court Record, Page 89—5 September, 1695: Elizabeth Roberts, Atty. to John Roberts of Long Island, Plntf; Samll Spencer, defendant. In an action of the Case for that he hath illegally entered into & doth hold possession of a certain house and Land in Hartford which of right doth belong to sayd John Roberts in right of his Wife Elizabeth above sayd, she being heir at law to the sayd house & Land, which is bounded by the High way south, & Doctor Hooker's or a chart Lane east, Zachary Sandford's Land North, Mr Way's Land west, to a surrendery of the sayd house & Land into possession of sayd Elizabeth Roberts, wth damage & Cost to the value of Twenty pownds. In this action the Jury find for the defendant with costs of Court.

Page 198.

Sadd, John. Died 20 December, 1694. Invt. £1901-05-10. Taken 1st January, 1694-5, by Joseph Wadsworth, Ciprian Nichols & John Merrells. A Child: son Thomas Sadd, 4 years of age 10 March next. Will dated 26 July, 1694.

I John Sadd of Hartford, Tanner, doe make this my last Will & Testament: My Will is that my Funeral Charges & all my Just Debts which I owe be truly and fully paid out of my Estate. And unto my son John Sadd in England I give all my Money & all my Money Debts, whatsoever are owing or shall be owing unto me, excepting only the Sume of £120, that is to say, I give unto each of the Children of my sd. son John Sadd the sume of £10 in New England Money, and all the residue of my sd. Money and Money Debts, excepting the £120 before excepted, I give my sd. son and his heirs forever. And my Will is that the sd. Money or the effects thereof be sent into England to my sd. son and his Children at his and their adventure, or be remitted to them by Bills of Exchange or otherwise, or that it be paid to them or their Order in New England, according to the Discretion of my Executors. I give unto my son Thomas Sadd, if he live to the age of 21 years, all the residue of my whole Estate not otherwise disposed of by this my last Will. I give & bequeath unto my sd. son Thomas Sadd all my Houseing & Lands, Chattells, Goods, Stock, Debts, or other Estate what soever to me belonging & remaining as abovesd., to be to his Use for his Bringing up and Christian Education in Comely manner. And in particular I give unto him the above reserved sume of £120 in Money or Money Debts. But it is my Will that if my Executors be put to take any out of my money Debts in any other Specie than money, that then so much of those Debts as shall be paid in other Specie than Money shall not be paid my son John Sadd in England or his Children, but to my son Thomas Sadd, still within the sd. sume of £120, & that this sume be (with all my other Estate) given to my son Thomas Sadd in this my last Will, in my Executors' hands to improve as they see Best for my sd. son Thomas his use till he come of age. And my Will is that my sd. Executors hereafter named doe see my sd. son Thomas well educated and brought up out of my sd. Estate hereby given him. And further my Will is that the Executors of this my last Will shall in the first place (upon or after my decease) take Care and provide out of my Estate provision for my loving wife & her Child my sd. son Thomas Sadd for one year. And lastly, I doe make and appoint my trusty friend Mr. William Pitkin sen., Ensign Zachary Sandford and Deacon John Wilson of Hartford to be the Executors of this my last Will.

Witness: *Caleb Stanly Jr.,*   JOHN SADD. LS.
   John Downe.

Note: [*The Original Will was written "Wm Pitkin senior," and afterwards was written over to read "Junior."*]

Court Record, Page 78—1st January, 1694-5: The Witness testify that an Alteration had been made in the Will by substituting Wm Pitkin Jr. for Wm. Pitkin senior. Yet Capt. Caleb Stanly and John Easton did both Testify that John Sadd, immediately before his death, in their presence, caused Mr. William Pitkin Jr. to be put in Room of William Pitkin sen. in said Will. He having neglected his Wife in a maner, alloting her no considerable portion of his Estate, & this Court finding by Testimony that sayd Sadd, Immediately before his death, did grant that his Wife should have a third part of the Estate of the deceased, both personal and real, during life, and the personal to be to her heirs forever, excepting £150 [a Recorder's Error] *(£120)*, which John Sadd reserved for his son in England [a Recorder's error, see above Will] with consent of his wife Hepzibah sometime since, The remainder to be disposed of according to the Will, only the profits of the youngest son Thomas Sadd his Estate shall be to the Widow for the Maintenance of her son Thomas till he come of age or be married, & returned to her yearly by the Executors. The Will thus Confirmed.

Page 88.

Saunders, George, Windsor or Simsbury. Died 16 November, 1690. Invt. £85-03-00. Taken 24 February, 1690-1, by John Fyler, Sargt. John Williams, John Higley and Thomas Barber. The children: Mary, age 13 years, Abiah 6 years.

Court Record, Page 32—3 September, 1691: Adms. to the Widow Mehetabell Saunders and John Roberts, who were appointed to return to the Court in March next an Accot of the Debts, that so the Court may come to a Dist. of the Estate.

Page 70—12 April, 1694: The Adms. of George Saunders' estate exhibited an account of their Adms., and found that by Loss of the Estate and Debts, & Spent by the Widow on the Children, so much that brought

	£	s	d
the Estate that remains to be	42	01	10
In Land,	30	00	00
In Gozard's Bill,	4	02	00
In John Roberts' Hands,	5	14	10
In the Relict of George Saunders Hands in Goods,	2	05	00

There are 3 Children: The 2 eldest Children's ages are in the Inventory, & Hannah, born after her father's death, will be 3 years old the 23rd of May next. Dist. as followeth:

	£ s d
To the Widow,	14-00-00
To each of the daughters,	8-13-04

Page 116.

Scott, Edmund sen., Waterbury. Invt. £10-12-16. Taken 16 April, 1691, by Abraham Andrews & Thomas Judd. Invt. in Farmington, £17-11-06, which is in the Hands of Widow Porter, was taken by John Lee & John Orton. The children of the Deceased Edmund Scott are: Joseph, Edmon, Samuel, George, Jonathan, David, Robert, Elizabeth & Hannah.

Will in the Form of a Deed of Gift, dated 11 June, 1690: This present Writing witnesseth, that I Edmund Scott sen. of Waterbury, in the County of Hartford & Colony of Connecticut, for Good & Lawfull reasons mee moving thereunto, have given, & by these presents doe give, grant, bequeath, bestow upon, alienate and pass over unto my well beloved children as followeth: I give to my son Joseph Scott 20 acres of Land in the West Swamp in Farmington. I give to my son Edmund Scott, besides what I have formerly given him, my Lott in the Neck which adjoins Daniel Porter North & John Brunson South, in Waterbury. I give to Samuel my son, and my son Jonathan Scott, my whole Right & Title in Farmington of Houseing, Barn, Homelotts, Orchards, Meadows and Uplands, with the whole Rights belonging thereunto, both of Lands already divided or undivided, excepting what I have heretofore mentioned as given to my son Joseph, and 2 Divisions of Land in the East Division of Farmington Bounds, butting on Wethersfield Bounds & Hartford Bounds. The Division on the North side of the Path that leads to Hartford I give to my daughter Elizabeth Davis, and after her death to her son John Davis, to him & to his heirs forever. The South Division, that is, south from Hartford Path butting on Wethersfield Bounds, I give to my daughter Hannah Brunson and to her heirs forever. I give to my sons, George Scott, David Scott & Robert Scott, my whole Right and Title in the Township of Waterbury, both of Houseing, Barn, Homelott, 3-Acre Lott, all my Meadows & Upland, divided or undivided, belonging to me, with all the Rights thereunto belonging, except what I have herein given to my son Edmund Scott. I give to my son George Scott, Jonathan Scott, David Scott & Robert Scott, all my Moveable Estate, quick and Dead, both of Stock & Moveables. I the abovesd. Edmund Scott sen. doe by these presents freely, fully and forever remit, release & surrender all my Right, Title, Claim & Interest in all the Premises herein mentioned, to these my Children, to have and to hold from the day of the date hereof forever, & deliver into possession of these my Children, their Executors, Administrators or Assigns, not to make alienation or Sale of any Lands during my Natural life without my Consent, that is, of any of the Lands herein specified.   As Witness my Hand.

Witness: *Thomas Judd sen.,*   EDMUND X SCOTT SEN. LS.
   Thomas Judd Jr.

Acknowledged this 12th of June, 1690, before
                         Thomas Judd, Commissioner.

Court Record, Page 32—3 September, 1691: Invt. Exhibited. The Estate is ordered to be distributed amongst the Children: To the Eldest brother a double portion, £3-10-00, and to the rest of the Children £1-15-00.

Page 157.

Scranton, Nathaniel, Wethersfield. Died 13 March, 1692-3. Invt. £36-17-00. Taken 16 March, 1692-3, by Joseph Wright and John Welles. Will dated 13 February, 1692-3.
   I Nathaniel Scranton of Wethersfield doe make this my last Will & Testament: My Will is that my loving friend William Goodrich shall have the peice of Land that I had of Capt. Robert Welles, lying and being in the Township of Wethersfield and abutts on Nathaniel Cole of Hartford and a Highway South, the sides on Land of Thomas Bunce of Hartford East, & Ephraim Goodrich West. The sd. William Goodrich paying all my Just and Due Debts, paying himselfe in the first place. My Will further is yt my loving friend Thomas Fitch would be Executor.

Witness: *Thomas Fitch,*   NATHANIEL X SCRANTON.
   Jonathan Buck.

Court Record, Page 53—30 March, 1693: Will Proven, & Thomas Fitch accepted the Executorship.

Page 58.

Sension, Nicholas, Windsor. Invt. £11-17-00. Taken 8 April, 1690, by Timothy Phelps sen and James Ennoe.
   Court Record, Page 14—9 April, 1690: Adms. to Samuel Willson. Dist: To the Eldest son living, a pewter platter and a Coverlid; and to the Wife of Josiah Gillett, all her wearring Clothes & Skillet; the remainder of Nicholas Sension's Estate is past over to Samuel Willson. Approved.
   Note: *Nicholas Sension married Isable (   ) 12 June, 1645. Nicholas Sension died 18 September, 1689. Isable, wife of Nicholas Sension, died 2nd October, 1689.*—(W. R.)

Page 33-4.

Shear, Sarah, Windsor. Invt. £128-16-06. Taken 1st November, 1689, by John Fyler, Samuel Cross and John Cross. Will dated 16 October, 1689.

I Sarah Shear, being very sicke, doe see Cause to make this my last Will: I give my Still to Dr. Hastings. I give to Nathaniel Dickinson's wife my black wascoat, & Cloth wascoat with silver lace, and my silver Thimble & Seale, & fower red earthern panns, & my silck scarfe and Hood. I give to Hannah Palmer my Brass Kittle, & my great Iron Kitle, & my litle pot, & one pewter platter, two saucers, & two porringers, & three spons, & Stocks of Bees, & my riding Hood. To Nathaniel Dickinson's Wife I will my best bed & bedding, & two Poringers Marked S. S. Also, to William Persons I will about 6 yards of Occum Cloth. Also to Samuel Forward, all my Cooper's Tools. My Cross-Cut Saw I will to Stephen Loomis & Timothy Hosford & Samuel Forward. Also I will to John Grihms my Cow & two small pigs or shoates. To my Cousin Jacob Gibbs I give all the rest of my Estate, both Houseing & Lands, and all moveables, & my desire is that my cousin Jacob Gibbs be my Executor, that he pay my lawful debts & bury my body in a comely manner. I desire Benajah Holcomb & Michael Tayntor to be Overseers.

Witness: *John X Williams,*   SARAH X SHEAR.
          John Hosford.

Court Record, Page 6—11 November, 1689: Will Proven.

Page 94-5-6.

Skinner, Corpll John, Hartford. Died 15 September, 1690. Invt. £874-08-06. Taken by Caleb Stanly, Ciprian Niccols & Stephen Hosmer. Will dated 18 July, 1690.

I John Skinner of Hartford doe see Cause to make this my last Will & Testament: I give to my wife Mary Skinner *(with special Privileges of House and Home)* all my Moveable Estate of what kind soever, she paying out of the same such legacies as I shall appoint her unto my Children, makeing her sole Executrix. I give to my Eldest son John Skiner the one-half of my home lott on which my dwelling house standeth, he to have the North side next to his Uncle John Easton's Land. I give to my son Joseph Skiner the other half of my house lott. I doe give unto my son Joseph Skiner all my right & Interest I have in a wood Lott that was formerly my Father Skiner's Lott in the ox pasture ajoyning on Mr. Haynes his Land South, on the river on the West, & on Thomas Cadwell's Land on the North, & upon Mr. Hooker's Land on the East. Joseph Skiner to pay his Brother Nathaniel Skiner £10, also to pay his brother Richard Skiner £10, Also to pay his brother Thomas Skiner £10. I give to my son Thomas Skiner 24 acres of Land which I bought of Mr. Steven Hollister, Richard Hall and John Welles of Wethersfield, as it stands recorded to me in the Book of Records of Land for the Towne of Wethersfield, to him and his heirs forever. I give to my daughter Mary Skiner £30. I give to my daughter Sarah £30. I desire my loving brother John Easton, my friend Caleb Stanly, & my brother Joseph Easton to be Overseers.

Witness: *Caleb Stanly,* JOHN SKINNER. Ls.
    Joseph Easton.

Court Record, Page 24—5 March, 1690-1: Will approved.

Page 209.

Skinner, Mary, Widow, Hartford. Died 18 June, 1695. Invt. £291-00-06. Taken by Ciprian Niccols & Thomas Bunce. Will dated 18 June, 1695.

I Mary Skinner of Hartford, being weake in Body yet sound in mind, do make this my last Will & Testament: I give to my son John Skinner one Cow, 4 Sheep & 40 Shillings. I give to my son Joseph Skinner all the Trooper's furniture, with the best of the Horses, which he shall choose. I give to my son Nathaniel £3 in Money, being part of what is in his Brother Joseph's Hand. I give to my son Richard one Cow, 2 Steers, 2 yearlings, one Horse, also 8 Sheep, also 40 Shillings in Money. I give to my son Thomas Skinner one Cow, 2 yerling Calves, one Horse, 12 Sheep and 40 Shillings. I give to my daughter Mary Carter £3, and to my gr. daughter Mary, the daughter of Mary Carter, £8. I give to my daughter Sarah Skinner £20 in Money, in her Brother John's Hand. I give to my son Joshua Carter 4 Sheep. I appoint my son Joseph to be my Executor.

Witness: *John Easton,* MARY X SKINNER.
    Joseph Easton.

Court Record, Page 88—9 July, 1695: Will approved.

Page 52.

Smith, Joseph, Hartford. Invt. £170-13-00. Taken 20 February, 1689-90, by Nathaniel Stanly & Jacob White. Will dated 13 June, 1689.

Whereas I, Joseph Smith of Hartford, being very sicke and weake, yet of perfect memory and Understanding, to prevent any future troubles, I doe ordain this my last Will & Testament: I give and bequeath unto my wife Lydia Smith all my Estate, both Personal & Real, during the terme of her natural life, only my Just Debts being paid out of the same; and then my Estate to be disposed to my Children as my wife shall see Cause. I ordain my dear and loving wife my whole & sole Executrix, and desire Mr. Thomas Hooker & Nathaniel Stanly to be Overseers.

Witness: *Stephen Hosmer,* JOSEPH SMITH. Ls.
    Sarah Stanly.

Court Record, Page 11—6 March, 1689-90: Will proven.

508 PROBATE RECORDS. VOL. V,

Page 197.

Smith, Joseph, Haddam. Died in Barbadoes, 1693. Invt. £49-01-07. Taken 3 January, 1694-5, by James X Welles and Tho: X Clarke. Will dated 30th May, 1693.

In the name of God, Amen. The last Will & Testament of Joseph Smith of Haddam, on Connecticut River: First, my Lands to my Brothers & Sisters in equal proportion. 2ndly, The Money in my Brother William Ely's Hand to be equally divided amongst my Brothers & Sisters, & what Money is due to me from Capt. John Joes (Ives) shall likewise be divided amongst my Brothers & Sisters as before. And a Broad Cloth Coat and a Caliminco Jacket & Breeches and 2 paire of Stockings and white Neck Cloth to be divided amongst the rest of my Estate, and my Mother to have an Equal Share of all that has been mentioned.

Witness: *Abraham Gording,*   JOSEPH SMITH. Ls.
Benjamin Savage, Samuel White.

The Cloth at the Francklin's, in Boston, where he did lodge when he was in Boston.

Part of the Inventory of Mr Joseph Smith of Haddam:

	£ s d
By Cash in his Brother Ely's Hand,	15-00-00
By Cash in his Brother John Smith's Hand,	6-11-07
By a Broad Cloth Sute,	6-00-00
By Land at Mattamodus, 60 acres,	15-00-00
By Land on the River side,	6-10-00
By a 3-acre Lott on the East side of the 30-Mile Island,	
	49-01-07

Court Record, Page 79—30 January, 1694-5: Will approved. Adms. to John Smith with the Will annexed.

Page 44.

Smith, Richard, Hartford. Invt. £21-07-06. Taken 9 December, 1689, by James Steele, Ciprian Niccols & Stephen Hosmore.

Court Record, Page 9—20 January, 1689: An Invt. of the Estate of Richard Smith was exhibited in Court, and Oath made by the Relict that she hath made a true presentment of the Estate of the Decd to the Apprisers so far as at present is known, and if more comes to her knowledge it shall be added to the Inventory.

On File. (Not found on Record.)

Smith, Simon, Haddam. Will dated 11 November, 1687: I Simon Smith senior of Haddam, being aged and being sensabell of my mortalyty, and at This time being visited with sickness, doe give my body to the dust in hopes of a Glorias reserecktion, and my Spirit to God that gave it. Doe make this my Last will and Testament, being sound in meamorie: I give to my Loveing Wife The use of my dwelling houss and two rowes of Apples Trees in my horchard, she takeing her choyes, and five poundes per yeare during her Widowhood, to be paid bv my sonns according to their proportions That they shall have of my Es'ate, and one Cowe to be kept yearly by my Sones, and fowr Shepe to be kept yearly for her use, and fowr poundes in good marchantabell Corne, Rie and Indian, to be paid her the next spring, and as much of the houeshould stores as she hath need of. I give to my sonn John my Lott by his in the Comon fild, and five pounds out of my Estate as it shall be inventoried. I give to my son Simon my upper Lott in the upper meadow. I give to my son Joseph my Cow, meadow Lott, and my swamp on the east side of the great River, and my Lott in the equall deuishon, and all my right at Machamoodas. I give to my Sonn benjamin my hows and barn and all my homested, and my meadow Lott in the hom medow, swamp and upland. I give to my daughter Elizabeth eaighten pounds, and to my daughter Susanah Sixten pounds, and to my daughter Mary Sixten pounds. And my Will is that my two Lottes in the upper medow be left for part of their portions. And if any of my Sonnes will take the above said Lotes as they shall be inventoried, and pay my daughters, they shall have Liberty; and the rest of their portions shall be paide out of my Estate as it shall be inventoried. And if their be any over pluss, it shall be equally disposed of amongest them. Also my Will is that my sonn benjamin be my Executor to se This my Will full filed.

Test: *George Gates,*   SIMON SMITH.
  John Bayle.

Hartford, 8 March, 1687-8: At a Court of Common pleas there held, George Gates & John Bayley, upon their Corporate oathes, Testified that Simon Smith in their prsence signed and declared the above written to be his Last will & Testament, and that he was of good memory when he did the same.

Page 171.

Starr, Comfort, Middletown. He Died October, 1693. Invt. £89-08-00. Taken December, 1693, by William Cheeny, Samuel Collins and John Hall. The children: Comfort, age 24 years, Joseph 17, Benjamin 15, Thomas 7, Daniel 4, Mary Starr 22, Hannah 20, Rachel 10. Mary Starr, the Widow, presented the Invt. in Court. Adms. to the Widow, Mary Starr. *(No other Rec. found.)*

Page 45.

Talcott, Lt. Col. John. An inventory of the Estate of John Talcot Esq., Lieutenant Colonall & one of his Matie's Justices of the Peace &

Quorum for the County of Hartford, who died 23 July, 1688, the total amount of Personal Estate being Inventoried at £282-03-06. Taken the 18 of September, 1688, by John Gilbert & Jonathan Ashley. In Lands, £1941-00-00. Taken 3 November, 1689. Also 2 Negroes, an Indian Boy and an Indian Girle, & a Bull, £41-00-00. Total: £2272-03-06.

Court Record, Page 8—20 November, 1689: The Personal Estate Distributed by the Adms. & Nathaniel Stanly. The Real Estate to be left for the Consideration of the Court of Assistants until May next.

Note: *The eldest son surviving made claim to the whole of the realty as his by right under English law.*—(C. W. M.)

Two parcells of land, given by Joshua Sachem, not divided. Contents unknown.

Page 122-3-4.

Talcott, Capt. Samuel, Wethersfield. Died 11 November, 1691. Invt. £2180-01-06 (£361-01-06 Personal Estate and £1820 in Lands). Taken 21 December, 1691, by John Deming, Daniel Rose, Benjamin Churchill & Nathaniel Foote. Will dated 22 April, 1691.

I Samuel Talcott of Wethersfield doe make this my last Will & Testament: I bequeath unto my wife Mary £10 per Annum and the Use of one lower room in my house, which she shall choose, with convenient Celerage and Use of an Oven or ovens in the same, with suitable Land for a Garden as she shall desire, and the Keeping of one Cow both Winter and Summer. All these particulars specified are according to our Contract & Agreement before marriage, and to continue only during her Widowhood. I give to my son Samuel Talcott the south side of my Homelott, which lott butts upon High Street West, the Great Meadow East, John Deming's Land North, Thomas Bunce his Homelott South, with the House, Great Barn, & the Buildings thereon; Land in the Great Meadow, bought of Samuel Sherman; Land in the Wet Swamp, bought of Richard Gildersleaue; also Land that butts upon Thomas Williams and William Colfax, other Land adjoining John Nott, and Land against Capt. Robert Welles. To my son John Talcott I give part of my Homelott, part of that Lott which was Mr. Crabb's, butting on High Street West, on the Meadow East, Siding on Mr. John Deming's Homelott North, and Samuel Talcott South; Lands bought of Mr. Richard Lawes. I give unto my son Eleazer Talcott Land in the West Field adjoining William Goodrich; Land in Beaver Meadow and my 50-acre Lott in the West Division, next Farmington Bounds. I give to my son Joseph Talcott, 30 acres in the West Field and 12 acres I bought of Samuel Sherman. To my son Benjamin Talcott, half of my Land on the East side of the Connecticut River bought of Mr. Samuel Sherman and Mr. Richard Gildersleaue, part of my Undivided Land lately purchased of the Indians on the East side of the River, also 200 acres given me by the General Court near Middletown Bounds, joining Mr. Willis his Land and Mr. John Whiting. I give to my son Nathaniel Talcott half my Lott at Naubuck. I give unto my daughter

Hannah Chester £90, and to my daughter Rachel £80. I appoint my son Samuel to be Executor, and desire Capt. Robert Welles and Ensign Samuel Butler to be Overseers.   SAMLL TALCOTT.

Court Record, Page 37—23 January, 1691-2: Will & Invt. Exhibited. *And his hand being so well known, he having wright it all with his own hand, the Court accepted of it, together with the Inventory.*

Taner, Rebecca. Court Record, Page 15—31 July, 1690: Rebecca Taner informs this Court that her husband is willing to deliver up the Estate that belongs to her Children, she desireing that her brother Thomas Shaylor and Amos & Samuel Tinker may take care for the safe keeping for the Children. This Court so order, and they give standing security to this Court.

Taylor, John. Court Record, Page 73—6 September, 1694: John Taylor presented to this Court a paper purporting to be a Will of his late Father John Taylor deceased, signed by himself and Bray Rossiter. This Court grant Adms. with the Will annexed to John Taylor.

Page 33.

Taylor, Widow of Stephen. [Elizabeth Nowell, married 25 October, 1649 (2nd wife). She Died 5 Aug., 1689.—W. R.] Invt. £14-09-06. Taken 11 November, 1689, by Samuel Grant sen. and Samuel Grant Jr.

Court Record, Page 7—11 November, 1689: Adms. to Stephen Taylor. Order to Dist. the Estate equally among her children. Stephen Taylor, the Husband, died 1st September, 1688. (W. R.)

Page 114-115.

Terry, Lt. John, Simsbury. Died 30 April, 1691. Invt. £548-17-06. Taken 16 June, 1691, by Joseph Wadsworth, John Higley and Peter Buell. The children: Stephen 25 years, Samuel 13, John 7, Daughter Elizabeth 27, Sarah 22, Mary 17, Abigail 5, Widow Elizabeth. Will dated 18 April, 1690.

The last Will & Testament of John Terry: I being weake in Body but having my Understanding, I think it best to set in order that little which God hath left me as followeth: Item. I give my beloved son Stephen Terry my house & Homested & Barn & half my Land lying within the Fence which I bought of Joseph Persons, with all my Stock of Cattell, Horses, Sheep & Swine & Household Goods, with whatever

Moveable Estate is truly mine, with half my Share in the Mills.   This I give him on the Conditions following: that is to say, he shall provide for & honourably mayntayne my beloved wife during the time of her natural life, & also pay as followeth: To my daughter Elizabeth £30 with what she hath already received, & to my daughters Sarah, Mary, & Abigail, £30 apiece, provided they live with their brother Stephen until they are married, & he shall provide for them during the time of their abode with him; but if either of my daughters goe from their brother Stephen without his free Consent before they be married, then he shall pay them But £20 that so leave him; & my aforesaid son Stephen shall mayntayne & bring up all my Children decently.   I give to my sons Samuel & John Terry all my lands not before mentioned, with half my share in the Mills.   I Constitute my son Stephen Terry sole Executor.   I appoint Mr. Edward Thompson and Lieut. Joseph Wadsworth my Overseers.

Witness: *Samuel Wadsworth,*   JOHN TERRY. LS.
　　　　 John Wadsworth.

Court Record, Page 31—3 September, 1691:   Will approved.
　　Page 108—(Vol. X) 7 December, 1725:   This Court appoint Benjamin Addams, John Humphrey & John Case of Simsbury to Dist. the Lands of Lt. John Terry, sometime of Simsbury, Decd, according to the last Will.
　　Dist. File: 12 November, 1729-30:   To Stephen, to Samuel, to John Terry.   By John Humphrey & Benjamin Addams & John Case Jr.

Page 203.

Thompson, John, Middletown.   Invt. £73-12-00.   Taken 6 December, 1694, by William Cheeny, John Hall & William Sumner.
　　An Account of what Margaret Thompson had pd for her decd husband:

	£ s d
To his Coffin,	0-10-00
For Digging the Grave,	0-05-00
For Rum for his Funeral,	0-05-04
For a Town Rate, was due 3 years past,	0-08-00
And 2 Town rates not yt paid, & a Country rate not yt pd,	0-08-03
Paid the Minister's rate,	0-10-04
For my Winter's Wood,	4-00-00
The Corne which was given to my Children by Mr. Richd. Blackledge of Strafford, which my husband had for his Use and promised to pay again to my Children,	10-00-00

£15-18-08

Court Record, Page 85—10 April, 1695: Adms. granted to Margaret the Relict and Lt. Wetmore.

Page 95—19 February, 1695-6: Joseph Leonard moves this Court to appoint an Adms., the former Adms. not accepting. This Court grant sd. Leonard Adms.

Page 126—4 March, 1696-7: Edward Turner of Middletown, Plaintiff, as Adms. to the Estate of John Blake; Joseph Leonard of Springfield, as Adms. to the Estate of John Thompson, late of Middletown decd, by attachment in Action of Debt to the value of 44 Shillings wth Damages. The Jury find for the Defendent the Cost of Court, and this Court accepts the Verdict and refer the Issue of the Case to Capt. Hamlin, the papers to be delivered to him.

Page 144—(Vol. IV) 10 April, 1695: Adms. was granted unto Joseph Leonard upon the Estate of John Thompson. He now appears & gives an Account of his Adms., and there remains due to him £22-01-08. He prays this Court that his Bonds may be cancelled. They grant his Request and give him a *Quietus Est.*

Page 148—11 March, 1696-7: Whereas, Joseph Leonard of Springfield did at the Last Court obtain his *Quietus Est.* from his Adms. on the Estate of John Thompson, it appearing that he sd. John Thompson died non-solvent: This Court grants Adms. on sd. Estate yet remaining to John Hamlin Esq., and he to attend the Direction of this Court: 1st, that upon Receipt of the sd. Estate, he to pay to Edward Turner of Middletown, if it appear to be due, in Right of his wife, what it is, and the rest to be distributed according to Law.

Page 111.

Tudor, Owen, Windsor. Invt. £294-07-00. Taken 3d March, 1690-1, by John Moore sen. and John Porter. Will *Nuncupative.*

John Loomis, aged about 39 years, Testifieth & saith: I was watching with Owen Tudor sen. about 3 nights before he dyed, & I Judged him to be in his right mind, & He declared to me and others that the girls should have £10 apiece, & Samuel & Owen should have the rest, only Samuel should have a double portion; & further Sayeth not. Rosamond Elmer Testifyeth the same. Abraham Colt testifyeth the same.

Court Record, Page 27—March, 1690-1: Will proven & ordered to be recorded.

See W. R., also "Lands," Sec. State Office:

Owen Tudor & Mary Skinner were married 13 November, 1651.
Samuel Tudor, son of Owen Tudor, born 5 December, 1652.
Sarah Tudor, daughter of Owen Tudor, born 5 December, 1652.
Owen Tudor, son of Owen Tudor, born 2 March, 1654.
Anne Tudor, daughter of Owen Tudor, born 16 October, 1657
Jane Tudor, daughter of Owen Tudor, born 16 October, 1657.

Wade, Robert. Court Record, Page 115—3 September, 1696: Inventory of the Estate of Robert Wade of Windham exhibited by Peter Cross. This Court grant Adms. to Peter Cross and Jonathan Ginnings. Also appoint Lt. John Fitch and Ensign Crane to assist in the Management of the Estate.

Page 8-9.

Wadsworth, John Esq., Farmington. Invt. £1398-06-00. Taken 6 November, 1689, by John Stanly sen. & Samuel Cowles. The legatees: The Widow Sarah Wadsworth; Samuel, age 29 years; Sarah 31, John 27, William 18, Nathaniel 15, James 12, Thomas 9, & Hezekiah 6 years; Timothy Root, age 8 years, & John Root, 4 years of age. Will dated 9 September, 1689.

The last Will & Testament of John Wadsworth: I being weake in Body yet through the Goodness of God having my Understanding, my Mind is to dispose of that little God hath lent me as follows: Imprimis. I give to my Wife Sarah Wadsworth the use of my dwelling house and HomeLott, with barn & outhouses, during the time of her natural life; also £12 a year to be paid out of my Lands during her life; also I give her £100 out of my personal Estate in what she shall chuse, as her own proper Estate to dispose of as she seeth cause; & also I give my negro man to my wife. It. I give to my son Samuel Wadsworth the hous and hom lot I bought of Thomas Orton; and also half my ten-acre pece lying in paquabok medow, buting northward on Samuel Gredly, & Southward on Samuel hooker, and East wardly on the River, & west wardly on a brook; and also half that pece caled shade Land lying between samuel hooker & Stephen Root; and five acres of grass Land at the lower end of the medow, next samuel gredly; also three acres & three Roods, be it more or less, Lying between samuel hooker and samuel gredly. These parcels of Land, except his hom Lott lying in paquabok medow, this I give to him & his heirs forever. It. I give to my daughter sarah Root & her heires £60 besids what she hath already. It. I give to my sons Thomas, Jeames an hezekiah, £10 apeace besides their proportion with the Rest of their brethren. It. I give all the Rest of my arable Land to my sons John, William & nathaniel & Jeames & Thomas & hezekiah, to be equally divided amongst them; also my hous & homsted after the decease of my wife. My Will is my son John should have the Lott I bought of John bronson, with the hous that stands upon it, as part of his portion. My lott lying in the Town between Stephen hart and daniel andrus to be divided as the arable Land within the medow. I constitute my wife sole Executrix, & my sons Samuel & John my Administrators, they to pay 40s apeace to John & Timothy Root, my daughter's Children. Capt. John & Ensign Nathaniel Standly to be Overseers.

Witness: *Samuel Cowles,*   JOHN WADSWORTH. Ls.
        Thomas Porter.

Court Record, Page 5—6 November, 1689: Will approved. Capt. John Stanly & Samuel Cowles are desired by this Court to Dist. the Estate according to the Will.

Page 58-9.

Ward, William sen., Ensign, Middletown. Died 28 March, 1690. Invt. £603-15-00. Taken 3 May, 1690, by Nathaniel White & Ensign Samuel Collins. Legatees: The widow, Phebe Ward; Thomas Ward, Anne Warde, Dorothy Ward, Susannah Ward. And William Ward, son of Thomas Ward. Will dated 25 December, 1688.

The last Will & Testament of William Ward sen. of Middletown, being in health of Body and having the perfect Use of my Understanding and Memory, yet not knowing the day of my death, and willing to leave peace in my family after my decease, is as followeth: I give to my wife Phebe Ward my Dwelling house, Homsted & all my Medow & swamp in the long meadow, & halfe my household goods which are properly so, during the time of her Widowhood. I give to my Eldest son Thomas Warde the remainder of the Homested where he dwells, at my decease; and after his mother's, so much more adjoyning to that as comes downe to a ditch and straight over from his Father Tapping's to Ensign Cheeny's. I give to him, for his son William, my Lott in the wester most range of Lotts. I give one-halfe of my fulling Mill and one-halfe the Land belonging to it, & halfe my Carpenter's tools, to him my said son. I give to my son William Warde, Land after his Mother's decease or marriage, one Loom, & halfe of my Weaver's tools, half my fulling Mill and halfe the Land belonging to it. I give to my son John Warde, after his Mother's decease or Marriage, if he be of age, my houseing and the remainder of the Homested, one Loom, one-halfe of the Weaver's tools, my part of my Bake house, with Lands. I give to my daughter Phebe Hall £5, to my daughter Sarah Hand £15. I give to my three daughters, Ann, Dorothy & Susannah, the remainder of my Stock. I give to my son William my fowling piece, one Musket & Cutlass. I give to John one Musket and a Sword; To Thomas, my Hulbard & Musket and a sword. I appoint my wife Phebe Administrator, and my two sons, Thomas & William, Overseers.

Witness: *William Cheeny,*   WILLIAM WARDE. Ls.
    John Hall sen.

A Codicil, dated 27 March, 1690: I give to my sons-in-law, Samuel Hall and Benjamin Hand. Finding his fulling Mill is bettered and his Estate increased, he gives more to his wife and daughters, as well as to his son William, now come of age.

Witness: *William Cheeny,*   WILLIAM WARDE. Ls.
    John Hall sen.

Court Record, Page 14—27 May, 1690: Adms. to Phebe, the relict, and to the 2 sons, Thomas & William Warde, with will annexed.

Page 62.

Warner, Robert, Middletown. Invt. £415-05-06. Taken 5 June, 1690, by Nathaniel White, Francis Wetmore, William Sumner & John Hamlin. The legatees: Seth Warner, age 32 years, John 28, Samuel 27, Elizabeth 30, Mary 26, Sarah 20, Mehetabell 17, Ruth 15, Bethiah 10.

Court Record, Page 16—4 September, 1690: Adms. to the Widow and to Seth, the eldest son. Francis Wetmore and Sargt. John Warner to be Overseers.

Page 18-19.

Warren, William, Hartford. Invt. £321-04-06. Taken 1st November, 1689, by William Pitkin and John Meekins. Will dated 24 October, 1689.

I William Warren sen. of Hartford do make this my last Will & Testament: I give unto my wife what by law is due unto her as Dower. My Will is that the Land that I now live upon be divided into two parts. I give to my son John Warren all of the Land south of the Line. I give to his brother William the Land North of the line. I give to him the use of 30 Apple trees, to the fruit of them, the Northernmost ones, for the space of ten years after the date of this my Will, provided he pay £10 to his brother Thomas Warren. I give to my son Thomas Warren two working Oxen, to be delivered to him the next spring, and £10 to be paid to him by his brother William When his time of apprenticeship is ended. I give to my four youngest children Three score pounds, to be paid to them as they Come of age. Also it is my Will that £5 be paid, at the discretion of my Executors, towards the bringing up of my youngest son. It is my Will that, in regard to the infirmity of my wife, that the three eldest Children I have had by my last Wife be placed abroad & bound out in good service ; that the girls be bound until they are 18 years of age, and that they be decently clothed by my Executors. And that Abraham be bound until he is 21 years of age, & that it be done with their Mother's Consent. The youngest child I leave at my wive's dispose, unless she prove so unkind or otherwise disabled that it be not well provided for, then I leave it to my Executor. I appoint my son John Warren Executor. WILLIAM X WARREN. Ls.
Witness: *William Pitkin, sen.,*
John Meekins, Daniel Crow.

Court Record, Page 5—6 November, 1689: Will approved.

Page 92.

Watson, Nathaniel, Windsor. Died 19 August, 1690 (W. R.) Invt. £229-00-00. Taken 11 December, 1690, by Return Strong and Abraham Phelps. The children: A daughter, Ann, 4 years of age, and Nathaniel, 6 months old. The Widow, Dorothy Watson.

Court Record, Page 24—5 March, 1690-1: Adms. to the Widow Dorothy Watson, and Return Strong & Corporal Daniel Hayden to be Overseers.

Court Record, Page 2—(Vol. VIII) 2 January, 1709-10. Nathaniel Watson, 20 years of age, son of Nathaniel Watson late of Windsor Decd, chose James Enno, Jr. of Windsor to be his Guardian.

Webster, John. Court Record, Page 82—7 March, 1694-5: This Court grant Adms. on the Estate of John Webster unto Mrs. Sarah Webster.

Page 80.

Welles, Jonathan, Hartford. Invt. £440-18-09. Taken 23 April, 1688, by Ciprian Niccols and Stephen Hosmore.

By his Excellency: The within Named Tho. Welles, Administrator to the Estate of Jonathan Welles deceased, appeared before me & made Oath that the within writing is a true and perfect Inventory of the Estate of the deceased so far as he knows or is come to his hands. Sworn the 12th day of November, 1688, before me,

John West, Deputy Secretary.   ANDROSS.

A Copy from the record, examined.
Isa Addington, Secretary.

Court Record, Page 19—4 September, 1690: Ichabod Welles, Samuel Welles, Joseph Welles & John Bidwell appeared in Court & desired this Court that they might have a Settlement of the Estate of their brother Jonathan Welles decd. The Executor, being summoned, did not appear.

Page 21—5 November, 1690: Invt. was exhibited in Court, and the Adms., Thomas Welles, ordered to pay or to make Dist. of the Estate of Jonathan Welles to his Brothers & Sisters.

Page 25—5 March, 1690-1: Ichabod, Samuel & Joseph Welles & John Bidwell in behalf of his wife Sarah, and James Judson in behalf of his wife Rebeckah, all survivors to Jonathan Welles, Plaintifs; *Contra,* Mr. Thomas Welles, defendent, to answer the complaynt for neglecting or refuseing to Dist. or pay unto them their several portions of the sayd deceased Estate according to Dist. & appoyntment of the Court 5 November, 1690.

Dist. File, 27 November, 1695: Estate Jonathan Welles. An Agreement for Division: John Olcott and Mary his wife, as Adms. on the Estate of Mr. Thomas Welles; Ichabod Welles, Jacob, Samuel and Joseph Welles, and Mr. James Judson in right of his Wife Rebeckah; Mrs. Sarah Bidwell, Adms. on the Estate of Mr. John Bidwell Decd. By William Whiting, Joseph Mygatt.

Page 217.

Welles, Thomas, Hartford. Invt. £589-07-02. Taken 8 November, 1695, by Joseph Wadsworth and Ciprian Niccols.

Court Record, Page 91—11 November, 1695: Adms. to John Olcott. Order of Dist: To the Relict, to the Eldest son, to the youngest son. The Administrators to have the benefit of the Children's Estate for their bringing up until they are 21 years of age.

Page 63.

Wetmore,* Thomas, Middletown. Invt. £200-13-04. Taken 29 August, 1690, by Nathaniel White, Thomas Rannie sen. and Francis Wetmore. The children: Elizabeth, b. 2 September, 1686; Thomas, b. 8 January, 1688-9.

Court Record, Page 17—4 September, 1690: Adms. to the Widow. Francis Wetmore & Richard Hubbard to be Overseers.

Page 7.

Whaples, Joseph, Hartford. Invt. £31-12-06. Taken 16 August, 1689, by Ciprian Niccols and Jonathan Bull. One Child, name Thomas, 2½ years old.

Court Record, Page 2—5 September, 1689: Adms. to Thomas Whaples, a brother of sd. deceased.

Page 5—6 November, 1689: Order to the Adms. to take Care that the Child be brought up and his Estate preserved.

Page 46-7.

Whiting, Rev. John, Hartford. Invt. £622-10-06. Taken 5 November, 1689, by James Steele, Stephen Hosmore and John Willson. The children: Sibbell Bryan, age 34 years; William Whiting, 30; Mar-

---

*Note: *Also written Whitmore.*

tha Bryan, 28; Sarah Bull, 26; Abigail Russell, 24; Samuel Whiting, 19; Eliza: Whiting, 11 years; Joseph Whiting, 8 years; & John, one year old.

Court Record, Page 8—20 November, 1689: Adms. to the Relict. Mr. Joseph Whiting and Stephen Hosmore are desired to take account of the debts and report.

Page 36—3 December, 1691: Deacon Stephen Hosmore & Thomas Bunce are appointed to Dist. the Estate: To William Whiting, the house & lot bought of Richard Smith; to Samuel, £68-14-00; to Joseph Whiting, £68-14-00; to John Whiting, £68-14-00; to Sibbell Bryan besides what she hath, £44-16-00; to Martha Bryan, £37-13-04; to Sarah Bull, £45-12; to Abigail Russell, £31-01-00; to Elizabeth Whiting, £58,-14-00.

Page 46-47—1 September, 1692: A Second Distribution: To William, £80-00-00; to the Relict, £136-19-08; to Samuel, £46-16-08; to Joseph, £46-16-08; to John, £46-16-08; to Sibbell, £27-18-08; to Martha, £20-16-00; to Sarah, £28-14-08; to Abigail, £14-03-06; to Elizabeth, £41-16-08. The 2nd Dist. a discount.

Page 166-7.

Whitmore, Catorn (Katharine), Middletown. Invt. £108-01-00. Taken 20 October, 1693, by William Southmayd, ffrancis Whetmore and Israhiah Whetmore.

The Last Will & Testament of Catorn Whitmore of Middletown is as followeth: Imprimis: I give to my son William Roborts £10, to Samuel Roborts £10, to my son John Roborts £10. I give to my son Benjamin Whetmore £6, which is besides what he hath by his Father's Will, and to my two loving daughters, Abigail and Hannah, they having ten pounds apeice by their Father Thomas Whetmore. If my Estate is more than sufficient to pay my debts & Legacies, the remainder to be Equally divided among all my sons & daughters. I request my son-in-law, Beriah Wetmore, to be Overseer.

Witness: *John Hall sen.,*   CATORN X WETMORE.
Beriah Wetmore.

Court Record, Page 63—6 December, 1693: Will & Invt. Exhibited. Adms., With Will annexed, to Beriah Whetmore & Wm Roberts, & appoint Wm. Southmayd to distribute.

Page 77.

Willcox, Israel, Middletown. Died December, 1689. Invt. £344-02-00. Taken by David Sage, Samuel Willcox and John Savage. The children: Israel, 10 years of age; John, 8 years; Samuel, 5 years; Thomas, 3 years; Sarah, b. 30 November, 1689.

Court Record, Page 19—5 November, 1690: Adms. to the Widow; John Savage & John Wilcox to be Overseers.

Page 53-4 (Probate Side, Vol. IX): A Dist. or Division of the Estate belonging to the heirs of Israel Wilcox, sometime of Middletown, Decd, set out to and among the surviving heirs. And for the Confirmation of the above and within written, We, the Adms. and Legatees, have hereunto set our Hands & Seals.

Witness: *Josiah Willard,*
Jane Hand.

SARAH WILCOX, Ls.   SAMUEL WILCOX, Ls.
ISRAEL WILCOX, Ls.   THOMAS X WILCOX, Ls.
JOHN WILCOX, Ls.   SARAH WILCOX, Ls.

Court Record, Page 10—3 April, 1716: Sarah Wilcock, Widow, Israel, John, Samuel, Thomas & Mary (Sarah) Wilcox of Middletown, exhibited an Agreement and acknowledged the same to be their free Act and Deed. This Court confirm the same and order it recorded and kept on file.

Page 97.

Willett, Daniel, Windsor. Invt. £10-06-00. Taken 27 December, 1690, by John Porter and Joseph Loomys *(Carpenter.)*

Court Record, Page 24—5 March, 1690-1: Adms. to John Wolcott.

Page 3.

Willoe, (Willey), John, Haddam. Died 2 May, 1688. Invt. £269-13-06. Taken by John Bate, Thomas Hungerfoote and Alexander Rollo. The children: Isaac, age 18¾ years; Isabell 17, John 14¾, Miriam 12, Allyn 9, Abell 6, Mary 4 years.

Court Record, Page 3—6 November, 1689: Adms. to the Widow. Mr. Alexander Rollo & Thomas Hungerfoote to assist as Overseers.

Page 44.

Williams, Jane (Mrs.), Hartford. Invt. £18-11-00. Taken 3 January, 1689-90, by William Pitkin sen. and John Meekin. Will dated 23 December, 1689.

I Jane Williams, having by my husband's Will the dispose of certain parcels of real Estate at my decease, My Will is that my son Gabriel shall have the lott which was bought of Capt. John Allyn, provided he

mayntayne his Sister Ruth and her Children until they are in a Capacity to help themselves; & for the rest I will that it be equally divided amongst all my Children. I appoint my son Gabriel sole Executor. Overseers as in my Husbands Will. JANE X WILLIAMS.
Witness: *Thomas Olcott,*
William Williams.

Court Record, Page 9—20 January, 1689-90: Will & Invt. approved.

Page 41-2-3.

Williams, William sen., Hartford. Invt. £298-08-00. Taken 3 January, 1689, by William Pitkin and John Meekin. Will dated 4 February, 1687.

I William Williams of Hartford doe make this my last Will & Testament: After my Just & Lawful Debts are satisfied, I doe give, bequeath and Will to my beloved wife Jane Williams my whole Estate that I shall die possessed of. I mean the profits & Improvement of it during her natural life, excepting what I have already given to 3 of my sons, viz., to William, John & Jonas, the Homelotts with the Houseing thereon which I have already put them in possession of. I give my wife my Upland Lott which I bought of Capt. John Allyn, to be at her own dispose forever. To my son William I give Land I bought of John Church, all there is to my Meadow (excepting that which I bought of John Halloway). I give to my three sons, viz, John, Jonas & Gabriel, to be equally divided between them, that Lott I bought of John Halloway. My Will is that my son William pay to my son Samuel £12. My Will is that the highway which I made from the Meadow to the Upland shall remain for my Children, William, John, Jonas, Samuel, Gabriel, and Thomas Adkins. I give to my four daughters, Elizabeth, Jane, Ruth & Mary, £10 apeice. My Will is that if William Adkins, with his parents' Consent, remain in our family until he come to the age of 21 years, then I give to him £10. I constitute my wife sole Executrix, and appoint Capt. Caleb Stanly & John Marshal to be Overseers.
Witness: *Thomas Olcott,* WILLIAM X WILLIAMS.
John Olcott.

Memorandum: What was paid to any of the Children since William Williams sen. signed his Will:

	£	s	d
To Mary Biggs, one Cow at	4-00-00		
To so much Indian paid them,	4-00-00		
To a Blankett,	1-00-00		
To a Kettle,	1-00-00		
Total:	10-00-00		

Court Record, Page 9—20 January, 1689-90: Will & Invt. Exhibited. The said Williams having a daughter that is infirm and very Ill, with some small Children, and He having declared to his sons that it was his mind his infirm daughter should be provided for out of his Estate till her Children are put forth, This Court Order £86 to be lodged in the hand of William, John, Jonas & Gabriel Williams, for the relief of the infirm daughter and her Children. The Executrix being now deceased, Adms. to the 4 sons with the Will annexed. The Adms. are to expend the Estate of Ruth Williams for her maintenance first.

Page 139-40.

Willson, Phineas, Hartford. Invt. £2576-01-01. Taken 6 June, 1692, by Thomas Bunce & John Marshal. Will dated 6 May, 1691.

I Phineas Wilson of Hartford, within the County of Hartford, in Connecticut Colony, Merchant, at present so journing in Boston, doe make this my last Will & Testament: I give unto my wife, in lieu of her third, £150. I give to my only son Nathaniel Willson all my Estate of Lands and Houseing Lying within the Township of Hartford that were formerly the Estate of his Grand Father Mr. Nathaniel Sandford. I give to my two daughters, Hannah and Mary Willson, £200 to each, With Furniture and Household goods not otherwise disposed of. I give to my three sisters, Hannah, Margaret and Jane, all living near Hull, in Yorkshire, England, the sum of £10 apeice, to be paid to their order in New England. I give to Mrs. Whiting, Widow, Relict of Mr. John Whiting, late minister of Hartford, deceased, the sum of £20. I give to Ephraim Turner, my Apprentice, & to his heirs and assigns forever, all that lott of Land Lying in Wethersfield commonly Called Rocky Hill Lott, formerly belonging to one of the Goffs; my best Hatt and £10 in pay, provided he faithfully serve the remainder of his time. I give to my Wive's daughter, Abigail Warren, £10 in money. I give to John Kelley two Coates of my wearing apparell. I nominate Mr. Nathaniel Stanly, Deacon Stephen Hosmer and Mr. Joseph Bull my Executors. I appoint my beloved Wife, Doctor Thomas Hooker, Deacon John Willson, & Mr. Benjamin Mountford of Boston, to be my Overseers, also Guardians to my son Nathaniel and my two daughters Hannah & Mary.

PHINEAS WILSON. Ls.

County of Suffolk, in the Province of Massachusetts Bay, in New England.

Court Record, 6 July, 1692—Probate of the Will of Phineas Wilson, Decd:

William Stoughton, Esq., Commissionated by his Excellencie Sr. William Phipps, Knt., Captain Generall & Governor in Cheife in and over their Maties provence of Massachusetts Bay, in new England, with the advice and Consent of the Councill for granting of probate of Wills and

granting of Letters of Administration within the County of Suffolk, etc:—
     To all to whom these presents shall come or may concerne, greeting:
Know Yee that on the Eleventh day of July, one thousand Six Hundred
Ninty two, before mee at Boston, the will of phineas Willson, late of Hartford, Merchant, deceased, to these presents annexed, was proved, approved
and allowed.
     Isa Addington, Regs., & WILLIAM STOUGHTON, *Ls. At Boston.*

     Court Record, Page 47—12 October, 1692: Will & Invt. Exhibited.
Adms. to the Relict with the Will annexed. Nathaniel Willson appeared
in Court and made Choice of his Mother, Mrs. Elizabeth Willson, Mr.
Thomas Hooker, Deacon John Willson and Mr. Benjamin Mountford to
be his Guardians. Approved.

Page 1. (Vol. IX).

     Elizabeth Wilson, Widow, Administratrix Estate of Mr. Phineas
Wilson, deceased: Release from Mr. Joseph Rowlandson, and Hannah
his wife, of Wethersfield, who was Hannah Wilson, daughter of said
Phineas Wilson. Date, 18 August, 1698.
Witness: *Samuel Rockwell,*   JOSEPH ROWLANDSON,   LS.
         Nathaniel Fitch.   HANNAH ROWLANDSON,   LS.

Legacy, £955-12-00.

Recorded from the Original, 2 May, 1716, by *Tho. Kimberly, Clerk.*

Page 2.

     Mr. David Jesse and Mrs. Mary Jesse: Acquittance unto Mrs.
Elizabeth Wilson, Administratrix Estate of Mr. Phineas Wilson: We,
David Jesse of Boston, Goldsmith, and Mary Jesse, wife of sd. David
Jesse, have received from Mrs. Elizabeth Wilson, Widow, Adms. on the
Estate of Mr. Phineas Wilson, deceased, The sum of £955-12-00 in full
of a legacy given by Phineas Wilson, in his Will, to Mary Jesse alias Mary
Wilson, daughter to the said Phineas Wilson.   Signed:
Witness: *Richard Lord,*   DAVID JESSE, LS.
         Caleb Stanly Jr.   MARY JESSE, LS.
                                  18 August, 1698.

Copy of the Original Record, 2 May, 1716, by *Tho. Kimberly, Clerk.*

Page 3.

     Nathaniel Wilson's Release and discharge to Elizabeth Wilson, 29
January, 1699-1700: Know all men by these presents, that I, Nathaniel
Wilson, of the Town of Hartford, Have received from my Honoured
Mother-in-law, Mrs. Elizabeth Wilson, of the same Town of Hartford,

Widow, Administratrix on the Estate of my late Honoured Father Mr. Phineas Wilson, sometime of Hartford, deceased, do by these presents acknowledge myself fully satisfied and contented, and do fully acquit, exonerate and discharge the sd. Elizabeth Wilson forever. 30 January, 1699 alias 1700.

NATHANIEL WILSON, Ls.

Recorded 2 May, 1716.   *Thomas Kimberly, Clerk.*

(See Nathaniel Sanford, on page 358 of this volume.)

Page 214-215.

Wolcott, Samuel, Wethersfield. Died 14 June, 1695. Invt. £1137-02-08. Taken by John Chester Jr. and John Curtice sen. Legatees: Mrs. Judith Wolcott, Samuel, age 16 years, Josiah 13, Hannah 9, Sarah 9, Lucy 6, Abigail 4, Elizabeth 3, Mary, 1 year old.

Court Record, Page 90—5 September, 1695: Adms. to the Relict, Mrs. Judith Wolcott, with Mr. Henry & John Wolcott & John Chester, Overseers.

Pr. Special Court, Page 19—31 July, 1690.

Whereas, Complaint hath been made by Hugh Peck that his master Mr. Samuel Wolcott hath dealt cruelly with him in beating and abuseing of him most unreasonably sundry times: The Court having heard the case & Examined the Witnesses, do find that Mr. Samuel Wolcott did in a cruell maner (when he had stript his boy naked and tyed him to a stadle) he with three great sticks beat him till he had bruised and wounded him in a grevious maner, & being examined about it he sayd he will beat him worse; & sayd Mr. Wolcott Justifying himself & pleading the Law allowed him so to beat his servant, this Court doe see good reason to lay a fine of three pounds upon him for his cruelty, & order that the servant boy shall not return to his master whoe hath soe abused & threatned to deal worse with him upon his return to him, but that he remayne in the Constable of Wethersfield's Custody till his master shall procure another master for him (to sattisfaction of any two of the Assistants), with whom he may serve the remaynder of his time.

Page 37.

Wolcott, Simon. 26 March, 1688: Know Ye that I, Simon Wolcott, son and heir of Simon Wolcott late of Windsor Deceased, for and in Consideration of my Natural Care to my Natural brothers, Henry Wolcott, Christopher Wolcott, William Wolcott and Roger Wolcott, have given, granted & Confirmed unto Henry Wolcott & John Wolcott of Windsor and William Pitkin of Hartford, as Feoffees in Trust for the aforementioned Henry Wolcott, Christopher Wolcott, William Wolcott & Roger Wolcott, all and singular the Lands, Tenements & Hereditaments which, in the Township of Windsor aforesaid, or Elsewhere in New England, did belong or ought to belong to my Honoured Father Simon Wolcott at the time of his decease, & so did in law descend or any ways belong to me the said Simon Wolcott as his heir, excepting only that lott or those lotts usually Called by my father Lower Lott or Lotts on the East side of the Connecticut River in the Township of Windsor, being eighty-one rods in breadth in the meadow and fifty-five rods in breadth in the upland, and reserving a full Double Share & portion with each one of my other brothers in and to all such Lands as may hereafter appear to belong to the heirs of my said Father Deceased which are not yet laid out or divided, together with all the appurtenances, privileges, profits & Advantages whatsoever belonging to or arising from said Lands, Tenements & Heredtaments not before Excepted for them the said Henry Wolcott, John Wolcott & William Pitkin as Feoffees in Trust for the above named Henry, Christopher, William and Roger, My Brothers, to have and to hold From and after the day of the date hereof till the said Henry, Christopher, William & Roger shall severally be of the age of twenty one years, & for them the said Henry, Christopher, Willaim and Roger Wolcott's only use and behoof; & after that my said Brothers shall severally attain the said age, then they severally to have and to hold, use, occupy, possess and enjoy the same, as also their heirs, Executors & assigns, forever.

Witness: *Benjamin Newbery,*   SIMON WOLCOTT. Ls.
       Samuel Mather.

I bind myself to pay out of my proper Estate £40 of the debts due from my deceased Father's Estate. I do leave intire my Mother's right of Dower in my father's estate. Finally, it is the intent of these presents to enable my said Mother to give what she shall see cause, out of the moveables, to my sister Elizabeth Cooley and my sister Joanna Wolcott.

Court Record, Page 7—11 November, 1689: Whereas, Mr. Simon Wolcott deceased, the Invt. of his Estate is Exhibited in Court, & no Dist. being made by this Court, Simon Wolcott, son of the deceased, with consent of the Children of age, and of the overseers of the children not yet of age, have settled a Dist. of the Estate of the aforesayd Mr. Simon Wolcott among themselves: This Court approve this settlement, and appoint Simon Wolcott Adms., With Mr. Pitkin, Henry Wolcott & John Wolcott.

Page 130-1.

Woodroffe, John sen., Farmington. Invt. £353-09-06. Taken 16 May, 1692, by John Orton & Samuel Newell. The children: John, age 23 years, Joseph 13, Mary 25, Hannah 21, Phebe 16, Margaret 10, & Abigail, 8 years. Will dated 18 April, 1692.

I, John Woodroffe, being weake in Body but sound in minde, doe make this my last Will & Testament: I give to my son John Woodruffe my house & Homested with all its Appurtenances, only I give to my wife convenient room in my House and part of my Barn and Homelott, as much as shall be for her conveniency, so long as she shall bear the name Woodroffe. I give unto my sons John Woodroffe and Joseph Woodroffe all the Land in the Great Meadow. I give to my son John Woodroffe my East Division of Upland layd out against Wethersfield Bounds. I give to my gr. son John Root my East Division of Upland laid out against Hartford Bounds. I give to my son Joseph Woodruffe 2 acres of Land in the Little Meadow, & 40 or 50 acres in any of my other Uplands where he shall choose it, and the rest of my Outlands to be divided between my 2 sons John & Joseph, only my 4 acres of Land which I bought of Jonathan Smith, which shall be sold for the payment of my Just Debts. I give to my 4 daughters, namely, Hannah & Phebe (feebe) and Margaret & Abigail, all my Personal Estate. My Will is that my daughter Mary Roote shall have £5 out of my Estate. I make my two sons John & Joseph whole & sole Executors. I request my brother Samuel Woodruffe and my Cousin John Orton to be my Overseers.

Witness: *John Orton,*   JOHN WOODROFFE.
            Thomas Orton.

Proven on the 23rd day of May, 1692, at Farmington, before
                    Thomas Hart, Commissioner.

Page 120.

Woodroffe, Matthew, Farmington. Invt. £334-08-02. Taken 18 November, 1691, by John Orton and John Lee. The children: Matthew, age 23, John 19, Samuel 14, Nathaniel 5, Joseph 2 ½ years, Mary 21 (Infirm in her leggs), Sarah 17, Hannah 10, Elizabeth 12.

Court Record, Page 35—3 December, 1691: Adms. to the Relict & John Woodroffe, with Order to Dist. the Estate:

	£	s	d
To the Widow, 1-3 of the Real Estate during her life,	43-00-00		
& of Personal Estate,	72-06-00		
To Matthew, Eldest son,	60-12-00		
To the other 4 sons, to each,	30-06-00		
To Mary, because of her infirmity,	40-00-00		
To Sarah, Hannah & Elizabeth, to each,	24-00-00		

To be divided by Ensign Thomas Heart and Deacon Thomas Bull, Distributors. The 7 Eldest children by the 1st wife the Court placed under the Guardianship of John Woodroffe; the youngest left with the Mother. The Relict relinquishes all further Claim on the Estate.

Page 43—24 May, 1692: John Woodruffe having taken the Adms. on the Estate that belongs to Matthew Woodroffe's Children, those he had by his first wife, and the sd. John Decd, this Court grant Adms. on that Estate to Samuel Woodruffe, brother of the Decd, and to his Eldest son John, who are to take care thereof accordingly.

Page 126.

Woodruffe, Widow Sarah, Farmington. Invt. £105-02-11. Taken 2 February, 1691-2, by Thomas Heart and Thomas Bull. The children: Nathaniel, 5 years old May next; Joseph, 3 years May next.

Court Record, Page 38—3 March, 1691-2: Adms. to John Woodroffe & Joseph North, & appoint Thomas Heart & Thomas Bull to divide the Estate, that of the Eldest son to be secured in the hand of Joseph North, and that for the youngest son in the hand of John Woodroffe.

Page 56—12 April, 1693: This Court being requested by Joseph & Samuel Woodroffe, in behalf of John Woodroffe, who is the Adms. of Estate of Sarah Woodroffe Deceased? Reply: John Woodroffe, the Adms., being deceased, the other Adms., Mr. Joseph North the Surviving Adms., we esteem to be the sole Administrator.

Page 49-50.

Wright, Ensign Samuel, Wethersfield. Invt. £1082-09-00. Taken 27 February, 1689-90, by Samuel Butler, John Welles & Benjamin Churchill. The children: 3 of them married; David Wright, almost 13 years of age. Will dated 17 January, 1689-90.

I Samuel Wright sen. of Wethersfield doe make this my last Will & Testament in manner following: I give to my Eldest son Samuel Wright that Homelott where his present Dwelling house now stands, and all my Land adjoining to the Same that I purchased of Jonathan Smith. I give unto my son David Wright my present dwelling house and Homelott with the Appurtenances and Buildings thereunto belonging. I give to my son Samuel a small parcel of Money made up in a Bag marked S. W. To my daughter Mary another parcel of Money marked M. F. To my daughter Hannah another parcel of Money marked H. B. I give to my Kinswoman Hope Butler, that sometime dwelt with me, a Heifer 2 years old. I make my son Samuel Wright and my son-in-law Daniel Boreman, Executors. I desire my Brother Joseph Wright and my Brother-in-Law Samuel Butler to be Overseers. I doe hereby request and impower my sd. Overseers to place and bind out my son David in a convenient time to some honest Master, that he may learn some useful trade.

Witness: *Isaac Boardman,*   SAMUEL WRIGHT. Ls.
Samuel Butler.

Court Record, Page 11—6 March, 1689-90: Will & Invt. approved.

Page 14-15.

Wrotham, Simon, Farmington. In\t. £143-08-02. Taken 5 November, 1689, by John Thompson & Daniel Porter. Will dated 28 November, 1686.

I Samuel Wrotham of Farmington think meete to state that Little which God hath given mee in this world at a stay: I give to my daughter Hofe's Children, William Hofe, Susannah Hofe and Samuel Hofe, my Swamp and Upland, in all 40 acres more or less, with my 22-acre Lott in that Division that abutts upon Wethersfield Bounds, to be equally divided to them. I give to Susannah Houfe my Brass Kettle, at the age of 18 years, and my daughter Newell to have the Use of it till she comes to that age; and if it should want mending, my daughter to get it well mended for her. And I leave my son Samuel Houfe a feoffee in Trust to see my Will performed in reference unto the abovesd. Land given to his Children. Item. I give to my daughter Newell the north end of my Houselott, together with my House. I give to my son Simon the remaining part of my Houselott. I give to my son Simon a 4-acre Lott which I bought of Thomas Richeson, also a 4-acre Lott I bought of Goodman William Higgenson. I bequeath unto my daughter Newell a soldier's Lott containing six acres, and a 4-acre Lott I bought of Daniel Warner. I give to my Prentice boy my Hanger or short Sword. I give my Cloak to my son Simon, the rest of my wearing cloathes to be made suitable for my prentice to wear. I give my prentice to my son Simon, in case he use him as an apprentice ought to be used, all his time (except that for the three first sumers I give him to my daughter Newell—from the 1st of April to the 1st of November, annually, for 3 years); & in case Simon doe not use him well, I assign him wholly to my daughter Newell & her Children. I make my son Simon, my son Newell, my daughter Newell, & their Children, Thomas & Simon Newell, Executors; and Samuel Cowles & John Thompson to be Overseers.

Witness: *Thomas X Newell,*   SIMON WROTHAM. LS.
Samuel Cowles, John Thompson.

Court Record, Page 4—6 November, 1689: Will proven.

Page 93—(Vol. XIII) 1st July, 1741: Whereas, Simon Wrotham of Farmington, deceased, did in and by his last Will & Testament give to his son Simon Wrotham several peices or parcels of Land in sd. Farmington, and ordered that if his sd. son Simon died without issue that then the sd. Lands so given should descend to his sister Hough's & his sister Newell's Children, some of the Executors named in sd. Will now being deceased and the other refuseing to Dist. & divide sd. Lands to sd. Heirs according to sd. Will, Whereupon Jonathan Lewis of sd. Farmington, being married to Elizabeth Newell, one of the heirs to sd. Simon in Right of his wife, moves to this Court that Freeholders may be appointed to

Dist. or divide sd. Lands to & among the heirs of his sd. sister Hough's and his sister Newell's Children, to be equally divided among them, Whereupon this Court do appoint & impower Capt. Thomas Curtiss, Deacon Anthony Judd & Mr. Joseph Smith of sd. Farmington, or any 2 of them, to divide sd. Lands accordingly, being first sworn as the law directs, & make return of their doings to this Court.

VOLUME VI.

1695 to 1700.

This is the Sixth Book of the Records
of the Acts of the County Courts and
Courts of Probates in the County of
Hartford, and of Wills and Inventories.

No. 6.

MEMORANDA:

Some of the Acts of the County Courts and
Courts of Probates which should have been entered in Book No. 5, or else in this Book, No. 6
(because they relate to several wills and inventories that are recorded in this Book), are entered
in Book No. 4, between pages *136* and *160*.

PROBATE RECORDS.

VOLUME VI.

1695 to 1700.

Page 125-6.

Abby, Samuel, Windham. Died March, 1697. Invt. £58-08-00. Taken 9th May, 1698, by Joseph Carey and Jeremiah Ripley. Legatees: The Relict Mary, daughter Mary, age 25 years, Samuel 23, Thomas 20, Eleazer 18, Ebenezer 16, Marcy 14, Sarah 13, Hepzibah 10, Abigail 8, John 7, Benjamin 6, Jonathan 2 years of age.

Court Record, Page 93—5 July, 1699 (The Prerogative Court held in Hartford for Probate of Wills and granting Administrations): Exhibit of Invt. Adms. to Abraham Mitchell, who had married Mary the Relict of the said Abby. Rec., £60.

Dist. File: Samuel Abby's Estate, 1 August, 1699: To the widow relict Mary, to Samuel Abby, to Thomas Abby, to Ebenezer Abby, to John Abby, to Benjamin Abby, to Jonathan Abby, to Elizabeth Abby, to Mary Abby, to Marcy Abby, to Sarah Abby, to Abigail Abby, to Hepzibah Abby.

Page 6—(Vol. VII) 18 December, 1700: There was presented to this Court a Dist. of the Estate of Samuel Abby by Abraham Mitchell, who married the Relict and became Adms. of the Estate.

Vol. V, P. C., No. 194.

Adams, Samuel, Fairfield. Intestate Estate. Invt. taken 7 February, 1693-4. (Amount & names of Apprisers not given.) Exhibited in Special Court, 15 February, 1693-4. The Widow Mary Adams, Daniel Meaker & Abraham Adams Adms., and they may place the Children out as they may & shall think best.

Nathan Gold, Clerk.

No. 195. Elnathan Hanford of Fairfield was Summoned to Court as Adms. on the Estate of Samuel Adams, Jr., late of Fairfield, Decd, to answer Abraham Adams, Adms. on the Estate of Samuel Adams sen., 15 March, 1698-9, on an appeal to 26 April, 1700.

Tho. Staples, Constable.
Nathan Gold, Assistant.

No. 196. Abraham Adams, Daniel Meaker & Mary Lyon. Estate of Samuel Adams sen. Decd. Report of Adms. 1st November, 1698, and Daniel & Mary refuseing to act any longer, Abraham Adams now sole Adms., & Daniel Meaker was empowered to bind out Abraham Adams, son of the Decd, to his Uncle Abraham (Adms.) *Samuel Adams, ye son of Samuel Adams, was born 5 January, 1678.*

Nathan Gold, Recorder (also Clerk.)

Page 27-8-9.

Allyn, Edward sen., of Boston, and Lydia his wife, Convey their Messuage or Tenement in Boston, wherein they Dwell, to Capt. Robert Clapp of Castle Island and Joseph Brigham of Boston, Tanner, as Feoffees, in trust for the Benefit of their son Edward Allyn, that he may obtain a loan from William Turner of Boston by Mortgage, the sum of £83. A life use is made secure to Edward Allyn sen. and Lydia his Wife, and £30 to their daughter Martha Allyn, the Estate being held for this additional £30. *Stated thus, it appears that Edward Allyn sen. of Boston & Lydia his Wife conveyed to son Edward by Trust Deed their Certain property, reserving life use and a legacy of £30 to their daughter Martha Allyn, to Enable their son Edward Allyn to borrow £83 of William Turner of Boston for 5 years, with £6 per year to be paid for its use.* Signed:
Witness: *Joseph Mygatt,*		EDWARD ALLYN, Ls.
William Caddey, Thomas Seamore.		RACHEL ALLYN, HIS WIFE. Ls.

Page 106.

Andross, Joseph, Hartford. Invt. £9-11-11. Presented in Court 15 February, 1698-9, by Thomas Bunce and Richard Lord.
Court Record, Page 69—15 February, 1698-9: Invt. Exhibited by the Father Mr. John Andross, who is made Conservator over the Estate, which appears Insolvent. Creditors to be paid *pro. rata.* Debts, £16-00-09.

Page 46.

Baker, John Jr., Hartford. Died 26 April, 1697. Invt. £40-16-00. Taken 10 May, 1697, by Ciprian Nichols & Zachary Sandford. Mary Baker, the widow, presented the Estate to the apprisers. The children: Joseph, age 7 & 6-12 years; Elizabeth 4 & 10-12, & John 2 & 8-12 years of age.
Court Record, Page 18—3 March, 1697-8: Invt. of the Estate of John Baker Jr. exhibited in Court, Oath being made thereto before Nathaniel Stanly, Esq., by the Widow.

Will on File.

Bailey, John sen., Haddam. Invt. £186-10-06. Taken 29 August, 1696, by Daniel Cone, Timothy Spencer & James Welles. Will dated 17 June, 1696.

I John Bailey sen. of Haddam, in the County of Hartford, doe make this my last Will & Testament: I give half of my Lands, both Meadow & Upland, to my eldest son John, to be his on an equal division with his two brothers Benjamin & Nathaniel, to whome I doe give the other half to be equally divided between them two. I mean all that my Land at a place in Haddam Bounds called Higganum. I give unto my son John 20 acres of that 40 acres of upland I have in the upper Meadow on the East side of the Great River. Also I give to my daughter Lydia 20 Shillings. I give unto my two sons Benjamin & Nathaniel all my other Land in Haddam and all Rights, to be divided equally between them, only that Nathaniel shall have that Lott whereon the house stands, & the house I now dwell in, as part of his division, and Benjamin the other half, the house to be Nathaniel's. And It is my Will that my daughters Susannah and Mary shall continue in the house until one or both of them marryeth or when they see cause of their own Will to leave the same; and when Susannah marryeth I would have her take the Care of Mary and let her live with her until she be married away. It is my Will to give to my daughter Susannah £8. My Will is that my two Executors shall pay 40 Shillings yearly until she marry away; and if in seven years she marryeth, I give her £7. My sons Benjamin and Nathaniel I appoint to be my Executors. And my neighbors Timothy Spencer & James Brainard to be Overseers.

Witness: *Jeremiah Hobert,*   JOHN BAILE.
         James Welles.

Upon the other side of the paper, Haddam July 3d, 1696 (was written): Account of my several debts wch I will my Exequators to pay unto the several Creditors after my decease. Imprs. I owe to Samll Stone of Salem fiftie four Shills in pay, & 6 shll in money. It. Debts to the Widd Mrs. Waie of Hartford, two pounds 16s & six pence in pay. It. To Ensign Stanly of Hartford, seventeen Shills & odd pence, to be payd by my Exequtors out of my small share of Hartford mill, viz, the rent for it; & the rest of the soms aforesayd to be payd & made up to him pr my Exequators, the wholl in pay. It. To my son John ten shills given him pr his grand father to buy him a Bible. It. To my Daughter Lydia ten shs given her pr ditto to buy her a Bible with (all). It. To my Daughter Elizab. Clark fifty shills in pay for a weding gown I promised her. It. To my son Thomas Clark pr an old debt of five pounds 5s, & for work of himself & teame thirty six shills; both added together make in all seven pounds one shs in or pay. It. Debts to Thomas Dunke deceased, ye sum of fourteen shs in pay. These are the principal of my debts as far as I know at present, which I require you to pay or cause to be payed, as witness my hand on the day of the date hereof.   JOHN BAILY.

(Copied from original Paper on file.)

Court Record, Page 114—(Vol. V) 3 September, 1696: The last Will now exhibited and Proven. Nathaniel Bailey, Executor, accepted of being Executor with his Brother in Court.

Page 78-79-80.

Barnard, Bartholomew, Hartford. Invt. £970-09-10. Taken 16 March, 1697-8, by Joseph Wadsworth, Aaron Cooke and John Pratt. Will dated 9 March, 1691.

I Bartholemew Barnard of Hartford declare this my last Will & Testament: I give to my wife Sarah Barnard, during her natural life, my now dwelling house and Lands, to be improved by her and my son John, and she to receive the one-halfe of the profits thereof for her subsistence, with the one-halfe of the benefits or profit of my stock. I also give her £30 to be at her own dispose forever. And after my decease and my wive's decease, to my son Joseph and to my son John I give all My houseing and Lands. I give to my daughter Hannah my House & Lott comonly called Kelor's Lott, & £40. I give to my daughters Elizabeth Wadsworth, Sarah Steele & Mary Bunce, £20 to Each. My son John to be Executor.

Witness: *John Allyn,*   BARTHOLEMEW BARNARD.
    Aaron Cooke.

Court Record, Page 38—13 April, 1698: Will Proven 15 April, 1698, by Testimony of Aaron Cooke, one Witness (Col. Allyn) being deceased.

Page 57.

Beckley, Nathaniel, Wethersfield. Died 30 October, 1697. Invt. £200-09-00. Taken 13 April, 1698, by William Warner and Ebenezer Deming. The children: Daniel, age 4 years, Joseph 2 6-12, Mary 1 year old.

Court Record, Page 27—13 April, 1698: Adms. to the Relict and her Uncle Ebenezer Deming.

Page 18—(Vol. VII) 4 September, 1701: Ebenezer Deming presented to this Court an Account of his Adms. on the Estate of Nathaniel Beckley Decd:

	£ s d
The Debts,	13-16-00
The Loss upon the Estate,	23-11-00
To be added from his Father's Will,	10-12-00

Page 19—4 September, 1701: Whereas, the sd. Nathaniel Beckley was Executor to his Father's Will, Richard Beckley Decd, and the sd. Nathaniel being decd, and the Will of the Testator not being executed,

and the Estate undivided, this Court appoint Deacon Warner, Capt. Robert Welles and Jonathan Belding to divide the Estate of the sd. Richard Beckley according to the Will.

Page 9—(Vol. IX) 3 April, 1716: Thomas Morton and Comfort Morton of Wethersfield, Adms., Exhibit an accompt, and there appears in Loss and debts paid the sum of £37-05-00. There remains to be distributed Real and Personal Estate of £171-02-00, besides a lot of Land belonging to that Estate called the 50-acre Lott not Inventoried. Account allowed and order to Dist. to Comfort Morton, formerly Beckly, Relict of the sd. Deceased, the use of 1-3 part of the houseing and Land during her natural Life, and the Personal Estate, £45-05-08, to be her own forever. And the rest of the Estate to be divided among the Children as follows: To Daniel Beckly, eldest son, £85-11-00; to Joseph Beckly and Mary Beckly, younger Children, to each £42-15-06, which is their single portions. And appoint George Stilman, Jonathan Belden and Joshua Robbins 2nd, of Wethersfield, Distributors, and also to apprize and divide equally among the said Children the aforesd. 50-acre Lott. And Joshua Robbins of Wethersfield, Esqr, is desired to Administer to the said Distributors the Oath provided by Law.

Page 188—(Vol. X) 2 April, 1728: An Agreement for the Settlement of the Estate of Nathaniel Beckley, late of Wethersfield, was now exhibited, under the Hands and Seals of the Relict and Children of sd. Decd, and acknowledged to be their free Act and Deed, which is by this Court accepted. See Agreement per File: An Agreement with the Consent of our Father-in-Law Thomas Morton and our Mother Comfort Morton: To Daniel, to Joseph Beckley, to Thomas Hoskins, and to Mary his wife.

Page 94-5.

Benton, Edward, Wethersfield. Died 19 February, 1697-8. Invt. £342-10-00. Taken 26 March, 1697-8, by William Warner and Ebenezer Deming. The children: Samuel, Eldest son, Edward, Rebecca, Mary, Ellen, and Dorothy Benton (all of age except Edward).

Court Record, Page 54—13 January, 1698-9: Adms. to the Widow Mary, with Order to Dist. And appoint Ebenezer Deming and Benjamin Gilbert, Distributors.

Page 6.

Betts, John, Formerly of Wethersfield, late of Huntington, Long Island, now deceased. Estate in the Colony of Connecticut, in Lands, £188. Taken by John Chester sen. and Nathaniel Foote.

Court Record, Page 147 (Vol. IV)—4 March, 1696-7: Invt. Exhibited by John Betts Jr. Adms. to John Betts Jr. & Nathaniel Foote. Rec. in £200 for faithful Adms. of the Estate.

Page 25-6.

Beven (Beuen?), Arthur, Glastonbury. Died 15 December, 1697. Invt. £269-10-09, and £45 in Middletown. Taken 31 December, 1697, by Jonathan Smith, Joseph Smith and William Miller. Test: 19 January, 1697-8, by Mary Beven, the Relict of Arthur Beven, in Court. The children: John, b. 1676, Mary 1678, Grace 1679, Mercy 1681, Thomas 1682, Desire 1684, Arthur 1686, Joanna 1687, Elizabeth 1690, Abigail born 1692, Sarah 1694, Anna 1696.

Court Record, Page 12—19 January, 1697-8: Adms. to Mary the Relict & John the Eldest son. Mr. Eleazer Kimberly & Lt. ffrancis Wettmore to be Overseers.

Page 43 (Vol. VII)—7 April, 1703: John Bevin, Adms. on the Estate of his father Arthur Bevin of Glastonbury, presented an Account of his Adms., which the Court accepts and grants a *Quietus Est.* The sd. John Bevin being of age, this Court appoint Ensign Ephraim Goodrich & Thomas Treat to set out to John Bevin a Double share of the Real Estate. The debts being not all paid, the Court appoint the 2nd son, Thomas Bevin, Adms.

Page 120—(Vol. VIII) 12 February, 1712-13: Thomas Bevin of Glastonbury, Adms., exhibits now an Account of Payment of the remainder of the Debts due from that Estate, and the sd. Thomas Bevin declared and set forth to this Court that he has paid all the Debts. Whereupon this Court grant the sd. Thomas Bevin a *Quietus Est.*

Page 122.

Bird, Samuel, Farmington. Invt. £113-01-06. Taken 11 March, 1698-9, by Samuel Newell and Samuel Woodruff.

Court Record, Page 92—12 April, 1699: Adms. granted to the Widow. And this Court appoint Ebenezer Deming and Stephen Kelsey to assist the Widow in her Adms.

Page 56—(Vol. VII) 12 April, 1704: This Court appoint Lt. John Stanly of Farmington to be Guardian unto Samuel & Esther Burd, minor Children of Samuel Burd, late of Farmington, Decd.

Page 53.

Birge, Daniel, Windsor. Died 26 January, 1697-8. Invt. £254-07-00. Taken 3 March, 1697-8, by Timothy Phelps and James Ennoe. Legatees: The Widow; the Children (Deborah, Elizabeth and Mary were married): Daniel, Eldest son, age 18 years; Abigail 13, John 8 6-12, Cornelius 3, Hester 16 weeks.

Court Record, Page 21—5 April, 1698: Adms. to the Relict, with her Father Cornelius Gillett.

Page 35—13 April, 1698: Order to Dist. Sergt. Job Drake & James Ennoe to be Overseers, and to assist the Widow in her Administration.

Dist. File, 29 November, 1699: To Gerrard Spencer of Haddam, to Cornelius Gillett, to Moses Ventrus, to Daniel Birge, to Abigail Burge, to John Burge, to Cornelius Birge, to Esther Birge, (and) Receipts from Mary Birge, Hannah Birge, John and Jeremiah Burge, Children of John Burge Decd.

Page 36—(Vol. VII) 2 March, 1702-3: Report of the Dist. Accepted.

Page 34.

Birge, John, Windsor. Died 2 December, 1697. Invt. £314-08-00. Taken by Henry Wolcott, Abra Phelps and Daniel Hayden. The children: John Birge, age 18 years, Hannah 16, Jeremiah 12, Mary 10 years of age.

Court Record, Page 15—3 March, 1697-8: Adms. to Lt. Daniel Hayden & Sergt. Nathaniel Gaylord. John Birge chose (being 18 years of age) Mr. Henry Wolcott to be his guardian.

Page 57—1 September, 1698: Order to Dist. the Estate by the Adms., Daniel Heydon and Nathaniel Gaylord.

Dist. File: To John Birge the Dwelling house, Barn & Homelott, £80; also 7 ½ acres in the Great Meadow, £67; he paying to his 2 sisters £10 apeice to make up their portions, As also to Jeremiah by a lot on the east side of the Great River £40, also a lot near Pine Meadow £13. Also the remainder in pay to make up his portion. Receipts on File from Hannah Birge, 1705, and Mary Birge, 1707, for their portions; also from John and Jeremiah Birge.
Nathaniel Gaylord sen.,
Lt. Daniel Haiden.

Page 124—(Vol. VII) 4 April, 1709: Lt. Daniel Heydon & Lt. Nathaniel Gaylord, Adms. on the Estate of John Burge of Windsor Decd, exhibit an Account, & having paid all Debts known, are granted a *Quietus Est.*

Page 95-6.

Bissell, Benjamin, Windsor. Died 5 May, 1698. Invt. £334-00-06. Taken 2 June, 1698, by Samuel Grant sen., Return Strong sen. and Job Drake sen.

Court Record, Page 55—1 September, 1698: Adms. to the Widow, Mrs. Abigail Bissell.

See File: An Agreement made betwixt Thomas Bissell, John Bissell, Isaac Bissell, Ephraim Bissell & Nathaniel Gaylord in behalf of his wife, all of Windsor, and Daniel White in behalf of his wife, living in Hatfield, on the one part; and Abigail Bissell, Relict of Benjamin Bissell, late of Windsor, the other party, concerning the Settlement of the sd. Benjamin

Bissell his Estate: This 7th February, 1698-9, We, Thomas, John, Ephraim & Isac Bissell, Nathaniel Gaylord & Daniel White, do joyntly agree that our sister-in-Law, Abigail Bissell aforenamed, shall have all the Moveable Estate that doth or did belong to our Brother Benjamin Bissell Deceased, she paying his just Debts. And further, we do for ourselves joyntly give and resign up unto our beloved sister, Abigail Bissell aforenamed, her heirs & Assigns forever, all that Right & Title we now have or that we or any of our heirs in time to come might have in that peice of Land which our Brother Benjamin Bissell bought of Henry Chapman on the East Side of the Great River, as will more fully appear by sd. Henry Chapman's Deed. And further, we do agree to pay to our sister Abigail Bissell £6 a year in Country pay or £4 in money for the space of 5 years next ensueing. It is to be understood that upon this Agreement Abigail Bissell doth resign up her husband Benjamin Bissell's house and the remainder of his Lands to his Brother *emedyatly*.

Witness: *Return Strong sen.,*   THOMAS BISSELL, LS.
         Matthew Allyn.   JOHN BISSELL, LS.
                               EPHRAIM BISSELL, LS.
                               ISAAC BISSELL, LS.
                               NATHANIEL GAYLORD, LS.
                               DANIEL WHITE, LS.
                               ABYGALL BISSELL, LS.

Know all men by these presents, that we, John Stoughton, Joseph Bissell and Benoni Bissell of Windsor, Children of Joseph Bissell & Elizabeth Stoughton alias Bissell, late of Windsor deceased, do fully agree & consent to the above Agreement.

                               JOHN STOUGHTON, LS.
                               JOSEPH BISSELL, LS.
                               BENONI BISSELL, LS.
                           ————— ————LS.

Hartford, 19th May, 1713: Received of the parties within named (John Bissell only excepted), that is to say, each one their proportionable part of the within mentioned sum of £30, we say received per us:

                 JOHN WILLIAMS & ABIGAIL X WILLIAMS.

Court Record, Page 140—(Vol. VIII) 18 May, 1713: Daniel White, a party to an Agreement in Settlement of the Estate of Benjamin Bissell, with Thomas, Ephraim & Isaac Bissell, Nathaniel Gaylord, Abigail Bissell alias Williams, John Stoughton, Joseph Bissell & Benoni Bissell, all appeared & severally acknowledged the Agreement.

Page 54.

Bissell Samuel Jr., Windsor. Invt. £140-14-00. Taken 19 March, 1697-8, by John Moore sen. and Matthew Allyn.

Court Record, Page 22—5 April, 1698: Adms. to Mary the Widow, and further order to fix up the house, and what she shall pay out upon it of her part of the moveables shall be reimbursed.

Page 140.

Blackleach, John Jr., Farmington. Invt. £145-10-00. Taken 8 April, 1700, by Thomas Chester and Benjamin Churchill. Presented to the apprisers by John Olcott.

Court Record, Page 3—10 November, 1697: Whereas, Mr. John Blackleach Jr. being gone to sea and his wife Taken away by death in his absence, and no person appearing to preserve his Estate until his return or further order, Mrs. Elizabeth Blackleach moveing this Court that Ciprian Nickolls and Mr. John Olcott should take the estate into their hands for its preservation, this Court Joyn in Samuel Hooker with them.

Page 27—13 April, 1698: Capt. Ciprian Nichols and Mr. John Olcott, as Conservators to the Estate of Mr. John Blackleach, appeared in Court and desired that a caution might be entered against that part of the agreement made by the Children of the above sd. Mr. Samuel Hooker that respects the Estate belonging to Daughter of Mr. William Hooker, at Least that the said agreement be not confirmed by the Court in that particular until Mr. John Blackleach his returne or that the case be further heard.

Page 56—1st September, 1698: Mrs. Elizabeth Blackleach requests this Court to appoint Mr. John Olcott Guardian to the child of Mr. John Blackleach, whose name is John, about 2 ½ years Old.

Page 67—17 January, 1698-9: Adms. to Mr. John Olcott on the Estate of John Blackleach Jr. of Farmington Decd.

Page 139—10 April, 1700: Invt. Exhibited.

Note: *Mrs. Elizabeth Blackleach, mentioned above, was the widow of John Blackleach, senior, and daughter of Benjamin and Christian Harbert. See pages 46, 276 and 316 of this volume.*

Page 72.

Burr, Samuel, Hartford. Died 4 March, 1698. Invt. £297-18-06. Taken 14 April, 1698, by John Baker sen. and Thomas Burr sen. The children: Samuel, 7 years of age, Martha 4, Basey 2 years of age.

Court Record, Page 33—13 April, 1698: Adms. to Mercy, the Relict, & by her desire this Court appoint Major Jonathan Bull & Capt. Niccols to be Overseers.

Page 55—(Vol. VIII) 6 February, 1711-12: Samuel Burr, a minor 13 years of age, son of Samuel Burr, chose Samuel Church of Hartford to be his Guardian.

Page 93—6 October, 1712: Baisey Burr, a minor, age 17 years, son of Samuel Burr, chose his Mother Mercy Burr to be his Guardian.

Page 98.

Butler, George, Wethersfield. Died 5 May, 1698. Invt. £49-11-08. Taken 15 August, 1698, by William Goodrich and Joseph Churchill.

4th September, 1698: George Butler, being of Wethersfield, decd, and having left a certain Estate, We the Brethren of sd. Butler concluding that the sd. Estate ought to be disposed of to ourselves, have mutually agreed that there be an equal Dist. of the same, if the Honourable Court accepts, in manner as followeth: That Samuel Butler & Samuel Buck shall have that 10 acres of Land in the Little West Field and all the Moveable Estate according to Inventory, they paying £19-01-08 to their Sisters. 2ndly, That James & Jonathan Butler shall have the 8 acres of Land in the West Swamp, they paying 20 Shillings to their Sisters, who are Elizabeth Emmons, Mary Hopkins & Dorothy Kilbourn.

> SAMUEL BUTLER,
> JAMES BUTLER,
> JONATHAN BUTLER,
> SAMUEL EMMONS,
> SAMUEL BUCK,
> EBENEZER HOPKINS,
> JOSEPH KILBOURN.

Test: *William Whiting.*

Court Record, Page 58—5 September, 1698: Invt. exhibited by Benjamin Churchill. And whereas it appears, by a Writing under the Hands of the Brethren and sisters of the Decd, that they have agreed about the Dist. or settlement of the Estate, the Court confirms the sd. Agreement and order it to be recorded.

Page 83-4.

Butler, Nathaniel, Wethersfield. Died 9 February, 1697-8. Invt. £232-03-00. Taken by Ebenezer Deming and William Goodrich. The children: Samuel, Eldest son, William, Hannah Butler, alias Case, Ann Butler, alias Rily, Abigail Butler alias Walker, Ruth Butler.

Court Record, Page 40—11 May, 1698: Adms. to the Relict. Order to Dist. the Estate.

Page 22 (Vol. VII)—11 November, 1701: The children apply for a Dist. of the Estate. It was found that the Adms. had not rendered account, therefore a Citation or Order was Issued to the Adms., or to Philip Olcock in Right of his wife, to perfect their Adms. and make Return thereof to this Court.

Page 23—1st January, 1701-2: Philip Olcock and his wife, Adms. on the Estate of Nathaniel Butler, late Decd, exhibit an Account. This Court appoint Capt. Chester, Capt. Thomas Welles and Lt. Benjamin Churchill Distributors.

Page 24—1st January, 1701-2: This Court now discharge Philip Olcock and Sarah his wife from their Adms. And whereas, the Adms. is not wholly perfected, the Court appoint Isaac Riley and Samuel Walker Adms.

Page 26—9 March, 1701-2: This Court dismiss Isaac Rylie from his Adms. on the Estate of Nathaniel Butler, and grant Letters of Adms. to Ensign John Stedman, with Samuel Walker.

Page 33—8 September, 1702: Stedman and Walker, Adms. on the Estate of Nath: Butler decd, presented a further Accot of their Proceedings in paying Debts &c., Amt. to £23-18-10, which the Court accepts.

Page 56—29 June, 1704: John Stedman and Samuel Walker, Adms., presented to this Court an Account, which this Court accepts and order to be put on File, and grant them a *Quietus Est.* And Philip Olcock of Wethersfield exhibited in this Court an Account against the sd. Adms. and their Accompt, Whereupon this Court order that sd. Philip Olcock shall be heard upon the Matters of sd. Complaint before the sd Adms. be fully discharged. And for as much as all the Debts due from the Estate of the sd. Nathaniel Butler are not yet paid, This Court do now grant Letters of Adms. on the sd. Estate to Samuel Butler, eldest son of sd. Decd, Joseph Butler & Samuel Buck. Recog. £100.

Page 94—2 June 1707: This Court issue a Writ to the Constables of Wethersfield and Glastonbury to summons Joseph Butler and Samuel Buck, Bondsmen for Samuel Butler, Adms. on the Estate of his Father Nathaniel Butler Deceased, to appear and render account of his Adms.

Page 96—4 May, 1707: Joseph Butler of Glastonbury and Samuel Buck of Wethersfield appeared before the Court and prayed for longer time to produce the Account of the Adms. of Samuel Butler on the Estate of Nathaniel Butler Decd.

Page 112—7 June, 1708: Whereas, the Court, on the 29th of June, 1704, granted Adms. on the Estate of Nathaniel Butler of Wethersfield to his son Samuel Butler of Southampton, L. I., and the sd. Samuel died before he had rendered Account of Adms., Sarah Butler of sd. Southampton, Widow, appeared and Letters were granted to her on the Estate of Nathaniel Butler Decd, and gave Bond.

Butler, Thomas. Court Record, Page 9—15 December, 1697 (Special Court): Thomas Butler presenting to this Court an Attested Copy, under the hand of the Clerk, bearing date 5 July, 1690, of the Distribution of the Estate of his Father Thomas Butler, late of Hartford Decd, And the original Distribution not being entered in the Court roles, This Court do order that this Coppy be recorded: To Thomas Butler the houseing & a peice of the home Lott, being about halfe of it, and 8 acres. To Samuel an 18-acre Peice. To Joseph & John the other part of the home Lott below Collier's at the end of the home Lott, and 14 acres that was Mr. Gilbert's. Edward Cadwell, John Day, Thomas Cadwell, John Porter, Margaret & Hope Butler to have the 30 acres bought of Mr. Way. Susannah, 5 acres in the neck. Cornelius Holybut to have halfe the 70 acres and halfe the 4 acres, besides a Cow, and a bed he hath already. Ann, the other halfe of the 70 acres and the half of the 4 acres, and £5 to be paid her as followeth: 40 shillings by Thomas and 20 shillings apeice from the other 4 brothers. The Widow to have the remaining moveables forever, and one-third of the houseing and Lands during Life. Agreed to by Thomas and Samuel Butler, John Day, Edw. Cadwell and Thomas Cadwell. And ordered by the Court to be the Distribution of Thomas Butler his Estate, and Thomas Butler is Continued as Adms. 5 July, 1690.

Vera Copie, John Allyn, Clerk.

Dist. File, 5 July, 1690: Estate Thomas Butler, Wethersfield: To the Widow, to Thomas Butler, to Samuel, to Joseph, to John, to Edward Cadwell, to Jo. Day, to Thomas Cadwell, to John Porter, to Margaret and Hope Butler.

Page 101.

Cakebread, Isaac, Hartford. Invt. £17-02-00. Taken 4 November, 1698, by James Steele and Ciprian Nickols.

Court Record, Page 61—3 November, 1698: Adms. to Thomas Hill. Isaac Cakebread, son of the deceased, being about 18 years of age, chose Mr. Joseph Bull & Thomas Hill to be his guardians. Mary Andrews, about 17 years of age, having some Interest in the Estate, chose Joshua Carter to be her guardian. Thomas Bunce & Samuel Kellogg were appointed to distribute the Estate.

Page 64.

Chester, Capt. John, Wethersfield. He died 23 February, 1697-8. Invt. £1133-00-00. Taken 25 March, 1698, by William Warner and Thomas Welles. Will dated 21 February, 1697-8.

I John Chester of Wethersfield doe by this my last Will & Testament give as followeth: To my Eldest son John Chester, my dwelling house and all my buildings, with my home lott and Land adjoyning, to him and his heirs male forever; and in default of male heirs descending from my said Eldest son John, I give and bequeath said house and buildings, with home Lott and Land adjoyning, to my son Thomas Chester and to his heirs male forever. And this is all the Estate which I give Conditionally. All the remainder I give positively. I give to my Eldest son John Chester my Grist Mill; also Land lying at the Landing near my brother's Warehouse; also halfe my farme which the General Court gave me wch was laid out by Doct. John Brockett and Capt. Thomas Yale. I give to my son Thomas Land flanking upon Nathaniel Boreman North, upon the heirs of John Coltman south, in part, and in part south upon Lands given to my son Stephen Chester. I give him my gold ring that was given me at the funeral of Mr. Whitwell. I ratify unto the heirs of my son Stephen Chester, Deceased, all those Lands which I gave him. I give to my wife soe much of my Lands, houseing and Pasturing as I am now in possession of as she shall see meet to improve during her natural life. I give to her all my plate, viz, Tankard, Porringers, Wine Cup and Silver Spoons, to her and to be at her dispose to give hereafter to such of her children as she shall please. I order and appoint that each of my daughters, Sarah, Prudence & Eunice, their sums of one hundred pounds be paid to them in Current Country pay, viz, what is yet behind of any of their portions. I give and bequeath to my daughters, to the children of my daughter Mary (the former wife of Mr. John Wolcott) in lieu of their Mother's Twenty-five pounds, to Sarah £25, to Prudence £25, to Eunice £25, to be paid in Current Country pay either before or after their Mother's decease, as she my said wife be willing to part with the moveable estate. I give to my brother Stephen Chester £5 in Country pay to be for his Comfort & maintenance. I appoint my sons John & Thomas Chester my Executors. I give to the Towne of Wethersfield the Land at the burying yard which I bought of Samuel Willis Esq., Reserving a benefit and privilege therein for my own family and successors.

JOHN CHESTER, SEN. Ls.

Witness: *Stephen Chester,*
        Peter Bulkeley.

Court Record, Page 32—13 April, 1698: Invt. Exhibited by Sarah Chester, widow. Will proven 6 May, 1698.

Page 76.

Chester, Stephen Jr., Wethersfield. Died 9th February, 1697-8. Invt. £1140-00-00. Taken by William Warner and Ebenezer Deming. The children: Dorothy, born 5 Sept. 1692; Sarah, b. 5 March, 1693-4; Mercy, b. 26 October, 1696; & a posthumous son born 14 February, 1697-8.

Court Record, Page 34—14 April, 1698: Adms. to the Widow Jemima Chester, with Thomas Chester & Mr. James Treat Jr.

Page 169—(Vol. VIII) 4 January, 1713-14: Marcy Chester, a minor about 17 years of age, daughter of Stephen Chester Jr., late of Wethersfield Decd, made choice of Ephraim Goodrich to be her Guardian; and Stephen John Chester, about 16 years of age, chose Mr. James Treat to be his Guardian.

Page 174—1st Feb., 1713-14: Upon the Motion of Mrs. Jemima Chester of Wethersfield, Widow & Adms. on the Estate of Mr. Stephen

Chester, late of Wethersfield Decd, do now order that the Estate of the sd. Decd, both Real & Personal (except what is justly expended and disbursed towards payment of the Just Debts and necessary charge), shall be dist. and divided to and among the Relict and Children of the sd. Decd in manner following: To the Widow Jemima Chester, the Use & Improvement of 1-3 part of the Houseing and Lands during the time of her natural life, and 1-3 part of the Personal Estate forever; and the rest of the Estate, to the Eldest and only son of sd. Decd a double portion, and to each of the daughters a single portion. And appoint Lt. Jonathan Belding, Mr. Nathaniel Burnham and Isaac Ryly Distributors.

Dist. File: 5 April, 1714: To the Widow Jemima, to Stephen John Chester, to Dorothy, to Sarah & to Mercy Chester.

Page 66—(Vol. IX) 3 June, 1718: Capt. Ephraim Goodrich, Guardian to Mercy Chester, produced a Writing under her hand and witness, directed to this Court, informing that the sd. Goodrich had discharged his Guardianship to her the sd. Chester to her satisfaction and Content, whereupon this Court do discharge the sd. Ephraim Goodrich from his Guardian Bond for sd. Mercy Chester.

See File: An Agreement made the 14th day of June, 1738, being joyntly, severally and unanimously agreed to by Martin Kellogg & Dorothy his wife of Wethersfield, and by Joseph Lamb and Sarah his wife of Southhold, in Long Island, in the County of Suffolk and Province of New York, and Mercy Chester of Wethersfield, the only surviving heir and Co-heirs of Stephen John Chester of sd. Wethersfield. And the above parties, for themselves, their heirs and assigns forever, have given, granted and released unto each other by these presents the several Claims or Demands that they have or might have in or to the Estate aforesd. or any part thereof other than what in the above Dist, or partition is to them set out. In Witness whereof the parties to these presents have hereunto set their Hands & Seals this 27th day of June, 1738.

MARTIN KELLOGG, LS.
DOROTHY KELLOGG, LS.
JOSEPH LAMB, LS.
SARAH LAMB, LS.
MERCY CHESTER, LS.

Page 139.

Churchill, Joseph, Wethersfield. Died 5 April, 1699. Invt. £461-00-00. Taken by William Goodrich and Thomas Wickham. The widow, Mary. The children: Nathaniel, age 22 years, Mary Edwards age 25, Elizabeth Butler 21, Dina 18, Samuel 11, Joseph 9, David & Jonathan 7, Hannah 3 years old.

Court Record, Page 126—9 March, 1699-1700: Invt. & Nuncupative Will Exhibited by Nathaniel, in which Nathaniel was appointed Executor.

Page 140—11 April, 1700: Will not allowed. Adms. to Mary, the Relict, and Nathaniel, Eldest son.

Page 26—(Vol. VII) 9 March, 1701-2: This Court appoint Nathaniel Churchill to be Guardian to David & Jonathan Churchill, minors, 8 years of age, Children of Joseph Churchill. Recog. £100. This Court appoint John Francis to be Guardian to Samuel, Joseph & Hannah Churchill, minor Children of Joseph Churchill, deceased. Recog. £150.

Dist. File: 1701-2: To Nathaniel, to Samuel, to Joseph, to Hannah, to Jonathan, to Mary Edwards, to Elizabeth wife of Richard Butler, to Dinah Churchill. By Thomas Wickham & Benjamin Churchill.

Page 48.

Clarke, Joseph, Hartford. Died 7 February, 1697-8. Invt. £186-00-06. Taken by Aaron Cooke and Nathaniel Goodwin. The children: Mehetabell, age 3 years, 17 September, 1697; Jonathan, one year, 14 October, 1697.

Court Record, Page 19—16 March, 1697-8: Invt. Exhibited by Ruth the Relict.

Page 87—(Vol. VII) 13 November, 1706: This Court appoint Ruth Clark, Widow, to be Guardian to her daughter Mabell Clark, a minor, age 12 years, daughter of Joseph Clark, deceased.

Page 30.

Collier, Abell, Hartford. Invt. £61-16-02. Taken 9 November, 1697, by Joseph Wadsworth and Obadiah Spencer.

Court Record, Page 6—12 November, 1697: Invt. Exhibited by Zachary Sandford. This Court Order the Estate to be equally divided amongst Abell Collier's Brothers & Sisters. Lt. Sandford & Robert Sandford to Distribute to the Legatees.

Page 130.

Crow, Benoni, Simsbury. Invt. £15-15-00. Taken 23 November, 1699, by Timothy Phelps & Job Drake.

Court Record, Page 112—6 December, 1699: Invt. presented by Samuel Crow; Adms. to Thomas Burr of Hartford.

Page 30—(Vol. VII) 4 September, 1702: Thomas Burr, Adms., exhibits Account and is granted a *Quietus Est.*

Page 39—2 March, 1702-3: This Court grant Letters of Adms. unto John Clark of Windsor, who presents a peice of Land belonging to the Estate, lying in Greenfield, value £30 in the Invt. of Edward Bartlett, formerly of Windsor Decd (Benoni Crow as the Legatee). This Court order to Dist. the Estate to the two Brothers and four sisters, Children of Christopher Crow, viz, Samuel Crow, Thomas Crow, Mary, Hannah, Martha and Margaret Crow.

Inventory on File.

Davis, Hannah, Hartford. Invt. £12-19-06. Taken 26 November, 1697, by Joseph Wadsworth, Cyprian Nichols & Zachariah Sandford.

Court Record, Page 18—4 March, 1697-8: Invt. of the Estate of Hannah Davis, the Relict of Evan Davis, was now exhibited in Court by Mrs. Sarah Howard. This Court grant Letters of Adms. unto Ciprian Nichols, and also order that he pay the Debts, and the remainder of the Estate to be reserved for ye Child.

Page 8—(Vol. VII) April, 1701: Thomas Davis, a minor son of Evan Davis, formerly of Hartford, Decd, chose Samuel Spencer of Hartford to be his Guardian.

Page 15.

Day, Joseph, Hartford. Invt. £21-11-00. Taken 11 August, 1697, by Joseph Wadsworth & Aaron Cooke.

Court Record, Page 133—(Vol. V): Invt. exhibited by John Day, a brother of the Decd. This Court grant Adms. to John Day upon the Estate of Joseph Day, Decd.

Page 56—(Vol. VI) 1st September, 1698: John Day, who was by this Court appointed Adms., is now ordered to pay the Debts, £18-16-06, & the remainder, £2-14-06, this Court allow him for his pains in the Adms. of sd. Estate.

Page 135-6-7-8-9.

Deming, Jonathan sen., Wethersfield. Died 8 January, 1699-1700. Invt. £550-14-04. Taken by Jonathan Boreman, Ebenezer Deming and Jacob Williams. Will dated 27 March, 1696.

I Jonathan Deming sen. of Wethersfield doe make this my last Will & Testament: I give to my wife Elizabeth Deming the Use of all my Real & Personal Estate during her Widowhood, excepting what I have given to my Children. I give to her the Use of all my Improved Lands, with my House & Barn, & 1-3 of all my Moveable Estate, & so much of the Benefit of my Team that she shall need for the Improvement of my Lands. I give to my son Jonathan Deming the House & Land that he lives on, and about 5 ½ acres, and also 2 acres of Land in the Mile Meadow. I give to my son Thomas Deming that Lott I bought of Joseph Andrews, in that Division made for the List of Estate for the year 1693. I give to my sons Charles & Jacob the West half of my Lott that I live upon, to be equally divided between them, the east part to Charles & the West part to Jacob. I give to my sons Charles, Benjamin & Jacob, that 10 acres of Land that I bought of Ezekiel Buck, to be equally divided between them. I give to my son Benjamin my Dwelling house & Barn and all the remainder of my Lott that I now live upon as it is now fenced. I give to my daughter Sarah Rylie 10 Shillings with what she hath already had. I give to my son-in-law John Williams 1 Shilling together with what he hath had already. I give to my daughters, viz, Comfort, Elusia, Elizabeth, Mary & Ann, all the rest of my Moveable Estate when my wife has had her thirds, to be equally divided between them. I give to my brother John Deming a convenient highway in Mile Meadow by the Side of Mr. Lord's Lott to his own Land. All the Estate that shall happen to fall to me by my sd. wife Elizabeth out of the Estate of her father Josiah Gilbert, late deceased, I give the same to my sd. wife Elizabeth and to the Children I had by her, to be equally divided amongst them. I give my Land in the Indian Purchase to all my Children, except Sarah Rylie and John Williams. I appoint my wife Elizabeth Deming and my son John Deming to be Executors. In Case of their Decease, my son Thomas Deming to succeed to be Executor when he shall be 21 years of age. I also appoint my son Jonathan Deming and Mr. Jonathan Boreman to be Overseers.

Witness: *John Deming sen.,*   JONATHAN X DEMING SEN. LS.
Jno. Welles.

Court Record, Page 125—9 March, 1699: One Witness, viz, John Welles, late of Wethersfield, being removed out of the Country before the Exhibition of the Will, the Court do approve the same upon the Testimony of John Deming sen., the other Witness, and order the Will to be recorded.

Page 90-1-2.

Dickinson, Obadiah, Wethersfield. Died 10 June, 1698. Invt. £678-08-08. Taken 7 July, 1698, by William Warner, Joseph Churchill & William Goodrich. Will dated 7 June, 1698.

I Obadiah Dickinson of Wethersfield, concerning what Estate God in his Goodness hath bestowed upon me, I give the same as followeth: I give to my three sons, Daniel, Eliphalet & Noadiah Dickinson, all my Lands & Houseing in equal proportion. It is my mind that my son Eliphalet should have my 5 acres of Land lying by John Belding, to him & his heirs forever. I give to my daughters Sarah Smith and Mehetabell Dickinson, to each £40, not Counting the Wearing apparrell or the Child's Cloths that were her mother's my former Wife. I give to my Wife Mehetabell Dickinson the use of my houseing and house lott, wth a third part of all my improveable Lands, and the use of my moveable Estate, for her Comfort and the bringing up of the two children I had by her, so long as she remains my Widow. I give to my wife the improvement of the Estate of my son Noadiah until he come to the age of 21 years, and my daughter Mehetabell's Estate until she come to the age of 18 years or shall be married. I know not if my son Obadiah be living. If he be living, it is my Will that he have an equal share of my Estate with my other sons. I give to my servant Sarah Couch a young cow, to be paid her within one year after my decease. I make my son Eliphalet (with the advice and help of my wife) my Executor.

Witness: *Capt. John Chester,*   OBADIAH DICKINSON. Ls.
    Samuel Northam.

Court Record, Page 51—1st September, 1698: Will & Invt. Exhibited. Attest: the Widow Mehetabell Dickinson. Proven.

Page 2—(Vol. VII) 7 September, 1700: This Court appoint Capt. John Chester, Lt. William Warner and Nathaniel Foote to Dist. the Estate of Obadiah Dickinson according to a request of Daniel and Eliphalet Dickinson, sons of the sd. Decd.

Page 7—8 March, 1701: Report of the Dist.

Page 26—9 March, 1701-2: Whereas, Obadiah Dickinson did in his Will leave the Care of his 2 younger Children with his wife and put their Estate into her hands for the Bringing them up, and the wife being deceased, and thereby the Children exposed to difficulties, the Court do therefore appoint Daniel & Eliphalet Dickinson, sons of the sd. Decd and Brethren to the sd. Minors, Guardians to them, and put their Effects into their Hands to be improved for the Benefit of the two Children, whose names are Noadiah and Mehetabell Dickinson. Recog. £100.

Page 4—(Vol. IX) 1st January, 1715: Thomas Sheldon of Northampton, Atty. for Mehetabell Dickinson, daughter of Obadiah Dickinson late decd, cited hither Daniel & Eliphalet Dickinson, Guardians to sd. Mehetabell during her minority, to render an Account of their Transactions & Management of the Estate of sd. minors put into their hands. The sd. Daniel & Eliphalet appeared and prayed this Court that they might have longer time, which this Court grants them.

Page 6—7 February, 1715-16: Thomas Sheldon of Northampton having cited hither Daniel and Eliphalet Dickinson of Wethersfield, Guardians of Mehetabell Dickinson during her minority, to render an Account to this Court of their transactions, the parties attended and their pleas heard on both sides, and seeing that it don't appear to this Court that the sd. Daniel & Eliphalet did ever receive into their Hands any Estate of the sd. minor, do therefore order sd. Sheldon to pay the present Costs of Court.

Page 22—17 September, 1716: Daniel & Eliphalet Dickinson now appeared and rendered an Account of their Guardianship of the Bodys and Estate of Noadiah and Mehetabell Dickinson. Eliphalet Dickinson had received £48-13-06 and had disbursed £23-13-00 on account of Noadiah's Estate. There remains still due to the sd. Noadiah, £19-14-00. Daniel Dickinson had in his hands the Estate of Mehetabell amounting to £5-12-06, and paid, toward a legacy of £40, £28-16-06, and was still due £11-03-06. This Court order them to make their payment to the sd. minors as soon as can be.

Page 43-4.

Dix, Leonard, Wethersfield. Died 7 December, 1697. Invt. £53-08-00. Taken 17 January, 1697-8, by William Warner & Ebenezer Deming. Will dated 24 March, 1696-7.

I Leonard Dix of Wethersfield doe make this my last Will & Testament: Besides the Estate that I have already given to my two sons Samuel & John, as by their Deeds of Gift may appear, I do give unto my son John my great Brass Kettle & an Iron Pott, the Ketle that was Mr. Gardner's. I do give to my son Samuel the ½ of all the Iron Work and Tackling belonging to my Teame. I do give to my son Samuel the last Division of Land granted to me by the Inhabitants of the Town, and the Division of Land on the East Side of the Great River, being the Indian Purchase; also my great Musket and the long Fowling peice. Item. To my daughter Mercy my square, 2 broad Chisels, and a black heifer 2 or 3 years old. Item. To my daughter Hannah my warming pan and my Boston Kettle, a table wth a Drawer in it, and a meal Trough. Item. To my daughter Elizabeth a young brown mare. Item. To my son-in-law John Ffrancis, besides what he hath had already, 5 Shillings in pay. I give to my wife, the terme of her natural life, 1-3 part of the Lands for her maintenance, and which room in the house she sees cause to have, and also a Cow. Further, it is my Will that the Kettle given to Samuel and the two Kettles given to John that my wife shall have the use of them the time of her life. And further my Will is that my son John shall have my sorrill Horse. And further my Will is and I make my son Samuel my Executor.

Witness: *James Treat,*   LEONARD X DIX. Ls.
        Thomas Fitch.

Court Record, Page 17—4 March, 1697-8: Will proven.

Page 99-100.

Drake, Enoch, Windsor. Died 21 August, 1698. Invt. £372-05-00. Taken by John Moore and Timothy Phelps sen. Legatees: Sarah Drake, age 17 years, Enoch 15, Nathaniel 13, Hannah 3 years of age.

Court Record, Page 61—3 November, 1698: Adms. to the Widow, Mrs. Sarah Drake. Rec., £200, with John Moore.

Page 27—(Vol. VII) 12 March, 1701-2: Sergt. Josiah Barber, who married the Widow of Enoch Drake, late of Windsor, moves this Court for a Dist. of the Estate of Enoch Drake. This Court appoint Timothy Loomis and Capt. Matthew Allyn Distributors. Enoch Drake, Eldest son of the Decd, chose Capt. Matthew Allyn to be his Guardian; and Nathaniel Drake, another of the sons, chose Timothy Loomis for his Guardian. And for as much as the youngest Child is but 6 years old, the Court appoint Sergt. Josiah Barber, with the Mother of it, for its Guardian.

Dist. File: 16 June, 1702: To the Widow Sarah, now wife of Sergt. Josiah Barber, to Nathaniel, to Enoch, to Sarah, to Hannah. By Matthew Allyn & Timothy Loomis.

Page 35—11 November, 1702: Sergt. Josiah Barber, Adms. in Right of his wife on the Estate of Enoch Drake, did present an Account of their Adms. so far as he hath proceeded therein. There remain unpaid Debts, which the Court order shall be paid. Also presented an Account of the Dist. of the sd. Estate to the Relict & Children according to an Order of Court formerly given under the Hands of Capt. Matthew Allyn and Timothy Loomis. Accepted and ordered to be filed.

Vol. V, P. C., No. 209.

Dunk, Thomas, Saybrook, Tanner, Heir of Thomas Dunk of Saybrook. Tanner. Decd. Power of Atty. to Ensign John Stedman of Wethersfield, 9 Sept., 1699.   THOMAS DUNK. LS.
Witness: *John Dunk,*
          John Chandler.
Acknowledged 29 Sept., 1699, before *Danll Taylor, J. P.*

No. 210. John Stedman, Atty., makes application to the Court, being agrieved in the Dist. of the Estate of Thomas Dunk, late decd., per order of Court at New London, 20 November, 1683, of the Estate of my late Hond. Father, T. D. This against Benjamin Lord, Adms. Estate of Lydia Post, late of Saybrook, Decd.

A Letter from Thomas Buckingham to the Court of Probate:
No. 211. The case depending between Tho: Dunke and Benjamin Lord, as administrators to the Estate of Lidia Post, late of Saybrook, Deceased, I suppose to be about the distribution of the Estate of Tho. Dunke, late of Say Brook, deceased. And concerning the case, it being now about seventeen years since It was acted, It cannot bee expected that I can bee very particular. But if anything I can say may be of any good use, I hold myself bound as a friend to truth and righteousness, and in obedience to authority, to offer it Impartially. The sd. Lydia Post was sometime the wife, afterwards the relict, of sd. Tho. Dunke, late of Say Brooke, and she was prudent and industrious in her place; nor have I heard of any Contentio between the husband Dunke & her. Shee brought with her five or six children, the eldest of them between fourteen and fifteen years of age. Hee, the sd. Dunke, had with her the Improvement of between four and five hundred pounds Estate (as I am informed), most of it real estate, the most of which was fit for Improvement. The improvement of the personal Estate was so much the more, because utensils in the house of the sd. Dunke were not very plentifull before he was married to the sd. Lidia. And thus they lived comfortably and credibly for the space of between foure and five years, and until the decease of sd. Dunke. I have understood from them both that they had descorsed of a bargain between them that their Estates should be distinct, so that which of them should happen to die first should have the disposal of the Estate formerly belonging to the

dying one, their marriage notwith standing. And the woman being in her apprehension like to dy first (being very sick), shee showed herselfe that it might be according to these proposals, and Committed so to a friend to use his wisdom and interest that it might bee so. But after her recovery her friend had none occasio to negotiate in thee affairs, nor did he hear more from her of the matter. When the man came to ly upo his death bed hee was put in minde to make some alteratio in his will, because hee now had a wife but had none when hee made his will. Hee answered that his wife was to have her owne Estate and he was not farther obliged, but at length granted that something was meete and necessary to have done, but being under greate extremity hee said hee could not do it then, nor was there found a time to do it in. By which I could understand there had been something verbally passed between them about a bargain, and unto which neither of them was unwilling when they thought of dying first, yet nothing brought to that head as would oblige the survivor to set down by It, no, not in the Cort of Conscientio. When the sd. Dunke was deceased his widdow came to mee as guardian to the person of the heir, and advised what shee should doe. I cannot give a particular account of the discourse that passed between us. The Issue was that shee would be contented if her owne Estates were returned and such a summe as I proposed out of the sd. Dunke his Estate to bee allowed to her as his relict. And I engaged to her that I would write to the Corte and endeavor it might bee so, and that her children might bee comfortably cloathed out of the Estate besides. But after this and Immediately before ye Corte (and of which I knew nothing untill after the Corte) shee did meete with other advice, which prevailed with her, to inquire after, and the Corte allowed her more. And what the Corte saw cause to allow her hath been received by her unto a small matter, which hath been made up to foure sons since her decease, as doth appear under their hands. When the Corte made that distribution, the Estate of ye sd. Dunke was represented greater by not a few hundreds of pounds than indeed It was, as hath been evidenced to the satisfactio of the Corte, and as Captn. Chapman is able to demonstrate, and is upon record in the case depending, I have been informed. This is the substance of what I do remember that may bee usefull in the case depending. And such of It as may bee thought testimonial I am ready to affirme unto you upon the highest assurance, as witness my hand ye 30 Septemr, 1700.

THO. BUCKINGHAM, SENIOR.

Page 16.

Eaglestone, Thomas, Windsor. Invt. £114-06-06. Taken 5 May, 1697, by Daniel Haiden, Abraham Phelps and Job Drake.

Court Record, Page 155—(Vol. IV) May, 1697: This Court grant Adms. on the Estate of Thomas Eglestone of Windsor, Decd, unto his Brother Benjamin Eglestone, and grant him full power to receive and pay Debts, and also to prepare an Inventory against the Court in September next, then to render an Account of his Adms.

Page 132—(Vol. V) 2 September, 1697: Invt. exhibited by Benjamin Eglestone. This Court appoint Capt. Timothy Phelps, Lt. Daniel Hayden and Lt. Abraham Phelps to Dist. the Estate to Benjamin Eglestone, Brother, and to the wife of Jno Pettebone sen. of Simsbury, a sister of the Deceased.

Dist. File, 28 August, 1701: Estate of Thomas Eglestone. An Agreement for Division to Benjamin Eglestone, to John Pettebone, to John, to Thomas, to Nathaniel, to Isaac Eglestone.

Page 4.

Fowler, Jonathan, Windham. Died 12 June, 1696. Invt. £259-17-10. Taken 1st July, 1696, by John Fitch & Thomas Bingham. Elizabeth Fowler, the Widow, by letter, requested this Court to allow her Adms., and appoint Joseph Dewey sen. of Lebanon with Thomas Huntington of Windham to be Overseers.

Court Record, Page 147—(Vol. IV) 4 March, 1696-7: An Invt. of the Estate of Jonathan Fowler of Windham Decd was presented to this Court, whereto Oath being made by the Widow before Joshua Ripley, Comr, the Court grant Adms. to the Widow And appoint Josiah Dewey of Lebanon and Thomas Huntington of Windham to be Overseers.

Page 134—(Vol. V) 2 September, 1697: Mrs. Elizabeth Fowler gave Account of Adms. Order to Dist. the Estate to the Widow and the Children, to Elizabeth, to Joseph, to Sarah, to Jonathan Fowler. And appoint Deacon Josiah Dewey and Thomas Huntington to Dist. the Estate accordingly.

Page 16.

Freeman, Frank (Negro), Farmington. Invt. £72-02-00. Taken by John Hart and Daniel Andrews sen.

Court Record, Page 85—16 March, 1698-9: Adms. to the Widow, Maryland. Order to pay the debts and to keep the rest in her owne hands.

Page 130. (Court Side.)

Galpin, Philip. An Indenture of Bargain and Sale of House & Lands: Philip Galpin of Bristol, Somersett Co., England, Marriner, son of John Galpin of Rey, in the County of Fairfield, Colony of Connecticut: John Galpin, with free consent of his wife Mary, for a certain sum of money to them paid by Nicholas Hoppings of Rey, in the county of Westchester, Province of New York, Marriner, by indenture bearing date 5 March, 1697-8, did sell to the said Nicholas Hoppings House & Lands bounded North on County Road, S-E. on the Harbour, East on John & Joseph Horton Jr., West on Memoroneck River, late in the possession of John

Galpin and Mary his Wife, with other lands, etc. Philip Galpin came into possession of part of above premises by a Deed of Gift from John Morgan of Rey, in the County of Fairfield, Husbandman, 9 October, 1670, and Quit-Claims to said Nicholas Hoppings 29 April, 1700.
Witness: *Mary Jacksone.*   PHILIP X GALPIN. Ls.
  Acknowledged 10 July, 1700, before *Timothy Prout.* Suffolk.

Page 128.

Gaylord, John, Windsor. Died 29 April, 1699. Invt. £432-12-00.
Taken 31 May, 1699, by Job Drake and Nathaniel Gaylord. The children: John, Mary & Ann.
  Court Record, Page 104—7 September, 1699: Adms. to Mary the Relict & Job Drake. Recognizance, £300.
  Page 124—7 March, 1699-1700: Job Drake and Mary, the Relict of John Gaylord deceased, present to the Court an account of debts due from the Estate. And Whereas, Jedediah Watson hath married the Relict of John Gaylord and thereby become obliged as an Administrator on the fore sd. Estate, in Court he accepted that Trust with Bond of £300.
  Page 95—(Vol. VII) 7 July, 1707: Ann Gaylord, a minor, 15 years of age, daughter of John Gaylord, late of Windsor Decd, appeared before this Court and made choice of Jedediah Watson, her father-in-law, to be her Guardian.
  Page 103—7 January, 1707-8: John and Mary Gaylord made an Agreement for the Division of the Estate of their Father John Gaylor Decd, which the Court doth allow.
  Page 5—(Vol. VIII) 6 February, 1709-10: John Gaylord of Windsor, son of John Gaylord late of Windsor decd, and Ebenezer Bliss of Springfield, who married Mary Gaylord, daughter of sd. Decd, made Application to this Court for an Order of Division of that part of the Estate which was allotted to and intended for Ann Gaylord, now Decd. This Court order 2-3 thereof to John Gaylord and 1-3 to Ebenezer Bliss and Mary his wife.

Page 6.

Gilbert, James. Invt. £53-00-00. Taken 4 March, 1696-7, by Joseph Wadsworth, Ciprian Nichols and Lt. Zachary Sandford.
  Court Record, Page 140—(Vol. IV) 4 March, 1696-7: Invt. exhibited by Joseph Gilbert. Adms. granted to Thomas & Joseph Gilbert.

Page 96-97.

Gilbert, Jonathan, Middletown. Died 1st February, 1697-8. Invt. £202-19-02. Taken 16 July, 1698, by Nathaniel White, John Hall sen. and

Nathaniel Stow. Dorothy, his Wife, died 4 July, 1698. The children: Mary Gilbert, age 18 years, John 15, Jonathan 12, Nathaniel 5, Ezekiel, Sarah 3, Ebenezer (posthumous) about 5 months.

Court Record, Page 56—3 September, 1698: Israhiah Whetmore & the daughter made Oath to the Invt. Adms. to Israhiah Whetmore.

Page 1—(Vol. VII) 5 September, 1700: Israhiah Wetmore, Adms., reports that the Personal Estate is not sufficient to pay the Debts.

Page 34—11 November, 1702: Order to Dist. the Estate.

Dist. File: 4 February, 1702-3: Dist. of the Estate: To John Gilbert, to Jonathan, to Nathaniel, to Ezekiel, to Ebenezer, to Mary, to Sarah. By Nathaniel White, Alexander Rollo & Thomas Stow.

Page 63—6 March, 1704-5: Nathaniel Gilbert, a minor son of Jonathan Gilbert, chose John Bacon to be his Guardian. And this Court appoint Thomas Stow to be Guardian unto Ebenezer Gilbert, another son of Jonathan Gilbert.

Page 70—6 September, 1705: This Court now discharges Thomas Stow, Guardian to Ebenezer Gilbert, and appoint Israhiah Wetmore of Middletown to be his Guardian.

Page 129-30.

Gillett, John, Windsor. Invt. £88-09-06. Taken 1699, by Cornelius Gillett sen., Samuel Barber, Josiah Barber and Daniel Pratt. Will (Nuncupative) of John Gillett, Windsor: We whose names are underwritten, being at the house of Widow Abigail Kelsy in Windsor with John Gillett in his last sickness whereof he dyed, and we desired him to settle his Estate that there might be no trouble concerning the same after his death, upon which desire he made a nuncupative will as followeth: His Just debts being paid, he gave his Estate that was left to his three brothers and sister in equal proportions. And also gave the Widow Kelsy, in whose house he lay sick, One heifer about a year and ½ old, which he gave for her pains in tending him in his sickness; also, that if he should continue long sick he would have her further satisfied. He desired that John Allyn and his Brother Thomas Gillett should be his Executors. This was sometime in the month of July, 1699. To the truth of the above written we do affix our names this 8th of September, 1699.   DANIEL PRATT,
                                                         JOSIAH BARBER.

Court Record, Page 106—7 September, 1699: Invt. exhibited by his Brother, Thomas Gillett. It appearing to this Court by the Testimony of Daniel Pratt & Josiah Barber that the said John Gillett did upon his death bed make a Nuncupative will Wherein he did dispose of his Estate & also appoint John Allyn and his brother Thomas Gillett Executors, who accept of that Trust, which dispose of his Estate this Court see cause to Confirm, it being made to his three Brothers and Sister by an Equal proportion. Approved. Proven 7 September, 1699.

Page 254—(Vol. VIII) 14 April, 1715: John Bissell of Windsor, Attorney for Samuel Gillett of Suffield, moved this Court for a Division of Land in Windsor, about 28 acres, to which Samuel Gillett had acquired a Right to ¼ part, being part of the Estate of his Brother John Gillett Decd.

Page 49-50.

Gillett, Jonathan, Windsor. Died 27 February, 1697-8. Invt. £360-13-00. Taken by Capt. Timothy Phelps & James Enno. The children: William, age 24 years, Mary Bissell 31, Hannah 16, Jonathan 13, & Miriam Gillett, 10 years of age. Will dated 25 August, 1694.

I Jonathan Gillett of Windsor doe make this my last Will & Testament: I give to my son William all my Houseing & Lands lying in the Township of Simsbury, except 5 acres of Marsh lying under the Mountains. I give to my sd. son William half my Marsh lying in the Township of Windsor at Wash Brooke which adjoins Simon Drake. I give him 10 acres of Woodland which my Father gave me that abutts south on the Land of Thomas Barbour. I give him a Gunn and a Sword. I give to my wife Miriam the benefit of all my Houseing and Lands in Windsor (except what is befor given to my son William) until my son Jonathan is 21 years of age, and then ½ of my Houseing and Lands during her natural life. And if she see Cause to marry again, I give her £3-10 per Annum, to be paid by my son Jonathan, and 1-3 of my Moveable Estate. I give to my son Jonathan all my Houseing and Lands at Windsor (except those given to son William), and also the Land I bought and am to have of Father Dibble, he to enter upon ½ of sd. houseing and Lands at 21 years of age, and the other half after the decease of my wife. I give to my daughter Mary 10 Shillings besides what I have already given her. I give to my daughters Hannah & Miriam, to each of them, 1-3 part of my Moveable Estate except 10 Shillings, to be taken out of their part. I appoint my wife Miriam to be sole Executrix.

Witness: *Henry Wolcott sen.,*   JONATHAN GILLETT, Ls.
Nathaniel Gillett.

Court Record, Page 21—5 April, 1698: Will proven.

Page 140—17 May, 1700: Miriam Gillett, the Relict of Jonathan Gillett, request this Court that ½ acre of Land not disposed of by the Will be allotted to her to aid in the Payment of Debts. There being no provision in the Will for the payment of Debts, she, being Executrix, is necessitated to pay them out of her own particular Legacy. (The Court gave her the Land.)

Page 112—(Vol. IX) 6 October, 1719: Upon the Complaint made by Jonathan Filley, Josiah Filley, John Filley and Thomas Gillett of Windsor, and Joseph Gillett of Hartford, a Sumons was Issued to cite Jonathan Gillett, John Graham and his wife Priscilla, Cornelius Brown of Windsor, and Josiah Gillett of Colchester, to show reasons, if any they have, why Adms. should not be granted on some part of the Estate of said complainants' grand Father, Jonathan Gillett, sometime of Windsor, Deceased. Not granted.

Page 21-22.

Gilsman, Richard. Died 28 September, 1697. Invt. £230-18-06. Taken 27 October, 1697, by Joseph Olmsted sen. & Roger Pitkin. The children: Solomon, age 21 years, Richard 18, Mary 25, Sarah 23, & Hannah 13.

Court Record, Page 4 & 5—10 November, 1697: Adms. to the Relict and Solomon the Eldest son. An Agreement was presented to the Court by the Legatees wherein the three sisters were to receive £20 apeice in Moveables at Inventory price and good Country pay. And that our brother Richard shall have an equal portion of the Estate with Solomon.

Witness: *Roger Pitkin,* Signed: SOLOMON GILSMAN, Ls.
Joseph Easton. MARY X GILSMAN Ls. SARAH X GILSMAN Ls.

Page 123.

Goff, Jacob, Wethersfield. Invt. £136-03-06. Taken 12 November, 1697.

Court Record, Page 67—17 January, 1698-9: The Court order the Clerk to send a writ to the Townsmen of Wethersfield requiring them to take an Inventory of the Estate of Jacob Goff Decd, and the same to exhibit in Court March next.

Page 92—12 April, 1699: An Invt. of the Estate of Jacob Goff of Wethersfield, Decd, was exhibited in Court by Margery, the Relict, and Oath made before Capt. John Chester, J. P. Adms. to the Relict, and order Ebenezer Deming and Stephen Kelsey to assist with their Advice.

Page 186—(Vol. VII)—Probate Side: Whereas, the Honoured Court of Probates held at Hartford, 2 February last past, did Order and appoint us whose names are under written to make a distribution of the Estate of Jacob Goffe, late of Wethersfield, deceased, and being mett together on that occasion, do distribute the said Estate as followeth:

		£ s d
Imprs. To Margery Buck, relict of the said Goffe,		15-00-00
To Mabell, one of the daughters, personal Estate & 46½ acres of Land,		10-00-00
To Mary, one of the daughters, personal Estate and 26 ½ acres of Land,		10-00-00
To Unis Goff, another daughter, Personal Estate, 26 ½ acres of Land,		10-00-00

Signed: 16 February, 1707-8: *Samuel Walker, Joseph Kilbourn, Stephen Kelsey.*

Page 102—2 February, 1707-8: Jonathan Buck of Wethersfield and Margery his wife, Widdow relict of Jacob Goffe Decd, Adms. on Estate of sd. Jacob Goffe, presented to this Court an account of Adms. Allowed and approved and granted a *Quietus Est.* An Order to Dist. the Estate to Margery Buck, relict, and to Mabell, Mary and Unis Goffe, daughters of sd. Decd. And this Court do appoint Samuel Walker, Joseph Kilbourn & Stephen Kelsey Distributors. This Court appoint Jonathan Buck Guardian unto Eunis Goffe, a daughter of Jacob Goffe; and Mary Goffe, also daughter of the Deceased, made choice of Thomas Morton to be her Guardian.

Page 106—11 March, 1707-8: Report of the Distributors.

Page 83—(Vol. VIII) 7 July, 1712: This Court now discharge Thomas Morton of Wethersfield from his office of Guardianship to Mary Goffe, and order that his Bond be cancelled and burned, which was done accordingly this 7th of July, 1712.

Page 126-7.

Grave, George, Hartford. Died 20 June, 1699. Invt. £165-03-03. Taken 8 July, 1699, by Thomas Bunce sen. & Ebenezer Hopkins. Will dated 3 May, 1699.

I George Grave of Hartford doe make and ordain this my last Will & Testament: I give and bequeath to my sister Elizabeth Mitchell £10 in Current Country Pay, to be paid within 3 years after my decease. I give & bequeath unto my brother John Grave 10 Shillings in Pay. I give & bequeath my Wearing Apparrell to my Cousin John Mitchell. I give & bequeath to Robert Shurley, whom I make my only and sole Executor, all and singular my Moveable Estate and all my Land, by him freely to be possessed and injoyed forever, in recompense for the Great Trouble and Charge that I have been to him in the time of my Sickness. And I doe hereby ratify and confirm this to be my last Will & Testament.

Witness: *Hezekiah Wyllys,*   GEORGE GRAVE, Ls.
    Nathaniel Arnold.

Court Record, Page 93—10 July, 1699: Will & Invt. Exhibited. The executor accepts the trust, and doth account himself obliged for the payment of the debts due from the Estate of Marshall George Grave, father to the deceased Testator, as well as the Debts due from the Estate.

Page 152.

Grave, John. Whereas Robert Shurly of Hartford, in the Colony of Connecticut, in New England, has by an Instrument under his Hand & Seal bearing date wth these presents fully and wholly quit his Claim to and resigned all Right & Interest in and to the whole Estate of my Brother

George Grave Decd, as more fully doth appear by the sd. Instrument: Know all Men by these presents, that I John Grave of Hartford, in the Colony of Connecticut aforesd., doe hereby bind myself, my heirs, Exes & Adms. unto the aforesd. Robert Shirley, his heirs, Exes & Adms. & Assigns, in the penall summ of £100 Silver Money of New England to save harmless the sd. Robert Shurly from all manner of Debts, Dues, Demands, Obligations, Judgements, Executions & all manner of Costs and Charges of & upon the Estate or the Estates of George Grave senior or George Grave Jr., late of Hartford Decd. The true Intent & meaning of this Obligation is that the sd. John Grave shall pay all manner of such damages if the said Shurly, his heirs or administrators, shall meet with or be put to any such charge.

Witness: *Richard Burnham,*   JOHN GRAVE. LS.
        John Seamore.

Page 18.

Henbery, Arthur, Hartford. Invt. £108-06-04. Taken 18 August, 1697, by Joseph X Wadsworth and Cyprian Nicholls. The children: Mary, Hannah, Elizabeth age 17 years, Susannah 15 years. Will dated 25 June, 1687.

I being now neer forty one yeares old, and being now upon my sick beed and for ought I know my dyeing beed, my estate I will and bequeath unto my Children, my Estate what is left after My burriall and other debts are payd. I will to ech child, haveing but only five & they being daughters, in maner as followeth: to each a lik in portion to be distributed equally, only my daughter Lidia Henbery I bequeath to my Father and mother hill to bring her up till she Come of ye Age of eighteen years. The said lydia being of a wekly body, and being my father & mother Hill's desire, so it also is my will, that what remaynes of my wife's portion shall be given and added to what shall be of her portion of my Estate. And further I the said Arthur henbery do ordain & appoynt and constitute and give full power by vertue of these presents to my Honnored father Hill and My loveing and trusty friends peter Buell and John Slater to take a care of my Estate, to pay my debts out of the same, and also to distribute to my children of the remaynder of my Estate to ech an equal proportion as they come of agg. This is the Will and testament of me, Arthur henbery, as witness my hand.   ARTHUR X HENBERY.

Witness: *Abiah X Slater,*
       Mary X pryor.

Court of Assistants.

John Slater, of the town of Symsbury, personally appeared in Court 16 October, 1697, and Gave oath that to his Certain Knowledge Arthur Henbury, the devisor above mentioned, Signed and subscribed the above written Instrument and declared it to be his last Will & Testament.

Test: Eleazer Kimberly, Secretary.

4 September, 1697 : Abiah Slater & mary prior appeared in Court and owned that they had set these marks, etc., but could not give the evidence of witnesses that Arthur Henbery had declared the above to be his Last will.

Attest: Caleb Stanly, Assistant.

These may certifie this honnored Court, that on that very day wherein the Widow Bement was Married to Arthur Henbery I was personally present with them, where upon sd. Widow desired the afforsd. Arthur henbury to declare before me and the Wif of Luke Hill senr, as I tuk it, the conditions which he promised her in case they were Married together, which accordingly sd. Henbery did in my hereing, Which take as follow : First, in case she and he did marry together, that he did give unto her sd. Martha Bement the full and free possession of his house and house Lott in Simsbury durring the time of her natural life if she out lived him, or at least so long as she durred in the state of widdow hood and bear his name. Secondly, she should have the use of the Meadow Lott durring the time of her Widow hood and so long as she bear his name. And Further, that he the sd. henbery dide engag to her the 3d part of his other estat according to Law. There were some other passages between them which I cannot so perfectly remember the Circumstances there of, therefore do omit the relation of them. The abovesd. engagements made to the sd. Martha was before her Marraig to Arthur henbery. The time of sd. Agreement was about nine year ago the Last february. Further saith that there was an Instrument of conveyance of sd. his house and Land as abovesaid, and subscribed and asignd by him before us Witnessess. The above written being attested.   *P. John Slater, senior.*

Dated at Hartford, 11 October, 1697.

John Slater, the deponent abovenamed, personally appeared in Court and gave oath to his above written testimony.

Test: Eleazer Kimberly, Secretary.

Court Record (Vol. V) Page 134—10 November, 1697 : Adms. to the Widow Martha, & Joseph Mygatt gave bond, £60.

Page 4—(Vol. VI)—10 November, 1697 : Whereas, Adms. was granted to the Relict of Arthur Henbury, and Mr. Joseph Mygatt gave bond, she now gives an account of her Adms. and is granted a *Quietus Est.*, Adms. being granted to William Long upon the said Estate by the Court of Assistants in October Last.

Page 107—(Vol. VII, Probate Side) : An Agreement of Legatees, dated 8 November, 1704 : John Frisbie & Benjamin Frisbe to have Land in Windsor, east side of the Great River, about 306 acres. That William Long shall have 100 acres that lyes in the Township of Simsbury on the east side of the Mountain called little Phillips. That Samuel Richards shall have 80 acres also east side of the Mountain called Little Phillips.

Signed :   JOHN X FRISBE, Ls.
                BENJAMIN S. FRISBE, Ls.
                WILLIAM LONG, Ls.
                SAMUEL RICHARDS, Ls.

Test : *William Whiting, Clerk.*

Page 60—8 November, 1704: John Frisbe and Benjamin Frisbe, of the Town of Branford, and William Long and Samuel Richards, of Hartford, who Married the four daughters of Arthur Henberry Decd, appeared in Court and exhibited an Agreement in Writing under their Hands & Seal respecting the Estate of Arthur Henberry, who died Intestate, which this Court allow and approved.

Page 87-8.

Hall, George, Hartford. Invt. £95-17-02. Taken 23 May, 1698, by John Merrells and Samuel Webster. Will dated 28 February, 1697-8.

The last Will & Testament of George Hall is as followeth: I give to Mr. Thomas Buckingham 40s, to Mr. Stephen Hosmer 40s, and to Mr. Timothy Woodbridge 40s; to Ebenezer Benton 10s; And a Red Heifer to the Widow Mitchell; my bed and bedding to Joel Marshall. I give the improvement of my Land to John Camp sen. for 3 years, and after to return to Mr. Willys. I give my Iron Pot to Mary Camp, and after my lawful debts are paid I give the remainder to the south Church. I appoint Mr. Nathaniel Cole and Bevel Waters to be my Adms. I doe give to the Widow Cole 40 Shillings.

Witness: *John Camp Jr.*   GEORGE X HALL.
       Nathaniel Cole.

Mr. Bevel Waters and Sarah his wife appeared in Court and made Oath that they heard George Hall say and declare that whereas he hath given in his Will his Bed & Bedding unto Joel Marshall, now he sees Cause to make an Alteration in that part of his Will, and did give the Bedd & Bedding unto Samuel Wheeler in consideration as part of his watching and attending upon him in the time of his sickness. Moreover the abovesd. Bevel Waters and Samuel Wheeler made Oath that they heard George Hall say that he did give unto the Widow Mitchell his best Garments, viz, a Coat, Jacket and Wascoat.

Sworn in Court, 25 May, 1698. Test: *William Whiting, Clerk.*

Page 17.

Hart, Samuel, Farmington. Invt. £125-08-08. Taken 20 August, 1697, by Thomas Porter Jr. & Daniel Andrews sen. Will dated 5 August, 1697.

The last Will & Testament of Samuel Hart is as followeth: I give unto my brother Stephen Hart my Lott at the Mountains commonly called the Andrews Lott, and also my Cuttlash. 2ndly: I give unto my brother Thomas his two sons Stephen & Thomas all my Meadow Land on the West side of the River, equally divided between them at the age of 21 years. I give unto my Brother Thomas his Eldest son Stephen my

Shoo buckells and my silver (Shirt) Buttons, and also I give unto my brother Thomas my Cart, Hoopes & Boxes. 3rdly: I give unto my Brother John Hart my Mill, Swamp Lott, and my Interest in Lands & Buildings at Syderbrook, and also my Plow & Plow Irons and Timber Chain. 4thly: My Just Debts being paid out of the rest of my Estate, what remains my Will is that it be equally divided between my brethren and sisters, and in particular my Will is that my Cousin Ephraim Smith, with whom I am, be sufficiently rewarded for his Trouble and Paines now in the time of my sickness, according to the Judgement of my Honoured and loving Uncle Thomas Hart and my Cousin John Hart, whom I appoint Executors.

Witness: *Capt. Thomas Hart,*   SAMUEL HART.
Ensign John Hart.

Capt. Thomas Hart and Ensign John Hart appeared in Court and gave Oath that they saw Samuel Hart subscribe to the above written, and heard him declare the same to be his last Will & Testament. 2nd September, 1697.   Attest: *Caleb Stanly, Assistant.*

Court Record, Page 135 (Vol. V.) 2 September, 1697: Will exhibited in Court and proven.

Page 60-1-2-3.

Hilliyer, Andrew, Symsbury. Died 22 January, 1697-8. Invt. £192-16-10. Taken 25 January, 1697-8, by John Higley sen., John Slater sen., John Moses & Joseph Phelps. *His daughter Hannah, in her 17th year. Extracted from Simsbury Records, Liber 2d, Folio: 32, 11th April, 1698. John Slater, Register.* Will dated 16 February, 1692-3.

I Andrew Hilliyer of Symsbury, in the County of Hartford, doe make this my last Will & Testament: I give to my daughter Hannah Hilliyer, being all the living Children I have, whome I make my only and sole Executrix, all and singular my Lands, Messuages & Tenements here in Symsbury. I give & bequeath all my other Estate, Personal & Real, Moveable or Immoveable, of what kind soever, as Cows or Cow kind, Horses or Horse kind, that belong to me, whether pewter or brass, Iron or Tyn, as also those clothing that was her Mother's, as also all that Estate that is at her Uncle Thomas Burr's at Hartford given to her natural Mother by her grand father Burr, makeing her sole Heir and Executor. I desire Sergt. Samuel Willcoxson, Samuel Humphry & Sergt. Peter Buell to be my Overseers to assist my daughter.

                    ANDREW HILLYER, Ls.

Witness: *John Slater, Register,*
John Slater Jr., John Tuller.

Codicil. In Case of the death of my daughter without Issue, the Descent to James Hillyer, the son of my brother James Hillyer. If he die before he come to the age of two and twenty years, Descent to his brother Nathaniel Hillyer, or next, to two of my sister Crowfoot's sons, Daniel Crowfoot & David Crowfoot. His daughter Hannah now in her 17th year.

Witness to Codicil:
John Slater sen.,
John Moses.

Court Record, Page 31—13 April, 1698: Will Exhibited by James Hillyer.

Page 124—7 March, 1699-1700: An Agreement between James & Hannah Hillyer, by the Court recorded, and Hannah Hillyer was placed in full control of her Estates.

Page 85-6.

Hooker, Roger, Farmington, He died 28 April, 1698. Invt. £556-02-11. Taken 18 May, 1698, by John Wadsworth and Daniel Andrews. Will dated 28 April, 1698.

Mr. Roger Hooker, being very weak in body yet of sound mind, did in the presence of us, the subscribers, declare this following to be his last Will & Testament: He gave his house and shop in Hartford to Mary Stanly. He gave all the Improvement of his Lands in the south Meadow in Hartford to his Mother, Mrs. Mary Hooker, during life, the reversion to his Brothers & Sisters. As a particular Legacy he gave to his Eldest Brother, Mr. Thomas Hooker, his lott lying on the Road going to Farmington, next to the Land of John Merrells. His part of Outlands in Farmington he gave to his Brothers & Sisters, equally divided between them. All his Goods & Chattells now at Farmington he gave to his brother Nathaniel Hooker, except a Bill of £6 Money due from [   ] Gunn of Westfield, which he gave to his sister, Mrs. Mary Hooker. All the Money due from his Uncle Mr. Andrew Willett he gave to his Brother Daniel Hooker. Appointed Mr. Nathaniel Stanly & Thomas Hooker to be his Executors.

Witness: *Timothy Woodbridge,*   ROGER HOOKER, LS.
Ephraim Turner, Samuel Webster.

Court Record, Page 40—25 May, 1698: Will & Invt. exhibited & proven.

Page 58.

Hooker, Rev. Samuel sen., Farmington. Died 5 November, 1697. Invt. £1007-00-07. Taken 6 December, 1697, by Thomas Bull, John Hart and Daniel Andrews. Invt. in Hartford, £294-00-00. Taken 8 March, 1695, by Nathll Cole and Samuel Kellogg.

Court Record, Page 27-8-9—13 April, 1698: Adms. to John & Nathaniel Hooker. Daniel & Sarah Hooker chose Mr. Nathaniel Stanly to be Guardian.

An agreement of legatees:

Mrs. Mary Hooker the Relict, with the two daughters Mary & Sarah Hooker, accepted the personal Estate except the Library. That the Widow Mary Hooker with Nathaniel Hooker Joyntly have the improvement of all the real Estate during her life time which the said Samuel Hooker stood possessed of at his death, excepting that on the east side of the Great River belonging to Hartford and a Division of outlands against Wethersfield in Farmington. In consideration thereof they do engage to be at the charge of what is necessary for the perfecting of Daniel Hooker in Learning. That all the Lands belonging to the Estate in Hartford, together with that Division against Wethersfield, be divided between Thomas, James and Roger Hooker. That Daniel Hooker is to have the Library and be perfected in his Learning; also to receive £50 in money, to be paid him within one year after his Mother's decease. The Lands in Farmington, except the division against Wethersfield, to be divided between Samuel, John & Nathaniel Hooker at their Mother's decease. The £50 to be paid to Daniel Hooker, £20 to be paid by Thomas, James & Roger Hooker, and £30 to be paid by Samuel, John and Nathaniel. The Land & Homested sometime in the Improvement of William Hooker Decd should be settled upon Susannah Hooker, the only child of William Hooker deceased. In Witness whereof we have set to our Hands this 13th of April, 1698.

THOMAS HOOKER,	ROGER HOOKER,	DANIEL HOOKER,
SAMUEL HOOKER,	NATHANIEL HOOKER,	MARY HOOKER JUNR,
JOHN HOOKER,	MARY HOOKER,	SARAH HOOKER.
JAMES HOOKER,		

Page 7—(Vol. VIII) 6 March, 1709-10: Nathaniel Stanly of Hartford, as Guardian to Daniel & Sarah Hooker, did agree to a certain Agreement, made by the Widow and Children of the late Rev. Samuel Hooker of Farmington Deceased, for a Division of sd. Estate at the time wherein it was made, which bears date 13th April, 1698, and the sd. Nathaniel desired his declaration should be recorded.

Page 98—25 November, 1712: Whereas, all the Lands within the Bounds of Farmington, with the Buildings thereon, excepting a Division against Wethersfield Bounds, should belong to Samuel, John and Nathaniel Hooker and Mary Hooker, the Relict of the abovesd. Nathaniel Hooker, and that by reason of the death of the abovesd. Nathaniel Hooker the Division not being finished, pray the Court to appoint persons to divide sd. Estate. Whereupon this Court appoint Joseph Root, John Porter son of David, and Samuel Wolcott of Farmington, Distributors.

Page 105.

Hosford, John, Windsor. Invt. £330-08-06. Taken 14 December, 1698, by Michael Taintor, Samuel Cross and Jacob Gibbs.

Court Record, Page 65—17 January, 1698-9: Adms. to the Relict, Mrs. Deborah Hosford, & Lt. Samuel Cross. And Whereas, John Hosford was by the Will of William Hosford Decd Appointed sole Executor, he being dead and the will not executed, upon the desire of Deborah the Relict of the sd. John Hosford, this Court do desire and appoint Lt. Matthew Allyn & Michael Taintor to make up accounts with the Creditors of the Estate of William Hosford.

Page 141—17 May, 1700: The Children apply to the Court to appoint Lt. Samuel Cross and Sergt. Job Drake Adms. (Brothers & Sisters).

Note: John Hosford, who died 8 November, 1698, married Deborah Brown, 9 April, 1696 (W. R.).

Page 3—(Vol. VII) 22 October, 1700: Samuel Cross & Deborah, the Relict of John Hosford, presented an Account of their Adms:

	£ s d
Debts due from the Estate,	57-10-02
Loss on the Estate,	28-07-00
Due to the Estate,	7-15-00
Also due to the Estate,	4-04-00

Page 30-1-2.

Humphrey, Sergt. John, Simsbury. Died 14 January, 1697-8. Invt. £266-00-00. Taken 10 January, 1698-9, by Thomas Barber, John Slater sen. John Moses and Samuel Humphrey. The children: John, Thomas, Nathaniel, Samuel & Joseph Humphrey, Mary & Abigail Humphrey.

Court Record, Page 12—19 January, 1697-8: Adms. to Eldest son, John Humphrey, & Samuel Humphrey, a brother to the Decd.

Page 79—(Vol. VII) 8 March, 1705-6: Samuel Humphrey and John Humphrey of Simsbury, Adms. on the Estate of John Humphrey sen., late of sd. Simsbury Decd, exhibited Account of their Adms. on that Estate, which this Court allow and grant the sd. Adms. a *Quietus Est.* And appoint Deacon Nathaniel Holcomb, John Slater sen. and Deacon Cornish of Simsbury to Dist. the Estate.

Page 81—4 April, 1706: Report of the Distributors approved and ordered to be put on File.

Dist. File: To John, to Thomas, to Samuel, to Joseph, to Samuel Gridley in right of his wife Mary.

Humphrey, Michael, Windsor. Court Record, Page 151—(Vol. IV) 14 April, 1697: John Humphrys, Samuel Humphrys, Richard Burnham & Sarah his wife, Joseph Bull & Hannah his wife, Benjamin Graham and Abigail his wife, John Shipman & Martha his wife, John Lewis & Mary his wife, *Plantfs.,* all of them the heirs of Michael Humph-

rey of Windsor Decd; Ensign Joseph Welles & Ensign Benjamin Newbery, of Windsor, *Defendts.* In an Action of the Case for that you do un-
justly withold and keep the above named heirs, Children of the above
named Michael Humphrey, out of possession of their Lands lying within
the Township of Windsor on the East side of the Connecticut River,
containing by Estimation 60 acres and being 10 rods in Breadth be it more
or less, bounded west on the River and runs 3 miles from the River, and
North on the Land of Samuel Grant, and South on Land of Samuel Rockwell, which was the proper Estate of the aforesd. Michael Humphrys,
formerly of Windsor, late of Simsbury Decd. Jury find for the Defend-
ents, cost of Court.

Page 14-15.

Kates (Cates or Keates), John, Windham. Died 11 July, 1697. Invt.
£177-04-00. Taken by Joshua Ripley & Jonathan Crane. Will dated 5
May, 1696.

I John Kates of Windham, in the Colony of Connecticut, doe make
this my last Will & Testament: I give 200 acres of my Land not yet laid
out to the Poor of the Town of Windham, to be Intayled to sd. Poor for
their Use forever. I doe also give and Intayle 200 acres more of my Lands
not yet laid out to a scoole House for the Use of the above said Town forever. And further I doe give unto the Reverend Mr. Samuel Whiting
(Minister of the Gospel), of said Towne, I say I give unto him my Negro
Jo., one bed and bedd Clothes, one Chest, and my Wearing Clothes. And
further, I do give unto the Church of Windham ten pounds in Money. I
doe make Mary Howard my Executrix, and doe give unto herr all my
Estate not above mentioned, both personal and real. And I appoint Ensign Jonathan Crane and sergt. Thomas Bingham to be Overseers of this
my Will. Always provided that if any of my Children should Come over out
of England, then my Will is that they, he or she, should enjoy my Estate
notwithstanding what is above exprest. Otherwise, to stand Exactly in
all Points. The Negro Jo. an Exception.   JNO. X KATES.
Witness: *Exercise Conant,*
         Sarah Conant.   Proven 16 July, 1697.

Court Record, Page 2-3—10 November, 1697: Thomas Bingham
refuses to serve as Overseer. This Court Considered the Estate given to
Persons in England, and required a Bond of Mary Howard, who objected,
but agreed not to transact any business relateing to the Estate except with
the advice and approbation of Ensign Jonathan Crane.

Page 156—(Vol. IV) 20 July, 1697: Will proven.

A. W. Parkhurst writes of John Cates, the first settler of Windham,
as follows: "Windham's first settler was John Cates, an English exile.
It is only known for a certainty that after a weary wandering everywhere,
fearing the king, he came to Norwich, and thence through an untrodden
forest to his final retreat. With a faithful negro attendant, whom he had

purchased in Virginia, he dug a cellar in a rocky hillside a little north of
the present village of Windham, and in that forlorn spot spent the long
winter of 1688-9. That he had silver and gold, subsequent events fully
proved; but, miles away from a human habitation, it could at first contribute little to their comfort. Game was abundant, and the faithful Joe was
ever on the alert; so the winter wore away happily for the exiles.

"The proprietors of the tract that had afforded an asylum for the
English exile began to take measures for its immediate settlement. Cates
came forth from his hiding place, purchased land, and, with his servant,
built the first house in the township.

"Both Cates and the negro were buried near the place of their concealment, and a rough stone, rudely initialed, marked for a time the spot.
When the first cemetery was laid out, the body of Cates was removed
thither, and a stone, ample for the times, bore the following inscription:

In
Memory of
Mr. John Cates.
He was a gentleman, born in England,
And the first settler in the
Town of Windham.
By his last
Will and Testament
He gave a
Generous legacy
To ye first
Church of Christ in
Windham
In plate, and a generous
Legacy in land
For ye support of ye poor,
And another
Legacy for ye support
Of ye school
In said town forever.
He died
In Windham,
July ye 16th, A. D.
1697."

Page 111-112.

Kelsey, William, Windsor. Invt. £216-03-10. Taken 1st December,
1698, by Job Drake and Daniel Pratt. The children: Abigail, age 4
years, Joanna 2, Ruth about 6 weeks.

Court Record, Page 85—16 December, 1698: Invt. exhibited. Daniel Pratt & Daniel Loomis were appointed Conservators, and ordered to render Account to this Court.

On the 12th of December, 1698, Adms. was granted to Abigail the Relict.

Page 37—(Vol. VIII) 3 September, 1711: Abigail Kelsey, a minor daughter of William Kelsey, chose Thomas Olcott (son of Samuel Olcott decd) to be her Guardian.

Page 251—14 April, 1715: Abigail Kelsey, alias Watson, Adms., presented an Account of Disbursements. It appears the Moveable Estate is not sufficient to pay the Debts.

Page 263—3 August, 1715: By Act of the General Assembly, 12 May last past, this Court do order and direct Abigail Kelsey, alias Watson, Adms., to sell so much of the Land of the sd. Decd as will produce the sum of £12-08-00 Money.

Page 28—(Vol. IX) 2 September, 1723: Capt. Thomas Stoughton, Atty. to Abigail Watson, sometime Widow of William Kelsey, moved in her behalf that 1-3 part of the Land that was her late husband's, William Kelsey, that he died seized of, might be Dist. to her for Improvement during life. Before this Court appeared also Josiah Barbour, of Windsor, and pleaded "that if the sd. Abigail have any Right or Dower in sd. Lands, she should have brought her suit in the Comon Law, he having actual possession of sd. Land; and that this Court can't proceed to grant sd. Abigail's request for her Dower, and the Title this Court can't take Cognizance of, and therefore prayes Judgement." This Court is of the opinion that the plea is sufficient to barr the proceedings of the sd. Abigail & order she pay the Costs, allowed to be £0-04-05. Paid in Court.

On File.

Lewis, Ezekiel, Farmington. Court Record, Page 37—13 April, 1698: To all Christian people to whom these presents shall come: Know ye that I, Ezekiel Lewis, of ffarmington, in consideration of the fidelity and good service, to gather wth those sums of money and reasonable satisfaction that I have Received from Sampson, Negro, heretofore Servant to my Father William Lewis deceased, and of late in my hands and belonging unto me, until this time, under the aforementioned consideration have relinquished, acquitted and discharged the sd. Sampson, Negro, his wife and Children, from my service and all manner of right, Claim, Challenge and demand that I ever had or may hereafter have by virtue of any writing or Instrument made over unto me or in me, I say I do set at liberty and grant freedome to the aforementioned Negroes from my heirs and assigns forever. Given under my hand and seal this first day of August, in the year of our Lord 1698.

Witness: *Isaac Meacham sen.,*   EZEKIEL LEWIS. Ls.
Caleb Stanly Jr.

Page 142-3.

Loomis, Deac. Joseph, Windsor. Invt. £277-09-06. Taken 7 November, 1699, by John Wolcott, Matthew Allyn and Timothy Loomis. The children: Joseph, age 18 years, Hannah 21, Grace 15, Lydia 13, Sarah 6 years.

Court Record, Page 125 and 127: Adms. granted to the Widow, Hannah Loomis.

Page 8—(Vol. VII) 10 March, 1700: Sergt. John Marsh moveing this Court that a longer time might be granted unto the Widow Loomis, Relict of Joseph Loomis, late of Windsor Decd, for the perfecting of her Adms. on her sd. husbands Estate, it is granted.

Page 18—4 September, 1701: Hannah, the Relict of Deacon Joseph Loomis decd, presented to this Court an Account of her Adms. This Court defer the Dist. until March next.

Page 25—7 March, 1701-2: Extended the Dist. until March next.

Page 37—2 March, 1702-3: Hannah, the Relict, moves this Court for a Dist. of her deceased husband's Estate. This Court order that sufficient Estate be sequestered for the payment of Debts, which being done, the Court proceed to Dist. to the Widow and Children (no names given): To the Eldest son, all the Lands, he to pay to the daughters, at the age of 18 years, their portions.

Page 38—2 March, 1702-3: This Court appoint Mr. John Wolcott, Capt. Matthew Allyn and Timothy Loomis to apprise that part of the Land that shall fall to the daughters, and also to Dist. the Estate.

Dist. File, 7 April, 1703: To the Widow, to Hannah, to Joseph, to Grace, to Sarah, to Lydia Loomis. By John Wolcott, Matthew Allyn and Timothy Loomis.

Page 43—(Vol. VII) 7 April, 1703: Reprt of the Dist., and this Court grant the Widow a *Quietus Est.*

Page 5.

Lord, William, Haddam. Died 4 December, 1696. Invt. £141-02-00. Taken by James Bates and Daniel Brainard Jr. The children: William, age 16 years, Jonathan 11, Nathaniel 9, John 3, Mary 18, Sarah 14, Hannah 7, Dorothy, 9 months old. The Estate was indebted to John Arnold, Richard Christophers, William Eley, Samuel Joanes sen., Benjamin Scoville, Samuel Emmons, John Scovell and Thomas Shaylor to the full amount, including rates, £25-01-00.

Court Record, Page 141—(Vol. IV) 4 December, 1696: Adms. to the Widow and her Brother Thomas Shaylor.

Page 40—(Vol. VIII) 2 March, 1702-3: This Court order the Clerk to grant a Citation requireing Samuel Ingram of Haddam, Adms. in Right of Sarah his wife, & Thomas Shaylor, also Adms. on the Estate of William Lord Decd, that they appear at the adjourned Court to be holden in Hartford on ye 1st Tuesday of April next.

Page 102-3.

Mackmin, James, Windsor. Invt. £3311-05-12. Taken 9 January, 1698-9, by Abraham Phelps, Daniel Hayden and Alexander Allin. Will dated 27 June, 1697.

I James Mackmin of Windsor doe make this my last Will & Testament: I give and bequeath to my wife Elizabeth, after my Just Debts are paid, all the remainder of my Estate, both personal & Real, viz, all my houseing and Lands, goods, debts, Chattells or whatsoever doth of right belong to me here in New England, to be and remain to her, the above said Elizabeth, forever. I nominate and appoint my well beloved wife to be my sole Executrix.   JAMES MACKMIN. Ls.

Witness: *John Moore sen.,*
John Fyler.

Court Record, Page 65—17 January, 1698-9: Will approved.

Page 1.

Marshall, John, Wethersfield. Invt. £36-13-00. Taken 17 February, 1696-7, by Thomas Welles & Thomas Griswold. Will dated 1st February, 1693-4.

I John Marshall of Wethersfield, in the County of Hartford, in New England, intending to goe to Sea, for the Settlement of my Outward Estate I dispose the same in manner following: I give to my wife Mary during her Widowhood. If she bear me a child, then provision is made for that, either a son or a daughter. If no Child be born to my wife, then my wife Mary to have the Land during her Widowhood. But all the Houseing and Lands given me by my father Thomas Marshall, at my wife's Marriage or Deacease, to revert to my two brothers, Thomas and Benjamin Marshall. In Case I do not return home before my Decease, then I do Will the Authorities of this Colony, that shall then be, shall put in an Executor to this my Will.

Witness: *John Welles,*   JOHN MARSHALL, Ls.
Margaret Welles.

Thomas Seamore, aged about 20 years, and Robert Webster, aged about 20 years, certifieth and saith: That being in Boston in December last past, then met with Thomas Marshall, Brother to John Marshall, that married Mary North of Wethersfield, who went away to sea together, viz, Thomas Marshall and John Marshall aforesd., and Thomas Marshall had information that his Brother John Marshall was dead, that he died in France, and that he had creditable information that it was so, and that he did believe that his Brother John was dead according to the information he had received. Further he saith not.

On the 10th day of March, 1696-7, Thomas Seamore and Robert Webster personally appeared before me and made Oath to the above written Testimony.   *James Fitch, Assistant.*

The above written Inventory was presented to the Apprisers by Mary Marshall, the wife of John Marshall, late of Wethersfield, as she acknowledged in Court, 10th March, 1696-7. Attest: *Caleb Stanly, Assistant.*

Court Record, Page 146—(Vol. IV) 4 March, 1696-7: Whereas, Mary Marshall, the Widow of John Marshall of Wethersfield, presented an Inventory of her husband's Estate to this Court, with his last Will, and he having been absent a considerable time, and she hearing by Sundry persons that the sd. John Marshall dyed in France, and no Executor named in sd. Will, Adms. is granted to Mrs. Mary Marshall the Widow.

Page 132.

Marshall, John, Windsor. Invt. £183-10-04. Taken 4 December, 1699, by Daniel Hayden & Return Strong. Land in Middletown not Inventoried. One Child named Hannah, 5 years of age.

The Testimony of Elizabeth Strong & Elizabeth Grant, of sufficient age, saith: That when John Marshall laye upon his death bed we both were present with him and we heard him say: "Oh, Elizabeth, I am just agoing." I Elizabeth Strong asked him: "What makes you think so?" His answer was: "I feel all within me seem to faile me." Then I asked him What was his mind concerning his Child, whether it was his mind his Aunt Allyn should have her. His answer was: "Yes." Then I asked him Whether it was not his mind that the Child shall have all that he had. He answered "Yes."

Elizabeth Strong & Elizabeth Grant, each of them, gave Oath to the Truth of what is above written, this 16th January, 1699-1700.

Present: *Eliakim Marshall.* *Daniel Clarke, Justice.*

Court Record, Page 113—5 December, 1699: Adms. to Mrs. Hannah Allyn, Relict of Col. John Allyn Decd, and joyned with her Lt. Return Strong.

Page 139—7 March, 1699-1700: Nuncupative Will made by John Marshall, late of Windsor Decd, was presented in Court, as appeared by the Testimony of Elizabeth Strong & Elizabeth Grant, wherein he made dispose of his Child and of his Estate to her upon his Death Bed. Eliakim Marshall was present when the Will was read and had nothing to object against it. The Court approve, and order it to be recorded.

Page 73.

Mason, John, Hartford. Died 19 February, 1697-8. Invt. £245-11-00. Taken by John Merrells sen., Thomas Bunce and John Catlin sen. The children: Mary, age 20 years, Hannah 17, John 13, Joseph 10, Abigail 7, Jonathan 4, Lydia, 1 year old.

Court Record, Page 33—13 April, 1698: Adms. to the Widow, Hannah Mason.

Page 55-6.

Mills, John, Simsbury. Died 11 March, 1697-8. Invt. £117-10-06. Taken 13 April, 1698, by John Higley, Samuel Willcoxson sen., Peter Buell and John Slater sen. Wife Sarah: Children: John Mills, in his 8th year; Joseph and Benjamin, twins, in their 4th year; and daughter Sarah, in 2nd year of age.

Court Record, Page 27—13 April, 1698: An Invt. of the Estate of John Mills of Simsbury was presented by Samuel Pettebone. The Court grant Adms. to the Relict and Samuel Pettebone.

Page 30—13 April, 1698: Whereas, John Mills, late of Simsbury, was some years since chosen by the sd. Town for a Constable to collect the Country rates, and it appeareing to the Court that the rate is paid to the Treasurer and there remains considerable part of the sd. Rate yet unpaid to the sd. Constable in the sd. Town, Adms. upon the Estate of the sd. Mills being granted to Samuel Pettebone and the Widow, the Court do therefore invest the sd. Samuel Pettebone with the same power that he the sd. John Mills, Constable, had whilst living, and to execute the Treasurer as one to all intents and purposes as he might or could have done in order to the Gathering the remainder of the Rates for that year.

Page 168—(Vol. VIII) 4 January, 1713-14: Joseph Mills, a minor, 18 years of age, and Sarah Mills, age 16 years, children of John Mills, chose their Father-in-law John Humphrey to be their Guardian. Recog., £40. Benjamin Mills, a minor son of John Mills, chose James Hillier to be his Guardian. Recog., £30.

Page 171—4 January, 1713-14: John Humphrey & Samuel Pettebone of Simsbury, Adms. on the Estate of John Mills, late of Simsbury Decd, exhibited an Account of their Adms:

	£ s d
Inventory,	120-15-06
The Real part whereof is,	75-10-00
The Debts and Charges,	30-15-00
There remains to be distributed,	92-06-00
Account allowed. Order to Dist:	
To Sarah Mills, now wife of John Humphrey,	5-10-00
Also, to the Relict of the sd. Decd, her Dower in Lands.	
To John Mills, the Eldest son, his double portion,	34-12-02
To Joseph Mills, Benjamin Mills, to each of them,	17-06-01
And to Sarah Mills, now wife of Samuel Tuller,	17-06-01

And appoint John Pettebone, Joseph Case & John Slater, of Simsbury, Distributors.

Page 47.

More, Philip. Died 5 January, 1697-8. Invt. £39-08-04. Taken 10 January, 1697-8, by Joseph Talcott and Roger Pitkin.

Court Record, Page 19—3 March, 1697-8: Adms. to the Widow, Lydia More.

Page 3.

More, Ruth. (Colored Woman.) Died 27 August, 1696. Invt. £8-09-00. Taken by Joshua Carter & Thomas Richards. Will dated 21 August, 1696.

I Ruth More, Negro, of Hartford, doe make this my last Will & Testament: My Will is that all my Just Debts and Funeral Charges be paid. I give unto my daughter-in-Law Susannah, the wife of Cato, all the remainder of my Estate whatsoever.

Witness: *William Pitkin,*   RUTH X MORE, Ls.
   Hannah Cowles.

On the 8th of October, 1696, William Pitkin & Hannah Cowles made Oath that Ruth More signed, sealed and declared the above written to be her last Will & Testament, but afterward gave to Philip More's eldest daughter an Iron Pott and a Frying pan, which Susannah and Cato is willing she should have.   Attest: *Caleb Stanly, Assist.*

"*Col. Allyn, sen: What you see necessary to be done in Cato's affair, I doe freely allow of it. And his being in my service shall be no hindrance to him.*   Yours,   TIMO. WOODBRIDGE."

Page 74-5.

Mygatt, Joseph sen., Hartford. Invt. £412-08-04. Taken 31 March, 1697, by Jonathan Webster and Thomas King. The children: Joseph, 19 years, Susannah 17, Mary 15, Thomas 9, Sarah 7, Zebulon 4, Dorothy 2, and Sarah the Relict. Will dated 11 February, 1697-8.

I Joseph Mygatt sen. of Hartford, in the Collony of Connecticut, doe make and ordain this my last Will & Testament: I give to my beloved wife ½ of my moveable Estate. The other halfe I give to my four daughters, Susannah, Mary, Sarah and Dorothy, the Syder Mill and Press only Excepted in my personal Estate. I give to my wife the one-halfe of my House & Barne and Homelott and appurtenances, and the use of my Syder Mill & Press, so long as she remains my Widow; only my son Joseph shall have liberty to make what Syder he shall have occasion for. I give to my son Joseph Mygatt my House and Homestead, only excepting my wive's Interest therein. I give him a certain parcell of Land lying in the Crotch of the River which was given to me by the Town. I give to my son Thomas Mygatt all my Hog River Pasture. I give to my son Zebulon Mygatt all my Land at Suffield. My will is that my son Joseph shall pay as a legacy to my daughter Susannah £10 in Country pay when she comes to the age of 23 years, and to my daughter Mary £10 when she comes to the age of 24 years, and £10 each to my two younger daughters at their Marriage. I appoint my wife & my son Joseph Mygatt to be Joynt Executors, and desire Mr. Richard Edwards & Mr. Jonathan Bull to be Overseers.

Witness: *Jonathan Bull,*   JOSEPH MYGATT. Ls.
Richd Edwards, Daniel Clarke, Smith.

Court Record, Page 34—13 April, 1698: Will approved.

Page 93—(Vol. VII) 5 May, 1707: Thomas Mygatt, a minor, 18 years of age, son of Joseph Mygatt, chose Major William Whiting to be his Guardian.

Page 140.

Newbery, Thomas, Windsor. Invt. £280-00-00, Real Estate. Taken 10 April, 1700. One Item: ½ the farm given to his father by Mr. Allyn.

Court Record, Page 52—8 October, 1698: Adms. to Benjamin Newbery & Lieut. Matthew Allyn.

Page 124—7 March, 1699-1700: Ensign Benjamin Newbery presented an Inventory of the Real Estate of his deceased brother Thomas Newbery.

Page 67—(Vol. VII) 26 April, 1705: Joseph Leonard of Springfield and Benjamin Newbery of Windsor, Adms., are ordered to render an account of their Adms. September next.

Page 67—(Vol. VII) 26 April, 1705: Benjamin Newbery, son of the sd. Thomas Newbery, late of Windsor, Decd, appeared before Samuel Partridge Esq., Judge of the Court of Probate in the County of Hampshire, and made choice of Preserve Clapp of Northampton to be his Guardian. Recog. £20, with John Wolcott of Windsor.

Page 71—7 November, 1705: Joseph Leonard of Springfield, Adms., exhibited in this Court an Account of his Adms., which this Court allow and grant him a *Quietus Est.*

Page 123—7 March, 1708-9: An Agreement for the Dist. of the Estate of Thomas Newbery, late of Windsor, Decd, by Joseph and Benjamin Newbery, his two sons, and John Wolcott Jr., who married his daughter.

Page 125—4 April, 1709: Preserve Clapp, Guardian, now released from his Bond, the sd. Benjamin being of age. Exhibited and approved.

Newell, John. Court Record, Page 117—(Vol. V)—3 September, 1696: A Writing called by Thomas Newell and others the Last will and testament of John Newell, was exhibited in Court and Sundry witnesses to prove the same, which are very controdictary one to another, and are so cross each to other that we can not see reason to approve of the will, and therefore we order the Estate distributed as followeth: To the Eldest son a double portion of the Estate, and the rest his Brothers & Sisters equal portions. Adms. to Thomas & Samuel Newell, and appoint Mr. Samuel Wadsworth, Mr. Samuel Hooker and Lt. John Judd distributors.

Page 55.

Owen, John sen. Died 18 February, 1698. Invt. £29-01-00. Taken 5 April, 1698, by Lt. Hayden & Benajah Holcomb.

Court Record, Page 22—5 April, 1698: Invt. exhibited, being only personal estate, and that given to the Widow to be at her dispose, the children consenting.

Page 93.

Peck, Joseph, Hartford. Invt. £501-18-00. Taken 6 May, 1698, by James Steele sen. and Joseph Bull. The children: Joseph, 4 ¾ years of age, Ruth Peck 2 ¾ years of age.

Court Record, Page 51—1st September, 1698: Adms. to Ruth Peck, the Relict. Estate left in the Widow's hands until the children come of age.

Dist. File, 11 May, 1719: Receipt of Solomon Moss of Wallingford to his Mother-in-law Ruth Horskins, her husband John Horskins, and also to his brother-in-law Joseph Peck of Windsor, for the portion of my wife of the estate of her father Joseph Peck.

Signed: SOLOMON MOSS, Ls.
Witness: *Henry Stiles,*   RUTH X MOSS, Ls.
Israel Stoughton, Roland X Grant.

Page 104—(Vol. X) 5 October, 1725: Joseph Peck, formerly of Hartford, & Ruth Hoskins alias Peck, sometime Widow of Joseph Peck Decd, exhibited a Discharge from Joseph Peck and Ruth Moss, children of sd. Decd, for their portions of their Father's Estate.

Page 156—6 June, 1727: This Court grant the Adms. a *Quietus Est.*

Page 81-83.

Phelps, Ephraim, Windsor. Invt. £245-18-00. Taken 26 November, 1697, by Timothy Phelps, William Phelps. Invt. at Stamford, £55-04-03. Taken 26 November, 1697, by Daniel Schofield, John Holly and Jonathan Waterbury. Will dated at Stamford, 30 October, 1697.

I Ephraim Phelps of Windsor, in the County of Hartford, doe make and ordain this my last Will & Testament: I give to my Wife Mary Phelps the use and benefit & Improvement of my houseing & Lands, with all the appurtenances thereunto belonging, until my child shall come to the age of 21 years. If my wife then be my Widow, I give her one-half until her decease or marriage. Provision is made should another child be born. I desire my Uncles Samuel & John Cross of Windsor and Samuel Webb of Stamford to be my Overseers. Before signing, this was added: In Case his child or Children decease before he or they come of age to receive the Estate, then he gives it absolutely to his Wife Mary Phelps as her Property forever.   EPHRAIM PHELPS. Ls.
Witness: *Abraham Ambler,*
John Bates.

Know all men by these presents: That I John Copp of Stamford, in the County of Fairfield, in Connecticut, as Administrator to the Estate of

Ephraim Phelps, late of Windsor deceased, have the day of the date of these presents received & had of and from Mr. Samuel Cross & Mr. John Cross, of Windsor aforesaid, as they were appointed Overseers in the Last Will of the above sd. Ephraim Phelps Decd, all the real & personal Estate lately belonging to him the sd. Ephraim Phelps situate in Windsor, as it is Inventoried and apprised in Windsor since the sd. Ephraim Phelps Decd. And I the sd. John Copp. as Adms. do acquitt & discharge them the sd. Samuel & John Cross as Overseers from the same in every part thereof forever. 20 May, 1698.   JOHN COPP. Ls.

Court Record, Page 38—13 April, 1698: Will and Invt. Exhibited by Abigail Winchell, as no Executor was appointed. Adms. to the relict, with Samuel & John Cross conservators.

Page 56—1st September, 1698: John Copp Adms. by marrying the Relict.

Page 122—(Vol. VII) 7 March, 1708-9: Ephraim Phelps, a minor, about 16 years of age, son of Eaphraim Phelps, chose his Uncle William Phelps to be his Guardian.

Page 59—(Vol. VIII) 3 March, 1711-12: Josiah Phelps of Windsor is appointed Guardian to Ephraim Phelps, now 20 years of age, his former Guardian William Phelps being deceased.

Page 19-20.

Pinney, John, Windsor. Died September last. Invt. £107-16-06. Taken 25 October, 1697, by John Porter sen., John Drake & John Stoughton. Will dated 19 June, 1697.

I John Pinney of Windsor, being at present by the Providence of God called to goe into the War, doe now make this my last Will & Testament: I doe give, devise and bequeath unto Abraham Phelps Jr., son of Lt. Abraham Phelps of Windsor, my House or Allottment on which it stands in Windsor, with all the Appurtenances thereof, to be and remain to him, his heirs and assigns forever from and after the day of my decease. I give and bequeath unto Jonathan Pinney, the son of my Brother Isaac Pinney, my feather bed, Trammell, and what else soever I have now in my sd. Brother Isaac's House. And I appoint my Kinsman Abraham Phelps Jr. to be my Executor.

Witness: *Caleb Stanly Jr.,*   JOHN X PINNEY, Ls.
Nathaniel Down.

Court Record, Page 3—10 November, 1697: Will proven.

Page 107-8-9.

Porter, John, Sergt., Windsor. Invt. £849-06-00. Taken 2 February, 1698-9, by John Wolcott, Deac. Joseph Loomis and Lt. Matthew Allyn. Will dated 7 September, 1698.

I Sergt. John Porter of Windsor do declare this my last Will & Testament. I give to my wife, if she survive me, the use of all my houseing and homested on the east side of the highway before my Door until the heirs hereafter mentioned Come of age. Also I give her a third part of all my improved Land during her widowhood, excepting only my pasture by Mr. Allyn's. If she marry again, then my three sons, John, Daniel and David Porter, shall have liberty to pay to their mother £5 a year instead of a third of the land, or else she to hold of the land her life-time. Also I give her £50 out of my moveable Estate to her free dispose, and the use of my young Children's portions until they come of age. I give to my son John Porter, besides his house and Lands adjoining to it that I have given him a Deed of, I now give him 13 acres of my Land in Plymouth Meadow. I give him ½ of my 2 Woodlotts, the one called Poquanuck Path Lott, the other called the Woulfe pit Lott. I give to my son Daniel Porter all my House & Land on the East side of the Great River that now doth or hereafter may belong to my Estate, and my Pasture by Mr. Allyn's house as it bounds north & East on Mr. Allyn's Land, with all the Tackling and Arms provided him for Trooping, and 100 of Apple Trees that he shall choose out of my Nursery. I give to my son David Porter my Dwelling house and Barn, Orchard, Garden, Outhouseing, Cyder Mill & Press, wth the Furnis in the House, the muck in the Yard belonging to it, with the 4 acres of Homelott on the West side of the Highway adjoining Timothy Loomis his Lott. I also give him 5 acres of my Plymouth Meadow Lott. I give him the other half of my 2 Woodlotts mentioned in my son John's Legacy. As for the House & Homelott my son-in-Law Peter Mills now lives on, my Will is that he and his now wife shall have it their live's time, the property to remain as it is at present. And after the decease of the sd. Peter and his now wife, that house & Homested to be to their Eldest son, & to be reconed to my daughter Joannah at £13-10-00 of her portion. The remainder of my Moveable Estate, with 6 acres of Land bounding East on the 8 acres of Woodland I gave to David, that shall be equally divided among my six daughters. What I owe to be paid out of my Personal Estate, and what is due to me to belong to my Personal Estate. I appoint my wife and son John Executors. I desire my Brother Timothy Loomis and my son Thomas Moore to be Supervisors.

Witness: *Timothy Loomis,*   JOHN PORTER SEN., LS.
        Joseph Porter.

Court Record, Page 82—2 March, 1698-9: Will & Invt. exhibited by Joannah The Relict. Proven.

Page 50—(Vol. IX) 4 February, 1717-18: Upon Motion of Joannah Porter to the Court to set out of the Estate of John Porter to her according to the Will, Objection was made that there was no attested copy of a Will.

Page 53—4 March, 1717-18: This Court appoint Daniel Loomis, David Loomis and John Palmer to set out to her some Estate.

Page 36.

Porter, Thomas sen., Farmington.   Invt. £96-00-06.   Taken 13 December, 1697, by John Hart & Daniel Andrews.   Will dated 3 March, 1690-1.

The last Will & Testament of Thomas Porter sen. is as followeth: I give to my wife Sarah Porter, during her natural life, my now Dwelling house, wth half the Benefit of the Orchard, half the Garden behind the house, and Pastureing for a Cow during summer. Also my Personal Estate, within doors and without, to be disposed of by her among my Children that have the most need thereof. Also all the Divisions of Outlands given her by her Honoured Father Stephen Hart, to be disposed of by her and as she seeth meet forever. I give to my son Thomas Porter ½ of my House lott on the Side next to Mr. Wadsworth's houselott, and all my Land at the Round Hill that lyeth on the West side of the Way, the Cart way that now runneth through the Lott which is called the Farme Path, and also my whole Lott that runneth from the River across the Plaine West, on the North side of John Clarke's Lott. Also 12 acres up the Farme Brook, and also my whole Division of Upland abutting on Hartford Bounds. I do give to my son Samuel Porter the other half of my House lott, with the House that he now dwelleth in, and my part of the Barn, to be possessed by him immediately after my decease, except what I have before given to my wife, which he shall not possess until after the decease of my wife. Item. I do give to my daughter Dorothy Porter my Division of Lands lying against Wethersfield in the middle Division, on Condition that she shall make no alienations thereof, but shall first let her Brothers have the Refusal thereof. 5thly, I do give to my gr. son Timothy Porter my musket, Sword & Bandeliers. 6thly, I do further give my two sons, Thomas Porter & Samuel Porter, all my Divisions of Lands, divided & undivided, in the several Out-Divisions of Lands or elsewhere, to be equally divided between them, except what I have before given to my well beloved wife & to my daughter Dorothy Porter to each of them in particular. I say I do give to my two sons all my Out-Divisions as before mentioned, together with those before mentioned particular parcels of Land, to each of them and to their heirs forever, on the Conditions that they pay 40 Shillings apeice in Country pay to my wife and winter her a Cow yearly as long as her natural life shall continue, which 40 Shillings is to be understood to be paid yearly. I appoint my wife & two sons, Thomas Porter and Samuel Porter, Executors of this my Will.

Witness: *Thomas Hart,*   THOMAS PORTER, Ls.
       John Hart.

Court Record, Page 15—3 March, 1697-8:   Will proven.

Page 117-18-19-222.

Robbins, John, Wethersfield.   Invt. £2227-13-06.   Taken 21 November, 1699, by John Welles and Benjamin Gilbert.   Will dated 1st July, 1689.

I John Robbins of Wethersfield doe make this my last Will & Testament: I give to my son Joshua my Homelott with the Houseing thereupon, excepting so much of the sd. Lott as is afterwards given to John, which sd. Homelott or Messuage abutts northwest upon the Broad Street, South East upon ye Plaine, Northeast upon the Homelott lately belonging to John Betts decd, and Southwest upon the Homelott belonging to the Heirs of Nathaniel Grave late of Wethersfield Decd. Also a peice of Land lying at the rear of the Homelott, excepting only 5 acres given to John, which is bounded on the Homelotts of Lt. James Treat, John Betts, John Robbins and the sd. Nathaniel Graves North, South upon Land of Isaac Boreman and Joshua Robbins, West on John Graves & John Waddams, and East upon the Plain Lane. I give to my son Samuel 20 acres of Pasture Land in the South Field at Goff Brook, on the South side of the sd. Pasture, butting East on the Highway leading to Rocky Hill, West on the Common, North on that Part which I give to my son Richard, South on the Residue of my Father John Robbins his southermost Woodlott. I give to my son John part of my Homelott, on the North side thereof, with the Barn & the Lott, 7 Rods in Breadth at the Front next to Broad Street, and 9 Rods in Breadth at the Rear. I give to my son Richard Robbins 20 acres in my Pasture on the Highway leading to Rocky Hill and 5 acres of my Lott in Fearfull Swamp. My Lott on the East side of the Great River on the West side of Pahegansuck Hill, which I bought of Samuel Boreman, I give to my sons Samuel & Richard, equally; and also my part on the East side of the Connecticut River lately purchased of the Indians by several Inhabitants of this town of Wethersfield, of whom I was one, lying three Miles distant from the river, and which is not yet divided among the Purchasers, my part of it I give to my sons Samuel and Richard equally. I give to my wife Mary Robbins £100 in Current Country pay besides the thirds of the Estate and the use of the Children's portions until they Come of age. Should she decease before they come of age, the Custody of his minor children to be with his Brother-in-law Samuel Boreman and his Cousin Mr. John Chester, Esq. Also I give to my son Joshua 2 ½ acres of Land at the upper End of the Great Meadow, bounded North on the Highway leading to Churchill's Island, South on Land of Mr. Samuel Welles, East on Land belonging to my Brother Joshua Robbins. I desire my wife Mary Robbins to be sole Executrix.

Witness: *Gershom Bulkeley,*   JOHN ROBBINS. Ls.
        Peter Bulkeley.

Court Record, Page 87—7 March, 1698-9: Will & Invt. exhibited in Court by Mary the Relict. Witnessess not being present, we desire Capt. Chester to swear the Evidences and return the Will to the Clerk.

Dist. File, 3 January, 1713-14: Estate of John Robbins. An Agreement for a Division to Joshua, to Samuel, to Richard Robbins.

Witness: *Jonathan Belding,*
        Richard Nichols.

Sadd, John. Court Record, Page 70—27 November, 1695: By this Publique instrument of Substitution Be it known: That I Robert Calse of Boston, in New England, Merchant, by notice of a letter of Atty. & power to me given from John Sadd of Earls Colne, in the County of Essex, in England, Yeoman, bearing date the 10th of January, 1695, duely made before a notary publique in London and sworne to before Isaac Addington Esqr, Secretary for the province of the Massachusetts Bay, have as Well on behalfe of said Sadd as upon my proper and particular accot made, ordained and substituted, & by these presents do make, ordaine, substitute and appoint Capt. Samuel Ells of Hingham, in the County of Suffolk, in New England, mercht, my substitute, giving unto him full power and authority as attorney for the said Sadd, as well as agent or attorney for myself, or either of us, to ask, Demand & receive of and from Zachariah Sandford and William Pitkin, Executrs. of John Sadd, late of Hartford Decd, father of the above said Sadd, Whatsoever Legacys are due to the said Sadd or his Children or to me the said Calse.

7 October, 1698.

Witness: *John Watson,*   Robt. Calse. Ls.
John Valentine.   Notr's Publq.

Suffolk, Boston, Octb. 8th, 1698.

Mr. Robert Calse personally appeared before me, the subscriber, one of his Majst Justices of the peace for the County of Suffolk, & Acknowledged, etc.   John Eyre.

Hartford, 5 April, 1699: Then Received of Mr. William Pitkin & Mr. Zachary Sandford of Hartford, Executors of the Will of John Sadd, late of Hartford Decd, the sum of £100 in money for the use of John Sadd of Earls Colne, in the County of Essex, England, in part of what was given him by will, to be delivered unto Mr. Robert Calse of Boston, Atty. to sd. John Sadd, danger of Robbery Excepted, he paying for carrying the same. In Witness whereof I have set my hand to two Receipts, both of this tennor and date, one of which being accomplished the other to be void as to me Samuel Ells, substituted attourney by the said Robt. Calse for said John Sadd.

Witness: *Thomas Hooker,*
John Camp, sen.

Recorded 7 April, 1699: *Will Whiting, Clerk.*

Mr. Calse's Receipt to Capt. Ells is entered in this book, Fol. 142.

Page 142—April the 25th, 1699: Received of Capt. Samuel Eells the within Contents, viz, One hundred pounds, and then paid the charges. I say Recd.   Pr. Robert Calse.

Witness: *Ebenezer White,*
Mary Jones.

Page 42.

Saunders, George, Windsor. Died 5 December, 1697 (W. R.). Invt. £26-07-06. Taken 19 December, 1697, by Abraham Phelps, Michael Tainter & Daniel Hayden.

Court Record, Page 16—5 April, 1698: The Estate Insolvent. And this Court do appoint Nathaniel Bissell Conservator of the Estate.

Page 107—7 September, 1699: This Court order Lt. Samuel Cross & Mr. Nathaniel Bissell to make distribution of the estate to the creditors by a due proportion.

Page 93.

Segur, Richard, Simsbury. Died 14 March, 1697-8. Invt. £52-12-00. Taken 28 April, 1698, by John Higley, Samuel Wilcox and John Slater Jr. The children: John Segur, age 12 years, Joseph 7, Elizabeth 14, Abigail, one year old.

Court Record, Page 53—1st September, 1698: Invt. Exhibited by John Griffin. Adms. to Sergt. Samuel Wilcox, and order him to take the best care for the putting out of the children, the mother being also dead.

Page 123—(Vol. VII) 7 March, 1708-9: This Court do order that the Clerk do issue forth a writ to require Sergt. Samuel Wilcockson of Simsbury, Adms. on the Estate of Richard Segur, late of Simsbury Decd, to render an Account of his Adms. on that Estate to this Court on the 1st Monday of April next.

Page 128—2 May, 1709: Sergt. Samuel Wilcockson exhibited now in this Court an Account of his Adms., having paid to Creditors the sum

	£ s d
of	20-07-00
and Also delivered and paid to Elizabeth and Abigail, 2 of the daughters of the sd. Decd, their portions,	3-19-00
Both sums amount to	24-06-00

which is more than the whole of all the Moveable Estate by the sum of   2-14-00

And John Segur of Simsbury, eldest son of sd. Decd, now before this Court engaged to pay to the sd. Adms. the sd. £2-14-00, which makes an even balance of the sd. Account. Allowed, approved, and granted a *Quietus Est.*

Page 59—(Vol. VIII) 3 March, 1711-12: Joseph Seagur, 20 years of age, son of Richard Seagur, made choice of Thomas Griffin to be his Guardian.

Page 62—3 March, 1711-12: Upon the Request of John Segur, eldest son of Richard Segur late of Simsbury Decd, praying that this Court would appoint Distributors to distribute and divide the Estate of Richard Segur Decd, which by the Adms. Account appears to be £31-00, to be dist. to and among the Children; and that the same persons so appointed may also divide and dist. among the Children of the sd. Decd the sum of £11-10 that is lately descended to the sd. Children by the Right of their late Mother, who was daughter to Sergt. John Griffin, late of Simsbury Decd, and appears by Dist. lately made by Order of this Court and approved of, both which sums amount to £42-10. The Court order and appoint John Slater Jr., Sergt. Thomas Holcomb and Jonathan Holcomb of Simsbury to Dist. the sd. Estate:

| To John Seagur, Eldest son, | £ s d 17-00-00 | To Elizabeth, | £ s d 8-10-00 |
| To Joseph, | 8-10-00 | To Abigail, | 8-10-00 |

This Court appoint Samuel Wilcoxson to be Guardian unto Abigail Seagur, a minor daughter of Richard Seagur, late decd.

Page 108—6 January, 1712-13: Report of the Distributors.

Page 70-1.

Shepherd, Susannah sen., Hartford. Invt. £46-06-00. Taken 12 April, 1698, by John Marsh & Samuel Kellogg. Will dated 7 March, 1698-9.

I Susannah Shepherd sen., being in perfect memory, I doe comitt my Soule to God that gave it, and my body to an honourable buryall. I give to my daughter Susannah Pratt 2 Chests & two Boxes and all that is in them, the one a wainscott Chest, the other marked W. S. G. I give to John Pratt Jr. a little Pott, a quart Skillett, and a frying pan and a Table. And to my son William Goodwin's daughter Susan I give my great Brass Kettle and a bible & a Bodkin. I give the other Chest & all that is in it, between them, to my sons William & Nathaniel. I give to Nathaniel Goodwin's daughter Mehetabell a trundel Bedd, Boulster & 2 Blanketts. I give to Hezekiah Goodwin my bigest Iron Pott & a warming pan. I give William Goodwin's wife my wedding gown. And to my son Nath: Goodwin's wife my 2 gowns & a serge gown & a paragon Gown. And all the rest of my Woolen Clothes not mentioned I give my three daughters, to be equally divided.

Witness: *John Bigelow,*   SUSANNAH X SHEPHERD.
Jonathan Butler.

Court Record, Page 33—14 April, 1698: Will & Invt. exhibited. Adms. to William Goodwin & John Pratt with Will annexed.

Page 6.

Smith, Abraham. Died 11 April, 1695. Invt. £1-16-00. Taken 18 January, 1697, by John Porter and Thomas Griswold. (The former Invt. being lost.) The Invt. presented 17 February, 1696-7, & approved. Benajah Holcomb was desired to administer on the estate. Nathaniel Stanly, Caleb Stanly & Jno. Hamlin, Assistants.

Page 105. (Vol. V.)

Smith, Richard, Wethersfield. An Invt. so far as we can gain, on the Estate of Richard Smith, Deceased June, 1690: Imprimis: Received from Sargnt. John Welles & John Kilbourn, who formerly were desired to take an Inventory of the sd. Smith's Estate by his sons or Widow: To Apparrell; to the whole Moveable Estate in the house, as Brass, all pewter, all Woolen & Lining Cloath, Tackling for carrying on husbandry, Cattle & Sheep; To a Servant, Crop & Saw Mill, provision, etc. But they took noe Accot of Money, wch Accot or Invt. amounted to the sume of

	£	s	d
	330-00-00

being the best Accot they can give of their Proceedings.

To 50 acres of Upland by Estimation, with Buildings,	400-00-00
To Land purchased of Thomas Bunce, 240 acrs wth Buildings,	200-00-00
To several parcells of Land, apprissed at	240-00-00
To Land which Samuel Smith possesses, recorded to his Father, & we find no legal conveyance by Record to Samuel Smith,	40-00-00

1210-00-00

Wethersfield, the 10th of April, 1691. Pr us: *John Chester,*
Benjamin Churchill.

Court Record, Page 26—5 March, 1690-1: Upon the Petition of John Strickland and Richard Fox in behalf of their wives, daughters of Richard Smith: Whereas, the Widow of Richard Smith of Naubuck & one or more of her sons, have refused to give Entrance to the Townsmen of Wethersfield, & would not suffer them to take an Invt. of the Estate of sd. Richard Smith decd, this Court therefore order that the Marshall, with two of the Townsmen of Wethersfield, shall go over to Naubuck & take an Inventory of all Personal & Real Estate & present the same at the next Session of the County Court in Hartford. And if any doe oppose or hinder then in the due Execution of this Order, they are to seize them and bring them to the Common Goal, there to be secured till the Court be holden at Hartford the 2nd Wednesday of April next. The Clerk of the Court to issue out his warrant for the Attendance of this Order, & to impower the Marshall to take ayd with him for to accomplish the same.

Page 29—21 April, 1691: This Court having severall times by their officer demanded of the widow smith of Naubuck an Inventory of the Estate of Richard Smith deceased, which she hath refused us or at Least neglected to make presentation of the same to the Court, the Court therefore ordered the Marshall, with the Townsmen of Wethersfield, to take an Inventory of the sayd Richard Smith's Estate, & they have now presented an Inventory of the Estate amounting to £1210-00-00, in which there is no account of the crop on the Land or feild, nor what moneys were in the house. This Court accepts of the Inventory so far as it reacheth, & doe distribute the Estate: To the Widow a Third of the real Estate during her natural Life, & a Third of the personall to be to her & her heirs forever; & to the Eldest son a double portion, & to the rest of the Children equal portions; & the Court Grant Adms. to the Widow & her 3 sons, provided they accept thereof & signify the same to the Clarke within Ten days after notice hereof. But if they neglect this, the Court grant Adms. to Richard Fox & John Strickland. The sonns to have their portions in Land, provided they pay their Sisters their portions in good and currant pay of the country, or out of the Estate as Inventoried, In which the daughters have their just proportions. But if the sons neglect to doe this, the daughters to take their portions in Land, so much as shall be found wanting to make up their portions in other Estate. As also what portions any of the Children have received of their father formerly, & made to appear, it is to be added to the Inventory & accounted in the distribution.

Page 112-13 (Vol. VI):

Invt. of Richard Smith's Estate, who Died June, 1690. Invt. £590-00-00. Taken 2 March, 1698, by Jonathan Smith, Samuell Hale Jr., John Kilbourn & John Welles. Personal: Inventory not footed. Inventory in Lands as followeth:

	£ s d
His Lott bought of James Wright,	40-00-00
His Lott bought of Robert Rose,	45-00-00
The Lott he had of James Boswell,	180-00-00
The Lott purchased of Thomas Bunce,	145-00-00
His House with the Building upon it,	180-00-00
	590-00-00

In the year 1680 I, Richard Smith of Wethersfield, stricken in years and finding myself weake in body, thinke it meet and convenient to settle that little Matter which the Lord graciously hath given me in the World. Item. I give and bequeath to my wife 1 yoke of Oxen, to be sold for Money by my son Joseph Smith and the Mony delivered to my wife. Also she shall have two Cows, and my sons Joseph and Benjamin shall take care of and keep or maintain sd. Cows for sumer pastureing and winter fodder, or two other, during her life. I give to my wife one bed, the best now in my house, with whatever else belongs to it, to her and her heirs forever. I give to my wife the use and whole dispose of one of the rooms of my house, with the use of the seller chambers, during her natural Life, to be kept in repair so it may be comfortable for her. I give her what little mony I have in my hands (and) £15 in good Country pay, to be paid by my sons, Samuel, Joseph and Benjamin, equally. I give to my son Samuel my proportion of Land wch is on the East side of the great river wch ly in Comon undivided, wch was purchased by the towne In general of the Indians. Also, one-third part of a grant of Land given to Samuell Martin, all wch parcells of Land I give to my son Samuel Smith, to him and his heirs forever. I give to my son Joseph Smith that Lott which I bought of James Wright, abutting on the great river west, and north on Land belonging to Samuel Wells, and on the south upon Land belonging to James Wright, running east three miles. I give to my son Joseph one peice of Land I bought of Thomas Bunce. Also I give to my son Joseph one-third part of a peice of Land I bought of Samuel Martin. I give to my son Benjamin Smith my 50-acre Lott wch my dwelling house now standeth on, wth all my houseing thereon standing, that is to say, dwelling house, out-houseing, barnes, gardings, and Orchards. I give to my son Benja. Smith one parcell of Land lying on the east side of river, wch Land is forty rods, *sides* lying on the south side of Mr. Samuel Willis his Land, and on the north side of that Land before given to son Joseph, wch Land runneth to the upland. I give to my son Benja. Smith that devition of upland from the fence East ward to the highway, wch is the Country high-way. I say the devition to the highway of both lotts, that of ffifty and that of forty. And the remainder of these two Lotts be devided equally be-tween my sons Joseph Smith & Benja. Smith, except what I shall give to my son-in-Law Richd. Fox and John Strickland. I give to my son Benja. Smith one-third of that parcell of Land I bought of Samll Martin, to him and his heirs forever. I give to my son Joseph Smith what mony I have comeing to me in the bay, and also what time I have in the boy which liveth with me now, Thomas Buck. (Note: *Invt. as 4 years' time valued at £10. That indicates the age of Thomas Buck as about 17 years*). Item. Besides what I have already given to my daughter Hester Strickland in Brass & Pewter & Bedding and all other necessary Household Stuffe, and Cows & Swine, and what Mony I paid Blackleach, I say I give to my son-in-Law John Strickland the House wch he now liveth in, during the time of his natural life, wth also 4 acres of Land during the time of his natural life, and after his decease to return to his wife. I give to my daughter Beriah Fox, the wife of Richard Fox, in Pewter, Brass & Bedding and other Houseing Stuffe, and Cows & Swine, I give to my son-in-law Rich-ard Fox 6 acres of Upland lying in a place called by the name of Simmon's Plaine, next to Samuel Welles. I give to my daughter Bethia, the wife of Joshua Stoddar, besides what I have given and delivered to my daughter Bethia, as Cows & Brass & Pewter, Bedding & all other Houseing Stuffe, I say I give my son-in-Law Joshua Stoddar 2 Steers of one year old and the advantage. I make my wife Mary Smith and my son Joseph Smith sole Executors, and entreat Mr. Gershom Bulkeley and Samuel Steele to be ye Overseers.

Witness: *Samuel Steele.*   RICHD. SMITH.

A Prerogative Court for Probate of Wills and granting Administrations:

Page 87—7 March, 1698-9: The Last Will and Testament of Mr. Richard Smith, late of Glastonbury decd, was exhibited in Court wth the Testator's name affixed to it and Lieut. Samuell Steele as a witness. Sam-uell, Joseph and Benja. Smith, sons of the decd, made oath that they verily thought it to be their father's will, and they know no fraud therein, etc. The Court do accept it as a will and Order it to be recorded. An Inven-tory of his Estate was also presented & (oath) made thereto by the Relict before Mr. Kimberly, Justice of the Peace. Ordered to be Recorded. The Relict and Joseph Smith being made Executors by the Will, they do ac-cept of the trust.

Page 69-70.

Steele, John, Hartford. Died 6 March, 1698. Invt. £124-07-06. Taken 30 March, 1698, by Joseph Easton & Thomas Bunce.

Court Record, Page 33—13 April, 1698: Invt. exhibited by James Steele, Father of sd. Decd. Adms. to the Widow, Melletiah Steele.

Page 23—(Vol. VII) 23 June, 1702: Meletiah Steele, the Relict of John Steele, presented an Account of her Adms., which, not being perfected, was deferred.

Page 28—23 June, 1702: This Court appoint James Steele Jr. to be Guardian to the Children of John Steele decd, they being under age, viz, Bethia, John & Ebenezer Steele.

Page 105—(Vol. VIII) 15 December, 1715: Samuel Shepherd of Hartford, in Right of his wife Bethia, daughter of John Steele, moved this Court for an Order to Dist. the Estate of John Steele Jr., son of John Steele sen., who died in his minority. This Court order the Clerk to notify Melatiah Stevens of Killingworth, Widow, that she may appear and offer such objections as she may against sd. Order. Also signify to Ebenezer Steele, a minor son of John Steele sen., that he may appear and choose a Guardian.

Page 236—7 February, 1715-16: Ebenezer Steele, a minor, about 19 years of age, son of John Steele, chose Thomas Steele to be his Guardian.

Page 44-45.

Stocking, Samuel, Middletown. Died 2 December, 1697. Invt. £306-10-09. Taken 4 March, 1697, by Nathaniel White, John Warner & John X Clarke. Nuncupative Will, dated 5 February, 1691-2.

The Testimony of Capt. Nathaniel White, aged 60 years or thereabouts, and of Bethia Steele, 57 years of age or thereabouts, testifyeth and saith: That when Deacon Samuel Stocking made his Will we were present, and he fearing that his son John Stocking might be cut short of what he expected to be his Due and Right by Virtue of his Father Stocking's Will, that then his son John should have the ½ of his Lott or Division of Land lying on ye Et Side ye grt River, next Haddam Bounds.

Samuel Stocking personally appd and owned it, as sworn before me.
                                        Nathaniel Stanly, Assistant.

George Stocking, Daniel Stocking, & Thomas Stow in Right and behalf of his wife Bethia, did before this Court, on the 4th day of March, 1697-8, each one voluntarily declare that they are willing their Brother John Stocking shall possess and enjoy the Land mentioned given him by his Father.   Test: *William Whiting, Clerk.*

(See Vol. IV, Page 168-70—Will of Samuel Stocking sen., who Died 30 December, 1683.)

Court Record, Page 17—4 March, 1697-8: Whereas, there was a paper or Writing presented to this Court that was called the last Will &

Testament of Samuel Stocking of Middletown Decd, the Court, having well considered the same, do not see Cause to allow it as a Will, but do order that the Estate be equally divided amongst his brethren and Sisters, Debts due from the Estate being first paid. An Invt. of Samuel Stocking's Estate was presented in the Court by Thomas Stow and George Stocking. Adms. granted to George Stocking, who recognized in £150 to faithfully administer upon the Estate of his Brother Samuel Stocking Decd.

Page 7.

Stow, Ichabod, Middletown, Invt. £218-12-00. Taken 4 April, 1695, by Andrew Bacon & Thomas Allyn. The children: Abigail Stow, age 2 years, & Hope Stow, age 3 months. Will dated 18 January, 1694-5.

I, Ichabod Stow, being weake in Body yet of sound memory, doe see Cause to set my house in order and dispose of my worldly Goods as followeth: I give unto my wife the Use & Improvement of my House & Barn and all the Lands that I stand now possessed of legally, or afterwards shall be conveyed by my father, that lyeth here about my house, with the Use of all my Meadow Land, Stock, and other Personal Estate, for her comfortable subsistence during her Widowhood, and for the bringing up of my Children until they come of age. And my wife to have ½ of my Cellar and Barn and the other thirds of my Estate, both Real & Personal, during her life. I give to my eldest daughter Abigail ½ of my Houseing, Cellering and Barn when as soon as she hath occassion for it, & also 1-3 of my Real & Personal Estate when she marryeth, & the half of the third that my wife hath at her decease. To my other daughter Hope I give also 1-3 of my Real & Personal Estate, to possess and injoy, when she marryeth, or when she comes of age, if she needeth it, and that part of my Houseing, Cellering & Barne, and the half of that third of my Real & Personal Estate that I give to my wife during her life, to return to my daughter Hope after my wife's decease. I appoint my wife sole Executrix, and desire Mr. John Hamlin and Mr. James Pierpont to be Overseers.

Witness: *Samuel Collins,*　　　　　　　ICHABOD STOW, Ls.
　　　　　John Hamlin.

Court Record, Page 150—(Vol. IV) 14 April, 1697: Will & Invt. exhibited and approved.

Page 51-2.

Strong, John sen., Windsor. Died 20 February, 1697-8 (W. R.). Invt. £483-11-00. Taken 28 February, 1697-8, by Abraham Phelps, Daniel Hayden & Michael Taintor. The children: John Strong, age 32 years, Jacob 25, Josiah 19, Mary Stanly 40, Hannah Hopkins, 36 years of age.

Court Record, Page 21—15 April, 1698: Inventory exhibited. Adms. to John & Jacob Strong.

An Agreement on File: 3 March, 1697-8: An Agreement between Hannah Strong, late wife of John Strong, late of Windsor Decd, and John Strong & Jacob Strong, sons of the aforesd. John Strong: Wherein Hannah Strong has a part of the Homested & Lands during life, and a portion of the Personal Estate for her own Disposal. Further, we agree that our Mother-in-Law shall have Corne and Meat and Malt, with other things suitable for her sustinance, until the next December.

Witness: *Michael Taintor,*
　　　　Abraham Phelps Jr.

HANNAH X STRONG,　　JACOB STRONG,
JOHN STRONG,　　　　RETURN STRONG SEN.,
JOSIAH STRONG,　　　*Guardian.*

Agreement on File, 30 March, 1697-8: An Agreement between John Strong, Jacob Strong, Josiah Strong & Return Strong sen., Guardian to Josiah Strong, and Timothy Stanly & John Hopkins, referring to the Estate of their Father Strong Decd, which is to be divided amongst us. The abovesd. Timothy Stanly & John Hopkins shall have each of them the full sum of £55 apeice out of the Personal Estate, £42 apeice when the Court shall grant Dist., & the remainder £13 by Reversion.

Witness: *Return Strong sen.,*
　　　　Hannah X Strong.

JOHN STRONG,　　TIMOTHY STANLY,
JACOB STRONG,　　JOHN HOPKINS.
JOSIAH STRONG,

See Page 104-5 (Vol. VII., Pro. Side): An Agreement, dated 5 September, 1704, made by and between the heirs of John Strong sen., late of the Town of Windsor Decd, for a Division of Lands.

JOHN STRONG, Ls.
JACOB STRONG, Ls.
JOSIAH STRONG, Ls.

John Strong, Jacob Strong & Josiah Strong personally appeared in Court and acknowledged the above Agreement to be their free Act and Deed.　　　　　　　　　Test: *William Whiting, Clerk.*

Page 98.

Talcott, Cornet Samuel, Wethersfield. Died 28 April, 1698. Invt. £744-02-00. Taken by William Warner & William Goodrich. The children: Samuel, age 2 years; Ann, 7 years; & Mary, 8 months.

Court Record, Page 60—4 November, 1698: Adms. to the Relict, Mary Talcott. William Warner and Ebenezer Deming to be Overseers.

Page 148—(Vol. VIII) 6 July, 1713: Mary Talcott, a minor daughter of Samuel Talcott, chose her Uncle Joseph Talcott to be her Guardian. Samuel Talcott, son of the Decd, made choice of Capt. David Goodrich for his Guardian. Recog. £100.

Page 150—6 July, 1713: This Court do defer a Consideration upon the Account of Debts paid and made out of the Estate of Samuel Talcott Jr., late of Wethersfield Decd, Exhibited in Court by Mr. James Patterson of Wethersfield, who married with the Widow, Relict of sd. Decd, who was Adms. on the Estate.

Page 154—17 August, 1713: Mr. James Patterson of Wethersfield, Adms. on the Estate of Samuel Talcott in Right of his wife Mary, Widow, exhibited now in this Court an Account of Debts and Charges for several Disbursements due from that Estate, out of his own proper Estate, amounting to £11-03-01; and for nine years' service of himself takeing Care of the Children and improveing the Estate, at £10 per Annum, £90; and for nine years service of his Negro Man, at £8 per Annum, £72; and the sum of £32-11-06 for his wive's thirds. Capt. David Goodrich, Guardian to Samuel Talcott, objected to that for service of himself nine years and his Negro Man, etc. David Goodrich appealed from the Decree of the Court in allowing the sd. Court, unto the Superior Court.

Page 159—5 October, 1713: An Agreement between James Patterson, David Goodrich and Joseph Talcott, wherein James Patterson is allowed £76. This Court appoint Lt. Benjamin Churchill, Moses Crofts and Thomas Wright to Dist. the Estate.

Dist. File, 5 May, 1714: To Mr. James Patterson, to Samuel Talcott (only son), to Ann, and to Mary Talcott.

Page 200—7 June, 1714: Report of the Distributors.

Page 11-12.

Thrall, Timothy, Windsor. Died June, 1697 (W. R.). Invt. £797-14-07. Taken 25 June, 1697, by Daniel Hayden, Samuel Cross and Michael Taintor. Will dated 13 May, 1697.

I Timothy Thrall of Windsor, being of sound mind & in Health of Body, doe make my Last will & Testament: I give to my daughter Deborah Moses £10, to Elizabeth Cornish £20, to Mehetabell Clarke £20, to my daughter Martha Pinney £20, to my daughter Abigail Thrall £30. I give to my four sons, Timothy, John, Thomas and Samuel, all my right and Propriety in those Lands which Lye within the Township of Windsor which were appointed by the Towne to be divided to the proprietors, Inhabitants, by a comitte chosen for that end in the year 168-. I give and bequeath unto my son John Thrall, in the East side of my farm in Windsor, at a place Commonly Called Hoyt's meadow, Twelve rodds in breadth, bounding easterly in part on Samuel Gibbs, part by Samll Cross, south by the Riverlett, & to runn northerly til it comes to my north bounds. All the rest of my farm at Hoyt's Meadow, both upland and meadow, I give to my two sons Thomas & Samuel, to be equally divided betwixt them. And they shall each of them have a Yoake of Oxen or Steers, fitt for worke, and One Cow or Heifer a peice, three years of age at least, to be delivered within three years after my decease by my Executor afternamed. And all the Residue of my Estate and goods & Cattells not herein above bequeathed, after my debts and funeral expenses are discharged, I doe give and bequeath to my son John Thrall, whom I doe make sole Executor.

Witness: *Jacob Gibbs, sen.,*　　　　　Timothy Trall. Ls.
Abraham Phelps.

Court Record, Page 11-12—6 July, 1697: The Will and Invt. Exhibited and approved. At the same Court John Thrall and Thomas Thrall declared that Samuel Thrall & Abigail Thrall, being 15 years of age, made choice of Daniel Heyden to be their guardian.

Page 10-11.

Ventrus, Moses sen., Farmington. Invt. £17-15-00. Taken 12 April, 1697, by John Hart & Daniel Andrews sen. Will dated 15 June, 1693.

The last Will & Testament of Moses Ventrus sen. of Farmington: I having now for a long time been weake and infirm, and my only son and youngest daughter having taken special Care of me, I acknowledge the Goodness of God therein and think it my duty and in some measure to requite them according to my ability. Imprimis: I give to my daughter Sarah, the wife of John Brunson, a feather pillow & a pewter salt Celler, she having formerly received her portion. Item. I give to my daughter Grace, the wife of John Blakeley, a feather pillow, a little pewter dish and a little pewter Cup; & further I oblige my Executor, within one year after my decease, to pay her 20 Shillings and a Bible, she having already received her portion. Item. I give to my daughter Mary Ventrus my Bed and Bedding on which I used to lye, and one Cotton Pillow Beere, and 1-2 of all the Linen in the House, with 1-2 of the Bedds & Bedding not before mentioned, with all my Household Goods which is truly mine, except what is before or shall be hereafter mentioned in this Will. Item. I give to my son Moses Ventrus all my Right & Title and all the Neat (Catle), Sheep & Swine that is or was to be mine, with Household Goods, he paying the Legacies aforesd. I appoint him my Executor, and desire Samuel Hooker Jr. and John Wadsworth Overseers.

Witness: *William Wadsworth,*　　　Moses X Ventrus sen.
Nathaniel Wadsworth, John Wadsworth.

Court Record, Page 149—(Vol. IV) 12 April, 1697: Will proven.

Page 46.

Webster, Hannah, Hartford. Invt. £5-14-00. Taken 26 November, 1697, by Joseph Wadsworth, Ciprian Nicholls & Zachariah Sandford.

Court Record, Page 18—3 March, 1697-8: Adms. to Joel Marshall.

Page 88-9.

Wells, Capt. James sen., Haddam. Invt. £422-19-06. Taken 5 January, 1697-8, by John Smith, Daniel X Brainard and Timothy X Spencer. The children: James Welles, Thomas 15 years, Elizabeth Smith, Mary Arnold & Susannah Welles. Relict, Elizabeth Welles (?). Will dated 9 June, 1690.

I James Welles sen. of Haddam, being employed in the Country Service, doe think it my duty to set my worldly affairs in some Order. Item. It is my Will that my wife shall have my Homelott & House, and one of the 3-acre Lotts on the East side of the Great River, and my upper Lott in the Meadow, during her Widowhood; and if she marry again, then all to return to my son James. My son James shall have my Dwelling house & Homelott, and all the Land on the West side of the Great River, and all my Land in the Upper Meadow, & all my Rights on the Plaine on the East side of the Great River, he not claiming any right at Machamoodus. And my Will is that my son Thomas Welles shall have my Cow Meadow Lott, & all my Rights at Machamoodus. My son James shall have all my Moveables of Stock and all other things not above disposed of, and he my son James to pay to my daughter Elizabeth £10 besides what she hath already had. And to pay to my 2 daughters, Mary and Susannah Welles, when they come to age, £15 apeice.

Witness: *George Gates,*   JAMES X WELLES.
Thomas Gates.

Court Record, Page 44—22 June, 1698: The last Will & Testament of Capt. James Welles exhibited in Court, and Capt. George Gates made Oath that the Testator did in their presence sign and declare it to be his last Will. Accepted, proven, and ordered to be recorded. There being no Executor expressed by Will, this Court grant Adms. to James Welles to perform the Will of the Deceased.

Page 124-5.

Welles, Jonathan. Distribution of Estate, £440-18-09, 27 November, 1695. It is to be understood that the several Legatees, viz, John Olcott and Mary his Wife as Administrators on the Estate of Mr. Thomas Welles Decd, Ichabod Welles, Samuel & Joseph Welles for themselves, Mr. James Judson in right of Rebecca his Wife, and Sarah Bidwell as Administrator on the Estate of Mr. John Bidwell Deceased, do mutually agree to exchange the 12 acres of Land that was Jonathan Welles's, lying in the Oxpasture, for 12 acres of Mr. Joseph Welles his Land, lying in the same Oxpasture, and that the sd. Land be distributed.

JOHN OLCOTT &	MRS. SARAH BIDWELL, RELICT OF
MARY HIS WIFE,	JOHN BIDWELL DECD,
ICHABOD WELLES,	JAMES JUDSON &
SAMUEL WELLES,	REBECKAH HIS WIFE.
JOSEPH WELLES,	

Court Record, Page 92—12 April, 1699: Dist. presented in Court by William Whiting & Joseph Mygatt.

Note: This Agreement (as on file), dated 27 November, 1695, has Jacob placed between Ichabod (Jacob), Samuel & Joseph Welles.

Page 86—(Vol. VII) 5 August, 1706: Sarah Bidwell of Hartford, Widow, & Capt. James Judson of Stratford, complain to the Court that no Dist. of sd. Estate had been made. The case came before this Court, and Claim was made that Dist. had been made by an Agreement among the parties concerned.

Page 110-11.

Wells, Joseph, Hartford. Invt. £342-08-00. Taken 13 June, 1698, by Thomas Hooker, Ciprian Nicholls and Edw. Allyn. Children: One daughter, one year and 5 months old.

Court Record, Page 82—2 March, 1698-9: Adms. to Mrs. Elizabeth Wells, Widow.

Page 46—(Vol. XIV) 19 July, 1744: William Powell of Hartford in Right of his wife Elizabeth Welles alias Powell deceased, daughter and heir of Joseph Welles late of Hartford decd, now moved to this Court that the thirds of her Dowry in the Real Estate of the sd. Deceased may be set out to Elizabeth Welles, Widow of Joseph Welles decd, Whereupon this Court appoint Thomas Richards, Capt. Joseph Cook & Mr. Thomas Hooker of Hartford to set out to Elizabeth Wells, Widow, 1-3 part of the Houseing and Lands for her Improvement during life.

Page 8-9.

Whitmore, John, Middletown. Died 1st September, 1696. Invt. £267-18-06. Taken by Nathaniel Stow, Israhiah Wetmore and Edward Shepard. The children: Elizabeth, age 9 years, Mary 5, John 2, Ebenezer 3 months. Will dated 6 August, 1689.

I John Whitmore of Middletown doe make this my last Will & Testament: I give to my wife Mary the use and Improvement of my whole Estate during my Children's non-age, desireing and expecting that she, as God shall enable her, to see them brought up and educated in the fear of God, and it is my earnest desire that each one of them be instructed in reading and writing according to their Capacity. I give to my son Thomas Whitmore the one-halfe of my House and Land on both sides of the way at Home in Middletown, to be divided between my wife Mary and my son Thomas, according to the Quantity and Quality thereof, when my son Thomas shall arrive at the age of Twenty and one years. And the other halfe to remain to the use of my wife till her natural death. And then the whole of my aforesaid House and Lands to be for my son Thomas Wettmore & his heyres for Ever. Lands, one parcel of meadow at Wangonque containing about three acres according to my Father Thomas Whetmore's Deed of Gift to him. Also my three side arms, one short gun or Carbine, two fowling pieces, one sword, one Pike, with the rest of the implements thereunto belonging, when he comes to the age of 21 years. I give to my daughter Abigail Wetmore one peice of Meadow Land at Wangonque containing about two acres, with the pond adjoyning to it, as it is specified in Father Andrew Warner's Deed of Guift to me. I give to my daughter Elizabeth Whetmore one parcel of Meadow Land at Wangonque containing about 4 acres, to be to her according to the Tenour of my Father Whetmore's Will to mee. I will that a certain black stuff gown that was my former wive's, also her Bible, be given to my daughter Abigail. My Will is that that portion of Land that falls to my wife Mary from her Father Savage's Estate I leave to her solely to dispose of, only to be to her children by me if they shall survive. I ordain my Wife Mary to be sole Executrix of this my Will. I desire my two Brothers, Beriah and Joseph Wettmore, and my brothers-in-law, John Savage and Andrew Warner, to be Overseers. JOHN WETTMORE. Ls.

Witness: *Sarah Wilcock,*
Beriah Wettmore, Jonathan Gilbert.

Court Record, Page 154—(Vol. IV) 14 April, 1697: Will & Invt. exhibited & deferred to the next Court of Assistants.

Page 139—(Vol. VI) 11 April, 1700: It appeareing to this Court that the last Will & Testament of John Whetmore of Middletown, as also his Inventory, was exhibited in the Court about 3 years since, and through mistake there was no record made of the Exhibitions thereof, not withstanding which Omition the sd. Will & Invt. are recorded. Beriah Wetmore, appeareing in the behalf of the Wydo (the Children being under age), moves this Court that the Will might only be a Direction to the Court for the Dist. of the sd. Estate, and not to stand in force, but be null and void. The reason is because the sd. Testator had 3 Children born betwixt the time of makeing his Will and the time of his decease, and two of them are deceased that were alive when he made the sd. Will. The Court having considered the Case, do see Cause to defer until some other time, the Widow not being present.

Page 127—(Vol. VII) 2 May, 1709: Upon Consideration of the Application of Mary Wetmore of Middletown, Widow & Relict of John Wetmore late of Middletown Decd, at sundry times formerly and now again made to this Court, relating to a writing called the last Will & Testament of the sd. John Whitmore Decd, which by mistake was entered on the Records of this Court in Book No. 6, Pages 8 & 9, but was never proved nor approved nor allowed by this Court: This Court do not approve or allow the sd. Writing as the sd. John Wetmore's Will, but do disallow the same and order that it be wholly set aside as null and void. And this Court do now grant Letters of Adms. on the Estate of sd. John Wetmore, Decd, to sd. Mary Wetmore.

Page 129—6 June, 1709: Whereas, this Court, on the 2nd day of May last past, granted Adms. on the Estate of John Wetmore, late of Middletown, unto Mary Wetmore (now Mary Allyn), relict of the sd. Decd; and whereas, the sd. Mary doth refuse or decline to take the Trust, this Court doth now therefore grant Letters of Adms. on the Estate of John Wetmore unto Beriah Wetmore of sd. Middletown, Brother of the sd. Decd.

Page 130—6 June, 1709: Ebenezer Wetmore, a minor son of John Wetmore, chose Lt. John Savage of Middletown to be his Guardian.

Page 134—7 November, 1709: Beriah Wetmore, Adms., presented now to this Court an Account of his Adms: Paid in Debts and Charges, £28-03-11; and that there was more of Moveable Estate spent for the Building of a Barn, £14-00-00. There remains to be divided, £46-18-07. Account Allowed. Order to Dist. the Moveable Part of the Estate to Mary the Relict, now wife of Obadiah Allyn; to John Wetmore, eldest son; to Ebenezer Wetmore, 2nd son; to Elizabeth Elton, daughter. And appoint Capt. John Hall, John Bacon & Edward Shepherd, of Middletown, Distributors. John Wetmore, a minor, made choice of his Uncle Joseph Wetmore to be his Guardian.

Dist. File: 1st Monday in June, 1710:

	£ s d
To the Widow,	66-06-02
To John, the Eldest son,	65-19-06
To Ebenezer, the younger son,	32-19-09
To Richard Elton in Right of his wife,	32-19-09

John Hall sen., John Bacon & Edward Shepard, Distributors.

Whereas, Beriah Wetmore of Middletown, Adms. to the Estate of John Wetmore, late of Middletown Decd: We, Mary Allyn, the Relict of sd. Decd, and Richard Elton in Right of his wife, and John Savage, Guardian for Ebenezer, younger son of the sd. Decd, and Joseph Wetmore, Guardian for John Wetmore, eldest son of the Decd, all under-subscribe, having in Distribution and at the Hand of sd. Adms. received our full & Just proportion, both of Real & Personal Estate, which was assigned us to receive of sd. Estate at the Honourable Court of Probate, doe forever discharge, release and quitt Claim the sd. Beriah Wetmore, his heirs Executors & Adms., of all and singular every part and parcel of sd. Goods, Rights & Chattells, fully and absolutely by these presents, from the date hereof and forever. Signed with our own Hands, September 25, 1710.

<blockquote>
MARY X ALLYN,   JOSEPH WETMORE, Guardian.
RICHARD ELTON,   JOHN SAUAEGE, Guardian.
</blockquote>

Page 133-4.

Wickham, Sarah, Widow, Wethersfield. Died 7 January, 1699-1700. Invt. £31-11-00. Taken 7 February, 1699-1700, by Isaac Boreman & Benjamin Churchill, Selectmen. Will dated 15 December, 1699.

I Sarah Wickham of Wethersfield, Widow, doe make this my last Will & Testament: Whereas, I now am in a very weake and helpless Condition, and have been a long time at the great Charge and Care of my eldest son Thomas Wickham, and doe depend upon him under God for my maintenance and support while I live, I doe give & bequeath my whole Estate unto him my sd. son Thomas, excepting only such Legacies or Tokens of my Love as are hereafter mentioned. Whereas, the rest of my Children have had their portions that their Father and myself gave them in full, and whereas, my son William Wickham is indebted to the Estate of my husband, which was left to my disposal, the sum of £10 in Country pay, it is my Will that my son William shall pay the £10 to my sd. son Thomas for my daughter Sarah Hudson in part of the £20 which we intended for her. And I doe remit and forgive my sd. son William what rents he may be indebted to me for any Lands or farme he lives on, provided I have not necessity for it by Weakness & Sickness. And whereas, my sd. son William is indebted to me, for which my sd. son Thomas engaged to see it satisfied until the Money, £3-06, which was lent to him in the year '97, and in Wheat 3 Bushels at 5 Shillings per Bushel, my Will is that he shall pay that Money and Wheat to my son Thomas on Demand. And my Will is that if my daughter Sarah Hudson should die before the time of makeing Good of this Will, that the £10 above mentioned shall go to her son John Cherry, and the other £10 to be prised out of my Household Estate, if it remains after my decease and the decease of my daughter Sarah, then to go to John Cherry, each £10 to be prised in Country pay. I give to my son Samuel Wickham 40 Shillings in Silver, and doe remit my sd. son Samuel that Debt which he oweth me of £2 more. I give unto my son Joseph Wickham 20 Shillings in Silver besides that £5 which he received in Money Pay of Jonathan Strickland of Long Island. I give unto my gr. son John Cherry 40 Shillings in Silver. If my son John Wickham should be living and appear, I give unto him the sum of 40 Shillings in Silver. I make my son Thomas Wickham my Executor.

Witness: *Stephen Chester,*   SARAH WICKHAM, Ls.
Samuel Buck, Samuel Butler.

Court Record, Page 123—8 March, 1699-1700: Will approved.

Page 32-4.

Willett, Nathaniel, Hartford. Died 4 January, 1697-8. Invt. £450-09-04. Taken 11 January, 1697-8, by Thomas Bunce, John Merrells & Thomas Thornton. Will dated 13 July, 1697.

I Nathaniel Willett of Hartford doe make this my last Will & Testament: I give to my wife the Use of a third part of all my Lands during her natural life. And if she sees fit to live in Hartford, I give her the Use of my House, Barn & Homelott, besides the thirds, during her Widowhood. Also, I give unto my wife 2 Plows, 1-3 part of my Sheep, 1-3 part of my Household Goods, with the Provision in the House, in full of her Dowry, she keeping houseing and fences in repair. I give and release to my son Bishop the Debt of £12 in Money which he oweth me, as a particular Legacy. I give to my daughter Hannah my bigest Brass Kettle as a particular Legacy. I give all my Land, Meadow, Upland and Outlands whatsoever, to be equally divided between them, 2-3 after my decease, and the other third after the decease of my wife. I appoint my son-in-Law, Zachariah Sandford, to be my Executor, and desire Mr. Nathaniel Stanly and Major Jonathan Bull to be Overseers.

Witness: *Timothy Woodbridge,* NATHANIEL X WILLETT, Ls.
  Caleb Watson.

Court Record, Page 12—19 January, 1697: Will & Invt. exhibited. Zachariah Sandford refuses to be Executor. This Court grant Letters of Adms. to Zachariah Sandford & Basey Baker.

Page 17—(Vol. X) 2 May, 1723: This Court appoint Capt. Aaron Cooke, Thomas Seymour & Deacon John Skinner to divide and dist. the Lands in Hartford that the sd Nathaniel Willett died seized of, to and among his heirs according to his Will. John Bunce, who married one of the gr. daughters of sd. Deceased, appeals from the Judgement of this Court to the Superior Court.

Dist. File, 16 January, 1723-4: To John Whiting, John Bunce & Sarah Bunce, to Mrs. Baker, Relict of Basey Baker, Widow Hannah. By Aaron Cooke and John Skinner.

Page 38-9-40-1.

Willson, Deacon John, Hartford. Invt. £376-13-03. Taken 1st March, 1697-8, by John Marsh & Nathaniel Goodwin sen. Will dated 25 May, 1697.

I John Willson of Hartford doe ordain this my last Will & Testament: I give to my wife Lydia the Use of all my Houseing and Lands until my sons, that is, John and Stebbin, shall attain the age of 21 years. And then it is my Will that my wife, as long as she remains a Widdow, shall improve so much of the Houseing and Lands as shall be fore her comfortable maintenance while she abides a Widdow. Also I give to her, to be at her own dispose, 1-3 part of my Personal Estate forever, expecting she will be kind to fatherless Children. At the age of 21 years, I give to my son John my House, Homelotts, Gardens, with all the Appurtenances thereunto belonging. Also, I give to John all my Materials for his Trade, excepting Leather. Also I give to my son John my whole Pasture adjoining to Mr. Aaron Cooke. Also my upper Lott in the North Meadow, and half my lower Lott in the sd. Meadow. My Will is that he shall give to his Brother Stebbin £20 in Current Country Pay towards building him a House. I give to my son Stebbin, at the age of 21 years, the other half of my Lott in the Long Meadow, and also my Lott at Four-Mile Hill, and 2-3 of all my Woodland. But it is my Will that my son shall not divide the several Lotts, but one take one, and the other take the other, according to the several proportions above mentioned. I give to my daughter Hannah £40 of my Moveable Estate. I give to my daughter Mary, at the age of 18 years, £40 out of my Moveable Estate. What Estate I have after my wife's Decease that is personal Estate undisposed of, shall be equally divided between my four children, John & Stebbin, Hannah & Mary. I appoint my wife sole Executrix. I desire my brother Nathaniel Cole and my Cousins Edward Cadwell and Thomas Cadwell to assist my wife in the performance of this my Will.

Witness: *John Haynes,*   JOHN WILLSON, Ls.
             Edward Cadwell.

Court Record, Page 15—3 March, 1697-8: Will & Inventory exhibited by Lydia, the Relict. Proven.

Page 128—16 March, 1699-1700: John Wilson, a minor son of John Wilson, made choice of Edward Cadwell to be his Guardian. And Stebbin Wilson made choice of Nathaniel Cole for his Guardian.

Page 23-4-5.

Willson, Samuel, Windsor. Died 3 August, 1697. Invt. £430-13-00. Taken 28 September, 1697, by Timothy Phelps & James Enno. The children: Elizabeth, age 24 years, Mary 22, Abigail 13, Samuel 5, Mindwell, 1 & 1-2 year old.

Court Record, Page 6—12 November, 1697: Adms. to Mary, the Relict. By her request, Lt. Matthew Allyn of Windsor & Deacon John Willson of Hartford were appointed Overseers. And this Court also appoint them to make a Dist. of the Estate.

Page 22—5 April, 1698: Mary, the Relict of Samuel Willson, applying herselfe to this Court for Dist. of her husband's Estate, The Court order that the Debts be first paid, and then to Dist. the Estate as followeth: To the Widow, 1-3 part of the Real Estate during her life, and an equal share of the Personal Estate with the Eldest Child, to be to her and her heirs forever. To the Eldest son, a double portion, both of Real & Personal Estate. To the Rest of the Children, an equal part of the remainder of the Estate. The Court appoint Lt. Matthew Allyn and Michael Taintor, Distributors.

Page 127—7 March, 1700: Mary, the Relict of Samuel Willson, now the wife of Anthony Hoskins sen., presented a further Account of Debts due from the Estate:

	£ s d
Debts, with Loss,	19-15-05
Extraordinary Expense about a young child that died,	6-00-00
	25-15-05
Inventory,	434-04-00
Former Debts added,	52-10-00
Debts subtracted,	78-05-05
There remains to be distributed,	355-19-05
To the Widow,	88-19-10
To John, the Eldest son,	88-19-10
To Elizabeth, Mary, Abigail & Samuel, to each of them,	44-09-10

Dist. File: 8 April, 1702: To the Widow Mary (married, 2nd, Hoskins), to Mary, to Abigail, to Elizabeth, to John, to Samuel Wilson. By Matthew Allyn & Michael Taintor.

Page 66—(Vol. VII) 5 April, 1705: Mary Willson of Windsor, Relict of Samuel Willson, late of Windsor, exhibited a Dist. of the Estate of Samuel Willson under the Hands of Matthew Allyn & Michael Taintor. Accepted and ordered to be kept on File.

Page 141-2.

Winchell, Nathaniel sen., Windsor. Died in March. Invt. £540-09-10. Taken 30 April, 1700, by Benajah Holcomb sen. & Nathaniel Gaylord. The children: Nathaniel, age 32 years, Thomas 28 (Decd, leaving four Children), Stephen 22, John 20, Sarah 25, Mary 17 years.

These may inform the Honoured Court: That there is a peice of Land on which Thomas Winchell built a house and lived some years, and after his death, as we are informed, part of sd. Land was Inventoried as part of sd. Thomas his Estate, though not made over to sd. Thomas according to Law before his death, nor since unto the Surviving. So that the Land not being passed, neither by Will nor Deed, from the Old man to his son, nor to son's Children, we were in Doubt whether to Inventory sd. Land unto Nathaniel Winchell's sen. Estate or not. Now the Division of that Matter we leave with your Honours. If it must be put into the Inventory, we apprise it at £15.   BENAJAH HOLCOMB.

Court Record, Page 140—25 May, 1700: Invt. of the Estate of Nathaniel Winchell, late of Windsor, was exhibited in Court by Sarah, the Relict, and Nathaniel, son of the sd. Decd. Adms. is granted to Sarah, the Relict.

Page 1—(Vol. VII) 5 September, 1700: Sarah Winchell, Relict of Nathaniel Winchell, late of Windsor Decd, Adms. Recog., £200, with Josiah Phelps of Windsor.

Page 5—16 December, 1700: Prays for longer time to perfect the Adms.

Page 6—20 December, 1700: This Court orders that all the Lands belonging to the Estate of Nathaniel Winchell, except that parcel at Simsbury and one other parcel at Westfield, shall be dist: To the Widow, Sarah Winchell, 1-3 part during her natural life; and to the Children, or their legal representative, the remainder of sd. Estate. And appoint Lt. Return Strong, Michael Tainter and Sergt. Benajah Holcomb, Distributors. This Court appoint Capt. Abraham Phelps to be Guardian to John Winchell, a minor son of Nathaniel Winchell; and Atherton Mather appointed Guardian to Mary Winchell, daughter of sd. Decd.

Dist. File: 1701: Order to Dist: To the Widow, to Nathaniel, to the Children of Thomas, to Stephen, to John, to Mary, to Josiah Phelps. By Benajah Holcomb & Michael Taintor.

Page 16—4 September, 1701 : Report of the Dist.

Page 17—4 September, 1701 : The Court grant the Widow a *Quietus Est.* Nathaniel Winchell Jr. appeared in Court and appealed to the Court of Assistants. Recog., £10.

Page 18.

Winchell, Thomas, Windsor. Invt. £138-16-00. Taken 2 September, 1697, by Daniel Hayden, Abraham Phelps and Michael Taintor.

Court Record (Vol. V), Page 135—2 September, 1697: Adms. to Sarah Winchell, the Relict. Lt. Phelps of Windsor and Samuel Forward to be Overseers.

Page 1—(Vol. VII) 5 September, 1700: Samuel Forward presented to this Court an Account of Debts due to and from the Estate of Thomas Winchell, late of Windsor Decd. The Court accept, and ordered to be filed ; and also that the Relict, who is Adms., do perfect her work.

Page 6—20 December, 1700: This Court order that Capt. Abraham Phelps and Lt. Daniel Heydon be Guardians to the Children of Thomas Winchell, late of Windsor Decd.

INDEXES.

ERRATA.

Page 16. Thomas Hooker, second line, read 1649.
" 49. No. 165. John Cole, *son* of *James Cole*, incorrect.
" 97. William Belden, third line, read 1655.
" 118. John Goit, Invt., for 25 June, 1659, read 1661 (Coit).
" 120. Samuel Greenhill, first line, read Thomas.
" 194. Beget Eglestone, fourth line of Will—"Estate which is but small."
" 202. John Goodrich, Will not dated.
" 209. Anthony Howkins, Court Record, 1st April, 1664, read 1674.
" 223. Thomas Knapp, 22 January, 1699–1700, read 1669–70.
" 298. Nicholas Disbrow, for John Kelly read John Kelsey.

GENERAL INDEX.

This relates to other than Probate Records, and affords light upon the methods of trade, of equity cases, and criminal trials in Court, of pleas by attorneys, and of correspondence in the Colony and with England, the mother country.

INDEX TO ESTATES.

This refers to the names in black letters at the head of each article running throughout the volume, which enables one to turn at once to any will or estate without reference to the page figures in the index of names.

INDEX TO NAMES.

279, 280, 301, 307, 319, 327, 338,
351, 371, 372, 389, 396, 407, 408.
410, 413, 414, 438, 439, 440, 441,
461, 462, 482, 485, 493, 498, 513,
540, 551, 571.
Lydia, 573.
Martin, 79, 488.
Mindwell, 222.
Mr., 409.
Philip, 488, 489, 573, 574.
Ruth, 488, 489, 574.
Susannah, 574.
Thomas, 84, 578.
More, Ed., 22.
Morecock, see Moorcocke.
Morecock, Nicholas, 411, 412.
Morgan, Evan, 190.
James, 91, 123, 127.
John, 61, 555.
Isaac, 493, 494.
Morris, John, 83, 138, 222, 273, 453.
Joshua, 222.
Mary, 222.
Robert, 222, 337, 338.
William, 246.
Morton, Comfort, 537.
Samuel, 223.
Thomas, 537, 559.
William, 110, 418.
Moseley, see Maudsley.
Moseley, Henry, 190.
Moses, Deborah, 590.
John, 5, 338, 339, 394, 489, 563, 564, 566.
Margaret, 338.
Martha, 338.
Mary, 338, 339, 489.
Mindwell, 338.
Sarah, 338.
Timothy, 338, 489.
Moss, Solomon and Ruth, 576.
Mountford, Benjamin, 522, 523.
Mudge, Jarvis, 8.
Micah, 239.
Moses, 239.
Widow, 139.
Mumford, Thomas, 174.
Munn, Benjamin, 83.
Munning, Theophilus, 135.
Munroe, Andrew, 49.
Muscamp, George, 190.
Mygatt, Ann, 339.
Dorothy, 574.
Jacob, 190, 339.
Joseph, 32, 77, 83, 98, 146, 285, 339,
340, 378, 400, 404, 405, 438, 450,
452, 455, 470, 471, 488, 518, 534,
561, 574, 575, 593.
Mary, 574.
Sarah, 339, 574.

Susannah, 574.
Thomas, 574, 575.
Zebulon, 574.
Mylls, see Milles, Mills, Miles.
Mylls, Richard, 3, 231.

Napp, see Knapp.
Napp, Thomas, 223.
Nash, John, 44, 341.
Joseph, 152, 253, 340, 341.
Margaret, 340.
Rebeckah, 305.
Sarah, 340, 341.
Thomas, 446.
Neale, Edward, 320.
Nesacanett, Indian, 68.
Neschegen, Indian, 67.
Nethercoole, Christian, 276, 316.
Nettleton, Sarah, 138, 139.
Newbery, Abigail, 374.
Benjamin, 85, 94, 101, 114, 127, 129,
150, 172, 184, 199, 200, 208, 211,
218, 220, 221, 259, 268, 281, 300,
320, 323, 334, 350, 372, 374, 386,
388, 389, 489, 490, 525, 567, 575.
Capt., 192, 198, 218, 232, 247, 256, 280,
368.
Hannah, 85, 489, 490.
John, 85.
Joseph, 84, 489, 490, 575.
Mary, 85, 172, 374.
Rebeckah, 85.
Sarah, 85.
Thomas, 24, 25, 489, 490, 575.
Newell, Elizabeth, 528.
Esther, 490.
Hannah, 490.
John, 490, 491, 575.
Joseph, 490.
Mary, 490.
Mrs., 343.
Rebeckah, 490, 491.
Richard, 491.
Samuel, 343, 464, 479, 480, 490, 491,
493, 525, 538, 575.
Simon, 528.
Sarah, 490.
Thomas, 86, 92, 157, 189, 209, 233,
331, 490, 491, 528, 575.
Newman, Robert, 190.
Thomas, 92.
William, 99.
Newton, Benjamin, 228, 229.
Benoni, 229.
Mary, 17.
Mr., 106, 107, 116, 177, 288.
Roger, 86, 103, 132, 235.
Samuel, 288.
Susan, 133.

Hannah, 147, 227.
John, 85, 146, 147, 196, 227.
Joseph, 219, 227, 254.
Josiah, 91.
Lydia, 196, 197, 227.
Mary, 147.
Ruth, 196, 197, 227.
Samuel, 18, 454, 523, 567.
Sarah, 196, 197, 227.
Simon, 146, 147, 228.
William, 85, 335.
Wilmet, 147.
Rogers, Elezer, 288.
James, 123, 244.
John, 225, 226.
Mr., 178, 350.
Rollo, Alexander, 213, 214, 346, 363, 384,
    428, 473, 477, 483, 520, 556.
Roo, see Rue.
Roo, John, 63.
Root, Caleb, 356, 357.
Elizabeth, 406.
Joseph, 356, 357, 565.
Mary, 133, 356, 526.
Sarah, 514.
Stephen, 356, 468, 514.
Timothy, 514.
Thomas, 83.
Rootes, John, 93, 133, 190, 209, 233, 356,
    357, 476, 514, 526.
Rootsey, John, 190.
Rose, Daniel, 54, 181, 309, 311, 510.
Elizabeth, 310.
John, 300.
Robert, 10, 11, 86, 585.
Rosseter, see Rocester.
Rosseter, Bray, 25, 85, 243, 511.
Rossiter, John, 307.
Rowell, Thomas, 148.
Rowland, Henry, 87, 163.
Rowlandson, Hannah, 523.
Joseph, 357, 380, 523.
Mary, 357.
Rowley, Mary, 192.
Shubael, 430.
Thomas, 192, 198.
Royce, Robert, 95, 211.
Rudd, Jonathan, 148.
Rue, see Roo.
Rue, John, 342.
Rumble, Bethia, 148.
Thomas, 148.
Rusco, William, 83, 145.
Ruscoe, Joanne, 229.
Nathaniel, 75, 93, 182, 223, 228, 229.
Russell, Abigail, 519.
Daniel, 302.
James, 319, 388.
John, 64, 129, 134, 155, 225, 471.

Jonathan, 155.
Mabell, 319.
Mary, 388.
Mehetabell, 302.
Mr., 116, 155, 270.
Noadiah, 461.
Ryley, see Riley.
Ryley, Ann, 542.
Grace, 230.
Isaac, 230, 435, 543, 546.
Jacob, 230.
Jonathan, 230.
Joseph, 229, 230.
Lydia, 449.
Mary, 14, 230.
Sarah, 230, 549.

Sabell, John, 32.
Sachem, Joshua, 61, 68, 69, 282, 344, 494,
    497, 510.
Sadd, Hepsibah, 352, 501, 503.
John, 74, 352, 500, 502, 503, 581.
Thomas, 502, 503.
Sadler, Deborah, 230.
John, 94, 113, 116, 122, 230, 231.
Sage, David, 400, 459, 519.
Salmon, Mr., 328.
Saltonstall, Gurdon, 355, 356.
Jerusha, 355.
Sammis, see Samwise, Samwis.
Sammis, Johanna, 148, 149.
John, 148, 149.
Mary, 148, 149.
Sampson (a negro), 569.
Samuel (a servant), 164.
Samwise, see Sammis.
Samwise, Richard, 85, 131, 148, 149.
Sanders, see Saunders.
Sanders, Christopher, 370.
George, 232, 503, 581.
Mary, 232, 503.
Sandford, see Sanford.
Sandford, Andrew, 149.
Ann, 357, 358.
Ephraim, 198.
Mary, 149.
Robert, 31, 80, 222, 231, 352, 357, 358,
    429, 430, 501, 547.
Susannah, 358, 485.
Zachary, 119, 120, 211, 228, 231, 267,
    291, 298, 336, 357, 422, 425, 429,
    430, 453, 502, 503, 534, 547, 548,
    555, 581, 591, 597.
Sanford, see Sandford.
Sanford, Abigail, 231, 357.
Ezekell, 40, 228, 231, 357.
Hannah, 228, 231, 357.
Mary, 500.
Mrs., 224.

SUPPLEMENTAL INDEX.